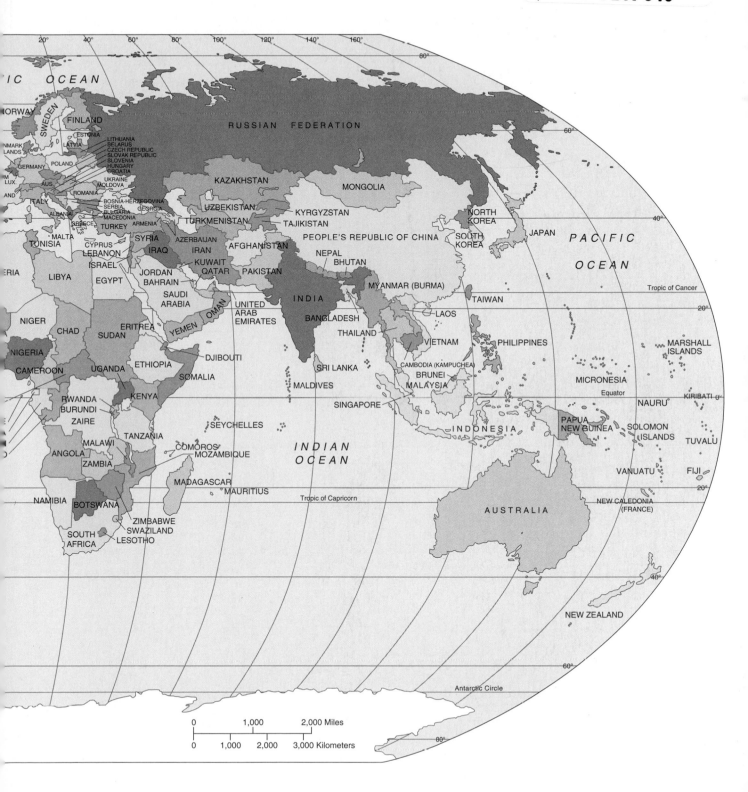

WORLD POLITICS

INTO THE TWENTY-FIRST CENTURY

WORLD POLITICS

INTO THE TWENTY-FIRST CENTURY

Unique Contexts, Enduring Patterns

ALAN C. LAMBORN
Colorado State University

JOSEPH LEPGOLD
Late of Georgetown University

Prentice Hall

Upper Saddle River, New Jersey 07458

Library of Congress Cataloging-in-Publication Data

Lamborn, Alan C.
   World politics into the 21st century : unique contexts, enduring patterns / Alan C.
Lamborn, Joseph Lepgold. -- 1st ed.
    p. cm.
   Includes bibliographical references and index.
   ISBN 0-13-032535-X (alk. paper)
   1. International relations.   I. Title: World politics into the twenty first century. II.
Lepgold, Joseph.   III. Title.

JZ1242 .L36 2003
327--dc21

2002030726

Editorial Director: Charlyce Jones Owen
Senior Acquisitions Editor: Heather Shelstad
Editor in Chief, Development: Rochelle Diogenes
Development Editor: Don McNamara
VP, Director of Production and Manufacturing:
   Barbara Kittle
Production Editor: Barbara Reilly
Copyeditor: Serena Hoffman
Editorial Assistant: Jessica Drew
Manufacturing Manager: Nick Sklitsis
Prepress and Manufacturing Buyer: Ben Smith
Director of Marketing: Beth Mejia
Marketing Manager: Claire Bitting
Marketing Assistant: Jennifer Bryant

Creative Design Director: Leslie Osher
Interior and Cover Design: Kathryn Foot
Art manager: Guy Ruggiero
Line Art Illustrations: Mirella Signoretto
Maps: Carto-Graphics
Director, Image Resource Center: Melinda Reo
Interior Image Specialist: Beth Boyd-Brenzel
Manager, Rights and Permissions: Zina Arabia
Permissions Coordinator: Nancy Seise
Photo Researcher: Jerry Marshall
Cover Image Specialist: Karen Sanatar
Cover Photo: UNDPI Photo/James Skovmand
Media Editor: Kate Ramunda
Media Production Manager: Lynn Pearlman

This book was set in 10.25/12 Janson by Interactive Composition Corp.
and was printed and bound by Von Hoffman Press.
The cover was printed by Phoenix Color Corp.

©2003 by Pearson Education, Inc.
Upper Saddle River, New Jersey 07458

For permission to use copyrighted material, grateful
acknowledgment is made to the copyright holders listed
on page 546, which is considered an extension of this
copyright page.

Printed in the United States of America
10 9 8 7 6 5 4 3 2

ISBN 0-13-032535-X

Pearson Education LTD., London
Pearson Education Australia PTY, Limited, Sydney
Pearson Education Singapore, Pte. Ltd
Pearson Education North Asia Ltd, Hong Kong
Pearson Education Canada, Ltd, Toronto
Pearson Educación de Mexico, S.A. de C.V.
Pearson Education-Japan, Tokyo
Pearson Education Malaysia, Pte. Ltd
Pearson Education, Upper Saddle River, New Jersey

For Jean and Will

*With love, respect, and a dad's passionate hope that the world gives you
a rich set of options for a fulfilling life and that
you play the hands you are dealt with wisdom, spirit, and humor*

**and for Joe's family, friends,
colleagues, and students**

*Who will keep Joe alive in their memories and in the ways
in which they understand the world around them*

Brief Contents

Contents

8   Security and the Uses of Force Today   223

13 The Politics of International Environmental Issues   404

Boxes

ENDURING PATTERNS

World Politics and the Individual

A Closer Look

Maps

Preface

Helping introductory students make sense of world politics matters. It matters because the issues that dominate world politics—the level of people's physical security, their place in the international political economy, the extent to which their human rights are respected, and the quality of the environment within which they lead their lives—are important politically, practically, and morally. It matters because world politics affects the life chances of each and every student in our classrooms, and they all deserve the opportunity to use a better understanding of the world around them to make more informed and effective choices about how to lead their lives. It matters because over the course of our careers we teach generations of students with the hope that informed and thoughtful citizens will produce a better world. Finally, how well our students learn also matters for narrow and personal reasons: It's a lot more fun to come out of a class on a high because your students "got it"; and looking forward to course evaluations sure beats dreading them.

While the incentives to invest in making our courses work well are clear, so too are the challenges. Perhaps the biggest challenge is that world politics is complex. Understanding the quest for security, the politics of international economics, the growing controversies over human rights, and the distinctive ways in which nature and politics collide to produce environmental issues involves making sense of a host of challenging concepts. It also involves learning an often overwhelming number of facts about the issues and the historical, cultural, and political contexts within which those issues play out. To overcome these challenges, students need to be willing to invest themselves in learning. That willingness, however, depends in turn on us: We need to show them how world politics affects their lives, to overcome the hurdles created by the wide variation in the quality of their preparation in such areas as history and economics, and to find a way to encourage an increasingly visual, "hunt-and-click" generation to read a sustained exploration of world politics.

All these challenges are complicated still further by the distinctive political culture of the discipline. The field of international relations is defined no less by *what* we study—world politics—than by deep and often passionately held differences about *how* we should study it. That creates a dilemma for faculty. If we teach just our own personal view of world politics, we do a disservice both to colleagues with whom we share legitimate differences and to our students, who will get a one-sided presentation. If, in an effort to avoid this problem, we use the field's differences as an essential organizing focus, we run the risk that we will inadvertently turn an introduction to world politics into an introduction to the field. When that happens we not only can lose sight of why we come together—to make better sense of the world around us—we can also produce a perverse unintended consequence: By stressing the differences in our intellectual tools and approaches, we can leave students with few tools they have any confidence in using.

We have tried to steer a course through these challenges that will make it easier for you and your students to focus on what really matters in an introductory course on world politics. The principles we used to steer that course are explained in the next sections of this preface. Along the way we relied both on our own sense of dead reckoning and on the immensely valuable reactions of many reviewers over a series of significant revisions and reorganizations. The reactions of the reviewers to the last drafts and the comments of students who used the preliminary edition are gratifying, but whether we have steered a course that works for you is not for us to decide.

The Conceptual Framework

We believe an introductory text should give students a set of tools they can use to make sense of world politics across a wide variety of issues, actors, and historical eras. We also believe that these tools should be designed to cultivate the largest piece of common intellectual and substantive ground available while simultaneously promoting an understanding and respect for intellectual and normative differences.

After decades of teaching and studying world politics, we are drawn to the conclusion that the largest piece of common ground available involves choice under conditions of strategic interdependence. All the major worldviews and virtually all of the principal intellectual traditions and research programs in the field sooner or later bump up against questions about the choices people make under conditions of strategic interdependence. Emphasizing this dimension of political life as an organizing theme gives students tools they can use without prejudging what worldviews and research traditions they will ultimately find most persuasive and interesting.

The second organizing theme is linkage politics. While there is a growing consensus that separating international and domestic politics is artificial and misleading, few texts reflect this emerging consensus and none does so in a systematic way. This failure not only makes it harder for students to make sense of world politics, it also makes it harder for them to see how world politics affects their lives. Unless they can see those connections, it is often hard for them to recognize why they should care enough to learn.

World Politics into the Twenty-First Century: Unique Contexts, Enduring Patterns has, therefore, two foundational features: It introduces students to world politics by focusing on enduring patterns in the politics of strategic choice; it integrates international and domestic politics throughout all the substantive topics in the text. By focusing on the process of strategic interaction in international and domestic politics—and on how they are connected—students can make sense of world politics even as the issues, actors, and contexts change. By focusing both on what political actors share in common and on how the reality of diversity creates meaningful differences, students can begin to learn how to walk in other people's shoes without feeling that they are being asked to give up their own values and perspectives.

This approach has another important advantage: It stresses patterns that are intuitive and makes complex concepts more accessible. Students make choices under conditions of strategic interdependence every day. The contexts in which they lead their daily lives may be far different from the contexts that characterize world politics, but many of the key underlying dimensions that drive the politics of choice are intuitive and resonate in ways that they can recognize. In addition to emphasizing what is similar about the politics of choice in world politics and in students' daily lives, we have tried to increase the accessibility of the material by using the theme of "unique contexts, enduring patterns" to connect factual and historical material with concepts and theoretical patterns. Students find it easier to make sense of world politics when they learn how to differentiate between what is unique to different contexts and what is common to the politics of strategic choice across those different contexts.

To promote these objectives, the four central issues in world politics—security, international political economy, human rights, and the environment—and their key concepts are all introduced in historical context. Doing that gives history a theoretically informed story line that not only makes it more interesting, it also leads students to consider the many ways in which ideas and worldviews have been shaped by historical and cultural roots. Whether it is free trade or balance of power, containment or preventive war, globalization or global warming, the ideas that dominate and inform contemporary debates in world politics reflect the efforts of real people to understand issues they cared about in distinctive historical, strategic, and cultural settings.

When one looks at world politics from the perspective of how unique contexts and enduring patterns combine, it appears that many competing intellectual traditions actually agree about how the *process* of political choice works. What they disagree about is the nature, frequency, and importance of different types of issues, actors, and strategic situations. Students will have a far easier time understanding and evaluating competing schools of thought when they can see a common set of assumptions about the process of politics buried underneath the debates about the relative value of the different approaches.

Finally, using the theme of "unique contexts, enduring patterns" to increase accessibility squares with the findings of a large body of recent educational research. It turns out that even the best students remember only 20 to 30 percent of the facts they learn for as long as two months. What they do retain is higher order learning skills—the capacity to think systematically and communicate effectively. None of this is to deny the central role of factual material in undergraduate education. But the purpose of "facts" is to convey essential background, to give students enough substance to hold their interest, and to illustrate and apply generalizations. A text that teaches students a way to think about world politics—while simultaneously giving them tools that can be used to evaluate both that perspective and competing ones—will help professors teach what students are capable of learning and retaining. It will also help students become more systematic and independent thinkers who can communicate their views more effectively.

The Organization of the Book

We discuss the plan of the book in detail at the end of Chapter 1 because we want students to know where we are going and why. In brief, the text is organized so that students are confronted immediately with the fact that world politics affects *whether* and *how* people live—that people's security, prosperity, health, and dignity are all shaped by the linkages between international and domestic politics. Given that world politics is worth understanding, the obvious next question is how? Chapters 2 and 3 introduce students to two quite different ways to make sense of world politics.

One approach is to examine the different intellectual traditions that have evolved and to choose the worldview the student finds most persuasive. Another is to look for common ground.

Having opted for an emphasis on common ground and the politics of strategic choice, we give students a detailed review of the key actors in world politics and the international institutions, norms, and laws that affect the origins and consequences of their choices. Because contemporary world politics is built around a state system, we begin with the state in Chapter 4 and then turn to interstate law, institutions, and non-state actors in Chapter 5.

After introducing the actors and the role of international law, institutions, and norms in Part I, we then integrate the treatment of law, institutions, norms, and the politics of choice throughout the substantive and theoretical chapters that follow. The eight chapters in Parts II–IV cover the key substantive issues in world politics: military conflict and the quest for security, international political economy, human rights, and the environment. Part V concludes the book with a discussion of how students might combine their growing understanding of the substance of world politics with a more self-conscious awareness of patterns in the politics of strategic choice to think more effectively about what the future might hold.

Pedagogical Features

In an effort to help students understand, evaluate, and use the book's conceptual framework most effectively, we have worked with the editors at Prentice Hall to develop a series of pedagogical features designed to reinforce the text's narrative, encourage active learning, and stimulate critical thinking.

Enduring Patterns Boxes   Placed throughout Chapters 6 to 13 of the text, these boxes show students how the enduring patterns in the politics of strategic choice explained in Chapter 3 can be used to help make sense of world politics across a wide variety of issues, actors, and historical eras. Each box illustrates one or more of the following five enduring patterns: (1) the connection between preferences and power, (2) the impact of varying beliefs about just relationships, (3) the effect of the shadow of the future, (4) the impact of discounting and risk taking, and (5) the impact of linkage politics. The specific topics of these Enduring Patterns boxes feature often counter-intuitive combinations of cases and issues. They include "Medieval Burghers, Modern Trans-State Business Enterprises, and Terrorists," "The Clash of Civilizations: Protestants and Catholics 400 Years Ago; the West and Islam Today," "NATO, Bismarck, and Global Terrorism," "Imagining Just Systems: India Today and the United States after World War II," "Taking Risks for Human Rights: NGOs, States, and IGOs," "The Montreal Ozone Protocol and the Kyoto Protocol on Climate Change," and "'Spaceship Earth,' Scientific Proof, and Politics."

World Politics and the Individual Boxes   These short boxed features provide a glimpse into how world politics has influenced individuals—both notable political actors and everyday people—throughout history and how individuals have in turn influenced world politics. The goal of the series is to help students think about the role of the individual in world politics and consider how the choices and actions of one can have a significant impact on many. Each box contains a brief introduction to the topic at hand along with suggestions for a critical reading of the full essay, which the students are directed to find at this book's Companion Website™, *www.prenhall.com/lamborn*. Individuals featured include Nikita Khrushchev, Kwame Nkrumah, Rosa Luxemburg, Matsuo Taseko, John Maynard Keynes, Jody Williams and the Vietnam Veterans of America Foundation, and workers and business people in Mexico during the 1980s debt crisis.

A Closer Look Boxes As the title of the series suggests, these boxes take a more in-depth look at a topic mentioned in the chapter. Topics include "What Is Bureaucratic Politics?" "United Nations Specialized Agencies," "The Evolution of the European Union," "The Evolution of a Trans-State Business Enterprise: The History of the Nestlé Company," "Bismarck's Alliances," "The Ottoman Empire," and "Lenin's Predictions."

Case Studies The text includes a series of extended case studies that focus on current issues in world politics. An introduction to the case study and several questions for analysis and discussion are provided in the relevant chapter; the complete case study is located on the Companion Website™. Examples include "India's Nuclear Weapons Choice," "Human Rights and Trade in the U.S. Policy toward China," "The Pinochet Case," "The United States, Global Warming, and the Kyoto Protocol," "Indonesia's and South Korea's Responses to the 1997 Asian Financial Crisis," and "A Tale of Two Environmental Protest Movements."

Full-Color Maps, Photos, and Charts Today's students are often very visual learners. Consequently, we have worked with the editors and designers at Prentice Hall to enhance the visual scope of the text in ways that draw attention to the substance of the material while also reinforcing conceptual and theoretical points. Over 24 maps provide students with the visual background they need to understand the evolution of the key issue areas, the implications of historical events, and even such abstract concepts as reference points and loss aversion in prospect theory. More than 90 photos have been carefully selected to enhance and illustrate important concepts in the text. Several charts, graphs, and other line illustrations help students analyze important statistical information.

Key Terms Most students learn better when the definitions of central concepts are not only clear and concise but also placed in highly visible locations throughout the text. Consequently, key terms and concepts are defined in detail in the margin of the page on which they are introduced, and they are listed again at the end of the chapter to help students review. A complete glossary also appears at the back of the book.

Chapter Summaries and Questions for Review We have drafted chapter summaries and questions for review that can be found on the Companion Website™ for this text. Students can download them to build their own study guides, organize their notes, and use them in group study sessions.

Teaching Aids for Instructors

Instructor's Resource Manual The Instructor's Resource Manual provides detailed chapter summaries, lecture outlines, questions for discussion, the case studies in their entirety, the World Politics and the Individual essays in their entirety, and other teaching tools that we believe will help you make use of the book as effectively and easily as possible.

Test Item File   This helpful aid provides numerous multiple-choice, short-answer, and essay questions organized by chapter.

Prentice Hall Test Manager   A computerized version of the Test Item File, this program allows full editing of the questions and the addition of instructor-generated items. Other special features include random generation, scrambling question order, and test preview before printing. It is available for use with Windows or Macintosh operating systems.

Study and Research Aids for Students

Companion Website™   The Companion Website™ includes a wide variety of active learning materials, including detailed chapter summaries and review questions, the complete case studies and the complete World Politics and the Individual essays referenced in the text, and interactive assignments. It will also provide an effective way to create links to material that will help faculty and students track current events as they unfold.

September 11ᵗʰ and Beyond   This supplement features a collection of essays by Prentice Hall authors. Perspectives span global economy, psychology, domestic politics, religion, and sociology.

Other Online Resources   The Prentice Hall Guide to Evaluating Online Resources includes a free access code for Research Navigator™, which features EBSCO's ContentSelect™ academic journal database, *The New York Times* 12-month Search-by-Subject Archive, and a complete guide to finding, citing, and writing research.

Acknowledgments

Many people have contributed to this project over the years. Beth Gillett Mejia signed us and has remained an enthusiastic supporter throughout. More recently we have benefited from the suggestions and professional insights of Heather Shelstad. At Georgetown, Joe had an extraordinarily supportive set of colleagues. For lending an ear (and often more) on this project in particular, we thank Tony Arend, Andy Bennett, Victor Cha, George Shambaugh, and Steve Wayne. Our thanks, too, to Lillian deValcourt, Mark Patton, and Geoff Taubman for their work preparing initial drafts of several of the cases we have placed on the website and to Renae Ditmer, who showed exceptional tenacity and poise in responding to our many requests for alterations in the charts and tables she prepared. At Colorado State, I benefited from the insights of Dimitris Stevis and Kathryn Hochstetler, colleagues who read substantial pieces of an early draft, and the general sideline support of Wayne Peak, Sue Ellen Charlton, John Straayer, and Bob Hoffert. I would also like to thank Bob DeLapp for his close reading of a draft of the manuscript, Lisa Dale for her collaboration when a late version of the text was used in a course we taught together, and Marni Berg for responding to a very last-minute request for help in researching some cases. Finally, there's Don McNamara, free-lance development editor extraordinaire, and Barbara Reilly, production editor at Prentice Hall. Without Don's superb grasp of the English language, exceptional ability to read a manuscript outside his field with intelligence and insight, and unfailing (well, almost unfailing) good humor, we never could have polished the writing and organization to the level it ultimately achieved. Without Barbara's coolly tenacious and gracious professionalism, we could never have brought the final project home sane and shipshape.

In addition, we would like to thank the many reviewers and students who contributed to the shaping of this text over the years. Their feedback was invaluable and we are truly grateful. Our thanks to Ross Burkhart, Boise State University; Jeffrey Pickering, Kansas State University; Vincent Auger, Western Illinois University; Bruce Cronin, University of Wisconsin, Madison; Alan Kessler, University of Texas, Austin; Richard Siegel, University of Nevada, Reno; B. David Meyers, University of North Carolina, Greensboro; Paul Sondrol, University of Colorado, Colorado Springs; Cameron Thies, Louisiana State University; Paul S. Vicary, Florida International University; Burcu Akan, American University; Karen Adams, Louisiana State University; Stephen Wright, Northern Arizona University; Robert DeLapp, Colorado State University; Miroslav Nincic, University of California, Davis; Mir Zohair Husain, University of South Alabama; Salvatore Prisco, Stevens Institute of Technology; John W. Outland, University of Richmond; Thomas E. Sowers, Florida State University; Timothy J. White, Xavier University; the students at the University of Wisconsin and Colorado State University who used the preliminary edition of this text in their courses.

The acknowledgments offered in the last paragraphs are the normal and long-anticipated thank-you's that come after a long project. What follows is anything but normal or anticipated. In the fall of 2001, Joe Lepgold traveled to Paris over his Thanksgiving break with his wife Nicki and son Jordan to give a series of invited lectures on European security. They were all overcome in a hotel fire the night before they were scheduled to fly home. How does one thank a co-author, close friend, and intellectual kindred spirit in the preface of a book he never lived to see?

Joe and I met in the spring of 1992 at the suggestion of a mutual friend who thought we were interested in similar ideas and might want to work together. He could not have been more right. Within an hour of sitting down to coffee late one afternoon at a convention hotel in Atlanta, we were finishing each other's sentences. For the first couple of years we simply read each other's manuscripts as we finished up already ongoing projects. Then we began what was to be a career-long series of projects together. This text was the first major one. The second project was designed to link theories of strategic choice with theories of the individual and social origins of cognition. The first article in this project came out in December 2001; two other manuscripts will soon be sent out for review. This second project was to lay the foundations for a third, which was designed to explore the ways in which an understanding of the interconnections between strategic incentives and the individual and social sources of cognition could help explain ethnic violence, terrorism, and enduring rivalries. After that we hoped to explore the value of using these theoretical connections to improve our understanding of other issue areas in world politics.

It was an extraordinary collaboration. We both shared a passionate—and often stubborn—commitment to the logical integrity of the ideas we used to make sense of world politics, an enthusiasm for theory, and a belief that research, teaching, and scholarly outreach ought to form a seamless web running throughout academic life. But while we discovered we shared these things, we also discovered that we were different in ways that mattered. I was more instinctively interested in looking for general theoretical patterns, and Joe was more interested in explaining the specific puzzles that preoccupied policy makers and dominated much of the scholarly literature. There were other differences as well. I was more interested in historical sweep and story line; Joe was more interested in tracking contemporary cases and the nitty-gritty details of examples that could bring general points to life. Finally, when we first began working together, Joe was more interested in the sources of cognition, and I was more interested in the politics of strategic choice. Over the years, in a series of long and often effervescent discussions about ideas, their meaning and significance, and how best to explain our conclusions and suggestions to students and colleagues, we each convinced the other. The result was an emerging synthesis of all these things.

Joe was an impassioned scholar and teacher who insisted that the theoretical and practical value of ideas must trump every other academic and career consideration. He loved classical music, baseball, Chicago-style deep-dish pizza, and Indian food. Above all he loved Jordan and Nicki.

Alan Lamborn

About the Authors

Alan Lamborn

Alan Lamborn is professor of political science at Colorado State University and, since 1999, also associate dean of the College of Liberal Arts. He has been a visiting professor at the University of Colorado, Boulder, and at the Graduate School of International Studies at the University of Denver. Before coming to Colorado State University, he taught at Smith College, where a nomination by his students led to his selection as a Danforth Associate by the Danforth Foundation. The Danforth Foundation describes the Associate Program as one designed to honor college faculty who are "interested and active in research, and concerned with the development of undergraduate students in terms of their values and social responsibility." In 1994 he was selected for a Pew Faculty Fellowship in International Affairs, a program based at the John F. Kennedy School of Government at Harvard, which promoted case-method teaching and active learning techniques. He received a Ph.D. and M.A. in political science at the University of Michigan and a B.A. in government from Oberlin College.

Professor Lamborn's scholarly work focuses on the politics of strategic choice, bargaining and conflict resolution, the linkages between domestic and international politics, the nature of power, and theories of world politics. He is the author of *The Price of Power: Risk and Foreign Policy in Britain, France, and Germany* (1991) and coauthor, with Stephen Mumme, of *Statecraft, Domestic Politics, and Foreign Policy Making* (1988). His principal articles have appeared in the *International Studies Quarterly* and the *International Studies Review*.

Joseph Lepgold

The late Joseph Lepgold was associate professor of international affairs and government in the Edmund A. Walsh School of Foreign Service and the Department of Government at Georgetown University, where he won the School of Foreign Service Award for the Best Teacher in Government in 1997 and the School of Foreign Service Teaching Award in 1993 and 1996. He was field chair of the international relations sub-field in the Department of Government and chair of the Faculty Field Committee for International Politics in the School of Foreign Service. He received a Ph.D. and M.A. in political science from Stanford University and a B.A. in international relations from the University of Wisconsin at Milwaukee.

Professor Lepgold's scholarly interests included multilateral security, theories of strategic interaction and of cognitive processes, and the link between theories of international relations and policy practice. He was the author, coauthor, or co-editor of five books dealing with alliance politics, regional conflict management, the uses of international relations theory in policy making, and burden-sharing: *Beyond the Ivory Tower: International Relations Theory and the Problem of Policy Relevance* with Miroslav Nincic (2001), *Being Useful: Policy Relevance and International Relations Theory*, edited with Miroslav Nincic (2000), *Collective Conflict Management*, edited with Thomas Weiss (1998), *Friends in Need: Burden Sharing in the Persian Gulf*, edited with Andrew Bennett and Danny Unger (1997), and *The Declining Hegemon: The United States and European Defense, 1960–1990* (1990). His articles appeared in *International Security, International Organization, Security Studies, Political Science Quarterly, Journal of Strategic Studies, Review of International Studies*, and *International Interactions*. He also contributed chapters to a variety of scholarly collections on security studies and international relations theory.

WORLD POLITICS

INTO THE TWENTY-FIRST CENTURY

The Central Questions

Whether and How People Live

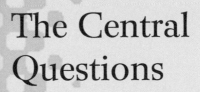

orld politics affects *whether* and *how* people live. At its best, world politics can provide a wide range of options for a successful and fulfilling life. At its worst, world politics can produce an utter desolation that strips people of meaningful choices, dehumanizing or destroying them.

Thomas Hobbes, who lived through civil war in England and watched the Thirty Years' War kill about 30 percent of the population in large areas of Europe between 1618 and 1648, painted a nightmare vision of life's choices when world politics is at its worst:

> In such [a] condition, there is no place for Industry; because the fruit thereof is uncertain; and consequently no Culture of the Earth; no Navigation, nor use of the commodities that may be imported by Sea; no commodious Building; no Instruments of moving, and removing such things as require much force; no Knowledge of the face of the Earth; no account of Time; no Arts; no letters; no Society; and which is worst of all, continual fear, and danger of violent death; And the life of man, solitary, poor, nasty, brutish, and short.[1]

While scholars debate the details in Hobbes's vision, no one debates the fact that war has been an all-too-common part of the human condition. As Table 1–1 shows, between 1816 and 1997 there have been 79 wars between states and 108 foreign wars between states and non-state entities (most of which were colonial wars). Even this extraordinary catalog of death and destruction understates in three important ways the true magnitude of the human suffering created by armed conflict. First, it omits over 200 civil wars (wars between the governments of states and domestic opposition groups). Second, the researchers who assembled this data did not count armed conflicts that resulted in fewer than 1,000 battle deaths. Third, Table 1–1 omits civilian deaths (16 million people in the armed services of the countries fighting in World War II died in battle but another 40 million civilians were killed).

Before the September 11, 2001, terrorist attacks that killed almost 3,000 people at the World Trade Center in New York City and several hundred others in Pennsylvania and Washington, D.C., world politics had dealt young people living and working in the United States a far better hand to play than the one in Hobbes's nightmare world of a war of all against all. Indeed, as one student told *The New York Times* two days after the attacks, "We grew up with nothing bad ever happening to us. Not the Bay of Pigs, not the cold war, not the threat of nuclear [war]."[2]

But while the sense of vulnerability and the fear of war within their own boundaries is new to younger generations in the United States, for long years before the September 11 attacks, Hobbes's nightmare had been a continuing reality for people in Bosnia, Kosovo, Afghanistan, Somalia, Liberia, and Rwanda. And it was not so long ago that almost 60 million people were dying in the battles, concentration camps, and the general carnage of World War II. Memorials around the United States pay tribute to the 435,000 Americans who died in their country's service, but it is in Europe and Asia that the magnitude of the suffering is clearest: over 20 million people in the Soviet Union, 8 million Germans, 6 million Poles, 5 million Chinese, and 3 million Japanese perished.[3]

"Continual fear, and danger of violent death" did not disappear with the end of World War II in 1945. From the late 1940s through the 1980s, people in the United

TABLE 1–1 ARMED FORCES BATTLE-RELATED DEATHS, 1816 TO 1997

INTERSTATE WARS

War	Years	Deaths	War	Years	Deaths
Franco-Spanish	1823	1,000	First Kashmir	1948–49	2,000
Russo-Turkish	1828–29	130,000	Palestine	1948, 1948–49	8,000
Mexican-American	1846–48	19,283	Korean	1950–53	909,833
Austro-Sardinian	1848, 1849	7,527	Russo-Hungarian	1956	4,002
First Schleswig-Holstein	1848, 1849	6,000	Sinai	1956	3,221
Roman Republic	1849	2,600	Assam	1962	1,853
La Plata	1851–52	1,300	Vietnamese	1965–75	1,021,442
Crimean	1853–56	264,200	Second Kashmir	1965	7,061
Anglo-Persian	1856–57	2,000	Six Day	1967	19,600
Italian Unification	1859	22,500	Israeli-Egyptian	1969–70	5,368
Spanish-Moroccan	1859–60	10,000	Football (El Salvador, Honduras)	1969	1,900
Italo-Roman	1860	1,000	Bangladesh	1971	11,000
Italo-Sicilian	1860–61	1,000	Yom Kippur	1973	16,401
Franco-Mexican	1862–67	20,000	Turco-Cypriot	1974, 1974	1,500
Ecuadorian-Columbian	1863	1,000	Vietnamese-Cambodian	1975–79	8,000
Second Schleswig-Holstein	1864	4,500	Ethiopian-Somalian	1977–78	6,000
Lopez	1864–70	310,000	Ugandan-Tanzanian	1978–79	3,000
Spanish-Chilean	1865–66	1,000	Sino-Vietnamese	1979	21,000
Seven Weeks	1866	44,100	Iran-Iraq	1980–88	1,250,000
Franco-Prussian	1870–71	204,313	Falklands	1982	910
First Central American	1876	4,000	Israel-Syria (Lebanon)	1982	1,235
Russo-Turkish	1877–78	285,000	Sino-Vietnamese	1987	4,000
Pacific	1879–83	14,000	Gulf War	1990–91	26,343
Anglo-Egyptian	1882	2,232			
Sino-French	1884–85	12,100			
Second Central American	1885	1,000			
Franco-Thai	1893	1,000			
Sino-Japanese	1894–95	15,000			
Greco-Turkish	1897	2,000			
Spanish-American	1898	3,685			
Boxer Rebellion	1900	3,003			
Sino-Russian	1900	4,000			
Russo-Japanese	1904–05	151,831			
Third Central American	1906	1,000			
Fourth Central American	1907	1,000			
Spanish-Moroccan	1909–10	10,000			
Italo-Turkish	1911–12	20,000			
First Balkan	1912–13	82,000			
Second Balkan	1913	60,500			
World War I	1914–18	8,578,031			
Russo-Polish	1919–20	100,000			
Hungarian-Allies	1919	11,000			
Greco-Turkish	1919–22	50,000			
Franco-Turkish	1919–21	40,000			
Lithuanian-Polish	1920	1,000			
Sino-Soviet	1929	3,200			
Manchurian	1931–33	60,000			
Chaco	1932–35	92,661			
Saudi-Yemeni	1934	2,100			
Italo-Ethiopian	1935–36	20,000			
Sino-Japanese	1937–41	1,000,000			
Changkufeng	1938	1,726			
Nomonhan	1939	28,000			
World War II	1939–45	16,634,907			
Russo-Finnish	1939–40	74,900			
Franco-Thai	1940–41	1,400			

FOREIGN WARS BETWEEN STATES AND NON-STATE ENTITIES

War	Years	DEATHS States	DEATHS Non-State
British-Mahrattan	1817–18	2,000	2,000
British-Kandyan	1817–18	1,000	10,000
Turko-Persian	1821–23	1,000	n.a.
British-Burmese of 1823	1823–26	15,000	5,000
British-Ashanti of 1824	1824–26	150	2,350
Dutch-Javanese	1825–30	15,000	20,000
British-Bharatpuran	1825–26	5,000	n.a.
Russo-Persian	1826–28	5,000	2,000
British-Zulu of 1838	1838–40	800	14,200
British-Afghan of 1838	1838–42	20,000	n.a.
Russo-Khivan	1839	5,000	n.a.
First Opium	1839–42	11,000	n.a.
Franco-Algerian of 1839	1839–47	15,000	285,000
Peruvian-Bolivian	1841	1,000	n.a.
British-Baluchi	1843	6,000	n.a.
Uruguayan Dispute	1845–52	7,500	3,500
Franco-Moroccan	1844	200	800
British-Sikh	1845–46, 1848–49	3,000	10,000
British-Kaffir	1846–47, 1850–53	4,000	n.a.
Cracow Revolt	1846	1,000	1,000
	1848–49	1,500	8,500
	1850–53	3,000	n.a.
British-Burmese of 1852	1852–53	1,000	n.a.
British-Santal	1855–56	15,000	n.a.

TABLE 1–1   (continued)

FOREIGN WARS BETWEEN STATES AND NON-STATE ENTITIES

War	Years	DEATHS States	DEATHS Non-State	War	Years	DEATHS States	DEATHS Non-State
Second Opium	1856–60	11,000	n.a.	Mahdi Uprising	1896–99	16,000	n.a.
Kabylia Uprising	1856–57	1,000	n.a.	British-Nigerian	1897	1,000	n.a.
Franco-Senegalese of 1857	1857	1,000	n.a.	Indian Muslim	1897–98	1,000	n.a.
Indian Mutiny	1857–59	3,500	11,500	Hut Tax	1898	2,000	n.a.
Franco-Indochinese of 1858	1858–62	4,000	n.a.	American-Philippino	1899–1902	4,500	8,000
Argentine-Buenos Aires	1859	500	500	Somali Rebellion	1899–1905	6,000	n.a.
British-Maorin	1860–70	10,000	n.a.	Boer War of 1899	1899–1902	22,000	13,000
Spanish-Santo Dominican	1863–65	7,000	12,000	British Conquest of Kano and Sokoto	1903	1,000	n.a.
British-Bhutanese	1865	1,000	n.a.	South West African Revolt	1904–05	2,000	78,000
British-Ethiopian	1867–68	75	1,000	Maji-Maji Revolt	1905–06	1,000	149,000
Spanish-Cuban of 1868	1868–78	100,000	100,000	British-Zulu of 1906	1906	5,000	n.a.
Franco-Algerian of 1871	1871–72	1,000	n.a.	First Moroccan	1911–12	1,000	n.a.
British-Ashanti of 1873	1873–74	100	1,400	Sino-Tibetan of 1912	1912–13	2,000	n.a.
Franco-Tonkin	1873–85	3,000	27,000	Second Moroccan	1916–17	2,000	n.a.
Dutch-Achinese	1873–78	6,000	17,000	Sino-Tibetan of 1918	1918	1,000	n.a.
Egypto-Ethiopian	1875–76	7,000	n.a.	Caco Revolt	1918–20	28	2,074
British-Kaffir of 1877	1877–78	1,000	n.a.	British-Afghan of 1919	1919	1,000	n.a.
Russo-Turkoman	1878–81	2,000	18,000	Franco-Syrian	1920	5,000	n.a.
Bosnian	1878	3,500	2,500	Iraqi-British	1920–21	2,000	n.a.
British-Afghan of 1878	1878–79, 1879–80	4,000	9,000	Italo-Libyan	1920–32	5,000	35,000
British-Zulu of 1879	1879	3,500	10,000	Riff Rebellion	1921–26	29,000	11,000
Gun War	1880–81	1,000	n.a.	Moplah Rebellion	1921–22	137	2,337
Boer War of 1880	1880–81	18,000	n.a.	Franco-Druze	1925–27	4,000	4,000
Franco-Tunisian of 1881	1881–82	10,000	1,000	Saya San's Rebellion	1930–32	10,000	n.a.
Franco-Indochinese of 1882	1882–84	4,500	2,000	British-Palestinian	1936–39	2,849	n.a.
British-Mahdi	1882–85	20,000	8,000	Indonesian	1945–46	1,400	3,600
Franco-Madagascan of 1883	1883–85	1,000	n.a.	Franco-Indochinese of 1945	1945–54	300,000	300,000
British-Burmese of 1885	1885–86	6,000	n.a.	Franco-Madagascan of 1947	1947–48	1,800	3,200
Mandigo	1885–86	1,000	n.a.	Malayan Rebellion	1948–57	13,000	n.a.
Russo-Afghan	1885	1,000	n.a.	Indo-Hyderabad	1948	1,000	1,000
Serbo-Bulgarian	1885	2,000	1,000	Sino-Tibetan of 1950	1950–51	1,000	n.a.
Italo-Ethiopian of 1887	1887	400	600	Franco-Tunisian of 1952	1952–54	3,000	n.a.
Franco-Dahomeyan	1889–92	3,000	n.a.	British-Mau Mau	1952–56	11,000	n.a.
Franco-Senegalese of 1890	1890–91	1,000	n.a.	Moroccan Independence	1953–56	3,000	n.a.
Belgian-Congolese	1892	20,000	n.a.	Franco-Algerian of 1954	1954–62	18,000	82,000
British-Ashanti of 1893	1893–94	1,000	n.a.	Cameroon	1955–60	32,000	n.a.
Dutch-Balian	1894	1,000	n.a.	Angolan-Portuguese	1961–75	8,000	47,000
Franco-Madagascan of 1894	1894–95	6,000	2,000	Guinean-Portuguese	1962–74	1,500	13,500
Spanish-Cuban of 1895	1895–98	50,000	250,000	Mozambique-Portuguese	1964–75	5,000	25,000
Japano-Taiwanese	1895	164	6,760	East Timorese	1975–77	6,000	10,000
Italo-Ethiopian of 1895	1895–96	9,000	10,000	Namibian	1975–88	1,000	19,000
Spanish-Philippino of 1896	1896–98	2,000	n.a.	Western Saharan	1975–83	12,000	4,000

Source: Correlates of War Project, version 3.0 data sets. Available at *http://cow2.la.psu.edu*
See also: J. David Singer and Melvin Small, *The Wages of War, 1816–1965* (New York: John Wiley, 1972); Melvin Small and J. David Singer, *Resort to Arms: International and Civil Wars, 1816–1980* (Beverly Hills, California: Sage Publications, 1982); and Meredith Reid Sarkees, "The Correlates of War Data on War: an Update to 1997," *Conflict Management and Peace Science,* vol. 18, no. 1 (2000), pp. 123–44.

The world was shocked when over a period of just a few months, hundreds of thousands of people were massacred in Rwanda in 1994 during fierce ethnic warfare.

States were told that their entire way of life and very survival were threatened by the Soviet Union and international communism. Over 2 million people died in the Korean War between 1950 and 1953. In the United States during the late 1950s and early 1960s, school children huddled under their desks in air raid drills, young men planned their lives around compulsory military service, and some frightened adults built bomb shelters in their basements or backyards. In 1962 the United States and the Soviet Union went to the brink of war over nuclear missiles in Cuba. The 1960s also brought the war in Vietnam and over 1 million battle deaths—including approximately 1,150,000 Vietnamese and 57,000 Americans. Then, as the Vietnam War drew to a close in the early 1970s, controversies over the sources of security swung back to debates about the threat of nuclear war between the United States and the Soviet Union. Was it better to design nuclear weapons to destroy cities or military installations? Would anti-missile defense systems such as President Reagan proposed in his Strategic Defense Initiative (nicknamed "Star Wars" by opponents) increase or decrease the probability of global war? Through the rest of the 1970s and most of the 1980s, questions like these provided a daily diet of news.

Contemporary World Politics: An Abundance of Issues and Unique Contexts

The United States

With the end of Cold War competition between the United States and the Soviet Union in 1989 to 1990 and the disintegration of the Soviet Union in December 1991, the threat of a new world war suddenly seemed to evaporate. Indeed, from 1990 to September 11, 2001, people in the United States faced relatively little direct military threat from any clearly identifiable enemy. The United States had non-threatening neighbors to its immediate north and south, and in the Western Hemisphere as a whole, only the small, militarily weak Cuba was an adversary.

Even so, security did not entirely disappear as a political and policy issue in the 1990s. Some argued that the absence of a global threat marked the beginning of a

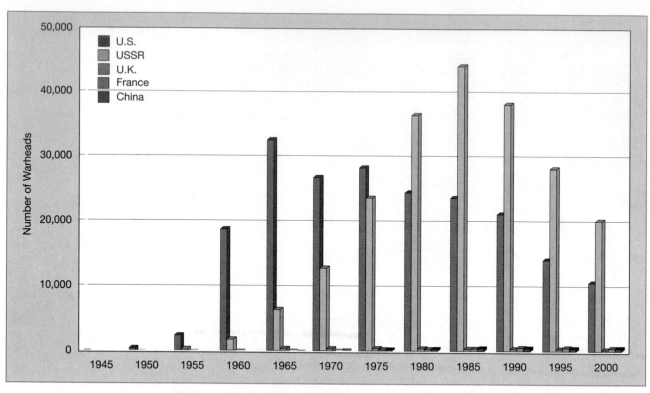

Figure 1–1   Nuclear Warheads 1945–2000: The United States, the Soviet Union (Russia), Britain, France, and China

The Soviet Union/Russia and the United States have produced about 98 percent of the more than 128,000 nuclear weapons built since World War II. (The incentives for producing this extraordinarily large number of warheads are discussed in Chapters 7 and 8.) In addition, Britain, France, and China have developed stockpiles of well over a hundred weapons, and Israel, India, and Pakistan are known to possess a few nuclear weapons.

Source: Reprinted by permission of *The Bulletin of the Atomic Scientists,* copyright 2002 by the Educational Foundation for Nuclear Science, 6042 South Kimbark, Chicago, Illinois 60637. A one-year subscription is $28.

prolonged period of peace. Others argued that the apparent peace of the post–Cold War period was merely a short time-out in a continuing struggle—a continuing quest—for security. Analysts taking the more pessimistic approach stressed that, while the Cold War's end had removed the greatest immediate threat to global security, it had also altered—and, in some cases, worsened—the problem of nuclear proliferation, the ways in which many regional security conflicts played out, and the likelihood of global terrorism.

Nuclear proliferation refers to the spread of nuclear weapons to actors that didn't previously have them. Historically, the major concern has been with the spread of nuclear weapons to *governments* (such as Pakistan, India, and North Korea) and the fact that more than 20 countries either have, or soon will acquire, the capacity to manufacture ballistic missiles that could deliver nuclear weapons anywhere around the globe (see Figure 1–1 for the number of warheads held by the traditional nuclear powers). During the 1990s, policy makers began to worry about the possibility that nuclear weapons or chemical and biological weapons of mass destruction might fall into the hands of small *groups of people*, not under the control of any central government, who were willing to use those weapons for personal or political purposes.

Meanwhile, regional security threats seemed to grow more common in the post–Cold War period. Those threats raised a variety of questions: How should one respond to Saddam Hussein's drive to build nuclear, chemical, and biological weapons of mass destruction? How should one evaluate the nature of the regional security threat created by India's decision to go public with a nuclear weapons test? How should one respond to North Korea's decision to test a missile by firing one over Japan? What should outsiders do when countries such as Yugoslavia, Somalia, Rwanda, and Zaire disintegrate into civil war and the specter of genocide returns? When should new generations of young people be sent into "harm's way" either to protect their own security or the security of others? With the end of the Cold War, the old answers to questions about the best paths to a more secure world no longer seemed to apply. But without them, how were policy makers and their constituents to differentiate between good and bad choices in their quest for security?

The September 11, 2001, attacks in the United States altered the ways in which these and other security questions are likely to be framed for the foreseeable future. The use of small knives and box cutters to hijack planes that could then be used as flying bombs to kill thousands of innocents on the ground makes it clear that mass murder on a scale equal to acts of war can be committed with low-tech weapons by shadowy networks of non-state actors. Moreover, the degree of coordination involved and the numbers of people who were prepared to die in pursuit of their cause are a signal that we might be far closer than previously thought to attacks by terrorists armed with weapons of mass destruction. With such threats, the line between living at peace and being at war is not likely to be easily or clearly established, even after the military campaign launched by the United States in reaction to the September 11 attacks ends.

While the events of September 11 put security issues back on center stage in the United States, it's important not to lose sight of the fact that world politics affects *whether* and *how* people live in many other ways than security. The jobs that will be available when young people graduate, the quality of the environment, and our understanding of the nature and importance of human rights and diversity are all affected by world politics. The United States remains more insulated from the world than many other countries due to its size, huge internal market, and location. But even in the United States, people in all walks of life are increasingly affected by developments originating in other parts of the world.

Consider first the connections between the U.S. economy and the world. As Figure 1–2 suggests, global mergers and acquisitions are tying the economic fate of business enterprises in different countries ever more closely together. Moreover, many jobs now depend on exports to foreign markets, which makes many more U.S. firms dependent on foreign sales than before. When people outside the United States suffer income losses and consequently spend less on U.S. exports, Americans producing those goods and services lose their jobs. Equally important, many more imports now enter the U.S. market as a percentage of all domestic sales. As consumers, Americans frequently want a wider range of choices than the domestic market supplies. Also, to buy American exports, foreigners need to earn dollars by selling in the U.S. market. But Americans are producers as well as consumers, and

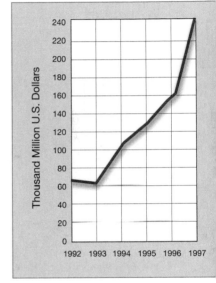

Figure 1–2 Growth in Global Mergers and Acquisitions, 1992 to 1997
The increasing globalization of international investment is dramatically demonstrated in this graph. The value of transboundary acquisitions tripled between 1992 and 1997. Meanwhile, according to the International Institute for Strategic Studies, the percentage of total direct foreign investment that can be attributed to mergers and acquisitions rose from 42 percent to 59 percent.

Source: International Institute for Strategic Studies, *Strategic Survey 1999/2000* (London: Oxford University Press, 2000), p. xxxii. Reprinted by permission of Oxford University Press.

foreign penetration of the U.S. economy has hurt some of the domestic industries that compete with the imports, especially the footwear and apparel industries. Finally, many U.S.-based firms that want to become more competitive internationally have been trying to reduce their costs by *downsizing*—firing large numbers of professionals and other middle echelon employees—or by locating their plants abroad to take advantage of lower labor costs. These trends have combined to make many Americans more economically vulnerable to changes in international economics than at any time since the Great Depression in the 1930s.

International businesspeople tend to see the implications of the U.S. role in the world economy quite differently from employees who have lost their jobs to downsizing and shifting production abroad. From the perspective of people responsible for the success of U.S. businesses, competition from the European Union (EU), Japan, and many newly industrialized countries (NICs) is so intense that managers must make business decisions with the global market in mind. Among other things, many have concluded that the notion of a "contract" with their American workers to provide lifetime employment—an implicit bargain that many U.S. firms made with their workers for several decades after World War II—is outdated. Managers now feel they must locate where production is economically most efficient, which is often abroad in lower-wage countries. In some cases, communities which for generations depended on employment from particular plants have lost the source of their livelihoods when those plants have relocated abroad. As a result, the interests of firm managers and stockholders have increasingly diverged from those of the communities where the firms have been located, producing sharp divisions between upper management and many American workers. For this reason, U.S. policy makers are caught between the preferences of local communities and workers, who worry about the negative effects of an increasingly global economy, and international business constituencies, who want to take advantage of globalization to increase profits.

In addition, the "information revolution" is changing Americans' connections to world politics in unprecedented ways. By early in the twenty-first century, most American households will have at least one computer, many hooked up to the Internet and "dot.com" businesses (see Figure 1–3). Worldwide, business is being transformed by the pervasive use of electronic information and data-manipulation systems (see Figure 1–4). For example, as early as the mid-1980s the value of international financial transactions—many of them computerized—was 25 times larger than the value of trade in goods.[4] Aside from its business applications, computer technology has completely transformed people's abilities to communicate across vast distances and obtain information through data banks, linked library catalog systems, and many other storehouses of data. It has linked individuals and groups within and across national boundaries, making it easier to share information and form coalitions.

The growth in tourism is another indicator of globalization and the extent to which the world is growing closer together. Every region in the world experienced a massive increase in inbound and outbound tourists between 1980 and 1997 (see Table 1–2 on page 10). Not surprisingly, the totals of outbound tourists are far higher from regions composed largely of rich countries than regions, such as sub-Saharan Africa, that are far poorer. As this example suggests, while globalization is a worldwide phenomenon, its patterns and effects are not always symmetrical.

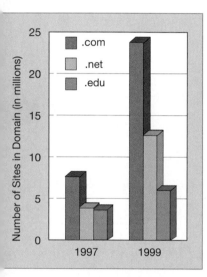

Figure 1–3   Growth in Internet Sites, 1997 to 1999 With the growth in commercial sites leading the way, Internet usage has exploded over the last several years. The countries with the largest number of top-level (primary) sites in October 2000 were: United States, Japan, Canada, Britain, Germany, Italy, Australia, the Netherlands, France, and Taiwan. As this "top-ten" list suggests, so far the host sites are very much concentrated in the world's richest countries.

Source: International Institute of Communications, *TeleGeography: Global Communications Traffic Statistics* (London: International Institute of Communications, 2000), p. 123. © TeleGeography, Inc., 2000. *www.telegeography.com*

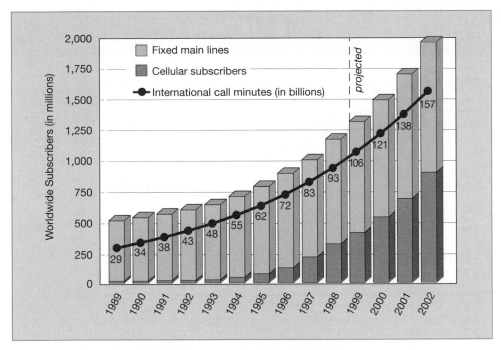

Figure 1–4   Growth in Global Telecommunications since 1989
Globalization is not simply an economic phenomenon; it also involves a revolution in trans-boundary communication. Trans-boundary communication is not only easier and faster than ever before; it's also being used by far more people.

Source: International Institute of Communications, *TeleGeography 2000* (London: International Institute of Communications, 1999), p. 141. © TeleGeography, Inc., 2000. *www.telegeography.com*

Controversies over immigration policy also make it clear how dependent Americans' lives are on the linkages between domestic and international politics. Perhaps more than any other nation in history, the United States is populated by immigrants and their descendants. To a large extent, American national identity was based on the belief that people could come here to seek a freer and more prosperous life than was available elsewhere. Indeed, between 1900 and 1930, approximately 11 to 15 percent of the U.S. population was foreign-born. Despite that history, with economic insecurity growing and publicly funded programs under political attack, recent immigrants face resentment from many established U.S. citizens, and there is pressure to close the door to new entrants. The reasons for such feelings are easy to see. First, after a long decline, the population that is foreign-born rose from 4.7 percent in 1970 to 7.9 percent in 1990.[5] Second, conditions in the countries these immigrants have left give them an incentive to work long hours for low wages, leading many observers to claim that they take jobs from established citizens, who are unwilling to work for such long hours at such low wages. Third, immigrants bring their languages and social customs with them, which leads some people to worry that U.S. society is in danger of losing a widely shared sense of community and identity. Immigration became a leading political issue during the 1996 presidential campaign season, with Republican hopeful Patrick Buchanan basing much of his platform on a strong anti-immigration policy.

TABLE 1–2	**THE GROWTH IN TOURISM: INBOUND AND OUTBOUND TOURISTS, BY REGION, 1980 AND 1997 (figures in thousands)**					

	1980			1997		
Region	**Inbound Tourists**	**Outbound Tourists**	**Total Inbound & Outbound**	**Inbound Tourists**	**Outbound Tourists**	**Total Inbound & Outbound**
East Asia and Pacific	9,570	3,339	12,909	49,748	37,471	87,219
Europe and Central Asia	17,935	15,522	33,457	91,125	89,019	180,144
Latin America and Caribbean	22,766	9,907	32,673	48,213	27,212	75,425
Middle East and North Africa	11,815	4,620	16,435	22,229	12,173	34,402
South Asia	2,086	1,259	3,345	4,068	5,040	9,108
Sub-Saharan Africa	3,328	370	3,698	14,889	5,175	20,064
High-Income Countries*	193,391	123,635	317,026	381,320	359,421	740,741

*Countries with per capita incomes over $9,266. Includes: Australia, Austria, Belgium, Canada, Denmark, Finland, France, Germany, Greece, Iceland, Ireland, Italy, Japan, Luxembourg, Netherlands, New Zealand, Norway, Portugal, Spain, Sweden, Switzerland, United Kingdom, United States.

Source: World Bank, *1999 World Development Indicators* (Washington, DC: The World Bank, 2000), pp. 324–26, 366–68.

No review of the ways Americans are linked to the world would be complete without a discussion of the impact of environmental issues. In the United States, the modern environmental movement began with the publication in 1962 of Rachel Carson's *Silent Spring*, which brought widespread attention to the damage caused by pesticide use in agriculture. Over the last 40 years, Americans have come to care more than before about the effects of pollution, the destruction of the atmosphere's ozone layer through the use of chemicals found in refrigeration systems and aerosol spray products, the effect of "greenhouse" gases on the earth's temperature, and the increasing extinction of many animal species by the destruction of the habitats in which they live. Almost all of these problems have trans-boundary dimensions: Air pollution spreads without regard to political boundaries; greenhouse gases emitted in one country rise into the global atmosphere; and any global warming, with the consequent melting of the polar ice caps that occurs, will raise sea levels of all countries with coastlines.

Societies have always been connected to each other in a number of ways, but until fairly recently, during times of peace these linkages were much less visible and typically affected only a small proportion of the population. Today the linkages that connect people across national boundaries are much deeper, wider, and more visible. In almost every society, people's life choices are deeply affected by the economic, military, and environmental policies of other countries. Simply put, world politics now affects more aspects of people's lives. It is hard to understand any political or social issue without seeing how it is connected to a variety of other developments, actors, and issues across national boundaries. As we move into the twenty-first century, the number of these linkages and the speed with which they are changing are increasing rapidly.

Whether the changing structure of world economics and politics is a threat or an opportunity depends on exactly how individuals are connected to world politics and how they play the hand they are dealt. Those connections—and the hands they create for people to play—vary immensely with the country individuals live in, as well as with their culture, gender, religion, and economic class. (See the box "*A Closer Look:* Dealing the Cards: Who Gets What Hand to Play?")

Snapshots from around the World

Russia   Consider what it means to be Russian at the outset of the twenty-first century. Russians have experienced enormous changes in their international and domestic situations during the last decade. Russia was once the principal component of the Soviet Union, a major multinational state and the key rival of the United States. While the standard of living of Soviet citizens was far lower than that of Americans, Soviet leaders were major international players because of their country's military capabilities, the role of communism as the primary ideological competitor of market capitalism and democracy, and the stability of their political system. All these assets are now gone. Today, Russia is struggling to implement a market economy and a pluralistic political system under disastrous economic, social, and political conditions. Per capita gross national product (GNP) has dropped dramatically since the 1980s, crime is rampant in Russian cities, and Russia no longer heads a major alliance or enjoys the diplomatic leverage it held before the Soviet Union collapsed in 1991. As shown in Table 1–3, life expectancy in Russia also has changed dramatically over the last hundred years. The low numbers in the early dates reflect both the country's poverty and the effects of war and internal repression. The years from 1958 through 1987 show the dramatic growth in people's life chances created by the decline in violence and the improvements both in health care and the standard of living. Sadly, the collapse of the Soviet Union and the birth of Russia's fragile democracy and market economy have, at least initially, reduced life expectancy.

Consequently, when Russians look at international economic and security issues, they see a bleak picture. During the Soviet era, Moscow had relatively little need for international *liquidity*—a stock of convertible foreign currencies that could be used to pay for essential imports—because the Russian economy was not tied to international markets in the way it is today. As a result, the Soviet Union did not depend to any great extent on foreigners to provide infusions of capital and could ignore outside pressures to reform its economy. Today, in contrast, many of Russia's most

---

TABLE 1–3   LIFE EXPECTANCY IN RUSSIA, 1896 TO 1995

Year	Men	Women	Year	Men	Women
1896	30.9	33.0	1987	64.9	74.3
1926	39.3	44.8	1990	63.8	74.4
1938	40.4	46.7	1991	63.5	74.3
1958	61.9	69.2	1992	62.0	73.8
1965	64.0	72.1	1993	59.0	72.0
1970	63.0	73.4	1995	58.0	72.0
1980	61.4	73.0			

Sources: Julie DaVanzo, ed., *Rand Conference Proceedings* (Santa Monica, CA: Rand, 1996), p. 116; World Bank, *World Development Indicators, 1997* (Washington, DC: World Bank, 1997), p. 87.

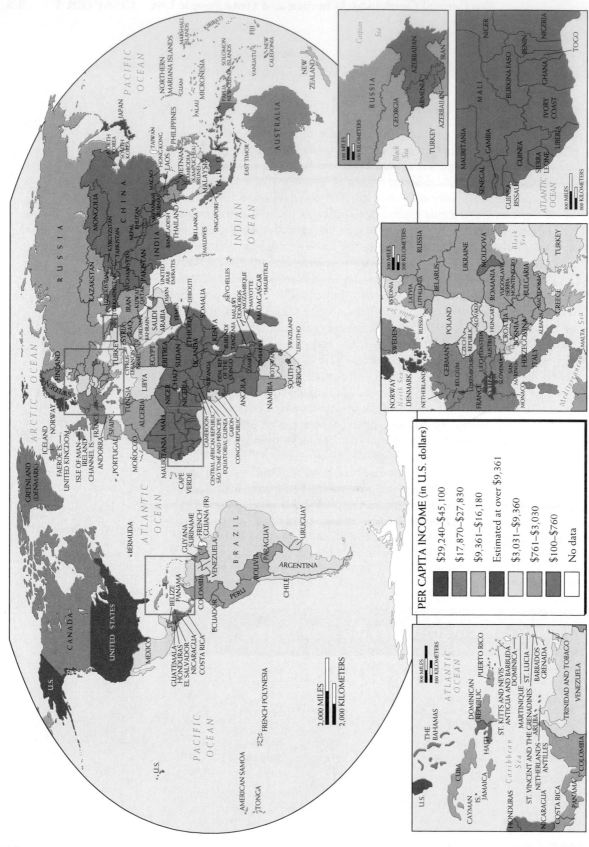

Map 1–1   The World by Per Capita Income Level, 1998

PER CAPITA INCOME (in U.S. dollars)

- $29,240–$45,100
- $17,870–$27,830
- $9,361–$16,180
- Estimated at over $9,361
- $3,031–$9,360
- $761–$3,030
- $100–$760
- No data

Source: Data from The World Bank, "GNP per Capita 1998, Atlas Method and PPP," World Development Report (Hong Kong: Asia 2000, Ltd., 2000 edition, CD-ROM.

A Closer Look

Dealing the Cards: Who Gets What Hand to Play?

What are the chances that you will be rich or poor? What are the chances that you will live in a country with a government capable of influencing the world around it, or live in a country that is routinely swept along by the choices others make? What are the chances that you will live in a society with a broad range of non-governmental organizations and groups that are active both at home and abroad?

In short, what are the chances that you will be dealt a good hand to play when you set out to lead a successful and fulfilling life? The answer is as clear as it is ethically troubling: The hands people are dealt in this life depend first and foremost on the lottery of birth.

Map 1–1 shows the distribution of average per capita income in different countries around the world. Almost all the countries in Africa have an average annual income below $760. Almost all the countries in North America and Western Europe have incomes above $9,361. Country-by-country data show even starker differences. Luxembourg and Switzerland, the countries in the world with the highest per capita incomes, are at $45,100 and $39,980. The United States, which ranks 10th in the world, is at $29,240. Most of the countries in Africa are at the bottom of the

table. The average annual income in Ethiopia is $100; Sierra Leone is at $140.

The picture of wealth and poverty is far more varied in Asia. Japan ranks 7th in the world with $32,350, and Singapore is 9th with $30,170. But Nepal has an average income of $210, India is at $440, and Pakistan at $470. Latin America shows fewer extremes. While Nicaragua, Haiti, and Honduras have quite low average incomes ($370, $410, and $740, respectively) and Uruguay and Argentina have much higher ones at $6,070 and $8,030, most countries in Latin America range between $1,010 (Bolivia) and $4,990 (Chile).

Individuals have a range of options for different choices, no matter what hand they are dealt. But as one looks at the way in which different income ranges are distributed around the world, it's clear that the number of options for living an economically comfortable life vary radically across different regions of the world. The number of workers immigrating to the United States from Mexico is easy to understand when one sees that the average income in Mexico ($3,840) is $25,000 lower than it is in the United States. Imagine the incentives in Haiti, with a per capita income of $410.

TABLE 1–4	INCOME INEQUALITY WITHIN SELECTED COUNTRIES IN AFRICA, NORTH AMERICA, AND EUROPE						
Country	**Gini Index[a]**	**Country**	**Gini Index[a]**	**Country**	**Gini Index[a]**	**Country**	**Gini Index[a]**
Sierra Leone	62.9	Madagascar	46.0	Switzerland	36.1	Germany	28.1
South Africa	59.3	Nigeria	45.0	Ireland	35.9	Finland	25.6
Zimbabwe	56.8	Kenya	44.5	France	32.7	Norway	25.2
Lesotho	56.0	Guinea	40.3	Ghana	32.7	Belgium	25.0
Senegal	53.8	United States	40.1	United Kingdom	32.6	Sweden	25.0
Mexico	53.7	Ethiopia	40.0	Spain	32.5	Denmark	24.7
Mali	50.5	Uganda	39.2	Canada	31.5	Austria	23.1
Niger	50.5	Mauritania	38.9	Netherlands	31.5		
Zambia	49.8	Tanzania	38.2	Italy	31.2		
Burkina Faso	48.2	Côte d'Ivoire	36.9	Rwanda	28.9		

[a] The Gini Index measures how equally a resource is spread across different groups of people. In this case, the Gini Index is being used to measure how equally income is spread across different countries. A Gini score of zero indicates complete equality; a score of one indicates the largest degree of inequality possible. For instance, the United States has a far higher score than other wealthy countries in North America and Europe because the wealthiest groups in the United States have a higher percentage of the country's income. The highest 20 percent in the United States gets 45.2 percent of the total income of the country; the lowest 20 percent gets 4.8 percent. In Austria, the highest 20 percent gets 33.3 percent; the lowest 20 percent gets 10.4 percent. (For ease of reading, all numbers in the table have been converted to percentages of one, the maximum possible.)

Source: World Bank, *World Development Report, 1999/2000* (New York: Oxford University Press, 2000), pp. 238–39.

Europe is experiencing similar in-migrations from Africa, Asia, Turkey, and the Middle East. The incentives to migrate to Europe from Africa are especially easy to understand when one compares the massive differences in average income in the two continents. But there is even more to the differences in economic chances than the averages indicate. Africa is not only poor; it also has a more unequal distribution of income within its countries. Consider the information on income inequality in Table 1–4 on page 13. This table lists the Gini indexes for selected countries in Africa, North America, and Europe. As the note below the table explains, the Gini index measures how equally income is distributed across different groups within a society. A score of zero indicates perfect equality (all the groups have the same income); a score of 1 indicates that the society has as much inequality as possible. (If you were to divide a society into five groups, you would get a Gini of 1 if the wealthiest 20 percent had 100 percent of the income.) With few exceptions, the countries with the highest Gini indexes (the most unequal income distributions) are in Africa.

The wide range of variation in countries' average income affects more than their citizens' chances to lead economically comfortable lives. It also affects the ability of their governments—and of non-governmental groups—to act effectively internationally. But when it comes to the ability to affect international events, it's important to look at more than just per capita income. The ability of governments and non-governmental groups to affect international politics depends on the relative scale of the total resources within their countries. If one were to compare the rank ordering of *per capita* income data that was used to construct Map 1–1 with the rank ordering of countries' *total* income in Table 1–5, one would see that Luxembourg is first in average income but only 68th in total income; not surprisingly, Luxembourg doesn't play a highly visible role in world politics. When you look at the others in the top category of average income, you'll see that there are quite a few that don't play highly visible international roles. The reason why is quite simple: Their populations are too small to make them major players across a broad range of issues.

There are only two countries in the top ten in both rankings: the United States and Japan. Three other major players in world politics—Germany, France, and the United Kingdom—rank 3rd, 4th, and 5th in total income; 13th, 20th, and 22nd in average income. Also important, but usually far more important regionally than globally, are countries with modest per capita incomes but large populations. China is 145th in average income; 7th in total. Russia ranks 97th in per capita income, but 16th in total income. India is 161st in average income; 11th in total. Brazil is 68th in per capita; 8th in total.

As you read the chapters that follow, you will find that the distribution of economic resources is only part of the story when it comes to understanding world politics. There is, however, no doubt that the range—and the attractiveness—of the choices available to individuals in different countries varies with the economic cards they have been dealt in the lottery of birth.

TABLE 1–5   TOTAL INCOME FOR COUNTRIES IN 1998

Ranking	Economy	Millions of U.S. Dollars	Ranking	Economy	Millions of U.S. Dollars
1	United States	7,902,976	16	Russian Federation	331,776
2	Japan	4,089,139	17	Argentina	290,261
3	Germany	2,179,802	18	Switzerland	284,119
4	France[a]	1,465,400	19	Belgium	258,968
5	United Kingdom	1,264,262	20	Sweden	226,454
6	Italy	1,157,001	21	Austria	216,697
7	China	923,560	22	Turkey	200,530
8	Brazil	767,568	23	Denmark	175,160
9	Canada	580,872	24	Hong Kong, China[b]	158,238
10	Spain	555,244	25	Norway	152,049
11	India	427,407	26	Poland	151,285
12	Korea, Rep.	398,825	27	Saudi Arabia	143,361
13	Netherlands	389,055	28	South Africa	136,868
14	Australia	387,006	29	Thailand	131,916
15	Mexico	368,059	30	Indonesia	130,600

TABLE 1–5   (continued)

Ranking	Economy	Millions of U.S. Dollars	Ranking	Economy	Millions of U.S. Dollars
31	Finland	125,091	97	Zimbabwe	7,214
32	Greece	123,394	98	Tanzania[c]	7,154
33	Portugal	106,391	99	Uganda	6,566
34	Iran, Islamic Rep.	102,242	101[d]	Ethiopia	6,169
35	Colombia	100,667	102	Latvia	5,917
36	Israel	96,483	103	Trinidad and Tobago	5,811
37	Singapore	95,453	104	Congo, Dem. Rep.	5,433
38	Venezuela	82,096	105	Georgia	5,281
39	Malaysia	81,311	106	Jordan	5,252
40	Egypt, Arab Rep.	79,185	107	Gabon	4,922
41	Philippines	78,938	108	Bahrain	4,909
42	Chile	73,935	109	Nepal	4,889
43	Ireland	69,322	110	Estonia	4,878
44	Pakistan	61,451	111	Botswana	4,795
45	Peru	60,491	112	Senegal	4,683
46	New Zealand	55,356	114	Yemen, Rep.	4,630
48	Czech Republic	53,034	115	Angola	4,578
49	Ukraine	49,207	116	Honduras	4,564
50	United Arab Emirates	48,673	117	Jamaica	4,481
51	Algeria	46,389	118	Mauritius	4,329
52	Hungary	45,660	119	West Bank and Gaza	4,263
53	Bangladesh	44,224	120	Papua New Guinea	4,104
55	Nigeria	36,373	123	Azerbaijan	3,821
56	Morocco	34,421	124	Malta	3,807
59	Romania	30,596	125	Guinea	3,777
60	Vietnam	26,535	126	Madagascar	3,741
61	Uzbekistan	22,900	127	Mozambique	3,478
62	Belarus	22,332	128	Zambia	3,234
63	Kazakhstan	20,856	129	Namibia	3,217
64	Croatia	20,786	131	Haiti	3,163
65	Uruguay	19,960	132	Cambodia	2,945
66	Slovak Republic	19,941	135	Albania	2,718
68	Luxembourg	19,239	136	Mali	2,646
69	Tunisia	19,193	137	Macedonia, FYR	2,584
70	Ecuador	18,450	138	Burkina Faso	2,575
71	Guatemala	17,759	140	Tajikistan	2,256
74	Syrian Arab Republic	15,532	141	Benin	2,252
75	Sri Lanka	15,176	142	Malawi	2,168
76	Lebanon	14,975	146	Niger	2,023
77	Dominican Republic	14,629	149	Congo, Rep.	1,899
80	El Salvador	11,207	150	Rwanda	1,864
82	Kenya	10,201	152	Kyrgyz Republic	1,771
83	Côte d'Ivoire	10,196	153	Nicaragua	1,756
84	Bulgaria	10,085	154	Fiji	1,748
85	Costa Rica	9,771	155	Armenia	1,728
86	Lithuania	9,411	157	Chad	1,658
87	Paraguay	9,172	158	Moldova	1,652
88	Cyprus	8,983	159	Lao PDR	1,583
89	Cameroon	8,736	160	Togo	1,453
90	Panama	8,275	162	Swaziland	1,384
91	Sudan	8,224	164	Lesotho	1,167
93	Bolivia	8,013	166	Central African Rep.	1,053
95	Iceland	7,626	167	Mauritania	1,033
96	Ghana	7,269	168	Mongolia	995

TABLE 1–5 (continued)

Ranking	Economy	Millions of U.S. Dollars	Ranking	Economy	Millions of U.S. Dollars
170	Burundi	911		Bermuda	...
174	Eritrea	781		Bosnia and Herzegovina	...
175	Sierra Leone	703		Brunei	...
176	Suriname	684		Cayman Islands	...
179	Guyana	661		Channel Islands	...
180	Belize	635		Cuba	...
182	Antigua and Barbuda	565		Djibouti	...
183	St. Lucia	556		Faeroe Islands	...
184	Seychelles	505		French Polynesia	...
185	Cape Verde	499		Greenland	...
187	Equatorial Guinea	478		Guam	...
189	Gambia	408		Iraq	...
190	Bhutan	354		Isle of Man	...
191	Solomon Islands	315		Korea, Dem. Rep.	...
192	Grenada	313		Kuwait	...
193	Maldives	296		Liberia	...
194	St. Vincent and Grenadines	290		Libya	...
195	St. Kitts and Nevis	253		Liechtenstein	...
196	Vanuatu	231		Macao, China	...
197	Dominica	230		Mayotte	...
198	Micronesia, Fed. Sts.	204		Monaco	...
199	Comoros	197		Myanmar	...
200	Guinea-Bissau	184		Netherlands Antilles	...
201	Samoa	181		New Caledonia	...
202	Tonga	173		Northern Mariana Islands	...
203	Kiribati	101		Oman	...
204	Marshall Islands	96		Palau	...
206	São Tomé and Principe	38		Puerto Rico	...
	Afghanistan	... [e]		Qatar	...
	American Samoa	...		Somalia	...
	Andorra	...		Turkmenistan	...
	Aruba	...		Virgin Islands (U.S.)	...
	Bahamas, The	...		Yugoslavia, FR	
	Barbados	...		(Serbia/Montenegro)	...

[a]Data include French overseas departments.
[b]Based on GDP estimates.
[c]Data refer to mainland Tanzania.
[d]Rank #100 is missing in the original table.
[e]... denotes data not available.

Source: World Bank, "Total GNP 1998, Atlas Method," *World Development Report 56* (Hong Kong: Asia 2000, Ltd. 2000 Edition), CD-ROM.

important loans need to be certified by the International Monetary Fund (IMF), an organization that helps countries qualify for international loans to improve their liquidity. As a result, Russian leaders must bargain with outsiders about the way they will run their economy. They can refuse such conditions, much as anyone seeking a loan can refuse a bank's demand for collateral, but they will not then get the help they need. For many Russians, such dependence on Western funds and institutions is not only hard to get used to, it's humiliating.

While not as immediate a concern as the economy is to many average Russians, their security situation is equally bleak. It was one thing for Russians to see the Warsaw Pact, their European alliance during the Cold War, fall apart. It is another for some former members of the Warsaw Pact (Poland, Hungary, and the Czech Republic) to join the North Atlantic Treaty Organization (NATO), their Cold War adversary, and for Russians to watch NATO bomb Serbia, a historic Russian ally. In addition, large parts of their former empire are unstable and embroiled in ethnic conflict that has spread to Russia itself. As we discuss in Chapters 8 and 17, there is some possibility that growing cooperation with the United States and other NATO countries in the struggle against terrorism—symbolized by a May 2002 agreement to create a special new organization that includes Russia and NATO—may reduce Russia's sense of vulnerability. However, even if that occurs, Russians still will face profound uncertainties.

Western Europe   The situation in Western Europe is different from that of Russia. The countries of Western Europe have long been America's closest economic and military allies. Since the end of the Cold War and the collapse of the Soviet Union, they have faced few immediate security threats by state actors. However, their willingness to stand by the United States after the September 11 attacks will almost certainly increase the chance that they will be targeted for attack by terrorist groups. Moreover, there are many serious continuing security problems in the Balkans, where Yugoslavia's collapse in the early 1990s produced a major war in the heart of Europe for the first time since the end of World War II. Although European leaders have talked about the desirability of doing more for their own defense, Europeans' initial failure to deal with the war in the Balkans until the United States made a major diplomatic and military effort to end it convinced many Europeans and Americans that Europe was not ready or willing to play an independent role in international security affairs. Prior to the September 11 attacks, policy makers on both sides of the Atlantic wondered about the value and durability of the U.S. pledge to maintain 100,000 troops in Western Europe under NATO command. With the post-attack revival of European interest in maintaining close cooperation with the United States on security matters, trans-Atlantic conversations about security are likely to shift from whether the tie should be sustained to how common objectives can best be pursued.

These conversations will be affected by how the European Union (EU, formerly the European Community, or EC) evolves. As we discuss in Chapter 5, France, Britain, and Germany are the major members of the European Union, which began as a common market in the 1950s. Members of a common market pledge to maintain open borders for one another's goods and services and a common tariff on imports from nonmember states. Thus, for purposes of international economic bargaining, they often constitute a single actor. But some Europeans believe that EU members should begin to integrate their political institutions as well. The result at some point could be a single European federal unit, organized something like the United States, with a common foreign and defense policy. Were that to happen, the nature of the defense relationship with the United States would have to change, since NATO has been based on the assumption that each member's defense ties to the United States were as important as any intra-European relationships. For these reasons, the future of European security relations depends not only on what happens in Russia, in the Balkans, and in the campaign against global terrorist networks but also on developments inside Europe itself.

In addition to the longer-range issue of political integration, European countries are divided about the pace and the extent of further economic integration. On January 1, 1999, the EU began its next major step in the long-debated and controversial process of moving toward economic union: the creation of a common currency (called the *euro*) and a common central bank. Euro notes and coins went into full circulation on January 1, 2002. The goal is to give EU members, who now have economies that are still governed mostly by national authorities, a single economic system. The move toward a common currency and central bank requires participating countries to act more like a *single* country on economic matters. They will need to decide *together* on policies to deal with inflation, unemployment, and borrowing. Since these policies are very sensitive politically, and members of the EU continue to have distinct economic traditions and problems—Germans, for example, fear inflation more than unemployment, while many other Europeans have the opposite preference—it remains to be seen how well the move to monetary union will play out. The fact that Britain, Denmark, and Sweden are not joining the others—Austria, Belgium, Finland, France, Germany, Greece, Ireland, Italy, Luxembourg, the Netherlands, Portugal, and Spain—in the move toward a common currency and central bank is an important indicator of the significant differences in the mix of international and domestic incentives confronting people in the different countries that make up the EU.

Japan   Japan's situation is similar to that of many of the principal European countries. Its economic and security systems have become very closely tied to those of the United States over the last half century, and it, too, is unsure about the nature of its post–Cold War relationship with the United States. As a result, the Japanese government, like many European governments, finds itself caught between U.S. demands for more access to its markets and higher contributions to joint security projects on the one hand, and domestic opposition to giving in to U.S. pressure on the other. Moreover, the end of the Soviet threat has left Japanese foreign policy makers as perplexed about the sources of security and the shape of the necessary trade-offs among different foreign and domestic objectives as are their American and European counterparts. And while the U.S. media have often presented Japan as if it were led by a unified elite pursuing an aggressive strategy for achieving long-term economic and political advantage, in many ways Japanese policy makers are burdened by a very small margin for error in both international and domestic politics.

On the international side, Japan faces challenges in maintaining both its economy and security. It is far more heavily dependent on imported oil and other raw materials than other industrialized countries; at the same time, Japan's standard of living depends on exporting a large percentage of the goods its factories produce. Japan also faces difficult security threats. The biggest question mark is China, the world's most populous country, whose people are being cross-pressured by an unstable mix of market reforms (which have generated massive economic growth), political repression, and uncertainty about their future choices. Experts debate whether China will fall apart or become the dominant military and economic power in the Far East—no small difference to a nearby neighbor such as Japan. Meanwhile, the Japanese must keep a wary eye on the political situation in North Korea. On the one hand, the North Koreans tested a multi-stage ballistic missile in 1999, and they are widely believed to be on the verge of building nuclear weapons. On the other hand, in the fall of 2000 U.S. Secretary of State Madeleine Albright made a widely acclaimed visit to North Korea to improve relations between the United States, North Korea, and its neighbors. That visit was followed in 2001 by the beginning of talks between North and South Korea on possible steps toward reunification.

These economic and security vulnerabilities are difficult to manage because Japanese culture, institutions, and politics make it hard to reach decisions quickly. The politics of choice are further complicated by a prolonged weakening of the Japanese economy through the 1990s and an often stalemated struggle to build a governing coalition that can replace the one that dominated Japanese politics and economics from the late 1940s into the early 1990s.

Post-Colonial Societies in Asia, Africa, and the Middle East; the Changing Face of Latin America   As one moves away from North America, Europe, and Japan, the ways in which the links between international and domestic politics affect people's choices become even more varied. Most of the countries in Africa and Asia were colonies until a wave of decolonization between 1947 and the mid-1960s largely ended formal empires. Consequently, while many of the countries on these continents look for ways to connect with Europe, the United States, and Japan to help their economies grow and to improve their security, they are worried that they do so from a position of weakness, thus compromising their recent and hard-won independence. In stark contrast to this widespread desire to avoid external influence, other countries, such as some of the former French colonies in Africa, are governed by coalitions that sometimes look to their former colonizers to intervene in support of their political and economic control. Jean Bedel Bokassa, the dictator of the Central African Republic from 1965 to 1979, provides a particularly infamous example of a post-colonial leader who depended on the influence of the former colonizer (France) to stay in power through a period of repression and exploitation—including spending one-fourth of his country's gross national product on his

The rapid growth in exports and GDPs in a number of newly industrializing countries (NICs) led to a tremendous building boom in their major cities' business districts. The change in the skyline of Hong Kong from the 1960s to the 1990s reflects that rapid economic growth.

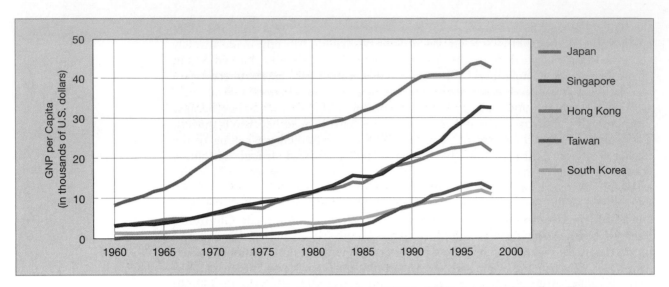

Figure 1–5   Economic Growth in Asia, 1960 to 2000: Japan and the Four Tigers
The growth in Asia's global economic role is symbolized by the extraordinary gains in per capita income by Japan and the "Four Tigers" (Hong Kong, Singapore, South Korea, and Taiwan).

Sources: For Taiwan: "Major Indicators at Current Prices," *National Statistics of Taiwan, The Republic of China.* Available at *http://www.stat.gov.tw/bs4/nis/EP1.xls* (November 15, 2000). For Japan, Hong Kong, South Korea, and Singapore: World Bank, *World Development Indicators. CD-ROM* (Washington, DC: World Bank, 1999).

coronation as emperor in 1976. One can also find, at the opposite extreme, elites determined to isolate their populations from outside influences as completely as possible—a task that has become increasingly difficult with the growth of the Internet.

Some of these countries pursued their linked domestic and international objectives within the context of rapid economic growth from the 1970s to the late 1990s (see Figure 1–5). Most often mentioned are the so-called "Four Tigers" in Asia (Singapore, Taiwan, South Korea, and Hong Kong), but there were also a relatively large number of other newly industrializing countries (NICs) in Asia (such as Indonesia) and Latin America (such as Brazil). All these countries have substantially altered both their citizens' lives and their regional political and economic power by tying their economies more tightly to the international market, promoting industrialization, and taking their chances with export-led economic growth. The stress on rapid economic growth in NICs, however, has given rise to a wide range of problems along with the economic successes. As industrialization has created major new sectors in the economy, thousands (in some countries millions) of people have migrated from rural areas to cities. The results have often been sprawling slums, the collapse of social and educational networks, abject poverty, and political instability. The political instability created by the growing slums has been increased by the large foreign debt accumulated in the rush to industrialize, by corruption and infighting among the elite over the division of new economic and political spoils, and by controversies about whether continued economic growth makes possible a transition from authoritarian to democratic government. Meanwhile, lurking in the background are a growing number of environmental catastrophes waiting to happen if nothing is done to deal with the deforestation, waste, and pollution generated by rapid industrial growth and mass population movements.

In the late 1990s the controversies created by these side effects of rapid economic growth in the NICs began to be pushed aside by a sudden and spreading economic collapse. Beginning in 1997 in Asia and spreading to Brazil in late 1998, many of the most important NICs have gone into deep recessions as foreign investors lost confidence in their economies and policy makers were unable to build coalitions to respond to the escalating economic problems. Policy makers in Brazil, for instance, faced a situation in which the Brazilian congress refused to accept the conditions negotiated by Brazil's president for a $41.5 billion loan from the International Monetary Fund. As a direct result of this domestic stalemate, in early January 1999 foreign investors began to withdraw huge amounts of money, and the value of Brazil's currency fell almost 20 percent in three days.[6]

That many people in other countries in Latin America, Africa, and Asia would not mind having the problems facing the NICs is a telling indication of the unattractive economic options available to large numbers of people in the world. Two quite different situations are common. In one, countries have products that foreigners want to buy, but almost all those goods are primary products and raw materials, such as jute, sisal, coffee, or bauxite. The problem is that the prices for primary products fluctuate wildly, creating boom and bust cycles that make it very hard to achieve steady, predictable economic growth. Even worse off are a large number of countries—such as Niger, Chad, Mozambique, Jordan, and North Korea—that have almost nothing the world wants to buy.

Increasingly, the great variety in the specific international and domestic situations confronting individuals in different countries is made even more complicated by growing controversies about religion and culture in world politics. As we discuss in the chapters that follow, modern world politics is very much a product of European political and economic expansion. The history of that expansion inescapably entangles questions of culture and religion with questions of economic and political power. Even when people want to achieve mutually agreeable outcomes, it is often hard to communicate effectively across different cultures. However, in other places the issue is not misunderstandings across cultures but fundamentally incompatible objectives. The revival of Islamic fundamentalism in North Africa, the Middle East, and parts of Asia spawned governments (most notably in Iran, the Sudan, and Afghanistan), violent opposition movements (in Algeria, Egypt, and Pakistan, among others), and terrorist networks (most notably, al-Qaeda) led by people determined to reduce the influence of Western culture, religion, and politics on their way of life.

It is precisely because international and domestic choices are so inextricably linked in world politics that these incompatible values are difficult to manage without coercion and violence. In Hobbes's time, Austria's drive for political and economic dominance in Central Europe combined with the struggle between Catholicism and Protestantism to produce the Thirty Years' War—also called the Wars of Religion. The Peace of Westphalia, which brought the Thirty Years' War to an end, was based on a formula in which the states in Central Europe would retain their independence and the people of those states would take the religion of their ruler. Of course, this arrangement gave the prince's subjects no say in the matter, but it did allow Europe's rulers to end the Wars of Religion by adopting a live-and-let-live policy regarding the religion of other states in the region.

Today, the daily confrontation of different cultures created by the information revolution, combined with the growing number of economic and political linkages that cut across state boundaries, makes it increasingly difficult to resolve basic differences in the values and objectives that frame people's ways of life simply by "agreeing to disagree." The prospects for achieving jointly acceptable peaceful outcomes become even more remote when the clash of civilizations becomes intertwined with regional security disputes—as is the case with the ways in which the al-Qaeda network has become connected with the Arab-Israeli dispute, the civil war in Afghanistan, and struggle over the future of Pakistan.

World politics is about people making hard choices that have real consequences. We have given you a short tour of the issues confronting people in different countries around the world. The next step is to introduce you to the cast of characters.

The Cast of Characters in World Politics

World politics is populated with a wide variety of actors. The most visible are states.

The Sovereign State

The **state** is a form of political organization that makes a claim to govern a specific piece of territory subject to no higher authority. That claim is known as **sovereignty** (or **sovereign territoriality**). The idea of sovereignty thus has both an internal (a domestic) face and an external (an interstate or foreign) face. The internal face of sovereignty asserts a claim to final legal authority within the state. The external face of sovereignty rejects the legitimacy of any external claim to an authority higher than the state. These twin claims to sovereign jurisdiction are *territorial* in the sense that they are both defined and limited by territorial boundaries.

The changing nature and role of the state is a central theme in the story of the evolution of world politics. The first significant agreement to recognize the sovereignty of states goes back hundreds of years to the Peace of Westphalia, which ended the Thirty Years War in 1648. However, for several centuries the state system remained largely a European form for organizing politics. Indeed, it wasn't until the period between the late 1940s and mid-1960s that most of Africa and Asia were reorganized into legally sovereign states. Today, everyone lives in some state or, in the few remaining cases of dependent territories, in places controlled by a state.

States have a legal and political status that makes them central international actors. States have the right to regulate by law anything occurring within their boundaries. Even though other international actors may at times get their way, legal control of territory gives states a form of leverage that can be highly useful in dealing with non-state actors. States also have a relationship with individual people that is distinct among international actors. A person who is a *citizen* of a state enjoys certain rights and privileges usually denied to non-citizens, such as voting in elections or owning land. States can also make claims on their citizens, such as tax and military-service obligations, that no other international actor can make. Under customary international law, only states can sign treaties and legitimately use physical force.

While clear in principle, the idea of sovereignty can get murky when applied to specific cases and historical periods. For instance, as we discuss in Chapter 6, the first claims to sovereign jurisdiction were made by *monarchs* who thought of

state A form of political organization that claims the exclusive right to govern a specific piece of territory.

sovereignty A legal and political principle that asserts a claim to final authority within the territorial boundaries of a state and denies the legitimacy of any higher authority outside the state.

themselves as individually sovereign. These rulers typically regarded the people who lived within their countries as their subjects and thought of the land and wealth of their countries as personal possessions. Several centuries later, norms about legitimate rule began to change. Sovereignty came to rest with the *people*—the citizens of a country. As a result, policy makers within the central government were increasingly expected to act as *representatives* (or agents) of those sovereign constituents, not as rulers of subjects. This shift in political values radically altered the nature of domestic politics; it also opened up a far wider range of variation in the ways in which the domestic face of sovereignty was intertwined with the interstate face. Those connections became even more complex when the growing demand that states represent people quickly became entangled with the question of whether those people needed to be part of *nations*.

States are not the same as *nations*, even though the two terms are often used interchangeably. A state is a *legal* entity defined by control over territory. As long as some permanent population lives within its boundaries, a state exists *de facto*, regardless of who those people are. A **nation,** by contrast, is a *social* entity—a group of people who have a *common identity* based on a belief that they have shared a past and should share a future. Sociologists call this a *we-they* feeling. *We* are distinct from other national groups, collectively designated as *they* (the others), and *we* should chart a destiny distinct from that of the others. The perceived or actual ties that create this group identity can be based on language, ethnicity, religion, or a sense of shared historical experiences.

When the members of a group share such an identity, the group is held together by a feeling of **nationalism.** National consciousness can be proclaimed by political elites and leaders, but to be politically effective it requires a mass base of support. Historians at times have asserted that this or that group constituted a nation when there was no evidence that ordinary people had that feeling. Only when enough people have asserted a national identity that can be used to mobilize large groups politically can a nation truly be said to exist.[7]

The fit between state and nation in world politics is often an uneasy one. Late nineteenth and early twentieth-century liberal thinkers, including President Woodrow Wilson, championed the idea of *national self-determination*, which held that self-proclaimed nations should have their own exclusive states. Some attempts were made to implement this principle in Europe after World War I, when the Ottoman (Turkish), Austrian, and Czarist Russian empires collapsed and some of the national groups that had been governed by imperial authorities were given their own states. Yet for several reasons, the principle of self-determination can only be taken so far. One reason is that many self-proclaimed nations are not large enough to be economically viable as states. For example, in Russia alone there are nearly one hundred national groups, at least 24 of them quite large.[8] Moreover, if every national group were to have its own independent state, the mutually exclusive claims over land and other assets would likely lead to intense, protracted conflict. India, which was created to be an officially secular home for Hindus in South Asia, comprises five major religions and ethnic groups that speak seventeen different languages. As a result, not every national group has its own state, and most states are not composed of a single nationality, even though that is the implication of the term *nation-state*. Of the 192 independent states in the international system in 1996, fewer than 10 percent are ethnically homogenous in the sense of having within them ethnic minorities that account for less than 5 percent of the population.[9]

nation   A group of people who share a common identity as a social entity.

nationalism   The feeling members of a group have when they perceive themselves as having a common identity based on a shared past and a commitment to a shared future.

Internal divisions among nationalities have led many political leaders to try to construct a common identity from scratch. Leaders find such an identity valuable, since it legitimizes the state's authority and promotes social integration.[10] But it can be hard to achieve. Not long after modern Italy was created in 1861 out of a wide variety of disparate states, an observer noted, "We have made Italy, now we must make Italians!"[11] The mismatch between state and nation is particularly dramatic in Africa. Colonial rulers in London, Paris, Brussels, and Lisbon drew boundaries in Africa for their own political and administrative purposes, without any reference to ethnic and tribal groupings. Few if any African states comprise one cohesive nation, with the result that African political leaders must often devote much of their attention to managing internal conflict.

Despite all these important reservations about the fit between the idea and the reality of the state, world politics is still built *around a state system*. Central governments of states continue to be key actors across an extraordinarily broad range of issue areas in world politics. States remain key actors in world politics for two inescapable reasons: first, leaders of states can make the claim that they are the legitimate voice for all citizens that live within their boundaries more effectively than any other actors in world politics; second, even though there is wide variation in the characteristics of individual states, as a group states are the largest and most widespread form of human organization that can both make and implement policy.

However, the central governments of states no longer monopolize high-stakes diplomacy in world politics. On economic, security, environmental, and human rights issues, diplomats representing governments' foreign, defense, and economics ministries, who used to dominate international bargaining, now routinely share the stage with other international players.

Non-State Actors in World Politics

Non-state actors play a key role in world politics and in our daily lives. One reason for this is that the number of intergovernmental organizations has increased dramatically, from 37 in 1900 to about 300 today. **International intergovernmental organizations (IGOs)** are formal international institutions that have states (and only states) as members. They are international because they include at least two sovereign states and regulate issues that cross state boundaries. They are formalized because they have some ongoing administrative structure, usually created by a treaty among the founding members. Although there are some IGOs, such as the North Atlantic Treaty Organization (NATO), that specialize in security questions, most deal with economic and social issues. The World Bank and the International Monetary Fund are two critically important economic IGOs. The World Health Organization (WHO) is an example of an important IGO that focuses on social issues.

While IGOs are *inter*-state actors, most of the other non-state actors are *trans*-state actors: private citizens living in different states who act together to achieve objectives that cut across the territories of two or more countries. Nongovernmental organizations and trans-state business enterprises are perhaps the two most important type of trans-state actors. **International non-governmental organizations (NGOs)** can be thought of as the private, non-state version of IGOs. Like IGOs, NGOs have distinctive substantive influence on issues concerning the environment, human rights, and economics. Examples would include Greenpeace, Amnesty International, and Global Trade Watch. Also like IGOs, NGOs claim that

international intergovernmental organizations (IGOs) Formal international institutions with an ongoing administrative structure that have states (and only states) as members.

international non-governmental organizations (NGOs) International organizations created by private individuals and groups.

they represent the preferences of their members as well as, at times, the interests of those non-members who are affected by policy choices in the substantive areas in which they specialize. The key difference is that unlike IGOs, NGOs are formal institutions made up of *private* individuals, or associations of such persons, from at least two states.*

Trans-state business enterprises (TSBEs) are firms with headquarters in one state and affiliates in at least one other state. You will often see these actors referred to as multinational corporations (MNCs) or transnational corporations (TNCs). We prefer the term *trans-state business enterprise* for two reasons. First, these actors must operate in a context set in large part by sovereign states because their activities cut across state boundaries. The "trans-state" designation highlights this point. Second, "business enterprise" is a more precise term than "corporation." As we shall discuss in Chapters 10 and 11, the actions of trans-state business enterprises—along with IGOs such as the International Monetary Fund—are at the heart of the controversies swirling around the globalization of the world economy.

The number and impact of international organizations, non-governmental organizations, trans-state business enterprises, and other non-state actors—such as environmental groups, human rights activists, religious organizations, terrorist networks, and international criminal organizations—have increased dramatically. However, since virtually everyone lives in a territory that is, at least in principle, legally controlled by a state, the effectiveness of non-state actors depends very much on their ability to make smart choices in a world that is still built around a state system. The relationship between state and non-state actors is, therefore, a central theme in our discussions of contemporary world politics.

The Plan of the Book

Facts and Patterns

We mentioned earlier that world politics is about people making hard choices that have real consequences. As this introduction to the cast of characters in world politics and the varying issues confronting people in different countries around the world suggests, individuals must make choices about a broad range of important issues in an extraordinarily wide variety of contexts. As a result, the "facts" of world politics are many and complex. To understand world politics, you will have to learn many of those facts: the distinguishing characteristics of particular historical periods, the substance of the issues, the nature of the actors, and the specific ways in which international and domestic politics are interconnected across different time periods, issues, and actors.

---

*Some international institutions mix public and private representation. The International Council of Scientific Unions and the International Telecommunications Satellite Consortium (INTELSTAT), to take two examples, include representatives from both governments and private organizations. But the IGO/NGO distinction remains useful since many international organizations are either completely private or public, and the two types have different kinds of constituencies. Amnesty International, for instance, is very cautious about accepting funds from any government, since doing so might appear to compromise its independence in identifying victims of human rights abuses.

trans-state business enterprises (TSBEs) Business firms with headquarters in one state and affiliates in at least one other state; also called multinational corporations (MNCs) or transnational corporations (TNCs).

But the facts of world politics—the issues, contexts, and actors—are only part of the story. The other part of the story is finding *patterns* in the facts. While there is an old expression that "the facts speak for themselves," that is misleading. Facts only have meaning when they fit—or don't fit—into larger patterns. Of course, facts sometimes *appear* "to speak for themselves." Facts appear to speak for themselves when people are so confident that they understand the significance of what they see that they don't bother to ask whether they are right or wrong. For centuries it was taken as obvious that the sun revolved around the earth. Standing on the earth and looking at the sun rise and set, how could the facts suggest anything else? Galileo's facts, which suggested quite the opposite, depended on a new way of thinking about the relationship between the sun and the planets, not on facts that spoke for themselves.

Political facts "speak for themselves" even less clearly than astronomical facts. People, after all, come in far more varieties than solar systems. People come in different cultures, genders, religions, and classes. People also have individual goals and perceptions of the world and how it works that they care about deeply. The sun and the earth don't care whether we understand which of them revolves around the other, but people do care about how they are understood by others and about whether their views of the world are right.

Because political facts don't speak for themselves, sooner or later you will need to decide *how* you are going to try to make sense of world politics. It will be an important decision because, when it comes to understanding the world around us, nobody naturally has 20-20 vision. We all must wear lenses to bring the world into focus, and what we see is a combination of what is "really" there and how our lenses are made. Choosing a different set of questions for analyzing world politics is like putting on a different pair of eyeglasses. It affects what you see. Consequently, being self-conscious about the choice of a lens for viewing the world is the price of learning to think for yourself.

Choosing a Lens

What lens should one use? We discuss two different routes to making sense of world politics in Chapters 2 and 3. One approach is to review the principal competing worldviews that have emerged from the struggle to make sense of world politics and then pick the one you find most persuasive. There is a lot to be said for this approach. Indeed, so many people make sense of the world around them by relying on these worldviews that they have become part of the fabric of political life. However, we are uncomfortable with asking students to choose among competing worldviews when they are just beginning their exploration of world politics. For that and a variety of other reasons that we will make clear as we go along, we believe it is better to introduce world politics by focusing on intellectual tools that can help you think about politics, no matter what substantive political issues you are interested in and no matter what your personal political values. In short, we're interested in providing a common ground for understanding world politics.

We believe that the broadest stretch of common ground available—the biggest and most versatile set of intellectual tools—can be found in the politics of strategic choice. All the worldviews discussed in Chapter 2 sooner or later get around to people making choices under conditions of strategic interdependence. Moreover, it is exactly because there is so much variety in what people care about and what they perceive that the easiest and most effective way to understand politics may be to focus on patterns in how people act *given* what they value and perceive.

Chapter 3 explains what it means to make a strategic choice and introduces a series of patterns in the politics of strategic choice. Political choices are driven by variations in the compatibility of people's goals, their notions about what is fair, and their relative power positions. Political choices are affected by how far people look into the future and their guesses about the consequences of different choices. Political choices are about trade-offs between trying to achieve an objective that is central to one part of a person's life as opposed to pursuing a goal basic to another. Political choices are about the risks people are willing to run—risks to their political position and risks to their policy aspirations—and whether they are willing to pay more to accomplish their goals sooner rather than later.

These variables *combine* in ways that are predictable. Because they do, there are a manageable number of enduring patterns in the politics of choice that you can recognize and use to understand world politics across different issues, actors, and time periods. Those patterns tell you not only what facts you need to know but also their political significance.

As these comments suggest, we believe you will be able to make far more sense of world politics when you learn to distinguish between what is *unique* to different strategic contexts and what is *common* to the process of politics across those different contexts. Much of what you read and see day-to-day about world politics is driven by the specific nature of the countries, political leaders, and issues involved and the specific ways in which international and domestic politics are interconnected. At the same time, the underlying *kinds* of reasons these events turn out the way they do are based on general principles about politics. Consequently, this text is organized around the theme of "unique contexts, enduring patterns."

Having made this case in Chapter 3, we complete Part I with a detailed overview of the key actors in world politics and a discussion of the role of interstate institutions, law, and norms. The idea of sovereign territoriality and the value and limitations of thinking of states as actors are covered in Chapter 4. In Chapter 5 we expand the discussion beyond state actors to take into account the choices of non-state actors and the effects of interstate institutions, laws, and norms. Chapter 5 also includes a comparison of the politics of strategic choice in state and non-state actors and explores their differing political assets, objectives, and responsibilities. The book then turns to the four central issue areas in world politics: military conflict and the quest for security, international political economy, human rights, and the environment.

The Importance of Context and Diversity

We begin our discussion of each topic historically, reviewing its evolution as an issue in world politics. We provide a fair amount of history on these issues for both educational and theoretical reasons. The first reason is that many contemporary issues are anchored in past events and how people perceive the historical record. Without knowing this background, you won't know whether certain issues matter at all, or to whom. Trying to understand contemporary world politics without a grounding in the history of the issues and the controversies they have generated is like trying to plan a game strategy with no knowledge of the history of the sport, the records of the opposing teams, or their personnel.

Second, history provides a database without which generalization is impossible. You need to know something about the history of world politics before you can see that there are patterns in the process of politics that transcend issues, place, and time. It is exactly because different historical periods, issues, cultures, and actors have unique dimensions that one has to look across them to see the patterns they share. Those shared patterns are highlighted in the "Enduring Patterns" boxes, which connect the patterns in the politics of strategic choice in the historical cases with issues facing the world today. A series of "World Politics and the Individual" boxes will, meanwhile, direct you to short cases on the text's website that emphasize unique examples of how particular individuals have affected, and been affected by, world politics.

Third, few students enroll in introductory world politics courses because they are interested in political science as an academic discipline. Most introductory students want to understand individual cases and issues long before they care about having an overall framework for understanding world politics. People usually develop an appreciation for the value of theory by seeing that their hunches about cause and effect cannot explain a series of cases or issues they care about. One of the best ways to gain that appreciation is to follow the story of people's efforts through time to understand the world around them.

Fourth, many of today's most widely held beliefs about cause and effect in world politics are based on inductively generated insights from particular historical periods; that is, people's understanding of specific historical cases and issues affects their larger outlooks about the world. We want to make this process of inference explicit, not only so that you can understand what has come before and evaluate the arguments of others, but also so you can evaluate what *you* think about cause and effect. The historical sections allow us to show that different ideas, theories, and intellectual traditions have typically emerged in response to particular combinations of problems and contexts. Once you see that people's perspectives about world politics are often rooted in issues that have arisen at specific times and places, you will be able to examine whether a particular perspective on the problem you are analyzing fits the case or cases to which you want to apply it.

Finally, approaching each issue in historical context makes it easier to stress two fundamental values: the value of theoretical generalization and the importance of understanding what is unique about different historical periods, issues, actors, and cultures. The initial sections show that there are key patterns in the process of politics that endure across time, actors, and issues. But they also show that you need to learn to look for the diversity in the human condition. You need to understand from the outset that what individuals and groups want to achieve is affected by their perception of their individual and collective historical experiences and that people vary in ways that matter: in their understanding of the central issues and actors in world politics, their beliefs about what is just, their time horizons, and their expectations about the future. In short, you need a theoretically informed sense of history to understand both what is unique and what is universal in the human condition.

As the historical sections in the discussion of each of these four issue areas show, contemporary world politics is built around a state system with European roots. That is not to say that Europe stands in a privileged position or that only states matter. To the contrary, world politics is no longer Eurocentric, state boundaries are far less meaningful than they were a century ago, and central governments must increasingly share international politics with non-governmental actors. But because the modern state emerged in Europe during the late Middle Ages and Renaissance, we begin our overview of the evolution of modern world politics there. Because the state system emerged in violence and evolved in response to military conflict, Part II (Chapters 6 to 8) begins our systematic discussion of the central issues in world politics with the quest for security.

The Four Issue Areas

Chapter 6 traces the connection between the quest for security and the evolution of the state system in Europe from the late Middle Ages to World War I. Chapter 7 takes a step back in time to pick up the story of European colonialism and the spread of the Eurocentric state system around the world. It then reviews the attempts to create state-based, global security systems from the end of World War I through the Cold War to the present. The distinctive security problems facing the world today are discussed in Chapter 8.

In Part III (Chapters 9 to 11) we turn to the second foundational issue in modern world politics: the politics of international economics. Political economy is central to an understanding of world politics. We talk about *political economy* rather than *economics* because functioning, real-world economic systems are based on political decisions about the structure, norms, and rules of "legitimate" economic activity.

Except during times of war or sustained security threats, the politics of international economics affects people's daily lives in far more obvious ways than security issues do. Domestic economic arrangements—and, hence, the economic opportunities individuals have—are shaped by the structure, norms, and rules of international economics. Moreover, variations in countries' relative economic capabilities have a profound effect on policy makers' ability to achieve a wide range of goals not only in economic policy but also in the areas of security, human rights, and the environment. It is, therefore, hardly surprising that international economics is a highly political activity not only in its origins and processes, but also in its effects.

The most enduring political issues in international economics involve questions about trade, the nature of the money that can be used for international transactions and as an international reserve asset (that is, for savings and investments), and the movement of capital across international boundaries. Depending on the time period and issue, the key actors in these issue areas include varying combinations of central governments, intergovernmental organizations (IGOs), and trans-state actors. Since our concern is with the political implications of these economic issues, we explore the underlying economic concepts only in the amount of detail necessary to understand how they become entangled in world politics and affect the linked international and domestic incentives that face policy factions.

Chapter 9 traces the politics of international economics from the mercantilist state-building of the 1500s, through the collapse of mercantilism and the rise of free trade in the 1800s, to the eve of World War I. This was a period of massive change, not only in policy makers' understanding of the sources of economic growth and in the international and domestic contexts for choice but also in the spread of Europe's political economy to the rest of the world. Chapter 10 takes the story from the end of the Eurocentric global economic system after World War I to the present. Chapter 11 analyzes the distinctive character of the politics of money, trade, and investment today.

Security and international economics are in many ways the foundational issues in world politics. They are not only fundamentally important; they also frame the ways in which other issues play out. Having reviewed them in Parts II and III, we are in a position to examine in Chapters 12 and 13 of Part IV the growing, but hotly contested, transnational obligations involving human rights and the environment.

Part V returns to the question first posed in Chapter 1: How might one make better sense of world politics today and tomorrow? Chapter 14 revisits the patterns in the politics of strategic choice discussed in Chapter 3 and shows how those patterns help explain the key cases discussed in Chapters 6 through 13. Given that there appear to be patterns in the politics of choice that endure not only across time but also across issue areas as different as military conflict, international economics, human rights, and the environment, we turn to a closer look at choice in Chapters 15 and 16. Faculty and students with a serious interest in strategic choice will, we believe, find the material in these two chapters to be of central importance. Others, however, may find it more useful to go directly from Chapters 14 to 17, which asks what the future might hold. We have written that concluding chapter so that it can be read on two different levels, either with or without the closer look at the nature of choice in Chapters 15 and 16.

This plan for the book reflects the ultimate educational goal of the text: to give you a set of intellectual tools for understanding world politics that you can apply on your own. That goal reflects our belief that the best test of textbooks and teachers is their ability to make themselves expendable by liberating people to think systematically on their own.

Key Terms

state
sovereignty (or sovereign territoriality)
nation
nationalism

international intergovernmental
  organizations (IGOs)
international non-governmental
  organizations (NGOs)

trans-state business enterprises
  (TSBEs)

To The Reader   QUESTIONS FOR REVIEW are available at
www.prenhall.com/lamborn

CHAPTER 2

Peace through Strength

Groups Make Ideas & Ideas Rule!

Individual Liberty = Peace and Prosperity

Competing Worldviews

Attempts to Answer the Central Questions

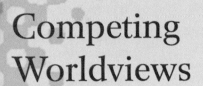

As we saw in Chapter 1, world politics affects people in many important ways. When you think about the number of high-stakes issues and the wide variety of historical and cultural contexts within which people have tried to understand those issues, it is not surprising that insights about world politics come packaged in very different intellectual traditions and worldviews. The two oldest are realism and liberalism. Realists emphasize the prevalence of conflict; liberals focus on finding ways to promote individual liberty and to identify and achieve common objectives. Dating almost as far back as the liberal tradition is the Marxist tradition, which analyzes class conflict and presents a normative critique of capitalism. In recent years, a number of new intellectual schools, such as feminism, have appeared alongside these older traditions.

A **worldview** is an intellectual tradition built on a distinctive set of ideas and arguments about political life. Each such tradition embodies a set of concerns—for example, security, wealth, liberty, or social justice. It also includes a body of causal reasoning about how the political world works, particularly in ways deemed relevant to explaining the identified concerns. Intellectual traditions tend to grow out of distinctive historical eras or cultural contexts as people ponder the ends and means of politics with a particular set of concerns in mind. Each tradition thus highlights certain types of issues, actors, goals, and types of relationships—typically those that defined the era in which the ideas originated and reflect the values of the advocates for these perspectives—while ignoring or deemphasizing others.

This chapter examines the major intellectual traditions that have emerged for analyzing world politics. It also explains the *"levels of analysis" problem*, which refers to a disagreement about whether world politics can be understood better by looking at characteristics of people, the nature and structure of social relationships, the norms and structure of the interstate political system, or a global level of analysis.

The Realist Tradition

Realism, as Robert Gilpin once observed, "is founded on a pessimism regarding moral progress and human possibilities."[1] From the realist perspective, incompatible goals and conflict are the defining features of world politics. Without enforceable international rules, decision makers have little choice but to compete with other states for security, status, and wealth. The competition is expected to be difficult, since the others are also likely to view their power resources and security positions in relative terms. According to Kenneth Waltz, realists thus expect "the necessities of policy [to] arise from the unregulated competition of states. . . . Calculation based on these necessities can discover the policies that will best serve a state's interests . . . [and] the ultimate test of policy . . . is defined as preserving and strengthening the state."[2]

The Pessimistic Assumptions of Realism

Realism—which has two major strands, classical realism and neorealism (also called structural realism)—is based on several fundamental assumptions. First, realists assume that politics is driven by the choices and actions of group actors that have competitive goals. As we shall see below, realists sometimes disagree about the

worldview A distinctive way of understanding political life that includes a set of central concerns that its advocates believe are defining aspects of political life as well as a set of cause-and-effect assumptions about how the political world works.

realism A worldview that assumes incompatible goals and conflict are the defining features of politics and therefore argues that actors must focus on relative gains, relative power, and security.

origin of those incompatible goals, even as they share the core assumption that incompatible goals, competition, and conflict are inescapable and defining features of world politics. The second core assumption that connects realist thinkers is the belief that politics takes place in an environment without a neutral authority that can enforce rules and decisions. The realist world is, therefore, a self-help world. As a direct consequence of these first two assumptions, realists are drawn to a third: actors must focus on relative gains, relative power positions, and security in order to compete effectively. In the case of states, this assumption leads to the conclusion that the leaders of states must put foreign policy considerations first; that they should try to achieve domestic goals only when doing so doesn't get in the way of achieving security objectives internationally.

The roots of realist thinking go back thousands of years. Thucydides' *History of the Peloponnesian War*, an account of the conflict between the ancient Greek city-states of Athens and Sparta, links those wars and their outcomes to arguments by the actors in which realist beliefs featured strongly. This led Thucydides to conclude that "what made war inevitable was the growth of Athenian power and the fear which this caused in Sparta."[3] Thucydides also attributed one of the most famous, and bleakest, observations in the Western intellectual tradition to an Athenian general besieging a far weaker force on the island of Melos: "For you know as well as we do that right, as the world goes, is in question only among equals in power, while the strong do what they will and the weak suffer what they must."[4] Less well known, but equally blunt, are the words of François de Callières, adviser to Louis XIV in 1713: "When a prince or state is powerful enough to dictate to his neighbors, the act of negotiation loses its value, for there is need for nothing but a mere statement of the prince's will."[5]

It is important to be aware that realist worldviews are not limited to Western thinkers. Realist assumptions about the nature of humans and the inevitability of

This painting by Goya, titled *The Shootings of May 3, 1808,* is one of the most visually powerful condemnations of war's violence against innocent civilians. It pictures a real event—the murder of Spanish civilians by Napoleon's army of occupation in Madrid. While the antiwar message is unmistakable, it simultaneously raises complex questions about how we should understand the world. On the one hand, it seems to suggest that the realists may be correct when they conclude, in the words of Thucydides, that "right, as the world goes, is in question only among equals in power, while the strong do what they will and the weak suffer what they must." But on the other hand, it's clear that Goya himself believed that this sort of violence was much more likely to happen when governments were unjust and tyrannical, an argument closely associated with liberalism and other nonrealist traditions.

conflict can be found in the writings of Chinese philosophers. And, several centuries before the birth of Christ, the Indian writer Kautilya counseled,

> Any power inferior to another should sue for peace; any power superior in might to another should launch into war; any power which fears no external attack and which has no strength to wage war should remain neutral; any power with high war-potential should indulge in invasion; any debilitated power should seek new alliances. . . .[6]

Classical Realism versus Neorealism: Two Different Sources of Conflict

All realists see conflict as prevalent in politics, particularly in world politics. But two quite distinct sources of conflict have been emphasized by different realist writers. **Classical realism** typically begins from a pessimistic notion of human nature. Self-interested, competitive, and power-hungry behavior is seen as rooted deeply in the human condition. To preserve himself, Hans Morgenthau argues, each person must, to some extent, act selfishly. Morgenthau believes that this tendency typically leads to conflict: "What the one wants for himself, the other already possesses or wants, too. Struggle and competition ensue. . . . Man cannot [therefore] hope to be good, but must be content with not being too evil."[7] In the same spirit, the Renaissance Florentine statesman and writer Niccolò Machiavelli argued that "how men live is so different from how they should live that a ruler who does not do what is generally done, but persists in doing what ought to be done, will undermine his power rather than maintain it."[8]

Out of these ideas has come an unsentimental approach to international strategy: prudent statesmen should avoid optimism about others' goals and should limit their objectives to those that they can sustain if things go badly. Thus Henry Kissinger cautioned Israeli and U.S. leaders to be wary of Syrian and Palestinian intentions in negotiating a Middle East peace settlement:

> It is likely that agreements will be reached . . . because the alternatives will, in the end, seem more dangerous. But when this happens, we must avoid euphoria. . . . An agreement will represent a strategic interlude for the Syrians and most of the Palestinians, not a commitment to a new world order.[9]

In short, classical realism sees competition and conflict as inevitable, with the roots of conflict in the nature of human beings. Human beings compete for scarce resources they value and desire power over their fellow people. Neither of these patterns can easily be overcome. Given these expectations about human behavior, classical realists often emphasize the importance of organizing individuals into groups that can protect their members through a focus on improving the group's relative power position over others.

A second strand of realist thinking, **neorealism** (also sometimes called **structural realism**), sees interstate conflict as rooted not in human nature, but in a specific characteristic of the interstate environment: the absence of legally binding rules. Neorealists argue that the absence of a neutral authority that can enforce rules and agreements creates an insecure, self-help situation in which all policy makers are pressured to act competitively, regardless of their individual natures or personal preferences.

classical realism A worldview based on the assumption that the principal sources of conflict in politics lie in human nature because people are self-interested, competitive, and power hungry.

neorealism (also called structural realism) A worldview based on the assumption that the anarchic nature of the interstate system is the principal source of conflict in world politics.

This detail from an engraving on the title page of the first edition of *Leviathan* (1651)—where each metallic piece in the king's coat of mail is rendered as an individual person—neatly symbolizes Hobbes's argument that the best way to prevent civil war is to unify all a country's people in the will of the sovereign ruler. While Hobbes proposed an absolute sovereign to enforce domestic peace, he saw no solution to the problem of war in interstate politics. His emphasis on the inability to prevent war because of the absence of a "common power" that can enforce agreements anticipates the neorealist focus on anarchy. However, Hobbes also believed that men had an innate drive for power. By combining this strand of classical realism with neorealism, Hobbes has, in effect, created a linkage politics interpretation of war: It is the nature of people interacting with the nature of the strategic environment.

This argument is not entirely new; it was a key theme in the work of seventeenth-century English thinker Thomas Hobbes. In his book *Leviathan*, written during the English Civil War, Hobbes contended that in a world without a common power that could guarantee security, people had a "right of nature" to use any means necessary to preserve themselves. But Hobbes also assumed that "all mankind . . . [has] a perpetual and restless desire of power after power that ceases only in death."[10]

The modern neorealist tradition drops the assumption that people desire power because of an innate inclination and focuses exclusively on the incentives created by the absence of a neutral authority that can enforce rules in interstate politics. Kenneth Waltz, for example, contends that the main cause of war must lie in some regularity at the level of the interstate system, rather than within particular leaders or states, since war has been waged for all sorts of specific reasons and by "good" as well as "bad" leaders.[11] That regularity, according to Waltz, is the *self-help* pressures created by anarchy. Without enforceable interstate rules, states must either resist possible domination by others through a policy of *balancing* against others' power capabilities, or by *bandwagoning*—joining a coalition that supports an aggressive state, in hopes of turning its aggression elsewhere. Waltz believes that large states have the capacity, and thus often the willingness, to resist the strength of others. The result, as he sees it, is a tendency for competitive policies among the major states regardless of their leaders' views or the nature of their domestic political systems.

Notice that the prediction contained in this argument does not differ from the one often made by classical realists. Based on their assumptions about people's natures, they also expect policy makers to act competitively. Where Waltz differs from many earlier realists is in the way he reaches his conclusion. The competitive pressure exerted on *all* national decision makers by the anarchic character of the interstate system, he contends, is the dominant influence on their behavior. Power-oriented strategies arise because political leaders need to compete for security, not because they desire power as an end in itself. Waltz sees states and leaders as more alike than different in this sense; all must adjust their strategies to the imperatives of self-help.[12] Where states differ is not in that objective but in the strategy for achieving it that their power positions make possible.

Realism has been an influential way to analyze world politics for hundreds of years, and it is easy to see why. Much of history has been laden with conflict. When states' goals conflict, one can expect leaders to pay close attention to their relative power positions. As you will see in Chapters 6 and 7, the classical realist worldview appealed to many statesmen during the period that states were evolving in Western Europe—an era rife with conflict, as medieval forms of rule broke down and rulers asserted new claims to authority against feudal lords or the Pope. It jumped to the United States when the experiences of World War II were followed by the onset of the Cold War. Neorealism later emerged when the bipolarity of the Cold War drew analysts' attention to the effects of the structure of the interstate system.

However, while realism has important insights to offer about some sets of circumstances in world politics, its value is limited when its distinctive assumptions about the nature of actors' objectives and political life don't fit as well. What happens to the value of realism, for instance, when actors value building legitimate relationships or when there is little conflict because they have compatible goals? What happens to the value of neorealism when policy makers' calculations are affected more by domestic considerations than by interstate security concerns? These limitations of the realist worldview are highlighted by liberalism, which is, in many ways, its mirror opposite.

The Liberal Tradition

Unlike realists, liberals are optimists about the human condition and the possibilities for cooperation. Instead of viewing world politics as a "jungle"—a metaphor commonly used by realists—liberals see it as a cultivatable "garden" in which peace as well as war can grow.[13] For liberals, the building block of politics is the individual acting alone or, more typically, as part of voluntary groups. The more liberty individuals have to pursue their goals within and across societies, the more harmonious and peaceful political life will be. Liberals view much of realist thinking as a self-fulfilling prophecy: If one expects competition and acts accordingly, others will tend to respond in kind. Liberals' main concern is to understand the conditions under which this cycle can be broken. As Michael Doyle points out, they expect this to happen when "the good of individuals has moral weight against the good of the state or nation."[14]

The Optimistic Assumptions of Liberalism

Traditional **liberalism** is based on the following fundamental assumptions: First, people writing in this tradition assume that actors' goals can be compatible and, consequently, that joint gains are possible. We can all get better off together. Second, they assume that people will act cooperatively as long as the environment makes it possible to succeed through cooperation. For liberals, the anarchic character of the interstate system does not imply that policy makers face an unchanging situation of international conflict. The prospect of economic, technological, and cultural benefits may give policy makers reasons to cooperate with other states. But the positive effects on politics that flow from these two assumptions are undercut by a third: that the existence of compatible goals and the possibilities for joint gains through cooperation are frequently blocked by misperception, a lack of understanding, and political structures that create false antagonisms. In particular, liberals worry that a lack of individual liberty within countries may block the opportunities for cooperation and productive exchange within and among states. Given these views, the liberal tradition emphasizes the importance of (1) making the world more transparent and thereby minimizing the likelihood of misperception, so the compatibility of actors' goals can be revealed; (2) eliminating institutions and norms that restrict individual liberty and promote false antagonisms; and (3) focusing on absolute, as opposed to relative, gains so we can all become better off together.

This liberal worldview has been shaped by many writers interested in democracy, peace, and individual prosperity. Liberals believe that the actions of states reflect internal bargaining among politically active groups. It follows from this, according to liberals, that states cannot focus on international problems and ignore domestic politics. Even in dictatorships, foreign policy significantly reflects domestic incentives. Based on this reasoning, liberals expect state behavior abroad to reflect the way citizens' rights are treated domestically. Consequently, the freer a state is internally, the likelier it is to be influenced by other like-minded societies. Also, liberals believe that the importance of military coercion in world politics has declined over time. As democracy, economic and social ties among societies, and international institutions have developed, liberals believe that force has become a *relatively* less effective tool of international statecraft. This does not imply a complete end to war, but it does suggest that a distinct "zone of peace" can develop among internally liberal, interconnected societies.

The Ebbs and Flows in the Popularity of Liberalism

Like realism, the persuasiveness of liberal arguments has varied with the circumstances that thinkers and statesmen faced over the centuries during which this tradition developed. Beginning in the seventeenth century, one group of thinkers conceived of liberty in terms of a small, unobtrusive government. This variant was introduced by Englishman John Locke and was later supported by the French philosopher Voltaire and early American thinkers such as Thomas Paine. For them, as for Adam Smith, David Ricardo, and Jeremy Bentham, who focused (during the eighteenth and nineteenth centuries) on the benefits to the individual and society from unrestricted international commerce, the goal was to give individuals as much freedom as possible, consistent with public safety and order. Among other things, this broad objective meant that individuals should be able to exchange goods and services freely across state boundaries. Living in eighteenth-century Prussia—a more

liberalism Traditionally, a worldview that emphasizes finding ways to promote individual liberty and to identify and achieve common objectives that create joint gains.

repressive political atmosphere than England or America at that time—Immanuel Kant contributed to liberalism the argument that war stemmed from authoritarian regimes, since governments based on popular consent were less likely to take actions that ordinary citizens would find costly in human lives and money.

Variants on these themes have been picked up and elaborated since the end of the nineteenth century. President Woodrow Wilson believed that German militarism in the decades before World War I reflected the authoritarian political patterns in that society. Only a world of democracies, he claimed, would ultimately be peaceful. In the meantime, he argued that an international organization devoted to keeping the peace—the League of Nations—could check the impulse to wage war by pledging to resist aggression before it could succeed. As the twentieth century wore on, various thinkers and statesmen championed the idea that international organizations, by taking some decision-making authority away from independent states, could ease the rivalries often associated with international self-help. Greater world peace *and* prosperity were expected to follow. This reasoning laid the foundation for creating the United Nations and many other contemporary international organizations, such as the World Bank, the World Health Organization, and the Food and Agriculture Organization.

Liberalism has thus come to signify at least the *possibility* of progress toward a more prosperous, freer, and safer world. In the words of Stanley Hoffmann, such hopes rest on "the possibility of devising institutions based on consent . . . [institutions] that will make society more humane and just, and the citizens' lot better."[15] Clearly, these are ambitious expectations. In part for that reason, liberal thinkers have tended to focus on distinct pieces of the overall process by which they believe that liberty and cooperation can be achieved. Let us examine more closely three of these strands of liberal thinking.[16]

The Emphasis on Free Trade

One important set of liberal arguments has focused on the benefits of free trade. Not only does trade make the actors directly involved better off; entire societies benefit too, since goods and services that cannot be efficiently produced at home can be obtained abroad. At times, various liberal writers have argued that international trade brings other advantages as well. In 1913 Norman Angell said,

> Even where territory is not formally annexed, the conqueror is unable to take the wealth of a conquered territory, owing to the delicate interdependence of the financial world (an outcome of our credit and banking systems), which makes the financial and industrial security of the victor dependent upon the financial and industrial security in all considerable civilized sectors; so that widespread confiscation or destruction of trade and commerce in a conquered territory would react disastrously upon the conqueror.[17]

Coming as it did on the eve of World War I, Angell's argument has since been attacked as naive. Today, analysts would be less likely to assume that leaders will always prefer the expected gains from trade to the expected gains from war. Still, free trade may at times foster the effects Angell anticipated. For example, the deep economic ties among the Western states since World War II have probably helped to prevent any remote possibility of war among the United States, Europe, and Japan.

Liberals also claim that trade can foster the development of democracy. Trade opens societies to new people-to-people connections and rewards innovative domestic groups, both of which erode the power of authoritarian leaders and increase the influence of those committed to an open society. Finally, liberals often argue that economic exchange fosters joint decision making and predictability among governments. When societies become economically connected, each has to take the likely behavior of others into account to achieve its own goals. As one liberal scholar put it, "The growing interdependence of the world economy creates pressures for common policies, and hence for procedures whereby countries discuss and coordinate actions that hitherto were regarded as being of domestic concern exclusively."[18]

The Emphasis on Democracy and Peace

A second strand in liberal thinking sees democratic states as more reluctant to go to war than non-democracies. Kant began this line of argument in 1795 with the publication of his *Perpetual Peace:*

> Now the republican constitution, besides the impeccability of its origin in having sprung from the pure source of the concept of right, has also the desired consequence in prospect, namely the eternal peace, for this reason: If assent of the citizens is required (as cannot be otherwise in this constitution) to resolve on "whether there shall be war or not," nothing is more natural than that they will much deliberate to start such an ill game, since they would have to bring down on themselves all the calamities of war. . . .[19]

Much effort over the last few decades has gone into testing Kant's hypothesis. Most of the evidence suggests that Kant was correct when it comes to wars *among* democracies, which seem to be far less common than would be expected among any types of states chosen at random.[20] Two explanations have been offered for this pattern. One, suggested by Kant himself in the passage above, is that political leaders in democracies cannot get popular support for war or fear the consequences for their hold on office if they choose war. A second explanation is that democratic governments respect others of the same kind as expressing the popular will in their societies, and thus deal with those societies in a non-coercive manner.[21] It is also possible that these two processes reinforce each other: *because* democratic governments can only choose policies that the people will support, other democracies see those states as belonging to a like-minded, rule-governed community. That bond is strong enough, from this point of view, to rule out the use of force.

The Emphasis on International Institutions

A third strand in liberal thinking views international organizations such as the Council of Europe, the World Bank, and the Arab League as helpful in achieving common purposes among states. Some thinkers who take this position contend that for such organizations to exist at all, the member states must already share important values. Once such organizations are created, they foster even deeper cooperation down the road.[22] Another version of this argument sees international organizations as limited tools through which governments can act together to deal with certain specific problems. They do this mainly by spreading information about members' behavior—particularly their behavior in carrying out agreed commitments. Armed with that kind of information, the members can use the organization to put pressure on states that violate the agreements, making it more likely that agreed objectives will be achieved.[23]

Karl Marx was one of the most influential thinkers of the nineteenth and twentieth centuries. Aroused by the injustices of nineteenth-century industrialization, Marx began his long writing career with scathing critiques of capitalism. Over the following decades he turned toward more analytical—and often ponderously intricate—theoretical treatises on the relationships between economic systems, class exploitation, and revolution.

Marxism   A worldview that uses an economic and historical analysis of the evolution of class conflict called *dialectical materialism* to identify the origins of revolution, peace, and justice.

Not surprisingly, the contributions and limitations of liberalism mirror those of realism. Liberals have analyzed important reasons for international cooperation and many of its implications. Having found reasons to open their societies to others, political leaders can "appreciate that the existence of other liberal states constitutes no threat and instead constitutes an opportunity for mutually beneficial trade and (when needed) alliance against non-liberal states."[24] But just as the value of realism is limited by the assumption that conflict and competition are the defining or essential issues of political life, the value of liberalism is limited by its inability to offer meaningful guidance for dealing with situations in which actors' objectives are not compatible. In those situations, actors' relative power positions *do* matter. Like realism, liberalism helps us interpret certain cases—those in which actors' goals fit its assumptions.

The Marxist Tradition and Critical Theory

As we explain in Chapter 9, Marxism became a highly influential way to analyze politics and society during the nineteenth and early twentieth centuries. Karl Marx (who wrote some of his work and publicized much of it with the help of Friedrich Engels, the radical son of a textile manufacturer) argued that political conflict stems from antagonistic relationships among socioeconomic *classes*—groups whose members share important economic, political, and perhaps cultural features. During the mid-nineteenth century, when Marx did his writing, *industrial capitalism*—an economic system in which the means of production and exchange are privately controlled—began to replace agriculture, with its often communal economic arrangements, as the dominant way of organizing the economy in much of Europe and North America. In historical terms, Marx saw this development as progressive. Industrial capitalism took power away from landed elites, who relied on inherited aristocratic privileges to maintain their positions, and fostered technological changes of long-term benefit to society. But while it was historically progressive, Marx argued that capitalism also impoverished and alienated workers. Fortunately, from Marx's perspective, capitalism carried the seeds of its own destruction at the hands of the working class and would be replaced by a classless, and just, communist society.[25]

A Different Set of Assumptions about What Is Important and How We Should Understand It

Karl Marx believed both that capitalism was evil and that it was a historically inevitable stage on the way toward a communist revolution that would produce a just, classless society. Traditional **Marxism** makes three basic assumptions: First, people's position in society is determined by the way in which they are connected to patterns of economic activity. In every society, the divisions between classes (peasants, landowners, merchants, and so on) are determined by what is produced, how it is produced, and how goods and services are exchanged. Second, everything else in society, including ideas, laws, and religion, reflects the economic structure. In other words, the foundation of society is seen as *materialist*; social life is run and transformed not by any independent set of ideas, but rather through the technological and socioeconomic forces at work in a given period. Marx emphasized that even the most creative ideas are ultimately products of the material environment in which they arise. This view led him to argue that industrial societies would necessarily generate far different notions of legitimate government, law, and social order than fishing or farming communities.[26] Third, Marxists see the world as evolving through a dialectical process. A *dialectic* is a process of development (and reasoning) in which progress occurs through stages. At each stage there is an ordered development of a *thesis* (a prevailing idea or set of relationships), an *antithesis* (the opposite of the prevailing system), and a *synthesis* (a new and superior thesis that resolves the previous contradictions between thesis and antithesis). Just as traditional agricultural-based economic systems were challenged by those based on skilled crafts and then industry, so capitalism would confront its own internal contradictions and be replaced by a new—and final—synthesis, communism.

In sum, Marxism argues that history moves through a process of dialectical materialism. **Dialectical materialism** assumes (1) that people's position in society—including not only their income but also their ideas and their ability to develop fully as human beings—is determined by the ways in which they are connected to patterns of economic production; (2) that a society's dominant ideas, laws, and institutions are all determined by its economic structure; and (3) that the world evolves through a predetermined sequence of thesis, antithesis, and synthesis.

Marx believed that these processes were at work in the development of nineteenth-century capitalism. Because he anticipated that the rate of profit would fall over time in developed economies, Marx expected factory owners, bankers, and other capitalists to continually increase the scale of their enterprises to survive. In doing this, Marx argued, weaker capitalists would be driven out of business and periodic depressions would occur when factories churned out more goods than the underpaid workers could purchase. At some point, the workers' frustrations would boil over and capitalism would be overthrown.

Marx did not spend much time analyzing the nature of the utopian society that would replace capitalism or any specific scenario by which revolution would occur. The presence of any detailed guidance on a revolutionary strategy probably seemed unnecessary to him. Capital was becoming concentrated in fewer hands and the working class was growing rapidly. It seemed logical to Marx that the remaining capitalists would eventually be reduced to such a small number that revolution would be all but inevitable.

Even though revolutionary political action would often be confined to specific states for tactical reasons, traditional Marxists saw the ultimate objective as worldwide revolution. To achieve that goal, they tried to understand how the stages of historical progress unfold and how societies relate to one another depending on their respective developmental stages.[27]

Lenin Shifts the Focus to Imperialism

In the early twentieth century, followers of Marx concluded that the historical progression of different means of production would require a close look at a topic Marx largely ignored—imperialism. Although Russian revolutionary V.I. Lenin is best known as the founder of the Bolshevik party and the first leader of the Soviet Union, he played a central role in shifting the focus of the Marxist tradition to the relationship between capitalism and imperialism (see the discussion of Lenin in Chapter 9).

Lenin's pamphlet *Imperialism: The Highest Stage of Capitalism* was written in Switzerland, where he was living in exile, in 1916. In this essay, he drew on the writings of several people: John Hobson, a British liberal economist (see Chapter 9);

dialectical materialism
Marx's theory that changes in people's relationships to the means of production drive the evolution of economic systems, the political systems that develop in response to those changes in the structure of the economy, and the ways in which people conceptualize the world around them.

Rudolf Hilferding, an Austrian socialist thinker; and Rosa Luxemburg, a Polish revolutionary thinker and activist. They had noticed two tendencies in the political economy of Europe beginning in the mid-nineteenth century. One was a resurgence in *imperialism*—the control by more powerful states over less developed areas. Another was the advent of *finance capital*. As modern corporations replaced family-owned firms, the capital needed by large businesses came increasingly from financial institutions such as banks and holding companies. Just as banks try to control the means of production domestically to maintain high and stable prices, they do the same with investments abroad.[28]

While these thinkers disagreed on whether imperialism was inevitable under modern capitalism, Lenin synthesized their work into an argument that made precisely that point, asserting that industrial firms and financial institutions needed to expand abroad. Industry needed guaranteed supplies of raw materials at stable prices to operate efficiently; banks needed profitable investment outlets. At first on their own, then acting through their governments, banks and industrial firms solved their problems by dominating and exploiting large areas of Asia, Africa, and South America.[29]

According to Lenin, imperialism would have two consequences. Workers in the underdeveloped areas would become a new target of opportunity for exploitation by

Ideas can have powerful political effects when they appear to explain important aspects of people's life experiences. Lenin's 1916 attack on imperialism resonated not only because of what it said about the exploitation of the working class in industrial societies, but also because of what it appeared to explain about European colonialism. Moreover, audiences in both the colonies and in Europe were primed and waiting for an interpretation of the causes of imperialism by the increasingly widespread awareness of atrocities committed in the name of profit. These two pictures were widely circulated in Europe about ten years before the publication of Lenin's book as part of a press campaign against King Leopold's control of the Congo. They purported to show the methods used by King Leopold's agents to force Africans to increase production on rubber plantations. In the picture at the left, a worker is whipped for not meeting the quota demanded. In the picture at the right, a father stares at the hand and foot of his daughter, cut off by sentries to punish him for violating company policy.

capitalists in developed nations. Until those workers took political control in their countries from the capitalists, their nations could expect to remain poor. And as the governments in the developed states—which, by this reasoning, were controlled by capitalists—realized that their firms needed new areas to exploit, conflict among those states for acquisitions abroad would follow.

Late Twentieth-Century Perspectives Sympathetic to the Marxist Tradition

The Dependency Perspective   In recent decades, analysts building on the Marxist tradition have gone in two notable directions. One, the **dependency perspective,** tries to explain the continued poverty in much of the Third World (see Chapter 10). Why is it, these analysts have asked, that despite impressive growth in the world economy as a whole, vast sectors of the population in these societies remain poor while the distribution of income has become even more unequal? Their answer is that despite attaining legal independence from their colonizers, these areas are still tied economically to the capitalist economies. As Theotonio dos Santos put it, "by dependence we mean a situation in which the economy of certain countries is conditioned by the development and expansion of another economy to which the former is subjected."[30] Many poor states rely on the wealthy ones for technology, financing, export markets, and basic imports. Because the most productive economic sectors in these societies tend to be controlled by business firms headquartered in the industrialized countries, there is little opportunity for independent economic development. Whatever benefits these firms bring in the form of technology or investment capital, more wealth tends to be taken out than created on a self-sustaining basis. Politically, the poor countries cannot break out of this bind, since local political elites typically depend for their support on domestic factions that are tied economically to the exploiters.[31]

Critical Theory   **Critical theory** is another influential set of ideas that builds on the Marxist intellectual tradition. Critical theory grew out of the work of a group of intellectuals in Frankfurt, Germany, beginning in the 1920s. This group rejected the assumption that the world can be understood objectively, arguing that the analysts' ideas and values are always embedded in their political and social observations: "Theory is always *for* someone and *for* some purpose."[32] Given this perspective, critical theorists analyze existing political and economic relationships with an eye toward determining who benefits from them at whose expense. In Robert Cox's words, critical theory

> stands apart from the prevailing order of the world and asks how that order came about. Critical theory, unlike problem-solving theory, does not take institutions and social and power relations for granted but calls them into question by concerning itself with their origins and how and whether they might be in the process of changing.[33]

As this quotation suggests, critical theorists ultimately want to change the world, not just to understand it. They seek to open dialogue with those who have been marginalized by existing arrangements and construct new kinds of communities that break down existing barriers.

dependency perspective An interpretation of economic development that views capitalism as responsible for keeping the countries of the Third World poor by forcing them to specialize in producing commodities and other primary products for export while importing expensive industrial and high-technology goods from rich countries.

critical theory A research approach that advocates using an understanding of the interrelationships among values, ideas, observation, and the structure of society to change the world in ways that will help the poor and politically weak.

As you might imagine, arguments in these traditions have been very controversial. On the one hand, the Marxist and critical theory traditions provide ethical lenses through which important issues can be examined. For example, one might ponder the legitimacy of a world economy in which 1.2 billion people (about one out of every six) lived in dire poverty in 1998. This was the same number (although a somewhat smaller percentage) as in 1990. During those eight years, global spending on assistance to poor countries dropped from $60 billion to $55 billion a year,[34] even though many developed countries, particularly the United States, enjoyed significant economic growth.

On the other hand, the Marxist and critical theory traditions can be critiqued on analytic grounds. Marx's major predictions—that capitalism would succumb to a worldwide revolution, and that the middle classes would drastically shrink over time—have missed the mark. Equally off target was Lenin's assertion that World War I was but the first of an inevitable series of wars of imperialist redivision. Dependency writers have largely avoided these kinds of sweeping predictions. But this perspective has been troubled by questions about whether an intellectual tradition that usually assumes that poverty and underdevelopment reflect exploitation from the outside should also take domestic influences into account. Some analysts in this tradition acknowledge that poverty typically reflects both a country's internal problems (such as a lack of marketable natural resources or a limited population on which an internal market for industrial goods can be built) as well as the way in which outsiders exploit those weaknesses. Many others assume that only the external dependencies really matter; however, that conclusion has been widely critiqued as simplistic.[35] Critical theorists also often seem to want to have it both ways: saying that theories of cause and effect in politics must be evaluated from the perspective of a particular set of values and objectives, at the same time as they appear to assert that their own interpretations about how the "prevailing order of the world . . . came about" should be exempt from the criticism that their conclusions are biased by their values.

Between 1 and 3 million Cambodians perished in Pol Pot's "Killing Fields" between 1975 and 1978, part of the Khmer Rouge's campaign to liquidate people the revolutionary group believed to be "class enemies."

Finally, critics of the Marxist tradition emphasize the injustices created in its name. Self-proclaimed Marxist governments have been responsible for tremendous cruelty and repression. Millions of people starved to death as a result of the famine deliberately created by Soviet leader Josef Stalin in the early 1930s. The famine was designed to weaken resistance to Stalin's dictatorship and to pave the way for the forced abolition of private agriculture. Millions of people spent time—often decades—in Soviet and other communist-run political prisons. In the communist People's Republic of China, Mao Zhedong's government similarly engineered a famine that killed millions as part of an effort to collectivize agriculture. And in Cambodia, a radical Marxist government that took power in the 1970s exterminated virtually everyone who might have been an opponent of the regime. The Cambodian nightmare was later portrayed in an extraordinarily powerful film, *The Killing Fields*.

Social Identity Traditions

Social identity traditions examine how people are shaped by the groups to which they belong. Social identity approaches focus on the group-based origins of people's values, preferences, perceptions of the world around them, and self-images.

All of us, of course, also have distinct identities as individuals. Our values and beliefs grow in part out of distinctive characteristics that are *not* shared with others. They are formed from the personalities, goals, and beliefs that make each person different from others. One of the authors of this book won't move to a better seat at a sports event than the one he paid for even when it is clear that the seat will otherwise remain unoccupied, while the other is much less scrupulous about doing that. In neither case do these values have a social basis; they seem to reflect our distinctive personalities. Yet some part of an individual's values and beliefs typically grows out of the social environment. People's identities, beliefs, and values often vary with the ethnic, national, religious, and cultural groups to which they belong.

Social constructivism is an academic perspective that believes an emphasis on how people's identities, goals, and ideas are "constructed" by their group affiliations is one of the best available ways to improve our understanding of the social, economic, and political world.

The Assumptions of Social Constructivism

From a constructivist standpoint, shared ideas provide the glue in social groups, promoting communication and creating a sense of group identity. Moreover, constructivists believe that actors create social reality in a more active way than realist, liberal, or Marxist analysts expect. While realists, liberals, and Marxists have very different views of the world, people in all three traditions are willing to make assertions about the objectively "true" nature of world politics and actors' goals. By contrast, constructivists see social life as much more open-ended, depending on how actors' beliefs and expectations about themselves and others evolve. As Alexander Wendt argues, shared understandings about the world shape the way in which action (either cooperation or conflict) is organized.[36]

Constructivist interpretations share three assumptions.[37] First, people's identities, ideas, and goals are "constructed" in large measure by their group affiliations. "Ideas" in this broad sense include *causal beliefs* about the world (for example, defenses against ballistic missiles will produce military stability, or will threaten stability) and

social identity traditions
Research approaches that assume individuals' self-images, values, preferences, and perceptions are principally determined by the characteristics of the groups to which they belong.

social constructivism
An approach that focuses on how people's identities, ideas, and goals are affected by their participation in social groups during particular historical periods and how their socially constructed understandings and perceptions in turn shape the ways in which political cooperation and conflict are organized.

principled beliefs (land mines should be banned because they kill innocent civilians). Constructivists argue that actors' identities—"who they are" in policy and political terms—evolve out of their participation in particular, socially defined relationships and institutions (for example, the belief that all Arabs belong to the same "nation," whatever state they live in). In Alexander Wendt's words,

> The commitment to and the salience of particular identities vary, but each identity is an inherently social definition of the actor grounded in the theories which actors collectively hold about themselves and one another, and which constitute the structure of the social world. Identities are the basis of interests. Actors do not have a "portfolio" of interests that they carry around independent of social context; instead, they define their interests in the process of defining situations.[38]

The second and third assumptions that guide constructivist interpretations reinforce this essential premise. The second emphasizes that group affiliations—and the meaning and importance of their shared ideas—reflect particular sets of historical circumstances. This assumption suggests that the way people define norms and view the world can change significantly over time, leading to the possibility that different values and goals will evolve. For instance, the notion that all states are independent of any higher legal authority had a somewhat different meaning in 1900 than it does today. A century ago, it was common for large states to bully or claim spheres of influence in places where the local authorities were too weak to resist. Today, while forcible coercion certainly still occurs in world politics, there is more of a tendency for states to be treated as legal equals. The second assumption then leads to the third, that these socially constructed understandings about the world shape the ways in which cooperation and conflict are organized. For example, it is not the distribution of weapons outside one's borders that causes insecurity as much as one's perception of the people who possess the weapons. U.S. officials welcome weapons in the hands of British leaders but fear weapons in Iranian or North Korean hands.

From this perspective, one can see why so many young men in contemporary Pakistan and Afghanistan are drawn to the beliefs of militant Islam. These boys are typically dirt poor; the *madrassahs* (Islamic religious schools) take better care of them materially and offer them more fellowship than they find anywhere else. In these schools, they are taught the need for a permanent *jihad*, or struggle with nonbelievers. Outside of these institutions, the young men continue to be devout Muslims, as their relatives and neighbors are. Inside, in the presence of teachers who passionately believe in the most militant form of Islam found in the contemporary world, they tend to emerge with a distinctively uncompromising Islamic identity.[39]

This interpretation, you might be thinking, amounts to saying that "no man is an island" (unless he chooses to live as a hermit). That is a good shorthand way to characterize the social constructivist worldview. From this perspective, to understand any behavior involving two or more people, we cannot look *just* at the experiences and thinking of the individuals involved, nor *just* at the types of groups or institutions in which they are operating. We must instead examine the social practices and rules that structure their activities and give them meaning. This line of thinking grows out of an extensive literature in social theory.[40] Just as there is no game of chess without a shared understanding and acceptance of the rules of chess, there would be no working system of states unless national policy makers understood that their legal authority stops where another country's borders begin. Likewise, unless officials understand and practice at least strict reciprocity toward others (I will do unto you as you have done unto me), diplomatic behavior would be difficult to interpret, and even the most basic diplomatic relationships would be difficult to sustain. Social life, in other words, is made up of the social rules, practices, and identities that people accept and that allow them to interpret what others are doing.

Key Questions Raised by Social Constructivism

Unlike the realist and liberal traditions, which had informed observers and practitioners for centuries, constructivism has gained influence only in the last few decades. The reason seems to be a sense that realist, liberal, and Marxist explanations *assumed* the true nature of actors' interests and incentives without asking how *the actors themselves* understood what they were doing, and why. Once these kinds of questions were put on the table, others followed. If shared understandings of the social world matter in what people see and want to achieve, how and when do those ideas and norms change? (We know they have changed; colonialism and slavery were perfectly permissible internationally one and two centuries ago, but now neither is considered acceptable.) Do actors ever actually *persuade* others to accept new norms and practices, or do the old ones change mainly when they are too costly in money or other material factors? Do important social bonds form across national boundaries, or do shared identities exist mainly within states?[41]

Constructivists have succeeded in raising important questions and providing some intriguing answers. The key question is where actors' values and preferences come from. As Martha Finnemore aptly put it, "states may not always know what they want or how to use their resources."[42] We saw earlier that realists, liberals and Marxists provide partial—but only partial—answers to this question. For Finnemore and other constructivists,

> State interests are defined in the context of internationally held norms and understandings about what is good and appropriate. . . . The normative context also changes over time, and as internationally held norms and values change, they create coordinated shifts in state interests and behavior across the system.[43]

Finnemore no doubt is partly right. It is hard to explain the recent resurgence of interest in internationally guaranteed human rights, or vigorous efforts to ban antipersonnel land mines, or the evolution of a shared European identity without invoking group-based ideas and beliefs. The key insight of constructivism is that "norms and understandings about what is good and appropriate" can help actors *tell them* what they want and even who they are.[44]

What the social identity tradition, and constructivism in particular, has not yet done is explain *how* actors get to their values and preferences, and from them to making choices. Simply saying that political actors are embedded in societal relationships is not enough; interaction and learning in groups can move individuals in varying directions, leading to different kinds of preferences or varying degrees of attachment to them. Even if we assume that shared norms can influence the choices people make, we need to understand how these processes work. Doing this is especially important when actors face other (perhaps competing) incentives *besides* shared norms or identities. So far, constructivists have succeeded in emphasizing the important point that choices are seldom made in a social vacuum. But unless we have some way to interpret the varying influence of norms across issues, actors, and situations—and how actors become attached to norms in the first place—we will miss key pieces of politics.[45]

The Feminist Tradition

Social identity is also a central concern in contemporary feminist thinking. In most cultures, women have traditionally been seen as societies' and families' nurturers, while men were seen as heads of families, breadwinners, and public authority figures. A sense of shared feminist identity is recent by historical standards and has by no means spread uniformly across the globe. Yet it has become an increasingly visible characteristic of Western thinking in recent decades, and there are signs that concerns about women's place in society and politics have begun to be felt in the Third World as well. Feminists believe that while women's traditional roles have always been valuable, those roles have been severely and unjustly limited by a male-dominated culture. Feminists want to make observers aware of the ways in which their understandings of the world have been narrowed by male-oriented cultures. They also believe that a more fully feminist understanding of world politics will in turn lay the groundwork for more just social, political, and economic arrangements.

The Role of Gender in Identity and Politics

The **feminist tradition** has many intellectual strands and draws on a wide range of assumptions about the social and political importance of gender.[46] But several ideas seem widely shared. In Ann Tickner's words,

> Since women have generally been outsiders, excluded from historical processes that have framed contemporary political and economic life, as well as from the development of knowledge that has interpreted these processes, most contemporary feminist approaches take identity as a starting point for their theoretical constructions. Conscious of the exclusion of women, feminists have been particularly concerned with the question of who are the collective "we" about whom the historical understanding of the world has been constructed.[47]

In other words, women have been ignored in mainstream thinking about world politics. Sometimes analysts have simply assumed that women are not important actors; other times they have assumed that men and women are involved in world politics in the same ways, in which case there is no need to make analytical distinctions based on gender.[48]

Feminist scholarship has critically examined both of these long-standing assumptions. What Christine Sylvester calls "everyday forms of feminist theorizing" involves locating what women have done as actors in world politics, even if it has not typically involved participation in high-level foreign-policy decisions.[49] For example, in the early 1980s female peace activists in Britain and the United States took the lead by chaining themselves to fences at military bases, dancing on missile silos, and otherwise drawing attention to what they saw as ill-advised military policies.[50] In Brazil, as Cynthia Enloe reported, many women during the 1970s and 1980s concluded that their country's anticommunist military government encouraged or at least tolerated domestic violence against women.[51] Sylvester admits that many observers may dismiss these sorts of stories as, at most, peripheral to the core concerns of world politics. Yet from a feminist perspective, these stories are important because they illustrate important sources of support and opposition to war, militarization, and exploitation.[52]

Many feminists also argue that men and women participate in, and are affected by, world politics in very different ways. The reason, they believe, is that men are far likelier than women to view themselves as independent, unconnected actors. Sylvester

feminist tradition A worldview and research approach that focuses on the origins and effects of socially constructed gender identities and roles; feminist interpretations argue that a more fully feminist understanding of world politics will lay the groundwork for more just social, political, and economic arrangements.

NATO's 1981 decision to deploy cruise missiles on U.S. Air Force bombers stationed at the Greenham Common airbase in Britain led to sustained protests by peace activists, including a feminist group that established the Greenham Common Women's Peace Camp.

and Sandra Harding argue that women typically see politics as being far more embedded in human relationships than do men, who characteristically understand politics as a series of interactions among individual, isolated actors. In Sylvester's view, men and women learn "different lessons on autonomy and obligation." Women learn a "relational autonomy," while "men learn to abstract 'individual will . . . out of the context of the social relationships within which it develops and within which it is exercised.'"[53] As Harding observes,

> Men are thought to conceptualize the self as autonomous, individualistic, self-interested, fundamentally isolated from other people and from nature, and threatened by those others unless the others are dominated by the self. . . . [To] women are attributed the concept of the self as dependent on others, as defined through relationships to others, as perceiving self-interest to lie in the welfare of the relational complex.[54]

There may be biological, in addition to cultural, reasons for this behavior. Even if one sets aside the impact of culturally defined roles in child rearing, the fact that it is women who bear children is an obvious potential biological source of different attitudes toward the importance of interpersonal relationships. Physiological studies have also shown that males and females react differently to stress: Men usually either confront such situations aggressively or flee—a pattern known as "fight or flight"—while women typically deal with danger by nurturing others and seeking their support. These differences reflect different hormonal reactions in men or women, patterns that may have developed through evolution as a way for females of various species to protect their offspring from predators.[55]

Insights about the biological and cultural origins of gender differences raise intriguing possibilities. Moreover, regardless of whether the sources of gender differences are biologically or socially constructed, the predicted patterns would have similar effects on politics. Finally, feminists raise still other important questions. They encourage us to examine world politics from the vantage points of those who lack an effective voice, wealth, or military resources.[56] They also suggest that while men might have an edge in political situations that call for relative strength or an ability to control others, women might be better in situations that call for cooperative outcomes and the resolution of conflicts.[57]

As we consider these ideas, it is important not to lose sight of still another possibility. The variations we see in people's tendency to cooperate rather than act competitively may result not from inherent group characteristics—either culturally or biologically induced—but from the nature of the situations in which actors find themselves. It may be that people behave in more nurturing ways when they are used to being in situations in which it is reasonable to assume that the other key actors have similar norms and compatible long-term objectives.

As this overview of the major intellectual traditions suggests, people use very different lenses to bring the world into focus. While each of these frameworks views the world in a coherent way, having multiple lenses on the world fragments our understanding of the world and makes it very hard to carry on productive conversations that can promote shared understandings of politics. We suggest a way to reduce these difficulties in Chapter 3, but before we do that, it is important to be aware of a second set of fault lines that make it hard to reach shared understandings—those involving different levels of analysis.

Understanding World Politics through Different Levels of Analysis

In any field of inquiry, observations can be made of the individual parts of a whole (such as trees in a forest) or of the whole formed by the aggregation of the parts (in this case, the forest), or the relationship between that whole and the larger world (the forest in its ecosystem). One can imagine "parts," "wholes," and "the system" created by the larger environment as arranged on a vertical scale, with many stopping points at varying levels of complexity. In world politics, the part, the whole, and the system would typically refer to the individual, the state (or other group actor), and the interstate system. Where one stops on this scale to observe and ask questions depends on the nature of the question and the kind of explanation one prefers. At each of these levels distinct actors and processes can be observed. The **levels of analysis** problem refers to a debate about whether world politics can best be understood by focusing on the characteristics of people (the individual level), states, the interstate system, or global economic, political, and ecological systems.

These distinctions have helped observers sort out and interpret the complex set of actors and processes that make up world politics. We need to be open to the possibility that we will find the causes and outcomes necessary to explain world politics operating at the level of the individual, the state or other group actor, or the international system. Levels-of-analysis distinctions give us a tool to organize our observations and interpretations. Let us briefly consider the factors that might influence behavior at each level.

The Individual Level

What impact do individual leaders have on politics and policy? To answer that question, consider this one: Why do particular individuals have distinct priorities and, at

levels of analysis
Different points on a scale of social or natural aggregation at which behavior can be observed and assessed.

times, make highly distinctive choices? If you examine your own behavior—for example, deciding whom to date or which university to attend—you would probably conclude that it reflects a mix of what makes you distinct as a person and the incentives you face in your personal, financial, or educational environments. When analysts consider the impact of the individual level of analysis in world politics, they examine those attributes of individual policy makers that distinguish them from others, such as their personalities, their beliefs about politics, or their images of certain other situations and actors. These factors may be distinctive enough to incline individuals to act differently from others, even in similar circumstances. Presidents Jimmy Carter and Ronald Reagan, for example, approached arms-control bargaining with Soviet leaders quite differently at the same point in the evolution of the Cold War. Particular individuals, then, *may* be distinctive enough to produce behavior that might not otherwise be expected.

The State (or Other Group Actor) Level

Of interest here is the impact that groups of individuals within collective actors can have on decision makers' incentives. That impact is felt not only in states. For example, when the heads of international institutions or terrorist groups make choices, their incentives may be significantly affected by key constituencies within their organizations. But because foreign policy is made only in states, and foreign policy has long been the chief interest of world-politics analysts, this level of analysis is often referred to as the *state level*.

Many specific factors can shape policy makers' incentives at this level: the kind of factions that form and their relative strength; differences in constitutional structure, such as that between presidential and parliamentary systems within democracies; the number, kind, and decision-making autonomy of bureaucratic organizations below the level of top political leaders; and the degree of pluralism inside the political unit (not just whether the state is a democracy, but the degree to which the press is free to probe state secrets, traditions of citizen activism, and so on). These variables are assumed to shape leaders' political and policy objectives (what they want to achieve in the first place) or leaders' ability to achieve whatever preferences leaders have formed for other reasons.

The Interstate Level

Here observers examine the distinctive character and effects of organizing world politics in a state system. Two distinctive features of interstate politics are emphasized: the norm of sovereign territoriality (which we explained briefly in Chapter 1 and discuss more extensively in Chapters 4 and 6) and the anarchic structure of the state system. Some see the norms that support the state system as operating independently of its anarchic structure; others see either the structure or the norms as the primary causal factor. However, whatever view is taken on this point, there is virtual unanimity among those that emphasize the interstate level of analysis that the norm of sovereign territoriality and the anarchic structure of the interstate system reinforce each other.

Analysts who stress the importance of the interstate level tend to focus on one or more of the following variables: the distribution of military capabilities among states; the distribution of wealth among states; and the nature of the economic, political, and military ties that connect states in more or less interdependent groupings. While analysts differ on which variables should be emphasized, they share a commitment to understanding world politics by looking for the effects of the characteristics of the interstate system. In doing so, they are making the assumption that the nature of the interstate system affects international outcomes in ways that overwhelm the effects of domestic political factors and the characteristics of the leaders involved.

Approaches that stress the effects of the interstate level of analysis usually talk about **international politics** rather than **interstate politics.** That usage is understandable because international and interstate have been used as synonyms for well over a century. However, while this usage is understandable, it's unfortunate. It's unfortunate because using the term international obscures the fundamental argument: that the interstate system affects the nature of world politics in fundamental ways. It's also unfortunate because, as we discuss below, international politics is probably the best term available to describe a level of analysis that takes into account the trans-state actions of both state and non-state actors. Since interstate so precisely describes the substantive points made by analysts who emphasize this level of analysis, we think the least confusing option is to use the term *interstate* whenever we are discussing approaches that stress the effects of the state system and *international* whenever we are including the trans-state actions of both state and non-state actors.

The Global Level

The growing interest in understanding world politics by examining a global level of analysis reflects two major trends: the increasing importance of environmental issues and the declining centrality of the state system in human affairs. The impact of environmental issues is easy to see. If major environmental issues arise out of the interrelationships between human activity and regional and global ecosystems, then the interstate system is as much a subpart of the global system as domestic politics is a part of interstate politics. State policy makers and their constituents must decide how they will react to the effects of the ecosystem; they cannot remain unaffected by them. Therefore, even though the global environmental system is subject to change over time as a result of both natural processes and human actions, in the short run it is even more a contextual "given" than the state system.

This reason for adding the global level to the list of levels of analysis is reinforced by another: the declining meaningfulness of state boundaries and the growing involvement of non-governmental actors in **trans-state politics.** It is not just environmental processes that cross state boundaries with little regard for the decisions of governments; increasingly it is also the flow of information, economic activity, and people that blur the distinctiveness of separate states and the societies within them. We no longer see international security as simply a product of what national governments do; non-state actors and trans-state terrorist networks operate in the crevices between different national jurisdictions, and many of them succeed—at least in the short run. And as we shall see in our discussion of the politics of international economic issues, debates about the impact of economic globalization partly reflect differences about how important state boundaries are, or should be, in regulating trade and especially financial flows.

As you might have guessed, different intellectual traditions make different assumptions as to which of these levels is most important. For example, neorealist Kenneth Waltz makes a case for emphasizing the interstate system, and particularly its lack of enforceable rules, as the factor most responsible for persistent rivalry and

international politics
Trans-border actions of state and non-state actors.

interstate politics   The interactions of states.

trans-state politics   The actions of non-governmental actors that have effects that cut across state boundaries.

war.[58] Classical realists, on the other hand, would begin with assumptions about the nature of human beings—that they are competitive and desire power. Marxists would examine the ownership of the means of production inside societies to interpret the relationships that develop between them. From this perspective, any focus on the motives of individual policy makers or international-level factors would simply cloud the real factors at work. Liberals would similarly look inside societies, though they would focus on a very different set of variables—the degree of economic and political liberty citizens are afforded. Environmentalists and those interested in the development of a global civil society naturally often incline toward an emphasis on the *global level.*

Given the intellectual origins of these perspectives, it is easy to see why they are drawn toward different levels of analysis. However, we believe it is more profitable to look at how phenomena are *linked* across different arenas. We argue in favor of examining linkage politics, rather than placing the focus on any one level, for two reasons. First, looking at all levels makes it easier to include the important insights of all the traditions we have reviewed. Second, we think linkage politics is how the world works. World politics inherently involves connections across levels; the leaders of both state and non-state actors have preferences and make choices that reflect a varying mix of individual, internal, international, and global reasons. Of course, at times factors at one of these levels will weigh significantly more heavily than those at the other levels.[59] But rarely are variables at any one level at such extreme states—either high or low—that they either dominate those in the other arenas or drop out altogether in importance. We therefore suggest an analytic approach based on the assumption of regular, systematic cross-arena connections.

Although we stress linkage politics throughout this book, we think it is important to make a small but significant change in the way in which the levels are presented to simplify the approach and to more effectively describe world politics. We think it is important to pay close attention to the ways in which state and non-state actors are interrelated. Because we do, we don't find it useful to restrict the third level to interstate politics. The effects of the interstate system are important, but they are best understood in relationship to the growth of non-state actors and the sorts of transstate networks that are emphasized by analysts interested in the possible emergence of a global civil society. Consequently, we suggest reconstituting the third level to include non-state actors and networks. Having made that choice, we call it the *international* arena. The international arena includes the interstate system, but they are not synonyms for each other. With non-state actors and trans-state networks in this broader international arena, the analytical value of adding a global political arena drops out. Global environmental processes are still there, of course, but the effects of global environmental considerations on world politics can be traced without adding a fourth level of analysis.

Conclusion

For centuries people have used different worldviews—and, more recently, different levels of analysis—to try to make sense of the world around them. Exactly because that is the case, widely held worldviews become part of the fabric of political life. Consequently, everyone who seeks to understand world politics begins a personal journey toward understanding in the context of whatever competing perspectives are popular at the time. This chapter has given you an overview of today's competitors.

Advocates of each perspective would, quite naturally, prefer that you see the world through their eyes. The question is what to make of the choices before you.

Ultimately you will need to answer this question for yourself. That is both the opportunity and the burden of independent thought. As you work your way toward a choice, we would suggest you consider the following points. First, all these competing perspectives have something of value to say about the world. Indeed, when you pause to think about it, it isn't very likely that a perspective that has captured the support of a lot of people over a long period of time would have *nothing* of value to say.

The problem with the competing-perspectives approach to understanding world politics is not that these perspectives aren't valuable. The problem is that they are useful only when a very specific and restricted set of conditions are met. Embedded within each worldview are assumptions about the facts (the nature of the actors and contexts in world politics), assumptions about what substantive issues are important, and assumptions about what the analyst should value either as a prudent decision maker or as a caring, moral human being. When you choose a worldview, you choose the distinctive package of assumptions that comes with it.

That being the case, we're inclined to look for alternative ways to try to make sense of world politics. We discuss the most intriguing possibility we can see—the search for common substantive and conceptual ground—in the next chapter.

Key Terms

worldview
realism
classical realism
neorealism or structural realism
liberalism
Marxism

dialectical materialism
dependency perspective
critical theory
social identity
social constructivism
feminist tradition

levels of analysis
international politics
interstate politics
trans-state politics

To The Reader   A CHAPTER SUMMARY and QUESTIONS FOR REVIEW are available at **www.prenhall.com/lamborn**

Searching for Common Ground
The Politics of Strategic Choice

We started Chapter 1 with the assertion that world politics affects *whether* and *how* people live. We concluded Chapter 1 with the promise that the ultimate educational goal of the text was to give you a set of intellectual tools for understanding world politics that you could apply on your own. One way to help people think independently is to introduce them to different worldviews and then urge them to pick the one that makes the most sense to them. Faced with that choice, you could either pick just one worldview—the one that makes the most sense to you overall—or use different frameworks on a case-by-case basis to analyze the issue before you.

This *competing-perspectives approach* is one of the oldest and most widely shared ways to make sense of world politics. The popularity of this approach is understandable. The major intellectual traditions have generated many insights, the debates among them are part of the fabric of political life, and evaluating their strengths and weaknesses is educationally valuable, providing the motivating energy behind many lively classroom discussions and interesting point-counterpoint books of readings.

While their centrality in the fabric of contemporary political life makes it essential that you understand these competing perspectives, we are not comfortable asking you to choose among them during your first course on world politics. Instead, we have decided to introduce world politics by searching for common ground. By searching for common ground, we mean looking for intellectual tools that can help you think about politics, no matter what substantive issues you are interested in and no matter what your personal political values are. We believe that the broadest stretch of common ground available—the biggest and most versatile set of intellectual tools—can be found in the politics of choice. All the worldviews discussed in Chapter 2, and all the substantive issues in world politics that are discussed throughout the book, sooner or later get around to people making hard choices that have real consequences.

Hard Choices with Real Consequences

Political choices are, by their very nature, choices under conditions of **strategic interdependence.** Saying that politics involves choice under conditions of strategic interdependence simply means that political outcomes depend on the goals, perceptions, and relative power of at least two actors. Put differently, people in interdependent relationships are simultaneously responsible—but only *partly* responsible—for the outcomes.

While politics involves choice under conditions of strategic interdependence, people vary a great deal in how they make choices. Not everyone sees the world around them in strategic terms. **Strategic choice** occurs only when people, believing that their ability to achieve their goals is constrained by the preferences and choices of others, evaluate the attractiveness of their options based not only on what they would prefer, but also on what they expect others to do. When those choices become part of a sequence in which two or more actors continue to evaluate their options based on what they expect the others to do, it creates a process of **strategic interaction.**

strategic interdependence A situation in which the outcomes generated by each individual's choices and actions depend on the choices and actions of the others.

strategic choice Choices made when people both believe that their ability to achieve their goals depends on the choices of other actors and evaluate the relative attractiveness of their options based on what they prefer and what they expect others to do.

strategic interaction A situation in which actors are involved in a sequence of interdependent strategic choices.

We discuss some of the reasons why people might or might not make choices strategically—and why they might make strategic choices more or less effectively—later in this chapter when we discuss perception and misperception. You will also find a far more extensive discussion in Chapter 15. At present, however, it's enough to recognize that the interconnectedness of people's lives means that politics is about trying to achieve interdependent outcomes—about making choices under conditions of strategic interdependence.

Strategic interdependencies in politics have, however, a very special character. Politics is not only about trying to achieve your goals given the norms and structure of the strategic situation in which you find yourself; it's also about whether those norms and structure are just. The connection between politics and questions about what is just is as old as the written record. In the fourth century B.C., Aristotle wrote, "man is by nature an animal intended to live in a . . . . [political association because] he alone possesses a perception of good and evil, of the just and the unjust."[1] The implication, as one modern scholar explains, is clear: "Within political settings, judgments of justice or injustice are distinct from judgments of personal policy preference and personal gain and loss."[2]

In sum, at its most basic level, politics is about people trying to achieve interdependent outcomes within a relationship *and* about perceptions of whether the relationship itself is just. Because the political choices people make depend heavily on their preferences, power, and perceptions, it's important to make sure that you are comfortable with exactly what those terms mean.

Key Concepts: Preferences, Power, and Perception

Preferences   People are political animals because they have *preferences* for particular outcomes, preferences anchored in their goals, values, and perceptions. Those preferences can be negative or highly general, as is the case when people fear vague or imagined threats to their security, status, or position. Those preferences can be determined largely by how people were socialized during childhood or by their unique genetic and biological makeup. The origins of a particular individual's preferences are, in short, as varied as the human condition. It is also the case that people vary greatly in how self-consciously they evaluate their preferences, how hard they work to identify different options for achieving their goals, and how carefully they examine the likely consequences of the different options they see. But even with all these reservations, it is hard to imagine politics without varying preferences about outcomes. Those preferences give politics a purposive, goal-oriented character.

Preferences, as we use the term, refer not to abstract "wants," but to the relative attractiveness of specific alternatives that may conflict with one another and thus require trade-offs among valued outcomes (which, in some cases, may not be easily reduced to the same dimension of value). The idea of preferences is, therefore, inherently comparative. It makes no sense to say that you prefer an outcome except in comparison to some other possible outcome. You would probably like to have a lot of money, be secure, and have the leisure to do whatever you want whenever the spirit moved you. Preferences come into the picture when you have to make trade-offs. Increasing your security might cost a lot of money or require that you take a lower-paying job in a safer neighborhood. You might also have to settle for earning less money in exchange for having more free time. It is such choices among different outcomes that reveal people's preferences.

preferences   A set of alternatives that an actor has ordered from most to least attractive.

It is important to distinguish between people's preferences for particular ends and their judgments about the means (the methods or instruments) by which those ends could be achieved. Strategic situations are defined by people's **preferences over outcomes** (ends). The strategic situation facing actors is heavily influenced—but not, as we discuss in this chapter, fully determined—by the compatibility of their preferences over outcomes. Given a set of preferences over ends, the next question concerns **preferences over policies**—the choice of the methods by which those ends can best be achieved. When people's preferences over outcomes change, the strategic situation changes. It was the shift in the Soviet Union's preferences over outcomes under Gorbachev that created a new strategic relationship with the United States and made possible the policies that led to the end of the Cold War. It was the remarkable continuity in preferences over outcomes during the several decades prior to Gorbachev that created a pervading sense of sameness and stalemate in U.S.-Soviet diplomacy, even as the specific policies (or methods) by which those ends might be achieved changed across different decision makers and over time.

The distinction between preferences over outcomes and preferences over different policies for achieving those outcomes makes it easier to recognize still another way in which the nature of actors' preferences affects political situations. Politics often involves building coalitions that bridge the preferences of different political factions. A **faction** is a group of actors who have identical preferences over *both* outcomes and policies. For purposes of predicting choice, factions can be treated as if they were individual people. A **coalition** is a group of two or more factions that have different ends but choose to come together temporarily because they happen to agree on a specific set of short-term policies. It is the compatibility of factions' preferences over policies that makes it possible for coalitions to form. Thus, while British and Soviet policy makers' preferences over ends could hardly have been more different during World War II, the shared policy goal of defeating Adolf Hitler brought them together in a wartime coalition. Britain's prime minister, Winston Churchill, drove this point home in a famous line defending his decision to ally with Soviet dictator Joseph Stalin: "If Hitler were to invade Hell, I would at least make a favorable reference to the Devil in the House of Commons."

However, while the existence of some shared objectives can bring factions together into a coalition, coalitions often need to give some of their members payoffs, called **side-payments.** When these side-payments involve policy concessions, coalitions can have difficulty making a series of internally consistent choices. The bargains that are struck on one policy choice may lean closer to one faction's long-term preferences, while the bargains struck on another lean toward another's. For example, the Carter administration (1977–1981) had a notoriously difficult time making internally consistent foreign policy choices—and sustaining the choices it did make long enough for them to work—because President Carter's principal foreign policy advisers led factions with different worldviews and policy preferences.

Power   **Power** refers to actors' ability to increase the probability that their preferred outcomes will occur. This definition of power is consistent with intuitive notions of both political and non-political forms of power. Non-political forms of power involve the ability of single actors to achieve independent, as opposed to interdependent, outcomes. For instance, people are sometimes described as "powerful"

preferences over outcomes   The relative attractiveness of different ends, as opposed to the methods by which those ends might be achieved.

preferences over policies   The relative attractiveness of the different means (or instruments) by which a specific end (or goal) can be achieved.

faction   A group of actors who have identical preferences over both outcomes and policies.

coalition   A group of two or more factions (or individuals) with different preferences over outcomes (ends) but compatible preferences on a specific set of policies that they agree to cooperate with each other to achieve.

side-payments   Concessions (or payoffs) given to members of coalitions to entice or reward cooperation.

power   Actors' ability to increase the probability that their preferred outcomes will occur.

The Carter administration (1977–1981) had a notoriously difficult time making internally consistent foreign policy choices and sustaining the choices it did make long enough for them to have a chance to work. One of the reasons why the administration seemed so inconsistent can be traced to the problems President Carter had in building coalitions within his own administration. Those problems can, in turn, be traced to the fact that his principal foreign policy advisers—Secretary of State Cyrus Vance, National Security Adviser Zbigniew Brzezinski (both shown with Carter, at left), and Andrew Young, U. S. Representative to the United Nations (with Carter, at right)—led factions with different worldviews and policy preferences.

swimmers because they can swim quickly, or "powerful" intellects because they can easily figure out complex problems. Similarly, the United States was said to be a technological "power" when it was able to put people on the moon. But none of these examples involves forms of power in the specific sense we are stressing here. *Political* forms of power describe actors' ability to increase the probability that preferred outcomes will occur in an *interdependent* setting, a setting in which the outcomes involve a process of strategic interaction.

Thus, political power is always *embedded within relationships*; it is not an attribute of individual actors. On this point, our language works against us. We are used to talking about actors *being* powerful, as if power were an individual trait. For example, since the collapse of the Soviet Union, the United States has been widely described as the world's only "superpower." Other states, meanwhile, are described as either major or minor powers. Usually these characterizations are based on the size of a country's economic or military resources—that is, its **capabilities**. But while an actor's power is usually affected by the relative size of his or her capabilities, capabilities and power are *not* synonymous. Indeed, an actor with very few capabilities can, if the situation is right, be placed in a quite powerful position.

Moreover, the stress on capabilities in discussions of power raises an even more important issue: capabilities to do what? The United States has the biggest economy on earth, but policy makers in Saudi Arabia probably have more influence over oil prices than officials in Washington. Similarly, while the United States has more military capabilities than any other country, it is not able to use those capabilities to equal effect everywhere in the world. Moreover, there are many policy areas where the size of an actors' economic or military capabilities is only very indirectly related to its ability to achieve preferred outcomes. The Irish Republic is small and weak in

capabilities The size of an actor's economic or military resources.

both economic and military capabilities, but it is highly influential in the bargaining over the fate of the British provinces in Northern Ireland.

These observations lead to another crucial point about power. The sources of power *vary*. They vary with the substance of the issues and preferred outcomes, the nature of the actors involved, and the context. People may be able to significantly improve the probability of achieving preferred outcomes in one issue area but not in another. Within the same issue area, a person may have more influence with one set of actors than with another. Even if the issues and actors are held constant, the context within which political interaction takes place can dramatically alter relative power positions, as when U.S. policy makers bargain with governments in international organizations where the votes are weighted by the size of a country's contribution (such as the International Monetary Fund and World Bank) versus organizations that operate on a one-nation, one-vote basis (such as the General Assembly of the United Nations).

For all these reasons, political power is always *relative* power—relative to a particular set of actors and outcomes. It is meaningful to talk about an actor's relative power position within a relationship. It is *not* meaningful to conceptualize political power as an individual attribute or possession that exists outside of a relationship.

Perception and Misperception   We mentioned earlier in the chapter that people may not always recognize when their choices are taking place under conditions of strategic interdependence and that, even when they are trying to act strategically, they may have trouble evaluating the strategic situation. Consequently, it is important to distinguish between an actor's **operational environment**—the setting in which a choice is actually taking place*—and an actor's **psychological environment**—the actor's mental image of the world around him.[3]

Several concepts are central to understanding how people's psychological environments function. **Perception** is the process of noticing and evaluating incoming information. A piece of information must be noticed to be evaluated, as opposed to being ignored amidst a mass of other data. Only then can its meaning and validity be assessed. Mistakes can occur when people fail to notice something that is present, think they see something that is not present, or draw an incorrect inference from a piece of data that is accurately noticed. Any such error can be called a **misperception** (a mistaken perception).

We discuss the origins of actors' perceptions and misperceptions more fully in Chapter 15. Here we will simply make the following key points. Perceptions reflect people's images of other actors, their beliefs about how politics works, the way in which their desires or fears shape those images and beliefs, and the guidelines they use to draw conclusions from limited or ambiguous data. The last of these points requires some elaboration. Information is costly to obtain and often hard to absorb and evaluate. The human mind can evaluate only a few pieces of information or courses of action at any one time. Ironically, too much data can impair one's ability

operational environment
The setting in which an actor's choice is actually taking place.

psychological environment   Actors' mental image of the world around them, sometimes quite different from their operational environment.

perception   The process of noticing and evaluating incoming information.

misperception   Error caused by the failure to notice something that is present or by an incorrect inference about something that is accurately noticed.

---

*As we explain later in this chapter—and discuss more fully in Chapters 15 and 16—any description of the "real" strategic situation necessarily involves making judgments. Those judgments require a more or less explicit theory of strategic incentives. However, while no one can *prove* what the *true* strategic situation is, the distinction between the operational and psychological environment remains a very useful one.

Calvin Contemplates the Meaning and Sources of Power   The problems Calvin discovers when he bases his claim to omnipotence on a pile of 200 snowballs reflect many of the theoretical points we have made about the nature of political power. Power describes actors' ability to increase the probability that their preferred outcomes will occur. Political forms of power are necessarily relational; they take place within strategically interdependent settings in which the outcomes depend, at least partially, on the choices and actions of other people. For all these reasons, the sources of power vary with people's goals, the nature of the other actors involved, and the strategic context. In this panel, Calvin starts out assuming that one set of capabilities (a pile of snowballs) can be used as a source of power across all the issues and actors he cares about. It doesn't take Calvin long to discover that it doesn't work that way. His boast soon seems empty even to him, because he stands alone, apart from any strategically interdependent relationship. People who believe the United States should always get its way because it is the world's only superpower (in the sense that it has the greatest economic and military capabilities) often make the same conceptual mistakes as Calvin without learning as quickly that it doesn't work that way.

to make decisions at least as much as too little. For example, during the Cold War Soviet negotiators knew that U.S. officials at times faced major domestic constraints in dealing with Moscow, but Soviet officials had so much data about the U.S. political climate that it was often of little use to them.[4]

An error that is the result of an actor's cognitive limits is called an **unmotivated or cold misperception.** An error that stems from an individual's emotions or the desire to make the world fit preconceived notions is called a **motivated or hot misperception.** Motivated misperceptions grow out of people's hopes and fears rather than an intellectual need for simplifying ideas, images, and heuristics. When people make a mistake in noticing or evaluating information because they want to avoid the emotional discomfort of an accurate assessment, a *hot error* has occurred. "Hawks" may discredit credible evidence of cooperation from adversaries on arms-control issues because they don't expect it (an example of a *cold error*). But they may also refuse to take such evidence seriously because it conflicts with policies with which they strongly identify (an instance of a *hot error*). "Doves" may similarly ignore or dismiss credible evidence that others are acting aggressively because they don't expect it *or* because it challenges policies they favor. Hot errors can thus produce many of the same results as cold ones, though for different reasons.

In conclusion, it's crucial to remember that actors' choices are driven by their perceptions. Indeed, actors' perceptions affect every key factor in the politics of strategic choice. Given the centrality of perception to politics, you should keep three

unmotivated (cold) misperception   An error created by cognitive (mental) limits on an individual's ability to process information.

motivated (hot) misperception   An error created by an individual's emotions or the desire to make the world fit preconceived notions.

points in mind. First, people's limited cognitive capabilities mean they need short-cuts in order to function effectively. As a result, what people "see" typically reflects their expectations and may also reflect their emotional needs. Second, images and beliefs are "sticky"; they usually change only under the pressure of undeniable contradictory evidence. People's preferred outcomes and policy options, then, often reflect durable mental and emotional "frames." Third, and related to this, in trying to explain what actors *choose*, whether and how much they *mis*perceive the situation is irrelevant. All that matters is how *they* have seen the situation. On the other hand, to explain the *consequences* of their choices—the outcomes of strategic interaction—the kind and degree of *mis*perception can be critical.

Enduring Patterns in the Politics of Strategic Choice[5]

We have stressed that politics is about people pursuing their goals in the context of their beliefs about just relationships. At this most basic level there is a fundamental similarity between the politics of strategic choice in world politics and the politics of the classroom, work, family, and friends. Consequently, the more quickly you can see a process of strategic interaction in your personal life, the more easily you will see it in world politics. The substance of the particular problems or issues at stake in world politics could hardly be more different. But underneath those differences, politics is politics.

The essential similarities in the process of politics can be most easily seen in five principles, or patterns, in the politics of strategic choice that we discuss in the sections that follow. By *principles* we simply mean a set of general assertions about how people's preferences and perceptions of the situations they confront affect the way they evaluate options and make choices. These principles tell you what to look for even as the specific, and often unique, "facts" of politics change over different issues, actors, cultures, historical periods, political arenas, and strategic contexts.

The Connection between Preferences and Power

As we noted above, politics is about the pursuit of interdependent outcomes, about what people *want* to achieve and *can* achieve. It is not at all surprising, therefore, that political observers often focus on actors' preferences and their relative power. But what matters most is how preferences and power are *connected*. People who are in a weak power position know that what really matters is what the stronger actors decide to do. Children try to manipulate their parents' preferences when they want something that costs a lot of money or want to go somewhere that requires driving or adult supervision because parents usually have the power to make such decisions. Low-level employees wonder about what the boss thinks and whether they are on her good or bad side. In feudal societies serfs worried about the nobility's intentions. The vulnerability of the weak to the choices of the strong is the central message in the old saying "When the elephants fight, it is the grass that is trampled." Of course, what the weak sense immediately—the importance of other people's preferences—the strong often ignore. Older children often run roughshod over younger siblings, just as adults used to getting what they want frequently pay little attention to how their choices affect people around them.

It is the same in world politics. It is the compatibility of U.S. and Canadian policy makers' overall objectives that makes the great difference in military power between the United States and Canada more an irritant than a major security threat to Canadians. Fidel Castro, who has opposed U.S. policies since he took over Cuba in 1959 and has been the target of assassination attempts and a U.S.-sponsored invasion by Cuban exiles, has a rather different view of the strategic implications of U.S. military superiority.

The first basic political principle (and the first enduring pattern in the politics of strategic choice) is, then, quite simple:

> *The strategic importance of power varies with the compatibility of actors' preferences: The more incompatible actors' preferences, the more strategically important their relative power positions.*

The "flip-side" of this principle is equally straightforward:

> *The strategic importance of differences in actors' preferences varies with the distribution of power: The weaker an actor's relative power position, the more strategically important the more powerful actors' preferences.*

In thinking about the implications of this principle, it is important to remember the points we made above about the meaning and nature of power. Power refers to actors' ability to increase the probability that their preferred outcomes will occur; capabilities and power are not synonyms; and *political* power is always *relative* power—relative to a particular set of actors, issues, and interdependent outcomes. Unfortunately, people who talk about the role of power in politics often forget that the sources of power *vary* with the issues and actors at hand. Instead, they tend to think of power as a *possession* of the strong and assume that whoever possesses the most resources—usually economic or military assets—gets what they want. But it makes little difference how wealthy a state is or how strong its military forces are if these assets are irrelevant to what its leaders seek to achieve. It also is the case that even those who have access to relevant assets can be defeated by actors who use lesser assets more effectively. All David had was a stone and a sling, but he slew Goliath. In the fable of the hare and the tortoise, the hare squandered its superior assets with exceptionally bad decision making. Likewise in world politics, small countries can use greater commitment and strategic skill to overcome immense disadvantages in resources, as Vietnam's defeat of the United States exemplifies. Consequently, when you think about the effect of power on politics, it's important to remember not only what power means, but also that the sources of power—and the effectiveness with which those sources are used—vary.

It is also important to recognize that the effect of this first principle in the politics of strategic choice depends on several additional factors: variations in how much the actors value building legitimate relationships; variations in actors' perceptions of the opportunities to create mutually advantageous patterns of reciprocity over a long-term relationship; and variations in risk-taking, discounting, and linkage politics. These observations lead to the next basic principle in the politics of strategic choice.

The Impact of Varying Beliefs about Just Relationships

The second fundamental principle describes the effects of variations in actors' beliefs about the importance and nature of just relationships. Politics is not simply about the pursuit of interdependent outcomes; it is also about people's beliefs and perceptions about what is just. You may not like the grade you get on an exam, the amount of help you get from your family to pay for college, or the decision your boss makes about your job schedule; but if you believe that the process that led to the decision was legitimate (the test questions reflected what you were told to expect, and the professor read your answers carefully), and if the outcome looks fair in comparison to what others received (your grade relative to those of your classmates), then you are far less likely to object.

As this example suggests, judgments about the legitimacy of political relationships reflect two underlying dimensions. **Process legitimacy** focuses on the process by which particular outcomes are reached. **Outcome legitimacy** focuses on the substance of the outcomes—who got what. The process and outcome dimensions of legitimacy interact with each other. Astute politicians sense these linkages and often attempt to reduce the level of opposition to unattractive outcomes by stressing the legitimacy of the process by which those outcomes were achieved.

Beliefs about just procedures and outcomes are thus important for two reasons: First, they provide direction for those who hold them, shaping and restricting both the order of their preferences and their strategies for achieving their preferred outcomes; second, they create a larger set of issues about what constitutes a legitimate community or relationship. Strategic interactions about particular substantive outcomes are, therefore, embedded within a larger set of interactions driven by actors' beliefs about the nature of just relationships.

The second basic political principle is as straight-forward as the first:

> *If people value creating and sustaining legitimate relationships*, and *if they think a political process and the outcome it produces are just, they are more likely to accept that outcome—even if they would have preferred something else. If they think either the outcome or the process is unjust, they are far more likely to oppose it.*
>
> *The lower the perceived legitimacy of a political process, the more important the legitimacy of the outcomes it produces. The lower the perceived legitimacy of political outcomes, the more important the legitimacy of the process that generated those outcomes.*

We see the impact of varying beliefs about process and outcome legitimacy operating all around us. Laid-off or downsized workers are not going to be happy regardless of how the decision was reached or how other employees were treated, but their hurt will turn into moral outrage if they think the decision was arrived at by self-interested executives trying to pad short-term profits, or if they see higher-ups who lose their jobs getting "golden parachutes" while they stand in unemployment lines. No citizens like to pay more taxes, but they are more likely to swallow hard and do it if they have had an opportunity to vote on the increase and if they perceive others as having to pay their fair share. In the early years of the Vietnam War, draft deferments for students enabled many young men from the middle and upper classes to avoid serving, while disproportionate numbers from the working class fought and died. As the war became more controversial, so did the question of whether student deferments were just, and they were dropped early in the Nixon administration. A few years later the draft itself was ended, but that simply altered the terms of the debate about justice and national service, with many arguing that volunteer armies were disproportionately composed of minorities and others who, because of a lack of economic opportunities, were forced to use the military for upward mobility.

process legitimacy   The perceived legitimacy of the procedures or means by which an outcome is reached.

outcome legitimacy   The perceived legitimacy of a particular result, as distinct from the process by which that result was achieved.

The impact of varying beliefs about the importance and nature of just relationships on the politics of choice can also help us think about some of the effects of gender and culture on choice. For instance, in Chapter 2 we mentioned that contemporary feminist scholars argue that women typically see politics as being far more embedded in human relationships than do men, who characteristically understand politics as strategic interactions among individual, isolated actors.

This possibility is completely consistent with the theoretical relationships outlined in the second principle in the politics of strategic choice. The feminist argument essentially asserts that there are gender-based differences in actors' beliefs about the importance and nature of legitimate relationships. If men are more likely to ignore the implications of their choices for the legitimacy of the relationships they are in, then cooperation among men will depend heavily on whether cooperation advances individual self-interest. Women, if the feminist argument is right, will be far more likely to assess the value of cooperation from the standpoint of creating or maintaining legitimate relationships. At an individual level, these differences might help explain predatory dating behavior by some men who try to manipulate women's willingness to invest in building relationships to satisfy their own desire for increased power and short-term gratification. At the social and international level, these differences might be used to link explanations of the frequency of conflict and war to the gender of the decision makers.

The notion that gender plays a role in creating different understandings of the strategic situations that confront people is, not surprisingly, highly controversial. Far less controversial is the possibility that these factors vary systematically across different cultures and ethnic groups. Many observers argue that European and North American culture is far more individualistic than the cultures of many parts of Asia and Africa. The Japanese stress on community, for instance, is likely to produce both a different set of preferences and a different bargaining style from those that are common in the United States. That cultural difference reinforces the effects of the institutional and political structure in Japan on the drive to achieve consensus quietly before making major policy changes. U.S. culture, by contrast, applauds the rugged individualist who refuses to be constrained by the community's prevailing norms (frequently described as "prejudices") and strikes out in new directions on his or her own. It is important to understand that this stress on individual initiative and leadership is a cultural trait, not a universal one.

As these examples suggest, it doesn't matter whether it is personal, domestic, or international politics: variations in actors' beliefs about the importance and nature of legitimate relations affect how people react to differences in their preferences and relative power positions. What does that mean for understanding the politics of strategic choice? It means that how this second principle plays out can alter the effects of the first. However, to assess the full implications of these first two principles, we must now consider a third.

The Effect of the Shadow of the Future

People pay attention not only to how power, preferences, and issues of legitimacy are related today but also to how they expect these factors to evolve over time. This aspect of choice is called the **shadow of the future.** It symbolizes the notion that different anticipated futures cast different shadows on choice. Looking just at how things are at one point in time, you might expect people to try to change situations

shadow of the future   The ways in which people's guesses about what the future may hold affect their judgments about the relative attractiveness of the different choices they are considering.

in which they are badly off, and to accept ones in which things are going well for them. But what if you expect the bad situation to improve dramatically even if you do nothing, and the good one to deteriorate in the absence of new policies? For instance, if you expect that a friend or business associate might double-cross you in the future, you might be looking at a different strategic situation than if you think that person can be trusted.

The third basic principle describes the effects of different anticipated futures on the decision to accept or challenge existing arrangements:

The more compatible people expect their preferences to become over time, the more co-operative and less power-based their strategic choices are likely to be. Conversely, the more incompatible people expect their preferences to become over time, the more competitive and power-based their strategic approach is likely to be.

Some of the most famous debates in world politics have reflected different perceptions of the shadow of the future. Consider, for instance, Neville Chamberlain's decision to appease Hitler in the 1930s. Chamberlain hoped that a policy of *appeasement*—giving in to Hitler's demands—would eventually lead Hitler to stop making new demands. Put differently, appeasement was designed to convert Hitler from a dissatisfied to a satisfied actor. Winston Churchill's opposition to appeasing Hitler was also based on his judgment about the effects of policy choices on the future, but he believed that Hitler's preferences were irretrievably incompatible with Britain's interests. Thus the fundamental question was whether appeasement would lead over time to a mutually acceptable set of policy preferences and relationships. If yes, concessions that increased Hitler's future power would be less dangerous because the strategic importance of differences in power decreases as the compatibility of actors' preferences increases. If one expected that the future would bring only incompatible preferences and values, then the strategic importance of power—and, hence, the dangers of appeasement—would rise dramatically.

In a time when the world is changing, what people see lying ahead may often vary with their **time horizons,** how far into the future they look. The length of actors' time horizons reflects both individual and situational factors. For instance, in the United States politicians tend to be far more interested in policy options that can produce rapid results—especially those that can be accomplished before the next election—than those that require years to bear fruit. That being the case, their view of the probable consequences of policy choices is likely to be different from that of policy makers in countries such as Japan and Britain, whose political systems (for quite different reasons**) encourage them to look further down the road.

The underlying similarity between the factors that affect the high-stakes decisions of policy makers and the factors that go into the small decisions of daily life is captured on page 67 in cartoonist Bill Watterson's portrayal of Calvin's struggle to choose whether to study or go sledding through fresh snow.

How the connections among these three basic political principles play out across different issues, actors, and historical periods will be discussed in the chapters that

time horizons   How far people look into the future when assessing the possible implications of a choice they are considering.

**Japan has a norm of consensus building; Britain has a highly centralized policy-making structure. Oddly, both encourage longer time horizons. The Japanese system encourages people to pay attention to sustaining a consensus; the British system makes it possible for determined policy makers with long-term goals to overcome opposition.

Calvin Contemplates the Impact of Different Time Horizons on Choice

follow. What is important to recognize now is that *the strategic incentives that confront people in a particular situation are a product of how these first three principles combine:*

- The strategic significance of different relative power positions depends on the compatibility of actors' preferences.
- The implications of that mix depend, in turn, on actors' views about the importance and nature of legitimate relationships.
- Add the length of actors' time horizons and their guesses about the future, and you have a picture of the strategic situation buried underneath the surface differences in world politics.

Being able to recognize the underlying strategic situation confronting people tells us most of what we need to know in order to anticipate their choices and the outcomes that are likely to flow from those choices. It does not, however, take us quite as far as we need to go. The reason is simple. People vary in how they react to the risks built into a strategic situation. Moreover, politics almost always involves linkages that cut across multiple political arenas. We need, therefore, to add two final sets of principles.

The Impact of Risk-Taking Preferences and Discounting

Strategic choices are, by their nature, risky choices. They are risky in two senses. First, the outcomes that result from strategic choices are seldom certain. There is almost always some chance that people will not achieve their goals even if they choose the best option available and implement that choice as effectively as possible. Second, strategic choices usually involve an investment in resources, time, and political capital. Some choices are politically dangerous only when they fail; others create political damage even when they succeed. The elder George Bush's decision to challenge Saddam Hussein after the invasion of Kuwait in 1991 was politically dangerous, but his popularity soared when Operation Desert Storm succeeded. In the United States, the political implications of policy choices involving abortion are quite different; even if you win, the issue is so polarizing that the political cost is high.

The political investment actors must pay in order to make strategic choices is the price of admission, with no refunds if you don't like the result. Strategic choices, therefore, carry both a *policy* risk and a *political* risk. **Policy risk** refers to the probability that actors' substantive goals will not be achieved even if their policy choices are implemented effectively. **Political risk** refers to the likelihood that policy choices will have adverse effects on actors' political positions—on their ability to make and sustain their preferred policy choices.

How people react to the risks they face can have a major impact on the choices they make. Sometimes people are willing to run extraordinary political risks in an effort to achieve their policy goals, but in other cases people are so sensitive to any perceived threat to their political position that they shy away from any decisions that put them at political risk. How can we anticipate whether people are likely to be willing to run political risks to achieve policy objectives? The general patterns are simple and intuitively reasonable.

First, political risks are like any other capital investment; a costly investment requires a large expected return for the risk to be worth taking. Second, people's willingness to run political and policy risks is affected by how much control they have over policy choices and the ways in which those choices are implemented. Entrepreneurs generally prefer to retain close control over their investments in order to manage the risks they run when they invest their money and prestige in a new product. Similarly, people don't like being put in a position where they might have to pay large political bills for choices over which they had little control. It is one thing to put yourself at political risk; it is quite another to have your political future depend on the choices of others. Moreover, people care more about avoiding policy failure when they are visibly responsible for the outcome.

Actors' **risk-taking preferences**—their willingness to "take a chance"—thus vary with the value they attach to achieving a specific policy outcome and how much control they have over a policy choice and how it is implemented. This pattern is summarized in the first pieces of the fourth principle in the politics of strategic choice:

The higher the expected value people attach to an outcome, the higher the political risks they will be willing to run to achieve it. People are less willing to run political risks in support of policy choices as their control over choice and implementation declines. However, as their control over choice and implementation declines, they become more indifferent to policy failure—as long as policy failure is not politically dangerous.

How people react to risks also depends on when the costs and benefits attached to those risks are expected to arrive. People generally prefer to get the benefits of a choice quickly and to defer the costs as long as possible. Consequently, actors typically *discount* costs (including political risks) and benefits (including preferred policy outcomes) over time, generally preferring current benefits over future benefits and future costs over current costs. Benefits people have to wait for are valued less than those they can get right away. Costs that people can defer look less costly.

Discounting is a concept that comes originally from economics. Charging interest on loans is the most common and obvious example of discounting in daily economic decisions, but how people discount costs and benefits affects politics as well. Do you pay the costs of protecting the environment now in the hope that your children will have a better world at some distant point in the future? Do you send your loved ones into harm's way now to protect people on the opposite side of the world in the hope that an investment of blood and money today will make the world a better place in some distant tomorrow?

policy risk The probability that actors' substantive goals will not be achieved even if their policy choices are implemented effectively.

political risk The probability that policy choices will hurt actors' political positions.

risk-taking preferences Actors' willingness to take a chance that either their political or policy objectives may not be fully achieved.

discounting People's tendency to prefer current benefits more than future benefits and future costs more than current costs; they are likely to accept a higher cost in exchange for delaying when it has to be paid and a smaller benefit in exchange for receiving it sooner.

Calvin Contemplates the Impact of Discounting and Risk on Choice

Here again, the underlying theoretical continuity between the high stakes, often life-and-death, decisions of foreign-policy makers and the small decisions of daily life is brilliantly revealed by Watterson's portrayal of Calvin's struggle to choose between the small, but immediate and certain, pleasure of throwing snowballs at Susie and the large, but uncertain and future, benefits of being rewarded for good behavior at Christmas.

These last pieces of the fourth principle in the politics of strategic choice can be summarized as follows:

People generally prefer current benefits over future benefits and future costs over current costs.

However,

The higher the expected value actors attach to achieving a specific policy outcome, the less their choices will be affected by discounting. The less control actors have over policy choice and implementation, the more actors will prefer future costs over current costs and the more they will value current benefits over future benefits.

The connections between these general patterns in risk taking and discounting help explain why politicians in the United States so often appear to be driven more by political considerations than by questions of policy. While there are some exceptions, most major policy choices in the United States require large and complex coalitions that cut across both the executive and the legislative branches. Even presidents, who are often able to block choices they oppose, are seldom able to get their preferred policies adopted without building a coalition. With control over policy choice spread broadly and the political costs of leading the way on controversial issues likely to arrive far sooner than the policy benefits, individual actors are understandably reluctant to put their political position at risk in what often appear (at best) to be only long-shot attempts to achieve preferred policy outcomes. In such a decision-making environment, really controversial policy choices are likely to be made only when the short-term costs of doing nothing are even more unattractive than the short-term risks of trying to change the status quo. Thus it was that in the 1980s and early 1990s U.S. politicians began to work hard to find ways to reduce the national debt and fund Social Security only when the political risks of inaction had grown so large that they matched the dangers of making a controversial choice.

The Impact of Linkage Politics

Politics almost always involves linkages across multiple political arenas. At the same time as political actors deal with other individuals or organized groups, they need to pay attention to their relationships with their supporters and with any other policy makers they need on board to reach the policy decision they want. Factions on school boards bargain simultaneously with teachers, taxpayers, other local stakeholders (people who believe they have a stake in public education), and among themselves, knowing all the while that any bargain they reach may be undone by new local or state legislation. Meanwhile, members of city councils and state legislatures, the very entities that can impose new rules of the game on school boards, are involved in strategic interactions in multiple political arenas and vulnerable to changes generated by national politics.

Linkage politics and vulnerability to outcomes in larger political arenas over which one has little control are a fact of life in state and local politics. What may be less obvious is that policy coalitions at the national level face similar constraints. It is in many ways natural to assume that policy makers over whom one has little influence have a great deal of flexibility in pursuing the goals they want to achieve. It is also entirely natural to think of local, state, and national politics as forming a kind of food chain, in which those who are higher up prey on those below them. There is no doubt that *elites* (a minority of people within a group or political arena who have acquired—whether by birth, merit, or political success—unusually high levels of status or power) often behave in predatory ways. Their choices, however, are no less constrained by linkage politics nor less vulnerable to changes over which they have little control than are the actions of those with less status or power. Indeed, as we shall discuss in Chapter 7, the collapse of communism in the Soviet Union was very much the result of how international economic and technological changes connected with the growing unhappiness and disillusion of Soviet citizens. Linkage politics is, therefore, yet another generic aspect of the politics of strategic interaction.

These observations lead to the fifth basic principle in the politics of strategic choice:

Politics involves linkages across multiple political arenas. World politics is driven by the interaction of international politics, factional politics within the policy coalitions that

linkage politics Ways in which choices and outcomes in one particular political arena are affected by what goes on in other arenas.

control the choices of international (state and non-state) actors, and constituency politics (the relationships between policy factions and their mass and elite constituencies—the actors whose support factions need in order to continue in the role of policy maker).

Actors' preferences, power positions, beliefs about legitimate relationships, and guesses about the future are all affected by the links that connect these three political arenas. The choices actors make will vary with the mix of international and domestic incentives (created by factional and constituency politics) attached to different options and the ways in which linkage politics affects their risk-taking preferences, their time horizons, and how they discount costs and benefits. The outcomes will vary with how successfully those choices bridge international, factional, and constituency politics.

These five basic principles can seem a little daunting at first. And there is no escaping the fact that you will have to invest time and effort to understand the basic concepts and relationships that drive world politics and to become familiar with the substance of the central issues. But focusing on *enduring patterns in the politics of strategic choice* will greatly reduce the investment you need to make to understand the issues *and* make your investment pay off over and over again. You will be able to use the same analytical tools to make sense of political situations across different issues, actors, political arenas, cultures, historical periods, and strategic contexts.

Moreover, understanding how world politics works will increase the probability that the choices you make will bring you closer to achieving your objectives. Focusing on the basic patterns in the politics of strategic choice will help you gain a clearer idea of what you value and the situation in which you find yourself. It will help you evaluate not only the nature of the game you are in and how to play the hand you have been dealt, but also how to anticipate the probability that either your cards or the game itself will change.

If you're prepared for the possibility that what happens in world politics may change the key circumstances that affect your life, you'll have a strategic advantage in making choices. However, to use that advantage, you need an idea of what to look for and an understanding of the significance of what you find. As we said above, we believe that the simplest and most direct way for you to understand world politics and how it affects your life is to focus on basic principles about how the *process* of politics works.

Exploring Common Ground

It may be easier to see the value of using these intellectual tools to explore common ground in the study of world politics when you become comfortable with the difference between a worldview and a theory. A theory focuses on some specific aspect of social or natural life (for example, the long-term development of animal or plant species) and tries to make sense of that particular issue through assumptions about cause and effect (such as Darwin's notion of natural selection, often known as "survival of the fittest").

Stated more formally, a **theory** is an intellectual tool for examining questions about the world systematically through a number of linked "if-then" assertions about cause and effect. You place the facts in the specific cases being studied (technically, these facts are called the "initial conditions") in the "if" portion of the relevant "if-then" statement. The statement then predicts what will happen given those particular facts.

The "if-then" propositions in a theory make it possible to organize a mass of information into coherent patterns. At their best, theories state their assumptions pre-

theory An intellectual tool for examining questions about the world systematically through a number of linked "if-then" assertions about cause and effect.

cisely enough to deduce a set of implications that can be used to predict and explain outcomes. To explain a specific outcome, you show that it is a particular instance of the general patterns outlined in a theory. Often, but not always, the implications of theoretical assumptions about cause and effect can be stated in the form of hypotheses that can be evaluated empirically by looking at whether the data are consistent with the prediction.

The five principles in the politics of strategic choice illustrate (in a simplified form) these essential characteristics of a theory. First, they identify the central concepts (actors' preferences, relative power, notions of legitimacy, the shadow of the future, time horizons, risk-taking preferences, discounting, linkage politics) that will be used to organize the analysis. Having identified the key concepts, they then offer a set of general assertions about the ways in which those factors combine to affect people's political choices. For example, in the first principle, the strategic importance of power *depends on* the compatibility of actors' preferences. In the second, the likelihood that actors will accept or oppose an outcome *depends on* whether they think the outcome and the political process that produced it are just. These statements, and the others in the five principles, summarize the general theoretical relationships contained in the argument.

Why bother with a theory at all? Why not just collect the facts that seem relevant to your particular concerns? The answer is as simple as it is unsettling and inescapable: No one naturally has 20–20 vision when it comes to understanding the "real world." We do *not* have the option of seeing the world "as it really is." We all must wear lenses to bring the world into focus because theoretical lenses define the very concepts into which our sense perceptions are organized. In short, *theoretical lenses give data meaning.* Since each lens focuses on different concepts and asks different questions, different lenses generate different images of the world. As a result, what we see is a combination of what is "really" there and the way in which our lenses are formed.

Let's return now to the differences between theories and worldviews. Worldviews include theoretical assertions about cause and effect, but those theoretical assertions come prepackaged with assumptions about the facts, the defining issues in world politics, and what you should value. Consider first the assumptions the different worldviews discussed in Chapter 2 make about actors' purposes and values. Classical realists assume that people are competitive, power-hungry beings. Having made that assumption about the facts, classical realists see little reason to expect that people will make commitments to other people for anything other than very temporary, tactical reasons. Liberals make quite different assumptions about the facts. They see people as cooperative and interested in joint gains. Social constructivists, meanwhile, reject the individualism of both realists and liberals and assume that membership in and identification with groups is a fundamental aspect of what it means to be human. Feminists put a distinctive twist on this point, arguing that socially constructed gender roles make women more likely than men to value building mutually advantageous long-term relationships.

Consider next the assumptions worldviews make about the defining issues in world politics. For analysts working within the framework of a particular worldview, world politics is about certain *defining* kinds of issues and events, and they weave examples of those issues and events into narratives to teach about social and political life. Realists see "typical cases" as those involving the threat of military aggression and defensive reactions to that threat. During the twentieth century, for instance, realist interpretations of the origins of war and peace revolved around the "lessons" of World War I, the German and Japanese aggression that spawned World War II, and the onset of the Cold War. It's not that realists deny the possibility of cooperation; rather, they believe that conflict and preparing to deal with conflict get to the heart of what is distinctive about world politics. Liberals see defining issues in missed opportunities for joint gains. Those missed opportunities can be the result of misperception or the absence of personal freedoms and institutions that facilitate cooperation. For social constructivists, the "typical case" is often one in which actors develop new social habits and interaction patterns that allow them to "learn their way out" of dysfunctional situations. The development of a peaceful, prosperous Europe in the decades after World War II, based on a self-conscious rejection of war and aggression, has become an important example in constructivists' narratives. At other times, group-based identities can evolve in destructive ways. This process occurred in the Balkans in the 1990s, when the disintegration of Yugoslavia led Serbs, Croats, and other national groups to harden their feelings toward each other.

It's natural for people to make judgments about the essential facts and defining issues in political life. It's also natural that these assumptions come connected the way we find them in existing worldviews. The classical realist premise that people are fundamentally competitive fits their stress on security threats as the key issue in politics. Liberals' assumption that people will behave cooperatively whenever it is possible to succeed doing so fits their interest in the question of how one achieves joint gains in domestic and international systems. Constructivist and feminist assumptions about socially constructed identities fit their interest in the role of groups and gender in the origins and effects of people's preferences, perceptions, and values.

But when assumptions about the essential facts and defining issues of politics are intermixed with theories of cause and effect, it can become exceptionally difficult to carry on constructive conversations about how one should make sense of world politics. Moreover, being asked to choose between competing worldviews can often present you with highly unattractive options. What happens if you share the realists' interest in security but disagree with their assumptions about people? What happens if you share the Marxists' normative commitment to egalitarianism but disagree with their understanding of cause and effect?

Consequently, we find it useful to separate theoretical arguments about cause and effect from debates about the essential facts and defining issues of political life. We recommend separating them for the following reasons. First, it is obvious that one of the most fundamental differences between these worldviews is their assertions about the facts: Are people competitive or cooperative? Do people see themselves as isolated individuals or part of enduring interpersonal relationships, and so on? When the facts are the central issue in dispute, they must be ascertained, not assumed. Second, if the review of world politics in Parts II through IV of this text leads to any conclusion, it is that *the facts do vary*. Because they do, it's crucial not to assume away central questions about the facts. The "if" part of "if-then" statements needs to be alive and well when you try to make sense of world politics. Third, relying on a single worldview to make sense of world politics runs headlong into the problem that worldviews focus on distinctive sets of issues or problems. World politics presents real people with a far broader array of substantive issues and problems to address than they will find tools to handle in any single worldview.

For all these reasons, we believe you will find it less useful to look at world politics from the perspective of a particular worldview and its "typical cases" than it will be to invest in identifying and understanding theoretical patterns in politics that cut across the concerns of all these perspectives. Theories don't claim to provide a worldview. To the contrary, theories only claim to be windows on specific *parts* of the world. Theories don't claim knowledge about the true nature of people's values, goals, and essential nature—the "facts" of political life. Theories only present assertions about *particular implications* of the facts. Theories don't claim certainty. Theories are about tentative and contingent conclusions, about inviting conversations on whether particular arguments and interpretations are persuasive and useful.

If theories are more versatile than worldviews when one is trying to make sense of world politics across a wide range of issues and contexts, then the next question is obvious. What is a good theoretical lens to use when introducing world politics? Although there are many different theoretical approaches, we think the best place to start is with a lens that helps explain the largest piece of common ground we can see in the study of world politics: patterns in political choice.

Conclusion

Each worldview discussed in Chapter 2 assumes that people make choices under conditions of strategic interdependence. Moreover, each of these traditions identifies the *same key variables* as centrally important in understanding actors' choices. These variables include actors' preferences and perceptions, their relative power positions, their degree of commitment to shared norms or identities, their time horizons, the way they react to risk, and any linkages that are assumed to exist between international and domestic politics. Where these worldviews differ is in the assumptions they make about the nature and origin of actors' purposes and perceptions, the values that guide them, and the context in which choice takes place. Put differently, each of these worldviews has a picture of a distinct type of strategic environment and a distinct set of substantive problems for choice. All of these possible contexts can and do crop up in world politics. Focusing on theoretical patterns in the politics of strategic choice allows each distinctive worldview to be useful to you *when the conditions it assumes exist fit the strategic circumstances found in particular cases*. A focus on choice thus introduces you to world politics in a way that respects the particular insights of distinguished intellectual traditions, while allowing you to build common ground across them.

There are two final advantages to making sense of world politics through the politics of choice: It is intuitive, and it will help you more effectively navigate your own life's choices. The politics of your personal life, school, work, and community revolves around very different issues, contexts, and stakes than world politics. But with all that understood, there's still an essential truth in the observation that you live the politics of choice everyday. Because that is the case, looking for dimensions in the politics of choice that are similar to those in your life will create an opportunity to connect more intuitively—as well as intellectually—with what is going on around you in world politics.

Recognizing what is similar and what is different about the politics of choice in your life and in world politics will also make you a more sophisticated and effective analyst in both arenas. Learning to compare across arenas is, after all, very similar to learning to compare situations within arenas. The issues, contexts, and stakes vary greatly within world politics. To understand world politics, you need to identify the effects of those varying issues, contexts, and stakes on choice. Having done that for world politics, you will be better positioned to evaluate the implications of the distinctive situations in which you find yourself.

In sum, it is impossible to avoid using some sort of conceptual lens when you try to understand the world around you. We offer the politics of strategic choice for your consideration, both because we find it the most useful and versatile way to begin making sense of politics and because we believe it will provide a valuable foil if you choose to go in another direction.

Key Terms

strategic interdependence	power	outcome legitimacy
strategic choice	capabilities	shadow of the future
strategic interaction	operational environment	time horizons
preferences	psychological environment	policy risk
preferences over outcomes	perception	political risk
preferences over policies	misperception	risk-taking preferences
faction	unmotivated (or cold) misperception	discounting
coalition	motivated (or hot) misperception	linkage politics
side-payments	process legitimacy	theory

To The Reader   A CHAPTER SUMMARY and QUESTIONS FOR REVIEW are available at **www.prenhall.com/lamborn**

States and the Politics of Foreign Policy

This chapter is the first of two on the key types of international actors that are active in world politics today. By **international actor** we simply mean any individual or group that attempts to achieve objectives across the territories of two or more countries. Given the range of the issues in world politics and the number of people who have a stake in the results, it's not surprising that an extraordinarily wide variety of individuals and organizations are actively engaged in trying to affect outcomes they care about. Consequently, a large part of political analysis consists of identifying the relevant actors and understanding what they are trying to achieve.

This chapter focuses on states and foreign policy; the next examines non-state actors and the effects of interstate law and institutions. When you have finished both chapters, you will have been introduced to the cast of characters that populate contemporary world politics, their different historical roots, and some important patterns in the ways in which they define and pursue their objectives. In addition to states, we will examine international intergovernmental organizations (IGOs), international non-governmental organizations (NGOs), and a variety of other non-state actors such as trans-state business enterprises, religious organizations, and terrorist and criminal groups. In each of these categories, the numbers have grown during the twentieth century, though the increase has been much steeper in some of them than in others. In 1900, the number of independent states was 47; today it is 192. At the beginning of the twentieth century, there were 37 IGOs; today there are 260.

We have two goals in this chapter. The first is to familiarize you with the idea of the sovereign state and the variety of state actors. The second is to introduce foreign policy in a way that highlights *general patterns of political choice*. Highlighting these general patterns will help lay the groundwork for making sense of the behavior of states across a wide variety of issue areas, geographical regions, and historical periods. For example, because their international positions and the preferences, norms, and expectations of their constituents usually differ, states often make foreign policy with distinct kinds of objectives and styles. Nevertheless, the ways their leaders make choices and bargain—given their unique mixes of preferences, norms, and strategic incentives—typically reflect the same set of enduring patterns in the politics of strategic choice. For this reason, we urge you to think of specific historical and contemporary cases as *examples* or *illustrations* of more generic patterns of strategic interaction. In doing this, you can use your understanding of historical cases to help explain the present and anticipate the future.

The Sovereign State

We begin with the state for two central reasons. First, everyone lives in some state or, in the few remaining cases of dependent territories, in places controlled by a state. Second, states have a legal and political status that makes them central international actors. States have the right to regulate by law anything occurring within their boundaries. As we discussed in Chapter 1, the **state** is a form of political organization that makes a claim for **sovereign territoriality**. The internal face of sovereignty asserts a claim to final legal authority within the state. The external face of

international actor Any individual, faction, or coalition that attempts to achieve objectives across the boundaries of two or more countries.

state A form of political organization that claims the exclusive right to govern a specific piece of territory.

sovereign territoriality A legal and political principle that asserts a claim to final authority within the territorial boundaries of a state and denies the legitimacy of any higher authority outside the state.

TABLE 4–1	THE LARGEST AND SMALLEST STATES IN AREA, POPULATION, AND WEALTH

SMALLEST STATE		
Area	**Population**	**Total Wealth**
Monaco 0.75 sq. mi. (1.95 sq. km.)	Tuvalu 9,400[a]	Tuvalu $8,750,000

LARGEST STATE		
Area	**Population**	**Total Wealth**
Russia 6,592,800 sq. mi. (17,075,400 sq. km.)	China 1,206,600,000[b]	United States $6,738,400,000,000

[a] Latest estimate: midyear 1995. Most recent census: 9,043 (1991).
[b] Latest estimate: midyear 1995. Most recent census: 1,133,682,501 (1990).

Source: Encyclopedia Britannica, 1996 Book of the Year (Chicago: Encyclopedia Britannica, 1996), pp. 445, 584, 699, 735, 742.

sovereignty rejects the legitimacy of any external claim to an authority higher than the state. These twin claims to sovereign jurisdiction are *territorial* in the sense that they are both defined and limited by territorial boundaries.

It is important to remember that *states* are not the same as *nations*. A state is a *legal* entity defined by control over territory. As long as some permanent population lives within its boundaries, a state exists *de facto*, regardless of who those people are. A **nation,** by contrast, is a *social* entity—a group of people who have a *common identity* based on a belief that they have shared a past and should share a future.

States vary widely in size, wealth, and natural resources. The largest in terms of the size of its territory, Russia, is over *nine million* times the size of the smallest, Monaco. Very small states (sometimes defined as those with populations of 250,000 or less) are often called *microstates* to emphasize how tiny they are compared to most other states. Some states are very wealthy overall or in per capita terms, while others are desperately poor. Table 4–1 presents data on the largest and smallest states on several key dimensions.

Despite these important differences, all independent states share one key attribute as international actors: **juridical (legal) sovereignty.** The root of the word sovereignty is *reign*, from the French word for "rule"; the prefix is from the Old French for "over." This linguistic root signifies that a sovereign actor is one who "rules over" a land. More specifically, a sovereign state is a political unit with a *constitution* (written or unwritten) that is independent of any other constitution. Such constitutional supremacy gives sovereign states ultimate legal control over some territory.[1] In other words, a sovereign state is legally subordinate to no other political unit. For example, Russia is now a sovereign state, as was the former Soviet Union, but the Commonwealth of Independent States—a grouping of Russia and the former non-Russian Soviet republics—is not sovereign, since it has no authority independent of its members. Sovereignty means that all independent states are legally equal.

nation   A group of people who share a common identity as a social entity.

juridical (legal) sovereignty   The right under international law and custom to make choices free from the legally binding control of other actors either within or outside the state.

Variations in norms about the sources of sovereignty affect world politics in significant ways. So does the fact that states can either exist in fact before they exist in law, or they can exist in law but not in fact. As we explain in Chapter 6, rulers made effective internal claims to supreme authority within the territories they ruled before those claims were recognized by the key external actors with which they had to deal in order to survive. Juridical sovereignty requires, first, a system of states (a group of states that interact with each other), and, second, an agreement by the policy makers in the central governments of those states on a set of rules for recognizing each other as sovereign.

Historically, **empirical sovereignty**—the ability to make an effective internal claim to sovereign control—came before there was a state system with a set of shared norms and rules for granting legal recognition to claims of sovereignty. Today, with world politics built around a state system, there are many states that have been granted juridical sovereignty but have no government that can exercise effective sovereign control within the state's borders. For instance, the Democratic Republic of the Congo (formerly Zaire) went through one civil war in the mid-1990s only to disintegrate into another in August 1998, when Uganda and Rwanda began backing new groups of rebels. It took until early 2001 to put a plan in place for restoring peace and creating an effective central government, but according to an April 16, 2001, UN Security Council report, that plan was soon undermined by Uganda and other neighboring countries, who preferred a weak Congolese government so they could continue to plunder the country's natural resources.

Even those states with governments that can make effective claims to being the final legal authority (such as the United States) increasingly have political and economic sectors in which that control is very shaky: namely, in some of the ghettos in major U.S. cities, along stretches of the borders with Mexico and Canada, and in the flow of information and economic activity across boundaries. The increasing erosion of empirical sovereignty—exemplified both by the inability of some governments to exercise final authority within their countries and by the decreasing meaningfulness of states' territorial boundaries—is one of the major reasons why some observers question whether the idea of sovereignty can continue to be the organizing principle for world politics much longer.

Despite all these important reservations about the fit between the idea and the empirical reality of the state, central governments of states continue to be key actors across an extraordinarily broad range of issue areas in world politics. States remain key actors in the strategic interactions that drive world politics for two inescapable reasons: (1) states can make the claim that they are the legitimate voice for all citizens that live within their boundaries more effectively than any other actors in world politics; (2) even though there is wide variation in the characteristics of individual states, as a group states are the largest and most widespread form of human organization that can both make and implement policy.

States as Actors in World Politics

States (in the sense of political institutions that govern specific territories) have existed for thousands of years in various forms, including the city-states in ancient Greece. States reemerged in Italy during the Renaissance, but a *system of sovereign states* came into being only after the norms and practices of sovereignty became widely accepted among the key actors in seventeenth-century Europe. Prior to that time, there were few mutually accepted rules of the game about how states should

empirical sovereignty An actor's ability to make an effective internal claim to sovereign control within the boundaries of a state.

deal with each other. As a result, interstate politics in Renaissance Italy resembled something close to the law of the jungle. Fortunately, during the sixteenth and seventeenth centuries, a wide range of rules and practices (starting with the rights of ambassadors) began to emerge. Then, in 1648 at Westphalia, the first mutually agreed-upon principles for a system of juridically sovereign states were accepted by most of the key actors in Europe. Following that agreement, the growth of rules and norms accelerated, including the recognition in one state of legal acts that occurred in other states. These rules and practices constitute *public international law* (see Chapter 5).

As we noted above, the state is a set of institutions that exercises final authority over a specified territory. Consequently, individual states are demarcated by very precise boundaries, and state officials take very seriously the notion that they control mutually exclusive pieces of territory. If state X controls a certain piece of real estate, state Y by definition cannot do so. The importance attached to exclusive territorial claims was illustrated strikingly in 1993, a few years after the disintegration of Yugoslavia into its constituent parts of Serbia, Bosnia, Croatia, Macedonia, Slovenia, and the Federal Republic of Yugoslavia (which contains as subunits Serbia and Montenegro). At that point, there were many conflicting claims regarding who rightfully controlled certain pieces of territory. A visitor to the office of the Slovenian prime minister was present when the country's foreign minister telephoned to say that some Croats were building a border post 50 meters inside Slovenia's claimed territory. The prime minister treated the news as an emergency, rushing to the scene to demand that the frontier post be relocated entirely outside the boundaries claimed by Slovenia.[2] Similarly, when U.S. police officials or bounty hunters "just run across the border" into Canada or Mexico to capture a fugitive, they are violating those states' autonomy by illegally exercising police power within a foreign sovereign state. The government that has suffered such an intrusion almost always issues a strong protest and typically is satisfied only by an official apology from U.S. diplomats. An apology from police officials or private individuals who committed the infraction is not sufficient because the action violated the state's sovereign rights and is, therefore, an issue of international principle.

Juridical sovereignty has two dimensions that directly affect how states act. One is *internal autonomy*. No other entity may make rules for the people in a sovereign state or exercise any jurisdiction on its territory. With only a few exceptions, states have complete legal jurisdiction within their territorial borders and such other possessions as embassies abroad and ships at sea, but no jurisdiction anywhere else. This constraint helps us understand why officials care so much about which states control exactly which pieces of territory. Under present international norms, territory confers the right to make rules in a particular place and to be free from rules made by others.

Because states exist in a world of other states, basic norms are needed about how they will relate to one another. A second dimension of juridical sovereignty, *external autonomy*, fulfills part of this function. External autonomy means that states have no legal obligations to other international actors that they do not choose to assume. States can decide which alliances or intergovernmental organizations (IGOs) to join, whether and when they will make trade or cultural agreements with other states, and even whether they will allow foreigners to enter their territory. India and Israel, for instance, have refused to accede to the Nuclear Nonproliferation Treaty, which would obligate them to dismantle their nuclear weapons. External autonomy means that they are under no obligation to do so. It also means that states need not extra-dite an alleged criminal to another state (that is, return him or her to that jurisdic-tion for trial) unless those states have signed a treaty with another state specifically requiring such an act. External autonomy even means that states need not have any links at all to the outside world. Japan had cut itself off from the Western world until the United States opened it up by force in the mid-nineteenth century. China simi-larly cut itself off from almost all other states during the Cultural Revolution of the late 1960s.

Of course, neither internal nor external autonomy means that states can do what-ever they want without incurring any penalty. Just as most individuals refrain from taking certain actions because the situation they are in constrains them, states are also, in most cases, situationally constrained. Because they face retaliation from oth-ers if they act outside accepted international "rules of the game," states often restrain their behavior accordingly. Virtually all states are subject to some forms of pressure from others, depending on the issue at stake and the actors involved. How states ma-nipulate these opportunities to alter others' behavior is a large part of what world politics is about in the international arena. Yet the internal and external dimensions of juridical sovereignty remain very important, for they give state officials the right to make final, authoritative choices about how they will deal with those pressures. This legal autonomy provides the underlying basis for international regimes and for public international law.

Even though all independent states are by definition juridically sovereign, they are *not* all equally viable as political units that can guarantee order, security, and eco-nomic well-being within their boundaries. Empirical sovereignty—that is, sover-eignty that is viable in everyday practice—does not follow automatically from legal sovereignty. It has been argued that political units that satisfy the latter but not the former standard should be thought of as either "failed" or "quasi-states."[3] Quasi-states are internally weak because they lack one or more of the following three char-acteristics: a coherent "we-they" feeling, political elites who have broad legitimacy within the society, or politically effective administrative structures. In extreme cases, central leadership is virtually absent, there is little public order, and various ethnic or tribal groups, gangs, and private militias take the law into their own hands, often outnumbering the central state's armed forces in firepower and zeal. As K. J. Holsti observes, such failed states retain "the fig leaf of [juridical] sovereignty for external purposes, but domestic life is organized around local politics."[4] Because these polit-ical units cannot effectively define and implement rules within the territory they claim to rule, they fail a basic, practical test of empirical sovereignty.

Failed states have attracted much international attention in recent years, since they have produced appalling violence and, in some cases, have required external intervention to restore order. Lebanon and Somalia illustrate such situations. Lebanon was created by France out of territory it had controlled since the 1860s, first as a protectorate, and later under a League of Nations mandate. The creation of Lebanon as an independent state was opposed by groups in Syria (also a former French mandate under the League of Nations), who argued that the territory ought to be part of a greater Syria. That opposition, plus the grave problems created by the Arab-Israeli dispute, created a very difficult international environment for building a viable state. Those international problems soon became entangled with political divisions within Lebanon. From the beginning, the Lebanese central government was designed to balance the rights and privileges of various religious and local

authorities, whose major political concerns were to ensure their groups' representation in the central government's decision-making bodies and their share of the goods and services the government controlled. A formula was carefully devised to divide decision-making authority and governmental services among the various Christian and Islamic constituencies. This arrangement might have produced stability over the long term (within the framework of a weak central state) had not the Islamic population grown much faster than the Christian groups, and had those groups not been radicalized by the Arab-Israeli dispute. By the 1970s the original formula for dividing jobs, government contracts, and other public goods among these groups was hopelessly outdated, but the Christians refused to revise it. A violent civil war ensued, during which central authority disintegrated, and order was produced only by Syrian intervention.

Somalia provides another example of a failed state. Somalia has been a legally sovereign state since 1960, but it has been without a government that can exercise effective control for most of the time since 1991. Some of the sources of Somalia's political instability can be traced directly to a long history of foreign intervention during and after colonialism, but here—as in Lebanon—some of the sources are clearly domestic. In Somalia, as in many other African states, ethnic clans have provided the main means of group identification. A socialist regime in the 1970s tried to modernize the state in "Western" terms, instituting legal rights to protect women and improve the position of low-status clans. When some internal actors resisted these policies, the government resorted to massive coercion. A civil war began in 1988. In 1991 the government collapsed and Somalia disintegrated into clan warfare. By the end of 1992 widespread starvation prompted intervention by the United States and later the United Nations to feed people and restore some order.

As the Lebanese and Somali examples suggest, a large part of the reason why so many fragile states exist can be traced to the history of European colonialism. Colonialism is covered in Chapters 7 and 9; here it is sufficient to mention that when

The Democratic Republic of the Congo (formerly called Zaire) is an example of a state that has disintegrated into civil war multiple times since it achieved independence in 1960. International efforts to resolve the most recent conflict, which began in 1998, were still underway in the middle of 2002.

colonialism fell into international disfavor after World War II, it also became clear that many colonies in Asia and Africa were *not* politically legitimate or coherent national entities. This created a dilemma for the retreating colonizers. Either they would have to admit that some form of international trusteeship would be required for some time, or they would have to grant the colonies juridical sovereignty and hope for the best. Juridical sovereignty won out for two reasons. First, the doctrine of *national self-determination* had come strongly into favor worldwide. In the Western world, acceptance of this doctrine reflected guilt over colonialism and the triumph of liberal Enlightenment ideas. It became politically unsupportable in democratic societies to insist that colonial units had to meet foreign standards of readiness for independence before it would be granted.[5] The second reason is perhaps even more fundamental: The rise of mobilized opposition to foreign rule in the colonies raised the costs of external control to unsustainable levels.

Juridical sovereignty is an either/or characteristic: Either a political unit has attained legal independence, or it is ruled by some other unit. Empirical sovereignty, in contrast, comes in degrees. States vary widely in their ability to administer their internal affairs effectively, a fact that has crucial implications for how we think of states as actors.

The many degrees of empirical statehood illustrate why this book stresses a *world politics perspective* that explores how various state, substate, interstate, and trans-state actors deal with one another. As we indicated above and stress again in Chapter 5, while states are key actors across a wide variety of issues in world politics, they are not the only actors. For instance, international economic IGOs such as the International Monetary Fund (IMF) can have a critical impact on economic development through the conditions they attach to assistance. The resulting policies inevitably affect the fortunes of different groups within states in different ways, helping some and hurting others. This, in turn, may strengthen or weaken various domestic factions and thus the composition and policies of governing coalitions.

The discussions in this section raise two important questions: Who actually speaks for "the state"? Does the state speak in one voice or many?

Controversies about the Legitimate Voice of Sovereignty: Who Speaks for the State?

Juridical sovereignty is a package of rights that states possess by virtue of being subject to no higher authority. But which individuals or groups within states, if any, actually "own" these rights? Theory and practice have evolved significantly on these questions over the past several centuries.

In the Middle Ages, before the rise of the interstate system, Church law stipulated that only the pope had the "fullness of power" to govern Christendom. Parts of that power were delegated to various other authorities, but according to Church doctrine, which was accepted as authoritative by many Christians, power rightfully resided in the pope as God's representative on earth. A number of philosophers and statesmen, most notably the sixteenth-century French thinker Jean Bodin, began to argue that "absolute and perpetual power over citizens and subjects in a commonwealth" should be transferred to a single *secular* ruler—specifically, for Bodin, the French king. This development in political thought coincided with the culmination of a centuries-long effort throughout Europe, especially in France, to increase the king's power at the expense of actors who had held so much power during the feudal era. Bodin did not want to destroy such actors as the guilds and nobility, for he saw

Writing in the sixteenth century, Jean Bodin was one of the most important early advocates of the idea that sovereignty had to reside in a single person.

them as a valuable source of advice for the king.[6] But Bodin insisted that sovereignty was indivisible and thus had to reside in a single *person*. The king thereby became *the* sovereign, and all others were thought of as his subjects. The belief in the *divine right of kings* to rule legitimated this idea.

As surprising as this sounds today, royal possession of sovereignty was a progressive idea in early modern Europe. It was part of a gradual secularization of state and society, reflecting the decline of the universalist religious authority that had prevailed in the medieval era.[7] It also had a pragmatic rationale. At a time when interstate alliances shifted quickly and many short wars were fought, centralizing the authority to make foreign policy in a monarch allowed the state to act rapidly and decisively.[8] But this view of sovereignty did not remain unchallenged for long. In overthrowing the monarchy and the social system that supported it, the French Revolution removed legal privileges from nobles and churchmen and gave political rights to the middle classes. Where formerly they had merely been the king's subjects, people became genuine citizens. France thus ceased to be simply the domain of its monarch and was transformed, at least rhetorically, into a place where "the people" were sovereign. Sovereignty was still considered to be indivisible; once the people's representatives decided on a course of action, there could be no internal challenge to their right to act. But that authority was now thought to reside ultimately in the people, rather than in any specific person or persons.[9]

It became more common in Europe during the nineteenth century to argue that "the people" should have a voice in state policy, including foreign policy. But the impact of this view on policy makers developed slowly. As late as July 1914, just before the outbreak of World War I, few leaders appeared to care what their people thought about the international situation, but the terrible costs of that war changed those attitudes.[10] No longer could political leaders ignore what their constituents wanted, especially if their policies carried large risks or entailed major sacrifices. Those who governed had become their people's representatives rather than their rulers. Today, in such non-democracies as North Korea, Iraq, and the People's Republic of China (PRC), rulers pay only lip service to the notion that they derive their authority and legitimacy from the people. But this pattern is becoming less typical as the number of democracies increases worldwide.

Democratization has raised two difficult issues involving the delegation of political authority. First, how can leaders identify what the people want? Second, are leaders bound to carry out their constituents' wishes? These questions are called **principal-agent problems.** A *principal* is some person or group that has ultimate authority to decide policy. An *agent* is some actor that operates on the principal's behalf in making day-to-day decisions. In publicly traded companies, for instance, the stockholders are the principal and the company's board of directors is the agent; in situations when a company's board of directors instructs the chief executive officer to implement a particular policy, the board can be thought of as the principal and the CEO as its agent. The same holds for government policy makers. From the perspective of democratic theory, the people are the ultimate principal; however, in day-to-day governance, high officials are often the principals, while lower-level bureaucrats who implement the policy are the agents.

Principal-agent problems arise because agents must often use their discretion to carry out policy, and they may use that discretion to make choices that differ from the ones the principal would have preferred. Agents' choices will differ if they have different preferences and incentives to act, such as their own private interests, or if

principal-agent problems Difficulties that arise either when agents have trouble identifying the wishes of their principal, or when principals have difficulty getting their agents to do what they want.

they think they know better than the principal what should be done. For example, managers care about profits, as do directors and stockholders, since all benefit when a firm does well. But stockholders may prefer conservative strategies designed to produce long-term growth, while managers may prefer riskier strategies designed to make a quick profit. Unless a principal is willing and able to monitor an agent's behavior closely, such problems of delegating authority to an agent cannot be completely solved.[11]

For purposes of understanding basic principal-agent processes, we assume here that principals and agents are **unitary actors;** that is, each of them has, or at least acts as if it has, a single set of preferences. (We will relax this simplifying assumption later in the chapter, when we discuss whether and when the state can, in fact, speak with a single voice.)

Principal-agent problems can arise for several reasons. Agents can pursue their own private political objectives instead of following the objectives of the electorate or politically responsible officials. This can occur, for example, when politicians running for election pander to the electorate's emotionalism on an issue rather than trying to use the campaign as an opportunity for reasoned debate, or when lower-level officials implement policies according to their own bureaucratic incentives rather than "national" goals. Alternatively, political leaders might act against their principal's (the electorate's) wishes for the opposite reason: because they think that they, rather than the public, truly understand the state's policy needs. In analyzing who rightfully speaks for the state on some issue in a democracy, then, it is important to ask whether the principal (the electorate) and its agents (political officials) have the *same goals*. Of course, since people often do not have well-thought-out views on international issues, and leaders often hide their real views, it may be difficult to determine how closely principals' and agents' goals coincide. The issue of legitimate delegation of authority is not problematic when these goals are similar, but important policy, political, and constitutional problems can arise when they differ.

Consider an example. In mid-1941, when the United States was not yet fighting in World War II but Nazi Germany had almost subdued Europe, U.S. foreign policy makers favored more active aid to Britain than the public and Congress seemed ready to accept. President Franklin D. Roosevelt feared the collapse of Britain, which would further isolate the United States with respect to Germany. While U.S. public opinion sympathized with Britain, it remained opposed to outright intervention in the war. To help safeguard Atlantic supply lines to Britain, Roosevelt proceeded to conduct an undeclared naval war against Germany in the Atlantic. He expected this policy to produce a hostile encounter with the German navy, which he hoped would bolster public support for aid to Britain. Such an incident occurred on September 4, 1941. In a radio speech a week later, Roosevelt implied that a German submarine had hit a U.S. ship in an unprovoked attack. In fact, the German U-boat had fired in self-defense. The Germans, remembering that attacks on U.S. ships had brought the United States into World War I, never intended to hit U.S. ships in the Atlantic. British officials, if not Americans, knew this at the time.[12] Thus the president, in his capacity as the people's agent, deliberately deceived Congress and the public (his principal) for what he thought was the larger good.

Any political system that limits its head of government in the conduct of foreign policy creates conditions that make such deceptive practices more likely. If leaders play by the constitutional rules, they risk making foreign commitments that may be repudiated by internal actors (such as the U.S. Senate) whose approval is legally

unitary actors Actors that have a single set of preferences over both outcomes and policies; individuals and factions are, by definition, unitary actors, but coalitions are not.

required. This happened to President Woodrow Wilson after World War I when he could not get the Treaty of Versailles through the Senate because the unpopular League of Nations Covenant was attached to it. Scholars call this type of problem **involuntary defection.** It occurs when the political leaders who make bargains with other international actors intend to uphold them but are prevented internally from doing so. Contrast this problem with **voluntary defection,** which occurs when political leaders fail to cooperate as promised because they see an advantage in defecting and do so on purpose.[13] Aside from the political embarrassment it causes, leaders fear involuntary defection because it tends to give the political unit they represent a reputation as an unreliable partner. Leaders thus sometimes turn to secrecy and deception to conceal their actions.

Problems can also arise for a political agent when its domestic constituencies demand policy outcomes that the agent finds hard to implement. Leaders need the support of their constituents to stay in power and govern effectively. When key constituencies demand outcomes that conflict with an agent's preferences or are difficult to deliver without creating opposition, the agent's political risks rise. Such problems frustrated President Bill Clinton's efforts to craft an economic policy toward China during his first term. In 1989, Americans were shocked when Chinese leaders brutally suppressed the pro-democracy movement in the massacre at Tiananmen Square. In his 1992 presidential campaign, candidate Clinton criticized President George Bush for "coddling" Chinese leaders and promised to hold China to a higher human-rights standard. Soon after Clinton won the election, this pledge was tested. U.S. officials had to determine what conditions, if any, they would attach to renewal of China's most-favored-nation (MFN) trading privileges with the United States. States enjoying MFN status can export goods to the United States at normal—that is, non-punitive—rates. (For a more detailed explanation of the meaning of the most-favored-nation principle, see Chapter 10.) Organized labor and human-rights groups wanted the U.S. government to attach tough conditions to MFN renewal, such as an end to Beijing's use of prison labor to make goods sold abroad and an easing of repression in Tibet. Clinton was reluctant to antagonize organized labor, which he needed to pass key pieces of his domestic program. In addition, prominent congressional Democrats were strong supporters of U.S. human-rights groups, who increasingly had become identified with Chinese political exiles and political prisoners still in China.[14] But it soon became evident that U.S. economic pressure on Beijing to change its human-rights policy was likely to fail, and that U.S. business groups, which Clinton had also courted, would oppose any such policy. Efforts to resolve these differences between the administration's business and human-rights constituencies failed.[15] Meanwhile, Clinton had become convinced that a trade war with China would make it more difficult to cooperate on such strategic issues as an easing of tensions on the Korean peninsula. After months of wavering, he finally decided to separate the issue of MFN renewal from China's human-rights performance, and to grant China renewal.

This example illustrates another point about the relationship between political leaders and their domestic constituencies. As societies have become more prosperous and more of them have moved toward democracy, the number of politically mobilized groups has tended to rise. This has made it more likely than before that leaders will be cross-pressured by groups with incompatible demands. Such cross-pressures, in turn, make it hard for leaders to assemble coalitions and to make and sustain coherent policy.

involuntary defection
A situation in which policy makers are unable to honor an agreement even though they want to.

voluntary defection
A situation in which policy makers decide not to honor an agreement even when they could.

These trends have made it more difficult over time for leaders to "sell" their foreign policy choices within their states. The need to legitimize their policy choices domestically raises both practical and normative issues for political leaders. Without legitimization, their day-to-day choices may be subjected to intense media and interest-group scrutiny. Such pressure can make it difficult for them to pursue their long-range policy objectives coherently and consistently.[16] In normative terms, the need for policy legitimacy raises the question of how much and when leaders should *follow* factional and constituency opinion, as opposed to *leading* it. When the political risks of action are high, leaders may prefer to reflect the existing consensus within their state rather than try to move that consensus to a different point. But this tendency can mean that opportunities to improve policy outcomes will be missed.

The State as Unitary Actor or Coalition: Does the State Speak in One Voice or Many?

As we have seen, principals and agents may have different preferences. For this reason, we must take care when discussing states or other complex actors in world politics to identify whether policy makers are speaking in one or several voices. To do this, we need to examine how coalitions, as opposed to unitary actors, make choices. That question, in turn, will lead us to ask what exactly it means to talk about state or national interests.

Choices are made either by unitary actors or by coalitions. By definition, unitary actors have a single set of preferences over outcomes and agree on the best available policy steps for achieving those goals. A unitary actor may be either a single individual or a *faction*—a group of people with identical preferences. A *coalition* is a set of factions that come together because they temporarily agree on means, though *not* on ends. For example, a defense minister in a particular state is necessarily a unitary actor. Depending on whether or not they have identical preferences, decision makers for the Army, Navy, and Air Force (or some subgroups within those organizations) could be factions. The military establishment as a whole could, but need not, constitute a coalition. How might such a coalition form? Let us assume that the defense minister's goal is to build the most militarily effective armed force for the least money. Assume further that the three services have different views on how to achieve that goal and how much money each should get. In such a situation, the three factions may engage in *logrolling*, supporting one another's top priorities. The military establishment would then be a coalition rather than a faction because the actors within it agree temporarily on policy choices (means), but not on the ultimate ends each seeks for itself. If the services could not reach agreement on either ends or means, then it would be inappropriate to treat the group as an actor.

Government policy is rarely made, much less implemented, by a single unitary actor. The reason is simple. There is rarely a need to make policy in areas in which there is complete unanimity among all the actors. Consequently, political choices typically involve objectives over which actors disagree and over which they seek to achieve their preferred solutions in the face of contrary views. Such groups are found not only within the government bureaucracy and legislature, but also outside of government. A faction may also contain elements from two or more of these arenas. In Israel, for example, a religious faction typically includes Orthodox rabbis within both the Knesset (parliament) and non-government organizations. Policy is made by coalitions of such factions.

With this in mind, it would seem that the state as a whole is only on very rare occasions a unitary actor. For unity to occur, what is at stake would either have to be so trivial that most people would be indifferent to the outcome, or they would all have to be affected equally and in the same way, so that their objectives naturally coincided. Such situations do occur, but only infrequently. Consequently, the notion of the "state as actor" is a figure of speech. While the term is an acceptable shorthand expression, it is important to remember that the state as such does not act; instead, the state refers to the factions and coalitions that act in its name.

Foreign Policy, Linkage Politics, and the "National Interest"

The Impact of Linkage Politics

If most political choices are made by coalitions, it should not be surprising that world politics is a coalition-building process. This process takes place across three linked political arenas. The first is the **international arena,** in which state and non-state actors try to achieve goals across the boundaries of two or more states.* What goes on in international politics is linked to two other arenas: a **policy-making arena,** in which factions within governmental and non-governmental actors form coalitions that can act in the name of a particular international actor, and a **constituency arena,** in which policy factions interact with their constituents and political backers. We call the coalition-building process that takes place in the policy-making arena **factional politics** regardless of whether those factions are in state or non-state actors. We call the politics that takes place in the third arena **constituency politics.**

Policy factions need political support within both the policy-making and constituency arenas to be effective. Because they do, factional leaders typically try to assess how the different policy options they are considering may affect their political standing with other factions and with their constituencies. The Congressional Black Caucus, for instance, was an important faction in many policy coalitions assembled

international arena The collection of interstate and trans-state relationships and strategic contexts within which international politics takes place.

policy-making arena The collection of relationships and strategic contexts within which factions form coalitions that can act in the name of an international actor.

constituency arena The collection of relationships and strategic contexts within which policy factions interact with their mass and elite constituencies—the actors whose support those factions need in order to continue in the role of policy maker.

factional politics Interactions of policy-making factions within international actors.

constituency politics The relationships and interactions that connect policy-making factions with their constituents and political backers.

---

*The term *international* needs to be used with some care because, as we explained in the discussion of different levels of analysis in Chapter 2, there is a long tradition of using *international* and *interstate* as synonyms. This practice is unfortunate both because states and nations are quite different entities and because the political entities that gave rise to what is commonly called the international arena are *states,* not *nations.* If states were the only key actors in international politics, it would be easy to clear up this terminological confusion by replacing *international* with *interstate.* However, while world politics is still built around a state system, it involves far more than the choices and actions of people who claim to speak for the state. Given the wide range— and growing number—of non-state actors involved in trans-state politics, it seems best to reserve *interstate* for the interactions of states and use *trans-state* when focusing on the cross-boundary actions of non-state actors. That leaves the question of what we should call the larger umbrella category that includes both interstate and trans-state politics. While creating a new term might describe this category more precisely, *international politics* is so widely used that the value of any increased precision is more than offset by the cost of using new and unusual terms. Therefore, it seems best to continue the traditional practice of using *international* to refer to this political arena.

Members of the Congressional Black Caucus formed a politically important faction in many of President Clinton's coalitions.

by President Clinton during his two terms. When members of the caucus were consulted on U.S. foreign policy decisions (such as those toward Haiti and Nigeria), it is highly likely that they examined not only their feelings about the substance of the issues before them but also the political ramifications of different choices. How might their response affect their power within Clinton's coalition and, thus, their ability to bargain successfully in the future on other issues they cared about? How would their choices be seen by members of their constituency base? Factional leaders value strong support from their constituencies because it helps them retain power within the group and provides leverage when they bargain with other factional leaders.

The coalition-building processes in each of these three political arenas can be examined using principal-agent relationships as an analytical tool. Assume that the policy-making factions have coalesced behind a particular policy option. A key question then arises: Can the leaders of these factions sell this policy option to their principal—that is, to their constituencies? Consider first what might happen if the leaders' constituents have expressed strong opinions in support of a different option. For instance, during President Richard Nixon's first term, solid majorities of the public favored a prompt withdrawal of U.S. forces from Vietnam. Although Nixon agreed with the public's ultimate objective of leaving Vietnam, for various reasons he rejected a quick withdrawal. Consequently, he found himself in a position in which achieving his preferred outcome required either changing public opinion or finding a strategy that would enable him to work around it. He tried to sell a more gradual policy, relying heavily on symbolic appeals that depicted advocates of a faster withdrawal as foolhardy and unpatriotic. His overwhelming reelection suggested that these tactics succeeded. Had not the Watergate scandal intervened, he would likely have had solid constituency support for his foreign policies in a second term.

It is also possible that policy factions will discover that there is as yet no consensus among their constituents for any particular policy option. For example, for years Israeli society had been divided almost evenly between those willing to return a significant portion of occupied territory to the Palestinians as part of a peace settlement and those who refused to consider such a concession. In several elections during the 1980s, policy factions supporting and opposing a negotiated solution to the conflict on these terms drew nearly equal strength from voters. Under such conditions, even policy makers who believe that they have a way to solve the diplomatic problem may conclude that no solution to the domestic coalition-building problem can be found. For this reason, Israeli policy toward the Palestinians changed hardly at all during the 1980s, even though Palestinian leaders appeared at times to be willing to move in a more conciliatory direction. By contrast, an agent may believe that while no winning coalition currently exists at the constituency level, steps could be taken to build support for a solution. Yitzhak Rabin had this belief when he became Israel's prime minister in 1992. He concluded that a majority of his constituents would accept a land-for-peace trade if Palestinians were seen to accept Israel's existence and cooperated with Israel on security issues. Here, an agent decided to try to move constituent groups to a new point rather than simply accept the existing deadlock.

In situations in which policy makers have a clear idea of what they want to accomplish internationally but see those choices as being politically risky, they will need to weigh their political risks against the possibility that a less risky policy will fail to achieve their substantive objectives. President Clinton found himself in this position in mid-1997, when international and domestic support grew for a total ban on military antipersonnel land mines. It is estimated that 110 million mines lie buried in at least seventy states and that they result in five hundred deaths a week, many of them civilian. One hundred and ten states—and fifty-nine of the one hundred members of the U.S. Senate—favored a total ban on all types of land mines. Clinton, however, agreed to support such a ban only if two exceptions were made: mines that self-destruct after forty-eight hours would be allowed; and all types of mines could be kept indefinitely on the Korean Peninsula. Clinton could not get U.S. military commanders to support any policy that did not meet those conditions. He was apparently unwilling to risk his future relations with the military by supporting a policy it rejected, even though the compromise that enjoyed the support of U.S. military leaders was unlikely to be acceptable to other states.[17]

Many scholars use the term **bureaucratic politics** when they discuss how multiple agents within a government relate to one another on issues where they represent different organizational factions. We explore the value of this term in the box "*A Closer Look:* What Is Bureaucratic Politics?"

Because policy making in world politics involves a three-level coalition-building process, the composition of coalitions greatly affects the coherence of policy and its stability over time. Policy becomes incoherent when the factions that leaders believe must be included in a coalition favor actions that are either internally inconsistent or that conflict with leaders' other objectives. Let us examine first how domestic coalition-building can affect the internal coherence of a state's policy choices.

Consider what happened in Imperial Germany in the decades preceding World War I. From the 1870s to the early 1900s, German foreign policy makers worked very hard to minimize the possibility that they would have to fight a two-front war. To achieve that goal, they needed to isolate France diplomatically (France was assumed to be permanently hostile to Germany after the Franco-Prussian war) and to maintain good relations between Germany, Russia, and Britain. However, by the late 1890s it had become clear that the conservative coalition governing Germany needed the domestic political support both of agricultural and industrial elites to survive in office. The agricultural groups demanded high tariffs on grain to close out

bureaucratic politics
A situation in which the preferences and choices of government policy makers are driven by their desire to protect the interests of the agency they represent and advance their personal political power.

A Closer Look

What Is Bureaucratic Politics?

Scholars who analyze bureaucratic politics usually make three claims about government policy making. First, it appears that people's responsibilities within a government agency strongly influence their policy positions, and thus the factions that form in interagency bargaining. Second, the policy choice that results from this bargaining reflects actors' commitments not only to their agencies' substantive agendas but also to maintaining or improving their agencies' budgets and relative political position. Third, the relative power of factions across these bureaucratic units helps to determine who wins such bargaining encounters.

A bureaucratic politics perspective would, for example, lead one to expect that a state's trade and environment ministries would evaluate a proposed environmental treaty quite differently. Part of those differences would reflect the fact those in the trade ministry would assess its costs and benefits to the state's export industries, while those in the environment ministry would care about its effect on environmental quality. But according to bureaucratic politics arguments, agency positions would also be affected by pure budgetary and political self-interest, and the winner in this process would be the agency with the most influence on top leaders.

Several important criticisms have been leveled at these claims. First, it has been argued that *bureaucratic position* is not necessarily the main determinant of people's policy preferences. Second, it is not clear that bargaining among bureaucratic factions is necessarily a crucial determinant of policy choice, especially in areas where top political leaders have strong policy views of their own. Third, while bureaucratic agencies greatly influence how a policy is implemented (because here they become top leaders' agents), this influence is lessened when leaders have a large stake in a particular policy choice and thus monitor implementation closely themselves.[a]

Much research has explored bureaucratic-politics arguments.[b] It finds that they best explain cases in which differ-

ent policies have clear implications for agencies' budgets.[c] Overall, however, support for these arguments has been mixed. In some cases, as the critiques suggest, factions are not defined by organizational or suborganizational interests. In others, the political beliefs and substantive preferences of top leaders matter much more than agency positions in explaining ultimate policy choices.[d]

In sum, scholars who have investigated bureaucratic politics processes are dealing with important aspects of policy making. Clearly, factions and coalitions do form in and around government agencies when it comes to questions both of policy choice and implementation. Nevertheless, it is misleading to assume that one can identify actors' preferences solely on the basis of the institutions they represent, since this reduces policy and political stakes to a single dimension. It is better to investigate the sources and nature of actors' preferences, rather than relying on assumptions about them.

[a]Two influential critiques of the key claims about bureaucratic politics are Robert J. Art, "A Critique of Bureaucratic Politics," in Robert J. Art and Robert Jervis, eds., *International Politics: Enduring Concepts and Contemporary Issues*, 3rd ed. (New York: HarperCollins, 1992); and Stephen D. Krasner, "Are Bureaucracies Important?" in G. John Ikenberry, ed., *American Foreign Policy: Theoretical Essays*, 2nd ed. (New York: HarperCollins, 1996).

[b]Particularly influential pieces of work include Graham T. Allison, *Essence of Decision* (Boston: Little, Brown, 1971); and Morton H. Halperin, *Bureaucratic Politics and Foreign Policy* (Washington, DC: Brookings Institution, 1974). A good collection of readings can be found in David C. Kozak and James M. Keagle, eds., *Bureaucratic Politics and National Security: Theory and Practice* (Boulder, CO: Lynne Rienner, 1988). A useful review of the literature is David A. Welch, "The Organizational Process and Bureaucratic Politics Paradigms: Retrospect and Prospect," *International Security* 17, no. 2 (Fall 1992): 112–46.

[c]Allison, *Essence of Decision*, p. 176; Art, "A Critique of Bureaucratic Politics," p. 432.

[d]For cases in which bureaucratic politics propositions are evaluated, see the country-specific chapters in Andrew Bennett, Joseph Lepgold, and Danny Unger, eds., *Friends in Need: Burden Sharing in the Gulf War* (New York: St. Martin's Press, 1997).

Russian competition; at the same time, the industrial elite demanded high tariffs on manufactured goods and a continuation of the naval arms buildup that produced large government contracts for ship building. These policies kept the governing coalition together, but they conflicted sharply with the fundamental diplomatic objective of maintaining good relations with Britain and Russia. High tariffs on grain angered Russian leaders, whose constituents wanted to export to the German market. Meanwhile, the tariffs on manufactured goods and the naval ship-building program dramatically worsened relations with Britain.[18] The factions that German leaders needed to have on board for domestic political reasons thus led to policy choices that were inconsistent and self-defeating internationally.

This example of German policy making illustrates a set of policies that was stable for long periods, even if it lacked internal consistency. If the factions that leaders need in order to govern change frequently, a different problem may appear: Policy may be coherent at any given time, but very unstable over time. For example, soon after President Clinton took office, he chose to increase the U.S. commitment to Somalia that had been made at the end of the Bush administration. Bush had intervened militarily to protect the international agencies distributing food in Somalia, but these efforts were stymied by fighting among local warlords for political control of the country. The UN Security Council authorized member states to apprehend Mohammed Adeed, a warlord who was believed to be responsible for an attack on members of the international relief force. At the request of the UN, U.S. forces sought out Adeed and his key followers. Congress at first supported this policy, at least passively. But when eighteen U.S. Army Rangers were killed, congressional support for UN operations evaporated almost overnight. Realizing that he could not hold on to a congressional coalition for his foreign policy unless he reversed course, Clinton quickly promised to withdraw from Somalia and instituted more selective criteria for any future humanitarian interventions.

You may have noticed how much factional preferences can vary even within the same state. In Imperial Germany, some factions always favored free trade; other factions, such as the large industrialists, were sometimes free-traders and at other times

President George Bush decided to send U.S. troops to Somalia in late 1992 in an effort to stabilize the situation enough for humanitarian relief supplies to be delivered. They were met on the beach by camera crews from the media, but it wasn't long before expanding objectives (called "mission creep" by critics), misjudgments about the nature of the security threats U.S. troops faced, factional disputes within the U.S. government, and miscommunication between U.S. officials and the United Nations all combined to create a policy-making fiasco that led to the deaths of eighteen U.S. Army Rangers.

were not; and the major landowners never supported free trade. In the early 1990s many factions in Congress favored U.S. participation in UN peacekeeping operations, but opposition grew sharply after the Army Rangers were killed. How can we explain these contrasting and shifting preferences?

First, even within the same state, different factions often see the world differently, and thus have quite different policy incentives. For instance, between the end of the Cold War and the September 11, 2001, attacks, some U.S. interest groups and congressional factions saw few external threats to U.S. safety and thus few reasons to spend lives or money on UN operations or modernizing the military. Other groups saw a world filled with terrorists and failed states in which innocent people starved or were slaughtered because there were no institutions within their states that could provide order. While these groups were both more internationalist than factions who saw neither a security threat nor a humanitarian obligation to intervene, they stressed different problems and consequently usually advocated different foreign policies.

Second, variations in actors' preferences within countries can occur when factions depend on different constituencies for political support. For instance, in the pre-World War I period, German policy makers who were dependent on support from industrialists knew that their constituents were often ambivalent about a high-tariff policy because at least some of them wanted to sell abroad, and high tariffs made it likely that they would be shut out of foreign markets. Meanwhile, policy makers who represented agricultural interests knew that German landowners were much more uniformly threatened by foreign competition; they did not have a comparable interest in exporting, and therefore supported protectionist trade policies more consistently.

Third, the preferences of different domestic factions may vary because they assess the risks of alternative policies differently. Factions' risk assessments can vary because their constituents are affected differently or because they have a different view of the international stakes. For instance, as we discuss in a case study on the text's website, referenced in Chapter 8, factions within the U.S. Congress that support building a national missile-defense system estimate both the political and policy risks of deploying such a system quite differently from those that oppose it.

If distinct groups within the same state can differ so much about foreign policy objectives, you might wonder whether states have "national interests" in foreign policy at all. It has long been claimed that states do have such interests, but that argument has come under criticism in recent years.

Debates about the "National Interest"

The **national interest** refers to matters that are claimed to be very important to a state as a whole, usually in foreign policy. Sometimes the term is defined narrowly to include only the physical security of those living within a state's boundaries; other times it is defined to include the promotion of a country's culture, values, institutions, and economy. The idea that states have such collective interests goes back to the early state-builders of the Renaissance. At that time, the doctrine of *raison d'état* (reason of state) was influential among statesmen and thinkers. According to this doctrine, the ability of a state to survive in a competitive international environment depended heavily on its relative economic and military power. Consequently, survival and power represented predominant values. It was argued that because states cannot guarantee

national interest The idea that all the people in a state have some core collective concerns.

their security in such a world, their leaders must do whatever is needed to protect vital territorial, economic, and diplomatic interests. In practice, *raison d'état* then meant that the ends justified the means, and that the king and his ministers would (and should) provide security with no questions asked. Niccolò Machiavelli, in *The Prince*, was among those who articulated this view (see Chapter 6).

The idea of the national interest has remained a key part of the realist tradition in international relations up to the present. Realists focus on the lack of enforceable rules above the level of sovereign states and conclude that states must focus on relative power in order to protect their basic values. Reflecting this tradition, Hans Morgenthau defined the state's interest in international affairs in terms of power. To Morgenthau, power was so vital that it became an end in itself: the state must act to protect its power position.[19]

However, toward the end of the twentieth century the notion of the national interest became increasingly controversial. Alexander George and Robert Keohane, for example, argue that while policy makers may need a general standard by which to judge a state's objectives, "the national interest" is too vague to serve that diagnostic function. States have many goals, they contend, and to claim that some have higher priority than others begs the question of how the trade-offs among competing values should be made. In practice, they say, "the national interest" has been used as much to justify as to determine state behavior in foreign policy.[20]

While decision makers, policy factions, and factions' constituents have preferences and objectives, the notion that states as entities have interests rests on several questionable assumptions. First, it assumes that the principal-agent problem is trivial: that those who act for states inevitably do so for public rather than private political motives; and that whenever they disagree with their constituents, the agents are right. Second, this notion assumes that only the international arena matters in determining a state's policy objectives. Strategic objectives at the international level may be important, but how political leaders balance those incentives against domestic needs arising from factional and constituency arenas matters as well. Third, it assumes that states are governed by unitary actors. For there to be an unambiguous national interest, the people who speak in the name of the state must have the same preferences over outcomes and, ideally, also agree on the best policy instruments by which those outcomes can be achieved. But states are rarely governed by unitary actors, and there is seldom only one overriding solution to policy and political problems. States are normally governed by coalitions. By their very nature, coalitions are composed of factions that have different preferences and perceptions. For all these reasons, the notion of "the national interest" seems to have little analytic value.

Conclusion

To analyze world politics, we need to identify the major actors and their preferences. For several hundred years after the Westphalian settlement in 1648, it was commonly believed that states virtually monopolized the resolution of most world political issues. Today states are no longer the only effective actors, but they remain the central actors in some issue areas and, even when they no longer dominate outcomes, they are usually important participants. Consequently, if you are going to try to make sense of world politics, it is still crucial to pay attention to states, who speaks for them, and whether the people who speak for a state speak in one or many voices.

While states remain important actors, on most international issues today it is common to find states, IGOs, NGOs, and other non-state actors bargaining with one another, each seeking to achieve distinct goals. As a result, it is usually difficult to understand contemporary outcomes in world politics without taking the positions of each of these types of players into account. Fortunately, as we discuss in the next chapter, while there are many different types of actors in world politics, they share a common set of patterns in the ways in which they react to the politics of strategic choice.

Key Terms

international actor	principal-agent problems	constituency arena
state	unitary actors	factional politics
sovereign territoriality	involuntary defection	constituency politics
nation	voluntary defection	bureaucratic politics
juridical (legal) sovereignty	international arena	national interest
empirical sovereignty	policy-making arena	

To The Reader   A CHAPTER SUMMARY and QUESTIONS FOR REVIEW are available at **www.prenhall.com/lamborn**

Beyond the State

*Interstate Law
and Institutions
and Non-State Actors*

S tates affect central aspects of world politics, but it is important to go beyond the state—to take into account the effects of interstate law as well as the preferences and actions of non-state actors. Interstate law, by tradition called **international law,** is the body of rules designed to regulate activities that occur across or among states. The rules established under international law can ultimately only be enforced by the actions of states, but there are usually strong incentives to follow established legal rules. Moreover, states that willingly and visibly violate established legal norms usually pay a political price.

Non-state actors also play a key role in world politics and in our daily lives. Terrorist groups affect people's security. International relief organizations may mean the difference between life and death for refugees in war-torn states. Trans-state business enterprises shape people's standard of living by relocating existing jobs or creating new ones. It is very difficult for a state to get new loans from foreign banks or to refinance old foreign debt unless the terms are approved by the International Monetary Fund (IMF), a key IGO, even though the IMF rarely contributes any of the funds itself. These examples are, moreover, but the tip of the iceberg: it is now a rare case in world politics when states monopolize policy making.

We begin this chapter with a discussion of the nature and importance of international law. We then examine international governmental organizations (IGOs), international non-governmental organizations (NGOs), and other trans-state actors. After defining each type of actor, we discuss its purposes, how it affects political outcomes and people's welfare, and how coalitions are built in and around it. We conclude with a comparison of the politics of choice in state and non-state actors.

The Nature and Importance of International Law

It is common to distinguish two branches of international law, private and public. **Private international law** deals with the rights and duties of individuals and other non-governmental actors as they are affected by their location within different states. If, for instance, a business firm operates in more than one state and those states impose incompatible legal obligations on it, some set of legal procedures is required to resolve the jurisdictional conflict. **Public international law** deals with the legal rights and duties of sovereign states. Such rules, for example, would identify the limits of permissible actions that one government could take against the territory or people of another state in retaliation for terrorist acts committed against the first state. Because world politics is built around a system of sovereign states—organizations that exercise legitimate and exclusive legal authority within their borders—any legal obligations they assume to govern their relationships with other states must be mutually acceptable. For that reason, most of the important *political* questions involving international law concern *public* international law, and that is our focus in this section.

The Sources of International Law

According to Article 38 of the Statute of the International Court of Justice (the principal judicial organ of the United Nations), there are five main sources of international law: customary practice, treaties, general principles of law, judicial decisions,

international law   Rules designed to regulate the interstate activities of state and non-state actors.

private international law The interstate rights and duties of individuals and other non-governmental actors.

public international law The legal rights and duties of sovereign states.

and the writings of international legal scholars. Although Article 38 does not establish any of these as intrinsically stronger than the others, treaty-based and custom-based rules are thought to override rules derived from the other sources, since they show direct evidence that states have accepted the rules in question.

Custom in this context refers to repeated behavior by diplomats and political leaders over time. It is the oldest source of international law. For example, as it became useful for governments to communicate about commercial and alliance matters on a regular basis, resident ambassadors were established in Renaissance Europe at the major royal courts. It was quickly recognized that ambassadors could most effectively serve as conduits between governments if they were not subject to the local law of the state in which they were serving. Without such protection, they could easily have been legally harassed as a way to put pressure on their governments. Envoys thus came to be seen as political and legal extensions of the ruler they represented abroad—a person who would not be subjected to local legal rules if he happened to visit another state. In this way, the doctrine of *diplomatic immunity* developed. Today, it means that the ambassador, his or her family, and a few other resident members of an embassy are immune from the application of local law unless their home government voluntarily suspends their immunity. (If they violate local law, they are typically asked to leave the host country.) Although diplomatic immunity has been codified in treaties, it is rooted in a centuries-long pattern of customary behavior. Customary legal rules are considered binding on all states unless their governments have consistently objected to the rule.

Bilateral and multilateral treaties are a second major source of international law. Treaties have the same function in international law as contracts have in domestic law: They identify for the parties what each has a legal right to expect from the others under various conditions. As you might imagine, diplomats and lawyers draft these documents very carefully, so that their states are obligated to do only very specific things in well-defined circumstances. Traditionally, most treaties have included only a small number of states and have dealt with commercial, security, or cultural matters of direct concern only to those parties. In recent decades, this pattern has shifted somewhat. Today, a growing number of *multilateral treaties*—those subscribed to by a substantial number of states—set out to create more general and wide-ranging legal obligations. Such treaties—for example, the Genocide Convention, which makes extermination of particular groups of people an international crime, regardless of where or by whom it is committed—are often designed to set down in writing an emerging general principle of law. While these law-making treaties are technically binding only on the states that sign them, there is often significant diplomatic and moral pressure on governments not to violate them, even if those governments do not accept the legal obligation in a strict sense.[1]

The other three sources of international law provide indirect indicators of legal obligations. General principles of law are those found within many domestic legal systems. One example is that legal obligations must ordinarily be *reciprocal;* the parties to an agreement cannot expect others to be bound by rules they themselves do not accept or implement. The widespread acceptance of this principle means that it is often used to develop or interpret treaties, even if the word "reciprocity" does not appear in them. Decisions of international or domestic courts are also at times used to identify an international legal rule. But such decisions have limited applicability for legal decisions in future cases, since states typically do not recognize precedents from prior legal rulings unless those rulings have been reinforced by treaty or widespread customary practice. Finally, the published work of legal scholars has also been used to identify the legal status of international rules. But such writings are at most an indirect indicator of state practice, which is the guiding criterion for identifying a rule of international law.

By observing how international law is created, we see that while moral rules and legal rules are both important types of social norms, they differ in a key respect. **Moral rules** involve freely accepted obligations that limit people's options when choices need to be made. If I believe that it is morally wrong to lie, I must not lie even when doing so would be more convenient than telling the truth. Moral rules are accepted voluntarily by individuals and groups; they are not seen as obligations that derive from some political process. They are thus not enforceable as purely moral rules by political authorities. By contrast, **legal rules** are created by political authorities. As such, they are the products of a political process and enforceable through a political process. So even though many legal rules derive from moral rules, the existence of a moral rule does *not* necessarily signify a corresponding legal rule.[2] This explains why, for instance, one might recognize a moral obligation to resettle wartime refugees in other states, even though those states are under no legal obligation to take them in.

Our discussion might be summarized as follows. To know whether an international legal rule exists, we must find out whether a significant group of states have explicitly said so or repeatedly acted as if it was so. Even then, because there is no world government, legal rules cannot be legally enforced at the international level. These features of the international environment have convinced some analysts that international law is not really law at all. Law, they say, must have its origins in a government of some kind, and it must also be enforceable by designated government institutions. Because each recognized state is sovereign, there is no institution legally superior to them that can carry out these tasks.

We recognize, of course, that there is no world government. But we disagree with the above conclusion. Even though international law is created and applied in a way that differs from law within most societies, that does not mean that international law lacks legal character. If political actors say that they accept certain practices and obligations as legally binding, and they act in a way that coincides with such statements, those rules have legal force for them. Even though violations of such obligations draw a lot of attention, they do not constitute typical behavior. Almost all governments observe their international legal obligations almost all the time, since to do otherwise would disrupt the orderly international relationships most of them value and subject them to criticism at home and abroad.[3]

The absence of a world government does, however, have implications for the nature and application of international law. In world politics, legal rules are produced in a fragmented way by the same actors to which those rules will most often apply— sovereign states. As a result, there is no single, legally authoritative source that lays out all the rules. In cases where there is no clear treaty or customary obligation, much of the work of international lawyers involves finding and interpreting the applicable principles and rules from past cases and policy decisions.

The Historical Development of International Law

The first roots of public international law derive from ideas prevalent in ancient Rome. The early Roman law (called *jus civile*, or civil law) applied only to Roman

moral rules   Freely accepted obligations based on people's understanding of right and wrong, which are not enforceable by political authorities unless they are supported by a companion set of legal rules.

legal rules   Binding obligations created by a formal political process that identifies both the substance of the laws and the governmental agencies that have the right and responsibility to enforce them.

citizens and was designed to serve the needs of a small city-state. As Rome began to conquer other peoples, a legal system was needed that could govern both relations among Rome's foreign subjects and between foreign subjects and Roman citizens. A system of legal rules known as *jus gentium* (law of peoples) was gradually developed for this purpose. Over time jus gentium overrode jus civile, which ceased to exist. Jus gentium became the common legal code of the Roman empire and was viewed by Romans as universally applicable.[4]

The structure of contemporary public international law dates from the beginning of the modern state system. As we discuss in Chapter 6, beginning with the Peace of Augsburg in 1555 and then reinforced by the Peace of Westphalia in 1648, the state system took the form of a set of legally independent entities, each of which was free to order its internal affairs as it saw fit. Consequently, states were no longer subject to higher compulsory legal authority. The seventeenth-century Dutch scholar Hugo Grotius was a key intellectual figure in developing a doctrine of international law based on the sovereign nature of states. His major substantive contribution was the notion that the high seas must be free for use by everyone; they could not be appropriated for the exclusive use of any state.

Grotius's ideas reflected the tradition of **legal positivism**—the idea that only those rules grounded in the consent of states would be binding on them. Freedom of the seas met this test, at least in the emerging European context. Dutch business and political leaders, whose society earned its primary living from ocean-based commerce, found Grotius's ideas useful.[5] The converse also applied: According to legal positivism, states need not follow rules based on moral reasoning if there is no pattern of state practice supporting them. Historically, a tension has existed between this tradition and one based on natural law. According to **natural law,** there is a fundamental set of universal principles, based on divine will, that existed prior to any state and that binds them whether or not they have specifically consented. As we discuss in Chapter 12, modern notions of human rights—notions that often must be asserted against the policies and traditions of state actors—are often rooted in this alternative legal tradition.

From the early seventeenth century through the nineteenth century, the state system—which was still overwhelmingly Eurocentric—constituted a fairly homogenous group of actors. Most of them had a common (Christian) religious background, and while some were more free internally than others, there was less variation in attitudes about the appropriate relationship between the state and the economy within the Euro-centered system than between that system and the rest of the world. Moreover, policy makers in the interstate system regarded the use of force as a fully legitimate tool of statecraft. They also believed that it was legitimate to acquire and hold colonies.

Each of these beliefs was challenged, if not shattered, during the twentieth century, and each change had important implications for international law. The 1917 Russian revolution legitimized a socialist alternative to prevailing capitalist systems of economic organization and provided some governments an excuse to seize private property—including the property of foreign nationals—for state use. Two brutal world wars and the advent of weapons of mass destruction have narrowed (to self-defense) the grounds on which states can legitimately use force outside their borders. The biggest changes have involved the delegitimization of colonial empires and the gradual assertion of individual human rights against authoritarian state practices. States no longer have legal "rights" to hold colonies, and an emerging

legal positivism
A tradition that asserts that states are only bound to honor rules they accept either through formal treaty or long-established custom and practice.

natural law   A tradition that asserts that there are universal principles—usually based in religion but sometimes also in nature—that exist independent of states and the political process.

human-rights regime (discussed in Chapter 12) has begun to qualify the absolute rights of rulers to treat their citizens as they see fit.

In a world in which social, economic, and technological change can occur very rapidly, it often seems as if international law cannot keep up. In recent years a number of problems—trans-state crime, trans-state terrorism, and destructive ethnic conflicts—have emerged that are difficult to address within the framework of a state system. While national policy makers increasingly agree that such problems must be solved, achieving agreement on legal rights and responsibilities is difficult. Yet this situation is not unique to international politics; rarely does the law within states instantaneously reflect the recognition of new problems or produce a workable solution. The response internationally may be slower still, but the problems involved in devising legal remedies are similar. And progress does sometimes occur, despite the obstacles. Over the last several decades, the problem of terrorism has prompted states to cooperate more closely on criminal investigations and on measures to prevent terrorist groups from attacking innocent people. Treaties providing for the extradition or prosecution of those accused of terrorism outside a state's territory have multiplied and now cover such crimes as money laundering and drug trafficking.[6] The September 11, 2001, terrorist attack on the United States will likely deepen this trend.

International Intergovernmental Organizations (IGOs)

The effects of the growth of international law on the evolution of the state system have been complemented and reinforced by the expanding number of international institutions. In any area of social life, **institutions** are "persistent and connected sets of rules (formal and informal) that prescribe behavioral roles, constrain activity, and shape expectations."[7] While it is easiest to see formal institutions that operate out of a specific headquarters and have a permanent staff, it is important to look for sets of informal rules that become so well established ("institutionalized") that they structure people's perceptions and behavior. Institutions help to bring order to an area of human activity or codify the order that has arisen on its own, so that people know what to expect of one another. Such "rules of the road" help people cooperate to achieve shared goals. For example, you and three friends might eat together every Saturday night, with each person in turn preparing dinner or organizing a potluck meal. This is a *social* institution; it is clear who participates, what the institution's purpose is, and how decisions are made. People also join formal gourmet clubs, which generally have more explicit rules that lay out who prepares the dinners and the obligations (if any) of the other members. The difference between these arrangements is that the first consists of informal understandings, while the second specifies the rights and duties of membership more precisely, often in writing.

International intergovernmental organizations (IGOs) are formal international institutions that have states (and only states) as members. They are international because they include at least two sovereign states and they regulate issue areas that cross state boundaries. They are formalized because they have some ongoing administrative structure, usually created by a treaty among the founding members. This structure, or secretariat, is what distinguishes IGOs from an ad hoc series of international conferences; it provides continuing staff support for the organization's

institutions Organized sets of rules that structure people's roles, expectations, and behavior.

international intergovernmental organizations (IGOs) Formal international institutions with an ongoing administrative structure that have states (and only states) as members.

activities. The IMF secretariat, for example, helps to draw up and then monitor the economic plans that states agree to follow as a condition for receiving bank loans. The UN secretariat monitors and coordinates the activities of UN-authorized peacekeeping operations around the world. IGO secretariats provide continuity to their institutions and an outlook not identified with the preferences of any one state.

IGOs began to develop when states realized that managing their growing interdependence more systematically could foster economic growth.[8] During the early nineteenth century, technology was rapidly breaking down barriers to communication and commerce. Steamships were replacing sailing ships, railroad trains were making stagecoaches obsolete over long distances, and the telegraph was introduced. In 1821, the first modern IGO, an international commission to regulate use of the Elbe river, was created. Commissions for the Rhine and the Danube followed in 1831 and 1856. These regional bodies were followed by a geographically broader group of institutions called the Public International Unions. The International Telegraphic Bureau (now called the International Telecommunications Union, or ITU) was created in 1868 to standardize telegraph messages. The Universal Postal Union (UPU) was founded in 1874 to set general rules for mail delivery across state boundaries. Organizations to standardize weights and measures and fight communicable diseases soon followed.

As we discuss in Chapter 7, a worldview called *functionalism* began to affect these developments in the first half of the twentieth century. Functionalism held that states could cooperate on economic and social problems even without addressing the political differences that often divided them. In practical terms, this idea reached its highwater mark after the two world wars, with the creation of the International Labor Organization, the many functional organizations in the United Nations system, and the European Coal and Steel Community (later part of the European Economic Community and then its successor organization, the European Union, or EU). Fewer IGOs have been developed to deal with security issues, in part because political leaders have tended to believe that it is difficult to arrive at compatible preferences on diplomatic and security issues, and in part because it is more common to organize responses to security threats through alliances. The Concert of Europe did help the European great powers coordinate their diplomatic and military actions for a time after the Napoleonic Wars, but it lacked a permanent secretariat and thus was not an IGO.

The League of Nations was the first major security IGO. It was designed to safeguard the Versailles Peace Settlement of World War I, to create a collective security system that would radically reduce or eliminate war, and to manage some of the nationalities problems associated with the breakup of the Russian, Ottoman, and Austrian Empires. In Chapter 7 we discuss why the League was not able to implement a system of collective security that was up to the demands placed on it. The UN also failed in its efforts to implement collective-security arrangements in the decades immediately after it was established in 1945. More recently, the UN has had some successes in the security area, which we discuss in more detail below.

The number of IGOs has increased seven-fold during this century, from 37 in 1909 to 260 in 1996.[9] Most of them deal with economic and social issues. This growth reflects a major increase in economic, social, and cultural transactions across state borders. The industrialized countries are more heavily represented in IGOs than the less economically developed countries (LDCs),[10] even though many IGOs have been created to promote economic growth in the LDCs.

		Breadth of Purpose	
		Single Purpose	**Multiple Purpose**
Scope of Membership	**Universal**	International Atomic Energy Agency	United Nations
	Regional	North Atlantic Treaty Organization	Association of South East Asian Nations

Figure 5–1   **Classification of IGOs, with Examples**

So far, we have distinguished among IGOs in terms of breadth of membership (regional as opposed to global) and purpose (economic, social, or security). These points require some elaboration. First, IGOs can comprise states of one region or they can be open in principle to all states. Distinguishing between regional and global organizations tells us more than just the likely number of members. Since states within a region often share concerns that are not shared by all states, regional IGOs typically have more specific objectives than global IGOs.[11] Second, whether they are regional or global, IGOs can serve one purpose or multiple purposes. This classification scheme yields four types of IGOs, as indicated in Figure 5–1.

We will discuss each of the organizations in Figure 5–1 as examples of how an IGO's breadth of membership and stated purpose help to create distinct organizational identities. Bear in mind that these are only examples of each type; many more organizations belong to each of the four types.

Single-Purpose, Universal Membership IGOs

Some IGOs have a single purpose and allow any state that shares it and assumes the obligations of membership to join. The International Atomic Energy Agency (IAEA) illustrates this type of IGO. Under the terms of the Nuclear Nonproliferation Treaty (NPT), the IAEA—the only global IGO devoted entirely to security matters—monitors the possession and potential use of fissionable materials (enriched uranium and plutonium), which are key ingredients of nuclear weapons. The IAEA grew out of a widespread belief in the 1960s that some way had to be found to deal with the problem of "horizontal nuclear proliferation"—the spread of nuclear weapons to states that did not previously possess them.* The Nuclear Nonproliferation Treaty (NPT), which entered into force in 1970, provides that all

---

*Horizontal proliferation differs from vertical proliferation, which refers to growth in the nuclear arsenals of existing nuclear states. The NPT has dealt with vertical proliferation by requiring existing nuclear-state members to reduce and eventually dismantle their arsenals of these weapons, though only recently have there been any major reductions. For most NPT members, horizontal proliferation remains the more significant of the two problems.

non-nuclear weapons states that sign it must submit their peaceful nuclear-energy programs for inspection by IAEA officials. All nuclear reactors, nuclear research and development facilities, and sites where uranium is mined or stored fall under this obligation. Since 1992, *any* state that receives nuclear-related equipment or supplies has also had to agree to IAEA inspections in order to receive exports from the group of states known as the Nuclear Suppliers Group. The rationale for making the NPT a global agreement is that many people believe that every additional nuclear-weapons state increases the risk of nuclear war to some degree. However, a number of known or suspected nuclear proliferators (India, Pakistan, Israel, and Iran) have not accepted the IAEA's jurisdiction over their nuclear programs. The IAEA thus regulates effectively only those states that choose to be regulated.

Multiple-Purpose, Universal Membership IGOs

The United Nations and its predecessor, the League of Nations, define what this entire category is about. While each was created by the victors after a cataclysmic war—the League after World War I and the UN after World War II—and initially excluded the defeated states and others that did not meet the victors' standards for legitimate partners, they had an announced goal of universal membership. They also were designed to help achieve a wide range of outcomes. As one might expect given the historical contexts that led to their creation, security ranked first in priority. But the founders of both organizations saw peace as being inescapably intertwined with the creation of open international economic systems and the promotion of at least some minimal human rights standards. When concerns about the environment grew into international issues in the 1960s, the UN became active in that area as well.

The UN is also officially charged with coordinating the work of a large number of specialized agencies and affiliated organizations (see the box "*A Closer Look: United Nations Specialized Agencies and Other UN-Affiliated Organizations*"). Each one of these organizations has its own charter, budget, and staff. Some, such as the International Telecommunications Union and the Universal Postal Union, were created long before the UN itself. Others, such as the International Monetary Fund (IMF) and the World Bank were created around the same time as the UN or much later. In each case, these are single-purpose IGOs with substantially global membership. Nothing about their mission is region-specific. In practice, the UN's supervisory role with regard to these agencies varies considerably. At one extreme are the IMF and World Bank, which are essentially autonomous organizations that report to UN bodies only in a perfunctory way. At the other are organizations such as the United Nations Industrial Development Organization, which functions in close harmony with the UN's voting majority of Third World states.

When one combines the UN's goal of universal membership with an agenda that includes the four most important issue areas in world politics—security, political economy, human rights, and the environment—one is immediately drawn to the question of whether such a large group of actors will be able to work together effectively. The sheer numbers involved make coordination hard enough, but the challenges go beyond numbers. As states, every member of the UN asserts a claim to sovereign territoriality, which means in the case of an international intergovernmental organization such as the UN that members are only responsible to carry through on the obligations they specifically agree to. A universal organization of states runs immediately into another problem as well: the power to achieve different goals is very unevenly distributed in world politics.

United Nations Specialized Agencies and Other UN-Affiliated Organizations

Food and Agriculture Organization (FAO) works to increase food production, raise rural standards of living, and help states cope with emergency food shortages.

International Bank for Reconstruction and Development (IBRD, known as World Bank) lends money to governments (or to private enterprises, if the government guarantees repayment) for specific agriculture and rural-development projects. Also supports projects to develop countries' infrastructure (ports, roads). The World Bank Group incorporates the following four institutions:

> **International Development Association** provides interest-free credits to the world's poorest states for fifty years.

> **International Finance Corporation** lends money to private corporations without government guarantees.

> **Multilateral Investment Guarantee Agency** guarantees investments in developing countries against such risks as war and nationalization.

> **International Center for the Settlement of Investment Disputes** mediates between developing countries and trans-state business enterprises, encouraging TSBEs to invest by improving the investment climate.

International Civil Aviation Organization (ICAO) works to facilitate and promote safe international air transportation by setting binding international standards and by recommending efficient flight practices. (ICAO regulations govern international flights.)

International Fund for Agricultural Development (IFAD) lends money on concessional terms for agricultural development projects, primarily to increase food production by the poorest rural states.

International Labour Organization (ILO) formulates international labor standards and provides technical assistance training to governments.

International Maritime Organization (IMO) promotes international cooperation on technical matters related to shipping and provides a forum to discuss and adopt conventions and recommendations on such matters as safety at sea and pollution control.

International Monetary Fund (IMF) provides technical assistance and financing to countries that are experiencing balance-of-payments difficulties.

International Telecommunications Union (ITU) promotes international cooperation in telecommunications, allocates the radio-frequency spectrum, and collects and disseminates telecommunications information for its members.

United Nations Educational, Scientific, and Cultural Organization (UNESCO) pursues international intellectual cooperation in education, science, culture, and communications, and promotes development by means of social, cultural, and economic projects.

United Nations Industrial Development Organization (UNIDO) serves as intermediary between developing and developed countries in the field of industry and as a forum for contacts, consultations, and negotiations to aid the growth of industrialization.

Universal Postal Union (UPU) sets international postal standards and provides technical assistance to developing countries.

World Health Organization (WHO) conducts immunization campaigns, promotes and coordinates research, and provides technical assistance to countries that are improving their health-care systems.

World Intellectual Property Organization (WIPO) promotes the protection of such intellectual property as patents and copyrights. Encourages adherence to relevant treaties, provides legal and technical assistance to developing countries, encourages technology transfers, and administers the International Union for the Protection of Industrial Property and the International Union for the Protection of Literary and Artistic Works.

World Meteorological Association (WMO) promotes the exchange and standardization of climatic information through its World Weather Watch; conducts research and training programs.

World Trade Organization (WTO) oversees rules by which trade across state frontiers is conducted and it has a dispute-settlement procedure to determine when and how those rules apply in contested cases. Incorporates and supersedes General Agreements on Tariffs and Trade (GATT).

International Atomic Energy Agency (IAEA) promotes peaceful uses of nuclear energy, and by agreement with the parties to the Nuclear Nonproliferation Treaty, carries out inspections to ensure that weapons-grade nuclear material is not diverted to military purposes. (The IAEA is not technically a specialized agency under the UN's definition, but functions much like one.)

Source: United Nations Association of the United States, "The United Nations at a Glance," available at the website for United Nations Association of the United States (*UNAUSA.org*).

The UN General Assembly has been called the "talking shop" of the world, because members can discuss almost any issue.

The League of Nations, the first major multipurpose IGO with aspirations to universality, tried to address these problems in two ways: It adopted a requirement of unanimity on all binding decisions (as opposed to expressions of opinion which could be made on a majority vote), and it gave the major military powers a special role on security issues in a smaller, non-universal council. The UN dropped the principle of unanimity but kept the two-chamber organizational structure—the entire membership in the General Assembly and a far smaller Security Council—and gave the five permanent members of the Security Council a veto. In clear recognition of the uneven distribution of military capabilities in the world, the permanent members of the Security Council were the major military powers in the victorious coalition in World War II: the United States, Britain, France, the Soviet Union (now Russia), and China.

Politics being politics, designing an organization for sovereign states is not just about establishing rules for legitimate expressions of preferences, it is also about gaining access to the resources necessary to implement any policy decisions. Here the framers of the UN also had to deal with the implications of the principle of sovereignty and the reality that resources were very unevenly distributed. The principle of sovereignty led to the decision to make a distinction between recurring expenditures for things like the salaries of the Secretariat, the international civil servants who work for the UN, and expenses for special projects, such as peacekeeping operations or special funds for development. Recurring expenditures for the "normal" operations of the UN organizational infrastructure are paid through annual assessments which states have a treaty obligation to pay by virtue of their agreement to become members. Special expenditures are paid either by voluntary contributions or by special assessments authorized by a vote on the specific policy or operation. The problem of the massively unequal distribution of resources was addressed by creating an assessment schedule based on a formula that took into account total national income, per capita income, and the ability to earn foreign exchange.

In spite of these efforts, financing the UN's continuing and special programs has remained a difficult and frequently controversial problem. Both the United States and the Soviet Union have at different times—the USSR during the 1960s and the United States through much of the 1990s—refused to pay their full recurring and special assessments. Not surprisingly, all these instances occurred after either the United States or the USSR had been outvoted on initiatives it opposed. That happened much more to the Soviet Union in the first decades of the UN's existence, when it was on the winning side of General Assembly votes only between 34 and 55 percent of the time. The United States, in stark contrast, went from feast to famine: voting with the majority 60 to 74 percent of the time until 1960, 32 to 55 percent of the time between 1960 and 1980, and 12 to 14 percent of the time between 1981 and 1990.[12]

The intensity of U.S. unhappiness at being outvoted has been reinforced by the magnitude of its contributions. The initial formula for annual assessments made the United States responsible for 50 percent of the cost of the UN. That was immediately reduced to 40 percent and, over the years, it has gradually been lowered still more, first to 33 percent, then to 25, and most recently to approximately 22 percent (the United States pays a slightly higher share for authorized peacekeeping operations). While these are significant reductions, they still leave the United States paying by far the largest share. That creates continuing opportunities for controversy: within the United States whenever it is outvoted, and around the world whenever the United States tries to use the size of its contributions to get its way.

The UN's involvement in security, international political economy, human rights, and the environment will be discussed in the chapters that cover those topics. In the chapters on security you will find that security operations have been strongly affected by shifts in the ability of the permanent members of the Security Council to identify shared goals. While all UN members can discuss any dispute, identify the conditions they believe led to it, and urge the parties to negotiate, it is the Security Council that specifically deals with threats to the peace and can impose economic or military sanctions. During the Cold War, the Soviet Union or the United States would often veto or threaten to veto efforts by the UN Security Council to deal with breaches of the peace through economic or military coercion directed at one of the parties. The only significant exception was in 1950, when the Soviet Union missed an opportunity to veto a Security Council resolution supporting U.S. involvement in the Korean War because its representative was boycotting the session over another issue (whether the Nationalist government on Taiwan or the communist government of People's Republic of China should have the China seat). That was the last time a permanent member made the mistake of missing an opportunity to veto a policy it adamantly opposed. To sidestep the resulting impasses, UN Secretary-General Dag Hammarskjold promoted peacekeeping operations during the 1950s as an alternative to full-scale UN enforcement activities. These operations feature lightly armed troops who are deployed, with the consent of the parties, to supervise and monitor truce agreements, separate the combatants, and so on.** A number of successful UN peacekeeping missions took place during the Cold War, notably in Cyprus and the Middle East, but better Russian-American relations after the Cold

---

**These operations presume that a truce will be in place before peacekeepers are sent and that their principal responsibility will be to monitor it. That requirement, as we shall see, has not always been met.

War's end led to a dramatic increase in these operations in the 1990s. For instance, in 1997 the Security Council imposed sanctions on UNITA, an armed faction seeking to overthrow the government of Angola. The sanctions required UN members to bar the entry, transit, or residence of senior UNITA family members and to ban all flights to any location inside Angola unless those flights were authorized by the Angolan government.[13]

The Cold War also had significant effects on the UN's ability to respond to economic and human rights issues. Through much of the Cold War the UN was hamstrung by the fact that the United States and its allies in the West had very different understandings of legitimate economic systems and of appropriate human rights standards than did the Soviet Union and its allies. However, both these issue areas were at least as heavily affected by decolonization as by the Cold War. When the UN was created after World War II, the overwhelming majority of its member states were in Europe or in North and South America. The collapse of the European empires changed all that, and by 1960 the General Assembly had a voting majority of post-colonial societies. As we discuss in Chapter 10, that "new majority" led a concerted attack on the Western economic system from 1960 through the late 1980s. The attack largely failed, but during this same period the new majority also organized a far more successful campaign against racial discrimination in South Africa and elsewhere that had a significant effect on the UN's role in addressing human rights issues.

As these examples suggest, it is impossible to understand the evolution of the UN's multidimensional roles in the world without paying attention to the impact of the Cold War and decolonization. Completing this overview requires that we add three additional historical transformations: the growth of an international environmental movement, which literally created the UN's fourth major issue area; the development of the feminist movement, which immediately altered debates about human rights and has the potential to change existing understandings of how to promote economic development and security; and the massive increase in non-state actors, which is changing the composition of UN-sponsored conferences and the direction of the UN's activities in almost all areas.

Single-Purpose, Regional Membership IGOs

Because many sets of concerns in world politics are region-specific, 72 percent of IGOs are regionally oriented.[14] Most of them are single-purpose organizations. The North Atlantic Treaty Organization (NATO) illustrates this type of IGO.[15] Under the North Atlantic Treaty (NAT), the United States and a number of Western European states have since 1949 pledged mutual defense against armed attack. Although the Soviet Union was not named as NATO's adversary, preparation for a possible conflict with the USSR was NATO's major Cold War purpose (see Chapter 7). NATO is thus an alliance, but it is the most heavily institutionalized alliance in history, with an elaborate set of agreed-upon decision-making procedures and extensive military and diplomatic bureaucracies to implement its decisions. It has an integrated peacetime military command. Its troops train and fight as members of multinational units, and military equipment is designed to be usable by soldiers of every member state. No other alliance has had these features. They give NATO more continuity and organizational coherence than traditional, non-institutionalized military coalitions have.

With the end of the Cold War, NATO made three major changes. It will now consider undertaking peacekeeping operations outside the territories of its members at the invitation of the UN Security Council or the Organization for Security and Cooperation in Europe (OSCE). Efforts to guarantee the settlements that ended the Bosnian and Kosovo wars are examples of such operations. During the Cold War, various NATO members undertook military action in places such as Suez and Vietnam, but the organization as a whole did not endorse these missions. Today the major threats to European stability are likely to originate outside NATO members' borders, as they did when Yugoslavia disintegrated in the early 1990s and when the threat from global terrorist networks expanded dramatically in 2001. Addressing these threats has become NATO's major military challenge.

NATO has also begun to admit, on a selective basis, some members of the former Warsaw Pact—the Soviet Union's Cold War alliance. Two rationales for doing so have been offered: NATO membership will for the first time allow these states to be part of an effective international security structure of their own choosing; and joining an organization of democracies will help them complete the transition to democratic and free-market economic systems. If NATO is indeed intended to promote internal change of this kind, it has taken on a new purpose in addition to mutual defense. But this nation-building objective remains unofficial; on paper, NATO remains a heavily institutionalized but otherwise traditional military organization.

The third significant change in NATO reflects both the growing importance of terrorism as a security threat and the diplomatic complexities created by the expansion of NATO into Eastern Europe. In May 2002, the nineteen member states in NATO and Russia signed an agreement creating a NATO-Russia council. The council is designed to have responsibility for a restricted but very important set of issues: terrorism, the proliferation of weapons of mass destruction, and theatre missile defense. While falling far short of making Russia a full member, the agreement simultaneously involves Russia in discussions about three critical security areas and makes it easier for supporters of NATO to argue that the alliance is not targeted against Russia. If the collaboration works, it will also make it easier for President Vladimir Putin to overcome domestic opposition to his effort to move Russia closer toward the West.

Multiple-Purpose, Regional Membership IGOs

The Association of Southeast Asian Nations (ASEAN)—and the European Union, which we discuss in detail later in this chapter—illustrate IGOs whose several purposes have been strongly shaped by their members' shared regional history. Until the late 1960s, East Asian states had developed few IGOs. This reflected a pattern in which some state outside that region (at various times, China, Japan, or the United States) had typically exercised a *sphere of influence* over those countries, making independent choices about economic and military cooperation difficult or impossible.

ASEAN was established in 1967 by Indonesia, Malaysia, Singapore, the Philippines, Thailand, and Brunei. It later added Vietnam, and by the end of 1997 also included Burma, Laos, and Cambodia. ASEAN was officially designed as a means for promoting economic, scientific, and cultural cooperation, but the more immediate aim in the 1960s was regional security. The Vietnam War was then at its height, and the ASEAN states, worried about the involvement of outside powers in that conflict, sought to take control of their own security agenda.[16]

Regional security concerns within this group have continued, especially concerning Vietnam's occupation of Cambodia and the growth of China's military capabilities. Yet ASEAN members have also been concerned with the major economic changes that have occurred in East Asia during the past few decades. After Deng Xiaopeng became China's top leader in the 1980s, major parts of the Chinese economy were opened to outside investment. This helped to spur a rapid expansion of trade and investment throughout East Asia. As a result, states in the region deepened their economic ties, and ASEAN has become more involved in promoting economic cooperation.

ASEAN has developed into a major collective voice within its region. During the 1980s, it often functioned as a bloc in regional and global forums. When China hinted that it might use force to back up its claim to an oil-rich island also claimed by the Philippines, ASEAN members stood behind the Philippines and nudged China into negotiations over the issue.[17] ASEAN has also been used to create a free-trade area, and the ASEAN Post-Ministerial Conference has become an institutionalized way to converse with seven key trading partners from outside the region (Australia, Canada, the EU, Japan, New Zealand, South Korea, and the United States).[18] ASEAN has continued to focus on regional security, mainly by hosting an annual Regional Forum specifically on such issues.

The Four Roles of IGOs

Now that you are familiar with some examples of IGOs, we can assess how the existence of these institutions affects world politics. While not all IGOs are equally weighty actors, in general they play four roles.[19] First, by providing a predictable location and format for meetings and putting dependable staff support at the service of the group, IGOs can offer an efficient environment in which actors can bargain. Bargaining of any kind involves **transactions costs**—that is, the costs of trying to reach any agreement at all. These costs include arranging meetings, preparing and distributing the needed documentation, and so on. If participants had to organize many meetings *ad hoc*, instead of relying on a framework supplied by permanent organizations with fixed procedures, the costs of bargaining would increase, and the number of agreements would likely decline.

Second, IGOs often make it more likely that states will actually comply with the agreements they make. In some cases, compliance is achieved or made more probable by the threat or imposition of group sanctions. Bosnian Serbs, for instance, engaged in fewer violations of cease-fire agreements after NATO agreed to enforce such truces at the Security Council's request. Enforcement in world politics is typically carried out by individual states or groups of states that coordinate their actions informally. But IGOs can make enforcement more credible by providing predictable rules and ways to impose them. In addition, some agreements include systematic procedures for resolving disputes about the meaning of the rules. The World Trade Organization (WTO), for instance, has mechanisms to resolve disagreements among the parties. States may not actually use these procedures in settling disputes and instead act on their own outside the IGO, but they must then prepare for the possibility of collective sanctions.

The rules for making IGO decisions vary according to the issue at hand, the IGO in question, and the particular part of the organization making the decision. IGOs make decisions in five ways: by simple majority vote (50 percent of those voting

transactions costs The direct cost of reaching and implementing an agreement, whether those costs are financial, political, or human.

plus 1), by special majority (votes higher than a simple majority), by qualified majorities, by weighted vote, and by unanimous vote.[20] Many IGOs now permit nonbinding recommendations to be made by simple majority vote; this procedure is followed in the UN General Assembly. Qualified majorities are used in the UN Security Council, where each of the permanent members has a veto. In weighted voting systems, actors' votes can vary with states' financial contributions and, in some situations within the EU, on states' populations (to ensure that the more populous states cannot be outvoted by the smaller ones). In the IMF, weights are combined with a special majority rule, and the United States has had a weighted vote large enough to prevent the special majority from being reached. As a result, the United States has what is, in effect, a veto on IMF decisions. In a few IGOs, such as the EU Council of Ministers, key decisions require unanimity. The more consequential a decision and the more legally binding it is on member states, the more common it is that the IGO's rules will have been written in a way that makes it easy for one or a few states to block action.

The third role of IGOs is to signify the members' approval of some practices and ideologies in world politics and their disapproval of others. This political role is similar to what happens in domestic political arenas, where political leaders try to legitimize their objectives and actions so that they can achieve their aims and minimize their political risks. Domestic actors know that it is far easier to govern and remain in office if one's actions are widely seen as justified than if they are not. Global IGOs have similarly become a major forum for justifying certain actions, claims, and policies, and delegitimizing others.[21] In the early 1990s, President Bush felt that he needed explicit Security Council approval to lead a military coalition against Iraq's occupation of Kuwait, even though Kuwaiti leaders had requested that help. Bush apparently believed that the use of force against Arabs by wealthy European and North American countries would be seen as illegitimate unless it had the UN's blessing. Weaker states have also frequently used the UN in an effort to change international norms and perceptions to advance their policy objectives. For instance, in the first decades after World War II critics of colonialism used the UN to delegitimize colonization and to pass resolutions signifying international approval for various national liberation movements. The Palestine Liberation Organization (PLO) used these precedents in its move to gain permanent-observer status in the UN and build international support for its claim to represent all Palestinian people. The UN was also the most important forum for the Third World critique of the international economic system in the 1960s and 1970s.

Fourth, IGOs help to build coalitions on many issues in world politics, often through the involvement of secretariat personnel as facilitators or sources of expertise. In 1987, secretariat involvement helped shape intergovernmental agreement on measures to protect the earth's ozone layer from being depleted by the emission of chlorofluorocarbon (CFC) chemicals. More than other atmospheric components, ozone absorbs solar ultraviolet radiation that is extremely harmful to humans and other animals. CFC chemicals, which at one time were used in many common products such as refrigerators and aerosol sprays, release chlorine that depletes ozone irreparably. Beginning in the early 1980s, officials of the United Nations Environmental Program (UNEP), a UN agency, helped build a consensus that CFCs should be phased out of production and replaced by environmentally safer alternatives. Mostafa Tolba, an Egyptian scientist who headed the UNEP, worked hard to bridge gaps between the position of the United States, Canada, and the Nordic countries, whose firms were ready to stop producing CFCs, and Britain and France, whose firms were more reluctant to do so. Because the EU states operate as a bloc on many issues, continued French and British opposition to strong international controls over these substances would have precluded a meaningful treaty to deal with the problem. Tolba helped build support for strong controls by sponsoring conferences that brought together government officials and scientists. His scientific credentials provided credibility with researchers. At the same time, his Third World background allowed him to voice the concerns of many LDCs, which sought financial help from the wealthier countries in making the transition to safer chemicals as well as guaranteed access to the new technologies. He managed to sell a strong Ozone Treaty to a skeptical Third World faction because UNEP, under his leadership, assumed a key role in encouraging and distributing the aid, and because he created a strong sense of obligation on the part of the developed countries to contribute extra resources for this purpose.[22]

The Evolving Roles of a Major IGO: The European Union

In this section we take a close look at the European Union, both because it is one of the most important IGOs in the world today and because it provides a key case study in the ways in which an international institution can simultaneously respond to the goals of its member states and alter the environment within which state leaders pursue their international and domestic objectives. The European Union (EU) consists of closely linked institutions that have fostered common policies in many issue areas over the past 50 years. Integrated commercial, agricultural, financial, social-development, environmental, and human-rights policies have been developed through EU institutions. These policies have moved many issues that used to be subject to national jurisdiction to the jurisdiction of the EU. As a result, the EU has effectively pooled much of the sovereignty of its member states. The EU has also nurtured the beginning of a common European identity, and in doing so it has reinforced the belief that war among its members is virtually unthinkable. Having begun their institutional experiment during the early Cold War era, EU member states and societies now face the challenge of adapting their institutions to the distinctive problems of a post–Cold War world.

The EU's Historical Development

Even though Europe is the birthplace of modern nationalism and the sovereign state, the idea that Europe's peoples belong to a common civilization and would benefit from closer links across state boundaries is a very old one. In its modern version, Europeans began to raise the possibility of a united Europe after the shock of World War I led some political elites (and no doubt some ordinary citizens) to question the value of having separate and often competing states in Europe. These doubts were reinforced by the destructiveness of World War II. During that war, groups favoring the creation of a federal government in Europe once the fighting ended gained influence among some of the national movements that resisted the Nazi occupation. But commitments to traditional nationalism and the state were too deep for the most ambitious European integration plans to succeed in the late 1940s.[23] If a process of

European integration was going to begin at that point, another institutional formula had to be found. (See the box *"A Closer Look:* The Evolution of the European Union.")

That formula involved gradually integrating specific sectors across national lines, with the idea that the cumulative effect might eventually tie Europe as closely together as the United States of Europe championed by the federalists. The Schuman Plan, named after the French foreign minister who promoted it, was the first such effort, and the European Coal and Steel Community (ECSC) was its product. The plan provided for French and West German coal and steel production to be placed under a supranational High Authority (one that would have legal powers over specific affairs within the signatory states). For French leaders, the ECSC ended Germany's independent ability to make war by removing from national control key economic sectors needed in wartime. German leaders accepted the proposal as a way to reassure France that they were now "good Europeans." Belgium, the Netherlands, Italy, and Luxembourg also joined the ECSC at its inception in 1951. Britain was invited but declined to join.

In 1957, two other European IGOs were created by the Treaties of Rome: the European Atomic Energy Agency (EURATOM) and the European Economic Community (EEC). At a time when the use of nuclear power for peaceful purposes was becoming commercially viable, EURATOM was designed to promote cooperation across Western Europe in developing nuclear power facilities. The EEC was designed to implement a common market among its members; they would abolish trade barriers among them and adopt a common external tariff. The latter development allowed the EEC to bargain as a unit in global trade talks held under the auspices of the General Agreement on Trade and Tariffs, known as GATT (for a discussion of GATT, see Chapter 10). The EEC also created a Common Agricultural Policy (CAP), which was designed to promote a common European market for agricultural products, give preference to European agricultural producers over foreign producers in setting the external tariff for farm products, and share the costs of agricultural subsidies equitably among members. In practice, the CAP guarantees all member states' farmers the same price for their goods, regardless of supply and demand conditions.[24] Because many French farmers have been relatively inefficient producers, France insisted on including the CAP in the policy package agreed on at Rome. Britain was invited to join the Treaties of Rome, but again declined. In 1967, the three distinct European institutions (EEC, ECSC, and EURATOM) merged to form the European Community (EC).

During the 1950s, Britain's unwillingness to join the European institutions reflected deep ambivalence about its ties to continental Europe. British nationalism had increased during World War II, making an independent posture toward Europe more popular after the war.[25] Moreover, British leaders saw their ties to Washington and the Commonwealth (former British colonial) states as more important than their links to the continent. As Winston Churchill put it, Britain saw itself as "with" but not "part of" Europe. Both Conservative and Labour Party politicians also worried that submitting Britain to the jurisdiction of supranational European institutions would undermine a centuries-old tradition of Parliamentary supremacy on policy matters. While that attitude persisted in some circles of British opinion, Britain finally applied for membership in the EC in 1963 and 1967, only to see its bid rejected by France. It was not until 1973 that Britain was able to join the EC.

A Closer Look

The Evolution of the European Union

September 19, 1946	Winston Churchill invokes the need for a "kind of United States of Europe" in a speech at Zurich University.
May 14, 1947	The United Europe Movement is created.
June 5, 1947	The Marshall Plan is announced.
April 16, 1948	The Organization for European Economic Cooperation (OEEC) is instituted to coordinate the Marshall Plan.
January 28, 1949	The Council of Europe is established by France, Great Britain, Belgium, Luxembourg, and the Netherlands.
April 4, 1949	The North Atlantic Treaty is signed in Washington, D.C.
August 3, 1949	The Council of Europe enters into force.
May 9, 1950	"Schuman Declaration"—French Foreign Minister Robert Schuman proposes that France, Germany, and any other European countries desiring to do so should create a common pool of their coal and steel resources.
April 18, 1951	Treaty of Paris—Belgium, France, Germany, Italy, Luxembourg, and the Netherlands ("The Six") sign a treaty establishing the European Coal and Steel Community (ECSC).
March 25, 1957	Treaties of Rome—"The Six" establish the European Economic Community (EEC) and the European Atomic Energy Community (Euratom).
January 1, 1958	Treaties of Rome enter into force and the EEC Treaty is created. The nine-member EEC and Euratom Commissions are set up in Brussels and designed to share The Parliamentary Assembly and Court of Justice with the ECSC as per the Treaties of Rome. In addition, the EEC Treaty engenders the European Investment Bank (EIB) and the Economic and Social Committee (ESC).
July 1, 1967	Treaty merging the executives of the three Communities—the ECSC, EEC, and Euratom—signed in April 1965, enters into force creating the European Community (EC) with a single Commission and a single Council. Though independent, the Commission and Council will continue to act in accordance with the rules governing each of the three Communities.
January 1, 1973	Denmark, Ireland, and the United Kingdom join the EC.

Even among the continental countries, there were key differences about how to proceed with further integration. Under the leadership of the nationalist Gaullist party, French leaders insisted on an intergovernmental conception of EC policy making during the 1960s and 1970s. From this perspective, the IGOs in the EC should have little autonomy in proposing or implementing policy. Instead, policy initiatives would be accepted or rejected depending on what the separate member governments of the EC could agree on by bargaining among themselves. Other EC members were more willing than the French to accept a greater degree of supranational legal control over their affairs. During the 1970s, policy initiatives reflected French preferences. They grew out of bilateral negotiations between the EC heads

December 4–5, 1978	The European Monetary System (EMS) and its companion European Currency Unit (ECU) are established.
June 7 and 10, 1979	The First European Parliament is elected by direct universal suffrage.
January 1, 1981	Greece joins the EC.
February 14, 1984	The European Parliament passes the draft treaty on the establishment of the European Union.
January 1, 1986	Spain and Portugal join the EC.
July 1, 1987	The Single Europe Act, signed in February 1986, enters into force.
May 29, 1990	The European Bank for Reconstruction and Development (EBRD) is established.
February 7, 1992	The Maastricht Treaty is signed.
November 1, 1993	The Treaty on European Union (EU) enters into force.
January 1, 1994	The European Monetary Institute (EMI) is created.
January 1, 1995	Austria, Finland, and Sweden join the EU.
December, 1995	The European Council names the single currency created by the Maastricht Treaty the *euro*.
June, 1997	Regulations establishing the legal status of the *euro* and the creation of an exchange rate mechanism for currencies not participating in the *euro* area are approved by the European Council.
March 25, 1998	Eleven countries agree to participate in the *euro* currency area: Belgium, Germany, Spain, France, Ireland, Italy, Luxembourg, the Netherlands, Austria, Portugal, and Finland.
January 1, 1999	The European Council irrevocably fixes the conversion rates of the participating currencies for the *euro* when the *euro* becomes the official legal currency and national currency of the eleven participating member states.
July 1, 2002	All existing national currencies and coins cease to be valid, and remaining national currencies and coins must be withdrawn from circulation and replaced with the euro. However, holders of national currency will be allowed to exchange national currency for the euro at national central banks for a long period of time.

Note: This chronology is based on information posted at the European Union website (*http://europa.eu.int*).

of state rather than the central EC institutions in Brussels.[26] For example, close collaboration between French President Giscard d'Estaing and German Chancellor Schmidt was needed to create the European Monetary System (EMS), under which the exchange rates of the separate currencies would be allowed to vary only narrowly relative to one another. Even so, the EMS paved the way for the single European currency initiative in the late 1990s.

The French attitude toward further integration changed significantly in the mid-1980s. When Socialist François Mitterrand was elected French president in 1981, he put in place economic policies that raised workers' salaries and benefits without any commensurate increase in their productivity. The resulting inflation threatened to destroy the EMS policy of carefully managed currency exchange rates. At that point, Mitterrand's domestic incentives were incompatible with France's commitments to EC monetary collaboration, and perhaps to further European economic integration as a whole. Faced with these incompatible objectives, Mitterrand reversed course and adopted tough anti-inflationary policies. His choice was as much to move European integration forward as it was a reversal in his own economic policy. Once French policies in this area became more closely aligned with those of other EC members, further steps to integrate the economies of EC members could be contemplated.[27]

Two major initiatives followed over the next decade. In 1987, a proposal was adopted to create a single European market by the end of 1992. In such a market, all barriers to the movement of goods, services, and labor within the EU countries had to be removed. Several hundred specific measures have been required to achieve this goal.[28] In 1993, the Maastricht Treaty on European Union was ratified. EU members, as they were now called, agreed to pool their sovereign decision-making autonomy to a fairly radical degree. There would be an independent European Central Bank (ECB), compatible policies on price stability, and a common currency, which was scheduled to go fully into effect by 2002. Again, British leaders were reluctant to go along fully and opted out of the common currency.

EU Institutions: Structure and Functions

At present the EU consists of five linked institutions. The European Commission is ultimately accountable to EU member governments, but its three functions give it a key part on its own in making and enforcing EU rules. First, in most areas of EU policy, it is the only institution that can initiate the formation of new rules. In this sense, the Commission serves as an agenda-setting body. Second, it oversees the implementation of rules within the member states. Since member governments may have incentives not to fully implement certain EU measures their officials dislike, the Commission's oversight role is crucial. Third, the Commission manages the EU's budget. The Commission's thousands of bureaucrats, of course, are charged with the day-to-day performance of these three tasks, but they are overseen by twenty commissioners named by member governments. These officials—usually former high-ranking ministers in their home states—have distinct portfolios of responsibility within the Commission, such as environmental policy and industrial policy. Collectively, they function as the EU's cabinet, which is headed by the president of the EU Commission. In this role, an official who wants to take an initiative in charting new paths for EU action has a broad mandate and substantial administrative support.

The European Parliament (EP), as its name suggests, is a quasi-legislative body. It began as a group of people who served as delegates in their national parliaments and served in the EP in addition to that role. EP members began to be directly elected in 1979. These elections occur within the member states, with each member's share of the total number of legislators roughly proportional to its share of the total EU electorate. The members run as representatives of Europe's political parties. There are Socialist, Christian Democratic, and Liberal members. The EP's role in EU policy making is rather complex. It has progressively gained authority within the overall EU institutional structure, so that it now shares authority with the Council of Ministers (described below) on how to respond to legislative initiatives that originate with the Commission. But this authority varies by issue area, so that in practice the EP remains much weaker than a national parliament in a democracy. For this reason, public interest in the EP is low, with turnout rates for EP elections averaging below 50 percent.[29] (These rates would not be considered unusual in many U.S. elections, but in Europe, where voter turnout tends to be higher, they are seen to reflect an otherwise atypical degree of public apathy.)

The EU Council of Ministers is, along with the Commission, the EU's primary mechanism for drafting or amending agreements and legislation. Although it has come to share this role with the EP, on many issues it maintains the dominant voice. The identity of the ministers varies according to the issue under discussion; the composition of this body would be different, for instance, if the subject were environmental policy as opposed to defense policy. The presidency of this body is shared among EU members, rotating once every six months.

Along with the EU Commission and the EP, the European Court of Justice (ECJ) has supranational authority over EU members: Its rulings have the force of law within those states without a need for further approval at the national level. The ECJ's role within the EU is similar to that of the U.S. Supreme Court: It settles disputes among member states over the applicability or implementation of EU rules and disputes arising between EU members and one of the other EU institutions. While the Treaties of Rome did not specify that EU law would override national law when the two conflicted, several key ECJ rulings have established this rule in practice, much as the early nineteenth-century U.S. Supreme Court established itself as the guarantor of the U.S. Constitution.[30] The ECJ has thus grown in authority and prestige since 1957, ensuring that the European Union ultimately functions according to the rule of law. Since interstate law is often considered to be less reliable than national law, for reasons discussed earlier in this chapter, the ECJ in this sense has had a major impact on Europe's political, economic, and social life.[31]

The European Central Bank (ECB) is the newest of the primary EU bodies. It was created to manage the common monetary policy that came into being with the introduction of the euro as the EU's common currency. In this role, the ECB plays a role comparable in many ways to the United States Federal Reserve Board, setting European interest rates and controlling the money supply. While day-to-day implementation of these tasks is carried out by an executive board that is one step removed from the control of member states, important decisions, such as changes in interest rates, are in the hands of the ECB's Governing Council, composed of the heads of the national central banks of EU member states. As is true of the Commission, the ECB thus mixes some elements of supranational control and intergovernmental control of policy.

What Does the Future Hold for the European Union?

It is widely agreed that the EU experiment has succeeded remarkably well over the last fifty years. A deep and durable peace has been built among the EU countries, their economies are now tightly intertwined to their mutual benefit, and a progressive notion of individual human rights has been widely accepted within the region. For all of these reasons, the EU has become a magnet for aspiring democracies and has helped Spain, Portugal, and Greece build durable democratic institutions. In trade and finance, the single market seems to operate relatively smoothly, while in other areas, such as taxation and various aspects of social policy, policy discretion at the state level has been retained. This mix of pooled and state-level sovereignty seems to work well for most EU members.[32] During the 1960s, when the European integration experiment was still new, a number of analysts wondered whether such integration might also occur in other regions of the world. Three decades later, while regional trade organizations have appeared in other regions, the European experiment still seems distinctive in its broad membership and in the range of issues regulated by its institutions.

Despite—or even perhaps because of—this success, the EU faces two major challenges over the next few decades. One concerns how many of the aspirants for EU membership can plausibly be absorbed into its existing institutions and programs. The EU has promised to accept qualified formerly communist states in Central and Eastern Europe as members, and ten of them (Bulgaria, the Czech Republic, Estonia, Hungary, Latvia, Lithuania, Poland, Romania, Slovakia, and Slovenia) were negotiating entry as of midyear 2001. Three other countries (Cyprus, Malta, and Turkey) are also negotiating the terms on which they might join. The problem is that successful applicants must not only be able to show that they can accept the economic obligations of membership—including acceptance of the single commercial market and, increasingly, a common monetary policy—they must also show that they have developed the durable democratic institutions and the respect for individual human rights that have become EU hallmarks. Turkey's official policies, for instance, treat visibly observant Muslims in ways that might not survive close human-rights scrutiny. Even if all of these countries could satisfy the EU's extensive and demanding criteria for full membership, the costs for existing members would be substantial, since many EU programs involve redistributing resources from richer areas within the Union to poorer ones.

Whether the EU will develop a capacity for regional self-defense that can be used independently of the United States is a second challenge. Since most EU members (and all of the large ones) are also NATO members, the question did not arise during the Cold War. At that point, it was almost inconceivable that the major EU countries would want to use military force together in any major crisis that did not also involve the United States.

The international incentives facing the key actors may now be changing. U.S. leaders are increasingly preoccupied by security issues outside of Europe or issues that are broader in scope than Europe: a possible military rivalry with China, the destruction of international terrorist networks, and the global implications of missile defense. Moreover, during the 2000 U.S. presidential campaign, George W. Bush suggested that under his leadership the United States might not want to participate in peacekeeping operations such as those in Kosovo and Bosnia with the NATO allies. Although Bush softened his position on this issue once he took office—and revised it still more after the terrorist attacks on September 11, 2001—Europeans are well aware that Americans are very reluctant to commit ground troops overseas for peacekeeping operations. Such missions are unpopular with some U.S. policy factions—especially those from which Bush draws political support. Before the Kosovo War, British Prime Minister Tony Blair consistently supported a more vigorous military response to Serbian atrocities than U.S. officials felt they could support,[33] and Blair was embarrassed that Europeans could not muster more potent military forces on their own for the Bosnia and Kosovo missions. A perceived lack of U.S. dependability in such situations could induce EU political leaders to think more seriously about a common defense policy to go along with the common foreign policy they have developed over the last several decades.

The crucial question is whether EU leaders can fashion the domestic support for the enhanced military forces this option would require. Public support for a common European military policy is surprisingly strong—especially in Germany, where it actually exceeds support for the common EU monetary policy.[34] It is not clear that support would persist at these levels if new taxes were needed to pay for a genuinely European army. Yet forty years ago, few would have predicted that the EU would have integrated as much of European life by the early twenty-first century as is now the case. A common EU defense policy, supported by significant joint military forces, might just be conceivable in the foreseeable future.

Trans-State Actors

Whereas IGOs are _interstate_ actors, various other participants in world politics are _trans-state_ actors. **Trans-state actors (TSAs)** are private citizens living in different states who are connected _across_ (rather than _through_) government channels. However, for TSAs to operate anywhere, the consent of at least one state is needed. This need for access to territory gives states some bargaining leverage in dealing with TSAs. Nevertheless, TSAs may have significant leverage of their own in bargaining with other actors, depending on the issue. This means that we can analyze the behavior of TSAs using the same theoretical framework as we did for states and IGOs. Just as in states and IGOs, stable policy in TSAs requires bargains that bridge differences across the constituency, factional, and international arenas. In this section, we discuss NGOs as well as trans-state business enterprises, religious organizations, terrorist groups, criminal organizations, and miscellaneous other trans-state actors.

Non-Governmental Organizations (NGOs)

International non-governmental organizations (NGOs) have developed as the functional counterparts of IGOs. Like IGOs, NGOs have distinctive functions. Also like IGOs, NGOs claim that they represent the preferences of their members as well as, at times, the interests of those non-members who are affected by policy choices in the substantive areas in which they specialize. The key difference is that unlike IGOs, NGOs are formal institutions made up of _private_ individuals, or associations of such persons, from at least two states.*** NGOs typically have a permanent staff and some organizational identity. Their political activities, including lobbying states and IGOs, resemble in some ways the lobbying done by organized factions within states. Politically prominent NGOs include Amnesty International, a human-rights group, and Greenpeace, an environmental organization. Many others, such as the International Federation of Automobile Experts and the Association of Dental Dealers in Europe, attract little outside attention.

***Some international institutions mix public and private representation. The International Council of Scientific Unions and the International Telecommunications Satellite Consortium (INTELSTAT), to take two examples, include representatives from both governments and private organizations. But the IGO/NGO distinction remains useful, since many international organizations are either completely private or completely public, and the two types have different kinds of constituencies. Amnesty International, for instance, is very cautious about accepting funds from any government, since doing so might appear to compromise its independence in identifying victims of human-rights abuses.

trans-state actors (TSAs)
Private individuals, groups, and organizations located in two or more states that maintain their relationships without depending on government organizations and channels of communication.

international non-governmental organizations (NGOs)
International organizations created by private individuals and groups.

World Politics and the Individual

Jody Williams, the Vietnam Veterans of America Foundation, and the Treaty to Ban Land Mines

A treaty to ban land mines went into force on March 1, 1999. One of the most unusual things about this treaty was that it was promoted by a coalition of non-governmental actors that began work only a few years before. How were non-governmental actors able to put the idea of a treaty to ban land mines on the agendas of states? Why, once it was on the agenda, did it move toward acceptance and ratification so quickly? Why, in spite of the widespread international support, did the United States government refuse to sign the treaty?

For an overview of this case and links to other relevant sources on the Web, see **www.prenhall.com/lamborn**

NGOs predate the existence of IGOs. It seems that the first NGO was the Rosicrucian Order, a mystical education group that formed in the seventeenth century. However, as recently as 1850 only five NGOs existed. They then multiplied rapidly because people had more time and resources to participate in voluntary associations as the middle classes expanded, and new ways to communicate with people in other countries made such associations feasible.[35] By 1909, there were 176 NGOs, as compared to 37 IGOs; by 1996, there were 5,472 NGOs, as compared to 260 IGOs.[36] These large numbers reflect the specialized purpose of most NGOs, which have been formed to promote almost every group goal imaginable.

NGOs can affect outcomes in world politics in two ways. First, they help set political agendas and build constituency support for policies they favor. A political agenda is the set of goals and policies that are up for decision or are being promoted seriously by government officials and non-governmental actors at any one time.[37] **Agenda setting** is the series of steps by which issues come to command such attention. Not all significant problems make it onto key actors' political agendas. Environmental problems, which are examined in Chapter 15, were not a significant political issue before the 1960s. Problems tend to be placed on political agendas when people's preferred patterns of life seem threatened. For instance, Third World NGOs have tried to redefine development policies that seem likely to displace local villages or damage the local ecology. A coalition between U.S. environmental NGOs and Brazilian opponents of rainforest destruction helped stop a World Bank project to build roads through virgin areas of the Amazon Basin and reverse local plans for giving tax incentives to farmers and ranchers to develop these areas.[38] As this example suggests, NGOs often try to influence issues within states by bringing together local constituencies and outside groups that care about the problem. In doing this, their activists may have the advantage of long professional experience on an issue and a broader range of useful contacts than is typically found within a Third World government or IGO secretariat.[39]

Second, NGOs may have a key role in implementing policies. Doctors Without Borders and the Red Cross, for instance, have aided many victims of armed conflict. When the Russian government was suppressing the Chechnyan rebellion in 1997, the Red Cross was the only supplier of fresh water to Grozny, Chechnya's capital, and reconstructed the city's sewage system to prevent the spread of epidemics.[40] At

agenda setting The process by which issues become identified as topics worthy of analysis and action by policy makers.

times the UN or other IGOs use NGOs as their agents to deliver services in the field. This typically occurs when an NGO has some specialized expertise that an IGO or individual governments lack, when those who are affected by the policy trust an NGO more than other actors, or when hiring NGO personnel offers more flexibility than using IGO personnel. NGOs are likely to be asked to work on time-sensitive issues such as disaster relief and on such politically sensitive issues as aid to refugees and family-planning projects.[41] Whether justifiably or not, NGOs may be vulnerable to the charge that they are compromising local sovereignty when they perform services within a state. For that reason, detailed negotiations are sometimes needed about what an organization may do and how.[42]

Trans-State Business Enterprises (TSBEs)

Trans-state business enterprises (TSBEs) are firms with headquarters in one state and affiliates in at least one other state. You will often see these actors referred to as multinational corporations (MNCs) or transnational corporations (TNCs). We prefer the term *trans-state business enterprise* for two reasons. First, these actors operate across state boundaries. The "trans-state" designation highlights this point better than "multinational" or "transnational." Second, "business enterprise" is a more precise term than "corporation."

Firms that simply trade goods or services across state frontiers are not truly trans-state *enterprises*. To belong in this category, a firm must own or effectively control a business abroad. Such control is called *foreign direct investment* (FDI); it is distinct from *portfolio investment*, which involves owning shares in someone else's business. For example, Polygram Classics, which produces compact discs and music videos under various labels, is headquartered in Europe but owns processing plants around the world.

Direct ownership of foreign enterprises has gone on for centuries. As early as 1200 AD, Venetian and Genoese merchants established banks abroad to finance the trade carried by their ships. Five hundred years later, large corporations such as the British East India Company (headquartered in London, but largely operated out of British India) were responsible for much international commerce. In 1914, just 7 percent of the U.S. gross national product involved earnings from foreign affiliates of domestically based firms. After 1945, growing investments by U.S. and then Japanese, European, and Third World firms massively increased the global level of FDI. In the 1990s, at least 37,000 TSBEs in the agriculture, banking, manufacturing, retail sales, raw materials, and technology sectors controlled over 206,000 foreign affiliates.[43] (See the box *"A Closer Look:* The Evolution of a Trans-State Business Enterprise.")

TSBEs are controversial actors. Labor unions in TSBEs' home countries argue that they "export" workers' jobs to low-wage countries. Many of the jobs TSBEs create in lower-wage Third World assembly plants do represent one-for-one losses from factories in higher-wage countries. In the host countries, it is often claimed that TSBEs do little to train the local workforce in new skills or technologies, that they often avoid paying a fair share of the state's tax burden, and that they contribute little to the host state's trade balance because they often import components from the firm's subsidiaries in other countries rather than obtaining materials from local sources. Indeed, when they set up affiliates in developing countries, TSBEs at times receive concessions on matters such as tax rebates and investment allowances that

trans-state business enterprises (TSBEs) Business firms with headquarters in one state and affiliates in at least one other state; also called multinational corporations (MNCs) or transnational corporations (TNCs).

A Closer Look

The Evolution of a Trans-State Business Enterprise: The History of the Nestlé Company

1866	Charles Page, an American consul in Zurich, establishes Anglo-Swiss Condensed Milk Company in Cham, Switzerland.
1867	Henri Nestlé begins selling "Farine Lactée Nestlé," a replacement milk for infants who refuse breast milk.
1872	Anglo-Swiss expands its manufacturing facilities by establishing a new factory in Chippeham, England.
1874	Anglo-Swiss expands by purchasing the English Condensed Milk Company.
1881	Anglo-Swiss opens its first U.S. factory.
1898–1900	Nestlé acquires a Norwegian condensed milk company, then opens factories in the United States, Britain, Germany, and Spain.
1904	Nestlé enters a partnership with the Swiss General Chocolate company.
1905	Nestlé and Anglo-Swiss merge to form the Nestlé and Anglo-Swiss Milk Company.
1906	Nestlé begins manufacturing in Australia.
1914–1918	World War I creates new demand as governments attempt to supply troops with nonperishable products. By the end of the war, world production has doubled, and Nestlé now operates 40 factories worldwide.
1920	Nestlé acquires controlling interest in three Australian companies and expands production into Latin America.
1921	Nestlé comprises more than 80 factories plus 12 subsidiaries and affiliates.
1923	Nestlé merges with Peter, Cailler, Kohler Chocolate Suisses, S.A., adding 13 chocolate plants to its corporation.
1930	Subsidiaries and production centers are established in Argentina, Cuba, Denmark, Moravia, and Czechoslovakia.
1933	New legislation that sets minimum prices and conditions of sales reduces Nestlé's competition in the United States.
1936	Nestlé and the Anglo-Swiss Company become a holding company comprised of twenty companies on five continents. Unilac, Inc., is created to act as a second holding company in Panama.
1938	Nestlé introduces the Crunch Bar and Nescafé instant coffee.

are not given to domestic entrepreneurs. This can further polarize societal divisions between rich and poor that are already severe.[44]

But TSBEs bring advantages as well. They pay local taxes in host states that would not otherwise be paid; they create at least some wealth that is not repatriated to the parent company; and, under pressure from some host governments, they have trained host-state residents in management skills and offered them management positions that would not otherwise exist. Moreover, even home states that lose jobs to foreign plants typically gain new ones from incoming FDI. The United States, for

1941–1945	During World War II American armed forces' demand for Nescafé, evaporated milk, and powdered milk increases Nestlé's sales dramatically. By 1945 sales have jumped to $225 million.
1947	Nestlé merges with Alimentana, S.A., which manufactures Maggi seasonings and dehydrated soups, and becomes "Nestlé Alimentana Company."
1948	Quik drink mix hits the market.
1950–1960	Nestlé expands into the manufacture of preserves and canned foods with its acquisition of Cross and Blackwell in Britain.
1963	Nestlé buys Findus frozen foods in Scandinavia, then merges its German, Italian, and Australian Findus branches with Unilever.
1966	Taster's Choice freeze-dried coffee is introduced.
1971–1977	Nestlé acquires Libby, the U.S. fruit juice maker, Stouffer's, and Alcon Laboratories, and becomes a major shareholder in L'Oréal Cosmetics.
1977	A U.S. boycott of all Nestlé products begins in response to charges that Nestlé irresponsibly promoted its baby food to mothers in developing countries, causing infants to eventually starve to death when their mothers mixed formula with polluted water or overdiluted infant formula.
1979	Nestlé, S.A., is officially adopted as the company's name.
1981	Nestlé complies with World Health Organization demands to cease promoting its infant formulas through advertising and free samples in developing countries.
1984–1988	Nestlé acquires Carnation—at the time, the largest takeover in the history of the food industry. Acquires Hills Brothers, Rowntree, and Buitoni, among others.
1991	Nestlé and Coca-Cola join forces to market concentrates for their coffee, tea, and chocolate beverages.
1994–2000	Nestlé adds San Pellegrino in 1997 and Spillers Petfoods of the U.K. in 1998, but it also divests itself of Findus, Hills Brothers, MJB, and Chase Sanborn in order to focus its U.S. coffee strategy on a new premium line of Nescafé in 1999. At the close of the century, Nestlé is the undisputed largest packaged food manufacturer in the world, with 500 factories in 70 countries, sales exceeding 70 billion Swiss francs, and with a portfolio holding more than 8,500 brands.

Sources: Susan Boyles Martin, ed., *Notable Corporate Chronologies,* Vol. 2 L–Z, Indexes (New York: Gale Research, 1995), pp. 1246–47; Nestlé, Inc. *Our History* (http:// www.nestle.com/all_about/history/h-home.html, August 30, 2000); Jay P. Penderson, ed., *International Directory of Company Histories,* Vol. 28 (Detroit: St. James Press, 1999), p. 312.

example, now hosts 15,000 foreign affiliates of TSBEs.[45] The controversy will likely continue because TSBE actions have *both* positive and negative effects, depending on which arena or constituency group is being considered.

Trans-State Religious Organizations

Trans-state religious organizations are groups that organize across state frontiers to nurture or propagate their faith. Historically, religious creeds have tended to arise

trans-state religious organizations Religious groups that organize across state boundaries to promote their faith.

in one place and then spread to others through migration or the work of missionaries. Christianity arose in Europe and spread to every continent; Islam arose in the Arabian peninsula and spread to North Africa and Central Asia. This dispersion has created pockets of those who share the same faith in a wide number of countries. The Shia branch of Islam, for instance, is a majority in Iran but a minority in most other places in the Middle East, where Sunni Islam continues to maintain its historic position as the dominant branch of Islam. Since Shiites (followers of Shia Islam) are ardent missionaries and often reject the legitimacy of religious and political leaders tied to the Sunni tradition, states with majority populations of Sunni Muslims often find the presence of a large Shiite minority threatening.

The Roman Catholic Church is a particularly large and well-organized transstate oganization. As of early 1997, it had 220,117 parishes in 218 states and dependent territories worldwide.[46] The Church played a major role in the European-based state system that existed before 1648 (see Chapter 6). At times it functioned as a secular political and legal authority *above* the level of local rulers. The Protestant Reformation removed a number of states from this control, and the norm of sovereignty that developed soon thereafter further restricted the authority that Church officials exercised in domestic politics. However, the Church continues to play a major moral and political role in the constituency, factional, and international arenas. At the constituency level, Catholic teaching inspires opposition to abortion in many states. At the factional level, a number of Catholic-based parties have been key parts of governing coalitions in European states. Internationally, Pope John Paul II has spoken out for human rights and against abortion, and Catholic groups have vigorously lobbied UN bodies and conferences on these issues.

Trans-State Terrorist Organizations

Terrorists use violence or the threat of violence against innocent bystanders to achieve political purposes.[†] As the attacks on the World Trade Center demonstrate, terrorist attacks are often purposefully indiscriminate. Terrorists want to put pressure on policy makers by making people they care about, or are responsible for protecting, vulnerable. Consequently, the targets and tactics terrorists choose are intended to draw attention to their demands and to produce fear in the audience they are trying to influence. Terrorists do not usually distinguish between the people who have the ability to make the concessions they demand and innocent bystanders; any person or installation that is a useful target (often for symbolic reasons) is vulnerable. Terrorism today is often tied to ethnic and religious conflicts, but the political use of kidnapping and violence is not new. The term *terror* originated with the Reign of Terror during the French Revolution. Russian anarchists also used terror, as did the Sons of the American Revolution during the revolt against Britain.

Terrorists typically have one of four objectives.[47] One is to force governments to change existing policies. Osama bin Laden's al-Qaeda network clearly intends to use

---

terrorists Individuals or groups who use violence or the threat of violence against innocent bystanders to achieve political purposes.

[†]The U.S. State Department's *2001 Report on Foreign Terrorist Organizations* lists 28 organizations around the world. Designating particular organizations as terrorist is, not surprisingly, a very controversial decision. Because people on different sides of conflicts often have very different views about who is innocent and who is a legitimate target, it is often hard to get agreement on whether specific people are, or are not, terrorists. Nowhere is that more true than in the Middle East, where Israelis and Palestinians have very different views of what is and is not a terrorist act.

Terrorism has become an almost institutionalized part of the political struggle over the fate of Northern Ireland. At the left, victims of a 1998 car bomb explosion in Omagh are treated. At right, parents and their children run for cover in 2001 after a bomb was thrown at a school in Belfast.

attacks on the United States and other Western targets to change U.S. policy on the Middle East and to alter the overall relationship between the West and the Islamic world.

A second common objective of terrorists is to overthrow or radically transform governing arrangements within some state. Northern Ireland (also known as Ulster) was kept in the United Kingdom when most of Ireland was given its independence in 1921. Since that time it has suffered through waves of assassinations and other forms of political violence as both the Irish Republican Army (IRA), founded in 1919 during the Irish War of Independence against British control, and Protestant extremists (who want Ulster to remain in the United Kingdom) have struggled to control how Northern Ireland will be governed. Acts of terrorism have also been an enduring part of the Arab-Israeli struggle since the partition of Palestine over a half-century ago. Indeed, the Irish and Arab-Israeli situations are examples of conflicts in which terrorism has become an institutionalized part of the political struggle. Terrorist attempts to transform governing arrangements are not, however, always embedded within such long-term struggles. While the evidence presented at the trials of the two individuals convicted for the 1995 bombing of the federal building in Oklahoma City suggests that the bombers were trying to undermine the U.S. central government, it also suggests that they were acting largely on their own.

A third common terrorist purpose is to create a state for a national group that lacks one when existing states refuse to consider its claims. Kurdish groups have fought the Turkish and Iraqi governments for decades, hoping to wear down resistance to the creation of a Kurdish state.

While the first two forms of terrorism target states, states themselves have been behind many terrorist actions. This possibility leads to a fourth important type of terrorism: the use of political violence by government leaders and groups they control to suppress political opposition or to undermine governments in other countries. During the 1980s and 1990s, the Iranian government was suspected of assassinating a number of political exiles living abroad. Far more extensive and widespread examples of state terrorism occurred in Nicaragua, El Salvador, Guatemala, and Argentina at different times during the 1970s and early 1980s. State terrorism against civilians also played a large role in Slobodan Milosevic's ethnic-cleansing policies after the collapse of Yugoslavia.

Most forms of terrorism are very hard for governments to fight. Efforts to stop government terrorism against its own citizens quickly run up against the norm of sovereignty and the practical problems associated with outsiders intervening in another county's internal affairs. Efforts to organize international pressure against such governments also run the risk that they will begin a process that escalates into war. Controlling terrorism by non-state actors is often even more difficult. Terrorists are passionately committed to their goals, and government agents have great difficulty infiltrating their cells. But because terrorists usually need a territorial base from which to operate, they may be susceptible to capture if the states that protect them are vulnerable to diplomatic, economic, or military pressure from other states. For example, the terrorist known as Carlos the Jackal was widely hunted for many years, but he always managed to elude capture. At various times he was apparently protected by the Syrian and Sudanese governments, among others, who gave him fake passports, a place to live, and disguises. When these governments decided they needed better ties with the West more than they needed Carlos, they arranged for him to be delivered to French authorities in 1997.[48]

Over the last several years many commentators have added **cyberterrorism,** the threat to destroy computer-based information and communication systems, to the traditional forms of terrorism. The problem is real, but so far there has been very little terrorism in cyberterrorism. We say this for two reasons. First, most of the publicized attacks on computer systems have not been part of an attempt to hold society hostage in exchange for political or policy concessions; they were, instead, acts of cybervandalism. Second, attacks with political purposes have not been on innocent third parties; instead, they have been directed at the command and control facilities of the government and armed forces. As such, they are more an unconventional form of warfare than a form of terrorism. Of course, the fact that we have not yet seen many examples of genuine cyberterrorism does not mean it is impossible.

Trans-State Criminal Organizations

Trans-state criminal organizations are similar to terrorist organizations in several ways: They are typically hierarchically organized with specific rules for membership and operation; they use violence to achieve their goals; and they can operate fairly easily across international frontiers. Many of these organizations operate within weak states whose governments cannot resist them effectively. They are most closely identified with the drug trade, but they are also involved in other kinds of trans-state smuggling, corruption, and extortion. Prominent examples include the drug cartels in Colombia, which have virtually created a criminally directed "state within a state" in that country. These organizations control huge amounts of money. The Colombian cartels at times have more liquid cash than virtually any government in the area, and their annual earnings are greater than the national tax revenues of the South American states in which they are based.[49]

Trans-state crime has mushroomed in recent years, in part due to the growth in legal trans-state economic activity. The ease of travel and communication across

cyberterrorism The destruction of computer-based information and communication systems.

trans-state criminal organizations Networks of criminal activities in two or more states.

state frontiers and the tight links that exist among international banks and credit markets have created a single worldwide market for illegal as well as lawful goods and services. So much money, so many people, and so many commodities now move among states that law enforcement and customs officials are overwhelmed. They can inspect only a small proportion of the people and cargoes coming into their territories.[50] The impact has been substantial. With their widespread use of force, trans-state criminal organizations challenge government authority, weakening both the states in which they operate and citizens' perceptions of their security.

Other Trans-State Actors and Activities

Other kinds of trans-state actors play a part in world politics as well, even though they do not fit neatly into any of the major categories we have just discussed. In the 1996 presidential campaign, for instance, it seems that U.S. fund-raisers received contributions from foreign non-governmental actors and (perhaps indirectly) from foreign governments. Such sources for campaign contributions have long existed, but the increasing expense of campaigns has driven up the demand for them. Lobbyists who work for foreign state or non-state actors similarly try to affect governments' policies toward one another. U.S. firms have long hired lobbyists to work for "fair" treatment for their companies under EU regulations; European lobbyists might some day seek a similar objective in North America if the Mexican, U.S., and Canadian economies develop tighter links. And with the end of the Cold War, many U.S. and Western European consultants have tried to help government and non-government personnel in states of the former Soviet Union build democratic institutions, civilian-controlled militaries, and market economies.

The Politics of Strategic Choice in Non-State Actors

States, IGOs, and trans-state actors all share a fundamental similarity as international actors: To make effective policy, they must build coalitions that bridge the strategic interactions in the constituency, factional (policy coalition), and international arenas. Consider the effect that constituency and factional politics have had on the role of human-rights NGOs in world politics. Traditionally, many human-rights NGOs ignored the specific concerns of women—including domestic violence and sexual abuse—preferring to focus on the protection of such rights as freedom of worship and freedom of the press. Likewise, for years the factional and constituency politics of many women's NGOs led them to ignore broader human-rights concerns while they focused on enlarging the opportunities for women to succeed economically. During the 1980s, however, factional and constituency politics within these organizations began to change, and by the time of the UN's Second World Conference on Human Rights in 1993, the two sets of constituencies represented by these NGOs were cooperating closely.[51]

The same process of linkage politics takes place in trans-state business enterprises. To the extent that governments allow them to do so, TSBE managers try to treat the various states in which they operate as though they were part of a single, integrated market.[52] Beginning in the late 1960s, Gulf Oil found it difficult to do so in Angola. Gulf had a huge investment in Angola, having spent fourteen years exploring and getting ready to pump oil there before production finally began in 1968. At that time Angola was a Portuguese colony, and resistance to Portuguese control was mounting in America and Europe as well as in Angola itself. Various U.S. church groups organized boycotts of Gulf products to protest its involvement in a colonial situation, and a group of Gulf stockholders asked its managers to withdraw from Angola. During 1972 and 1973, Gulf tried to build an African American constituency in the United States that would support continued operations in Angola. Although its managers offered support to a number of black charitable, fraternal, and business enterprises, these efforts failed. The situation grew more complex when the Portuguese regime was overthrown in 1974 and the new government granted independence to Angola. A civil war erupted there, with a Soviet-backed faction fighting two others that had support from the United States, Zaire, China, and South Africa. Only when the faction favored by Moscow took effective power in Angola's capital and U.S. leaders gave Gulf officials the green light to pay royalties to it did Gulf's incentives at the constituency, factional, and international levels become compatible.[53]

Trans-state religious organizations must also build bridges across the three political arenas. The Catholic Church, for instance, has traditionally maintained an officially neutral stand in international conflicts. Within the framework of this general strategy, Church officials who have conducted the Holy See's relationships with other states have had to build an effective coalition among various Vatican factions for whatever specific policies they wished to pursue. During the late 1940s, Monsignor Giovanni Battista Montini (the future Pope Paul VI) was a Vatican undersecretary of state. He sought a somewhat closer relationship with the United States than official Vatican policy called for at the time. He believed that for political reasons in the United States, closer links required a more "ecumenical," or tolerant, policy toward other religious faiths than some Church constituencies favored. Montini gradually made progress toward his preferred policy by carefully cultivating ecumenically minded constituencies in the Church, gradually winning over the Church administration to this view.[54]

Trans-state terrorist and criminal organizations must likewise build cross-arena coalitions to make effective policy. For instance, the terrorist network organized by Osama bin Laden included a wide range of governmental and non-governmental actors (including a large number of TSBEs) in Sudan, Kenya, Afghanistan, and many countries in the Middle East. Similarly, the success of drug cartels depends on their ability to gain the cooperation of the factions within the cartel, as well as a wide variety of actors in the countries where the drugs are produced, the countries through which they are shipped, and the countries in which they are distributed.

To sum up, *any* international actor must be able to bridge the strategic interactions within the constituency, factional, and international arenas in order to make stable and coherent policy.

Conclusion

State and non-state actors continually try to influence each other's choices. Consequently, each is part of the other's strategic environment. Taking account of the participants in our environment is something we all do every day. Your strategic environment—the context in which you operate—includes family members, friends, professors, and perhaps an employer. A change in the situation or objectives of any of these actors (for example, a friend becomes emotionally distant; a parent or sibling becomes very ill) can affect your ability to pursue your objectives. At the same time, you are part of these other actors' strategic environment.

Representatives of a wide range of state and non-state actors assembled for the 1997 UN Global Warming Conference in Kyoto, Japan. Each brought different political assets and limitations to the bargaining over the final conference agreement.

With this in mind, consider what it means to be a non-state actor in a system of sovereign states. One major consideration in this regard is that the legal and normative obligations of states are different from those of non-state actors. As we discussed in Chapter 4, state officials are responsible for regulating the interactions between their state and the international arena. This typically gives them a set of strategic objectives different from those of the leaders of non-state actors. After all, unlike state officials, the heads of TSBEs do not have to worry about protecting territory from possible aggression or providing unemployment or welfare benefits for workers who lose their jobs as a result of economic shifts. States' political assets are also different from those of non-state actors: They have the right to control what goes on in their territory. Finally, states have a powerful symbolic asset: They can claim to represent "the national interest," something no non-state actor can do.

Now consider what it is like to be a state in a world that also includes IGOs, NGOs, and trans-state business, religious, criminal, and terrorist organizations. When these actors oppose a state's policy and have resources that allow them to resist it effectively, it may be difficult for state leaders to achieve their aims. Why would this be so? First, domestically based non-state actors are often these leaders' constituents. State leaders may choose to pursue their own objectives regardless of what their constituents want. But they will pay a political price for doing so; they may even find that domestic groups can act in ways that make government policy less likely to succeed. For instance, a French president who wants to cut the subsidies the EU pays to farmers is likely to lose the support of that voting bloc in the next election and, perhaps, lose political office as a result.

Second, depending on the issue, particular IGO or trans-state actors may need to be part of a state leader's coalition in order for the policy to work internationally. In the fall of 1990 President Bush considered UN Security Council approval of the actions of the Desert Storm coalition crucial for diplomatic (though not for military) reasons. And today it would be difficult for a state leader to conclude a treaty on antipersonnel mines without dealing with the problems of land-mine survivors, due largely to the work of such NGOs as the Landmines Survivors Network.

Third, in dealing with IGOs, state leaders need to take account of whether they are autonomous actors with distinct agendas of their own or simply agents of the states that compose them. Sometimes the EU Commission has its own political goals, distinct from those of its member states; at other times it follows the lead of state actors. State leaders may be able to overcome the Commission's opposition even if it does have its own purposes, but they must, in any case, take account of what those objectives are and the Commission's ability to pursue them.

In recent decades, it has often been argued that states are losing the privileged position they have held in world politics since the seventeenth century. For example, international financial organizations and banks now routinely participate in setting some states' economic policies. Other IGOs try to tell governments how to treat people living in their sovereign territory. These trends are indeed important, but too much is often made of them.

While non-state actors play important roles, world politics is still built around a state system. States are still the key actors in the evolution of international law. Moreover, only states combine juridical sovereignty with control over specific pieces of territory. Taken together, these attributes mean that state officials can choose to regulate what occurs within their borders. The combination of sovereignty and territorial control can provide a key source of leverage. Any actor needs access to other territories if it wishes to operate across state boundaries. State decision makers have a key role in determining what access, if any, other actors will have to their territory. In a sense, these decision makers have responsibilities that place them at the intersection where the state and the trans-state arena meet. They are charged with regulating the interaction between the two—for example, deciding how many and what kinds of imports enter the state, and how much official foreign assistance leaves it. This responsibility involves choices about the benefits and costs of dealing with other actors. These choices can pose difficult trade-offs, but state leaders have the right to make them. Thus, if member states are truly losing authority to the EU, it is still the states in the EU that have decided when authority will be exercised by state and non-state actors. For these reasons, while non-state actors bargain with states on many issues, they usually do so from a position of some institutional weakness.

Key Terms

international law
private international law
public international law
moral rules
legal rules
legal positivism
natural law

institutions
international intergovernmental
    organizations (IGOs)
transactions costs
trans-state actors (TSAs)
international non-governmental
    organizations (NGOs)

agenda setting
trans-state business enterprises
    (TSBEs)
trans-state religious organizations
terrorists
cyberterrorism
trans-state criminal organizations

To The Reader   A CHAPTER SUMMARY and QUESTIONS FOR REVIEW are available at **www.prenhall.com/lamborn**

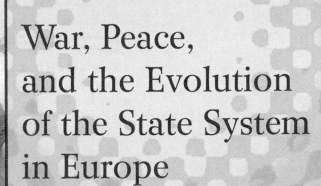

CHAPTER 6

War, Peace, and the Evolution of the State System in Europe

The modern state system emerged out of the violence that racked Europe between the start of the twelfth century and the end of the seventeenth; the ways in which it has evolved since then have been very closely tied to military conflict and the quest for security. The prominence of armed conflict in the history of the state system makes it crucial that we take a close look at the relationship between the evolution of the state system and military conflict.

The state system has been around for such a long time that it is easy to think of it as a natural way to organize world politics. The sense that organizing world politics around a state system was somehow inevitable reflects, however, an *ex post facto* (after-the-fact) view. While it may be hard when we look back down the historical path that world politics has traveled to imagine arriving at anything other than a state system, we got to a state system because people made choices. Moreover, life's choices are made *ex ante* (before the fact) from a range of perceived options, with only more-or-less informed guesses about the consequences of different choices. States began to replace existing forms of political organization in the late Middle Ages in Europe when key actors, responding to a diverse set of political and economic incentives, formed coalitions that undermined one set of political arrangements—feudalism—and gradually replaced it with another—the sovereign state.

It is important not to let our distant perspective on the origins of the state system lead us to overlook two crucial facts: The state was not the only available alternative to feudalism, and it took centuries for the state to emerge as the winning alternative. The state had begun to emerge in some parts of Europe by early in the twelfth century, but it wasn't until the mid-fifteenth century that enough of the key political actors began to look like states to talk meaningfully of a state *system* in parts of Europe. Even then, it would be another two hundred years—until the Peace of Westphalia in 1648—before the key states in that system agreed on a set of norms that made the state system the organizing principle for European politics.

Europe's state system was subsequently grafted onto quite different indigenous forms of political organization around the world through a process of military and economic expansion—seen most visibly in the history of European colonization and decolonization—that lasted almost five centuries. Ironically, although the process of grafting the European state system onto the rest of the world was completed only very recently (during the decolonization process that took place in the decades after World War II), an increasing number of people are wondering, for different reasons, whether the state system remains an effective way to organize world politics today. This is not the first time doubts about the state system have led some to consider alternative arrangements; indeed, there is a longstanding concern that the state system may itself be the principal cause of war. To that historic concern has been added a broad range of questions about the technological and economic viability of states in the modern world. Whether these concerns create enough reinforcing incentives for powerful actors to coalesce around new arrangements for organizing world politics remains to be seen, but we will have a far better chance of evaluating the probability that such changes will occur if we first understand the origins of the sovereign state system.

The Rise of the Sovereign Territorial State

The territorial state replaced feudalism, a very distinctive set of political arrangements that dominated most of the Middle Ages in Europe. Learn what was distinctive about feudalism, the manorial system that supported it, and the reasons for its collapse in "The Rise of the Sovereign Territorial State," which can be found at the text's website **www.prenhall.com/lamborn**. It's an extraordinary historical story, one in which the dominant actors of the period—the pope of the Roman Catholic Church and the emperor of the Holy Roman Empire—exhausted both the Church and the empire in a centuries' long struggle for ascendancy. At the same time as the key actors in the old system were locked in this debilitating struggle, a massive increase in long-distance trade created new actors (merchants and other townspeople called *burghers*) who used their growing wealth to form coalitions in support of new political systems. The exhaustion of the old political system and the rise of powerful coalitions that supported new ones created a strategic opportunity for system change. How the specific choices different coalitions made and differences in their strategic assets led to the triumph of the state provides an intriguing case study that suggests the conditions that might be necessary to produce an end of the state system in the twenty-first century.

The Origins of the Westphalian State System

It took more than half a millennium—from about 1100 to the mid-1600s—for the modern state system to emerge in Europe. The sovereign territorial state replaced the feudal political arrangements that had prevailed throughout the Middle Ages for a simple reason: The state was better than the two other principal alternatives to feudalism—city leagues and city-states—at organizing the economy, mobilizing internal resources in support of preferred policy outcomes, and creating a set of mutually acceptable, long-term relationships that could manage how the political units in Europe interacted with each other. Put differently, the state had a competitive advantage because it turned out to be better than the alternatives at connecting politics and policy, both *within* the principal political units (what we today call domestic politics) and *between* them (what we today call international, or interstate, politics). Once the emerging state system began to develop some momentum, the selection process became self-reinforcing. Leaders of states began to treat non-state entities—such as communes and city-leagues, which had no defined territorial boundaries—as inferior and unworthy of recognition on the same terms as states. Meanwhile, the combination of this "de-selection" process and the visibility of the competitive advantage that states had over alternative forms of organization led more and more key actors to prefer the state.[1]

While the state came to dominate European politics, it would be centuries before the key actors in the evolving state system developed even a primitive set of legitimizing principles and norms. Until the leaders of states could agree on new

6.1 ENDURING PATTERNS

The connection between preferences and power
The stronger actors' relative power positions, the more strategically important their preferences.

The impact of linkage politics
World politics is driven by the interaction of international, factional, and constituency politics.

Medieval Burghers, Modern TSBEs, and Terrorists

The expansion of trade in Europe between 1000 and 1300 made burghers (merchants and other townspeople) much more useful coalition partners, and thus far more powerful politically. With the burghers' rise in power, their preferences became more strategically important. In the Late Middle Ages, burghers were key factions in the coalitions that moved Europe away from feudalism toward the principle of sovereign territoriality.

Trans-state business enterprises (TSBEs) grew in political importance along with the expansion of global trade and investment in the second half of the twentieth century. With their growth in relative power, their preference for weaker government controls over trans-state economic movements became more strategically important. Similarly, when the political power of trade unions in the United States deteriorated badly during the last two decades of the twentieth century, their preference for stronger government controls over trans-state investment became less strategically significant than the preferences of more powerful trans-state business enterprises with a stake in the declining meaningfulness of state boundaries. Views about the value of sovereign territoriality (and, especially, the value of the state's ability to control movements across its borders) changed after the September 11 attacks on the World Trade Center and the Pentagon. With those changes, the range of potential coalition partners for groups skeptical about the value of globalization has increased.

---

legitimizing principles, the collapse of feudal arrangements left policy makers without any agreed-upon standards of legitimate rule either within or between the key actors in Europe.

Interstate Politics without Shared Principles of Legitimate Rule

As we discussed in Chapter 3, shared norms and principles can lead people to accept situations they might otherwise challenge. Shared norms also strengthen the basis for reciprocity and reduce the attractiveness of relying on power to achieve valued goals. From the time the first interstate system emerged in Renaissance Italy during the 1300s until 1648, when the Peace of Westphalia ended the Thirty Years' War, Europe's states lacked any shared principles for legitimate rule that could fill the moral vacuum created by the disintegration of feudal standards of legitimacy. The result was a surge in military conflict. Historian Garrett Mattingly sums up the situation:

[with the collapse of papal authority in Renaissance Italy,] power was temporal in the strictest sense of the term. It was naked and free, without even the most tenuous connection with eternity. Fundamentally it was illegitimate, . . . [and] the pragmatic and provisional nature of power made all temporal authority quite literally temporary authority. . . . Therefore the state, depending for its survival on power, was compelled constantly to seek more power. . . . The shortest way to these objectives was by war.[2]

In his classic history of the period, Jacob Burkhardt commented on the violence of the Italian city-state system during the Renaissance, observing that "the foundation of the system was and remained illegitimate, and nothing could remove the curse which rested upon it."[3]

Machiavelli and Renaissance Diplomacy   It is important to recognize that while great political philosophers at times possess a genius that escapes the rest of us, they typically share a trait common to us all—an interest in the most prominent political issues in the world around them. Consequently, their writings usually reflect a synthesis of timeless insights and observations about what is peculiar to the times in which they write. Consider Niccoló Machiavelli, who had been a diplomat for Florence, one of the most significant city-states in Renaissance Italy. The times in which Machiavelli lived encouraged him to focus on questions of power and security, but the ways in which he analyzed the quest for security reflected not only what was distinctive about his time but also his understanding of patterns in the politics of strategic interaction that transcend time and place.

Machiavelli wrote *The Prince* and *The Discourses* in the first decades of the 1500s, while he was in exile after the overthrow of the government in Florence and the invasion of Italy by France, Spain, and the Holy Roman Empire. As the earlier quote by Garrett Mattingly noted, it was a time without agreed-upon standards, a time when power was "naked and free." Given that context, Machiavelli's stress on the quest for security and survival made perfect sense.

For where the very safety of the country depends upon the resolution to be taken, no considerations of justice or injustice, humanity or cruelty, nor of glory or shame, should be allowed to prevail. But putting all other questions aside, the only question should be, what will save the life and liberty of the country?[4]

A prince should therefore have no other aim or thought, nor take up any other thing for his study, but war and its organization and discipline.[5]

The absence of agreed-upon norms greatly worsened three other aspects of the strategic context in Renaissance Italy. First, the size of the Italian city-states (see Map 6–1) gave policy makers very little time to recover from an unexpected attack. There were no large stretches of territory that one could temporarily concede while preparing for a counterattack. Instead, invaders were quickly, and quite literally, at the gate. (The absence of any significant geographical buffer zone gives Israel much the same strategic problem today.) Second, the distribution of power was fluid and hard to predict. Because the city-states were relatively small and vulnerable, it didn't take a very large increase in military resources to produce significant changes in relative power. Those changes occurred frequently, and this instability in the cities' relative military power was accentuated by the frequency with which alliances were made and broken. Finally, these negative features of the strategic context were

Map 6–1   The Italian City-State System during the Renaissance
The absence of agreed-upon standards of legitimate rule combined with the number and compact size of the city-states in the Italian peninsula to create incentives for ambitious rulers to make and break alliances in an effort to expand the territory they controlled.

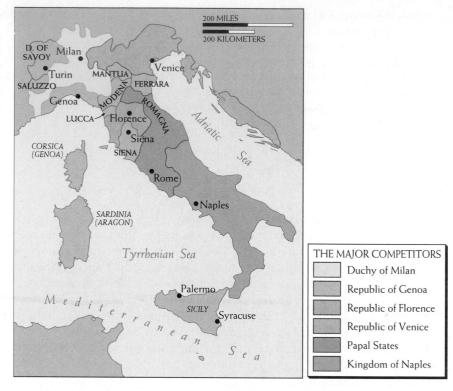

greatly worsened by a third factor: invasion by France, Spain, and the Holy Roman Empire in the late 1490s.

The conclusions Machiavelli drew about the security implications of this strategic environment were affected by his assumptions about people:

> For it may be said of men in general that they are ungrateful, voluble dissemblers, anxious to avoid danger and covetous of gain. . . . All those who have written upon civil constitutions demonstrate . . . that whoever desires to found a state and give it laws, must start with assuming that all men are bad and ever ready to display their vicious nature, whenever they may find occasion for it.[6]

Given his assumptions about humanity's essential character and the fact that Renaissance Italy had no widely shared norms of legitimate conduct, Machiavelli concluded that it was dangerous to trust others or to rely on reciprocity to produce jointly acceptable outcomes.

> It is much safer to be feared than loved. . . . Men have less scruple in offending one who makes himself loved than one who makes himself feared; for love is held by a chain of obligation which, men being selfish, is broken whenever it serves their purpose; but fear is maintained by a dread of punishment which never fails. . . . Men act right only upon compulsion.[7]

Machiavelli advised against relying on alliances. He argued that the selfishness of allies would give a strong single enemy a wedge to break any alliance and that, even if an alliance held together to victory, states would use any benefits achieved by the coalition to turn on their former allies. As for dealing with people more generally, Machiavelli advised "that men must either be caressed or else annihilated; they will revenge themselves for small injuries, but cannot do so for great ones; the injury therefore that we do to a man must be such that we not fear his vengeance."[8]

Both critics and admirers of Machiavelli often evaluate his arguments on the basis of whether or not they think his assumptions about people and his strategic advice are in some sense universal truths. What is too often missed is the *contingent* nature of his analysis. *If* one starts with the assumptions he makes, and *if* the linked diplomatic and domestic contexts that one confronts resemble those facing policy makers in Renaissance Italy, *then* the proposed strategic choices follow logically.

From the Reformation and Counter-Reformation to the Thirty Years' War

Whatever side one comes down on in the enduring debates about Machiavelli's assumptions, it is historically accurate to say that the new forms of diplomacy spread beyond the Italian peninsula into central and western Europe after the intervention of France, Spain, and the Holy Roman Empire in the Italian wars during the late 1490s. These new forms included not only Machiavelli's emphasis on relative power positions and constant maneuvering in pursuit of survival but also the increasing reliance on permanent resident ambassadors to facilitate information gathering and coalition building.

But while the spread of the state system in this period makes it appropriate to begin to talk about a new form of linkage politics, the European system was still without any widely agreed-upon norms that could legitimize either domestic political arrangements or the relationships among states. Moreover, the domestic political position of European monarchs continued to depend upon how shrewdly they managed the coalitions that had been patched together to simultaneously reward their supporters and buy off potential opponents among the nobility, many of whom still had the right to raise private armies. Those coalitions unraveled under the combined pressure of a renewed drive by kings to expand their domestic control and the effects of the Reformation (the Protestant challenge to the hegemony of the Catholic Church) and the Counter-Reformation (the Catholic attempt to reassert the Church's dominant position) on linkage politics throughout Europe. The result was a century of war from the mid-1500s to the mid-1600s.

The Protestant Reformation, led by Martin Luther, began in 1517 and was centered in northern areas of the Holy Roman Empire. A second wave began under John Calvin in Geneva in 1536 and spread rapidly to his native France (where Calvinists were called Huguenots). The coalitions that formed during the struggle between Protestants and Catholics varied with the substance of Calvinist and Lutheran teachings and the power and preferences of the key actors in different countries. Of the two strands of Protestantism, Calvinism carried the more politically subversive message: Calvin rejected both centralized religious hierarchies and monarchical rule. In 1579, that principle was extended to include an announced right of localities to rebel against tyrants and to invite the intervention of foreign princes who shared their values. In France, where the nobility retained significant military resources, Calvinism provided a religious justification for armed rebellion at the same time as the Counter-Reformation justified the brutal suppression of Huguenots. The result was a half-century of civil war involving various domestic factions and their external allies.

Lutheran doctrines and the different strategic situation in the Holy Roman Empire initially produced a different outcome. While Luther advocated religious reform, he argued that legitimacy of religious and secular authority were separate questions, and that it was a sin to rebel against lawful temporal government. Consequently,

6.2 ENDURING PATTERNS

The connection between preferences and power

The more incompatible actors' preferences, the more strategically important their relative power positions.

The impact of varying beliefs about just relationships

Shared norms and principles can lead people to accept situations they might otherwise challenge. Shared norms also strengthen the basis for reciprocity and reduce the attractiveness of relying on power to achieve goals.

The impact of linkage politics

World politics is driven by the interaction of international, factional, and constituency politics.

The Clash of Civilizations: Protestants and Catholics 400 Years Ago; the West and Islam Today

Europe's states lacked any shared principles of legitimate rule from the time the interstate system emerged in Renaissance Italy until the Peace of Westphalia in 1648. The result was a widespread emphasis on achieving what power made possible. The conflicts that resulted were made even more bitter and destructive by the Reformation and Counter-Reformation because there were Catholics and Protestants scattered throughout most of the countries in Europe. As a result, conflicts among states became connected to conflicts within states. When the Holy Roman Emperor decided to try both to centralize the internal administration of the empire and to crush domestic Protestant resistance to Catholicism, the clash of civilizations within the empire turned into an interstate war that convulsed Europe for 30 years.

In the late twentieth century, observers began to worry about the growing possibility that there would be a "clash of civilizations" between the West and the Islamic world. In discussions about that possibility, some analysts stressed not only the differences in key actors' policy preferences and legitimizing principles, but also the possibility that those differences might get entangled in ongoing interstate rivalries and domestic conflicts among different ethnic and religious groups. More optimistic observers stressed a more positive possibility for linkage politics— one in which the increasingly multiethnic and multicultural character of societies in the West would lead to greater mutual understanding.

Luther opposed political revolution, and when it threatened, he supported local nobles who suppressed revolt. The emperor, meanwhile, was cautious not to challenge the decentralized arrangements for managing the Holy Roman Empire that had been agreed upon in the Golden Bull of 1356. The result was the Augsburg Settlement of 1555, in which the princes of the empire were allowed to choose either Lutheranism or Catholicism. People who did not like their prince's choice could sell their property and move to a more congenial part of the empire.

The situations in sixteenth-century Spain and England were quite different. In Spain, King Carlos I's principal coalition partners clearly favored a dominant position for the Catholic Church, but their appetite for a larger share of royal revenue encouraged the king to seek greater central control over the resources in those parts of his kingdom that were controlled by other factions. The result was protracted revolt and war. In England, Henry VIII chose to bolt from the Catholic Church without committing himself to the Protestant camp. The result was the Church of England, a national church with the monarch as its head. After two short-lived attempts to reestablish Catholicism, Henry's coalition was reassembled by his daughter, Elizabeth I.[9]

The Augsburg Settlement came unglued in 1618, when the Holy Roman Emperor tried to consolidate his political control by reasserting the ascendancy of the Catholic Church in his hereditary domains in Bohemia (see Map 6–2). Protestant nobles in Bohemia and several other important principalities in the Holy Roman Empire revolted. The emperor decided to crush them and centralize the empire. Besides posing a fundamental threat to Protestantism, the emperor's objectives also raised the prospect of a centralized state large enough to dominate Europe. Consequently, the emperor's attack on Protestant princes was met by a coalition that included not only Protestant states but also several Catholic ones (most notably France). The coalition's members feared that the Holy Roman Empire would become a *hegemonic state*, a state so strong that it could not be defeated even by a grand coalition of all the other major military powers. The conflict (known both as the Thirty Years' War and the Wars of Religion) convulsed the continent, killing over 30 percent

Map 6–2   The Holy Roman Empire on the Eve of the Wars of Religion
The religious cleavages of the Reformation and Counter-Reformation created a very unstable political situation in the Holy Roman Empire. Under the Augsburg Settlement of 1555, the princes in the empire were allowed to choose the official religion for their area, but many continued to have substantial minorities.

of the population in many areas—more people (as a percentage of Europe's population) than were killed in World War I and II *combined*. In 1648, after extended negotiations held in the Westphalian towns of Münster and Osnabrück, the principal combatants signed two treaties that came to be called the Peace of Westphalia.

The Significance of the Peace of Westphalia: Agreement on Interstate and Domestic Norms

While fighting would continue between France and Spain until 1659, the Peace of Westphalia ended the wars in central Europe triggered by the emperor's drive for religious and political hegemony. Those negotiating the two treaties were simply trying to find a way to end the war, but their "live-and-let-live" solution to the conflicts over religion and political influence had a fundamental, if largely unanticipated, impact on the evolution of world politics. The political deal that was made in Westphalia created a set of agreed-upon principles for legitimate rule that provided the normative basis for the modern state system. As we have seen, there had been states led by elites claiming exclusive internal jurisdiction over a defined territory since the end of the High Middle Ages. There had also been collections of interacting states—and, hence, state systems—since the rise of city-states in Renaissance Italy. What there had *not* been before Westphalia was agreement on a set of principles for recognizing which rulers had the right to govern which pieces of turf and for resolving the continuing conflict over the role of religion in politics.[10]

The provisions in the Peace of Westphalia were straightforward, but the political principles that guided those provisions reflected a set of revolutionary legitimizing principles and norms for organizing European politics. The signatories to the peace agreed to recognize the independence of over 300 states in the Holy Roman Empire; they were allowed to make alliances and did not have to pay taxes to the emperor. They also set the boundaries for the principal combatants. Finally, they agreed to stop fighting about religion. (The formal Latin phrase was *Cuis regio eius religio*, which translates as "He who reigns chooses the religion.") In agreeing to these terms, the signatories established the following principles for the European state system:

- States and their rulers would acquire legitimacy through mutual recognition.
- States would no longer use religious differences as a justification for war or as the basis for decisions to honor or annul their treaty obligations.
- Agreements settling competing territorial claims would be ratified in treaties signed by the major military powers.

With the exception of the provision about religion, these principles were not explicitly stated in the treaties. They were simply implicit in the underlying logic of the agreement. The rulers of states had recognized each other, identified the boundaries of their separate domains, and guaranteed the treaties' provisions. No higher authorities were asked to sanctify the agreement; no domestic groups were granted standing to question it. The joint assertion of sovereignty—and the first set of legitimizing principles for the state system—stuck not because they represented the natural order of things, but because there were no non-state actors that could mobilize coalitions with enough people and resources to challenge it. Thus, while Westphalia was an agreement born of an attempt to end a specific military and religious conflict, its implied principle of sovereign territoriality has survived to the present day (see Map 6–3).

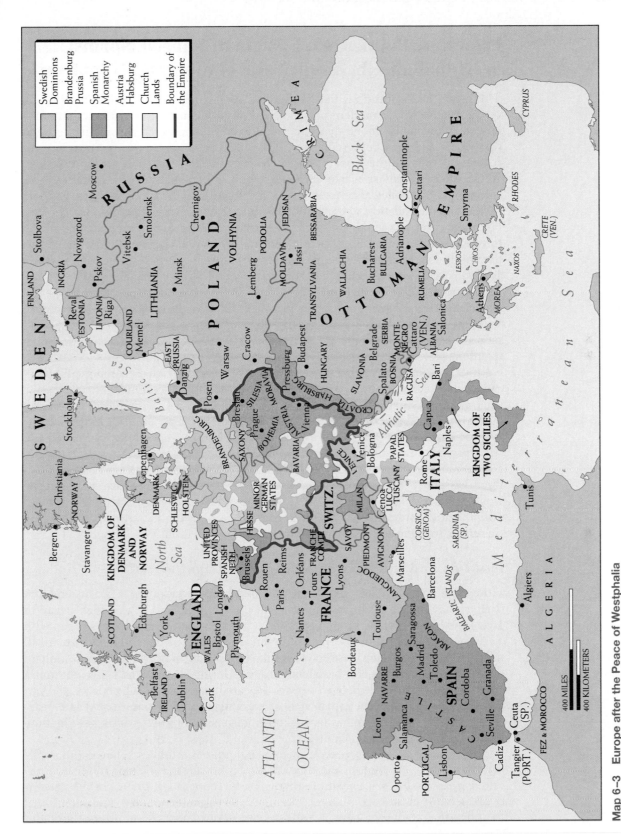

Map 6–3 Europe after the Peace of Westphalia

Most historians and political scientists place the birth of the modern state system—and the acceptance of the principle of sovereign territoriality—at the Peace of Westphalia. The map of Europe in 1648, however, looks quite different than it does today. Notice how far the Ottoman Empire extends into Europe, the multiple states in what is now Italy, and the absence of a unified Germany. The norms of the period were also quite different. For instance, the Hohenzollern dynasty governing Brandenburg ruled East Prussia because the family inherited it from a relative in 1618.

Interstate Politics in a System of Shared Norms: Westphalia to the French Revolution and Napoleon

The norms and institutions that shaped linkage politics in this period do not look very attractive from a modern perspective. Political legitimacy was a function of interstate agreements among dynastic rulers, *not* of domestic arrangements between the people and their representatives. The rulers were sovereign; the people were subjects. Moreover, the monarchs used the principle of personal sovereignty to create what looks eerily similar to a modern "cult of personality"—one that could be used to generate allegiance to the state and legitimize the monarchs' increasingly successful consolidation of control over domestic and international policy choices. Finally, sovereigns used this growth in centralized control and perceived legitimacy to fund standing armies under their personal command. No longer dependent on the nobility's private armies, monarchs now had direct control over enough military assets to crush domestic opponents or pursue a policy of territorial expansion.

But while these are very unattractive norms from a modern perspective, the appropriate standard for judging this period is what had existed *before* Westphalia. Since the collapse of papal authority and the disintegration of feudalism, Europe had suffered through the chronic violence of the Italian city-state system in the fourteenth and fifteenth centuries; the almost continuous warfare in the sixteenth and early seventeenth centuries as monarchs sought to crush (rather than buy off) powerful nobles, who, in turn, brought external allies into the conflict; and, finally, the cataclysmic destruction generated by the combination of the emperor's drive for military preponderance with the struggle between Protestant and Catholic Europe in the Thirty Years' War. It was with this bloody history—recently experienced and still a prominent possibility—that Thomas Hobbes published the *Leviathan* in 1651, a justification for absolute monarchs whose principal responsibility was to protect their subjects' right to live without continual fear of war. The fear that Europe would slip back into "a war of all against all" haunted policy makers' efforts to build a diplomatic system that would make the Peace of Westphalia work. It is useful, therefore, to begin the discussion of this period with Hobbes.

Hobbes and the Fear of a War of All against All

Hobbes's argument reflected a synthesis of his observations of the world around him (the carnage of the Thirty Years' War and the English Civil War, which began in 1642) and his theoretical assumptions about people and politics. Hobbes began with a crucial assumption about people's preferences: "I put for a general inclination of all mankind, a perpetual and restless desire for power after power, that ceaseth only in death." As for politics, Hobbes assumed "that during the time men live without a common Power to keep them all in awe, they are in a condition which is called War; and such a war, as is of every man against every man. . . . The nature of War, consisteth not in actual fighting; but in the known disposition thereto, during all the time there is no assurance to the contrary."

Given these assumptions about people and politics, Hobbes believed the implications for strategic choice were clear: "There is no way for any man to secure himself, so reasonable, as anticipation; that is, by force, or wiles, to master the persons of all men he can, so long, till he see no other power great enough to endanger him." In short, the only way a person could become secure was to dominate others. But while Hobbes regarded this strategy as a "right of nature," he was brutally frank about its implications: "In such condition . . . [there is] continual fear, and danger of violent death; and the life of man, solitary, poor, nasty, brutish, and short."[11]

Hobbes had a proposal for escaping a war of all against all within societies: a *social contract* that established an absolute sovereign. He did not, however, have a suggestion for solving the quest for security in interstate politics.

Escaping from a Hobbesian World: Longer Time Horizons, Reciprocity, and Westphalian Norms

The Westphalian principles for recognizing legitimate rule can be thought of as the first successful effort to institutionalize a set of norms that could move the European state system out of a Hobbesian "state of nature." War would continue, but it was increasingly war for incremental advantage *within* a system, not war *about* the system. As a result, wars were usually fought for limited aims, and treaties were negotiated with an eye toward compromise and jointly acceptable outcomes that would last over a long period of time.[12] A modern diplomatic historian has observed that the literature on diplomacy remained pretty much the same from the 1400s to the 1700s except for one major change:

> By the last decades of the seventeenth century a much heavier emphasis than ever was being placed on the need for honesty, for the diplomat to behave in a way which inspired confidence in those with whom he dealt. This, it was now increasingly argued, would be far more effective in the long run than any amount of sharp practice. . . . In place of an unbridled power struggle in which almost anything was permissible and extreme instability in relations between states was the norm, it was now being asserted that the task of diplomacy was not to deceive or even perhaps to defeat an opponent, but rather to reconcile conflicting ambitions and help different states to coexist.[13]

In such an environment it was possible to build long-term relationships and a norm of reciprocity. Writing in 1716, in language starkly contrary to what one finds in Machiavelli and Hobbes, François de Callières argued that "men will do as they are done by; reciprocity is the surest foundation of friendship."[14] Significantly, de Callières's advice reflected not so much different assumptions about people as an understanding of how the new strategic context would lengthen actors' time horizons and help create a norm of reciprocity that made it easier to find jointly acceptable outcomes:

> We must think of the states of which Europe is composed as being joined together by all kinds of necessary commerce, in such a way that they may be regarded as members of one Republic. . . . [Therefore,] the negotiator will bear in mind that he will be engaged throughout life in the affairs of diplomacy, and that it is . . . [in] his interest to establish a reputation for fair and plain dealing. . . . A lie always leaves a drop of poison behind, and even the most dazzling diplomatic success gained by dishonesty stands on an insecure foundation.[15]

These lengthening time horizons reinforced the growing sense of community that began to build around the legitimizing principles accepted at Westphalia. In time, these changes in the context of linkage politics in Europe would lay the groundwork for public international law. Such law was virtually impossible to develop under either the amoral conditions of the Machiavellian state system or the competing universals of the Thirty Years' War. After Westphalia—with time horizons growing longer and more value being placed on finding jointly acceptable outcomes and norms—public international law gradually did become possible.

The principal exception to this picture of evolving community standards was the War of the Spanish Succession. With King Carlos II of Spain ill and impotent between 1665 and 1700, the question of what dynasty would take over Spain when he died was a recurring concern for policy makers. King Louis XIV of France was worried about a possible union of Spain and Austria (the seat of the remainder of the old Holy Roman Empire) under the Habsburg dynasty. The leaders of the other key states in Europe were worried that Louis would try to make France preponderant by linking Spain to the French royal family. A series of moves that convinced policy makers around Europe that Louis was angling to gain control of the Spanish monarchy led to war in 1701 between France and a grand coalition of opponents determined to block him. The blocking coalition won, but only after the most destructive war Europe would experience between the Peace of Westphalia and the French Revolutionary and Napoleonic wars (1792–1815). Moreover, Peter the Great, the Russian tsar, used the war as an opportunity to expand Russia's territory to the Baltic Sea and become, for the first time, a key actor in European diplomacy.

Because the stakes, costs, and consequences of the War of the Spanish Succession were so high, the reaffirmation of Westphalia's norms in the Peace of Utrecht (the 1713 treaty that ratified the successful containment of France in the war) is frequently regarded as crucial to the consolidation of the sovereign state system. Consequently, many scholars consider Utrecht to be second only to Westphalia as a milestone in the evolution of the European state system.

Given this context, dynastic rulers sought to acquire more territory and subjects to rule, but at the same time they worried that competition might either drop them back into a Hobbesian war of all against all or give one state the opportunity to gain enough power to dominate Europe. This particular mix of preferences combined with the existing distribution of power, norms, and time horizons to foster the growth of the classical balance of power system.

The Classical-Balance-of-Power System

The term **classical balance of power** refers to a system for managing interstate politics that emerged in Europe after the Peace of Westphalia. The classical balance of power was designed to prevent **preponderance** (also known as **hegemony**). After nearly collapsing during the wars that followed the French Revolution and Napoleon's rise to power, it was rebuilt in a much altered form (the Concert of Europe) after Napoleon's defeat. It finally disintegrated in the mid-nineteenth century. It was a highly decentralized system run by the dynastic rulers that dominated European politics in this period, and its diplomatic techniques reflected a simple goal: to preserve the independence of the key states by preventing any one state from becoming so powerful militarily that it could dominate all the others. That goal is referred to either as "preventing preponderance" or "preventing hegemony." Either way, the message was the same. All the key actors shared an interest in preventing any other state from growing so powerful that no opposition coalition could contain it. This common objective required foreign policy makers to be willing to go to war against a state that appeared to be growing too powerful *even if* they had no other quarrel with its leadership. Classical balance of power also required that

classical balance of power A decentralized system for managing interstate conflict that emerged in Europe after the Peace of Westphalia.

preponderance (or **hegemony**)   A situation in which one state is so strong that it can dominate all the others.

Map 6–4   The Partition of Poland
After the partitions of 1772, 1793, and 1795, Poland ceased to exist as an independent country until after the end of World War I.

Partitions:	1st 1772	2nd 1793	3rd 1795
To Prussia			
To Austria			
To Russia			

victors in these wars of containment exercise moderation in victory. Defeated states needed to be rehabilitated not destroyed, so that they would be available as potential alliance partners against any new threats in the future. The classical-balance-of-power system involved a stronger commitment to the welfare of the major powers as a group than had existed before.

It is crucial to understand that peace was *not* the primary goal of the classical-balance-of-power system. Many modern commentators talk about "maintaining the balance" to preserve the peace, but the aim of classical balance of power was to prevent preponderance. Wars of containment were a central mechanism for achieving that goal. It is also important to know that classical balance of power protected only the *key* states—that is, the countries that had the military capacity to affect the outcome of major European wars. The small states, especially the many principalities in central Europe, were considered expendable. Indeed, contemporary practice emphasized **reciprocal compensation,** the practice of using the territory of the smaller states to adjust the balance among the major powers after wars. The rulers of many small states lost their lands in the process of reciprocal compensation. Even a few large states that had become too weak to play a significant military role were dismembered. The most famous example was Poland, which was too weak politically and militarily to prevent its partition by Russia, Austria, and Prussia in 1772, 1793, and 1795 (see Map 6–4). Poland did not reappear as an independent state until the peace settlement after World War I.

Finally, it is important to understand the critical role that alliances played in the classical balance of power. Alliances compensated for the fact that the major states were not really equal in military power and therefore needed to form coalitions to

reciprocal compensation
The practice of reshuffling the territory of smaller states to rebalance the distribution of military power after wars.

contain expanding states. Alliances were also a more general hedge against uncertainty. If an actor could start a war at any time, one needed a hedge against attack at a moment of vulnerability. To serve these purposes, balance-of-power alliances needed to be assembled quickly when war threatened, had to hold together through the war of containment, and then had to lapse after the system was rebalanced. There were supposed to be no permanent friends or enemies; all the major powers had to be available as potential alliance partners for one another.

Classical balance of power never worked perfectly. Prussia, for instance, managed to expand from a very small state to one of the greatest military powers on the continent. It started off in a small area on the eastern Baltic far from Berlin, merged with the state of Brandenburg (which had the territories around Berlin), gobbled up parts of Poland in the late eighteenth-century partitions, fought some wars with Russia and the Austrian empire that gained it still more territory in spite of the efforts of several blocking coalitions, and expanded still more as part of the settlement after the Napoleonic wars.

But while classical balance of power was an imperfect diplomatic system, it worked reasonably well for a century and a half. The reason for its relative success is historically simple and theoretically significant: It fit both the preferences of the key policy makers and the linked international and domestic arenas within which they operated. Balance of power assumed policy makers wanted to expand but, when push came to shove, would defer short-term gains in a long-term effort to prevent any other state from becoming preponderant. What that meant in practice is that they would turn down a chance to get a share of the spoils by **band-wagoning**— allying with the side that was about to win—*if* there was a dominant state in the coalition that had the potential to become preponderant. In such a situation, policy makers were to reject the short-term temptation to band-wagon and choose, instead, to ally with the weaker side in an effort to form a successful blocking coalition— the essence of **balancing** behavior. Classical balance of power assumed, in other words, that while policy makers looked for opportunities to gain marginal advantage in territory and military power, they were committed to maintaining the system. In that sense, they were ultimately defensive seekers of security, rather than system-threatening challengers of the status quo.

The majority of the key states' policy makers shared these objectives, so when they had to choose between short-term and long-term gains, they typically preferred balancing over band-wagoning. Moreover, these specific strategic objectives were nested within a larger set of shared political values about the legitimizing principles for the state system. As Hans Morgenthau and Edward Vose Gulick, two great scholars of this period, argue:

> [C]ommon moral standards and a common civilization as well as common interests . . . kept in check the limitless desire for power . . . and prevented it from becoming a political actuality. Where such a consensus no longer exists . . . the balance of power is incapable of fulfilling its functions.[16]
>
> The balance of power system was . . . an old and oft-repaired machine, which creaked badly enough as it was; without a lubricating homogeneity [of values] it might well have broken down.[17]

The compatibility of the actors' preferences is, however, only one of the prerequisites for the success of a diplomatic system. Those objectives also need to fit within the range of what the domestic and international arenas make possible.

band-wagoning
A strategy of allying with the stronger side during a conflict.

balancing A diplomatic strategy of allying with the weaker side during a conflict to form a blocking coalition that could prevent the strongest states from becoming too powerful.

6.3 **ENDURING PATTERNS**

The impact of risk-taking preferences

(1) The higher the expected value people attach to an outcome, the higher the political risks they will be willing to run to achieve it; (2) people are less willing to run political risks in support of policy choices as their control over choice and implementation declines.

The impact of discounting

People generally prefer current benefits over future benefits and future costs over current costs. However, (1) the higher the expected value actors attach to achieving a specific policy outcome, the less their choices will be affected by discounting; (2) the less control actors have over policy choice and implementation, the more actors will prefer future costs over current costs, and the more they will value current benefits over future benefits.

Classical Balance of Power, Modern Conflict Management, and Anti-Terrorism

Classical-balance-of-power wars involved paying a high current cost (fighting a war to prevent another state from growing more powerful) in order to achieve a future gain (reducing the probability that a state would become preponderant at some point in the future). The high value classical balance of power attached to preventing preponderance and the tight control decision makers had over policy choice and implementation in this period made the risks of fighting balance of power wars more acceptable. The high value attached to the objective and the level of control over choice also made it easier to overcome the normal tendency to discount; that is, to prefer current benefits over future benefits and future costs over current costs.

By the mid-twentieth century, the growth of domestic involvement in policy making in the Western democracies had substantially altered policy makers' calculations about their ability to sustain decisions that involved paying high short-term costs to achieve long-term gains. Efforts at collective conflict management after Yugoslavia disintegrated in the 1990s initially floundered, partly because the key actors were unwilling to take the political risks of paying high short-term costs to achieve uncertain long-term gains. The same underlying problem undercut the League of Nations' collective security system in the 1920s and 1930s (see Chapter 7). In each case, the value policy makers attached to achieving the goals was not high enough to justify the political risks involved.

After the September 11, 2001, attacks on the United States, President George W. Bush announced a long-term campaign against global terrorist networks, in which he emphasized that the people in the United States should expect the anti-terror campaign to be long, costly, and difficult. This announced willingness to pay high short-term costs to achieve valued long-term goals reflects a very different strategic calculation than the ones described in the previous paragraph.

Balance-of-power strategies presuppose a linked international and domestic context in which policy makers can measure military power reliably and prevent significant changes in power by preventing territorial expansion. Balance-of-power strategies also assume that policy makers can extract enough resources from their domestic systems to remain competitive internationally. Both were possible in pre-industrial, dynastic-rule Europe. Without industrialization to generate massive increases in the amounts of resources within a state's boundaries, there were only two major sources of significant changes in military capabilities. With territorial expansion, monarchs could acquire more people (to tax) and land (to skim a share of the value it generated). With a revolutionary restructuring of the state's bureaucratic apparatus, monarchs could increase their ability to extract resources to pay for mercenaries. However, territorial expansion could be stopped by forming a blocking coalition; and revolutionary restructurings of the state were rarely possible. Indeed, the very difficulty of creating a revolution from the top down is why those rare monarchs—such as Louis XIV (France), Maria Theresa (Austria), Frederick the Great (Prussia), and Peter the Great (Russia)—who were able to increase central control and dramatically raise the state's revenues became famous. Relative military power was also comparatively easy to estimate in a period before nationalism made the zeal of soldiers a key variable and before industrialization along with other technological changes produced great variation in the efficiency with which armies could be organized, moved, and supported.

Finally, balance of power presupposes another characteristic of the international and domestic political arenas that was in high supply in dynastic-rule Europe: great flexibility in policy making. Balance-of-power strategists need to be able to make decisions based on estimated changes in military power without regard to domestic agendas and actors. They also need to be able to make and break alliances easily and quickly, exercise moderation in victory, and rebalance the system through reciprocal compensation without regard to the wishes of the people being moved from one ruler to another.

All of these prerequisites for an effective balance-of-power system existed between the Peace of Westphalia in 1648 and the French Revolution of 1789. All of them then gradually disappeared under the combined pressures of the Industrial Revolution, the growth of nationalism, and the demand for democratic governments.

The Old Order Crumbles

The Impact of the French Revolution and Napoleon

The French Revolution signaled the beginning of the end of the classical-balance-of-power system and the interstate agreement on the legitimacy of dynastic rule that had been established at Westphalia. The legitimacy of dynastic rule was directly threatened not only by the demand for democratic representation that was at the center of the French Revolution but also by the nationalism it unleashed. Multiethnic states such as the Austrian Empire were most directly threatened by the principle of nationalism, but it indirectly undermined all dynastic rulers by suggesting that the people were sovereign, that countries were not the personal possessions of monarchs.

At the same time as the French Revolution undermined the principles of the old order, it unleashed a restructuring of domestic and diplomatic coalitions in ways that generated a drive for preponderance, thereby directly attacking one of the most cherished goals of classical balance of power. The initial wars generated by the French Revolution occurred when other European monarchs tried to crush the revolution. They feared revolutionary change and French expansion, but they also wanted to use the instability created by the revolution to grab long-desired pieces of territory. In addition, French revolutionary governments were themselves aggressively expanding. The French drive to expand reflected both ideological and financial incentives. On an ideological level, French policy makers desperately wanted to replace the norms of the old order, which assumed that the only legitimate rulers were dynastic sovereigns who had been recognized by other sovereigns in major-power treaties. Without a change in these norms, France would be an outcast. Spreading the norms embodied in the French Revolution to neighboring countries was, therefore, part of an effort to create an interstate environment with compatible legitimizing principles.

These ideological goals were reinforced by a narrow domestic incentive: the drive to avoid bankruptcy by *expropriating* (seizing without compensation) church and noble lands in other countries. This financial incentive figured heavily in France's decisions to invade Belgium in 1794, the Netherlands in 1795, Italy in 1796, and Switzerland in 1798. However, in spite of expropriating huge amounts (about 360 million francs between 1792 and 1799), political leaders in France were unable to solve their domestic financial crisis. As a result, they increasingly turned to their generals to raise the funds necessary to fight the wars. That, in turn, laid the groundwork for the shift in domestic coalitions that enabled Napoleon Bonaparte to take over in a 1799 coup d'état.[18]

The story of Napoleon's expansion and eventual defeat at the hands of a grand coalition that formed as he retreated from the frozen steppes of Russia in 1812 is one of the greatest in European history. In brief, Napoleon used both his military genius and the unprecedented numbers of soldiers he was able to mobilize to defeat most of continental Europe. (French revolutionary governments used nationalism to create the first mass draft; other European armies depended on mercenary armies that were willing to take far fewer casualties.) While he did not occupy Prussia, Austria, or Russia, at one time or another Napoleon forced all of them to sue for peace on his terms. At the time of his decision to invade Russia in 1812, only Britain remained in active military opposition. Consequently, it is fair to say that by 1812 Napoleon had come closer to making France a hegemonic, or preponderant, power than any policy maker since the Peace of Westphalia. The classical balance of power system was, therefore, a shambles at the time of Napoleon's decision to invade Russia.

The failure of the classical balance of power before 1812 is one of the crucial things to remember about the Napoleonic wars. The ability of Prince Klemens von Metternich, the Austrian chancellor, to use the invasion of Russia as the occasion to build a grand coalition that could finally defeat Napoleon and restore the balance is a second crucial part of the story. It is especially important, from the perspective of the evolution of major-power statecraft, to recognize that Metternich, as leader of the grand coalition that defeated Napoleon and organized the peace settlement, self-consciously attempted to restore the old order. He led Europe back to the legitimizing principles of the classical balance of power system, even as he altered the diplomatic strategies of that system in fundamental ways. The result was the Concert of Europe.

Trying to Restore the Old Order: The 1815 Peace Settlement and the Concert of Europe

The settlement that was negotiated at the Congress of Vienna in 1815 after the Napoleonic wars was in many ways a classical-balance-of-power peace. The norm of dynastic rule was reasserted by restoring the monarchy in France, and the central concern for maintaining the key actors was reflected in the decision to return France to its historic boundaries and let its new leaders return to the councils of the major powers. The goal of rebalancing the system through a complicated process of reciprocal compensation can be seen in the agreement to give Prussia and Austria enough new territory to deter threats from France and Russia, but to locate those territories in places that lessened the threat they posed to each other. Although Prussia and Austria shared an interest in being able to deter France and Russia, they were also competitors for leadership of the many small German states left over from the Holy Roman Empire, which had finally collapsed during the Napoleonic wars. Consequently, it was important that the territories Austria and Prussia received to counterbalance France and Russia were in locations that did not increase either country's vulnerability to the other (see Map 6–5).

All these moves reflected Metternich's commitment to classical balance of power and the legitimizing principles of the old order. But Metternich was also determined to change the diplomatic techniques used to support those old values. The Napoleonic wars had shown that the balance of power system was too decentralized to respond effectively to a challenge as sustained and powerful as Napoleon's. Therefore, in addition to rebalancing the system through reciprocal compensation, the makers of the peace settlement tried to increase the level of coordination among the key actors. They aimed to manage the competition between Prussia and Austria for influence among the German states, while simultaneously increasing the coordination among all of these states in the event of a threat from France or Russia. To do this, the peace makers created the *German Confederation*, a loose association of Austria, Prussia, and the thirty-four German principalities and four cities that remained independent states. Members of the German Confederation agreed not to go to war with each other, to submit disputes among themselves to mediation, and to coordinate their policies in the event of a war with nonmember states. Much to Prussia's dismay, the presidency of the Confederation's assembly—which was composed of representatives of the member governments—was given to Austria.[19]

While the German Confederation and the Austrian presidency of the assembly helped Metternich manage the relations among the German states, the key diplomatic innovation focused on relations among the great military powers. Metternich convinced representatives of these states that they ought to meet once a year—or more often if the occasion demanded—to identify any threats to the peace in Europe that required a collective response. The resulting meetings were called the Concert of Europe.

The initial version of the Concert included Britain, France, Prussia, Austria, and Russia. Britain withdrew in 1822 when it became clear that its understanding of what constituted a threat to the peace was different from that of the continental monarchs. Robert Viscount Castlereagh, Britain's foreign minister, had with great difficulty convinced the British cabinet to join the Concert in order to facilitate joint action in response to any state's effort to dominate the continent and thereby threaten Britain's economic and military security. But by 1822 it became clear that the dynastic rulers on the continent believed the greatest immediate threat to their security was domestic social and political reform—renewed pressure for nationalism and democracy. Fearing that demands for democracy and the creation of nation-states would undermine the legitimacy of dynastic rulers and multiethnic empires, the monarchs in Prussia, France, Austria, and Russia agreed to work together diplomatically (and, in some cases, through military intervention) to suppress efforts to

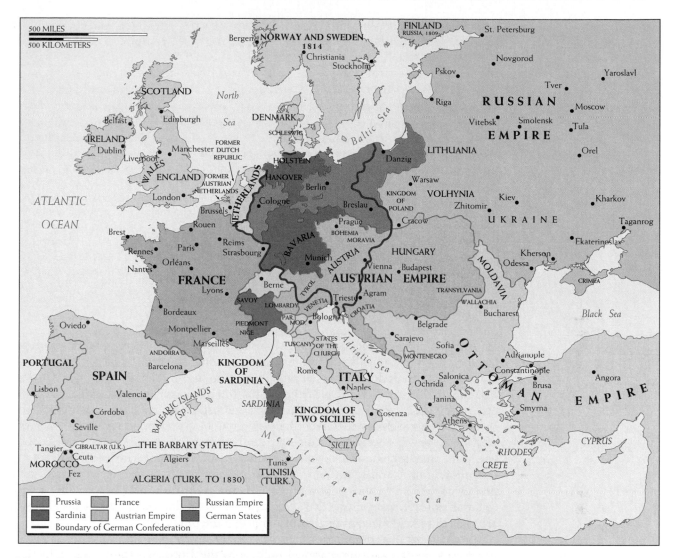

Map 6–5   Europe after the Peace Settlement at the Congress of Vienna
This map shows the ways in which the diplomats at the Congress of Vienna tried to rebalance Europe after the Napoleonic wars. The strategy was to increase Prussian and Austrian power relative to France and Russia in a way that did not give either Austria or Prussia an advantage over each other. When you compare this map to Maps 6–3 and 6–4, you will notice that both Austria and Prussia have grown, but you will also notice that one of Prussia's biggest additions was a separate piece of territory next to France (and far from Austria). The German Confederation, which included all the remaining small German states plus pieces of Prussia and Austria, was designed to reinforce this intricate balance by providing more coordination in the center of Europe without allowing Austria or Prussia to expand further.

create new constitutional monarchies in Europe. This view was directly opposed by the British, who were happy with their own constitutional monarchy and argued that the Concert was designed to deter external aggression, not to defeat domestic political reform. Unable to convince the continental monarchs not to intervene, the British decided to leave the Concert in 1822.[20]

Who Will Be My Ruler? Moving People to Rebalance the System

Classical-balance-of-power diplomats frequently reshuffled the boundaries and populations of small states to rebalance the distribution of military power after wars. The negotiations about how people should be moved around after the Napoleonic wars got so complicated that a Demography Committee was created to evaluate proposals. One of the most elaborate proposals came from Prussia. To see the table outlining Prussia's proposal for "Finding the Number of Subjects for the Prussian King" and to read a short discussion of the way Europe was rebalanced, go to **www.prenhall.com/lamborn**.

As you read these materials, consider how difficult it was to come up with a scheme that strengthened Prussia and Austria against France and Russia without giving either a military edge against each other. You also might want to think about what it would be like to live in a world in which people had so little say about who their rulers were—and about whether things have really changed that much since then.

Although the Concert of Europe was used to organize social repression, its leaders continued to pay close attention to international security. Indeed, their diplomatic and domestic agendas were mutually reinforcing, and for a very simple reason: Policy makers on the continent believed that major-power war was unlikely unless one of the major powers was captured by a new domestic coalition that supported social and political change. Given that logic, the best way to prevent major-power war was to prevent domestic change. From this perspective, the Concert of Europe was simultaneously innovative and profoundly conservative. Its innovations were in the international arena, where the major powers replaced the decentralized approach of classical balance of power with a standing alliance designed to enable them to act in concert. Its conservative agendas were in the domestic arena, where monarchs tried to save the legitimizing principles of the old order.

Notice what this combination suggests about the changing nature of the linkages between domestic and international politics in the European state system. In the classical-balance-of-power period, the stability of domestic arrangements facilitated competition for empire and the balancing behavior used to prevent preponderance. In the Concert of Europe, the stability of interstate arrangements facilitated cooperation to quash revolutionary change and preserve the domestic basis of the system. In the earlier period, the principal threats were in the interstate arena; in the second, the principal threats were domestic. But in both periods the two arenas were closely linked. Given the perceived linkages among social change, regime survival, and war, the Concert's continental policy makers pursued a ruthless strategy of joint intervention in an effort to prevent the spread of democratic institutions.

Collapse of the Old Order: The Impact of Economic, Social, and Political Changes

Just as diplomatic systems require a large number of mutually reinforcing factors cutting across international and domestic politics if they are to succeed for a long period of time, so it usually takes a large number of changes occurring more or less at the same time for longstanding arrangements to unravel quickly. By the mid-nineteenth century, both the European economy and widely held ideas about legitimate political relationships had been changing dramatically. The Industrial Revolution generated massive increases in the amount of resources available to policy makers without any need for territorial expansion. It also began to generate trade ties and other forms of economic interdependence that gave policy makers huge economic stakes in other countries. Consequently, they were often unwilling to make or break alliances solely on the basis of changes in relative military power. As for changing domestic incentives to act, the Industrial Revolution led to the rise of new domestic actors—first in the industrial and commercial elite, later in the middle and working classes—with enough resources to insist that their preferences be taken into account.

These changes in the composition and power of domestic actors were reinforced by a growing demand for new legitimizing principles. In place of dynastic rule by sovereigns over subjects, there were to be democratic governments that represented citizens from distinctive nationality groupings. The growth of nationalism combined with the Industrial Revolution to undermine the ability of strategists either to measure power reliably or to prevent major shifts in power by preventing territorial expansion. The rise of domestic actors who cared about nationality issues, the ideological disputes between monarchists and republicans, and the newly formed trade ties simultaneously undermined the ability of policy makers to make or break alliances easily, practice moderation in victory, and rebalance the system through reciprocal compensation.

In spite of the pressures created by these underlying changes, the Concert's conservative coalition held together from 1815 until the late 1840s, when the renewed pressures for domestic reform were brought home forcibly by a series of barely contained rebellions during 1848 in the major capitals of Europe. Symbolic of the perceived need for new approaches was the decision by the Austrian emperor to fire Metternich in an effort to appease domestic opponents. Divisions among the old allies in the Concert created by increasing fears about domestic instability after 1848 were then dramatically widened by a breakdown in cooperation over the Balkans. In 1853 the Russian government used the persecution of Christian minorities in the Ottoman Empire as an excuse to try to gain more land in the Balkans and increased control of the straits into the Black Sea. Determined to prevent Russia from expanding and worried about the Russian navy being able to gain easy access to the Mediterranean, Britain declared war. The ensuing war (called the Crimean War because most of the fighting took place on the Crimean peninsula) lasted from 1853 to 1856. It also drew France into the fighting and led to Austrian threats to intervene if Russia did not come to terms. Russia acquiesced, but the war shattered any remaining hopes that the Concert might be rebuilt.

Soon thereafter, the continuing search for new domestic strategies to legitimize the governments of the principal continental states led them in directions that reinforced their differences. The Russian and Austrian governments continued to try to hold together multiethnic, autocratic empires by suppressing demands for national self-determination and democracy. In contrast, Count Otto von Bismarck, who became chancellor of Prussia in 1862, used nationalism to unify Germany under Prussian control and introduced universal male suffrage in an attempt to build political support for the emperor. Indeed, the ways in which Bismarck connected his international and domestic objectives created a new and distinctive synthesis in the history of European linkage politics.

The Triumph of European Nationalism: Bismarck to World War I

Bismarck was a young politician from the Prussian agrarian nobility in 1848, when the Prussian emperor, Kaiser Ferdinand I, barely managed to suppress rebels calling for the creation of a unified Germany under a constitutional monarch responsible to an elected parliament. Viewing this near-miss with remarkable strategic insight, Bismarck drew the conclusion that the only way conservatives could maintain their dominant position was to capture German nationalism. Since the time of the French Revolution, nationalism had been a tool of the political left—of those demanding radical change in Europe's domestic political, social, and economic arrangements. Bismarck coopted German nationalism, turned it into a tool of the political right, and rode it to political power.

The Wars of German Unification

Most of the other major transformations in the European state system came only slowly over time, but the ones wrought by Bismarck came quickly in response to a rapid-fire series of strategic opportunities. The first came in late 1863, only a little over a year after he had become chancellor of Prussia. The new king of Denmark announced that he was going to take over an area called Schleswig-Holstein. The problem was that these duchies not only were right at the point where Denmark and the German-speaking states met, but they also included large numbers of ethnic Germans who had no interest in becoming Danes. Moreover, this was the second time in recent decades that a Danish king had made a move on these territories. The first had come in 1846 and led to a war between Denmark and Prussia that ended only when Britain mediated a settlement. Ratified in a major-power treaty, the settlement gave the crown of the duchies to the Danish king but left them administratively independent. Bismarck responded to the Danish king's 1863 announcement by forming an alliance with Austria, the other major power in the German Confederation, and attacking Denmark in 1864. The Danes quickly lost, but the question of what to do about governing Schleswig-Holstein soon turned into a struggle between Austria and Prussia over preeminence in the German Confederation. Talks broke down. Faced with this diplomatic stalemate and domestic pressures by his Hungarian provinces for greater autonomy, the Austrian emperor decided that he could best achieve both his international and domestic objectives by declaring war on Prussia, which he did in 1866. Austria was widely regarded as militarily superior to Prussia, but Bismarck used his far better understanding of technological innovations in warfare and the new logistical capabilities created by railroads to defeat the Austrians in one decisive battle. The speed of his victory is reflected in the Austro-Prussian war's other name: the Seven Weeks War.

Having won, Bismarck confounded international and domestic observers by declining to march on Vienna or extract an indemnity. Instead, he simply annexed Schleswig-Holstein and the German states that had sided with Austria and insisted that Austria leave the German Confederation. Having done that, the only independent German states that remained were in the southwest, between Prussia and France. Consequently, he manipulated a dispute with the French government to provoke a declaration of war in 1870 from the French emperor, Napoleon III. Once again, Bismarck's enemy was thought to be far stronger, but once again, Prussia won

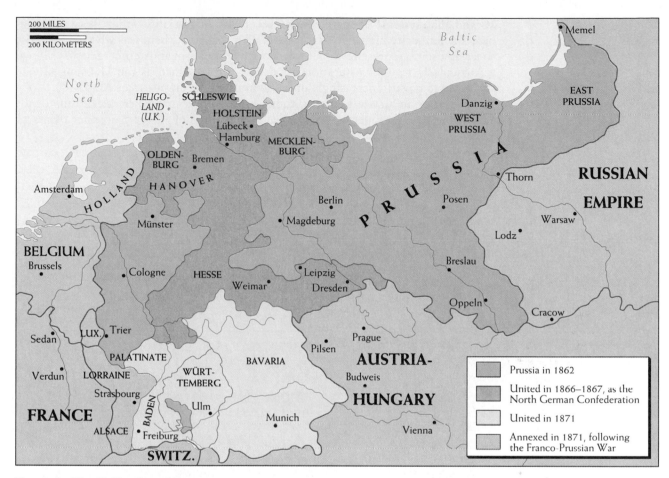

Map 6–6   The Unification of Germany
Bismarck used three wars to unify Germany: one in 1864 against Denmark; a second in 1866 against the Austrian empire; and a third in 1870–1871 against France.

in one decisive battle. This time Bismarck occupied the defeated capital city, refused to leave until the French paid an enormous indemnity, and annexed a key piece of French territory—the provinces of Alsace and Lorraine. He also informed the leaders of the last independent German states, now occupied by Prussian troops dropped off on the way to France, that they needed to offer the crown of a united Germany to the Prussian king (see Map 6–6).

The Bismarckian Synthesis after 1871

Bismarck's military successes put the last nails in the coffin of the old order. He based the legitimacy of a united Germany on two pillars: German nationalism and military power. He refused, moreover, to seek formal interstate approval for German unification through a major-power treaty. Nationalism was a mortal enemy of the old order, which based a regime's legitimacy on interstate agreements ratified by treaty. With its original, externally defined legitimizing principles gone, all that was left of the

Westphalian system was agreement on sovereign territoriality—the refusal to recognize any authority higher than the state. The question, then, was who would those sovereign states represent? What role would nationalism and democracy play? It was a particularly troubling question for dynastic rulers such as the Habsburgs, who struggled to govern increasingly unstable multiethnic empires (see Map 6–7).

Operating in a state system without agreed-upon principles of legitimate rule and facing French anger over its defeat and the loss of Alsace-Lorraine, Bismarck

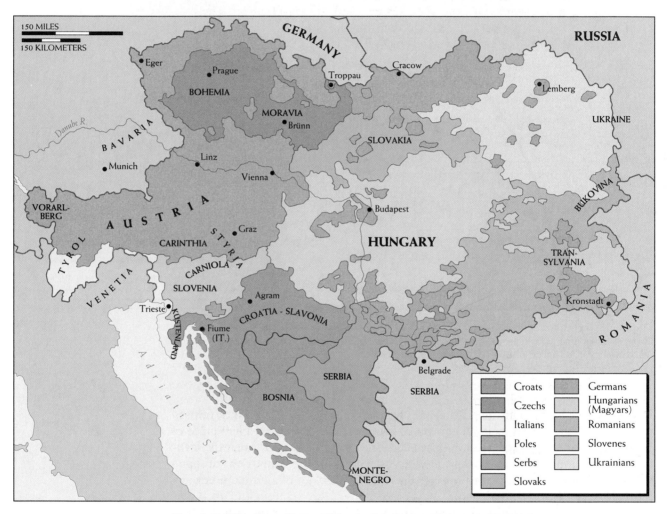

Map 6–7   The Many Nationalities in the Austro-Hungarian Empire
The Habsburgs' Austro-Hungarian Empire contained almost a dozen major ethnic groups. Longstanding demands for local autonomy and a more federal system grew stronger with the growth of nationalism in Europe. Hungarians were the strongest of the nationality groups and led the opponents of centralization. Foreign policy failures weakened the central government still further. In 1867, after the disastrous loss in the Austro-Prussian war, the Habsburg dynasty decided to split the Hungarian opposition from the other nationality groups by granting Hungary internal self-rule. The Austrian Empire was renamed Austria-Hungary (also called the Dual Monarchy). A joint administration handled foreign, defense, and economic policy. The emperor retained control of internal affairs in Austria and all parts of the empire outside Hungary.

constructed a diplomatic strategy designed to protect Germany's position. Bismarck regarded Germany as a satisfied (status quo) power, so his strategy now became defensive. He assumed that France would be permanently hostile but was too weak to attack Germany on its own. Therefore, he wanted to isolate France diplomatically to prevent it from picking up any powerful allies and to preserve the peace throughout Europe to avoid having Germany drawn into any wars. The problem was that there were ongoing controversies throughout Europe that might produce military conflict. He was particularly concerned about the collision of Russian and Habsburg ambitions for expansion into the Balkans (where the Ottoman Empire was losing control) and controversies involving Italy, France, and Austria-Hungary. His solution was to create a set of pre-targeted, standing, peacetime alliances that simultaneously deterred stronger parties and restrained weaker ones. All these alliances either included Germany as a signatory or were set up with Bismarck's urging. They were overlapping and complex, designed to entangle and restrain. The key alliances are briefly described in the box, "*A Closer Look:* Bismarck's Alliances."

The result of all these alliances was an extraordinary web of agreements that were qualitatively different from the alliances that had characterized the European state system before Bismarck. Alliances during the classical-balance-of-power period were reactive, ad hoc combinations formed by states with no permanent friends or enemies; they were temporary arrangements designed to assemble coalitions that could win an ongoing conflict and then lapse when the conflict was over. Bismarckian alliances were standing, peacetime agreements designed to prevent disputes from escalating into war by deterring the stronger and restraining the weaker. The classical-balance-of-power security system was decentralized and designed to prevent preponderance. The Bismarckian security system was an organized web of crosscutting alliances designed to prevent reinforcing grievances and antagonistic blocs, while simultaneously isolating France and preserving German preeminence (see Map 6–8 on page 159).

The Collapse of the Bismarckian Synthesis and the Onset of World War I

After Bismarck's forced resignation in 1890 (the new German emperor, Kaiser Wilhelm II, disliked Bismarck and also disagreed with him on both domestic and foreign policy), German policy makers adopted a fundamentally different set of international objectives. While Bismarck regarded Germany as a satisfied state after unification and preferred to focus on European rather than global politics, his successors wanted to expand German influence globally. Moving Germany from the role of satisfied to dissatisfied state was bound to be unsettling to its neighbors, but the diplomatic environment was further poisoned by their misreading of how Bismarck had used Germany's military and economic power. Bismarck was famous—many would say *infamous*—for using cold-blooded calculations of what power made possible to achieve his goals. Indeed, Bismarck was so well known for this approach that the German-language versions of the terms "realism" and "power politics" (*realpolitik* and *machtpolitik*) became part of the diplomatic lexicon. However, Bismarck's successors somehow missed the fact that Bismarck had been careful to challenge only those he could defeat. Equally important, once Bismarck had used war to unify Germany, he immediately switched from challenging other states to using German military power to maintain the status quo. In a world of conflicting preferences and few agreed-upon

A Closer Look

Bismarck's Alliances

1879 The Dual Alliance This alliance, which included Germany and the Austro-Hungarian Empire, was unprecedented. It was the first standing, peacetime defense pact in European history. It was negotiated in the aftermath of the First Berlin Conference on the Balkans, (which ended the war between Russia and the Ottoman Empire) and a prohibitively high 1879 German grain tariff that eliminated Russian grain exports into Germany. Both the settlement and the tariff enraged the tsar. The terms of the treaty called for Germany and Austria to help each other if either was attacked by Russia, but it required only benevolent neutrality if either was attacked by another power. The strategic effect was to deter Russia from attacking either Germany or Austria (because it was too weak to take on both) and to restrain the Austrians in the Balkans (because Austria was weaker than Russia and would get help under the treaty provisions only if it was attacked). The treaty also eliminated Austria as a possible alliance partner for France.

1881 The Three Emperors League Included Germany, Austria-Hungary, and Russia. The terms called for consultation on the Balkans and benevolent neutrality in case of war with a fourth power. Its effects were to reduce Russian-German hostility after the signing of the Dual Alliance; to restrain competition between Russia and Austria in the Balkans; and to make a Russian-French alliance less likely. Significantly, none of these provisions were inconsistent with the terms of the Dual Alliance.

1882 The Triple Alliance Included Germany, Austria-Hungary, and Italy. Italy had requested an alliance with Germany to protect it from France. Italy's leaders were worried about French expansion in North Africa after it imposed a protectorate on Tunis in 1881 and were also concerned about continuing French pressure on the Italian border. Bismarck insisted on including Austria over Italian objections because he wanted to use the treaty to lessen the probability of war between Italy and Austria. The terms called for Austria and Germany to aid Italy if it were attacked by France. Italy promised to remain neutral if Austria were attacked, but *not* if Austria initiated a war. This treaty had the effect of deterring France while restraining both Italy and Austria (who got help only if they were the victims of aggression and not if they initiated a war).

1887 The First and Second Mediterranean Agreements Included Italy, Great Britain, and Austria-Hungary. This treaty was organized by Bismarck, but Germany was not a signatory because membership was restricted to countries with a naval presence in the Mediterranean. The terms called for cooperation to preserve the status quo in the Mediterranean, Aegean, and Black Seas and for joint defense of the Balkans against Russian attack. It was designed to check French and Russian naval expansion in the Mediterranean and to deter Russia from pressing for any changes in the restrictions on access to the Bosporus and the Dardanelles, the straits between the Black Sea and the Aegean.

June 1887 The Reinsurance Treaty Included Germany and Russia. The terms called for neutrality in any war waged by the other. There were, however, two key exceptions: It did not apply to a Russian attack on Austria (this provision was crucial because it made the treaty compatible with the Dual Alliance). And it did not apply to a German attack on France (this provision was included simply for symmetry; Bismarck had no interest in attacking France). The strategic effect of the treaty was to remove Russia as a possible alliance partner for France while continuing to deter it from attacking Austria. It also was designed to draw Russia back toward Germany after making it the target of the Mediterranean agreements.

norms about legitimate behavior, his successors' decision to use power politics to demand a global role for Germany led to the collapse of Bismarck's intricate web of alliances and the diplomatic encirclement of Germany.

The shift in the European alliance structure began in the early 1890s, when Bismarck's successors decided they could gain more flexibility by letting the Reinsurance Treaty with Russia lapse. France, on the lookout for a strong ally against Germany since its defeat in the Franco-Prussian war, leapt at the opportunity to sign an alliance with Russia. The Russian government, worried by the change in Germany's attitude and desperate to gain permission to float loans on the Paris

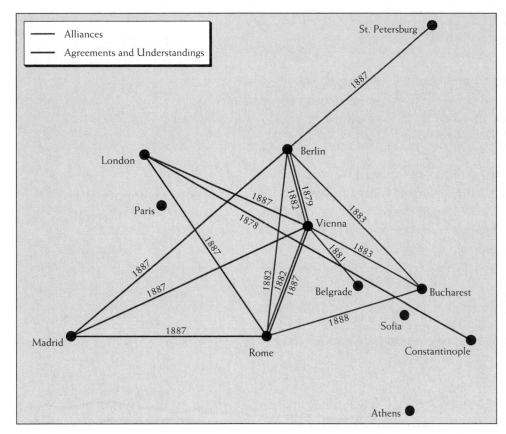

Map 6–8 Europe's Alliances and Alignments at the Height of the Bismarckian System
Bismarck's alliances were designed to create an entangling web that restrained the weak and deterred the strong. Bismarck also sought to isolate France, which had no formal allies in this period.

Source: William Langer, *European Alliances and Agreements,* 2nd ed. (New York: Knopf, 1966), p. 452. Reprinted by permission of McGraw-Hill Publishers, Inc.

exchange, was willing to comply with the French request. By 1894 France and Russia were allied in a defense pact against Germany.

Germany's strategic position soon grew even worse. As part of his goal of becoming a global military and economic player, Kaiser Wilhelm II decided to challenge British naval supremacy by building a battle fleet that could project German influence around the world. Unable to build enough ships to challenge Britain's naval power in all the major areas of the world, the German policy makers decided on a novel—and ultimately disastrous—strategy. They believed that if Germany built a battle fleet large enough to threaten Britain's home fleet (which patrolled the English Channel), they could successfully demand British concessions around the world. This strategy (called the Risk Theory because it was based on putting the British home fleet "at risk") had a fatal flaw. Instead of responding to the increase in German naval capabilities by making concessions to German demands for a place in the sun, the British built more battleships. The result was a naval arms race that poisoned British and German relations from the 1890s to 1914.

With France and Russia in an anti-German alliance and Britain increasingly hostile, the diplomatic encirclement of Germany was then completed by agreements that connected Britain both to France and Russia. In an interesting quirk of history, those agreements grew out of a war between Russia and Japan in 1904. When Russia and Japan went to war in 1904, leaders in London and Paris decided

B&K centered

6.4 ENDURING PATTERNS

The connection between preferences and power

The stronger actors' relative power positions, the more strategically important their preferences.

Germany before World War I and the People's Republic of China Today

Germany not only had one of the largest economies in Europe between 1871 and 1914; it also had the fastest economic growth rate. It used those growing economic capabilities to substantially increase its naval forces. Given rising German power, its preferences—and the compatibility of those preferences with the goals of the other key actors in Europe—were critical in any calculation of the strategic situation in Europe.

By the 1970s the People's Republic of China was being treated carefully diplomatically because it was seen as a potential regional and, ultimately, global superpower. By the end of the 1990s, it was clear any sustained improvement in China's economic growth would bring that day sooner rather than later. In that context, many have stressed that the key is making sure that Chinese preferences are compatible with those of its neighbors.

---

they needed to coordinate their policies to avoid being drawn into a war neither wanted. The result was an *entente*, an agreement to consult before acting. Three years later, Russia also negotiated an entente with Britain. The Japanese had sunk the Russian fleet during the war, and the tsar's advisers felt they needed to avoid antagonizing Britain until they could build a new one.

The combination of the 1894 defense pact between France and Russia, the 1904 entente between Britain and France, and the 1907 entente between Britain and Russia came to be called the Triple Entente. From the German perspective, it represented the encirclement of Germany by three of Europe's strongest military powers. Germany was left with the militarily and financially bankrupt Austro-Hungarian Empire as its only sure ally (Italy was allied both to Germany and to Britain). Given this alliance structure, it's not surprising that German planners concluded that all wars involving them would escalate into a two-front war (see Map 6–9). German strategists also assumed that the next European war would, like the Austro-Prussian and Franco-Prussian wars, be won in one decisive battle. That put a premium on each state's ability to mobilize its armed forces quickly at the first sign of possible conflict. German military strategists developed the Schlieffen Plan, which called for Germany to throw everything they had at France, defeat her quickly, and get the troops back on the train to the Russian frontier before Russia could mobilize for an all-out attack. The emphasis on mobilization schedules in the Schlieffen Plan put the German military on a hair-trigger in any crisis.

This situation almost produced a war in 1908 during the Bosnian crisis. In 1908, to Serbia's great anger, the Austro-Hungarian Empire annexed Bosnia, a province that it was allowed to administer but not annex under an agreement reached at the 1878 Berlin Conference on the Balkans. The Austrian emperor initially bought

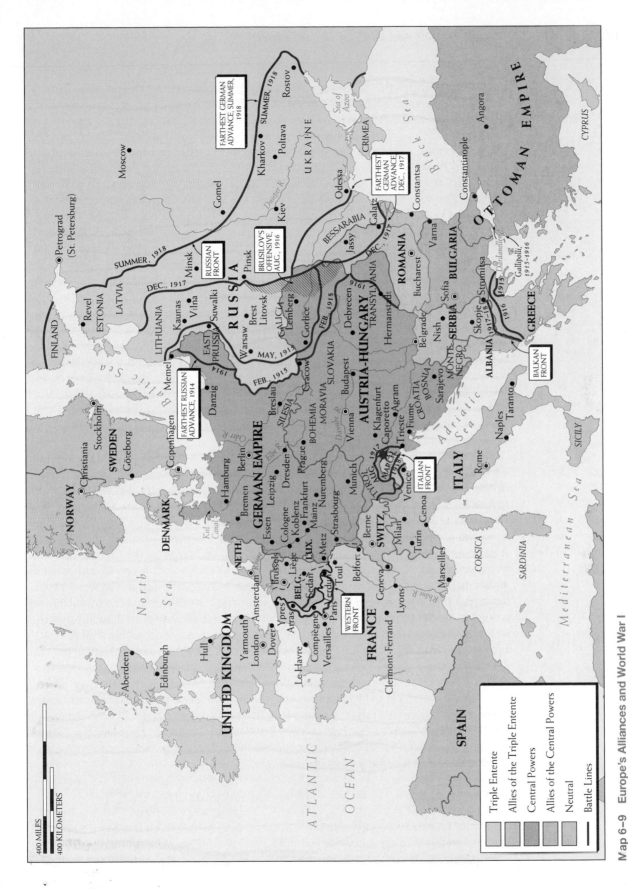

400 MILES
400 KILOMETERS

Map 6-9 Europe's Alliances and World War I
The collapse of the Bismarckian alliance system after his resignation in 1890 led to a dramatic shift in the structure of European alliances. From the web of commitments shown in Map 6–8, Europe moved to a set of antagonist alliances in which Germany and the Austro-Hungarian Empire (known as the Central Powers or the Dual Alliance) were encircled by the Triple Entente (composed of Britain, France, and Russia). The members of the Triple Entente were later joined by Italy, who hoped to expel Austria from its Italian provinces.

161

Russia's assent to the annexation of Bosnia by promising to support Russian demands for greater access through the Bosporus and Dardanelles straits connecting the Black Sea to the Aegean. Germany reneged on the deal, leaving Austria in control of Bosnia and the Russians without any gains in control over the straits. The Russians' anger over both the annexation of Bosnia and the double-cross over the straits led them to back Serbia's protests about the annexation. The Russian government also tried to use its alliance with France (originally designed to deal with Germany) as a basis for convincing the French to support them in a war over Bosnia. Russia backed off only when France refused to be drawn into a war over the issue.

In 1914 another crisis exploded in Bosnia, but this time Europe's antagonist alliance blocs spread the conflict from the Balkans into a cataclysmic war that engulfed the entire continent. The catalyst for the outbreak of World War I was the assassination of the Archduke Franz Ferdinand, Austrian heir to the throne, as he rode in an open car through the Bosnian capital of Sarajevo. The underlying causes of the war were far deeper than this incident. The Austrian emperor feared that the growing role of nationalism as a legitimizing principle would lead to the disintegration of the empire. He suspected that the Serb nationalists who killed the archduke had been supported by the Serbian government, and he decided to use the assassination as a pretext for crushing Serbia and nationalist pressures throughout the empire. He asked Kaiser Wilhelm for support. Unlike Bismarck, who had used alliances to restrain his allies from initiating any conflict that might draw Germany into a war, Wilhelm supported the Austrian emperor with his infamous "blank check"—an authorization to act as he saw fit.

Meanwhile, the Serbians asked the tsar for support, who in turn asked the French. With Germany involved and the implications for French security far grimmer than in the 1908 Bosnian crisis, the French decided to support Russia. With that support in hand, the tsar told the Austrians that he would attack if they invaded Serbia. The tsar initially ordered his military advisers to mobilize only against Austria, but they responded that they had only two plans available: a partial mobilization against Austria and a general mobilization that would include forces on the German border. Without a plan to get from a partial to a general mobilization and afraid of what would happen if the war spread, they convinced the tsar to order a general mobilization. German planners, terrified about what the start of the Russian mobilization would do to the timetables in the Schlieffen Plan, got the kaiser to demand that the tsar cancel the general mobilization. When the tsar refused, the Schlieffen plan was activated. Germany invaded France through Belgium; Britain declared war on Germany; and Russia confounded all of Germany's plans by not waiting for its mobilization to be complete before attacking Germany in support of France. In response to the unexpected Russian assault, German military planners stripped troops from the offensive in France and sent them to the Russian border. The offensive in the west then bogged down just outside Paris, and World War I moved from a war designed to be won in one decisive battle to a war of attrition. Nine million soldiers would die before the war ended in 1918.

Conclusion

The state system arose in Renaissance Europe in response to shifting coalitions that undermined feudal arrangements. It achieved its first set of legitimizing principles when the combatants' mutual exhaustion in the Thirty Years' War led to the Peace of Westphalia, an agreement to stop fighting about religion and to resolve the question of what dynasty had the right to rule which pieces of territory by a process of mutual recognition ratified by treaties signed by the major powers. The classical-balance-of-power system that evolved after Westphalia reflected the shared policy preferences and normative values of the relatively homogeneous set of elites that dominated European politics in that period. That system, in turn, collapsed under the twin pressures of economic change (the Industrial Revolution) and the spread of new legitimizing principles (nationalism and the demand for democracy).

The victorious coalition after the Napoleonic wars tried to put the genie back in the bottle by rebuilding the balance, reasserting the old legitimizing principles, and creating the Concert of Europe to enforce those linked domestic and interstate agendas. Their failure at mid-century led to the Bismarckian synthesis. Domestically, Bismarck coopted nationalism—changing it from a tool of the political left to the right—to undermine domestic threats to conservative dominance. Internationally, Bismarck worked to preserve the post-unification diplomatic position of Germany through a series of standing peacetime alliances designed to deter the strong and restrain the weak, thus preventing the enduring disputes that divided Europe from leading to war. Bismarck's synthesis collapsed when new leaders with different objectives tried to use the forces of nationalism and the techniques of realpolitik to change, rather than preserve, the status quo.

Faced with the carnage of World War I, policy makers approached the making of the peace determined to prevent another cataclysmic war. The question was how? Moreover, the interstate system was no longer only a European one. As a result of the spread of European colonialism between the late 1400s and 1914 plus the rise of Japan and the United States as major military powers, the European state system had "gone global." As we discuss in Chapter 7, the response of the peace makers to this changed strategic situation was to attempt radical change, both in the state system's legitimizing principles and in its principal diplomatic tools.

Key Terms

classical balance of power
preponderance, or hegemony
reciprocal compensation

band-wagoning
balancing

To The Reader   A CHAPTER SUMMARY and QUESTIONS FOR REVIEW are available at **www.prenhall.com/lamborn**

CHAPTER 7

The Interstate Security System Goes Global

Colonialism, the World Wars, and the Cold War

When World War I broke out in August 1914, many Europeans—recalling that the last wars among the major military powers in Europe (the Wars of German Unification) had been short—thought it would be over by the end of the year. Many observers outside of Europe thought that whether the war was short or long, it was none of their affair. Both of these notions were wrong. The war ended up following the bloody and exhausting trench-warfare model of the U.S. Civil War more closely than the decisive-battle model of the Wars of German Unification. It also drew in the United States and provided opportunities for Japan to expand in Asia. Moreover, troops from sub-Saharan Africa fought and died in the fields of Belgium and France, even as Indian troops were shipped to the deserts of the Middle East to fight the armies of the Ottoman Empire—allies of Germany and Austria. And when the war was over, those who assembled in Versailles in an effort to influence the peace treaty included not only representatives of the major military powers in the victorious coalition—Britain, France, the United States, and Italy (which had jumped in late, hoping for a share of the spoils)—but also delegates from the Middle East, Latin America, Asia, and Africa.

How did the state system evolve from the first *de facto* interstate system on the Italian peninsula during the Renaissance to the beginnings of a global state system at the Versailles Conference? The answer begins with the incentives for European colonial expansion in the late 1400s and Europe's collision with the rest of the known, and unknown, world.

Europe's Collision with the Rest of the World

Europe, the Islamic Arc, and Routes to Asia

The beginnings of this story are to be found in the competition between Christianity and Islam. As Map 7–1 shows, by 600 Christianity had consolidated its position in the Holy Land, spread around the Mediterranean Sea, and moved northwest into Europe. With the arrival of the Prophet Muhammad (570–632) and the growth of Islam, the tide quickly turned, and Christians found themselves expelled from the Holy Land, the Balkans, North Africa, and Spain by 750 (see Map 7–2). Christian Europe's response included the reconquest of Spain (a seven-hundred-year process that ended only in the late 1400s) and the three Crusades between 1096 and 1192 (see Map 7–3). As the dates of the Crusades and the size of the different stages in the reconquest of Spain outlined in Map 7–3 suggest, Europe's efforts to roll back the Muslim empires reached their peak at the same time as the expansion of trade between 1000 and 1200 generated the resources European policy makers needed to fund their efforts.

However, by the time of the Renaissance the force of this wave of European expansion was largely spent. The religious and secular incentives for expansion were checked by the limits of European military power and by strong economic incentives to reach an accommodation with the surrounding Islamic empires. The Islamic empires in this period had an immense heartland that spread from Morocco to Afghanistan (see Map 7–4). From that huge base, Islam had expanded still further. Turkish armies under a tribe called the Ottomans moved toward Europe, conquering, first, the old Byzantine Empire by 1453, and then the Balkans, reaching the

Map 7–1   The Spread of Christianity, 200–600

Between 200 and 600 Christianity spread rapidly from a few scattered pockets of believers to become the dominant religion around the Mediterranean.

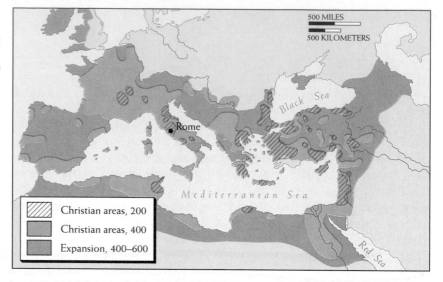

Christian areas, 200

Christian areas, 400

Expansion, 400–600

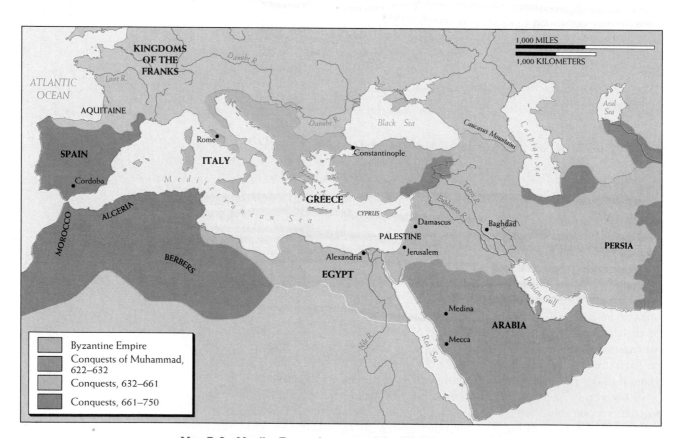

Byzantine Empire

Conquests of Muhammad, 622–632

Conquests, 632–661

Conquests, 661–750

Map 7–2   Muslim Expansion around the Mediterranean

The teachings of the Prophet Muhammad (570–632) and the military conquests led by him and his followers reversed the spread of Christianity around the Mediterranean with startling speed. Compare the expansion of Islam depicted in this map with the situation in 600 shown in Map 7–1.

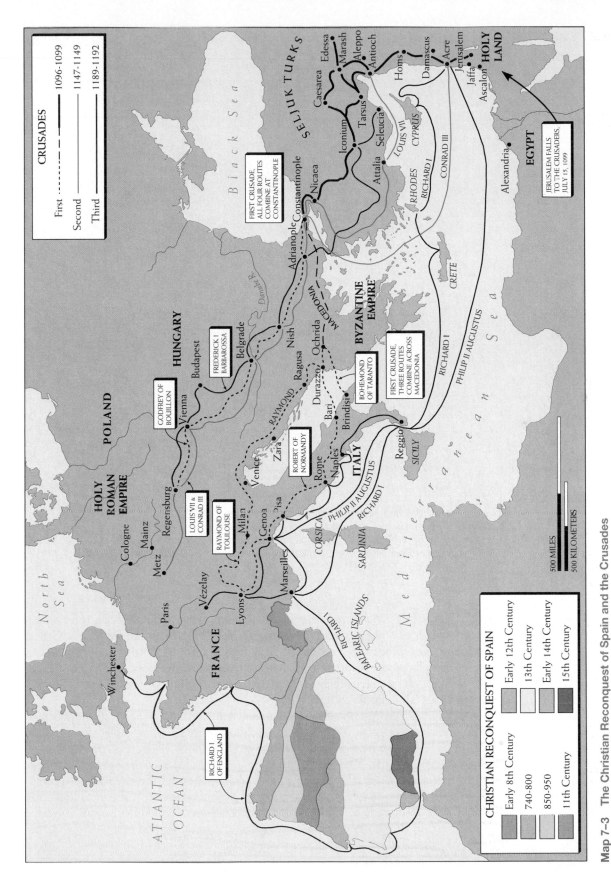

Map 7-3   The Christian Reconquest of Spain and the Crusades
The seven hundred years between the end of the eighth and fifteenth centuries saw a sustained struggle between Christians and Muslims for control of Spain and the Holy Land. The reconquest of Spain, along with the Inquisition (which began in 1480), cleared the way for Ferdinand and Isabella to expropriate the assets used to fund Columbus's voyages. The First Crusade, which sent 100,000 troops to the Holy Land, temporarily succeeded in achieving the pope's multiple purposes: retaking Jerusalem while using the combination of religious zeal and the promise of land in the conquered territories to distract an increasingly fractious nobility, thereby establishing peace in Europe. However, within forty years, Muslims began to regain control of the lands lost in the First Crusade, and the next two Crusades failed.

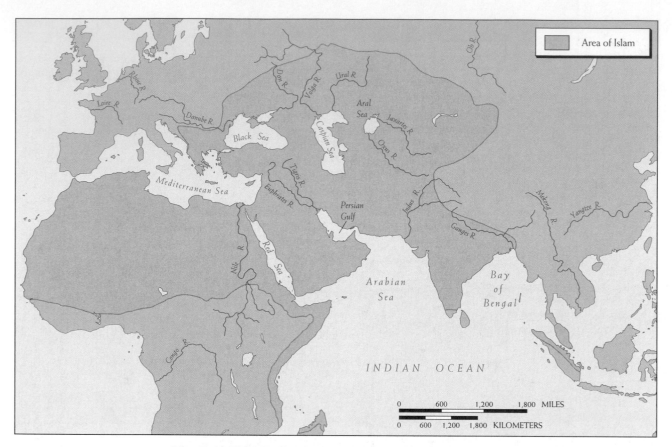

Map 7–4 The Islamic Arc at the End of the 1400s
At the end of the 1400s Islam controlled a huge swath of territory in North Africa, the Middle East, Southeastern Europe, Central Asia, and the Indian subcontinent. Significantly, that arc lay across all the known routes to the Orient, areas with which Europeans desperately wanted to increase trade.

gates of Vienna in 1526 and not beginning their slow, two-century-long retreat and disintegration until 1699 (see the box "*A Closer Look:* The Ottoman Empire"). Other Islamic empire builders moved from Afghanistan into the Indian subcontinent, where they replaced the Hindu rulers. Meanwhile, far to the northeast, the remains of the Mongol (also called Tartar) clans that had invaded Russia centuries before under Genghis Khan converted to Islam.

Given the competing universalist claims of their religions, their different political systems, and the long history of war between Muslim empires and Christian Europe, Islam's great arc from Morocco to the Mongolian plains created obvious security problems for Europeans. It also cut them off from all land routes to the Orient, which for Europeans in this period was equivalent to being cut off from the richest trading partners in the known world. Consequently, while Europeans continued to fight the Ottoman Empire outside of Vienna and in the Balkans, they had substantial incentives to find mutually acceptable arrangements for trade through the Islamic arc to the east. Muslim rulers, meanwhile, also had an incentive to reach an accommodation over trade; they would, after all, benefit greatly as the "middlemen" between Europe

A Closer Look

The Ottoman Empire

The first Ottoman principality was founded in 1280 in Anatolia, the plateau between the Mediterranean and Black seas that now includes the country of Turkey. After consolidating their control of Anatolia, the Ottomans began to expand their empire into Europe in 1356. While their conquest of Greece and the Balkans was underway, their armies also moved to the southwest along the Mediterranean coast. Between 1512 and 1520, they conquered Syria, Palestine, Egypt, Algeria, and the eastern coastline of the Red Sea down through Medina and Mecca. Only six years later, in 1526, they completed their conquest of the Balkans and began an unsuccessful three-year siege of Vienna.

At its peak between 1526 and 1683, when the Ottomans began a second unsuccessful siege of Vienna, the empire governed an extraordinary arc that ran from Algeria, through the Mideast and Anatolia to the Persian Empire, and then back up through the Balkans to Austria on the west and around the Black Sea to Russia on the east. With the failure of the second siege of Vienna, the Ottoman Empire began a 220-year retreat in 1699 with the cession of its Hungarian provinces to Austria.

The gradual collapse of the empire's European territories in the Balkans and along the northern coast of the Black Sea created many opportunities for conflict between the Ottomans, countries that wanted to expand into the Balkans (principally Russia and the Austrian Empire), and indigenous groups seeking independence. These conflicts brought in still other countries—Britain, France, and Prussia/Germany—that wanted either to prevent Russian and Austrian expansion or to manage its effects on European diplomacy. The resulting high-stakes problems lasted so long that they became known in European diplomatic circles simply as "the Eastern Question."

The principal dates in the disintegration of the Ottoman's European possessions are:

- 1699   Hungarian provinces ceded to Austria
- 1774   Crimean Peninsula lost to Russia
- 1812   Bessarabia lost to Russia
- 1821–1832   Revolt in Greece leads to Greek independence
- 1830–1833   Serbia gains autonomy
- 1878   Congress of Berlin agreements: Bulgaria given autonomy; Romania, Serbia, and Montenegro granted independence; Britain given Cyprus; Austria-Hungary granted rights to administer Bosnia-Herzegovina
- 1908   Bulgaria gains independence
- 1912–1913   First and Second Balkan wars lead to Albanian independence and transfer of most of Macedonia to Greece; with the exception of a small strip of land, Ottoman Empire expelled completely from Europe

But while the Balkans and the Eastern Question preoccupied European diplomats for over two hundred years, it was the decay of the Ottoman Empire's Middle Eastern and North African provinces in the nineteenth century that altered the face of colonial expansion. In 1830, the Ottoman Empire still had formal control of the southern Mediterranean to Algeria. In practice, however, the local rulers (called the *Dey* in Algeria, the *Bey* in Tunis and Tripoli, the *Khedive* in Egypt) were virtually autonomous. With no effective help available from the Ottoman Empire, Algeria was invaded by the French in 1830, Tunis was forced to accept a French protectorate in 1881, Egypt was taken by Britain in 1882, and Tripoli (now Libya) was seized by Italy in 1908.

The Ottoman Empire entered World War I with only its Middle Eastern possessions (the eastern coast of the Red Sea, Lebanon, Syria, Palestine, Jordan, Mesopotamia, and Iraq) remaining. As part of its war effort against Germany and its allies, the British government sent Colonel T. E. Lawrence and others to help organize Arab nationalist movements against the Ottomans, promising independence in exchange for help. However, the British simultaneously—and quite incompatibly—promised in the Balfour Declaration that they would support creating a Jewish homeland in Palestine.

The Ottoman Empire collapsed after its defeat in the war. Its Anatolian heartland was reborn as the country of Turkey in 1923. Meanwhile, the peace settlement after World War I reneged on the promises of independence made to the Arabs. Instead, the victors created a "mandate" system under the League of Nations that, while promising independence in the near future, gave control of Lebanon and Syria to France, and gave Palestine, Trans-Jordan, and Iraq to Britain. As for the Balfour Declaration, the British tried to walk a tightrope between honoring the pledge by allowing large-scale Jewish immigration into Palestine (which they did until 1936) and avoiding a full-fledged Arab revolt by refusing to create a Jewish state.

and the Far East. The result was a series of agreements that enabled European traders to locate in the Ottoman Empire and elsewhere through the Islamic arc.*

These accommodations created incentives for others to look for ways to circumvent the coalition between the Islamic rulers that sat astride the trade routes and the principal European cities that received the goods for transshipment to the rest of Europe. The problem confronting those who wanted to set up their own trade arrangements was the lack of any other known route to the Orient. In the early 1400s, Europeans' knowledge of the African continent ended at the Sahara, and the best guesses of the size of the ocean to the west put a direct route to China and Japan at well over 10,000 miles from the farthest known island outposts where ships could re-provision. That distance was far more than any contemporary ship could travel.

The problem of navigation routes would be solved by a combination of skilled persistence and luck. The skilled persistence would come from Portugal, where Prince Henry the Navigator organized over fifty expeditions down the west coast of Africa before his death in 1460. His successors continued the effort. The Cape of Good Hope, which revealed an alternate trade route to India, was discovered by the end of 1487. Vasco da Gama wouldn't use that route to reach India until 1499, but with the knowledge of the route in hand (and treated as the highest of state secrets), it is hardly surprising that the Portuguese quickly rejected Christopher Columbus's request to outfit a fleet to sail west. The Portuguese had a known route that allowed for re-provisioning, and his plan looked poorly thought out. His estimate of the voyage's length was only one-fourth that of the scientific consensus at the time and was, therefore, considered virtually suicidal. Spain's rulers, however, were in a position where even a high-risk venture looked better than their available alternatives. Having just consolidated their control over Spain by conquering Grenada and expelling all Jews and Muslims who refused to convert to Catholicism, Ferdinand and Isabella had both the domestic breathing space and the wealth (taken from expelled Jews and Muslims) to fund the expedition. With no existing routes of their own to the Orient and no other proposals on the table, they had a lot to gain if Columbus got lucky and very little to lose if he never returned.**

The combination of Portuguese persistence in opening up the route around the Cape of Good Hope to India and Columbus's extraordinary luck in finding the Americas about where he thought Asia would be did more than break the existing monopolies on trade routes to the Orient (see Map 7–5 for the voyages of discovery). It also signaled the beginning of a process of European colonial expansion into the Western Hemisphere, Africa, and Asia that would last until the middle of the twentieth century. That process would, in its turn, lead to the spread of the European state system to the rest of the globe.

Historians and political scientists usually break the four-hundred-year process of European colonial expansion into three periods: the old colonialism, running from the initial discoveries in the late 1400s to the Napoleonic wars; a lull in government-sponsored expansion that lasted until the 1870s; and the period of the new imperial-

---

*Consistent with contemporary Islamic customs, which assumed that only the faithful and other subjects of the sultan were to be held to local law, Europeans who resided in Islamic areas for purposes of trade were allowed to govern themselves under European law.
**Our thanks to Bruce Bueno de Mesquita for his insights on the domestic and strategic incentives for the Spanish decision to fund Columbus.

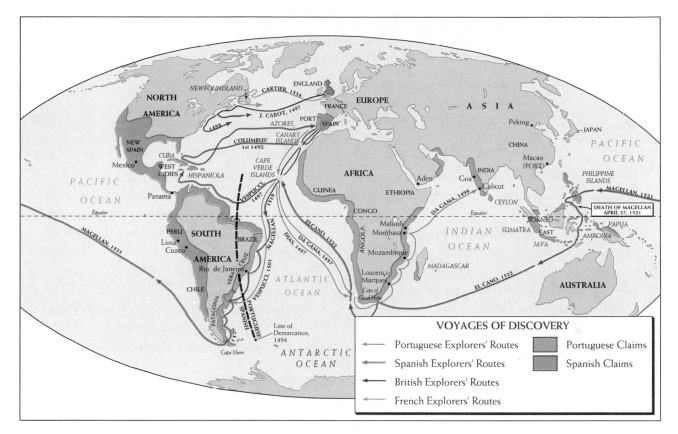

Map 7–5   European Voyages of Discovery: The Exploration of Sub-Saharan Africa and the Americas

With the land routes between Europe and the Orient controlled by Muslim middlemen, Europeans began voyages to find a sea route to India, China, and Japan. The Portuguese explored the coast of Africa south from the Sahara to the Cape of Good Hope. From there, they went up the east coast looking for a jumping-off point to cross the Indian Ocean. With funding from Spain, Columbus went west, finding islands in the Caribbean about where he expected to find Japan.

ism, from about 1880 until World War I, in which European governments scrambled to partition Africa and Asia. In the sections that follow, we look at these periods in more detail.

The Old Colonialism: From the 1400s to the Napoleonic Wars

The drive to expand during the **old colonialism** reflected the norms and preferences of European state builders during pre-industrial, dynastic-rule Europe. Indeed, because European governments sought empire throughout this period, one finds a startling continuity in objectives and methods, even as the European state system was transforming itself internally as a result of the legitimizing principles adopted at Westphalia. But while the drive to expand reflected European preferences, what actually happened when Europeans arrived on the shores of the Americas, Africa, and Asia was influenced by the structure, values, and power of the indigenous civilizations and their rulers.

old colonialism The period of European colonial expansion that began in the late 1400s and lasted until the Napoleonic wars.

7.1 ENDURING PATTERNS

The connection between preferences and power
The stronger actors' power positions, the more strategically important their preferences.

Expansion during the Old Colonialism; China Takes Tibet

During the period of the old colonialism, the indigenous regimes in Africa and Asia were more powerful militarily than the European explorers who arrived at their shores. Consequently, Europeans had to request opportunities to establish trading posts. In the Americas, indigenous societies were usually weaker militarily than the Europeans they confronted. Since the preferences of the Europeans ranked conquering the indigenous civilizations far higher than trading with them, this military weakness had catastrophic results for their security.

In 1950 the population of Tibet clearly preferred to remain independent of China. Policy makers in the People's Republic of China, however, strongly preferred taking over Tibet and integrating it into China. Faced with rebellions in 1959 and renewed opposition in 1988 to 1989, the Chinese government used force to maintain control and encouraged immigration by ethnic Chinese to change the composition of Tibet's population. With massively greater military resources at its disposal, the preferences of the Chinese government dominated the outcome.

Regional Differences in the Pattern of European Colonial Expansion A distinctive regional pattern emerged from these separate encounters. In the Americas, Europeans found a number of incentives to establish settlements. They found gold and silver in areas controlled by the large but militarily weak empires of the Incas and Aztecs. Elsewhere, they found vast forests and plains suitable for lumbering and agriculture populated by tribes that were dangerous to individual groups of explorers but collectively incapable of stemming the European tide. Finally, the Americas had a temperate climate that was attractive to Europeans. The result of all these incentives was a large migration of Europeans into the Western Hemisphere and a "settlement empire" (see Map 7–6).

In Africa, the other continent that was largely unknown to Europeans before exploration began, the pattern of expansion was quite different. With the exception of Dutch agricultural settlements that grew out of a re-provisioning base for ships traveling around the Cape of Good Hope, Europeans stayed on the coast of Africa from the late fifteenth-century discoveries until the 1880s. Europeans' decision to stay on the coast partly reflected the original impetus for exploration—the search for a route and supporting bases for the voyage to the Orient. However, the fact that Europeans did not venture into the interior in great numbers also reflected the disincentives created by climate and disease and the military power of many of the indigenous civilizations. Unlike the Incas and Aztecs, who had largely stone-age weapons, the Ashanti, Bantu, Xhosa, and Zulu were more than a match for Europeans before the Industrial Revolution. Europeans found little reason to challenge these military and climatic odds when they could stay on the coast and trade for slaves, gold dust, and ivory.

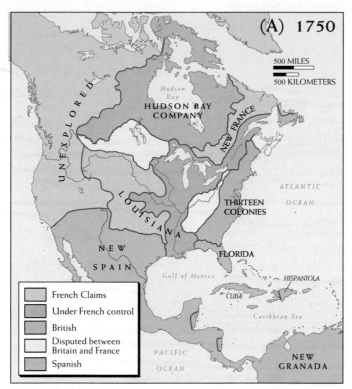

(A) 1750

500 MILES
500 KILOMETERS

Hudson Bay

HUDSON BAY
COMPANY

NEW FRANCE

U N E X P L O R E D

L O U I S I A N A

THIRTEEN
COLONIES

ATLANTIC
OCEAN

N E W
S P A I N

FLORIDA

Gulf of Mexico

HISPANIOLA

CUBA

Caribbean Sea

PACIFIC
OCEAN

NEW
GRANADA

	French Claims
	Under French control
	British
	Disputed between Britain and France
	Spanish

Map 7–6
The Colonization of the Western Hemisphere
Europeans created settlement empires throughout the Western
Hemisphere during the period of the old colonialism.

(B) 1780

DISPUTED BY
ENGLAND, RUSSIA,
AND SPAIN

St. Lawrence R.

Ohio R.

VICEROYALTY
OF
NEW SPAIN

EFFECTIVE FRONTIER OF
SPANISH SETTLEMENT

ATLANTIC
OCEAN

Rio Grande

Gulf of Mexico

Mexico City • • Veracruz

Santo Domingo
Caribbean Sea

Cartagena
Portobelo • • Caracas

VICEROYALTY OF
NEW GRENADA
Bogotá • Separated from
Viceroyalty of Peru,
1717,
1739

GUIANA

Quito •

Amazon R.

VICEROYALTY
OF PERU

VICEROYALTY
OF
BRAZIL

Recife •

Lima •

Bahia •

PACIFIC
OCEAN

Potosí •

São Paulo • • Rio de Janeiro

VICEROYALTY OF
LA PLATA
Separated from
Viceroyalty of Peru,
1776

1,000 MILES
1,000 KILOMETERS

Santiago • • Buenos Aires

AUDIENCIA
OF CHILE

ATLANTIC
OCEAN

	Spanish
	Portuguese
	Dutch
	Disputed by England, Russia and Spain

The situation in Asia, the part of the world Europeans knew about when the exploration began, was different from those in Africa and the Western Hemisphere. In Asia, Europeans found large and complex political systems. It is easy to fall into the habit of using the word *state* to describe any political entity with a government, but the political systems in India, China, and Japan (as well as in the Islamic arc) were qualitatively different from the European states, in that they did *not* claim sovereign territoriality. They were, instead, **suzerain systems.** Suzerain systems are different from state systems in two key respects: First, the rulers of the many smaller political entities that made up each regional suzerain system recognized an underlying hierarchy in authority relations that placed one of them, the suzerain, at the top; second, none of the rulers within each system claimed exclusive authority over the territory they ruled—although they did have considerable independence, including the ability to deal directly with outside governments.

Between the late 1400s and the early 1800s, the political elites in these Asian suzerain systems were internally strong enough—and the Europeans who could reach their shores isolated and militarily weak enough—to insist that Europeans *request* the opportunity to trade. The Japanese refused European requests for commercial access well into the nineteenth century. In contrast, the structure and norms of suzerain systems in China and India made it seem natural to grant requests by Europeans to establish bases that had the right to administer and tax specific localities under the nominal control of the Supreme Ruler. Hence it was that Robert Clive, one of the most famous English entrepreneurs in the Indian subcontinent, was given formal authority by the emperor of the Indian suzerain system to tax and administer all of Bengal, Bihar, and Orissa in 1765. While these grants were natural in a suzerain system that did not make a claim to sovereign territoriality, they had the effect of giving European actors a territorial base within the empire.

The long-term results for the indigenous political systems were toxic. With substantially different preferences and conceptions of legitimate political and economic relationships than their hosts, Europeans acted in ways that accentuated existing internal differences among indigenous elites. These pressures gradually undermined the authority and economic viability of suzerain systems throughout Asia. Thus weakened, all but Japan would collapse when the effects of these incompatible preferences and values were reinforced by a massive shift in relative economic and military power in the nineteenth century.

In sum, while Europeans had a dominant military edge over the societies they encountered in the Americas, during the period of the old colonialism the only significant technological edge they had over the major indigenous empires in Africa and Asia was in navigation. Europeans could get to sub-Saharan Africa, India, and China; their hosts were in no position to return the visit. But once there, Europeans had to bargain for access.

The Impact of Mercantilism The regional differentiation in the pattern of colonial expansion—settlement empires in the Americas and trading posts in Africa and Asia—is the first central feature of the old colonialism. The second is **mercantilism.** Because it is a distinctive type of political economy, we explore mercantilism in more depth in Part III, the section on the evolution of the global political economy. Nevertheless, it is impossible to understand the old colonialism and what came after it without knowing a little about mercantilist attitudes. Mercantilism assumed that there was a fixed amount of wealth available in the world, and that wealth could only be discovered, not created. The assumption that wealth could

suzerain systems Hierarchically arranged networks of semi-autonomous political entities; in which none of the rulers—not even the highest ranking—is sovereign.

mercantilism A set of beliefs about political economy that assumed that wealth could only be discovered, not created, and that the best way to accumulate wealth was in precious metals.

only be discovered was reinforced by the belief that acquiring precious metals and *specie money* (currency coined in gold and silver) was the best way to accumulate wealth. This belief led, in turn, to an emphasis on promoting exports (which generated specie money) and restricting imports (in which money was lost in the purchase of goods and services). The emphasis on specie and the assumption that shared economic growth was impossible led to a ferocious competition for empire and a drive to reorganize agriculture in the colonies, shifting it away from subsistence farming to products that had a high market value in Europe. The emphasis on reorganizing colonial economies to generate high-value exports, in turn, created pressure to find laborers to work on plantations in the New World. The solution, pioneered by the Portuguese and then widely copied by other colonizers, was to trade with African middlemen for slaves.

The Post-Napoleonic Lull in Government-Sponsored Colonial Expansion

The patterns that defined the first phase of European colonial expansion came unglued after the Napoleonic wars. The French, Spanish, and Portuguese lost control of most of their colonies after the war's end, and by the 1820s, Britain and Holland were the only two significant European colonial powers left. Holland, however, was pretty much restricted to its holdings in the East Indies (now Indonesia), having lost its colony next to the Cape of Good Hope to the British during the wars.*** Consequently, the story of European colonialism in the decades after Napoleon is really a story of changing British attitudes and capabilities. Three factors dramatically reduced the British government's interest in further colonial expansion.

First, the cost of controlling settlement colonies in North America had become too high. The rebellion of the thirteen colonies in 1776 had resulted, after long years of war, in independence and the founding of the United States. To the north, in Canada, the influx of loyalists from the United States had worsened divisions between French- and English-speaking settlers. The resulting controversies required more attention and resources than the British government wanted to invest. The conclusion in London was inescapable: Settlement colonies were not worth the trouble.

Second, attitudes toward slavery shifted dramatically in Britain. Estimates of the number of Africans forcibly transported as slaves range as high as 100,000 a year during the eighteenth century, but anti-slavery activists in England (led by Lord Wilberforce's Anti-Slavery League) finally convinced Parliament to outlaw slavery throughout the empire in 1807.[1] Over the next several decades, buying and selling slaves was outlawed by all the major European states. The end of legal slavery destroyed the basis for plantation economies in Britain's Caribbean colonies. It also led to a series of bloody conflicts between legally free workers and planters, who often tried to keep their workers enslaved, which troubled British policy makers and reduced their interest in empire still further.

The third and final transformation was in British thinking about political economy. Ever since 1776, when Adam Smith published his attack on mercantilism in

---

***While the Dutch colonies in the East Indies were dwarfed in international significance by the far larger British Empire, they were very significant within Holland because the Dutch monarch relied on tax revenue from those colonies to replace the revenue from the crown lands he lost when Belgium seceded from Holland in the 1830s.

7.2   ENDURING PATTERNS

The impact of varying beliefs about just relationships
If people value creating and sustaining legitimate relationships, and if they think an outcome is unjust, they are far more likely to oppose it.

The impact of linkage politics
World politics is driven by the interaction of international, factional, and constituency politics.

Ending the Slave Trade and Apartheid

While many groups in Britain benefited economically from the slave trade within the colonial empire, many other groups believed slavery to be a profoundly evil institution. Using arguments based on what was just—rather than what was profitable or convenient—the Anti-Slavery League organized a coalition that led a successful fight in 1807 to outlaw slavery in the British empire.

In the late twentieth century, African states in the United Nations organized a campaign to increase international opposition to the system of racial discrimination known as *apartheid* in South Africa. The United Nations declared apartheid an international crime in 1973. Even after that announcement, many policy makers in the United States were reluctant to put pressure on South Africa to end apartheid because the South African government had been very helpful in supporting U.S. strategic initiatives to contain the Soviet Union. Eventually, however, the domestic political price generated by supporting a regime that had such an unjust political system grew too high, and the U.S. government joined the trans-national effort to end apartheid.

The Wealth of Nations, a growing number of politically significant actors in Britain had begun to advocate abolishing mercantilist practices and moving toward free-trade principles. As we discuss in Chapter 9, Smith began a revolution in thinking about political economy by challenging the mercantilist view that shared economic growth was impossible. He argued that new wealth could be created if government interference in the economy were ended and individuals were left to act on their own economic incentives. Under free-trade principles, colonial control was not only unnecessary to create new wealth; it was positively counterproductive because it interfered with the cornerstones of wealth creation—people's freedom to make choices that maximized their economic advantages. The free-traders finally won the debate in Britain in the late 1840s, a victory symbolized by the abolition of the Navigation Acts (which established government controls on trade with the British Isles and all colonial possessions) and the Corn Laws (which restricted food imports to protect British agriculture from foreign competition).

These three changes all pushed in the same direction. Increasing opposition by settlers in the colonies raised the cost of empire at the same time as doubts about the legitimacy of slavery and the wisdom of mercantilism reduced policy makers' incentives to maintain existing colonies, much less acquire new ones. It is a classic

> ## World Politics and the Individual
>
> ### The French Conquest of Algeria:
> ### Debt, Pride, Culture, and Politics
>
> At the same time as the British government was rethinking the value of acquiring new colonies, the French government began the conquest of Algeria. That conquest would change the lives of people throughout North Africa in the nineteenth and twentieth centuries. Its aftershocks continue to reverberate today both in North Africa and France.
>
> The origins of the French decision to conquer Algeria (see the discussion at **www.prenhall.com/lamborn**) show both the importance of underlying strategic conditions—in this case massive differences in military power—and the importance of chance events that radically alter actors' preferences and their perceptions of the diplomatic and domestic stakes.
>
> Look for the impact of non-state actors in setting the scene in the mid-1820s, and think about what this example suggests about the importance of non-state actors in world politics 150 years before it became fashionable to study them. Consider the elements of farce in the tale of the fly swatter and, since it clearly didn't seem farcical at the time, what that suggests about the impact of culture and variations in actors' expectations about behavior in different historical periods. Finally, you might wonder whether the French would have invaded Algeria sooner or later during the nineteenth century, even without this specific event to trigger it. To answer this question, you will need to evaluate different assumptions about the underlying causes of French colonial expansion.

example of the impact of the linkages between international and domestic politics that drive world politics across different historical periods.

The decline in the British government's interest in formal empire was not matched by all the governments in Europe or by key actors in the colonies. Perhaps the most important exception among the European governments was France, whose politically vulnerable monarch saw substantial advantages in trying to conquer Algeria in the 1830s and began a process of expansion in North Africa that would take over a half-century to complete. Meanwhile, all the empires experienced pressures at one time or another from actors within existing colonies who wanted to expand. Often these pressures came from officials trying to consolidate their control (British security policy in India, for instance, was based on the notion of *defense-in-depth*, which called for continued expansion to protect areas already under British control). Other pressures came from settlers interested in more land, traders interested in more areas that could be forced open for European commerce, and missionaries interested in converting large populations to Christianity. However, with the exception of the French in North Africa and the British in India, European governments spent most of the years between 1815 and 1880 trying to keep local actors from dragging them into commitments and conflicts they did not want. The overall result was a lull in government-directed European colonial expansion.

The New Imperialism: 1880 to World War I

The **new imperialism** refers to the period between 1880 and the beginning of World War I during which virtually all of Africa and most of Asia fell under the

new imperialism   A period of renewed colonial expansion that began around 1880.

Map 7–7   Africa in 1880, on the Eve of Partition

With only a few important exceptions—Algeria (conquered by the French), the British Cape Colony, the Orange Free State and the Transvaal (settled by Dutch farmers who had trekked north from the Cape Colony)—almost all of Africa remained under the control of indigenous societies in 1880. The fact that Europeans were located largely in scattered coastal settlements reflected a combination of the goals of early mercantilist explorers, the relatively equal military power of European and African political systems before the Industrial Revolution, and the absence of strong incentives for Europeans to expand into Africa from 1815 to 1880.

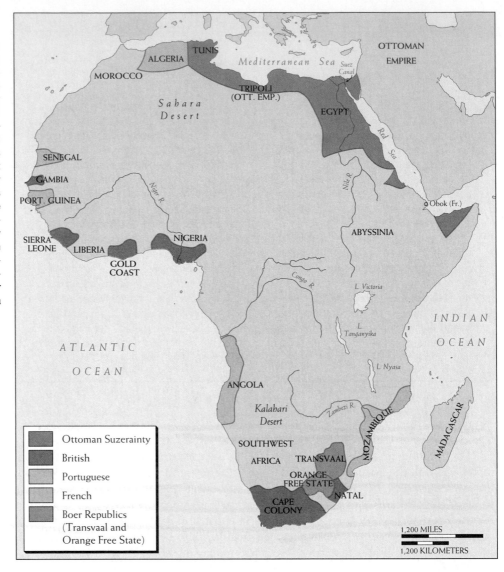

formal control of European colonizers[†] (see Maps 7–7, 7–8, 7–9). The only exceptions to colonial domination in Africa were Ethiopia and Liberia, and of these two, only Ethiopia was governed by an indigenous regime; Liberia was governed by the descendants of freed American slaves as part of a "return to Africa" movement. In Asia, the only countries to escape being either partitioned or colonized were Japan and Siam (now Thailand). Even China, which maintained a formally independent

---

[†]Writers analyzing this period sometimes build their assumptions about the causes of this expansion into distinctive definitions of imperialism (see, for instance, Lenin's unique definition in Chapter 9). Others use the word *imperialism* quite broadly to refer any situation in which economically and militarily strong states exploit weak ones. In the mid-twentieth century some observers also began to call the spread of Western ideas and culture throughout the Third World *cultural* imperialism.

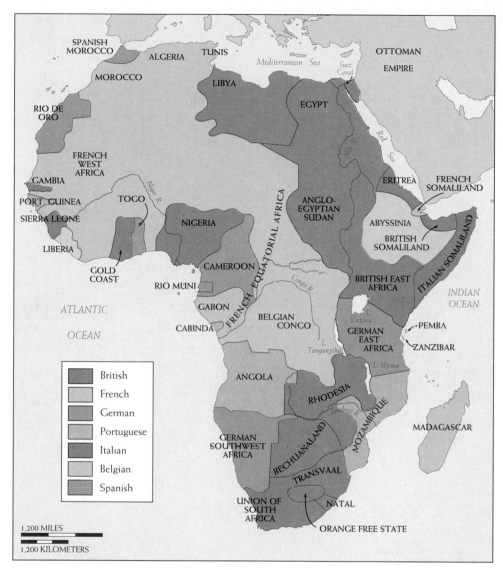

Map 7–8 Africa after the 1880–1914 Partition

Between 1880 and 1900, Europeans partitioned Africa, dividing almost all of it among themselves. By 1914 only Liberia and Abyssinia (Ethiopia) remained independent.

government, was subject to a series of partitions along its coastline in which the central government lost control of "Treaty Ports" to Russia, Britain, Germany, France, Portugal, and Japan.

The causes of this sudden burst of formal colonial expansion remain controversial. The perspective outlined in Chapter 3 leads us to look at how *linkage politics* in Europe, Africa, and Asia became intertwined in the late 1800s in ways that gave key European actors incentives to try to achieve their goals through a process of formal expansion. Approached that way, the following picture emerges.

The Impact of the Changing Distribution of Military and Economic Power With the massive increase in resources and sophisticated weapons generated by the Industrial Revolution, there was little question about Europeans' ability to conquer large areas in Asia and Africa. The question was whether there were

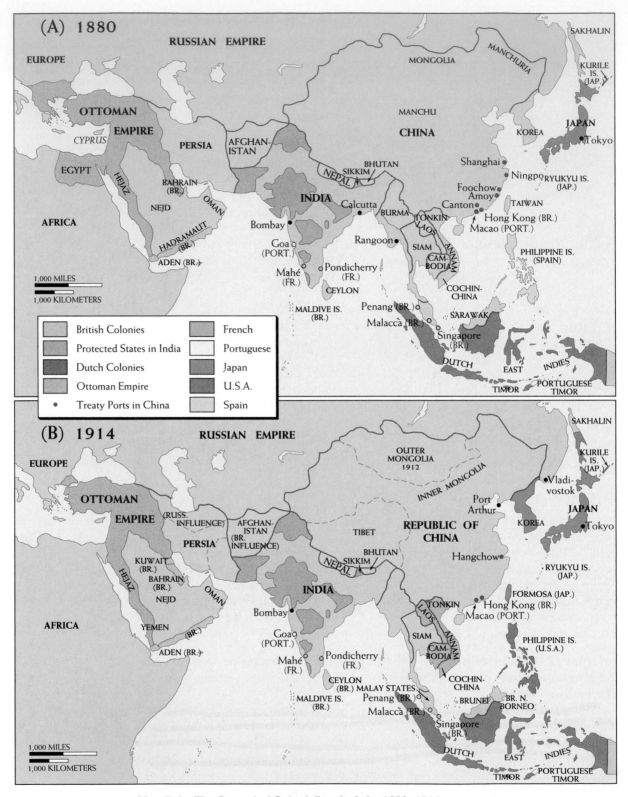

Map 7–9   The Spread of Colonialism in Asia, 1880–1914

As the top section of this map shows, Europeans already had a large presence in Asia by 1880, a presence reinforced by British settlement in Australia (which the British had used as a penal colony as early as 1788). What the new imperialism brought to Asia was an expansion in the territory controlled by long-term colonial states and an increase in the number of states competing for a sphere they could control.

incentives to go forward. The first set of incentives can be found in the changing distribution of military and economic power within Europe.

Recall the changing strategic context in Europe during the 1870s that we discussed in Chapter 6. The defeat of France in the Franco-Prussian War and the unification of Germany had radically altered the distribution of military and economic power. In the aftermath of the war, France was divided between advocates of *revanche* (from the French word for revenge), a direct attack on Germany when conditions permitted, and pro-colonial factions that wanted to gain resources for increasing French military and economic power by expanding into northern Africa and southeast Asia. Pro-colonial factions in the Third Republic's executive worked secretly with elements of the army, settlers, and traders to promote expansion behind Parliament's back. These unauthorized moves led to the acquisition of French Indochina (now Vietnam, Laos, and Cambodia) and a military operation conducted out of Algeria that forced the government in Tunis to accept French control in 1880. Parliamentary opponents were furious at being lied to, but were unable to muster a majority to undo these *faits accomplis*.

While less directly threatened than the French, the British were also worried about the military and economic implications of German unification. British concerns increased still more when first Germany (in 1879) and then France (in the early 1880s) increased import tariffs to the point where British exports—the key to British economic growth since the beginning of the Industrial Revolution—were put at risk. That led some factions in Britain to rethink the value of empire, both as a market for British exports and investment and as a source of raw materials. They concluded that trade with the empire was crucial to Britain's economic health and its ability to continue as a major military power. Their ability to sell this conclusion was increased by several important transformations in British society and politics.

The Impact of Electoral Politics and Racism   Britain had gone from a tiny electorate in the 1830s to full male suffrage in 1884. The size of the new electorate prompted political elites to form the first mass political parties and look for ways to win the votes of the new electorate. They found a broad and enthusiastic appetite for imperial expansion. The popularity of imperialism was reinforced by the growth of mass-circulation newspapers. The *Daily Mail* was first published in 1896, and by 1901, it was selling a million copies a day. As the historian William Langer reports, the opening editorial of the *Daily Mail* announced that "first and foremost" it would stand

> for the power, the supremacy and the Greatness of the British Empire.... Those who launched this journal had one definite aim in view.... To be the articulate voice of British progress and domination.... We know that the advance of the Union Jack [the British flag] means protection for weaker races, justice for the oppressed, liberty for the down-trodden. Our Empire has not exhausted itself.[2]

Yet another impetus for the domestic popularity of imperial expansion was the growth of Social Darwinism. **Social Darwinism,** sometimes also called *natural history*, was a perversion of Charles Darwin's ideas about evolution, natural selection, and survival of the fittest. Social Darwinists argued that civilization progressed through the struggle of race against race and nation against nation. The winners in this struggle, which many Europeans and North Americans confidently expected to

Social Darwinism (also called *natural history*)   A pseudoscientific adaptation of Darwin's ideas about evolution, natural selection, and survival of the fittest that argued that civilization advanced through the struggle of race against race and nation against nation.

be, were by definition mentally and physically superior to the losers. This racist doctrine created a pseudoscientific justification for white domination of Africa and Asia. Consider the following quotation from a pamphlet published by Karl Pearson, a renowned mathematician who had shifted from mathematics to natural history:

> History shows me one way, and one way only, in which a state of civilization has been produced, namely, the struggle of race with race, and the survival of the physically and mentally fitter race. . . . You may hope for a time when the sword shall be turned into a ploughshare. . . . But, believe me, when that day comes mankind will no longer progress; there will be nothing to check the fertility of the inferior stock; the relentless law of heredity will not be controlled and guided by natural selection. . . . The path of progress is strewn with the wreck of nations; traces are everywhere to be seen of the hecatombs [sacrificial slaughter] of inferior races, and of victims who found not the narrow way to the greater perfection. Yet these dead peoples are, in very truth, the stepping stones on which mankind has arisen to the higher intellectual and deeper emotional life of today.[3]

With these attitudes widespread at the time, there were few blocking coalitions that could form around the notion that imperial expansion was unjust. Meanwhile, the perceived deterioration in the military and economic position of France and Britain relative to that of Germany gave policy makers in London and Paris some Eurocentric strategic incentives to expand. But these European incentives may not have been enough by themselves to produce the new imperialism. We must add a series of changes in Africa and Asia to what was taking place in Europe in the late nineteenth century.

The Impact of Changing Conditions in Africa and Asia on Europeans' Incentives to Colonize   In Asia, changing conditions created a variety of incentives for European governments to resume colonial expansion. The continued weakening of the indigenous suzerain systems was creating a growing power vacuum that allowed European settlers, traders, and missionaries to move inland from their outposts and to call for the support of their governments as they migrated. The possibility that some European governments would support their nationals prompted other European governments to worry that they would be disadvantaged economically and militarily unless they got involved as well.

The drive to partition Africa was triggered by events in North Africa and in the Transvaal, an ethnically Dutch area in South Africa that had retained considerable internal independence but had been forced to cede its foreign policy to the British. The central catalyst in North Africa was the revival of Islamic fundamentalism. The key arena was Egypt, which was nominally still part of the Ottoman Empire but, as is the case in many suzerain systems, functionally independent. The leader of Egypt, called the *Khedive*, had allowed a French company to build the Suez Canal, linking the Mediterranean to the Red Sea, in the 1860s. Deep in debt even after selling off all his shares of stock in the canal, the Khedive was forced to give an international debt commission—composed of representatives of the countries in which most of the canal stock and bonds were held (Britain, France, and Germany)—control over Egyptian finances. That produced enormous resentment among Egyptians which, when combined with a revival of Islamic fundamentalism throughout the region, led to a nationalist revolt.

The French government, worried about a possible spread of the revolt in Egypt to Algeria, convinced the British to intervene. At this point domestic politics in

France dramatically altered the outcome. The French parliament, convinced that it was being lied to again by the executive just a few years after the secret move on Tunis, brought down the government. The French fleet was recalled by the new government, and the occupation of Egypt fell to the British alone. Furious that the British refused to share the spoils with them and encouraged by Bismarck (who was delighted to have the French and British angry with each other), the French government authorized its settlers and army units in West Africa to expand at the expense of adjacent British colonies. The British reciprocated.

After enjoying this dispute from the sidelines for several years, Bismarck moved to gain control of the outcome by calling a conference, which was held in Berlin in 1884.[††] The result of the 1884 conference was a series of agreements: the division of West Africa between the British and the French; the transfer of the Congo to the Belgian king; and an overarching **principle of effective occupation.** Under this principle, the European country that first effectively occupied an area in Africa had its claim recognized. The British, believing that they needed to control the Nile to its source in order to protect Egypt, drove south to Lake Victoria and from there to the African coast to establish a link to the sea. Bismarck, personally uninterested in Africa, felt compelled to respond to domestic pressure for a piece of the action by acquiescing to German control of areas in east and southwest Africa. (The eastern holdings were part of what is now Tanzania; the southwestern areas were in what is now Namibia.) The British and Germans, in turn, recognized French claims to huge tracts of North Africa.

The final pieces of Africa, all in the south, were partitioned in the aftermath of the discovery of gold and diamonds in the Transvaal. English settlers poured into the Dutch Republic and were denied the right to vote by the Dutch settlers (called *Boers* in South Africa), who were determined not to be submerged. British factions in South Africa, hoping to get rich, coalesced with foreign policy makers in London, who worried that they might lose control of the Cape Colony (and with it, control of the trade route around Africa to India) if the Boers were successful in recruiting Germany to aid their cause. The result was the Anglo-Boer War of 1899–1902 and European agreement on the boundaries for the rest of southern Africa.

The New Imperialism, World War I, and the Changing State System   Thus it was that when war broke out in Europe in 1914, Britain brought Indian troops to fight in the Middle East, and France brought African troops to fight the Germans in the trenches. Moreover, both relied heavily on a combination of contributions and taxes from the colonies to fund the awful cost of the war. Even with those colonial resources, they came out of the war bankrupt and facing a new strategic reality. The interstate system was no longer dominated exclusively by Europeans. Between the U.S. Civil War in the 1860s and World War I, the industrial capacity of the United States had surpassed that of all other states in the world. Furthermore, the need to borrow during the war had turned France and Britain from the world's largest

---

[††]This conference is sometimes called the Second Berlin Conference. The first one had been called by Bismarck in 1878 to negotiate a settlement that would reduce major-power conflict over the Balkans. It is interesting to note that although Bismarck had refused to submit Germany's victories in the wars of German unification to international ratification, he was more than willing to call a conference in order to get a place at the table when other countries' disputes were at issue.

principle of effective occupation An agreement among European colonizers to recognize the claim of whichever colonizer first gained control over a specific piece of Africa, which set off a scramble to partition Africa as quickly as possible.

creditor states to debtors, and the United States held most of that new indebtedness. Finally, the Europeans had to contend with a new Asian power, Japan. Driven by the domestic coalition that had dominated its politics since the Meiji Restoration in 1868, Japan was rapidly industrializing and building a formidable military that had easily defeated the Chinese in 1895, humiliated the Russian Empire in 1905, and conquered Korea.

The question for the peace makers at the Versailles Conference, then, was not only how to rebuild major-power politics to prevent a repetition of World War I, but also how to do it in the context of an increasingly global state system.

World War I and the Demand for Radical Change

In 1919, forty years after Bismarck created his first standing alliance, many policy makers and constituents concluded that whatever the immediate reasons for the outbreak of war in 1914, the structure and norms of the interstate system were ultimately at fault. This view was most closely associated with Woodrow Wilson, who called for radical changes in the structure and legitimizing principles of world politics. The Wilsonian critique was wildly popular among many Europeans, who felt that their policy makers' commitment to power politics and traditional instruments of statecraft had contributed to the outbreak of the war.

The Wilsonian Critique of the European State System

The principal elements of this critique can be summarized as follows: First, the European state system had been without an agreement on the substance of the norms for legitimate rule since the Westphalian consensus on the rights of dynastic rulers had been destroyed by the rise of nationalism and the demand for democracy at the end of the eighteenth century. It was this absence of consensus on the role of nationalism that had fueled Serbian expansion into Bosnia, fed the emperor's fear that Austria-Hungary would collapse, encouraged *jingoism* (militant nationalism) in Britain, France, and Germany, and sustained Alsace-Lorraine as a symbol of wounded French pride and hostility toward Germany.

Second, it was widely believed that the outbreak of war was largely the fault of dynastic rulers who governed autocratically and incompetently. The Austrian emperor's ultimatum to Serbia was designed to be rejected so he would have a pretext for war. The tsar's administration declared a general mobilization, which included Germany, because it had no plan to get from a partial mobilization to a general one. The German kaiser gave the Austrians a blank check to do what they felt necessary, went on a cruise on the Baltic, returned to discover Russia's mobilization and, unable to undo it, authorized the implementation of the Schlieffen Plan.

Third, it was believed that the system of diplomacy worsened these underlying inadequacies in the state system. The alliances that had characterized European diplomacy since Bismarck usually had secret provisions that made it difficult for outsiders to analyze their implications. Moreover, the antagonistic alliances that had evolved since France had replaced Germany in 1894 as Russia's principal alliance partner were believed to have fed the arms races between Germany, France, and Britain and to have spread a local conflict from the Balkans throughout Europe. Finally, the emphasis on mobilization schedules put the whole system on a hair-trigger.

Given the perceived link between the inadequacies of the European state system and the outbreak of World War I, critics proposed radical changes in the structure and norms of the state system. In the domestic arena, the former combatants were to end the debates over nationalism and democracy by accepting nationality as the basis for drawing interstate boundaries, by eliminating the last of the dynastic rulers, and by promoting democratic regimes. The German regime collapsed in the wake of the war and was replaced by the Weimar Republic, named after the city where the delegates met to write the constitution. The Austro-Hungarian Empire was dismembered, and as a result, Czechoslovakia and Hungary became independent countries, as did a catch-all kingdom of Croats, Serbs, and Slovenes that would later be called Yugoslavia. Poland resurfaced as an independent country for the first time since the 1790s. The Baltic republics—Lithuania, Latvia, and Estonia—were also created at this time (see Map 7–10).

Map 7–10   Redrawing the Boundaries of Europe after World War I

After World War I the victorious allies tried to redraw the boundaries of Europe to reflect the distribution of nationalities. Three Baltic states—Lithuania, Latvia, and Estonia—were created. Poland reemerged for the first time since the eighteenth-century partitions, but with East Prussia, ethnically German, remaining a part of Germany. The Austro-Hungarian Empire was dismembered into five separate states: Austria, Hungary, Czechoslovakia, Romania, and the Kingdom of Croats, Serbs, and Slovenes (later renamed Yugoslavia).

7.3 ENDURING PATTERNS

The impact of linkage politics

World politics is driven by the interaction of international, factional, and constituency politics.

The Collapse of the Austro-Hungarian Empire and the Soviet Union

Although the Austro-Hungarian Empire was dismembered after World War I, it was on the verge of collapse before the war and might have disintegrated even if it had not been defeated. The underlying causes show the significance of linkage politics. The empire was involved in international competition that created military commitments that were far more costly than its faltering economy could afford. Those international problems were compounded by the fact that its political system (an autocratic, dynastic empire controlling many different nationality groupings) was incompatible with the growing international emphasis on democracy and national self-determination.

In the 1980s, the Soviet Union found itself increasingly unable to pay the costs of competing in the Cold War. The international difficulties created by the regime's inability to sustain the economic and military competition with the West were compounded by the effects of the costs of that competition on the standard of living of its people and the legitimacy of the communist system. The threat to communism's legitimacy was worsened by the growing international popularity of market systems and the continuing difficulty Moscow had in convincing the many nationalities in the Soviet Union that communist solidarity was better than national self-determination.

The stress on democracy and nationalism did not extend to the colonial empires. In spite of the efforts of Ho Chi Minh, the Vietnamese nationalist, and others from Africa and Asia who traveled to Versailles to lobby for independence, the empires stood. All the victors were willing to do was to create a *mandate system* in which territories taken from Germany and its defeated ally, the Ottoman Empire, were divided among the victors under a trust (called a mandate) from the League of Nations.

Although the victors were unwilling to make major changes in the colonial empires, the twin emphases on democracy and national self-determination represented major changes in the principles of legitimate rule for independent states. These changes were to be complimented by radical alterations in the nature of security systems that were designed to make war impossible. Arms races, secret treaties, and peacetime alliances were all to be eliminated. Consultations were to be required prior to the use of force. And to make all these provisions work, the League of Nations was to create a **collective security** system.

The League of Nations' Collective Security System

The League of Nations was created as part of the peace settlement after World War I. The League was designed to bring all the independent states in the world together in an organization that could promote international peace and cooperation,

collective security   A diplomatic system designed to promote peace and guarantee the security of its members by promising help for any member who is attacked; unlike standard military alliances, which target actors outside the alliance, collective security systems are designed principally to deter aggression within the community.

and guarantee humane conditions of labor, trade, human rights, education, and health. The principle of universality—initially violated by the unwillingness to include Germany (because of its perceived responsibility for starting World War I) and the Soviet Union (because of its communist government)—was implemented most unambiguously in the Assembly, which included all members. A smaller body, the Council, was intended to include the major military powers (the United States, Britain, France, Italy, and Japan) plus four states chosen by the Assembly. Domestic opposition within the United States, which kept the United States from ratifying the Versailles Treaty and joining the League, reduced the number of original permanent members to four.

The collective security provisions in the League of Nations Covenant were straightforward:

1. Disputes among both members and nonmembers were to be subject to the collective security policies developed by the League.

2. Any dispute which seemed "likely" to lead to war was to be submitted "either to arbitration or to enquiry by the Council" (Article 11). All parties to a dispute were to "agree in no case to resort to war until three months after the award by the arbitrators or the report by the Council," which would have six months to complete its work (Articles 11 and 12).

3. Any member (or invited nonmember) that resorted to force without submitting the dispute to the League and waiting the required period for Council action "shall *ipso facto* be deemed to have committed an act of war against all other Members of the League" (Article 16).

4. An immediate trade and financial embargo would be imposed on aggressor states, with the possible addition of military action if the Council so recommended (Article 16).

5. All decisions by the Council had to be unanimous, but the parties to the dispute were ineligible to vote (Article 15).

The League's collective security provisions created the first diplomatic system in the history of the Eurocentered state system to establish peace as its preeminent goal. It was also the first to promise to protect all countries, not simply major powers, and to place the responsibility for fulfilling these promises in the hands of a permanent intergovernmental institution. However, while the League's collective security system was a historically important effort to achieve international peace, it did not work out the way its creators intended.

The Contradictions of Collective Security

The failure of the League's collective security system can be traced to a series of fundamental contradictions in its goals and procedures. First, the League defined "aggression" without regard to the substance and perceived legitimacy of the competing claims. An aggressor was quite simply any country that refused to follow the procedures outlined above. The problem with this approach is that people often care as much about the perceived legitimacy of an outcome as they do about the procedures that led to it. In the absence of an agreed-upon standard for judging the legitimacy of different outcomes, policy makers were caught in a politically unsupportable contradiction. They had to argue that there was no national objective for which the use of force was a legitimate option at the same time as they argued in favor of creating military capabilities that would be used to protect victims of aggression anywhere in the world. In short, peace was the only thing worth fighting for.

This essential contradiction was worsened by another. Collective security requires convincing key domestic policy factions and their constituents to pay substantial, visible, and *immediate* costs—going to war to protect another country from aggression—in order to gain possible *future* benefits—reducing the long-term probability of armed conflict. But people generally prefer immediate benefits over future benefits and future costs over current costs. Consequently, it is difficult to persuade people to incur immediate and certain costs in exchange for future benefits that may never be obtained. That essential difficulty looms even larger when the promised future benefit is a non-event—wars that *don't* happen. How are people to be convinced that they got the benefits they paid for when only the costs are visible?

These two fundamental political problems were aggravated by a third. For collective security to work, foreign policy makers needed to be confident that help will arrive in time to protect them from potential aggressors. Otherwise, they would need to look to their own defenses and do all the things the League's system was designed to prevent: negotiate standing defense pacts, build up their armies, and generally pursue individual security objectives rather than community obligations. But the only way to guarantee that the community would ride to the rescue in time was for the leaders of the key countries to promise to send aid without lengthy domestic consultations. Such a promise would create a fundamental contradiction between international obligations to support collective action and domestic obligations for leaders to be accountable to their domestic constituencies.

In addition to these three political problems, advocates of collective action faced a basic strategic problem. Military and economic power is very unevenly distributed in the world. That unequal distribution creates two questions: What is to be done about threats by major military powers? How are the burdens of collective enforcement to be shared when only the decisions of a very small number of major powers are critical to the success of collective security?

These issues must be resolved satisfactorily before any state-based collective conflict management system can be expected to work effectively. Whether or not they can ever be overcome, the League of Nations hardly had a chance. With the United States refusing to join, the majority of the permanent members of the Council in the crucial 1930–1935 period were anti-democratic, in favor of fundamental changes in the status quo, and willing to use force to achieve their states' objectives. The original permanent members were Britain, France, Italy, and Japan. Germany was added in 1926 and the Soviet Union in 1934; Germany and Japan left in 1935, and the Soviet Union was expelled after invading Finland in December 1939. The only status quo countries on the Council, Britain and France, were far from preponderant. Indeed, both were financially and emotionally exhausted after World War I.

The Collapse of Post–World War I Security Arrangements

The League's collective security system and the changes in the norms for legitimate rule (the recognition of nationalism and democracy) were the twin pillars of the attempt to transform the state system after World War I. Not surprisingly, many states continued to look to their own defenses in an effort to meet their individual security concerns. The story of the decade before the outbreak of World War II is the failure of both these collective and individual efforts.

Collective Security Fails

The League of Nations played a useful role in resolving conflicts short of war when the parties were looking for a jointly acceptable peaceful solution. By one scholar's count, the League helped settle thirty-five out of the sixty-six disputes brought before it.[4] What the League could not handle was incompatible preferences when some of the parties were willing to use force to prevail.[5] What it could not make work, in short, was collective security. The two most infamous failures are the Manchurian Crisis (September 1931 to February 1933) and the Italian invasion of Ethiopia (December 1934 to July 1936).

The Manchurian Crisis   Japan took advantage of the decades-long instability of the Chinese political system before and after World War I to coerce a ninety-nine-year lease to operate a railroad that opened up Manchuria, one of China's richest provinces, to Japanese companies. In September 1931, Japanese soldiers patrolling the railroad zone fought with Chinese troops. The Chinese government immediately requested an impartial, fact-finding investigation by the League. Japan initially succeeded in blocking a League decision to send an investigative team, but within a matter of weeks Japanese air and ground forces were involved in heavy fighting outside of the railroad zone. In response to the Council's demand that it withdraw back into its zone, the Japanese asked for a neutral commission of investigation. Four months later, in February 1932, the commission arrived to begin its investigation in Manchuria. It would not return its report until a year later, in February 1933, months after Japan had conquered the area (see Map 7–11) and established a puppet government for the newly renamed country of Manchukuo. When the League, finally in possession of its commission's report, formally demanded that it withdraw, Japan simply left the League.

The League's actions look pathetic, but consider who was available to help China. The Soviet Union was the closest major land power, but it was the successor regime to tsarist Russia, which had gobbled up huge areas of China throughout the nineteenth century. Could the Soviet Union be trusted to leave Manchuria once the Japanese were ousted? As for other potential sources of help, there were only three countries with the naval assets necessary to influence the outcome in Manchuria: the United States, Britain, and France. The United States was not even in the League. Britain and France were preoccupied with the political and economic effects of the Great Depression and had large antiwar movements determined to prevent a new war. Moreover, even if they had been willing to intervene, both France and Britain had unsavory imperial records in Asia that would have generated considerable doubts about their motives.

In short, major-power aggression like Japan's requires major-power defenders, and there weren't any available in this case. The procedural inadequacies of the League's investigation were symptoms, not causes, of the failure of collective security in Manchuria.

The Italian Invasion of Ethiopia   The League's response to the Ethiopian crisis showed an effort to learn from the Manchurian fiasco. It also showed an unprecedented shift in attitudes about the legitimacy of colonial expansion. But in spite of

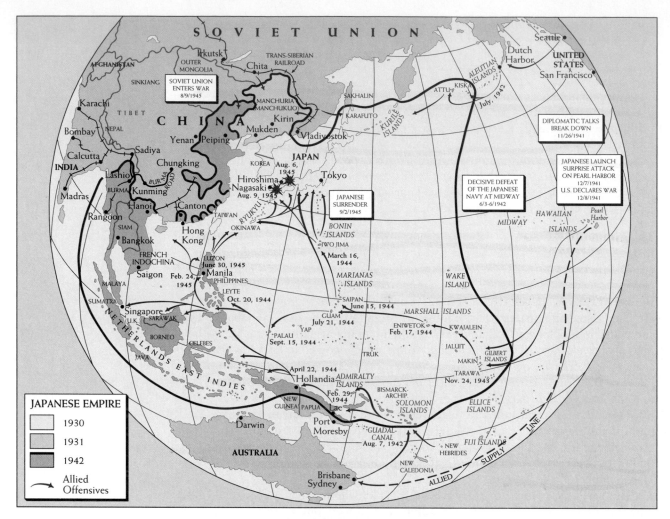

Map 7–11   Japanese Expansion in Asia, 1830–1942

The conflict in the Pacific during World War II was the culmination of a long competition between Japan, Russia, China, the United States, and the European colonial states. Japanese expansion in the 1930 to 1942 period came out of Japanese-controlled territories along the Chinese coast and in Korea. (After the Russo-Japanese War ended in 1905, Japan had expanded its control over Korea, annexing it in 1910.) As Admiral Yamamoto had promised the Japanese war cabinet before the attack on Pearl Harbor, Japanese forces were able to expand rapidly throughout Asia in the initial period of the war against the United States. However, starting with the Japanese defeat at Midway in June 1942, the tide turned.

these major changes for the better, the League's response to Italian aggression also sank under the weight of the underlying problems with collective security.

In December 1934, Italy announced that troops based in its colony of Eritrea (located between Ethiopia and the Red Sea) had been attacked by Ethiopia. Oddly, the Italians also announced the location of this attack—an oasis fifty miles inside Ethiopia! Ethiopia asked for arbitration; Italy countered by demanding apologies and reparations. In response to requests by the Ethiopian government for action by the League, Italy stalled by indicating a willingness to enter into arbitration. In October 1935, after the rainy season had ended, Italy launched a full-scale invasion.

This time the Council moved with extraordinary speed. Within ten days, it declared Italy the aggressor and imposed economic and financial sanctions. League members were asked to stop all arms sales to Italy, refuse credit to the Italian government and private companies, cut off all imports from Italy, and embargo the sale of raw materials and manufactured goods. Items that were available from nonmember states were exempt, however, and in the 1930s, the United States was one of the world's biggest exporters of capital, oil, coal, and steel.

In spite of this massive loophole, Italy was virtually bankrupt by July 1936, when the sanctions were ended. The announced reason for ending the sanctions was that Italian successes in overrunning all of Ethiopia had made the issue moot. The real reason was that Britain and France, fearing the growing power of Germany, hoped that ending the sanctions would prevent an alliance between Benito Mussolini's Italy and Adolf Hitler's Nazi Germany. It seems despicable, but the British and French had no one to turn to if Germany attacked them. Only major powers could help them against Germany, and as they were the only major powers in the area, they had to look to their own defenses.

The Failure of Traditional Security Systems

Perversely, just as the linkages between domestic and interstate politics in this period revealed that the new form of state-based security systems, collective security, had fundamental problems so, too, did linkage politics undermine the traditional methods for achieving security through deterrence. The classic cases here are the Munich Crisis of September 1938 and the Japanese decision to attack the United States in December 1941.

The Munich Crisis and the Failure of Defensive Military Alliances   The Munich Crisis has come to symbolize the failure of even well-conceived alliances and the dangers of appeasing aggressors by giving in to their demands. The key actors were the Czechoslovakian, German, French, and British governments. Czechoslovakia was one of the new states created as part of the Versailles settlement after World War I. It was widely regarded as one of the settlement's success stories. It was a model democracy and, for the times, quite prosperous. As for its principal security concern, Germany, Czechoslovakia had a highly trained army, one of the world's greatest armaments works, a series of well-thought-out fortifications along its mountainous border with Germany, and a defense pact with France that obligated the French to intervene in any war started by Germany. A small state in a world of big-state predators could do little more to protect itself.

The crisis began in late summer 1938, when Hitler claimed that ethnic Germans living in the Sudetenland, a fifty-mile-deep arc along the Czechoslovakian side of the border with Germany, were being abused by the Czech majority. Citing the principles of nationality that had been used to redraw European boundaries after World War I, he argued that the makers of the peace had erred in putting these Germans under Czech control and demanded that the Sudetenland be transferred to Germany. The Czechoslovakian government refused and turned to its French allies for support. France brought Britain into the discussions, and the two proceeded to search for a diplomatic solution—without paying much attention to the wishes of the Czech government or France's alliance commitments. Their unwillingness to immediately honor the alliance looks reprehensible, but one of the key lessons of the outbreak of World War I was that being too prompt in honoring alliance commitments can trigger a war. Furthermore, both the British and French governments faced strong domestic opposition to any moves that might bring a new round of war to Europe.

In September 1938, the British and French went to Munich to discuss Hitler's demands. In the end, they gave in to virtually all his demands and told Czechoslovakia that it had to give up the Sudetenland or fight alone. The Czechoslovakians reportedly came very close to deciding to fight in the hope that France would be shamed into honoring its alliance, but they ultimately decided that the risk was too high and acquiesced to the loss of the Sudetenland. The next spring, Hitler took over the rest of Czechoslovakia. In response, Britain and France promised to protect Poland, a far weaker and less defensible country, if Hitler invaded. The German attack on Poland brought war to Europe in the fall of 1939 (see Map 7–12).

The war in Europe turned into a genuinely global conflagration as Germany's drive for regional dominance in Europe became connected with the Japanese drive for dominance in Asia. Two factors linked the regional conflicts: the existence of European colonies throughout Asia and the role of the United States as both an Atlantic and Pacific actor. On the first point, Japan could not achieve its economic and military aims without expelling the Europeans from their colonial holdings in Asia. On the second point, President Franklin D. Roosevelt was convinced that the United States could not afford either a Japanese or German victory. The problem for

Map 7–12

Czechoslovakia and Poland Fall, 1938–1939

Starting with the forced but peaceful annexations of Austria (in the March 1938 *Anschluss*) and the Sudetenland (after the September 1938 Munich agreement), Hitler turned eastward. The September 1939 invasion of Poland and its partition between Germany and the Soviet Union was arranged in a secret agreement between Hitler and Stalin in August 1939. Hitler's decision to invade the Soviet Union in June 1941 was initially successful. By the end of the year, Germany had captured over 3 million Soviet soldiers, begun the siege of Leningrad, and was shelling Moscow. Ultimately, however, the invasion proved to be one of Hitler's biggest military miscalculations.

Roosevelt, other than the obvious strategic one of projecting military power into both Asia and Europe, was domestic. Roosevelt was unable to convince either Congress or the public that the United States ought to put itself in harm's way a second time.

The Japanese Attack on Pearl Harbor   The turning point in Asia came with the Japanese invasion of French Indochina in July 1941. Roosevelt, acting in combination with the British and Dutch governments, announced a freeze of Japanese financial assets in the United States and a sweeping embargo on exports from the United States and the British and Dutch colonies in southeast Asia. The embargo cut Japan off from its principal supplies of imported oil (for which it had no domestic sources), scrap iron, rice, tin, bauxite (used to make aluminum), nickel, and rubber. The embargo was to stay in place until Japan withdrew from Indochina and agreed to leave China. There was some confusion as to whether the demand that Japan leave China included Manchuria, but even if it had not, the ultimatum's terms were immensely unattractive to the Japanese government. Gaining access to assured supplies of raw materials was a central foreign policy objective of the government, and so was the drive to replace the Europeans as the dominant military and economic power in Asia.

These foreign policy objectives were inextricably entangled in Japanese domestic politics. Japan had been experiencing a prolonged period of political instability and assassination as ultra-nationalist factions fought to gain control of the government. In an effort to defuse that struggle, representatives of the two principal military factions, the army and the navy, had been given prominent positions in the cabinet. Each military faction was, therefore, uniquely essential to the stability of the government. The domestic stakes were immense because, if the government fell, many thought the entire political system would disintegrate into violence.

Faced with these linked interstate and domestic stakes, the Japanese cabinet debated the U.S. ultimatum. With only a sixty-day stockpile of oil to run the fleet, the navy faction demanded immediate access to petroleum, either by capitulating to the U.S. demands in order to end the embargo or by attacking the Dutch colonies to gain control of the oil fields in Sumatra. The army faction vetoed the idea of leaving China. With the collapse of the cabinet not a perceived option, the only thing the two factions could agree on was war with the United States. The attack on Pearl Harbor was designed to eliminate most of the U.S. Pacific fleet to buy time to defeat the European colonies and establish a defense perimeter. Minutes of the cabinet meetings indicate that Japanese policy makers estimated that U.S. military capabilities were eight times greater than theirs. What if the United States fought? The answer, given to the cabinet by Admiral Isoroko Yamamoto, the architect of the Pearl Harbor attack, was as follows: "In the first six months to a year of war against the U.S. and England I will run wild, and I will show you an uninterrupted succession of victories; I must tell you that, should the war be prolonged for two or three years, I have no confidence in our ultimate victory."[6]

From the perspective of Japanese policy-making factions, capitulation to the U.S. ultimatum would produce immediate, certain, catastrophic domestic and diplomatic consequences. In contrast, while attacking the United States would be costly, it would also produce immediate domestic and diplomatic benefits. Of course, if the U.S. government chose to fight a long war, the consequences were likely to be even worse; but those costs lay in the future and were not certain to happen.

The Strategic Context after World War II

It is hard to imagine any more compelling incentives to find a way to build a security system that actually works than those that drove policy makers after World War II. About 15 million soldiers and 40 to 50 million civilians—*55 million people*—perished in the war. Moreover, this was the second cataclysmic war in less than a generation; World War I had killed about 9 million soldiers and 6 million civilians. As if any more pressure were needed to get it right, the world had also entered the nuclear age when the United States dropped atomic bombs on Hiroshima and Nagasaki in 1945.

The perceived lessons of the interwar period were appalling. Neither the new forms of diplomacy (the League of Nations and its collective security system) nor the traditional forms of statecraft (such as alliances) had worked. Moreover, the presumed causes of World War II did not seem to produce the same lessons as the presumed causes of World War I. On the one hand, the outbreak of the first war was attributed to the inability to achieve consensus on nationalism as a fundamental principle of legitimate rule, the standing alliance system, the willingness to honor alliance commitments rather than negotiating a settlement, and the sustained and embittering arms races that divided Europe. On the other hand, the principle of nationalism had been used both by Hitler in his claim to the Sudetenland and by the Japanese government in its claim that it should lead Asia out from under European colonial domination. Meanwhile, the failure of appeasement at Munich suggested that alliances should be honored, that concessions simply increased the appetite for aggression, and that Britain and France should have stepped up their arms production in response to German rearmament, even if that decision resulted in an arms race.

The belief that catastrophic wars were increasing in frequency and magnitude, the prospect of nuclear annihilation, and the conclusion that both the new diplomacy of collective security and traditional forms of statecraft had failed in the interwar period generated a debate in the West about the state system and sources of security. This debate, which we discuss below, took place among not only policy factions but also opinion leaders in constituency groups outside government. It quickly evolved into a struggle for the hearts and minds of policy makers in the United States, Britain, and France. It was about as close to a widespread, public debate over first principles in politics as one finds in the record of the centuries-long quest for security.

While this debate raged in the West, key political actors elsewhere placed the quest for security in quite different conceptual and strategic frameworks. In the communist system—dominated at this time by the Soviet Union—security was understood from the perspective of Soviet leader Joseph Stalin's version of the Marxist-Leninist tradition. Whereas Lenin had predicted that recurring wars of "imperialist redivision" among the capitalist states would lead to revolution, the post–Cold War release of documents from the Soviet archives confirms that Stalin believed the Soviet Union would serve as the base for the defeat of capitalism and the expansion of communism around the world. As John Lewis Gaddis, a prominent historian of the period, observed, "The effect was to switch the principle instrument of revolution from Marx's idea of a historically determined class struggle to a process of territorial acquisition Stalin could control."[7]

In Africa, Asia, and the Middle East—the core of what, along with Latin America, was soon to be called the Third World—the weakening hold of the European colonizers led key actors to define the fundamental security issue as a question of whether empire would be replaced with sovereign states. Decolonization and the spread of the state system to Africa, Asia, and the Middle East then became intertwined with the different perspectives on the origin and nature of global security in the West and East. The intersection of these "three worlds" gave the quest for global security a distinctive character for almost fifty years after World War II. It began in a radically transformed strategic context.

A Survey of the Strategic Landscape

A survey of the strategic situation in the months immediately following the end of the war in August 1945 reveals an extraordinarily broad and interconnected set of security problems that demanded both short- and long-term strategic choices by foreign policy makers. Europe was in a shambles. With the exception of Britain and the Soviet Union, the governments of all the belligerents had to be rebuilt. Moreover, the economies of both victors and vanquished had been destroyed; millions of refugees were in need of temporary shelter and, often, permanent homes in new countries; and the armies of the victorious allies (the United States, Britain, France, and the Soviet Union) were facing each other in an uneasy mix of cooperation and hostility across a divided and occupied Germany.

The situation wasn't much better in Asia. Japan was occupied by the United States, which had refused Stalin's request for a joint occupation once the atomic bomb had eliminated the need for Soviet help in an invasion. Korea was, however, divided between U.S. and Soviet zones of occupation. Next door, in China, the civil war between the Communists and the Nationalists (the Guomindang), which had begun in the 1920s and was never far from the surface even during the temporary cease-fires arranged to fight Japan, was resuming even as the defeated Japanese armies were being disarmed and sent home. Farther south, in areas such as French Indochina and the Dutch East Indies, where the Japanese had presented themselves as liberators from European colonialism, the defeat of Japan raised a big question: Would peace mean freedom for the indigenous population or a return of colonial armies and administrators? In India the future of colonialism had been resolved by the British promise to withdraw after the war, but Muslims and Hindus argued with each other, as well as with the British, over the terms and the possible partition of the Indian subcontinent into separate Muslim and Hindu states.

Though not as badly battered as Europe and Asia, the Middle East faced significant security issues as well. The British and Soviets had divided Iran into zones of occupation during the war to prevent Iran from joining the Axis (the alliance between Germany and Italy), to assure access to oil, and to keep an eye on each other. With the war over, the questions shifted from occupation to withdrawal and rebuilding the independence of the Iranian government (while keeping an eye on who had how much access to oil). Turkey, meanwhile, was worried that the Soviet Union might exploit the instability of the post-war period and resume its drive to gain control over the Bosporus and Dardanelles, the two straits that connected the Black Sea to the Aegean. In Palestine, longstanding Arab concerns about the influx of European Jews and the Zionist goal of creating a Jewish state suddenly flared up with the growth of Jewish immigration after the Holocaust. Caught between competing claims and incompatible promises, the British (who administered Palestine under a mandate from the now-defunct League of Nations) looked for a way out as the violence among Palestinians, Jews, and British escalated. Far less complicated, but equally pressing, demands for the end of British and French mandates were also being made in what are now Jordan, Syria, and Lebanon.

To the west, in North Africa, many security problems were created by the combination of the need for post-war reconstruction and the pressure to address a series of specific issues. The most significant issues involved Egypt, the former Italian colonies, and Algeria. How could Egypt effectively shake off British influence, given the British desire to control the Suez Canal? What would be the status of Ethiopia and Libya now that Italy was defeated? What would be the fate of Algeria now that Algerians were mobilizing to eject the French, who had assumed they would stay indefinitely? In sub-Saharan Africa, there had been far less war damage, but even there the situation was unstable. Colonial control had been weakened by the German occupation of France and Belgium. Britain, even though it escaped invasion, had reduced the amount of power sharing it permitted in its colonies while it increased the resources it extracted from them. As a result, the burdens on the population increased at the same time as decision-making processes became even more arbitrary and illegitimate.

The countries in the Americas were the only ones in the world that came out of the war without pressing regional security concerns. They also had experienced little direct economic and political damage as a result of the war. Latin America had substantially increased its exports, and even those countries that had been formal belligerents had suffered comparatively few casualties. (Of the countries in Latin America, Brazil—with 1,000 battle deaths—lost the most people in combat.) The United States and Canada lost far more lives than the countries in Latin America— 408,000 for the United States and 39,000 for Canada—but like their southern neighbors, they benefited greatly from not being located in a war zone.

In sum, even a quick overview of the global post-war strategic situation reveals an unprecedented picture. With Japan and Germany occupied, France preoccupied with rebuilding its government and economy, Britain bankrupt and exhausted, China in the midst of renewed civil war, and most of Asia and Africa still under colonial control, the United States and the Soviet Union were the only two major military powers left. It was exactly this great gap in resources that gave rise to the notion that the post-war world had become bipolar, that there now were only two **superpowers.**

The Superpowers

The notion that World War II had led to the emergence of two superpowers had a basis in fact, but it was profoundly misleading, for two reasons. First, calling the United States and the Soviet Union *superpowers* makes it too easy to think of power as a property of a country rather than a characteristic of an issue-specific relationship connecting two or more actors. As a result, one is more likely to assume that superpowers will always get their way than to analyze what the relevant sources of power are, given the specific issues and actors involved. The second reason it was misleading to describe the United States and the Soviet Union as the world's two superpowers is less conceptual and more empirical: The military and economic assets available to the two superpowers were far from equal.

The contrast between the situations of the United States and the Soviet Union immediately after the war could hardly have been more marked. The United States emerged with an unprecedented share of the world's military and economic

superpowers   A term coined in the late 1940s to characterize the military capabilities of the United States and the Soviet Union, which dwarfed those of any other state.

resources. Militarily, the United States had the best-equipped army, the largest and best-equipped air force and navy, and the only successful atomic weapons program. Economically, the United States came out of the war astride the world's economy like a mythological Colossus. It was producing between 44 and 49 percent of the world's gross domestic product (a measure of the total amount of goods and services produced within a country's borders), had the only major currency that was widely accepted either in international trade and commercial transactions or as a reserve asset (that is, as savings), and was the largest source of trade and capital in the world. On top of all that, the United States had earned enormous prestige as a result of its economic, political, and military leadership during the war.

Though it had also been on the winning side, the Soviet Union had paid a far higher price than the United States. It had suffered well over 20 million dead (some estimates go as high as 25 million), including over 7 million soldiers—fully half of all the battle deaths in the war. While no country bordering the Soviet Union was in a position to defeat the Red Army without help from the United States, policy makers in the Soviet Union felt vulnerable relative to the United States (and to the West more generally) because of the weaknesses in their economy and their inability to project air and naval assets beyond the reach of their army.

While the Soviet Union had a significantly larger population than the United States (193 million as compared to 140 million), its national income was about one-fourth the size (42 versus 165 billion dollars). The dollar value of Soviet exports was 2.7 percent of the value of U.S. exports. Its farm production, which had to feed more people, was 23.8 percent of the value of U.S. farm production. Its bank deposits were 9 percent of those in the United States. Soviet industrial production shows the strongest results, but it was still only 38 percent of the U.S. figure.

The comparison of military capabilities after the war is equally striking. While the Soviet Union had significantly more ground troops, it had suffered grievously during the war. It lost over 7 million soldiers in combat and 3 million in prisoner of war camps, including all but 750,000 of an officer corps that numbered 2 million before the war. Moreover, it had no operational navy, its air force had been used largely for ground support in World War II, and fully 50 percent of the army's transport was still horse-drawn. The United States, in contrast, had over 45,000 combat aircraft, 10,000 utility and transport aircraft, and over 70,000 naval ships (including 262 submarines, 24 battleships, 92 cruisers, and 35 aircraft carriers).[8]

Given the magnitude of the security issues in the late 1940s, it's not surprising that policy makers in the United States and the Soviet Union believed the survival and prosperity of their countries depended on how world politics was reorganized in the post-war period. It's also not surprising—given the fact that each had more military and economic resources than anyone else—that they would each expect to play a central role in shaping the post-war world. The problem, of course, was that they had quite different visions of that world.

The essential problem for the post-war world was the incompatibility of the key actors' policy preferences and beliefs about the substance of legitimate economic and political relationships. Citing the experience of the 1930s (when economic protectionism had both deepened the Depression and accelerated the rise of fascism and militarism), the United States came out of World War II convinced that closed economic and political systems were recipes for economic collapse, political extremism, and war. This determination to rebuild the world's economy on free-market principles was utterly incompatible with Stalin's preference for a centralized, Marxist-style command economy. The U.S. preference for Western-style democracy was incompatible with Stalin's objectives of maintaining tight control both at home and in the buffer zone he was creating around the Soviet Union. Moreover, Western hopes that wartime cooperation with the Soviet Union had laid the groundwork for a mutually acceptable structure for organizing world politics were based on the assumption that Stalin was prepared to walk away from his commitment to communism and world revolution.

Given those different visions and the far greater economic and military capabilities of the United States, it was almost impossible to build a global security system that addressed Soviet and U.S. security aspirations in mutually acceptable ways. For instance, it is easy to see why the human and material costs of the German invasion of the Soviet Union and Stalin's views about the incompatibility of capitalism and communism led Stalin to create a massive buffer zone between the Soviet Union and any potential military threats from the West by installing "friendly" governments in Eastern Europe. But even if one is willing to think about Stalin's objectives as being largely driven by defensive concerns, the Soviet effort to consolidate control over Eastern Europe was dangerous to its Western neighbors—especially so given the size of the Soviet army.

Western efforts to increase their security decreased Stalin's. Scholars call this situation a *security dilemma*. According to John Herz, who coined the phrase, a security dilemma occurs when, "striving to attain security, . . . [people] are driven to acquire more and more power to escape the impact of the power of others. This, in turn, renders the others more insecure and impels them to prepare for the worst."[9]

In this strategic context it is perhaps surprising that the key actors reached any agreements on security arrangements at all. The most notable agreement—reached first by the Big Four (Britain, China, the Soviet Union, and the United States) at the Dumbarton Oaks Conference in 1944 and later ratified by fifty-one states at the San Francisco Conference as the war was ending in Europe—was to create the United Nations as a successor organization to the League of Nations and give collective security a second chance.[10]

The agreement to create the UN showed an understanding of the importance of building security arrangements that reflected both the power and the preferences of the key actors. They assumed that collective security systems could work only if the values and goals of the major powers were compatible. As Inis Claude, one of the most important analysts of the early UN, observed: "The security scheme of the Charter . . . was conceived as an arrangement against relatively minor disturbers of the peace, in cases where the great powers were united."[11] To make sure that the UN would try to act only when the great powers were united, the permanent members of the Security Council were given a *veto;* in Claude's phrase, "The veto is a deliberately contrived circuit breaker."[12]

Collective security largely failed during the long competition between the Soviet Union and the United States known as the Cold War because the authors of the UN system were right about the prerequisites for its success.[†††] "The cold war era

---

[†††]Those who call NATO a collective security alliance would disagree with the assertion that collective security failed in the Cold War. However, describing a standing, pre-targeted defense pact as "a collective security arrangement" eliminates the distinctive within-community-policing characteristic that defines collective security.

[did] . . . not represent a legitimate test of collective security because one of the key preconditions was missing. American and Soviet visions of an acceptable international order were simply incompatible."[13]

Those incompatible visions also undermined a second major dimension of the UN's approach to promoting security. The framers of the UN Charter believed they could reinforce the deterrent value of collective security by promoting more just economic and political arrangements. The Wilsonian connection between democracy and peace was broadened to include a stronger emphasis on decolonization, human rights, and social and economic justice. These features of the UN system would be hamstrung by the Soviet Union's and United States' competing claims about how the world should be organized politically and economically.

As a result of all these factors, the quest for a state-based security system would be organized around competing visions of a just order throughout the Cold War. The exact ways in which the Cold War developed, sustained itself for almost forty years, and then collapsed are discussed in the sections that follow.

The West's Debate about Sources of Security

In the West there were two important post-war debates about the sources of security. One was between constituency groups that advocated abolishing the state system and those people who argued that the state system would endure and the task was to learn how to use power wisely within that system. After the second group won the battle for the most important audience (policy makers), a far longer running debate developed between those who stressed security systems based on classical realist assumptions and those who stressed anticommunism.

Western Critics of the State System

In the years immediately following World War II, a large number of prominent constituency groups in the West argued that the state system is the principal cause of war. They assumed that the essential, innate character of people is good—that people will naturally avoid conflict as long as they can survive while behaving cooperatively.

From this perspective, the problem with the state system was two-fold. First, sovereignty meant that there was no way—other than self-help—to enforce interstate agreements. Wars occurred because there was no higher decision-making authority that could settle disputes among states. Second, states had been unable to meet their citizens' basic human needs. Critics argued that government policy makers had done a terrible job of alleviating poverty, social injustice, disease, and illiteracy. These failures meant that policy makers needed to find some other way to legitimize their political position. They found it, the critics claimed, by redirecting internal dissatisfaction toward foreign enemies. Thus the internal and external pathologies of the state system reinforced each other. Policy makers had domestic incentives to mobilize their constituents against external targets. At the same time, interstate anarchy made it difficult to find peaceful solutions to interstate conflict. Factions within this camp offered three different strategies for getting rid of the state.

The World Federalist Strategy   **World federalists** suggested that the United Nations should be turned into a world government, with member states becoming

world federalists Those who argue that the best way to create a more peaceful and just world is to create a federal system of world government in which existing sovereign states take on reduced roles analogous to states in the United States.

subordinate to the UN on security issues while retaining responsibilities for other issue areas. This idea, briefly popular after the war, was quickly defeated by four major objections: (1) a world government would promote global tyranny; (2) it would be too far removed from its ultimate constituents (the people) to be accepted as legitimate; (3) it would simply substitute civil wars for interstate wars; and (4) it would never be accepted by the key actors—policy makers in the central governments of states.

The Functionalist Strategy A second faction argued in favor of an indirect approach that would gradually render the state obsolete. Called **functionalism** because its advocates focused on economic and social functions that met basic human needs, this approach argued that the state system was too entrenched and politicized to be overthrown directly. Instead, functionalists advocated building a wide range of intergovernmental and non-governmental organizations led by independent experts devoted to meeting basic human needs. Cooperative actions by these organizations, they argued, could meet basic human needs far more easily and fully than could the actions of individual states. In the short run, these organizations would improve the quality of people's lives throughout the world by promoting economic growth, public health, education, and social justice. In the long run, as these organizations gradually took over responsibility for more areas that were central to day-to-day life, the state system would be rendered irrelevant and would simply fade away.

The functionalist argument had two fatal weaknesses. First, it was based on a very narrow notion of the sources of political conflict. Functionalists found the sources of political conflict in government actors and the institution of the state system. Indeed, they were so preoccupied with the ways in which governments and the state system could create false antagonisms that they believed turning over responsibility for meeting basic human needs to independent experts would eliminate conflict. In retrospect, the notion that issues such as economic growth, social justice, education, and public health could be solved in noncontroversial ways by apolitical experts seems utterly crazy. But the first functionalists lived in a period that had endured two world wars, the Great Depression, and the horrors of continued colonialism. In such a world it is not all that surprising that observers would be drawn to the possibility that interstate politics was the principal source of evil in the world. Having defined politics so narrowly that it was restricted to the choices and actions of government officials, early functionalists could then argue that getting rid of the state would rid the world of political conflict.

The second weakness in the original functionalist argument was its assumption that central governments would sit idly by while other organizations took responsibility for meeting their citizens' basic human needs. It is particularly perplexing that a group that included some of the best minds in North America and Europe would make this assumption, because it went against the entire weight of recent Western history. Ever since the expansion of suffrage and the growth of constituency politics in the 1800s, policy makers had increasingly relied on providing government-mandated services as a way to increase the perceived legitimacy of the state. Thus, during the 1880s, German Chancellor Otto von Bismarck, worried about the growth of the Social Democratic party and its demands for radical social and political change, tried to co-opt the loyalty of the working class by forcing through the first laws requiring that employers provide paid sick days and pensions. He even established the age of retirement at sixty-five. A few decades later, the British government enacted

functionalism An intellectual tradition that assumes that the state system is the principal cause of war and that if apolitical, non-state actors could help people meet their basic human needs, the state system would ultimately become irrelevant and disappear, creating a more just and peaceful world.

a wide range of laws mandating paid sick days and old-age benefits. British policy makers even established a centrally subsidized school lunch program.

Toward the end of World War II, electoral pressures and the visibility of their constituents' suffering led to the modern *welfare state* and promises that government would provide what Winston Churchill called "cradle to grave" coverage. Furthermore, one widely accepted lesson of the Great Depression held that even though free markets were indispensable institutions for creating wealth, they needed to be complemented by government regulation to lessen the adverse impact of the *business cycle*, periodic swings between growth and recession that seemed an inescapable characteristic of free-market systems. All these considerations pushed governments toward a wider role in promoting their citizens' human needs, not the smaller one envisioned by functionalists.

The Neofunctionalist Strategy   World federalists and functionalists were the most prominent Western critics of the state system in the post-war debates about the sources of security. Before we look at their principal antagonists, it is important to connect them to a group that emerged in the 1960s and is, in many forms, still alive and well.

The problems with the functionalist assumption that the responsibility for meeting basic human needs could be detached from the state and taken over by "non-political" groups were soon recognized by people who shared many of the functionalists' long-term objectives but disagreed on how those goals could be achieved. This insight led to a new school of thought called **neofunctionalism**, which argued that meeting human needs was an inescapably political activity. From the neofunctionalist perspective, the trick was not to attempt to do the impossible—to try to detach questions about how to fulfill human needs from the state—but instead to look for political and policy incentives for state and non-state actors to develop new intergovernmental and trans-state actors that could address these problems in ways that promoted international cooperation.

The neofunctionalist argument is far more conceptually sophisticated than the original version and helps explain the growth of European integration from the founding of the EEC in 1957 to its transformation into the European Union (EU) in the 1990s (see Chapter 5). Neofunctionalist arguments also contribute to key parts of modern debates about international political economy, the environment, and human rights. Any potential impact of these ideas on the evolution of security issues had, however, to wait for the end of the Cold War. Until the key actors' policy preferences and values began to converge in the 1980s, approaches built on assumptions of enduring conflict and the importance of military and economic power had a far greater impact on choices made by policy makers in the West.

Supporters of State Action to Achieve Security

Classical Realism Moves to the United States   No person did more to popularize classical realism in the United States than Hans Morgenthau. Morgenthau, a European expatriate and U.S. academic who wrote some of the most influential books on world politics from the late 1940s into the early 1970s, argued that there were two primary sources of conflict in politics: the competition for scarce resources and the desire for power.[14] Of the two, he felt the drive for power is much more dangerous. The competition for resources, Morgenthau argued, has limits; it can

neofunctionalism An intellectual tradition that shares the functionalist assumption that the state system causes war, but which also holds that because strategies to provide basic human needs are inescapably political, states must be given political incentives to rely on non-state actors.

ENDURING PATTERNS
7.4

The connection between preferences and power

The more compatible actors' preferences, the less strategically important their relative power positions.

The impact of varying beliefs about just relationships

If people value creating and sustaining legitimate relationships and if they think a political process and the outcome it produces are just, they are more likely to accept that outcome—even if they would have preferred something else.

The effect of the shadow of the future

The more compatible people expect their preferences to become over time, the more cooperative and less power-based their strategic choices are likely to be.

The impact of linkage politics

World politics is driven by the interaction of international, factional, and constituency politics.

Neofunctionalism from the 1960s to the 1990s

Neofunctionalism, which emerged in the 1960s, is sensitive to all the enduring patterns above. It looks for areas of shared international concern (to reduce the importance of the relative power positions among states) that are likely to become even more important over time (to increase the incentives created by the shadow of the future) and have positive effects on politically powerful domestic groups (to reduce the political risks and enhance the effects of linkage politics). It also looks for international and domestic contexts in which there is a growing concern for building mutually legitimate relationships (which makes it easier to get negotiators to accept less than they want).

While its analysis of the substantive areas it stressed is often theoretically subtle, neofunctionalism did not become as popular as many of its intellectual competitors. Its interest in cooperation and non-state actors simply did not fit the focus on competitive state security systems that preoccupied a Cold War dominated world in the 1960s.

The prevailing conditions began to change with the growing interest in international economic interdependence and in environmental issues during the 1970s, the end of the Cold War in the 1980s, and the rapid increase in the number of non-state actors. With those changes, neofunctionalism's emphasis on cooperation, non-state actors, and building mutually reinforcing international and domestic regimes became more relevant. There is no better example of the increasing value of neofunctionalist insights that these changing conditions created than in the ways it helps us better understand the evolution of the European Economic Community into the European Union during the late 1980s and 1990s.

also be muted by abundance. The drive for power, however, is limitless: "For while man's vital needs are capable of satisfaction, his lust for power would be satisfied only if the last man became an object of his domination, there being nobody above or beside him, that is, if he became like God."[15] Moreover, power is inescapably tied to actors' *relative* positions. Consequently, the drive for power creates immediate and visible conflicts between winners and losers.

It is important to note that Morgenthau did not like what he saw. He thought that trying to become more powerful than other actors was, in a very real sense, evil. Indeed, he wrote that "it is this ubiquity of the desire for power which, besides and beyond any particular selfishness or other evilness of purpose, constitutes the ubiquity of evil in human action."[16] But Morgenthau also thought that the drive for power was a fundamental aspect of human nature. Policy makers who assumed that people were essentially good were "blind and naive" because selfishness and the desire for power were there for all to see. Policy makers who thought otherwise were guilty of a "perversity of moral sense" because their choices would lead to far worse consequences than choices based on realist assumptions about the human condition. "Political ethics . . . must reconcile itself to the enduring presence of evil in all political action . . . Since evil there must be, [political ethics is the ethics of choosing] among several possible actions the one that is least evil."[17]

Morgenthau's bottom line was that statesmen ought to think and act in terms of the national interest, defined as power. If policy makers followed that advice, he believed they would find morality in politics by acting prudently to minimize the amount of evil done.

While Morgenthau's version of realism was controversial and subject to many scathing criticisms, it placed two important ethical issues before policy makers. First, he demanded that policy makers confront the fact that using power to achieve their policy objectives often creates profoundly troubling ethical dilemmas. Second, Morgenthau argued that attempting to achieve universal objectives in world politics was immoral and stupid, that ideological crusades would lead policy makers to accept terrible costs in causes that were bound to fail (Morgenthau was one of the most prominent early critics of U.S. involvement in the Vietnam war). It is this second injunction that separates Morgenthau, the European-trained classical realist, from the anticommunist strain of power politics that evolved in the United States during the early years of the Cold War.

The Anticommunist Variant of Power Politics   Perhaps the best exemplar of the ideological, anticommunist variant of power politics during the first decade after World War II is John Foster Dulles, Wall Street banker, important opinion leader for the Republicans in the late 1940s, and President Dwight Eisenhower's secretary of state from 1954 to 1958.

Whereas Morgenthau located the sources of conflict in the competition for scarce resources and in an innate drive for power, Dulles believed that international communism was the principal source of conflict in the world. Morgenthau urged policy makers to avoid ideological crusades, to act prudently and with a careful regard for the consequences of their choices; Dulles, in his influential book *War or Peace?* sounded the call for the crusade:

> There exists a great power—Russia—under the control of a despotic group fanatical in their acceptance of a creed that preaches world domination and that

would deny those personal freedoms which constitute our most cherished political and religious heritage. . . . They believe that it is their duty to extend that power to all the world. They believe it is right to use fraud, terrorism, and violence, and any other means that will promote their ends. . . . Soviet Communism starts with an atheistic, Godless premise. Everything else flows from that premise. If there is no God, there is no moral and natural law and the material world is primary. . . .

Power is the key to success in dealing with the Soviet leadership. . . . The despotism of Soviet Communism has great weaknesses . . . but they are weaknesses that are fatal only under pressure.[18]

State-based security systems that stressed power politics trumped the critique of the state system in the late 1940s, because their assumptions about the nature of the key actors and the level of incompatible preferences fit the prevailing conditions in the mid-twentieth century far more closely than did those of the world federalists and early functionalists. However, while both classical realism and the anticommunist variant of power politics stressed managing inescapable security threats, their understanding of the origins of conflict and their recommendations for pursuing the quest for security were radically different. The anticommunist variant became dominant in the United States partly because it responded to domestic perceptions of the threat posed by international communism. But there is more to this story than just the popularity of anticommunism. Going at least as far back as George Washington's Farewell Address—in which he warned Americans to avoid foreign entanglements and to be careful to stay out of European power politics—there has been a tradition of hostility in the United States to European-style classical realism, both because it requires an ongoing involvement in high-stakes diplomacy and because it appears to be based on amoral calculations of power. The anticommunist variant, in contrast, promised not only to protect Americans from communism, but also to provide for their security in a way that privileged U.S. values while avoiding any promises of long-term involvement once the crusade was won.

Into the Cold War

When one looks at the international and domestic incentives facing Soviet and U.S. policy makers at the end of World War II, it is easy to see why the wartime alliance quickly fell apart. The problem was as simple as it was stark: Policy makers in the United States and the Soviet Union both wanted to create a set of global arrangements that reflected their domestic economic and political institutions, but their visions of a just and secure world were fundamentally incompatible.

Competing Visions of a Secure World

The incompatibility of the key actors' worldviews put power center stage in the U.S.-Soviet relationship. It's important, therefore, to clarify the exact nature of the perceived security threat so we can identify the relevant sources of power for responding to that threat and then reflect on how the distribution of power affected the competitors' options. As several scholars have convincingly demonstrated, before 1949 U.S. policy factions thought the Soviet Union could threaten the United States militarily only if it gained control of the resources of Western Europe or Northeast Asia. Moreover, U.S. policy makers believed that Stalin was not prepared to start a war to gain that control, but instead was hoping that he could pick up the pieces after divisions within the capitalist world led to the collapse of Western control.

Recently released Soviet archives confirm this assessment. They reveal that, in Gaddis's words, "Stalin was determined to do nothing that might involve the USSR in another devastating war until it had recovered sufficiently to be certain of winning it." Consistent with Lenin's prediction that capitalism would collapse as the result of recurring wars of imperialist redivision, it was "Stalin's persistent belief, after 1945, that the next war would take place within the capitalist world."[19]

Consequently, the immediate security threat to the United States was more economic and political than military. Stalin's ability to gain control of those areas in Western Europe and Northeast Asia that he needed to achieve military superiority depended on whether the United States could rebuild the political economies of Japan and Western Europe along Western models before the destruction and suffering led groups in Europe and Asia to reject the market in favor of command economies.[20] This assessment suggests that U.S. policy makers were well positioned internationally to achieve their security goals. The international arena may have been bipolar in military capabilities, but it was unambiguously one-nation-dominant in economic capabilities.

Linkage politics created a complex set of incentives for policy factions in the United States. At the level of goals, there were reinforcing domestic and diplomatic incentives for sustained competition. Indeed, U.S. officials were convinced that their country's security required "an external environment compatible with their domestic vision of a good society."[21] Consequently, one of the most important characteristics of the Cold War was that it was simultaneously a high-stakes international issue and a high-stakes domestic issue. It was, after all, not only about war and peace but also about how countries would organize their domestic political and economic arrangements. But while the substance of the values to be achieved domestically and diplomatically reinforced each other, the means necessary to achieve those goals would require mobilizing domestic resources on an unprecedented level for peacetime, which would be both expensive and politically dangerous. Because they attached great importance to achieving their domestic and diplomatic goals, U.S. policy makers were willing to invest substantial resources and political capital. However, the structure and norms of the U.S. political system required them to get the support of an enormous number of factions in order to make and sustain policy. As we discussed in Chapter 3, actors particularly dislike running political risks in situations in which the size and complexity of the coalitions involved make it difficult to control policy choices and the ways in which those choices are implemented.

Given that situation, U.S. policy makers looked for tools that could be used to overcome domestic opposition. Several soon became part of the standard tool kit. The linkage between international goals and the "domestic vision of a good society" gave policy factions an enormous hammer with which to attack domestic opponents: the charge of un-Americanism. Because this hammer had a far heavier impact when U.S.-Soviet competition was framed within the anticommunist variant of realism—indeed, it didn't fit at all with the classical version—policy makers had strong political incentives to adopt the stridently anticommunist variant of realism.

U.S. policy makers had, in addition to the hammer, an important lever: their ability to manipulate the perceived security threat. Even if the international competition was fundamentally economic and political, the distribution of military capabilities was clearly bipolar and, consequently, the Soviet Union appeared to be a major threat

World Politics and the Individual

Nikita Khrushchev: Peasant, Premier, Pensioner

Nikita Khrushchev led the Soviet Union through some of the most tumultuous events of the Cold War, including several crises in Berlin, an extraordinary visit to the United Nations in which he pounded his shoe on the desk to show disapproval of a speech, and the Cuban missile crisis. The review at www.prenhall.com/lamborn covers his rise from peasant to premier.

Look for the effect of linkage politics and chance on his journey up the political ladder in Stalin's Soviet Union. Consider whether the personality traits and skills that aided his rise domestically contributed to his failures as premier. You may find it interesting to compare Khrushchev's story to Kwame Nkrumah's (see page 214).

to the West's military security. The experience of having just faced a tyrannical aggressor in World War II combined with the highly visible symbol of Munich and the dangers of appeasement to make this lever even more politically potent.

While leaders in the United States were cross-pressured—international policy incentives pulled them toward expensive foreign commitments while domestic political incentives pulled them in the opposite direction—Stalin's preferences for domestic and international control *reinforced* each other. Moreover, the Soviet political system gave him the ability to act on those preferences. Consequently, Stalin's response to the mix of international and domestic incentives confronting him in the immediate post-war period was to "try to strengthen further the security of his own regime, first by increasing safeguards against Western influences inside the Soviet Union; second, by tightening control over Russia's East European satellites; and finally by working to ensure central direction of the international communist movement."[22]

The perception that the Cold War created reinforcing diplomatic and domestic incentives for Soviet policy makers held, with one important exception, from the 1940s into the mid-1980s. The exception came in the years after Stalin's death, when Khrushchev attempted to reframe Soviet policy makers' understanding of the domestic political risks they were running and the implications of those domestic risks for the Soviet Union's international position. John Gaddis sums up the problem Khrushchev faced:

> Stalin's legacy . . . was to leave in place the structures for building a socialist order, but with no foundation of popular support. . . . Khrushchev worried a great deal about this. He understood clearly that unless socialism began to provide greater benefits, whatever support it had would disappear. . . . Khrushchev's single greatest priority was to humanize Marxism-Leninism, so that people would *want* to be associated with it.[23]

Khrushchev's reform efforts were defeated by linkage politics. Internationally, they were undermined by the pressures of a hostile international climate, which his own nuclear saber-rattling and propensity for high-stakes bluffing over Berlin greatly worsened. Domestically, they were undermined by the incentives built into the political system that Stalin had left in place. As Gaddis concludes, "Not until Gorbachev was a Soviet leader fully prepared to dismantle Stalin's structural legacy."[24]

Consequently, until the structure of linkage politics in the Soviet Union shifted under Gorbachev in the 1980s, the distinctive patterns in the linkage politics of the United States and the Soviet Union produced negative and self-aggravating diplomatic interactions. Each side's response to the linked international and domestic incentives it confronted led to choices that increased the other side's sense of vulnerability and threat.

Linkage Politics in the United States

Most of the key decisions on post-war relations with the Soviet Union fell to Harry Truman, who became president when Franklin Roosevelt died in April 1945, just as the war in Europe was ending. Policy makers seldom like taking high political risks in pursuit of foreign policy objectives, even when they know where they want to go. They are even less likely to accept political risks to sustain a policy that they don't value and had little role in creating. All of these conditions fit Truman's situation in 1945. Truman had been largely kept in the dark about the details of Roosevelt's post-war plans, and his advisers were divided on the prospects for developing an effective working relationship with the Soviet Union. Truman began to accept high political risks in pursuit of foreign policy objectives only after he began to reach closure on his diplomatic strategy during what Walter LaFeber calls "the awful year of 1946."[25]

In 1945 and early 1946, the Soviet Union pressured Turkey to grant it control over the Dardanelles. An apparent Soviet effort to stay in northern Iran prompted a January 1946 threat from Truman to send naval and ground forces to Iran if the Soviet Union did not withdraw the troops it had stationed there during the war. With the resolution of the controversy over Iran not yet clear, Stalin gave a major speech in February in which he called for a series of five-year plans that would boost Soviet industrial growth and weapons production. Stalin stressed the incompatibility of the two systems and the Leninist argument that true peace would be possible only after the end of monopoly capitalism.[26] Truman demanded answers about Soviet intentions from the State Department. One of the State Department's most experienced Soviet analysts, George Kennan, wrote a response that came to be called "the long telegram."

Kennan's conceptualization of Soviet intentions led to **containment,** a policy—adopted in 1946 by the Truman administration—of preventing Soviet territorial expansion. Kennan wrote that "Soviet power [is] . . . impervious to the logic of reason, and it is highly sensitive to the logic of force. . . . If the adversary has sufficient force and makes clear his readiness to use it, he rarely has to."[27] Moreover, Kennan argued, successful containment would eventually lead "either to the break-up or the gradual mellowing of Soviet power."[28] The goal of containing the Soviet Union resonated with Truman's values, and Moscow's retreat from Iran in April and Turkey in August 1946 suggested that Kennan was right about the Soviet Union's sensitivity to the logic of force.

However, while containment was to become the cornerstone of U.S. security policy, it soon turned out that there were two competing versions of containment. Kennan and Secretary of State George Marshall advocated a version of containment that stressed the value of defensive military preparations that would deter the Soviet Union from expanding, but put its primary long-term emphasis on the ability of the U.S. economy to outperform the Soviet Union and eventually "win" the Cold War. Another faction within the government, led by Paul Nitze and Dean Acheson, advocated a version of containment that argued that the Soviet Union could be

containment A term originally used to refer to the U.S. policy of preventing Soviet territorial expansion during the Cold War; the term has increasingly been used to refer to any strategy designed to keep a threat isolated (contained) within its current territory.

deterred and ultimately undermined only if the United States had overwhelming military superiority.

The Kennan-Marshall version of containment began to lose domestic political support in late 1946. Republicans won control of Congress in the November elections and proceeded to attack the administration for appeasing communism.[29] In this worsening domestic climate, Truman's diplomatic problems increased. In January 1947, Marshall's conclusion that the communists would almost certainly win the civil war in China led to the decision to end U.S. efforts to settle the dispute. In early 1947 noncommunist members of the Polish and Hungarian governments were forced out and, in some cases, turned up dead under very mysterious circumstances. Finally, in February a British note arrived warning the United States that the communists would win the civil war in Greece unless the United States was willing to assume the financial costs of supporting the royalist side. The result was the Truman Doctrine, the first pillar in Truman's evolving policy of containment.

The Truman Doctrine, presented to Congress in March 1947, called for U.S. military aid in "support of free peoples who are resisting attempted subjection by armed minorities or by outside pressures." It was a defining moment in the movement away from the Marshall-Kennan version of containment. In a crucial meeting with congressional leaders prior to going public with a request for funding to support aid to Greece and Turkey, Secretary of State George Marshall's focused and restrained analysis of the strategic stakes had produced little support from the factions Truman needed in a politically sustainable coalition. Sensing an opportunity, Undersecretary of State Dean Acheson intervened, asserting that the fall of Greece would, as a rotten apple infects an entire barrel, lead to the spread of communism throughout the world.[30] That got his listeners' attention and led to the famous "Vandenberg condition." Truman would get Republican support in Congress *if* he explained the stakes in Acheson's terms. According to Acheson's account, Senator Vandenberg warned, "the only way to get Congress and the public to support military assistance . . . was to 'scare the hell out of the American people.' "[31]

The language of the Truman Doctrine intentionally raised the diplomatic ante to gain domestic support. The second pillar of containment, the Marshall Plan—which called for massive U.S. economic aid to rebuild Europe—required less hyperbole because the large number of visible strategic, economic, and humanitarian incentives for rebuilding Europe made it easier to build a broadly based coalition. But the terms of the Marshall Plan also signaled the determination of the United States to ignore Soviet objections to the reconstruction of Europe's economy along market principles. The United States made it clear that the Soviet Union and the countries it controlled in Eastern Europe would receive aid through the Marshall Plan only if they changed their systems to meet Western standards for open economies. The United States also announced that it would include the West's zones of occupation in Germany within the Marshall Plan even though the Soviet Union had explicitly opposed rebuilding Germany's economy.

From the perspective of U.S. domestic politics, rebuilding Germany was a low-risk way to contain the Soviet Union. From the Soviet perspective, it was highly provocative. Stalin responded by blockading all land routes into West Berlin. The Berlin Blockade produced results exactly opposite to those Stalin intended. The United States responded with an airlift that kept West Berlin supplied with food, fuel, and other supplies for eleven months. With the airlift buying time internationally and a great political success domestically, U.S. planners accelerated the

7.5 ENDURING PATTERNS

The effect of the shadow of the future

The more incompatible people expect their preferences to become over time, the more competitive and power-based their strategic approach is likely to be.

NATO, Bismarck, and Global Terrorism

The founders of the North Atlantic Treaty Organization believed that their preferences were likely to remain incompatible with those of the leadership of the Soviet Union for as far into the future as they could see. Given that view of the future, they decided it was necessary to organize a standing, pre-targeted defensive alliance.

Between 1879 and 1890, German Chancellor Otto von Bismarck organized a series of standing pre-targeted defensive alliances to maintain the peace in central Europe. At the time, it was almost unprecedented to establish peacetime military alliances. Bismarck's policy innovation re-flected his judgment that almost all of the major military powers in Europe had incompatible preferences on one or more issues that were likely to endure for the foreseeable future.

In the fall of 2001, British Prime Minister Tony Blair and U.S. President George W. Bush began to campaign for the creation of institutionalized security arrangements to counter the threat of global terrorist networks. The desire to institutionalize those arrangements reflected the judgment that such threats were likely to persist for a long time into the future.

---

timetable for the creation of the Federal Republic of Germany (West Germany) and were able to build support for U.S. participation in the North Atlantic Treaty Organization (NATO), a defense pact against the Soviet Union that tied the security of Western Europe to the United States and Canada. NATO became the third pillar in the U.S. policy of containment.

Beginning with the success of the Berlin airlift, the fortunes of linkage politics underwent a startling reversal. Assertive statecraft suddenly became a political asset. In LaFeber's words, "Truman and Acheson used foreign policy to pull off a political miracle" in 1948, reelecting Truman and regaining control of Congress.[32] Truman's election victory reinforced his move to a hard-line anti-Soviet policy. It was soon followed by the ascendancy of the Nitze-Acheson faction's version of containment. Secretary of State Marshall resigned for reasons of health and was replaced by Acheson; Paul Nitze took over Kennan's old job as head of the Policy Planning Staff in the State Department.

In January 1948, Acheson and Nitze convinced Truman to authorize the building of a hydrogen bomb. Significantly, the debate hinged on different assumptions about the facts. Kennan had argued against building the hydrogen bomb on the grounds that it was not yet clear whether Soviet intentions made accommodation impossible. Acheson and Nitze argued that Soviet intentions were known, that they were fundamentally incompatible with American objectives, and that the strategic situation could not be improved over time by a search for jointly acceptable outcomes.

The H-bomb decision was followed by a National Security Council memorandum (NSC-68) in April 1950. Drafted under Nitze's direction, NSC-68 concluded that "The fundamental design of those who control the Soviet Union and the international communist movement is the complete subversion or forcible destruction . . . of the non-Soviet world and their replacement by an apparatus and structure subservient to and controlled from the Kremlin."[33] To defeat this threat, the United States would need to accept leadership of the "free world," launch a major military buildup, finish Europe's reconstruction, and be prepared to launch a preemptive military attack. At all times, it would have to be skeptical about the value of any negotiations with the Soviet Union. In addition to adopting these strategically risky policies, the United States would need to increase defense spending dramatically (to as much as 50 percent of GNP if necessary), cut domestic spending, and increase taxes.[34]

Truman signed off on NSC-68 but delayed sending a new budget to Congress. Indeed, it is hard to imagine a more politically explosive set of tax and spending proposals. Once again, policy entrepreneurs within the executive branch got unintentional help from their diplomatic adversaries. In June 1950, North Korea invaded South Korea. As Nitze observed later, it was only after the Korean war "had given concrete and bloody confirmation to the conclusions already produced by analysis [in NSC-68]" that its recommendations "were translated into specific action."[35]

With the onset of the Korean War and the implementation of NSC-68, U.S. foreign policy makers crossed a threshold. The objectives of containment were now global, and in addition to the original goal of deterring Soviet expansion into Western Europe and Northeast Asia, now included preventing subversion, revolution, and aggression throughout the Third World. In a colossal stroke of bad luck, the process of decolonizing Africa, Asia, and the Middle East was just getting underway. This historic unraveling of formal colonial control became entangled with the long U.S.-Soviet competition in ways that created problems for all concerned.

The End of Formal Empire

As we discussed earlier in this chapter, Europe's expansion into Asia and Africa began in the late 1400s. Almost five hundred years later, it ended with startling suddenness in the decades after World War II. Beginning with the independence of the Indian subcontinent and its partitioning into India and Pakistan in 1947, almost all of Asia became formally independent by the late 1950s. Most of sub-Saharan Africa (beginning with the independence of the British colony of the Gold Coast, renamed Ghana) achieved formal independence in a rush between 1957 and the mid-1960s. The principal remaining holdouts followed in less than two decades: the Portuguese colonies in the mid-1970s; Rhodesia (now Zimbabwe) in 1980; and Namibia (transferred to South Africa as a League mandate in 1920) in 1990 (see Map 7–13). Why did a five-hundred-year process end so rapidly?

Rising Opposition Overwhelms a Declining Willingness and Ability to Control

As always when major epochs end suddenly, our perspective leads us to look for a wide range of reinforcing international and domestic incentives that all push in the

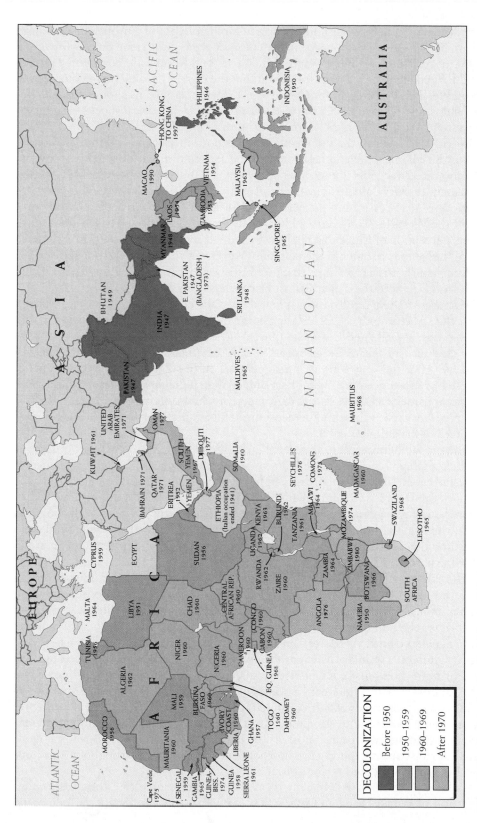

Map 7-13   Decolonization in Africa and Asia
The collapse of Europe's modern colonial empires began in 1947 on the Indian subcontinent. The partition of the subcontinent into the states of India and Pakistan was followed by the independence of Burma (now Myanmar) and Ceylon (now Sri Lanka) in 1948. Decolonization began later in Africa. The first sub-Saharan area to gain independence was the British colony of the Gold Coast (later Ghana) in 1957. Namibia, which had been given to South Africa under a League of Nations mandate after World War I, became independent in 1990.

same direction. The process underlying the rapid collapse of European colonialism is clear. Mobilized opposition within the colonies grew at the same time as European policy makers found it increasingly difficult to build domestic coalitions that believed that colonialism was legitimate and that the cost of holding on to colonies was acceptable. This essential shift in key actors' preferences, norms about legitimate relationships, and relative power was accelerated by three historical shocks to the colonial system: World War I, the Depression, and World War II.

World War I began the unraveling process both in Europe and in the colonies. Within the colonies, the emphasis on national self-determination and democracy in the announced war aims of the victors provided a publicly espoused set of legitimizing principles that could be used against European colonizers, even though their application to Africa, Asia, and the Middle East was hypocritically denied in the peace talks at the Versailles Conference. The war also weakened colonial ties by undermining the perception of Europe as a politically unified civilization whose power dwarfed that of indigenous peoples in the colonies. Moreover, the colonial troops in Europe saw first-hand both the cleavages that tore Europe apart and the ability of African and Asian troops to hold their own against Europeans. Finally, the mobilization of colonial resources to help pay for the war lengthened the colonies' long list of grievances.

At the same time that World War I contributed to the rise of opposition within the colonies, it weakened European power and resolve. Before the war, it was relatively easy for Europeans to believe in Social Darwinist ideas about their racial superiority. After the war, with an entire generation of soldiers dead in the trenches and the incompetence of many military and civilian policy makers brutally apparent, it became harder to believe in the legitimacy of white domination. Even as the war began to alter these values and perceptions, it also radically reduced the wealth and resources of the colonial states.

The global Depression of the 1930s intensified these linked changes. In Europe it struck another blow against European self-confidence and reduced still further the resources available to suppress or appease opposition within the colonies. In the colonies, the Depression not only highlighted the dangers of economic dependence and increased the suffering, but it also hurt the Europeans' principal collaborators within the colonies—those indigenous groups who had previously benefitted from the redirection of native economies away from subsistence and internal markets and toward exports to Europe.

The effects of World War II on the rise of opposition in the colonies were in many ways a replay of World War I. Once again, national self-determination and democracy figured prominently in the war propaganda of the Allies. Once again, Europeans relied on colonial troops and resources while revealing their own internal weaknesses and divisions to the world. But the second war added a new, and highly significant, wrinkle. Much as the Napoleonic wars had undermined Spanish and Portuguese colonial control in the Americas, so the occupation of France and Belgium by Germany and Japan's successes in Asia during World War II temporarily disrupted colonial control. It was much harder to regain that control after the war than it would have been to sustain it. Moreover, the knowledge that an Asian country had routed the Europeans (most visibly in the fall of the supposedly impregnable British fortress at Singapore) gave independence movements throughout Asia hope that the Europeans could be forced out.

As for the effects of World War II on Europe, here again the story was partly a repetition of World War I and partly new. The growth of anti-imperial values and the economic and military effects of the devastation echoed those of the earlier conflict. What was new was the rise of politically inescapable demands that governments redirect funds toward domestic agendas.

Just when these combined pressures were growing strongest, Europe's leadership role in world politics was eclipsed by the rise of the United States and the Soviet Union. Both, for quite different reasons, were initially opposed to the continuation of European colonial control in the crucial years immediately after World War II. With both colonial relationships and the global strategic environment so fundamentally altered, formal colonialism began to collapse.

Contributing Factors

Given the rise of organized opposition in the colonies and the decline in Europeans' ability and willingness to hold on to their empires, it is not surprising that colonial ties unraveled after World War II. But there was more to the speed of the outcome than the strength of the underlying shift in perceptions, values, and power. Europeans did not see the magnitude of these shifts and the stark choices they created until very late. Three reasons for this misperception stand out. First, many colonial administrators thought the opponents to colonialism were simply troublemakers and not typical of the general population. Many believed that the "real" people had no political agendas but only wanted impartial administration. They failed to see that the problem was inescapably political: the nature of legitimate rule. Second, many Europeans believed that indigenous African and Asian cultures were "backward" and practiced some gross offenses against human rights. While the hypocrisy in this view is obvious—and the failure to recognize their own human rights violations amazing—the clash of cultures was real and profound.

Third, Europeans had a very different view of nationalism and the preconditions for forming viable states. In the European context, nationalism meant a common culture, language, and (often) religion. None of these commonalities were present in the colonial territories, where Europeans had drawn the boundaries with utter disregard for the lines separating indigenous groups. What Europeans failed to grasp was the unifying effects of being ruled and exploited by foreigners. It was that shared experience that provided the basis for mobilizing opposition groups within the colonies.

The Cold War Intrudes on Post-Colonial Societies

The same factors that explain the rapid spread of decolonization help us understand the gloomy history of post-colonial societies in the decades immediately after independence. The essential problem is clear. Although these areas had enough in common to mobilize effectively against the continuation of colonial control, they had precious little else in common—and very few assets—when it came to organizing viable post-colonial governments and economies. Moreover, these areas achieved independence in the midst of an evolving Cold War in which the principal antagonists made competing claims about how international and domestic politics should be organized.

Superpower Intervention and the Non-Aligned Movement

The mix of Third World vulnerability and superpower aspirations to promote universal systems for organizing world politics was a recipe for disaster. Post-colonial

World Politics and the Individual

Kwame Nkrumah: A Nationalist's Odyssey

Kwame Nkrumah was one of the most important nationalist leaders in Africa during the decolonization struggle and the first decades of formal independence. He not only led the first black-African state to independence, he did as much as anyone to popularize the notion of neocolonialism (discussed in chapter 10).

You can read an overview of his life at **www.prenhall.com/lamborn**. Look for the origins of his distinctive understandings of

colonialism and the best ways to achieve independence. Try to identify what it was about the linked international and domestic situation after World War II that created opportunities for him to become such a successful leader in the nationalist movement. Consider why the strategy that worked so well in achieving independence was less well suited to the linked international and domestic contexts he faced as Ghana's president after independence.

societies became zones of competition between the United States and Soviet Union. We have seen strikingly similar situations in several earlier historical periods: the centuries-long conflict between the pope and the Holy Roman Emperor in the Middle Ages; the sixteenth and seventeenth-century struggle between Catholic and Protestant Europe that culminated in the Thirty Years' War; and the competition between supporters of the original legitimizing principles of the Westphalian system and advocates of nationalism and democracy that prompted the major-power interventions orchestrated by Metternich during the Concert of Europe. All these periods shared the following distinctive characteristics: a large number of militarily weak actors that were politically unstable because they lacked an internal consensus on legitimizing principles; and a pair of competing universalist doctrines promoted by major military powers led by policy coalitions that believed their internal and external security depended on the creation of a system of world politics consistent with their worldview. It is a situation made for meddling. Sometimes the initiative for intervention came from factions within the major power; other times from factions in the smaller state who were seeking powerful external allies. But whether invited from within or built from the outside, the result was the same: a trans-state coalition designed to control the organizing principles and policy choices of the smaller states.

These dangers were recognized by some of the most important Third World leaders in the 1950s: Jawaharlal Nehru, a leader in India during the decolonization movement and its prime minister from independence in 1947 until his death in 1964; Gamal Abdel Nasser, Egypt's prime minister and, later, president from 1954 to 1970; and Kwame Nkrumah, leader of the independence movement that brought the Gold Coast to independence in 1957, then Ghana's president until 1966. These three worked with Yugoslavia's Tito (who, though an ardent communist, had discovered the dangers of competing universals when Stalin tried to crush his independence in 1948) to form the **Non-Aligned Movement,** a coalition of countries brought together at the Bandung Conference in 1955 to promote neutralism as the best way to keep from being drawn into the Cold War.

Unfortunately for advocates of non-alignment, pressing international and domestic problems frequently gave factions in Third World countries incentives to

Non-Aligned Movement
A coalition of countries founded in 1955 that advocated remaining neutral in the Cold War.

violate their principles and bring in external coalition partners. Thus Nasser sought Soviet help in 1955, after being spurned by the United States, both to acquire modern arms and to build the Aswan High Dam on the Nile River. His successor, Anwar al-Sadat, expelled 20,000 Soviet advisers in 1972 and subsequently switched to U.S. patronage. Other Arab leaders, such as those in Syria and Iraq, also turned to the Soviet Union for military aid. Meanwhile, in the aftermath of the partition of British India into Pakistan and India (in which massacres of Hindus and Muslims killed thousands and produced 12 million refugees), continuing hostility with Pakistan and growing concerns about China in the 1960s and early 1970s led Indian policy makers to seek Soviet aid while Pakistan turned to the United States. Disputes left over from the ways in which boundaries were drawn during the break-up of the European empires also created opportunities for superpower competition in Africa, where the United States and the Soviet Union played a game of making and breaking alliances with different regimes and insurgent movements in the Congo, Namibia, Ethiopia, Eritrea, and Somalia.

The U.S. War in Vietnam and the Soviet Invasion of Afghanistan

Vietnam provides the most costly example of how decolonization became entangled with the Cold War. What started out as an attempt by Ho Chi Minh and other Vietnamese nationalists to prevent the French from resuming control after the Japanese defeat in World War II took a dramatic turn in 1949, when the victory of the communists in the Chinese civil war led U.S. policy makers to redefine the issue in Vietnam from decolonization to the expansion of international communism. Acting on that redefinition, the U.S. government began to subsidize the French effort to maintain control. When that failed and Vietnam was partitioned as a temporary solution in 1954, the United States then threw its support behind South Vietnam. Initially restricted to financial aid and military equipment, U.S. support escalated from 500 military advisers when Eisenhower left office in 1961 to 16,300 advisers under John F. Kennedy. In 1965, Lyndon Johnson committed combat troops, whose numbers rose dramatically to 536,000 by 1968 (see Table 7–1). By war's end in 1975 (the United States had withdrawn in 1973), the death toll was immense: 58,000 U.S. troops; 200,000 South Vietnamese troops; over 1 million Viet Cong and North Vietnamese combatants; and 2 million civilians.

Several years after Vietnam fell, the Soviet Union had its own humbling experience with a failed Third-World intervention in Afghanistan. Since British colonialists operating out of India first collided with the troops of an expanding Imperial Russia in the mid-nineteenth century, Afghanistan had long served as an important buffer state on Russia's (and later the Soviet Union's) border with the Indian subcontinent. In April 1978, a coup headed by a procommunist led Afghanistan out of the non-aligned camp and into the Soviet Union's. Armed opposition to the coup within Afghanistan led to still another coup and more fighting in the fall of 1979. Determined not to lose their newly acquired communist allies in Afghanistan, the Soviet Union invaded in December 1979. In the ten years of war that followed, over one million Afghans died and one-third of the Afghan population fled the country. The size of the Soviet commitment was "only" about 90,000 to 100,000 troops (compared to a maximum of 500,000 U.S. troops in Vietnam), but 15,000 Soviet soldiers died and over 73 percent of the 642,000 who served during the war were

TABLE 7-1	U.S. MILITARY BUILDUP AND MULTINATIONAL TROOP PRESENCE IN VIETNAM			

Year[a]	U.S. Military Advisers in Vietnam[b]	Total U.S. Military Personnel in Vietnam[c]	Total South Vietnamese Armed Forces	Other Allied Military Forces in Vietnam[d]
1956	65			
1957	70			
1958	71			
1959	76	760	243,000	
1960	83	900	243,000	
1961	893	3,205	243,000	
1962	1,136	11,300	243,000	
1963	1,239	16,300	243,000	
1964	2,412	23,300	514,000	
1965	3,529	183,400	514,000	22,420
1966	4,557	385,300	735,900	52,500
1967		485,600	798,000	59,300
1968		536,100	820,000	65,600
1969		475,200	897,000	70,300
1970		334,600	968,000	67,700
1971		156,800	1,046,250	53,900
1972		24,200	1,048,000	35,500
1973		50	1,110,000	0
1974		50	N.A.	0

(a) The war in Vietnam ended on April 30, 1975.

(b) The term "advisers" refers to U.S. military personnel assigned to assist the South Vietnamese armed forces prior to 1966.

(c) Number includes military advisers.

(d) "Other Allied Military Forces" includes forces from a total of 39 different nations besides the United States over the course of the war. Major force contributions came from South Korea, Australia, Thailand, New Zealand, and the Philippines.

Source: Jeffrey J. Clarke, *Advice and Support: The Final Years, 1965–1973* (Washington, DC: Center of Military History, United States Army, 1988), p. 523; Ronald H. Spector, *Advice and Support: The Final Years, 1941–1960* (Washington, DC: Center of Military History, United States Army, 1973), p. 252; Harry G. Summers, Jr., *The Vietnam War Almanac* (Novato, CA: Presidio Press, 1999), pp. 29–59.

wounded or fell victim to debilitating illness. To make matters even worse politically, the Soviet regime was still claiming as late as 1983 that there had been only six dead and wounded (by that time there had actually been 6,262 dead and 9,880 wounded). In 1989, the Soviet Union finally gave up and withdrew, with none of its objectives achieved.[36]

The combination of the U.S. experience in Vietnam and the Soviet Union's failed intervention in Afghanistan dramatically reduced the superpowers' appetite for armed interventions in the Third World. The end of the Cold War then eliminated the ideological incentives.

The Cold War Winds Down

To explain the end of the Cold War, our focus must turn to the linked international and domestic incentives facing the Soviet Union in the 1980s. Those incentives were, in turn, very much a function of the ways in which the United States managed the linkages between its own international and domestic priorities after it moved from a policy of regional containment to a policy of global containment in 1950.

Because the Soviet decision to change course in the 1980s took place in an international context that was very much the product of thirty years of U.S. strategic policy, we begin the story of the end of the Cold War with the long prelude during which U.S. policies on global containment played a critical role in setting the stage.

Setting the Stage

As we discussed earlier in the chapter, the United States embarked on a policy of global containment in 1950 in response to the recommendations of NSC-68 and the outbreak of the Korean War. The Eisenhower administration came into office in 1953 committed to continuing a strategy of global containment. However, given the costs of the Korean War and the open-ended commitment of resources envisioned under NSC-68, it was determined to achieve global containment without the twin costs of another war and an arms race. This mix of international and domestic incentives created a substantial problem. Somehow, the Soviet Union was to be deterred from expanding in the core areas of Western Europe and Northeast Asia at the same time as subversion, revolution, and aggression were to be stopped in the Third World. Moreover, these diplomatic objectives had to be achieved within the context of Eisenhower's understanding of constituency politics in the United States, where concerns about casualties, the economy, and taxes were dominating the domestic politics of strategic choice.

In an effort to bridge these competing pressures, Eisenhower introduced the *New Look*, a policy that stressed relying on nuclear weapons more than on conventional forces to contain the Soviet Union. Secretary of State John Foster Dulles expanded this idea further when he introduced the *Doctrine of Massive Retaliation*, under which the United States announced that it reserved the right to launch an all-out nuclear attack on the Soviet Union if it decided that the Soviets were behind aggression or subversion anywhere in the world. Taken together, the New Look and the Doctrine of Massive Retaliation were designed, as some advocates put it, to give the United States "more bang for the buck."

It's important to recognize that the Doctrine of Massive Retaliation was a threat to use nuclear weapons *first*. Whatever its other merits and liabilities, one thing is clear: Threatening to launch a first strike when one is invulnerable is quite different from using nuclear weapons when the other side can respond. When the Doctrine of Massive Retaliation was announced, the United States was essentially invulnerable to Soviet attack. While the United States had air bases in Europe that made it possible to hit the Soviet Union, the Soviet Union did not have planes that were capable of reaching the continental United States. Then in October 1957 the Soviet Union put a satellite—Sputnik—into space. A sudden sense of vulnerability swept the United States. Sputnik demonstrated that the Soviet Union had the capability to respond to any U.S. nuclear attack with a nuclear strike of its own. *Mutual vulnerability* buried the Doctrine of Massive Retaliation.

When he came into office in 1961, President Kennedy was already closely tied to groups that opposed massive retaliation and supported an increase in conventional weapons. Those different assumptions about the sources of security led Kennedy to quickly replace the Doctrine of Massive Retaliation, which had threatened an all-out attack on both civilian and military targets, with the *No Cities Doctrine*, which promised that the United States would attack only military installations with nuclear weapons and not target population centers. He also rejected Eisenhower's assumption of limits and invested heavily in increasing U.S. conventional forces at the same time as he modernized and enlarged the U.S. nuclear arsenal.

While both decisions were designed to fix the perceived problems with Eisenhower's strategic policies, they, in turn, created problems of their own. In the Third World, the U.S. emphasis on conventional weapons and a *flexible and graduated response* led to a major increase in the number of U.S. military advisers in Vietnam and the beginning of a long escalation in U.S. involvement there. The problem with the No Cities Doctrine, which would bedevil U.S. military planners until it was replaced in 1965, was that contemporary delivery systems for nuclear weapons were not precise enough to fulfill the promise of hitting only strategic military targets in the Soviet Union.

When Kennedy was assassinated in November 1963, Lyndon Johnson inherited both the war in Vietnam and the uncertainty over the role of nuclear weapons. In 1965 Secretary of Defense Robert McNamara announced the doctrine of *assured destruction* (which critics turned into *Mutual Assured Destruction* to produce the acronym *MAD*). This doctrine reflected two assumptions, one technological and the other a mix of scientific, strategic, and moral thinking. On the technological side, McNamara decided to accept the fact that it was not then possible to build *counterforce* nuclear weapons—weapons with delivery systems that were precise enough to avoid civilian areas and destroy only military targets. If it wasn't possible to build counterforce weapons, then it was unacceptable to build a U.S. strategic doctrine on the assumption that they existed. So Kennedy's No Cities Doctrine had to go. However, while McNamara rejected the No Cities Doctrine, that did not mean he and Johnson were willing to threaten to use nuclear weapons first, as Eisenhower had done under the Doctrine of Massive Retaliation. Instead, McNamara and Johnson went in the opposite direction, arguing that no country could survive a nuclear war at an acceptable cost. Consequently, mutual deterrence was the only appropriate role for nuclear weapons.

Mutual deterrence was to be achieved through both sides having a *second strike capability*, defined as the ability to survive a surprise nuclear attack with enough weapons to launch a response that would inflict unacceptably high levels of damage. To make sure the damage created by that second strike was truly unacceptable, cities would be targeted in any response to an attack. (The initiator's attack was called a *first strike* to distinguish an initial act of aggression from the victim's response.) The goal, once again, was to deter aggression while simultaneously making nuclear weapons unusable. It was a sophisticated compromise between the actors' policy objectives (deterrence), their beliefs about morality (that threatening to use nuclear weapons first was immoral), and their assumptions about the state of scientific knowledge (that it was technically impossible to build effective counterforce weapons).

Domestic critics of assured destruction opposed it on several grounds. First, they argued that the United States should not accept mutual vulnerability, that the proper goal should be to return the United States to its pre-Sputnik invulnerability. Second, they asserted that it was self-defeating to build weapons systems that were not usable; both military security and political influence depended on having weapons that could be used in a militarily effective way. Finally, they opposed the notion, implicit in mutual assured destruction, that U.S. strategic doctrine should be built on acceptance of a continuing central role for the Soviet Union.

When President Nixon came into office in 1969, criticism of assured destruction was growing and efforts to design an antiballistic missile (ABM) were underway. Nixon decided, however, to stick with mutual vulnerability as the basis for successful deterrence. That decision reflected both his understanding of what was technically feasible and his views about the best ways to deal with the Soviet Union. On the technical side, by the late 1960s U.S. officials had concluded that they could not protect against an all-out attack by Soviet intercontinental ballistic missiles (ICBMs). Trying to do so, they believed, would fuel the arms race in offensive nuclear weapons, as Soviet leaders would try to overcome any U.S. defense system. Since an ABM system could be so easily overpowered, strategic military superiority wasn't a possibility. Therefore, it was better to try to move the Soviet Union's preferences toward mutually acceptable outcomes.

Nixon's diplomatic strategy included offering the Soviet Union *essential equivalence* (equal status as a superpower), détente (a relaxation of tension), and an institutionalized strategic balance through the Strategic Arms Limitation Talks (SALT). This logic was accepted by both sides when the U.S. and USSR signed the Antiballistic Missile Treaty (ABM Treaty) in 1972. It limited each country to two ABM interceptor sites. A 1974 amendment to the ABM Treaty cut the number of sites for each side to one and limited the number of interceptor missiles at that site to one hundred. Soviet leaders chose to defend Moscow with their site; the United States chose to defend a Minuteman ICBM base in North Dakota but closed that site in 1975 when it became evident that the Soviets could deploy enough warheads to overwhelm it.

Ironically, at the same time as there was growing international acceptance of mutual vulnerability as the basis for stable deterrence, domestic criticism of essential equivalence and acceptance of mutual vulnerability continued to build in the United States. It came to a head after the Soviet Union invaded Afghanistan in December 1979. President Carter responded to domestic hostility to the Soviet Union and the perception that he was a weak president by scrapping the fifteen-year-old policy of assured destruction and replacing it with strategic doctrines built on counterforce targeting. As part of the decision to move toward counterforce weapons, Carter began the development of a new generation of nuclear weapons systems precise enough to destroy military installations.

President Reagan, already an advocate of counterforce and a staunch critic of accepting mutual vulnerability, continued the military buildup that Carter had begun in the last months of his term. He also added a commitment—called the Reagan Doctrine—to provide military aid to rebels fighting communist regimes in the Third World. With both these policies increasing the financial and military pressure on the Soviet Union, he announced a companion plan to eliminate U.S. vulnerability, calling for the deployment of a reliable missile-defense shield (formally known as the Strategic Defense Initiative but popularly known as "Star Wars"). While U.S. scientists and policy makers later concluded that it was not yet technically possible to build a reliable national missile defense (NMD), the combination of the military buildup begun under Carter, the Reagan Doctrine, and the announced commitment to radically reduce U.S. strategic vulnerability through national missile defense, substantially increased Soviet worries about their strategic vulnerability.

The Soviet Union Changes Course

Consider the linked political dynamics confronting Soviet policy factions in the mid-1980s. The Cold War had been built and sustained by incompatible policy preferences and different assumptions about legitimate arrangements, all of which made power of great strategic significance. The problem for Soviet policy makers in the 1980s was that the continued stagnation of the Soviet economy meant not only that the USSR was unable to compete economically with the West, but also that the government had to impose immense burdens on the Soviet economy and people to extract the resources necessary to sustain a level of military expenditures consistent with established goals. Since there was every reason to believe that the economic decline would continue if nothing was done, the incentives for policy innovation increased still further.

The question for Soviet policy makers was: What type of policy innovation? Should they try to challenge the United States or seek some sort of innovative accommodation? It was a choice in which almost all of the historical precedents suggested a last-gasp challenge. Indeed, going back to Thucydides' analysis of the Peloponnesian wars in the fifth century BC, analysts of major-power war have argued that the most dangerous time in a sustained competition between bipolar alliance systems is the moment when one side comes to believe that it can no longer keep up. Arms-race theorists have drawn similar conclusions from statistical analyses of the impact of the financial and political costs of arms races on the probability of war.[37]

That is not, of course, what happened. Instead of organizing an international challenge, Soviet leader Mikhail Gorbachev launched an opening to the West, called *glasnost* ("new thinking") and domestic economic and social reform, *perestroika*. Why accommodation rather than challenge? The answer to this question lies in a number of reinforcing factors in the politics of strategic choice. On the international side, the incentives to challenge fell with changes in the substance of key actors' preferences and new ideas about the nature of just international relationships. The effect of these changes on the desire to find a mutually acceptable outcome was solidified by the dramatic rise in the costs of major-power war. These shifts in international incentives then became linked with a shifting domestic context, both in the factional politics of policy coalitions and constituency politics.

Consider first the international picture from a Soviet perspective. Soviet policy factions reacted to the prospect of being unable to sustain the competition with the United States by seeking mutually acceptable arrangements with the West, partly because nuclear weapons had made it virtually unthinkable to initiate a war with countries that have a clear second-strike capability. All the historical precedents, which suggested war rather than accommodation, were pre-nuclear. Moreover, even without the nuclear dimension of possible war, the stagnation of the Soviet economy and its inability to respond to the computer-based technological revolution in weapons systems were dramatically undermining Soviet conventional military capabilities.

The problems with the Soviet economy were simultaneously undermining the domestic political position of Soviet elites and their capacity to achieve domestic policy objectives. Food and housing shortages were widespread and a chronic embarrassment to a regime whose legitimacy was based on increasingly implausible promises that communism was both more moral (in its treatment of workers) and more productive than capitalism. Higher standards of living had manifestly failed to appear for workers at the same time as special privileges and the corruption of elites was increasingly visible. These factors combined with the widespread view that many of the resources spent on the military had been wasted, and that the interventions during the 1970s and early 1980s—particularly in Afghanistan—had failed miserably.[38] As a result, there was growing support, particularly in urban areas, for cuts in military spending and domestic reform.[39]

In this linked international and domestic context, Gorbachev was able to bring new actors and coalition partners into the policy-making arena.[40] Some of those policy factions worried about the long-term international implications; others were worried about the domestic system. But while these long-term preference orderings differed, there was relatively broad agreement that in the short-run the Soviet government needed "a durable and predictable [international] framework for resource choices."[41] That agreement provided the necessary preconditions for new thinking about the West—*glasnost* and *perestroika*.

There were, then, reinforcing domestic and international incentives for the Soviet government to change its policy objectives. Once that change was made, there were few fundamental policy conflicts remaining between Gorbachev's governing coalition and the West. As a result, military power became far less strategically important than before. Moreover, these radical changes led many key factions in the Soviet Union to reconceptualize their understanding of legitimate outcomes and procedures. With different diplomatic and domestic goals, Soviet policy factions could compromise on arms and control over Eastern Europe without compromising on security. Finally, with military power less strategically important, Gorbachev's coalition could hope that it would be possible to free enough resources to achieve both their diplomatic and domestic goals.

Even well-thought-out policy choices can, of course, lead to outcomes that decision makers neither anticipated nor desired. In this case, Gorbachev's diplomatic and domestic initiatives led not only to the end of the Cold War, but also to the disintegration of the Soviet Union.

Conclusion

The twentieth century began with a cataclysmic war in Europe that soon affected people not only in North America but also throughout the European colonial empires. The magnitude of World War I—and the recognition that the European security system had gone global—led to an attempt to create a global security system that would simultaneously guarantee peace and promote democracy and national self-determination.

Both ambitions failed. The League of Nations' collective security system was not up to the demands placed on it in the 1930s. Meanwhile, the hope that security would be enhanced by promoting shared values about legitimate government also failed because, in two quite different senses, those values were not shared. They were not shared, first, because European colonizers refused to extend the principles of democracy and self-determination to the people in their colonies. Second, it turned out that the world's major military powers—Germany, the Soviet Union, Japan, France, Britain, and the United States—had competing visions of how the world should be organized.

The end of World War II brought another attempt to create a global security system, but it too quickly foundered as the world moved into the Cold War and the U.S.-Soviet competition became entangled in the decolonization process. The end of the Cold War and the collapse of the Soviet Union radically altered the nature of global and regional security issues in the 1990s. The events of September 11, 2001 shifted them yet again. We discuss how security issues play out in today's unique context in Chapter 8.

Key Terms

old colonialism
suzerain system
mercantilism
new imperialism
Social Darwinism (or, *natural history*)

principle of effective occupation
collective security
superpowers
world federalists
functionalists

neofunctionalists
containment
Non-Aligned Movement

To The Reader   A CHAPTER SUMMARY and QUESTIONS FOR REVIEW are available at **www.prenhall.com/lamborn**

Security and the Uses of Force Today

What does security look like in today's world? During the Cold War, almost everyone paid close attention to the U.S.-Soviet competition and worried about the possibility of global nuclear war. When the Cold War ended, the threat of global war disappeared, and with its end, most people felt more secure. But the sense that security issues were a thing of the past was short-lived. Throughout the 1990s *regional* security issues became increasingly prominent and widespread. Russia struggled with its security relationships with an expanded NATO, the countries around its border, and Chechnya. The Balkans, beginning with the disintegration of Yugoslavia, became increasingly violent and unstable. The Middle East continued to struggle under the weight of the Arab-Israeli dispute, the regional ambitions of Iraq's and Iran's leaders, the fissures within Islam, and the clash of Western and Islamic culture. Africa saw a revival of ethnic violence and civil war. India's and Pakistan's struggle over Kashmir intensified, and both countries tested nuclear weapons. China's relationship with Taiwan became increasingly heated and militarized, and international concern about China's broader regional aspirations grew.

For much of the 1990s, people in North America saw most of these growing regional security threats as raising the important, but ultimately voluntary, question of whether the United States should get involved. The September 11, 2001, attacks eliminated the perception that the United States could choose when to become involved in the world's security issues. Subsequently, the decision by the Bush administration to organize a sustained campaign against terrorist networks that had a global reach reintroduced the first global security agenda since the Cold War. That global agenda, however, quickly became intertwined with ongoing regional disputes and the centuries-old question of how Western and Islamic culture can nurture mutually legitimate relationships.

This chapter has two principal purposes. First, it explores the distinctive issues raised by the quest for security and the use or threat of force. What does it mean to say that people and the states they live in are "secure" or "insecure"? How much of security is a result of "objective" problems, and how much stems from people's subjective feelings and perceptions? When can military force be useful to deal with security problems, and for what kinds of purposes? When, by contrast, is the acquisition or use of military power likely to produce *less* security? The second key purpose of this chapter is to discuss some of the ways in which the international security situation has changed since the end of the Cold War and the reintroduction of a global security agenda after the September 11 attacks.

The Distinctive Nature of Security Issues

Security issues involve the threat, use, and control of force.[1] From the standpoint of any actor, the threat or use of force by others may be more or less of a problem, depending on the capabilities and objectives of potential adversaries. An actor may see force as part of the solution if he believes countermeasures are needed. To explore these points, this section begins by discussing the nature of security itself: What creates a sense of safety or danger for actors in world politics?

People seem intuitively to think about security much as dictionaries typically define it: (1) freedom from harm and (2) freedom from fear. In other words, people think about what could harm them or those they care about and threats to cherished values and possessions. They then think about what they can or must do to avoid such harm or deal with it if it occurs. Because people rarely are completely free from danger or suspected danger, security is seldom absolute; it is best thought of as the *relative* freedom from harmful threats. In world politics, security is usually discussed with reference to some entity or actor larger than an individual. That actor is often a state or group of states, but it may also be a non-state actor such as a terrorist group or a substate ethnic community. The relevant entity may even be the world as a whole; in this sense, we can, for instance, compare the degree of *global* security from the threat of nuclear war during and after the Cold War. Given this intuitive understanding of what security means to individuals, we can say that there are three routes to security: An actor in world politics is secure if it is reasonably confident that no one wants to attack it, *or* if it is capable of deterring (preventing) an attack, *or* if it believes it can defeat the enemy at an acceptable cost if deterrence fails.[2]

Security has both an objective and a subjective component. An actor's **objective security** depends on whether and how much another actor can hurt him and intends to hurt him. Thus, an actor's operational environment may be more or less safe for him, regardless of how he perceives it. For example, an increase in Pakistan's ballistic missile capability increases to some extent the objective danger to India, especially given the two countries' long history of war and the possibility that a war between them could begin accidentally. More important, though, is whether Pakistani leaders intend to use such a capability coercively against India. They could have acquired a new generation of ballistic missiles for an unrelated reason, such as to enhance their regional prestige, or primarily to deter or coerce some state other than India. The problem is that one actor rarely knows fully the incentives or plans of another. Typically, the best an actor can do is make educated guesses about the likely behavior of another actor. Given their past experience with Pakistan, Indian leaders may fear the worst about the plans for the new missiles, interpreting ambiguous information as indicating hostile Pakistani intent.

Subjective security is far more open-ended than objective security because there are no inherent limits on "how safe" people may want to feel, nor on the stakes they decide to protect. Consequently, what it takes to make people feel secure varies a good deal in breadth and substance across time and space, depending on the political and cultural context in which politics takes place. People's subjective sense of security depends on two factors: the degree to which they prefer security as compared to other objectives, and the degree to which they see others as threatening. Since complete safety is rarely possible, the usual question is how much an actor is willing to pay to gain additional increments of safety.[3] Many security debates within societies turn on this issue. For example, for almost twenty years beginning in the early 1980s, Israeli troops occupied a narrow band of southern Lebanon to keep Islamic fundamentalist guerrillas from shelling settlements in northern Israel. With every military casualty, public support in Israel for keeping the troops in Lebanon dropped. By late 1998, after seven soldiers had been killed in less than two weeks, even Israel's hard-line foreign minister supported withdrawal. The army chief of staff disagreed, predicting more violence if the troops were withdrawn.[4]

objective security   Actual, as distinct from perceived, security; an actor is objectively secure if no one wants to attack it, or if it can deter a threatened attack, or if it can defeat an actual attack at an acceptable cost.

subjective security
Actors' perceptions about how secure they are.

In an effort to stop guerilla infiltration into Israel from Lebanon, Israel kept a military presence inside Lebanon from 1982 to 2000.

Subjective feelings of security also depend on how threatening the environment is seen to be. Those who see another state as an adversary or see others more generally as menacing will seek to prepare more intensely for war and react more quickly to assumed provocations than those who view the strategic situation less grimly.[5] After World War I, French leaders, claiming that their country still faced danger from Germany, sought additional security guarantees from the other members of the victorious allied coalition, but the allies rejected what they felt were excessive French demands. They argued that they had to evaluate France's relative security for themselves. Having done that, British leaders decided to pursue a more conciliatory policy toward Germany on territorial matters than French officials preferred as a way to build German support for the postwar peace settlement.[6]

The U.S. war in Vietnam reflected an expansive notion of security, one that had only a weak (if any) link to the safety of U.S. territory or its population. It was hard for many Americans at the time (and even more since then) to understand how a very poor and small state such as North Vietnam could be seen as threatening the United States.

At times, the means used to implement foreign and security policies, such as foreign bases and friendly governments in key allies, become objectives in their own right that then seem to require protection. When this occurs, policy makers' security objectives tend to expand significantly. Yet states can also define the stakes they will protect by force in a far more limited and narrow way. Within states as well as across them, people in similar "objective" strategic circumstances often differ in what they seek to protect and the price they will pay for that protection.[7] By the mid-1990s, for example, there was vigorous debate in Germany about whether the country should shed its post–World War II reticence about using force outside German borders and contribute more fully to NATO military missions. Close to fifty years after World War II, many Germans still resisted the idea that security objectives outside their own territory were worth the threat or use of their armed forces.

In thinking about security problems, it is useful to distinguish between **strategic vulnerability** and a **threat.**[8] Vulnerability is some inherent weakness an actor has with respect to its environment. Poland, for instance, has no natural frontiers and thus has historically been vulnerable to invasion from Germany and Russia. A small or geographically isolated state such as Kuwait is likely to be vulnerable to a withdrawal of protection by a larger ally. States such as Japan that lack indigenous energy sources are vulnerable to economic coercion from their energy suppliers. Clearly, absolute security is rare; few (if any) states are completely invulnerable.

A threat, by contrast, is a situation of impending danger, the result of one actor's capacity and intent to harm another. Threats exploit vulnerabilities. The United States—and particularly its air travel industry—has been vulnerable to terrorist attack for years. Even as the response to September 11 reduces that vulnerability, the sense of threat remains far higher than it was before. Insecurity thus reflects a combination of an actor's vulnerabilities and the threats perceived by policy makers.[9] A state with few or minor geographical, economic, or sociopolitical weaknesses leaves adversaries little to exploit. On the other hand, even a highly vulnerable state may enjoy high subjective security if no adversary seeks to exploit those weaknesses. In such a case, the strategic importance of military power will be quite low.

Having defined security as an issue area, we can now examine the distinctive features that characterize the issues involved. Four features stand out.[10] First, security issues are capable of raising unusually high stakes for leaders and citizens. Unless a society's people, territory, and other critical values are judged to be safe, it is hard for either policy makers or ordinary citizens to focus on other political problems and issues. This comment should not be taken to mean that economic, environmental, or human-rights issues typically carry low stakes. But a threat to use force indicates that an important line has been crossed between typical interstate interaction and something much more coercive in nature. As such, when one or more actors tries to use military force as a source of power, who prevails often has major implications for policies and values people care about. Moreover, war itself carries very high and often unpredictable costs and risks.

Second, actors seldom use force or threaten force unless they believe their objectives are incompatible. Consequently, decisions involving the acquisition, threat, and use of military force are not only high-stakes issues; they are also distinctively competitive in nature. It is difficult, though not impossible, for adversaries to pursue mutually advantageous military policies. As Robert Jervis put it, "because military power meets its test in clashes between states, it is relative, not absolute."[11] There is one important exception to this generalization. The effects of some weapons are considered to be so horrible that the only purpose in having them is to deter others from using them. In such a situation, the relevant strategic question is *not* whether you have more weapons than your adversary, but whether you have enough to deter them. When it comes to nuclear weapons, this perspective has led some analysts to argue in favor of a security standard that stresses **second-strike nuclear forces.** Having enough second-strike forces to inflict unacceptably high levels of damage on an aggressor (called a "second-strike capability") is considered by many to be the essential precondition for stable deterrence. Advocates of this second-strike standard argue that states can feel safe from attack if no adversary can wipe out their nuclear arsenal in a first strike. (In nuclear strategy, an initiator's attack is called the "first strike" and the victim's response to the attack, a

strategic vulnerability The inherent weakness or strength of an actor's situation *if* it is attacked; actors that are vulnerable may still be relatively secure if no powerful actors want to attack them.

threat A situation of impending danger when an actor has both the power and intent (expressed or implied) to harm another.

second-strike nuclear forces Nuclear weapons designed and deployed in ways that make it possible for them to survive a surprise nuclear attack.

"second strike.") Policy makers who try to achieve security by building a second-strike capability will not feel a need to match the deployments of other nuclear-weapons states once they believe that their own arsenal can absorb a first strike and still be capable of unleashing an unacceptable level of damage in response. As we will see later in this chapter, there are other security situations in which the actors involved can agree that some form of regulation is preferable to unrestrained military competition. While these are important exceptions, policy makers generally believe that they need to have more or better military capabilities than their likely opponents.

A third characteristic of security issues is that they often aren't transparent. **Transparency** refers to an outsider's ability to know in a timely manner what some actor is doing. While governments and non-state actors alike often try to conceal many of their actions from others, concealment and deception are most typical of military policy, in which knowledge about capabilities and plans is presumed to benefit an opponent directly. As a result, leaders often cannot predict the forces they will face in battle or estimate accurately beforehand an enemy's will to fight.[12] The resulting uncertainty often increases pressures on political and military leaders to overcompensate by acquiring more military capabilities than they would otherwise claim to need. Ronald Reagan's well-known "trust but verify" refrain makes this problem of uncertainty clear. Policy makers seldom consider mutual restraints on arms production or deployments unless measures to force adequate transparency are built carefully and explicitly into the prospective treaty.

The **security dilemma** can be a fourth distinctive characteristic of security issues. The policies by which leaders try to protect their states *may* have the effect of making others feel less secure, even if that was not the intention behind the policy. For example, a powerful navy guaranteed British freedom of navigation and commerce during its imperial era, but that same navy also constituted a standing threat to disrupt the trade of any state with which Britain was at war. What Israeli officials see as the quick-reaction forces they need to avoid a prolonged war with more numerous opponents, those opponents perceive as a threat to their own safety. When actors' objectives are highly incompatible, such inferences may be quite logical. Because attack can be a militarily efficient way to pursue security, because many weapons can be used both to attack and defend against attacks, and because leaders' objectives can change more quickly than their military capabilities, policy makers often infer one another's objectives from their military capabilities.

Security dilemmas are a common international phenomenon because there is no legal authority above the level of sovereign states that can enforce interstate agreements. Within domestic society, people can take various measures to make themselves and their property safer without endangering others; they can purchase auto, home, or office alarms, relocate to a safer neighborhood, or hire a private security service. There is often no reason (and no way) for them to protect themselves by *pursuing* people they might fear, except for those who are actually intruders—and doing so is often illegal. By contrast, because there is no international government or police force, officials must protect their states from whatever threats they see and however they think necessary. Consequently, in an effort to protect what they have, they *may* act in ways that policy makers in other states see as offensive rather than defensive. The resulting dilemma is that security rivalries *may* leave policy makers without any good policy options. When one state increases its arms, its opponents

transparency An outsider's ability to know what an actor is doing quickly enough to make well-informed choices.

security dilemma A situation in which one actor's efforts to increase its security decreases the security of others, even when the first actor's choices reflected defensive motives.

*may** feel compelled to respond in kind, even though doing so will not necessarily increase the second state's security. Why would they do this? Since the specific purpose behind the first state's action in acquiring a new weapon is often unclear to the second state, that purpose is often inferred from the first state's military capabilities. For analysts in the realist tradition, much of international power politics stems from this ultimately futile attempt to find security through competitive policies.[13]

Actors in a security dilemma are often driven by the fear that a cooperative policy will yield a "sucker's payoff"—which happens when one actor behaves cooperatively while the other behaves competitively—rather than a jointly cooperative outcome. Except in situations like a game of "Chicken," where jointly competitive choices produce disaster, the sucker's payoff is the worst result an actor can experience. And even in Chicken—which many analysts think is similar to *brinkmanship* in world politics—the unattractiveness of the sucker's payoff may at times keep people from backing down in a confrontation. (The formal characteristics of the game of Chicken and the value and limitations of other situations commonly analyzed using *game theory* are discussed in Chapter 16.)

But the fear that cooperative security strategies will lead to a sucker's payoff may be unfounded or exaggerated in particular cases. Unless an opponent is irrevocably committed to aggression, it may make sense to reduce that actor's incentives to use coercion by taking his security and diplomatic objectives into account. To the extent that one actor believes that another actor values the benefits of a jointly cooperative outcome, the first actor has little reason to fear the sucker's payoff outcome. In such a situation, an actor is far more likely to cooperate by restraining his own security policies. If everyone involved comes to hold such a view, a severe security dilemma can be avoided.

Security, then, amounts to reasonable confidence that an actor's values and objectives can be protected. Protection consists of assessing one's known vulnerabilities and cutting to an acceptable level the risk that they can be exploited.[14] To do this, policy makers must ask whether effective means of protection are available at a cost domestic actors are willing to pay. Since one common means of protection is force, security as an issue in world politics, according to Lawrence Freedman, "addresses questions of force: how to spot it, stop it, resist it, and occasionally threaten and even use it."[15] In the next section, we discuss what objectives military force is used to achieve and how actors try to control it.

The Uses of Military Force

Military force is distinct in at least two ways from such other foreign-policy tools as diplomacy, economic assistance, economic sanctions, and espionage. First, the armed forces are the only policy instruments designed primarily for conflict with

---

*Note that the word "may" has been italicized several times in the previous two paragraphs. While some security rivalries *are* severe and thus very difficult to resolve, not all are. If actors' objectives are even somewhat compatible, the dilemma just discussed can be softened, perhaps considerably. In its extreme form, the security dilemma is driven largely by a fear that if one restrains one's own behavior—for example, by not reacting competitively to the other's arms buildup—the other actor will exploit that moderation by acting coercively.

8.1 ENDURING PATTERNS

The connection between power and preferences

The more incompatible actors' preferences, the more strategically important their relative power positions.

The impact of varying beliefs about just relationships

If people think an outcome or procedure is unjust, they are far more likely to oppose it.

The effect of the shadow of the future

The more incompatible people expect their preferences to become over time, the more competitive and power-based their strategic choices are likely to be.

The impact of linkage politics

World politics is driven by the interaction of international, factional and constituency politics.

Security's Distinctive Mix: Palestinians and Israel; India and Pakistan; China and Taiwan

The Arab-Israeli conflict, the confrontation between India and Pakistan over Kashmir, and the dispute over sovereignty between the People's Republic of China and Taiwan have very different historical origins and linked international and domestic contexts. However, while they differ greatly in the substance of the facts, all three share a critical similarity: the distinctly difficult mix of incentives in the politics of strategic choice that characterize enduring security disputes.

- The strategic importance of power is high because a security issue wouldn't exist unless actors had incompatible preferences.

- Security issues almost always involve overt or implicit threats of force which are seldom, if ever, seen as legitimate by their targets.

- Current threats to an actor's security are usually taken as evidence of future danger.

- It is easier to defuse disputes in the international arena if there are political incentives to reach an accommodation. However, perceived security threats usually make accommodation politically dangerous.

In all three confrontations, the range of possible international arrangements that are jointly acceptable from the perspective of the actors' preferences is very small. The actors also have very different views about just outcomes and legitimate procedures for guiding their negotiations. Finally, their evaluations of the shadow of the future are different, leading them to evaluate the security implications of different options differently. Linkage politics compounds all these problems. Even if coalitions of policy makers on both sides of these three disputes find arrangements that are jointly acceptable internationally, it is not at all clear that they will be able to sell those arrangements to their key constituents.

The enduring patterns reveal the political dynamics that make it hard to settle these security conflicts. Knowledge of the substance of the unique contexts of each dispute provides the insight necessary to imagine how one might move toward peace by changing the values of the key variables in those patterns.

other states. For example, only through military means can one state physically take control of the territory of another.[16] Second, force is usually a blunt instrument. Its coercive nature makes it hard for actors to use military instruments to achieve limited objectives, persuade in subtle ways, or achieve jointly legitimate outcomes.

What kinds of objectives, then, can force be used to accomplish? To address this question, it helps to begin by distinguishing between the *physical* and *non-physical* uses of military force. Force is used physically when an actor captures or damages some asset of another actor. Seizure of territory, missile or bomber attacks designed to retaliate for terrorist operations, and the defense of one's territory from military invasion or attack all illustrate the physical use of military force. Force is used peacefully when policy makers threaten to use it physically or when, simply by its availability, it accomplishes the same objective.[17] When NATO forces are used to patrol truce lines in a civil war, or when U.S. warships deliberately sail into a state's coastal waters to signal a rejection of that state's claim to a wide slice of the ocean as its territorial waters, force is being used peacefully. Much of the strategic bargaining and signaling that states conduct with the instruments of force—such as putting military forces visibly on a higher state of alert or placing an aircraft carrier off the coast of a state that is threatening a neighbor—occurs without any physical use of force. In such cases, armaments are prominently displayed in order to send a signal about their *potential use*—an outcome that may or may not occur, depending on the actors' subsequent choices as they interact. Within these two categories, force is used for three major purposes: deterrence, compellence, and defense.

Deterrence

Deterrence involves the non-physical use of force. **Deterrence** consists of a threat by actor A to retaliate if actor B does something that actor A considers unacceptable. During the Cold War, the United States tried to prevent Soviet military action against Western Europe by threatening nuclear and conventional retaliation against Soviet targets. Today, Israel uses its potent conventional forces, openly displayed, and its nuclear weapons, hidden but widely suspected to exist, to convince its adversaries that any military action that could lead to Israel's defeat would be a costly mistake. Deterrent threats are made so they *don't have to be carried out;* if force is used following the issuance of a deterrent threat, that threat, by definition, has failed. However, analysts cannot say with assurance that a deterrent threat has "succeeded" unless they *know* why policy makers in another state refrained from doing something. Because it is very difficult to explain why something has *not* happened, analysts are usually limited to concluding that deterrence either has or has not failed.**

All else being equal, deterrence is least likely to fail when the actor issuing a threat has the capability to retaliate effectively and the commitment to do so is seen as credible. *Capability* in this sense includes adequate military strength but is broader than that; military forces must be visibly ready to destroy assets that the target of the threat particularly values. During the late 1970s, for instance, U.S. officials concluded that American nuclear-weapons doctrine, which emphasized the destruction

deterrence   Threats of force to prevent actors from doing something they would otherwise do; for deterrence to work, there must be *both* a credible threat and a jointly acceptable peaceful alternative.

**Policy makers who want to justify their actions may argue that a deterrent threat that is not followed by a use of force is the same as success, but this may not be the case. The target of the deterrent threat may have refrained from challenging it for reasons that have little to do with the threat.

Even though the United States kept thousands of nuclear weapons—such as the Tomahawk cruise missiles stored in these silos at the Greenham Common airbase in England—in Western Europe during the Cold War to protect its NATO allies, many people held doubts about America's willingness to use them in the event of war.

of a certain proportion of the Soviet industrial base if Moscow attacked NATO allies, had failed to identify the best targets. It was important, U.S. officials reasoned, to put at risk assets that Soviet political and military leaders valued most highly. Thus, a greater proportion of U.S. weapons were gradually aimed at Soviet Communist Party headquarters, installations used by the KGB (the Soviet secret police), and those industrial assets that would be used to sustain Soviet forces in a war, on the grounds that these were the assets Soviet leaders valued the most.[18]

Credible commitments are those that policy makers in the target state believe *will* be honored, even at some substantial cost to the actor that makes them. Would a state, for example, really use nuclear weapons to retaliate for an attack on an ally at the possible risk of its own destruction? This problem threatened NATO's cohesion during the Cold War, when there were widespread doubts that U.S. promises to protect Europe would be honored in a crisis, and it was one reason that French officials left NATO's integrated military command in 1966. Other analysts, however, argued that the problem of deterrent credibility had been exaggerated. Unless a potential challenger was very highly insensitive to costs and risks, they said, even a moderate likelihood that a potent deterrent threat would be carried out should be enough to prevent a challenge from taking place.[19]***

Finally, it is crucial to remember that even credible deterrent threats will fail if the actors who are challenging the status quo believe that achieving their desired objective is worth the risk. For deterrence to succeed, there must be more than a credible threat; there must also be a jointly acceptable peaceful alternative.

***This reasoning helps to explain why suggestions that NATO should give up the option to use nuclear weapons first typically meet strong resistance within the alliance. In 1998, Germany's new Social Democratic foreign minister made such a proposal, arguing that it would make the Western position against the spread of nuclear weapons more believable by decreasing the West's own reliance on them. Critics argued that such a change in official policy could remove enough of the uncertainty about retaliation that nuclear or biological attacks on the United States or other Western countries might become less risky and thus likelier. (See "Continuity Please—Or Else," *The Economist*, December 5, 1998, p. 23.)

Compellence (Coercive Diplomacy)

Compellence (also known as **coercive diplomacy**) can involve either the non-physical or physical use of force. Here, instead of trying to *prevent* something from happening (deterrence), an actor tries to *make* something happen by using force or the threat of force to induce someone to *change* his behavior in a certain way. When U.S. leaders positioned forces in the Persian Gulf to strike Iraqi targets unless Iraq allowed UN weapons inspectors free access to suspected weapons sites, compellence was taking place just as much as if the forces were being used physically. In situations like this, it is presumed that the forces *will* be used physically unless and until an actor's demands are met. As Thomas Schelling put it, compellence "usually involves initiating an action . . . that can cease, or become harmless, only if the opponent responds."[20] Of course, whether the target responds in a way that the initiator thinks is satisfactory depends not just on how much coercion is applied but also on what incentives the target has to resist.

The critical difference between deterrence and compellence is between the passive and active use of force. Deterrence is passive; once a deterrent threat is made, nothing happens unless it is challenged. Compellence is more active; coercion tends to be applied *until* behavior changes. Thus, while deterrence may be easier to achieve than compellence (since the target does not have to back down publicly), demonstrating that it has worked is harder (because we usually have no way of knowing that the threat produced the behavior).

Defense

A third purpose for which military force is used is **defense.** Here, force is used physically to repel an attack or to strike first if policy makers believe an attack is imminent or inevitable. The distinction between defense and compellence has mainly to do with the point at which another actor's behavior is resisted. The objective in defense is to reverse an ongoing attack or stop an imminent one from occurring. Compellence seeks instead to *reverse* an existing state of affairs that would otherwise be a *fait accompli*, such as Soviet missiles that would otherwise have remained in Cuba or Iraqi troops that would otherwise have stayed in Kuwait.

Defense is possible without a capacity to deter, and deterrence may be achievable even when defense is not.[21] A state can have the military capacity to repel an invasion without being able to threaten enough devastation to inhibit an attack in the first place. Conversely, while nuclear deterrence seems to be effective, there is as yet no successful defense against incoming nuclear-armed ballistic missiles. Policy makers typically prefer a capacity to defend their key possessions and values from external threats, since that would take care of their vulnerability and make any threatening intentions less relevant. But if defense is not possible—as is the case with nuclear, biological, and chemical weapons—a capacity to deter typically becomes the objective when responding to threats and vulnerabilities involving state actors.

Even though nearly every state maintains some military forces for defense or retaliation, most policy makers are aware that these forces can have undesired consequences. They can, for example, trigger an accident that could lead to war. In December 1998, an armed anti-aircraft missile was accidentally launched from South Korea near the border with North Korea—the most heavily fortified border in the contemporary world. In a context this tense, North Korean leaders or military

compellence (or coercive diplomacy) The use or threatened use of force to make actors change their behavior.

defense The use of force to physically stop an ongoing or imminent attack.

The United States and the Decision to Build a National Missile Defense

In the fall of 2001, the U.S. Congress voted to fund work on a national ballistic missile defense system (NMD). While domestic opposition to this decision virtually disappeared in the United States after the September 11 terrorist attacks, George W. Bush had been on record in support of building a national missile defense in spite of widespread domestic and international criticism since the presidential campaign a year before.

A brief case study of this decision can be found at **www.prenhall.com/lamborn**. As you review this case, consider how the arguments for and against trying to build a national missile defense system are related to the debates about the relationship between mutual vulnerability and security during the Cold War. How did the relationship between vulnerability and security—and the relative importance of deterrence and defense—change with the end of the Cold War and the shift from fears of superpower conflict to fears of attack by rogue states and terrorists? Why, even with these changes, did many of the most important government leaders in Europe and Asia continue to oppose the development of a national missile defense? How did domestic politics in the United States affect the mix of incentives the Bush administration had for going forward with its announced intention to build an NMD system? Finally, what does this case suggest about the impact on the politics of choice of uncertainty about the reliability of complicated technologies, other actors' intentions, and the sources of successful deterrence?

officers could have interpreted the launch as part of an attack. Just as military forces can create the potential for accidents, they can also, as we have discussed, contribute to severe security dilemmas. The competition for better or more weapons can make the actors less secure (and poorer) than they would otherwise have been, even if it does not lead to war. For reasons such as these, *controlling* the instruments of force may help to contain conflict in world politics.

Security through Arms Control and Disarmament

arms control   Multilateral efforts to mutually limit the development, deployment, or use of weapons.

disarmament   Efforts to eliminate a particular type of weapon. Used by itself, the term typically refers to multilateral efforts toward mutual disarmament; when single states decide to disarm, regardless of what other actors do, it's called unilateral disarmament.

Arms control consists of procedures that limit the development, deployment, or use of weapons. The quantity of weapons, their design features, or both can be affected.[22] Such measures are designed to reduce the degree to which military forces may invite rather than inhibit attack and, somewhat secondarily, to restrain their destructiveness and costs. Whereas **disarmament** seeks to eliminate certain armaments altogether, efforts to *control* arms assume that weapons are necessary for security, but that some configurations of forces are less provocative or destabilizing than others. Just as state *A*'s weapons are a response to the vulnerabilities and threats its leaders perceive, *B*'s weapons are likely, in part, to be a response to those of *A*. Keeping the action-reaction portion of this process within limits is the central rationale for arms control.[23] The resulting policies thus tend to have at least one of these purposes: reducing the likelihood of war; limiting the scope or violence of a war if it occurs; reducing the costs of preparing for war.[24] These concerns have become more pressing as the destructiveness, speed, and cost of weapons have escalated during the twentieth century.

As the previous paragraph indicates, when actors are confronting an international strategic context that is highly conflictual, the major purpose of arms control is to stabilize their military relationship. Such stability makes it less likely that a war will break out inadvertently. A military relationship is far more stable when no set of policy makers believes a major military advantage can be gained from a **preemptive attack**—that is, from attacking an adversary first in the expectation that he will attack you imminently. The key danger is that such an expectation may be wrong—that is, the adversary had no intention of attacking in the first place. Arms control can reduce this danger by making it relatively less attractive to strike first rather than second and by convincing policy makers that they will not lose their arsenal if they pause before responding to the very first evidence that they have been attacked. By removing the element of "hair-trigger" actions from decisions to go to war, the likelihood of inadvertent war is reduced. In this way, even very incompatible actors can realize that they are *mutually* better off when their forces appear able to withstand a first blow, but are still capable of promising a credible deterrent response by delivering a crushing second strike. Since aggressors often see a political advantage in claiming that they are attacking first for purely defensive reasons, claims that an attack is preemptive are often viewed suspiciously.

Two conditions are necessary for arms control to succeed in reducing inadvertent wars. First, the actors involved must agree that war is the worst result they could face. They then have incentives to reduce the risk that either side will defect and break the agreement. This is likeliest when both sides have nuclear weapons. For this reason, U.S. and Soviet leaders took a number of steps beginning in the early 1960s to reduce the incentives to strike first. They put their ballistic missiles underground or on submarines, where they were harder to destroy than if they were above ground. In the 1972 Antiballistic Missile (ABM) Treaty, they agreed to ban any programs that might allow one side, but not the other, to construct defenses against incoming ballistic missiles. Most recently, in the second Strategic Arms Reduction Treaty (START II), they agreed to ban land-based ballistic missiles with more than one nuclear warhead, on the grounds that these would be most useful *if* one side wanted to destroy the other's arsenal in a preemptive attack. (When each missile carries just one or a few warheads instead of many, it becomes less attractive to risk using it in an attack than if each individual missile can be used simultaneously to hit many targets.) A second condition is that each side must *want* the adversary's forces to be hard to attack preemptively. This is a difficult requirement to fulfill when the states involved are fierce competitors, since they may feel that the effectiveness of their deterrent commitments requires a militarily vulnerable adversary. If so, each is likely to be more concerned that the other would use any invulnerability it achieved from arms control to commit other forms of aggression.[25]

preemptive attack
Situations in which actors, believing they are about to be attacked, strike first to gain a military advantage.

During the Cold War, Soviet-American competitiveness made the second condition for reducing inadvertent war hard to satisfy. With the Cold War's end, this condition is far easier to meet. With the collapse of the Soviet Union, U.S. officials worry that Russia's decaying strategic warning system might not be able to distinguish between an innocent missile launch and a military attack. This is no idle concern. In 1995, Russian military commanders misread data from the launch of a Norwegian scientific rocket as a sign of a possible attack from submarine-launched missiles. As a result, the United States is now using its satellite warning systems to notify Russian leaders about missile launches anywhere in the world.[26]

Limiting the scope or violence of war if it occurs is a second purpose of arms control. This strategy has most often been followed on a regional level. One of the more far-reaching efforts to limit the geographic scope of war has been the creation of nuclear-weapons-free zones (NWFZs) in Latin America, the South Pacific, and Africa. All states in the respective regions have signed the 1974 Treaty of Tlatelolco for a Latin American NWFZ, the 1985 Treaty of Rarotonga that created a South Pacific NWFZ, and the 1995 Treaty for an African NWFZ. Each of the officially declared nuclear-weapons states except India (the United States, Russia, China, France, and Britain) has pledged to respect these accords. Participants are committed to refrain from acquiring nuclear weapons (a pledge also provided by the Nuclear Nonproliferation Treaty, or NPT) and to refrain from storing such weapons on their territories. Proposals have also been made for NWFZs that would cover the Middle East and a broad area of Eastern Europe and the former Soviet Union. Were all of these areas to become NWFZs, much of the globe would be off-limits to nuclear weapons.

One ambitious effort to limit the destructiveness of war, the Chemical Weapons Convention (CWC), reached fruition in the 1990s. It prohibits the manufacture, acquisition, possession, and use of *chemical weapons*, which are gaseous, liquid, or solid chemical substances used to poison or asphyxiate humans and other living things. Examples include nerve agents (which come from the same family as insecticides), blister agents (which burn and blister the skin soon after exposure), and blood agents (which enter the body through the respiratory system, causing death by interfering with the use of oxygen by tissues). After terrible experience with these substances on the battlefields of World War I, the 1925 Geneva Protocol banned their use in war. But neither their production nor stockpiling was banned, and Italy used them in Ethiopia during the 1930s. When Iraq used them against poorly equipped Iranian soldiers during the war between those countries in the 1980s, heavy casualties resulted, and some suspected that Iran's request for a cease-fire was a direct result.[27] Fearful that other actors might see chemical weapons as an attractive "equalizer" on the battlefield, global negotiations to ban their production and use accelerated. The CWC was completed in 1992 and came into force in 1997. Of special interest in this treaty are its verification provisions, the most demanding ever for a security agreement of global scope. Not only must the signatories declare and dispose of their chemical armaments; signatories can be inspected on 120 hours notice to determine whether they have complied. While these provisions allow signatories to keep industrial secrets away from the inspectors, access to suspected weapons production and storage sites should suffice to detect any major breaches of the accord.[28]

When mutually agreed-upon arms reductions can be achieved, all the actors can enjoy the same level of security as before for less money. Nevertheless, cutting costs often tends in practice to be a fairly weak incentive for arms control. The savings that would result from canceling specific weapons systems or building a few less planes, ships, or tanks tend to be relatively slight. In a military budget of $250 billion per year, for example, few Americans would be likely to notice the effects of such reductions in terms either of reduced taxes or more money for other public purposes. But incentives to cut military costs tend to increase when the competition for budgetary resources is tight. In late 1998, for instance, a number of U.S. military and civilian officials argued for unilateral cuts in the nation's nuclear arsenal, on the grounds that a lot of money was being spent on weapons that the United States had already agreed to scrap under the START II accord with Russia. Keeping more nuclear weapons than are needed, it was claimed, made it difficult to modernize weapons systems that should be retained, as well as harder to fund other security needs such as fighting terrorism and maintaining an ability to intervene in ethnic conflicts.[29]

For arms control policies to be sustainable, the diplomatic and domestic incentives must coincide. These conditions are not easily or often met among actors that are adversaries, as you have probably realized. Most important, perhaps, policy makers who would find arms control attractive for one of the reasons just discussed may not trust the other parties enough to go ahead with an accord. As our discussion of the politics of strategic choice would lead you to expect, the time when wars begin and end depends largely on the compatibility of leaders' objectives—not primarily on whether vulnerable weapons systems spark preemptive attacks or tremendous suffering is occurring on some battlefield. Arms control thus has a limited strategic purpose: to reduce the *specific problems* caused by weapons systems *aggravating* existing political incompatibilities. Yet even if leaders recognize this purpose, key domestic factions must have incentives that reinforce these strategic motivations. As with any substantial public project, arms expenditures create a set of benefits that strengthen or even create key constituencies. Military personnel, contractors, military research laboratories—not to mention the communities that these sets of organized interests support—typically develop a stake in existing and projected arms projects. Arms control thus vividly illustrates the possibilities and limits imposed by linkage politics.

Over the course of the twentieth century, as weapons became much more numerous and destructive, those trends fueled efforts to limit the production and deployment of various types of weapons, some in specific locations. As Table 8–1 indicates, many, though not all, efforts to control armaments have focused on weapons of mass destruction.

From our discussion so far, you have seen that while actors' security concerns usually have an objective component, they tend at least as much to be a state of mind. An actor can't be hurt unless someone else has the capacity to hurt him, which requires that he has some weakness that can be exploited. But how an actor views such risks also depends on two other factors: what he considers an acceptable and achievable level of safety, and what he believes about others' intentions toward him. Military force can be part of a solution for such problems, but it can also be part of the problem itself. For many years, the way in which analysts thought about these issues was conditioned by the Cold War. The contemporary security environment, however, is quite different. Consequently, the quest for security in today's world raises distinctive concerns.

TABLE 8–1   MAJOR ARMS CONTROL TREATIES

Year	Treaty	Intent of Treaty
1959	Antarctic Treaty	Treaty signatories agreed that Antarctica should be restricted to peaceful purposes only and prohibited any measures of a military nature other than scientific investigation from being carried out on the continent.
1963	Limited Test Ban Treaty	Treaty signatories agreed to prohibit nuclear weapons testing and the release of radioactive fallout into the atmosphere, into outer space, and under water by any means. The treaty does not ban underground testing, and while permitting nuclear testing within the territorial boundaries of a state, it prohibits nuclear testing if radioactive debris violates state territorial boundaries.
1967	Outer Space Treaty	Treaty signatories sought to restrict the exploration and use of outer space to projects that benefit all humankind, to ensure that it could not be subject to national appropriation by claims of sovereignty, and to prohibit the placement of nuclear weapons or other weapons of mass destruction in outer space.
1967	Treaty of Tlatelolco (Treaty for the Prohibition of Nuclear Weapons in Latin America)	Treaty signatories agreed to exclude the testing, use, manufacture, production, and acquisition of any nuclear material for anything except peaceful purposes.
1968	Treaty on Non-Proliferation of Nuclear Weapons	The five acknowledged nuclear states (the United States, the Soviet Union, the United Kingdom, France, and China) agreed not to transfer nuclear weapons, other nuclear devices, or their nuclear technology to non-nuclear weapons states. Other non-nuclear signatories agreed not to acquire or produce nuclear weapons or explosive devices.
1971	Seabed Arms Control Treaty	The treaty prohibits parties from placing nuclear weapons and other weapons of mass destruction on the seabed and/or ocean floor beyond their 12-mile coastal zone.
1972	SALT I (Strategic Arms Limitations Talks)	SALT I talks, which began in November 1969, culminated with the signing of The Antiballistic Missile Treaty (ABM) and the Interim Agreement on the Limitation of Strategic Offensive Arms in May 1972 by the United States and the Soviet Union.
1972	Antiballistic Missile Treaty and Protocols (ABM)	The United States and the Soviet Union agreed to severely constrain their ability to deploy antiballistic missile defense systems and to limit their ballistic missile defense deployments to two sites per treaty partner.
1972	Interim Agreement on the Limitation of Strategic Offensive Arms	The United States and the Soviet Union agreed to limit both the number and type of land-based and sea-based strategic missile launchers already existing or under construction, but allowed for improvement of those already existing, with the option to extend the agreement.
1975	Biological Weapons Convention	The parties agreed not to develop, produce, stockpile, or acquire biological agents or toxins as weapons of war.
1979	SALT II Agreement	The United States and the Soviet Union for the first time agreed on the total number of strategic launchers and set precise limits on the total number of U.S. strategic bombers. It also provided for the destruction of all launchers above the allowed limits.
1991, 1992	START I and associated Protocols	Parties agreed to reduce strategic offensive arms to equal aggregate levels, over three phases to be carried out over seven years, with specific interim target levels for reductions for each phase.
1993	Chemical Weapons Convention	The treaty bans the production, acquisition, stockpiling, transfer, and use of chemical weapons by parties and provides for the monitoring of commercial facilities that produce, process, or consume dual-use chemicals to ensure that they are not diverted for any prohibited purposes. In addition, each party agrees to destroy any existing chemical weapons and to destroy any chemical weapons production facilities it owns or possesses. Finally, the treaty penalizes non-signatories by prohibiting their access to certain treaty-controlled chemicals.
1993, 1996 and 2000	START II (Strategic Arms Reduction Treaty II)	The intent of the treaty is to eliminate heavy intercontinental ballistic missiles (ICBMs) and all other multiple-warhead (MIRVed) ICBMs. It is also intended to reduce by two-thirds below pre-START levels the number of strategic nuclear weapons deployed by both countries.
1996	Comprehensive Test Ban Treaty	The treaty prohibits nuclear explosions, whether for peaceful purposes or not, and establishes an organization to ensure the implementation of the treaty.
Pending	START III	START III would limit, by December 2007, each of the parties to a maximum of 2000–2500 strategic nuclear weapons for each party, and would include increased transparency measures for inventory verification and/or destruction.

Sources: Most of the information came from the website for the United States Department of State (*http:www.state.gov/*). Information on the Comprehensive Test Ban Treaty and the Chemical Weapons Convention came from the website for the Council for a Livable World Education Fund (*http:www.clw.org/*).

The Contemporary Security Environment

As we said at the beginning of this chapter, today's global security environment represents a complex mix of three intertwined features: the rise of regional disputes since the end of the Cold War, the reintroduction of a global security agenda with the campaign against terrorist networks, and the centuries-old question of how Western and Islamic culture can nurture mutually legitimate relationships. These intertwined features affect three of the most important contemporary security issues: the proliferation of weapons of mass destruction, terrorism, and ethnic conflict. The discussion here focuses on how these three contemporary security issues and the growth in regional conflict have created distinctive security problems.

The Diffusion of Security Rivalries and the Rise of Regionalism

It is useful to recall that once the Cold War ratcheted up in the late 1940s, it was pretty intense and all-encompassing. As you saw in Chapter 7, Soviet and American policy makers wanted to create a set of global arrangements after World War II that reflected their domestic economic and political institutions. The problem was that those institutions and the visions that they reflected were incompatible. As a result, with a few exceptions such as limited nuclear arms control and joint opposition to nuclear proliferation, Soviet and U.S. officials opposed one another vigorously on most international issues from the late 1940s to late 1980s. What Soviet officials proposed (such as the neutralization of American-allied West Germany) U.S. leaders tended to reject, and what U.S. leaders favored (such as genuine elections in Eastern Europe) Soviet leaders typically dismissed. World politics tended to be characterized by opposition across the two blocs, and countries in Africa, Asia, the Middle East, and Latin America became zones for competition between the United States and the Soviet Union.

This intense rivalry had three major causes. First, as just noted, Soviet and American leaders were trying to achieve very different kinds of international environments. Thus, whether a state had a communist or a capitalist system was typically taken as a sign of whether Moscow or Washington had jumped ahead in the global competition for influence. To protect themselves from subversion or attack by the opposing bloc, the smaller capitalist and communist states tended to be allied either with the United States or the Soviet Union, respectively. A non-aligned group of states existed from the 1950s on, but Washington and Moscow each kept a distinct set of friends and clients. The U.S.-Soviet competition instigated this rivalry. Because their disagreements were so fundamental, Soviet and American officials defined their relationship in terms of the ability to deter and, if necessary, compel behavioral changes in the other. As they accumulated vast military arsenals, a severe security dilemma developed: Each set of leaders used its arms to try to control the other, which in turn fed the other's fears and led to further arms development. In this context, allies became military as well as ideological assets, since the members of one's international coalition were expected to fight on one's side in the event of large-scale war. Keeping one's coalition at least as cohesive and strong as one's rival was seen as critical.[30] Finally, linkage politics deepened these antagonisms. The international rivalry was fed by and, in turn, strengthened hard-line constituencies within each society—those most opposed to accommodation with the rival. In

8.2 ENDURING PATTERNS

The connection between preferences and power
The more compatible actors' preferences, the less strategically important their relative power positions.

The effect of the shadow of the future
The more compatible people expect their preferences to become over time, the more cooperative and less power-based their strategic approach is likely to be.

U.S.–Soviet Competition, U.S.–Russian Cooperation

During the Cold War, their incompatible preferences led U.S. and Soviet policy makers to evaluate the impact of security initiatives undertaken by the other side on their relative power positions. With the Cold War's end, and especially after the September 11 attacks on the United States, converging preferences reduced the strategic importance of their relative power positions. Thus it was that Russian president Vladimir Putin took the utterly unprecedented step of supporting the U.S. request to base military personnel in countries north of Afghanistan as part of the campaign against al-Qaeda and the Taliban later in the fall of 2001.

essence, the Cold War was a very concentrated set of mutually reinforcing rivalries and threats among the same actors.

With the end of the Cold War, rivalries have become much more diffuse across different issues and actors. Rarely today do states compete simultaneously over ideology, arms, and allies, as many did during the Cold War. However, as Table 8–2 suggests, many regional disputes create severe security problems for people around the world. Contemporary rivalries are typically located in the Third World and often reflect deep-seated ethnic disputes. In these cases, security dilemmas tend to be intense and very hard to resolve.

Many of the same processes that produced the Cold War—though this time operating in the reverse direction—have contributed to this situation. First, the collapse of the Soviet Union and the fall of communism in Europe eroded global ideological rivalry. While communist states such as Cuba and China still exist, they have either ceased to be Marxist-Leninist in much but name (China) or are so fragile economically that their ideology poses little attraction to outsiders (Cuba). As market capitalism has become the preferred socioeconomic system in more and more places, there are increasingly fewer reasons for states to compete militarily. Second, military competition among the largest states has moderated significantly, reflecting a sense that large-scale, sustained warfare has become obsolete. While this trend developed gradually, it accelerated during the 1990s.[31] Many of the major states have nuclear weapons, making the risk of war unacceptably high. The muting of ideological rivalries has, at the same time, reduced the gains to be achieved from victory in war. It makes little sense to prepare for war against societies with which your people

TABLE 8–2   ENDURING POST–COLD WAR RIVALRIES

Location	Type of Conflict (parties involved in the dispute noted in parentheses)	Duration/Status of Conflict
Afghanistan	civil war	1978–ongoing
Albania	civil violence	1997
Algeria	civil warfare (Islamic Militants)	1991–sporadic
Angola	civil war (UNITA)	1975–ongoing
Azerbaijan	ethnic war (Nagorno-Karabakh)	1990–1997
Azerbaijan, Armenia	international violence	1990–1994
Bangladesh	ethnic war	1975–1997
Bhutan	ethnic violence (Drukpas vs. Nepalese)	1991–1993
Bosnia/Yugoslavia	ethnic war (Serbs, Croats, Muslims)	1992–1996
Burundi	civil violence	1991
Burundi	ethnic warfare (Tutsis vs. Hutus)	1994–ongoing
Cambodia	civil warfare (Khmer Rouge)	1990–1997
Cameroon, Nigeria	international violence	1996
Chad	civil war	1965–1996 with sporadic violence
China	ethnic violence (Uighurs, Kazakhs)	1980–ongoing
China	repression of dissidents	1990–ongoing
Colombia	civil violence	1984–ongoing
Comoros	political violence	1999–sporadic
Congo-Brazzaville	civil warfare (Ninja)	1997–suspended
Congo-Brazzaville	ethnic violence	1993
Congo-Kinshasa, Uganda, Rwanda	poltical, ethnic, and international violence	1999–ongoing
Croatia	civil war	1991
Croatia	ethnic war (Serbs)	1991–1995
Djibouti	civil violence	1991–1994
Ecuador, Peru	international violence	1995
Egypt	civil violence (Islamic Militants)	1991–repressed
Egypt and Libya	international violence	1977–1991
El Salvador	civil war (FMLN)	1979–1992
Ethiopia	ethnic warfare (Eritreans)	1974–1991, 1998–ongoing
Ethiopia	ethnic war (Oromos)	1999–suspended
Georgia	civil war	1991–1993
Georgia	ethnic war (Abkhazians-Ossetians)	1991–1993
Georgia	ethnic warfare (Abkhazia)	1998
Ghana	ethnic violence	1994
Guatemala	repression of indigenous peoples	1966–1996
Guinea-Bissau	revolutionary war	1998–suspended
Haiti	civil violence	1991
India	ethnic war (northeast tribal groups)	1952–sporadic
India	ethnic warfare (Sikhs)	1983–1993
India	ethnic violence (Hindu vs. Muslim)	1991–sporadic
India and Pakistan	ethnic war (Kashmiris)	1990–ongoing
India and Pakistan	international violence	1992
India and Pakistan	international violence	1996–1997
Indonesia	ethnic warfare (Papuan-West Irian Tribes)	1963–1993; 1998–sporadic
Indonesia	ethnic violence (Aceh)	1975–1991
Indonesia	colonial war (East Timor)	1976–1992: 1999–suspended
Indonesia	ethnic rebellion (East Timor, Aceh)	1997–sporadic
Indonesia	ethnic violence (Muslim-Christian)	1999–ongoing
Indonesia	civil violence	1998–sporadic
Iran	civil war	1978–1993
Iraq and Iran	ethnic warfare (Kurds)	1961–1993

TABLE 8–2 (continued)

Location	Type of Conflict (parties involved in the dispute noted in parentheses)	Duration/Status of Conflict
Iraq	ethnic warfare (Kurds)	1996–suspended
Iraq, Kuwait, U.S. (Gulf War)	international violence	1990–1991
Israel	ethnic war (PLO, Arab Palestinians)	1948–ongoing
Kenya	ethnic violence (Kalenjin, Masai, Kikuyu, Luo)	1991–1993
Lebanon	ethnic war (various sects)	1975–1991
Lebanon, Israel	international war	1982–1990
Lesotho	civil violence	1998–suspended
Liberia	civil war (ECOWAS)	1990–1997 with sporadic violence
Mali	ethnic violence (Tuareg)	1990–1991
Mexico	ethnic violence (Chiapas Rebels)	1994–1997
Moldova	ethnic violence (Trans-Dniester Russians)	1991–1997
Mozambique	civil war (RENAMO)	1971–1992
Myanmar	ethnic war (Karn, Shan, and others)	1948–ongoing
Namibia	war of independence (South Africa)	1965–1990
Nepal	political violence	1996–ongoing
Niger	ethnic violence (Azawad and Toubou)	1990–1997
Nigeria	ethnic violence (Muslim-Christian)	1986–1993 with ongoing communal violence
Papua New Guinea	ethnic warfare (Bougainville)	1988–1998
Peru	civil violence (Sendero Luminoso)	1982–1997
Philippines	civil warfare (New Peoples' Army)	1972–ongoing
Philippines	ethnic warfare (Moros)	1972–ongoing
Russia	civil war (Chechnya)	1994–1996; 1999–ongoing
Rwanda	ethnic warfare (Tutsis vs. Hutus)	1990–1994
Rwanda	ethnic violence (Hutu genocide of Tutsis)	1994
Rwanda	ethnic warfare (ousted Hutus vs. Tutsi Regime)	1994–1998
Senegal	ethnic violence (among Casamance separatist groups)	1991–1999
Sierra Leone	civil/ethnic warfare	1991–ongoing
Somalia	civil war (among rival clans and warlords)	1988–sporadic
South Africa	ethnic/civil warfare	1983–1996
Spain	ethnic violence (Basque separatists)	1968–ongoing
Sri Lanka	ethnic war (Tamil separatists)	1983–ongoing
Sudan	ethnic war (Arab/Islamic groups vs. Christian and animist groups)	1983–ongoing
Tajikistan	civil warfare	1992–1997
Turkey	ethnic warfare (Kurds)	1984–ongoing
Uganda	ethnic violence (Langi and Acholi)	1986–sporadic
Uganda	civil violence	1996–1997
United Kingdom	ethnic violence over Northern Ireland	1969–1994
Yemen	warfare (South Yemenis)	1994
Yugoslavia	ethnic war (Kosovar Albanians vs. Serbs)	1998–1999
Zaire	ethnic violence	1992–1996
Zaire (Congo)	civil war	1996–ongoing

Sources: Monty G. Marshall, Center for Systemic Peace, "Major Episodes of political violence 1946–1999" (*http://www.members.aol.com/CSPmgm/ cspframe.htm*). Ted Robert Gurr, Monty G. Marshall, and Deepa Khosla, Integrated Network for Societal Conflict Research (INSCR) Program, "Peace and Conflict 2001: A Global Survey of Armed Conflicts, Self-Determination Movements, and Democracy" (*http://www.bsos.umd.edu/cidcm/peace.htm*).

agree on fundamentals. Finally, nationalist sentiment within the major states is increasingly directed toward economic and social rather than military outlets. Absent a direct attack—such as occurred on September 11—few domestic constituencies appear to regard the use of force abroad as anything but a sometimes necessary evil.

These developments have made rivalry and cooperation in world politics much more issue-, actor-, and situation-specific. During the Cold War, to agree on an issue such as mutual defense typically meant that the states involved cooperated on most other issues. Today, it is harder to predict whether a set of states can agree on common policies on one issue by examining what they've done on some other issue. American and Chinese leaders can agree on economic matters and some security matters while strongly disagreeing on others, such as Chinese human rights policies. Russia and China are substantially friendlier than they were before 1990, though hardly warm allies. Since both rivalry and cooperation tend to be more situation-specific than they used to be, contemporary alliances such as NATO and the Russian-Indian Cooperation Agreement are also looser than before. There is little reason to tie one's policies very closely to others' goals and actions if one is likely to agree with them in some situations but not in others.

As specific issues and situations play a larger role in defining international interactions, it's not surprising that the distinctive features of various regions are making themselves felt more as well. During the Cold War, both the United States and the Soviet Union acted to restrain local wars and insurrections out of fear that they might escalate out of control, perhaps even bringing on inadvertent global war. These incentives vanished with the end of the Cold War. Since 1990, we have seen some of the results: terror and ethnic cleansing in Bosnia and Rwanda went on unimpeded until the participants were exhausted or external help finally arrived.

Of course, governments in Latin America, Africa, and Asia need not be as passive as these particular outcomes imply. With outside intervention less likely, greater responsibility falls on local states to manage their own conflicts. We cannot predict whether they will do so, but there are some encouraging signs. In recent years, several regional IGOs that began as economic bodies, such as the Regional Forum of the Association of Southeast Asian Nations (ASEAN), have begun developing an interest in dealing with security issues in their areas.[32] And in NATO—which has always been a security organization but has traditionally acted on the basis of unanimity among its members—a recent initiative would allow subgroups within the alliance to intervene selectively in conflicts that do not involve defense of members' territories. The idea behind this policy is that the interested parties would be able to act flexibly on their own in humanitarian or peacekeeping situations, without needing approval from the larger group.

While it is important to know that security rivalries among the largest states are more diffuse now than during the Cold War, such an observation gets us only so far. To understand the contemporary politics of security, we must be able to identify and analyze the kinds of security issues that are on policy makers' desks today. If major war and the management of a potentially deadly U.S.-Soviet rivalry are off the agenda, what is on it? We turn next to these questions.

The Proliferation of Weapons of Mass Destruction

Security risks created by the proliferation of **weapons of mass destruction (WMD)** began to receive increased attention with the 1991 Gulf War. The level of attention

weapons of mass destruction (WMD) Nuclear, biological, and chemical weapons capable of killing enormous numbers of people.

skyrocketed after September 11, 2001. Nuclear, chemical, and biological weapons—as compared with ordinary bullets, bombs, and missile warheads—are distinguished by their enormous destructive capability, especially in relation to their size, and by their ability to cause tremendous damage to people and property that are not the direct targets of an attack. **Nuclear weapons** use an atomic fission or fusion process to create enormous heat and blast effects that destroy and irradiate targets. Radioactive fallout from a nuclear explosion can spread over a much greater area than the one affected by the blast and can cause serious illness and deaths for long periods afterward. **Chemical weapons** are poisons that injure, incapacitate, or kill people through their effects on the skin, eyes, lungs, blood, or nerves. **Biological weapons** are microorganisms such as bacteria and viruses that cause lethal diseases in humans and other animals. These substances are typically deadlier than chemical weapons: Laboratory tests on animals indicate that if anthrax spores (a form of disease-causing bacteria) are disseminated widely and then inhaled, ten grams (just over one-third of an ounce) can produce as many casualties as *a ton* (one million grams) of nerve gas.[33] Table 8–3 identifies how each type of WMD attacks human bodies.

Analysts believe that five broad developments have increased states' vulnerabilities to WMD coercion or attacks. First, more actors than before—including dissatisfied ethnic groups within states, terrorist groups, and perhaps even criminal organizations, in addition to states—may be able to get these weapons, particularly biological and chemical arms. The materials and knowledge needed to make many WMD have become easier to acquire. Not only can one find designs for making these weapons on the Internet or in catalogues; many of the products used in chemical and biological weapons can be acquired commercially. This is the problem of **dual-use technologies and products**—those that have both a military and civilian purpose. The same technologies and organisms used to produce pesticides, solvents, and vaccines can be used to manufacture chemical and biological weapons. As we saw earlier in this chapter, this is why the verification provisions of the Chemical Weapons Convention are so strict. (See the box "*A Closer Look:* The Wassenaar Arrangement on Export Controls" on page 246.) Since all of these technologies are old, states such as America and Britain that are established leaders in military technology have no particular advantage in acquiring and using them.[34]

A second reason for increased concern about WMD proliferation is that the means of delivery are now more numerous and even harder to counteract than before. During the Cold War, there was no defense against incoming ballistic missiles. Now, however, bombers or ballistic missiles are no longer needed to carry a weapon to a target; very destructive devices can be carried on small trucks or even in briefcases.

A third source of concern is continued nuclear proliferation. Even though the United States and Russia have dramatically cut their nuclear arsenals since the late 1980s, the fact that they continue to maintain such arsenals at all implies that nuclear weapons still play a role in providing security. As the case study on India's nuclear weapons policy described at the end of the chapter suggests, this may encourage or help to rationalize further proliferation. Moreover, the end of the Cold War has weakened the U.S. nuclear umbrella that covers countries such as Japan. While the pledge to come to their defense against an attack still exists, many wonder if it has the same force as it did during the Cold War, when America and Japan faced a common enemy. It is conceivable that even Japan—the only state ever hit by nuclear weapons—would develop them itself if the U.S. nuclear guarantee ever lost credibility or was withdrawn.[35]

nuclear weapons
Weapons that use an atomic fission or fusion process to create enormous heat and blast effects that destroy and irradiate targets.

chemical weapons
Gaseous, liquid, or solid chemicals used to poison, asphyxiate, or disable large numbers of people.

biological weapons
Weapons made of microorganisms that cause lethal or disabling diseases.

dual-use technologies and products Technologies and products designed for peaceful uses in civilian life that can be easily converted into weapons.

TABLE 8–3 LETHALITY OF WEAPONS OF MASS DESTRUCTION

Classification of Agent	Agent	Lethality (dosage per person)			Part of Body Affected and Consequences
		Skin (mg)	Inhaled (mg/min/m²)[a]	Digested (mg)	
Chemical					
Nerve Agents (Lethal)	Tabun (liquid/vapor)	1000	400	40	Respiratory system, eyes, salivary/sweat glands, heart, digestive, excretory and central nervous systems; causes paralysis
	Sarin (liquid/vapor)	1700	100	10	
Blister Agents (wounding or possibly lethal)	Distilled Mustard (liquid/vapor)	4500	1500	50	Eyes, skin, lungs, other internal tissues; causes bronchopneumonia
	Nitrogen Mustard (liquid/vapor)	4500	1500	50	
Choking Agents (lethal)	Phosgene (gas)		3200		Respiratory organs; victims drown in their own mucus
Incapacitating Agents	CN (vapor)		11,000		Eyes, skin, respiratory systems
	CS (vapor)		61,000		Nervous, respiratory, digestive systems
	BZ (vapor)		200,000		Heart, central nervous system; causes hallucinations and manic behavior
Biological					
Traditional	Anthrax, Lassa Fever, Typhus, etc.	Varies with individual			Varying lethality
Toxin Agents (lethal)	Butolin X or A (powder/liquid)	0.00007	0.1	0.7	Body tissues, central nervous system; causes desiccation and paralysis
	Saxitoxin TZ (powder/liquid)	0.5	5	0.5	Nervous system; causes paralysis
	Enterotoxin B (powder/liquid)	Unknown	200	500	Digestive and excretory systems, body tissues, lungs
	Mycotoxin (agricultural fungi)	Varies with individual			Possible agent of immuno-deficiency, possible carcinogen
Nuclear					
U-235 or plutonium detonated by a high explosive	Gamma radiation released by the fission of uranium or plutonium atoms into two lighter atoms, or by the fusion of helium atoms released by the collision of two deuterium atoms	0–25 RADs[b]			Practically no effect
		100 RADs			Slight nausea and sickness; noticeable changes in the blood
		200 RADs			Definite blood cell damage, nausea, vomiting, diarrhea, hair loss, livid skin spots, fevers, hemorrhages, extreme fatigue, possible heart failure; up to 25% mortality rate within 30–60 days
		400 RADs			Increased severity of above symptoms; up to 50% mortality rate within 30–60 days
		600 RADs			Very immediate severe symptoms; up to 75% mortality rate within 30–60 days
		800 RADs			Death likely and imminent with rapid malfunction of circulatory system and parts of nervous system; up to 99% mortality rate within days
		1000 RADs			Rapid onset of symptoms or immediate death within hours; 100% mortality rate within hours

[a]Milligrams per minute per square meter of air

[b]The use of RADs (Roentgen Absorbed Dose) as the standard for determining the lethality of a nuclear blast is somewhat misleading because a significant portion of the lethality comes from the heat of the blast as well as the radiation. In addition, length of exposure to radiation produces a cumulative long-term effect.

Sources: The Diagram Group. *Weapons: An International Encyclopedia from 5000BC to 2000AD* (New York: St. Martin's Press, 2000), 268–273; International Institute for Strategic Studies. *The Military Balance: 1988–1989* (London: IISS, 1989), 242–47. Food and Agriculture Organization of the United Nations, "What Are Mycotoxins?" http://www.fao.org/.

A Closer Look

The Wassenaar Arrangement on Export Controls for Conventional Arms and Dual-Use Goods and Technologies

Because some common products can be easily adapted for use in weapons production, the liberalization of international trade and other processes relating to globalization have frustrated efforts to deal with the proliferation of WMD. The Wassenaar Arrangement is an effort by a number of states to deal with this problem.

In April 1996, 33 countries[a] entered into an arrangement designed to "contribute to regional and international security and stability, by promoting transparency and greater responsibility in transfers of conventional arms and dual-use goods and technologies, thus preventing destabilising accumulations." To do so, this arrangement proposes to limit access to dual-use goods (chemicals and manufactured components), technologies, and munitions that might contribute to the development or enhancement of other countries' military capabilities.[b] Initially, this was to have been accomplished by prohibiting the sale, transfer, or diversion of several hundred items specified in the Arrangement which are known components of strategic military weapons or their manufacture, or which might be converted or adapted for such use. In 1998, however, at the request of the United States, the list was expanded to include a restriction on the export of certain classes of cryptography software as well.

The Arrangement was designed to complement and reinforce existing control regimes for weapons of mass destruction and their delivery systems, and to enhance cooperation. In addition, it provides a forum for the continual updating and dissemination of information on new technologies, as well as a procedure for the notification of transfers and denials of such. However, the decision to transfer or deny transfer of any item remains the sole responsibility of the individual signatories, as does the enforcement of any policy designed to do so. Thus, while the arrangement specifies the list of prohibited transfers, export controls in participating countries determine the means, penalties and methods of enforcement for compliance and non-compliance.[c]

[a]Argentina, Australia, Austria, Belgium, Bulgaria, Canada, Czech Republic, Denmark, Finland, France, Germany, Greece, Hungary, Ireland, Italy, Japan, Luxembourg, Netherlands, New Zealand, Norway, Poland, Portugal, Republic of Korea, Romania, Russian Federation, Slovak Republic, Spain, Sweden, Switzerland, Turkey, Ukraine, United Kingdom, and the United States. Conspicuously absent from the list are Brazil, China, India, Iran, Iraq, Israel, North Korea, Pakistan, and South Africa—all thought to be attempting to create and/or develop nuclear weapons and/or WMD programs.

[b]The list of items is extensive and can be downloaded from *http://www.wassenaar.org*.

[c]Interestingly, though co-signatories, both France and the Russian Federation voiced concerns that the Arrangement would instead become a shopping list for countries seeking the indigenous development, production or enhancement of conventional munitions capabilities.

Source: Secretariat of the Wassenaar Arrangement, "The Wassenaar Arrangement on Export Controls for Conventional Arms and Dual-Use Goods and Technologies," *http://www.wassenaar.org/*.

The fourth reason for growing concern over WMD involves **rogue states.** Several states have demonstrated a strong appetite for acquiring WMD and the ballistic missiles that could carry them to distant targets. While there is no universally accepted definition of a rogue state, Western policy makers and analysts tend to think of them as authoritarian states that continue to pursue conflicts with their neighbors and flout many of the norms that are commonly accepted by states, such as a rejection of terrorism. Iraq, Iran, North Korea, and Libya are often put in this category.

To take just one example, as a condition of ending the Persian Gulf War, the United Nations Security Council created the UN Special Commission on Iraq (UNSCOM). It was charged with guaranteeing that all of Iraq's WMD were found and destroyed. UNSCOM officials were given the authority to search anywhere in Iraq that they believed these weapons, weapons components, or weapons laboratories were hidden. Despite many obstacles that Iraqi officials put in the way of these

rogue states   Countries whose leaders appear to be trying to acquire weapons of mass destruction to aid terrorists or challenge existing international norms and institutions.

As a condition of ending the Gulf War, Iraq agreed to accept UNSCOM inspectors on its territory, charged with detecting illegal nuclear, chemical, or biological weapons.

searches, UNSCOM personnel found that Iraq had made major progress during the 1980s in acquiring a nuclear-weapons capability. According to UNSCOM's chairman, Iraq hid its weapons so well that its full WMD capability was generally unknown until late 1995, four years after the end of the Gulf War. It was then learned that during the war, Iraq had deployed at least 150 bombs and 25 warheads filled with various biological poisons. Most of the Iraqi WMD arsenal was produced from dual-use or outdated technologies and materials that were acquired legally under existing export laws in the 1980s.[36] While these laws have been tightened in response to the huge nonproliferation failure represented by Iraq's WMD program, Western policy makers still worry about a WMD threat from the rogue states listed in the preceding paragraph.

Iraq remains an especially severe security problem, due to the brutality of its regime and its intense disputes with neighboring states. In December 1998, the United States and Britain launched a four-day bombing campaign to destroy portions of Iraq's remaining WMD capability. U.S. officials characterized these air strikes as an effort to accomplish forcibly what the UNSCOM inspections were never able to achieve fully: preventing Iraq from reviving its nuclear, chemical, and biological weapons capabilities. Since it is difficult to find all of the materials that could be used to rebuild chemical and biological weapons, the strikes focused on delivery systems for these weapons, including planes, missiles, and facilities that manufacture missile components. Nevertheless, air strikes are a blunt instrument; they miss targets the attacker would want to hit, if they were known, and they cause unintended damage to non-military targets. There are also inherent limits as to what compellence from the air can accomplish so long as an adversary retains political power. Even though the Desert Storm coalition dropped over 88,000 tons of bombs on Iraq during the 1991 Gulf War—more than fell on Japan in the last six weeks of World War II—it took a massive land operation in southern Iraq to compel Iraq's surrender.[37]

The fifth reason for growing concern about the spread of WMD is the **"loose nukes" problem.** When the Soviet Union disintegrated in 1991, reports began to

"loose nukes" problem
Fears that nuclear material and weapons developed by states will fall into the hands of terrorists.

reach Western capitals about Middle Eastern governments that were approaching Russian institutions in search of WMD technologies and expertise. One potential purchaser was Iran, which is believed to be trying to build a new ballistic missile with a range of 1,300 kilometers (about 800 miles). Such capacity would allow it to strike targets in Israel, Saudi Arabia, and Turkey.[38] These reports were particularly troubling because many feared that some Russian scientists and suppliers might cooperate. By 1991, Russia's huge Cold-War military-industrial infrastructure was shrinking or in the process of conversion to civilian uses. Many Russian military laboratories, factories, and research institutions were looking for foreign partners to help them finance their new activities. These institutions began to display more autonomy from the government's control, and the personnel that worked in them seemed eager to accommodate potential customers. The problem was heightened because many Russian WMD specialists, who had enjoyed well-paying and prestigious positions before the collapse of communism, are now barely surviving below the poverty line. Would any of them (estimated at sixty thousand) be willing to sell their knowledge and experience to rogue states or terrorists determined to acquire nuclear, biological, or chemical weapons?[39] Given the tremendous economic difficulties in Russia and the apparent demand for WMD expertise, this problem is likely to demand high-level policy attention for some time to come.

In sum, WMD proliferation illustrates how the targets of security policy are shifting and expanding. What then can be done about this problem? Many analysts are pessimistic. The states that have signed and adhere to the NPT, the Chemical Weapons Convention, and the Biological Weapons Convention tend not to be those who pose security problems for others. Moreover, with the end of the Cold War, such rogue states as North Korea and Libya have lost their major source of international support, which used to be the Soviet Union. This has made their leaders more likely to feel encircled by enemies and to seek WMD. While the NPT will keep nuclear material from being sold on the open market, it is unlikely to impede access to it if the buyer is determined and willing to procure it in novel ways.[40] The Nuclear Nonproliferation Treaty was based on the assumption that all existing nuclear weapons and nuclear-weapons materials could be accounted for at any given time. In a number of countries, that assumption may not be correct, either because the government is trying to hide weapons development or because existing nuclear weapons cannot be accounted for. Table 8–4 outlines the dimensions of this problem.

Terrorism

Terrorism is one of the most critical security issues facing today's policy makers. **Terrorists** are usually thought of as people who commit criminal acts, typically involving attacks on innocent bystanders, for political purposes. Because people on different sides of conflicts often have very different views about who is innocent and who is a legitimate target, it is often hard to get agreement on whether specific people are freedom fighters or terrorists. Terrorists' political purposes include efforts to achieve an independent state (as in Palestinian attacks on Israeli targets); to take revenge for earlier attacks or atrocities (as in Armenian attacks on Turkish targets); or to demonstrate general resentment toward some state or its policies (as illustrated by the September 11 attacks on U.S. targets). The attacks tend to be indiscriminate because terrorists typically try to put pressure on governments by making their citizens—and any others who happen to be on their territory—vulnerable. As the

terrorists Individuals or groups who use violence or the threat of violence against innocent bystanders to achieve political purposes.

TABLE 8–4	UNDECLARED NUCLEAR WEAPONS AND NUCLEAR WEAPONS MATERIAL
Country	**Suspected Nuclear Status**
Algeria	Inadequate scientific, technical, and material resources to create nuclear weapons potential, though the potential for nuclear research remains. Active 15 megawatt (or more) heavy water nuclear reactor under IAEA scrutiny. Bilateral cooperation with China on nuclear development.
Argentina	Dependable raw nuclear material base; several nuclear power plants under construction or in operation; highly skilled scientific cadre; technologies for enriching uranium obtained, several nuclear research facilities. Member of IAEA, Tlatelolco Treaty, and NPT signatory.
Brazil	Dependable raw nuclear material base; several nuclear power plants under construction or in operation; highly skilled scientific cadre; technologies for enriching uranium obtained; several nuclear research facilities. Member of IAEA, Tlatelolco signatory, but not NPT signatory. Major, advanced nuclear research program for military purposes not under the scrutiny of IAEA.
Egypt	Plans for industrial incorporation, extraction, and enrichment of explored uranium deposits for use as fuel for atomic power plants. Reported development of nuclear weapons. Bilateral cooperation with India, Great Britain, Argentina, Germany, the United States, Russia, and China for projects for peaceful uses.
Iran	No convincing evidence of any coordinated, integrated military nuclear program, though international worries remain due to expertise of nuclear technology derived from extensive use of nuclear power generation. NPT signatory. Allows IAEA inspection of its 23 nuclear research and technology facilities. No uranium processing capability expected before 2005. Accusations of purchase of four nuclear warheads from Kazakhstan are unsupported.
Iraq	Doubts linger as to the status of Iraq's nuclear research program (which was reportedly destroyed in the Gulf War) and its highly enriched uranium (purportedly removed and now under IAEA safeguards). Long-term monitoring of nuclear research program sought by UN Special Commission delayed until verification of all WMDs in Iraq has been completed. Member of IAEA and NPT signatory.
North Korea	Dependable raw nuclear power base. Nuclear research and development for energy purposes since 1960s. Nuclear weapons program since the 1970s. Suspected ability to produce weapons-grade plutonium since 1986, and suspected diversion of enough Pu-239 to theoretically produce one or two warheads during 1989 shutdown. Withdrew from NPT and IAEA in 1994, alarming the West. An agreement with the United States for economic aid in exchange for the right for U.S. inspections of certain nuclear facilities in 1998 reduced tensions with West and opened up a new era of international cooperation with North Korea.
Libya	No suspected nuclear weapons and no reliable data to confirm that purposeful work is being done to pursue them. Little scientific cadre to support such research, although the potential for research remains due to presence of nuclear power facility since 1982. Open to IAEA inspections, NPT compliance.

Sources: Cato Institute, "Missile Defense System Needed to Deter Rogue States," *http://cato.org*; Federation of Atomic Scientists, "Nuclear Forces Guide," *http://www.fas.org/nuke/guide*.

attacks on the United States illustrate, it is difficult for a government to insulate itself or its people from terrorist attacks without turning public buildings and streets into fortresses.

Trans-state terrorism is hardly new, of course. The man who assassinated the heir to the throne of Austria-Hungary in 1914, thereby sparking the crisis that produced World War I, was a Bosnian Serb terrorist. What is new is the emergence of worldwide communications that make it easier to organize global terrorist networks and get instant, wide-ranging publicity for terrorist acts. Non-state actors were once limited to communicating by telephone and the ordinary postal system. Today, they can use cellular or satellite phones, e-mail, and sophisticated pagers, and they can quickly transport weapons and other supplies through various shipping services. As a result, people *are* more vulnerable than they were a decade ago.[41]

Today many people worry about the use of WMD by terrorists. While several people in the United States died from anthrax-contaminated mail in the fall of 2001, at the time of this writing there have been only two cases in which biological or chemical agents have been used in a form that could kill or injure large numbers of people. In June 1994 and March 1995, members of a Japanese religious sect carried out nerve gas attacks that killed sixteen people and injured over five thousand. In the past, terrorists tended to avoid using WMD for several reasons: The resulting death toll would lose them more sympathy than they would gain; violence was also possible using conventional weapons and guns; and acquiring and using WMD involved more risks that the terrorists themselves would be harmed or apprehended than if they used ordinary weapons.[42] These restraints, however, seem to be weakening. Today, at least some terrorists seem to be more inclined than before to resort to mass-casualty violence. In part, this development reflects a rise in religiously motivated terrorism. Terrorists driven by religious beliefs less often have a specific political agenda; rather they have the view that violence, often extreme violence, is necessary to cleanse an evil world. In addition, improved education levels and the growing amount of information available about WMD components make it easier than before for terrorists to assemble and use these weapons.

This trend also seems to reflect the increased frustration of some regionally based terrorists with America's political and military presence in their societies, a frustration heightened by the perception that there is no longer another major state willing or able to challenge what is seen as U.S. hegemony. For some of these groups, such as al-Qaeda, extreme measures are seen as necessary to drive the United States out of the Persian Gulf, where its presence has grown stronger since the 1991 Gulf War.

Terrorism can at times succeed in its objectives, especially over the long run. While attacks intentionally designed to kill innocents are never morally acceptable, it is important to recognize that stateless groups that cannot achieve their purposes in other ways have strong incentives to bring pressure to bear by attacking innocent bystanders. Palestinians, for instance, probably could not have brought the Israeli government to the negotiating table in 1993 had they not spent the prior seven years conducting the *Intifadah*, or "Uprising"—a costly and bloody series of riots and attacks against Israeli soldiers and civilians. By the early 1990s, even many hawkish Israeli policy makers had come to believe that a political solution to the conflict was better than a permanent situation of occupation and internal war. But terrorism can also produce the opposite result. It can stiffen a target population against any concessions to the perpetrators, even if their demands might otherwise be negotiable. To understand which outcome will result, it is necessary to examine how the international and domestic incentives come together in each specific case.

The targets of terrorism, of course, try to prevent or retaliate for such attacks. A distinction is sometimes made between *anti-terror* measures, which decrease the target's vulnerability to attacks, and *counter-terror* measures, which attempt to suppress the threat itself. Anti-terror measures include placing metal detectors in public

8.3 ENDURING PATTERNS

The connection between preferences and power
The stronger actors' power positions, the more strategically important their preferences.

Tracking al-Qaeda before and after September 11

As a torrent of leaks from the Federal Bureau of Investigation (FBI) and the Central Intelligence Agency (CIA) revealed in the spring of 2002, policy makers had long known that the leaders of the al-Qaeda network and the leaders of the major Western states had fundamentally and irretrievably incompatible preferences. But threat-assessment involves not only identifying what actors *want* to do; it also involves estimates of what they *can* do. What changed after September 11 was Western estimates of al-Qaeda's power to carry out terrorist attacks on a massively destructive scale. Given that reevaluation of al-Qaeda's power, the strategic implications of their preferences—and, consequently, the FBI's and CIA's threat assessment—changed dramatically.

buildings, inspecting baggage carefully at airports, and promoting cooperation among police forces across states. Counter-terror measures include economic sanctions against governments that support terrorism, finding and freezing the assets of groups with terrorist connections, and taking military action against the terrorist groups themselves.[43]

In response to the September 11 attacks, President Bush and Prime Minister Blair announced a fully integrated campaign of anti- and counter-terrorist measures that is unprecedented in the scope of its methods and the number of countries that agreed to participate. The military dimensions of that campaign face very real challenges. Because terrorists typically try to blend in with the surrounding population, even the most precise weapons are likely to kill innocents. Force is, as we said, a blunt instrument.

The problems created by using military instruments in counter-terrorism campaigns are not, however, the biggest challenges facing U.S. and British leaders. The biggest problems involve the ways in which the campaign against al-Qaeda are entangled in regional disputes and the difficult relationships between Western culture and Islam. There is substantial reason to believe that Russian support for the U.S. coalition reflects its leaders' concerns about Chechnya and the strength of anti-Russian feeling in Islamic areas around its borders. Meanwhile, Israel's government has put the Bush administration on notice that it does not want U.S. efforts to court Middle Eastern allies in the war on terrorism to lead to increased pressure on Israel to grant concessions to gain a settlement with the Palestinians. Another prominent regional dispute—the one between India and Pakistan—also became entangled with the campaign against al-Qaeda when the Indian government protested the increased U.S. reliance on Pakistan during the bombing of Afghanistan.

The large number of regional disputes that have become entangled in the campaign against al-Qaeda have created immense diplomatic challenges. The fact that enduring security rivalries are deeply embedded in the domestic politics of the states involved makes the challenges still more daunting. However, the fact that the global anti-terrorist security agenda is inextricably connected with so many linked international and domestic issues creates an opportunity to reframe many of the existing security threats in contemporary world politics. Whether, and how well, that happens will depend on how the key actors manage the politics of strategic choice. As the principles discussed in Chapter 3 suggest, the effectiveness of the counter-terror campaign will depend on how well relevant sources of power are used, the compatibility of actors' preferences and perceptions, their beliefs about legitimate outcomes, and linkage politics.

Ethnic Conflict

Ethnic conflict is one of today's most important security issues. *Ethnic conflict* can be defined as "a dispute about important political, economic, social, cultural, or territorial issues between two or more ethnic communities."[44] **Ethnic communities,** which are sometimes called *nations,* are those groups that have names for themselves (such as Scots, Armenians, and Kurds), believe in a common group ancestry, have shared historical memories and a shared culture, feel an attachment to a specific piece of territory, and think of themselves as an ethnic group.[45]

Two points need to be kept in mind here. First, ethnic conflicts are not always violent. The conflict between French-speaking and English-speaking Canadians is most often nonviolent, and the division of Czechoslovakia into two ethnically based states was entirely peaceful. By contrast, the conflict between ethnic Serbs, Croats, and Muslims within Bosnia was very violent. Second, not all internal conflict has ethnic roots. For example, the war between Peru's *Sendero Luminoso* guerrillas and the Peruvian government has no ethnic aspect, nor did an intense civil war in Greece during the 1940s. For purposes of this chapter, we focus on violent or potentially violent ethnic conflicts.

When ethnic conflicts began to attract a lot of attention in the Western media and international-affairs publications at the end of the Cold War, some people seemed surprised by the scope of the problem. They shouldn't have been. As of the late 1980s, 900 million individuals—about one out of every seven people in the world—were members of politically active ethnic groups, and three-fourths of the 127 largest states had at least one politicized ethnic minority group. By one count, twenty-two wars were being waged worldwide in 1993, and ethnic rivalries or challenges to an existing state contributed to the conflict in seventeen of them.[46] In other words, there has always been a potential for ethnic conflict simply as a result of the way ethnic groups are distributed across states.

However deep the underlying causes of these conflicts have been, it is clear that many foreign policy makers, analysts, and NGO as well as IGO officials are paying more attention to them than they did during the Cold War. There are reinforcing reasons for this shift in attention. The collapse of the Soviet empire and the end of the U.S.-Soviet global competition have intensified a number of ethnic conflicts. When multinational countries such as the Soviet Union or Yugoslavia collapse, the successor states are often breeding grounds for internal wars, many of which have an ethnic component. These new states often have contested borders, mutually hostile population groups, and governments that one or more of these groups consider illegitimate. If key segments of the population view a successor government as illegitimate, this sense of injustice may inflame group hatreds to build constituency

ethnic communities
(sometimes called *nations*) Groups of people who believe they have a common ancestry, history, and culture; usually, ethnic communities also share an attachment to a particular territorial homeland and a commitment to promote a shared future as a distinctive community.

support.[47] The loss of U.S. and Russian leverage on these regimes intensified some of these ethnic conflicts. When Moscow and Washington competed for the allegiance of regimes in Africa, the Middle East, and Latin America, they often supplied arms to friendly governments. With such help often came diplomatic leverage that could be used to restrain local conflicts. When the United States and Russia withdrew from these conflicts, the weapons remained even as the ability to restrain the local actors disappeared.

The diffusion of rivalries has also allowed people to become more aware of the scope and importance of ethnic conflict. The Cold War was based on a competition between two ideologies, each of which claimed universal applicability across regions and cultures. By their natures, neither doctrine attributed much importance to differences in values or objectives across ethnic groups. The international relations literature of the time reinforced this tendency, devoting much more attention to the East and West blocs than to key distinctions or tensions within them. As late as the end of the 1970s, few world politics texts discussed ethnic issues. As the Cold War faded, people were able to see how many conflicts worldwide had a significant ethnic component.[48]

One critical difference between ethnic conflict and either WMD proliferation or terrorism is that ethnic conflict *may* have few tangible effects on outsiders. If this is the case, outside intervention to contain or stop the conflict may not be very vigorous. In general, outsiders have two kinds of incentives to care about and perhaps take action regarding an ethnic dispute. One is humanitarianism, as exemplified by the efforts of UN peacekeepers to set up safe areas to protect Bosnian Muslims during the Bosnian War. In such cases, an actor or a coalition of actors intervenes to protect civilians at risk in the midst of an ongoing war, deliver relief supplies or protect militarily those who are providing them, or evacuate war-torn areas. Outsiders may also intervene to keep an ethnic conflict from spreading closer to their own borders or those of an ally, or to stem the flow of refugees. The United Nations saw this as the major rationale for the preventive-deployment force (UNPREDEP) that helped keep conflicts elsewhere in the Balkans from spilling over into Macedonia during the late 1990s. The second of these two incentives to intervene is closer to what analysts and policy makers generally consider "a security issue," but that does not mean governments are more likely to act on it. Intervention to contain or prevent ethnic wars is more ambitious than humanitarian intervention, since it generally takes more specially equipped troops who must stay longer on the ground.

One lesson some actors have learned in dealing with ethnic conflicts is that an ounce of prevention may be worth a pound of cure. An example occurred in Rwanda during 1994. Over a period of three months, more killing took place among individuals belonging to the Tutsi and Hutu tribes than occurred in *four years* in the former Yugoslavia between 1991 and 1995. The commander of the United Nations Assistance Mission for Rwanda (UNAMIR) asserted that a force of 5,000 troops inserted in the region two weeks after the violence erupted could have prevented much of the killing (estimated at up to 800,000 people) that eventually occurred there. With this tragic experience as a backdrop, an international panel of senior military leaders was convened to evaluate the commander's claim. While of course no one can be certain what "might have been," the panel concluded that a properly trained, equipped, and supported force of that size could have saved half a million innocent people.[49]

8.4 ENDURING PATTERNS

The impact of varying beliefs about just relationships

If people value creating and sustaining legitimate relationships and if they think a political process and the outcome it produces are just, they are more likely to accept that outcome—even if they would have preferred something else.

The impact of discounting

The higher the expected value actors attach to achieving a specific policy outcome, the less their choices will be affected by discounting.

Rwanda, Yugoslavia, and Afghanistan

With the sudden growth and visibility of ethnic warfare in places such as Rwanda and Yugoslavia during the 1990s, policy makers struggled with the question of whether they should participate in humanitarian interventions. Those interventions were costly and often involved sending their citizens into harm's way. Moreover, those costs were likely to come sooner while the benefits came later. As the enduring patterns above suggest, in the absence of a perceived security threat, debates about the human and financial costs of humanitarian intervention and nation-building—and the political risks those costs generate—are very much dependent on the value actors attach to creating and sustaining mutually legitimate

trans-state obligations. In their debates during the 2000 presidential campaign in the United States, Al Gore and George W. Bush came down on very different sides of the issue of investing U.S. resources in building multilateral international relationships that were regarded as mutually legitimate. Given those differences, it is not surprising that the candidate who preferred unilateralism—Bush—was vigorously opposed to investing in humanitarian intervention. While nation-building in Afghanistan carries costs that are even higher, it is far easier to gain support for investing in Afghanistan because successful nation-building there has the potential to improve U.S. security.

Why then is *preventive* deployment so seldom used to deal with budding conflicts? The answer seems to be a nasty combination of "might have beens" and linkage politics. Domestic actors rarely have incentives to enter potentially deadly situations *in advance of* major problems; it is easier to wait and see if the cure is needed. Until people's subjective security comes to include the suffering of others with different skins or languages, it will be hard to organize international coalitions to respond to these problems.

Conclusion

People are at their most secure when they have compatible preferences, believe it's important to build mutually legitimate relationships, share the same notions about

India's Nuclear Weapons Choice: Security Dilemmas, International Norms, and Domestic Politics

In 1998 India announced that it had successfully tested a nuclear weapon. Pakistan promptly responded with a test of its own. Why did the Indian government decide to end over twenty years of carefully cultivated ambiguity over whether it had nuclear weapons?

The evolution of India's nuclear-weapons policy from Nehru's advocacy of nuclear disarmament, through nuclear ambiguity, to the public weapons test is discussed in a case study at **www.prenhall.com/lamborn**. This case is representative of the ways in which all of the distinctive features of the contemporary security context can come together. It combines the diffusion of security rivalries and the rise of regionalism with the proliferation of weapons of mass destruction, terrorism, and ethnic conflict.

Look for the ways in which leaders' foreign policy goals can get entangled with domestic politics and how the intensity with which they hold their views affects their willingness to run political and policy risks. Look also for how the interrelationships between India, China, and Pakistan created security dilemmas. Finally, consider how hard it is to promote international norms—such as nuclear non-proliferation—when those norms leave some countries with nuclear weapons and others with none.

---

just relationships, and expect the future to develop in ways that reinforce that combination of circumstances. The problem, of course, is that there are many situations in which people have incompatible preferences, don't value nurturing mutually legitimate relations, have different visions of justice, and expect the future to make their situation worse rather than better. When that happens and some or all of the actors involved appear to be willing and able to use force to achieve their goals, security issues grow in importance.

Force plays two major roles in world politics. It can be used to threaten, but it also can be used to respond to threats. However, how people diagnose, evaluate, and deal with threats are as much a subjective as an objective process. Perceptions play a key role in the politics of international security, on every issue from the choice of weapons to choice of bargaining strategies and allies. Moreover, military sources of power are only one dimension in the politics of security and strategic choice. The ability to alter people's preferences and their perceptions of the stakes *and* the ability to build a sense of mutually legitimate political processes and outcomes are both as potentially significant sources of power in addressing security issues as are the effective uses of force.

Seldom have these interrelated sources of security been clearer than they are in today's security context, where the post–September 11 decision to organize a sustained campaign against terrorist networks has become intertwined with ongoing regional disputes and the centuries-old question of how Western and Islamic culture can nurture mutually legitimate relationships. Policy makers and analysts are only beginning to understand and seriously confront the question of how these challenges go together.

Key Terms

objective security

subjective security

strategic vulnerability

threat

second strike nuclear forces

transparency

security dilemma

deterrence

compellence (coercive diplomacy)

defense

arms control

disarmament

preemptive attack

weapons of mass destruction (WMD)

nuclear weapons

chemical weapons

biological weapons

dual-use technologies and products

rogue states

the "loose nukes" problem

terrorists

ethnic communities

TO THE Reader   A CHAPTER SUMMARY and QUESTIONS FOR REVIEW are available at **www.prenhall.com/lamborn**

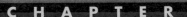

9

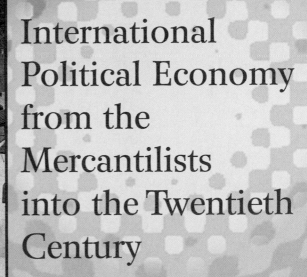

International Political Economy from the Mercantilists into the Twentieth Century

The global political economy is no longer Eurocentric, but it continues to show its European roots. The structure of the contemporary international monetary system, the shape of modern trade patterns, and the way capital moves across international boundaries are all affected by the ways in which Europe dominated the development of the global political economy in the four centuries before World War I. Moreover, the effects of this historical influence go beyond the structure of economic relations. The issues and concepts—the very terms of the debate—reflect their origins in the development of the Eurocentric system during this period.

We begin this chapter with a review of mercantilism, which was the dominant school of economic thought in Europe at the time the modern state system came into existence. In the next sections, we examine the reasons for the end of mercantilism and the rise of free-trade capitalism in the mid-nineteenth century. We then consider how radical changes in industrial and agricultural productivity in Europe combined with colonialism to consolidate Europe's central position in the global political economy in the sixty years before World War I. The chapter concludes with a discussion of how those changes then generated a new round of linkage politics that began to undermine that dominance even before the effects of the war ended the Eurocentric system.

Mercantilism and the Early State Builders

Mercantilist Assumptions about Wealth, Money, and Trade

Mercantilist ideas dominated the political economy of the emerging European state system until the late 1700s. As we mentioned in Chapter 7, **mercantilism** assumes that there is a fixed amount of wealth in the world and that the best way to accumulate, or save, that wealth is by acquiring precious metals such as gold and silver. This assumption encouraged European policy makers to compete ferociously for empire and ever-larger shares of interstate trade and led mercantilists to focus on ways to increase the number of items they possessed that were made of precious metals. They also wanted to acquire what is called **specie**—money coined in gold or silver. Alchemists' efforts to convert lead into gold having failed, three options stood out: finding new deposits that could be mined; expropriating the wealth of others; and running a favorable **balance of trade,** which refers to the net value of exports minus imports.

The first two options—mining and expropriating—provided incentives for colonial expansion. The third—running a favorable balance of trade—led to government efforts to organize the country's economic activities and those of its colonies in ways that produced a substantial surplus of exports over imports. The reason for favoring a surplus of exports over imports was quite straightforward: One could demand payment for the surplus in specie money. While domestic economies still relied heavily on barter or local currencies made of less valuable commodities, trade across great distances depended on coins cast in gold and silver. In a mercantilist world, there

mercantilism A set of beliefs about political economy that assumed that wealth could only be discovered, not created, and that the best way to accumulate wealth was in precious metals.

specie Money coined in precious metals, usually gold or silver.

balance of trade The net value of exports minus imports; a positive balance of trade is called a favorable balance of trade.

World Politics and the Individual

Privateers and Sir Francis Drake

Sir Francis Drake was one of the greatest of the privateers that plundered their way through the mercantilist trade wars and colonial competition of the sixteenth-century. Drake, a sixteenth century celebrity, was knighted by Queen Elizabeth in 1581. What kind of world makes it possible to use piracy as a route to prosperity and national honor?

An overview of Drake's life—and some possible answers to this question—can be found at www.prenhall.com/lamborn.

Look for how the honors bestowed on Drake were related, first, to the religious and political struggles between Protestants and Catholics, and second, to mercantilist assumptions about wealth, military power, and state building. As you consider these connections, look for the ways in which Queen Elizabeth's private resources were intermixed with those of the state's. How does this comingling of resources reflect contemporary ideas about sovereignty?

Buckland Abbey illustrates the wealth Sir Francis Drake gained as a pirate on the high seas. He purchased the estate with just some of the loot he had accumulated during his three-year circumnavigation of the globe.

were no questions about the worth of a country's international currency; it was literally worth its weight in gold (or silver).[1]

These views about the nature of wealth, money, and trade encouraged central governments to play a competitive and intrusive role in linking their domestic and international economic arrangements. Government economic strategies were highly competitive because the mercantilist assumption that wealth was finite ruled out the possibility of either creating new wealth or sharing in economic growth. The competition among governments drove them dangerously close to a *zero-sum* world, in which one actor's gain was necessarily another's loss. Economic sectors that generated exports were promoted at the expense of those that didn't, and governments often outlawed exports of machinery and emigration by skilled artisans to prevent a "loss" in their relative ability to export high-value items. Heavy **tariffs** (taxes on imports) were levied as part of the drive to create a favorable balance of trade. Artificially raising the prices of imports and suppressing exports of capital goods naturally created substantial incentives for smuggling. That, in turn, increased the role of the state's security forces in patrolling coastlines and other borders. Moreover, trade wars were common, and sovereigns authorized privateers—who, except for the fact that they were acting with the approval of the government, operated very much like pirates—to attack and loot foreign ships.

Government's role in economic activities was even more intrusive and ruthless in the colonies. When civilizations had significant sources of gold and silver, existing accumulations were simply stolen, and indigenous peoples were forced into the mines to dig for more. Agriculture was switched from **subsistence farming**—in which foodstuffs grown for the farmer and the local market were the principal products—to the production of commodities that had a substantial export value in Europe. Sectors of the indigenous economy that were producing goods that competed with European exports, such as textiles in the Indian subcontinent, were systematically undermined or simply outlawed. European governments also typically required that all merchandise traded between the colonies and European markets be shipped on

tariffs Government-imposed taxes on imports.

subsistence farming An agricultural system in which food is grown for the personal use of the farmer and for exchange in local markets; implies that farmers are able to produce little, if any, beyond what is necessary to survive.

9.1 ENDURING PATTERNS

The connection between preferences and power

The more incompatible actors' preferences, the more strategically important their relative power positions.

The effect of the shadow of the future

The more incompatible people expect their preferences to become over time, the more competitive and power-based their strategic approach is likely to be.

Mercantilism and Neomercantilism

Mercantilism assumed that the competition for increased wealth was zero sum, meaning that any increase in wealth by one set of actors inescapably reduced the ability of others to become wealthier. Moreover, they expected this zero-sum competition to persist as far into the future as one could see. Given these assumptions, mercantilists emphasized increasing the power of the state and using that power to control economic activity and, when necessary, fight wars for economic advantage.

In the 1970s, many policy makers came to the conclusion that their countries' long-term economic prosperity and employment levels depended on increasing their relative share of global exports. The emphasis on *relative* shares created an inescapable conflict of interest. That conflict led to an emphasis on using the economic and political power of governments to manipulate economic activity in ways that promoted exports and discouraged imports, an approach that was soon being called neomercantilism.

---

vessels owned by government-authorized companies, and that those ships dock only in authorized ports before the goods they carried could move on to their ultimate markets. These and other rules maximized central governments' ability to control colonial economic activity and to skim off a sizable percentage of the profits.

Spain led the way in the development of mercantilist colonial practices. Its holdings in Mexico and Peru were regarded by contemporary Europeans as some of the most valuable in the hemisphere. They provided vast amounts of gold and silver, mined at great human cost by the indigenous population, that were shipped back to Spain for the benefit of the crown and its domestic coalition partners. Spain also pioneered the mercantilist practice of monopolizing all colonial trade, requiring that it travel directly to Spain on Spanish-flag vessels. Finally, the Spanish were the first to reorganize agricultural holdings in the colonies, shifting them away from subsistence agriculture to the production of foodstuffs and other products that had a high market value in Europe.

Portugal was the second great innovator in mercantilist colonial practices. It was the Portuguese who developed the first extensive trading posts around Africa to support trade with the Orient. The Portuguese also organized the first systematic shipments of African slaves to the Americas. Disappointed by their inability to find precious metals in Brazil and unable to force the indigenous population to work on their plantations, the Portuguese traded with African middlemen for slaves who could be transported to the Brazilian plantations. In addition to the profits generated in trade, by 1700 Brazil's slave-based plantation economy was providing as much tax revenue for the Portuguese government as it was able to extract from all its domestic sources.[2]

Other European states copied the Spanish and the Portuguese to the extent that local conditions—and their ability to control the settlers—permitted. Thus it was, for instance, that the British government regarded the New England colonies as the least valuable of their American assets. They were difficult to control, wanted to compete with England by creating independent fleets, and often dragged the British into expensive wars with indigenous tribes. The plantation economies of the southern seaboard and Caribbean islands were the most valued parts of the British colonies in the Americas for the simple reason that they benefited the crown most directly. In between, both geographically and in perceived value, were the Middle Atlantic colonies, whose exports of foodstuffs helped feed the plantations.

Explaining Mercantilism's Durability

Mercantilist ideas framed European policy makers' preferences for almost three hundred years as a result of several mutually reinforcing economic and political factors. Consider first how mercantilism's monetary and trade policies reinforced each other. To function well, monetary systems must provide a way to buy and sell goods and services. This need for a medium of exchange is called the **transactions demand** for money. The more economic activity there is, the larger the supply of money must be simply to handle the increased number and scale of economic transactions. International monetary systems—indeed, all monetary systems—must also provide a means to accumulate savings and wealth in a predictable and safe way. This need creates a demand for money that can be used as a **reserve asset.** Mercantilism's reliance on specie met both the transactions demand for money that would be widely acceptable in trade and the need for a currency that could be used as a reserve asset for savings. Furthermore, it met those functions in ways that didn't present any problems with exchange rates. Gold was gold, no matter which country coined it. Consequently, while at any point in time a change in trade patterns might make one country's currency more widely used than another's, that increase simply represented the amount of specie money in circulation from the first country, not any differences in the confidence merchants had in the value of the two countries' currencies. Finally, while specie was used in interstate trade and transactions among governments, domestic economic activity still depended heavily on barter and more localized systems of exchange. This separation virtually eliminated one of the most vexing problems in modern international political economy: finding politically acceptable ways to adjust the domestic economy and the money supply in order to manage the value of a country's currency in international transactions.

The internal consistency of mercantilism's financial and trade policies was a key source of its durability. At least equally important was the fact that these policies—and mercantilist assumptions about the sources of wealth—happened to fit the prevailing conditions in the domestic and international environments for choice. The assumption that wealth could not be created and the reliance on specie for long-distance trade meant that the total amount of international economic activity that could take place was limited by the amount of gold and silver available for making money. That limitation would become a fundamental problem, however, only under

transactions demand
The varying need (demand) for money as a medium of exchange.

reserve asset   Money and other financial assets set aside as savings.

conditions of sustained economic growth. With agriculture still largely organized in subsistence farming and industrialization yet to come, there wasn't much growth to be constrained during the mercantilist period.

Mercantilism collapsed when the conditions that hid its limitations disappeared. The Industrial Revolution between the late 1700s and mid-1800s created explosive economic growth. That growth would, in combination with central governments' appetite for revenue to finance war, lead to a financial revolution in the way money was conceptualized and handled. At the same time, it made manifestly absurd even to the most casual economic observer the notion that the amount of wealth in the world was fixed. Moreover, the Industrial Revolution gave rise to a commercial and industrial middle class whose growth radically altered the character and relative power of the key actors in the domestic political arena, thus undermining the central government's ability to intrude extensively and competitively in economic activities.

These observations suggest a third basic reason for mercantilism's durability. Mercantilism survived as long as it did not only because of the mutually supporting character of its economic objectives and prevailing economic conditions, but also because of the fit between those economic considerations and policy makers' other principal objectives. Recall from Chapter 6 the nature of linkages between domestic and interstate politics in Europe during the spread of mercantilist ideas in the 1500s. This was the period in which monarchs were increasingly making claims to absolute control of a defined territory. To build such states, policy makers needed to break the control of regional magnates over local economies in order to reduce the nobility's capacity to oppose the crown, to extract enough resources to fund a centralized administrative apparatus, and to pay mercenary armies. Subsequently, the declining ability of local nobles to form blocking coalitions made it easier to sustain the intrusive and competitive role of the government in the domestic economy. These policies even acquired a veneer of legitimacy as a result of a growing consensus in Europe that dynastic rulers were sovereign and the people merely subjects. The mercantilist assumption of an economic world built on conflicting preferences was reinforced still more by the level of conflict generated by the struggle between competing religious universals during the Reformation and Counter-Reformation and the struggle created by Austria's drive for military hegemony during the Thirty Years' War.

Mercantilism was over 150 years old and well entrenched before the Peace of Westphalia began to create a set of shared principles that could moderate the level of competition in the state system. Moreover, while those principles moderated the use of violence by radically reducing the number of wars about the nature of the system, war and competition for marginal advantage did continue after the Peace of Westphalia (as we saw in Chapter 6, where we discussed the classical balance of power). Consequently, mercantilism's stress on conflicting economic preferences and on the extraction of resources for the benefit of state-builders was in essential harmony with the goal of increasing long-term military power. Jacob Viner, one of the greatest twentieth-century economic historians, summarized the compatibility of mercantilist attitudes about economics, politics, and military security this way:

> I believe that practically all mercantilists . . . would have subscribed to all of the following propositions: (1) wealth is an absolutely essential means to [military] power, whether for security or aggression; (2) [military] power is essential or

valuable as a means for the acquisition or retention of wealth; (3) wealth and [military] power are each proper ultimate ends of national policy; (4) there is a long-run harmony between these ends, although in particular circumstances it may be necessary for a time to make [short-run] economic sacrifices in the interest of military security and therefore also of long-run prosperity.[3]

The Effect of Linkage Politics on Mercantilist Policies in Britain, France, and Holland

The ways in which mercantilist policy preferences played out varied in response to the specific international and domestic situations policy makers confronted in different countries. For instance, during the last century of the mercantilist period, policy makers in France, Britain, and Holland (known then as the United Provinces) pursued economic and security agendas that reflected significant variations on mercantilism's principal themes. French governments placed a lower value on policies that increased trade than on policies that enhanced their land-based military capabilities. Holland was at the other extreme, stressing the pursuit of increased trade far more heavily than military preparations. Britain's position was more complex: putting a more nearly equal stress on trade and military capabilities than either Holland or France, but only when the military issues involved naval capabilities. On questions of land-based military capabilities and the distribution of military power on the continent of Europe, the British were willing to sacrifice their ability to project military power if that would help them achieve their commercial objectives.

These variations make sense when one looks at the varying structure of linkage politics in these countries. Whereas merchants played only a small role in French domestic politics, they were absolutely central to policy coalitions in Holland. But there was more to the differences between French and Dutch policies than domestic politics. Policy outcomes reflect the *connection* between domestic political incentives and the incentives created by the international arena. France had significant security concerns on the continent that could be met only if it brought substantial military assets to any alliances it formed. It could not, as a result, be a *free rider*, an actor that depends on others to provide the resources needed to achieve shared objectives. Dutch leaders, in contrast, had concluded after a sustained competition with the French and the British during the seventeenth century that Holland was far too small to achieve either its land-based or naval security requirements by its own actions.[4] With their naval security dependent on British preferences and their continental security dependent on French choices, Dutch policy coalitions had mutually reinforcing international and domestic incentives to stress economic policy over security concerns. Linkage politics created a different situation for British policy makers, whose policy coalitions were far more dependent on the political support of commercial groups than in France but were acutely aware that British trade depended on the British navy for protection. As a result, economic and security incentives reinforced each other whenever the security issue touched on naval capabilities, but the same could not be said of their ability to project power on land, hence the British willingness to subordinate security considerations to commercial objectives on the continent.[5]

In sum, mercantilism prospered for almost three hundred years for the same underlying reason that the classical balance of power worked more or less well between

9.2 ENDURING PATTERNS

The impact of linkage politics

World politics is driven by the interaction of international, factional, and constituency politics.

Mercantilist and Free-Trade Coalitions

While policy makers in Britain, France, and Holland shared the core ideas of the mercantilist perspective, there were significant differences in their international positions, the factions that needed to be on board (coalesce) to make policy choices, and the constituents they needed to keep happy. Those differences in international and domestic incentives led them to implement mercantilist ideas in different ways. As we discuss later in this chapter, during the mid-nineteenth-century free-trade perspectives began to replace mercantilism. However, the way shared ideas about the value of moving toward free trade played out varied with the specific domestic and international incentives confronting policy makers in different European countries. (See the discussions of Britain, France, and Germany on pages 268–72.)

After World War II, policy makers in the United States and Britain were united in their support of the principle of free trade. However, differences in their international positions and the domestic constituencies they needed to satisfy led to important differences of opinion on exactly how to move toward free trade. (See the section "Post-War Divisions and the Emergence of GATT"—particularly the discussion of the International Trade Organization and the Havana Conference—in Chapter 10.)

the Peace of Westphalia and the French Revolution: The preferences of policy makers were mutually reinforcing and were consistent with what the linked international and domestic contexts made possible. This is not to say that either mercantilism or classical balance of power was the most desirable policy choice from a moral or practical standpoint. At this stage of our discussion the questions are far simpler: Why did these strategic approaches to security and economics last as long as they did? Why, having survived so long, did they then fail? We have discussed why they lasted. The answer to why they failed is equally straightforward—the key actors' preferences and the linked domestic and international contexts within which they operated changed.

The Nineteenth-Century Transformation

The assault on mercantilism started with attacks on its ideas and logic. While the critics' arguments look compelling from a modern perspective, mercantilism held on for almost a century. It would take a major change in economic conditions—including the Industrial and Financial Revolutions—and the growth of politically powerful coalitions who accepted the critique to bring down mercantilism and replace it with a new system of political economy.

The Assault on Mercantilism's Ideas

A group of French economists called the **physiocrats** began the debate in the middle of the eighteenth century. They argued that tariffs and other government-imposed restrictions on trade raised the prices of goods far above their real market value while simultaneously reducing their quality and decreasing the potential for economic growth. They called for a policy of **laissez-faire**—French for "allow to act." Governments, they argued, should not try to control their people's economic choices. Internationally, that meant a policy of **free trade**—eliminating government controls and taxes on trade. While some provision was made for intervention necessary for security, the physiocrats assumed that economics and politics should be separated into autonomous spheres.

Adam Smith   Adam Smith—a Scottish economist, political philosopher, and teacher—joined this debate in 1776 with the publication of *The Wealth of Nations*, the first comprehensive, book-length treatment of political economy. It remains to this day one of the most widely cited books in the world. Smith argued that economic and political freedom, human progress, and order were all inextricably connected. If individuals were liberated from government interference and allowed to make their own economic choices, not just those individuals but society as a whole would benefit. Smith postulated, in short, a **harmony of interests** between the individual's pursuit of personal gain and the improvement of the economic and political health of society. According to this view, the best way to promote the collective interests of the whole community is to liberate individuals to do what they believe is in their self-interest. This harmony would be achieved naturally, "as if by an invisible hand." The only legitimate role for government was to provide for defense against external threats and internal law and order.

More specifically, Smith argued that the **division of labor** (a situation in which people specialize in different economic roles and activities) made it possible to *create*, rather than simply discover, wealth. It was the exchange of goods and services—produced by people whose distinctive skills and resources enabled them to produce those goods and services better and more cheaply—that generated new wealth and economic growth. In the area of international trade, this argument was formalized in the idea that every country had, at least potentially, an absolute advantage in one or more economic areas. By **absolute advantage,** Smith meant the ability to produce something better and cheaper than any international competitor. Specializing in those areas and then trading for goods that other countries could produce more efficiently would make everyone better off.

David Ricardo and the Doctrine of Comparative Advantage   Smith's ideas about international trade were taken a critical step further by David Ricardo, an English economist who lived from 1772 to 1823. In his 1817 book *Principles of Political Economy and Taxation*, Ricardo noted an important flaw in Smith's original analysis of international trade, namely that there were many countries that did not have an absolute advantage in any area. However, what initially appeared to be a basic problem in Smith's analysis became, in Ricardo's hands, an opportunity to greatly strengthen the essential logic in Smith's critique of mercantilism. The central economic mechanism in generating new wealth through trade was not absolute advantage, but *comparative* advantage. The doctrine (often called the "law") of **comparative advantage** states that a country (and, more generally, any economic actor) should specialize in

physiocrats   A group of eighteenth-century French economists who argued that government-imposed taxes and regulations on trade were both a violation of the natural order and counterproductive.

laissez-faire
A policy that calls for government nonintervention in the economy, except for the essential minimum required to protect security and establish the legal bases for free exchange.

free trade   A policy that eliminates government controls and taxes on interstate trade.

harmony of interests
A doctrine that assumes individual and community interests coincide; frequently serves as the basis for assertions that liberating actors to pursue their individual goals is compatible with achieving what is best for the community as a whole.

division of labor   A situation in which people specialize in different economic roles and activities.

absolute advantage
An assumption that every country will have one or more products that it can either make better or sell cheaper than any international competitor.

comparative advantage
A doctrine that asserts that every economic entity (whether it is a person, company, or country) will be better off in the long run if it specializes in producing what it can do best, even if others can produce the same goods more efficiently.

9.3 ENDURING PATTERNS

The connection between preferences and power
The more compatible actors' preferences, the less strategically important their relative power positions.

The effect of the shadow of the future
The more compatible people expect their preferences to become over time, the more cooperative and less power-based their strategic choices are likely to be.

Adam Smith and Globalization

Adam Smith's eighteenth-century argument that there was a fundamental harmony of interests between the individual's pursuit of personal gain and the society's economic and political well-being led logically to the conclusion that political power—especially the role of the government—ought to be unimportant in economics.

Liberal advocates of globalization in the late twentieth and early twenty-first centuries similarly base their support for open boundaries—and a minimalist role for national governments in economic regulation—on the assumption that there is a harmony of interests.

---

what it does best, even if other countries can produce the same goods more efficiently. From this perspective, the critical comparison is *not* between two or more actors' relative ability to make a product better and cheaper. The critical comparison is, instead, among the options available to any particular actor. This insight is similar to one we made in Chapter 3 about how any well-thought out strategic choice is made: If the goal is to maximize the chances of achieving your preferred outcome, then the proper comparison is among the options available to you.

The doctrine of comparative advantage does not promise that everyone will prosper equally. It only promises that choices made on the basis of comparative advantage will produce better long-term outcomes than any other available option. Being "the best of whoever you are" might still leave you far worse off than your compatriots, but you would be even worse off in the long run if you followed any other strategy. This point is easily lost because the term *comparative advantage* is often misinterpreted as suggesting a comparison of different actors, rather than a comparison of options available to single actors. This source of confusion is often compounded by forgetting that the predicted outcomes involve *long-term* results. In the short run, government protection and a variety of other interventions in the market could produce superior results. However, according to Ricardo and almost two centuries of laissez-faire economists after him, those short-run benefits create far more problems than benefits over the long haul.

Ricardo supported his analysis of the doctrine of comparative advantage with a simple example, the trade in wine and cloth between Portugal and England. A modern scholar summarized Ricardo's example in the following way:

Portugal, . . . [Ricardo] reasoned, could produce both wine and cloth more cheaply than England. However, since Portugal had a comparative advantage in the production of wine because its soil and climate enabled it to produce wine even more cheaply and efficiently than cotton, it would gain more by specializing in the production of wine and importing cloth from England. England [with an internal comparative advantage in cloth production] would gain by specializing in cloth and importing wine.[6]

This conclusion follows even though Ricardo started with the assumption that Portugal had an *absolute* advantage in both cloth and wine. In spite of that assumption, the argument suggests that it is better to allocate your time and resources to what you do best.

This approach, once again, has an important downside: *It makes no promises that the best option will be an attractive one.* Even though the doctrine of comparative advantage—and, more generally, the classical liberal economic doctrine represented by Smith and Ricardo—asserts that there is an essential harmony of interests between the pursuit of individual economic gain and overall social welfare, there are still winners and losers. Perhaps the easiest way to understand this apparently contradictory outcome is through the concept of **terms of trade,** which refers to a comparison of the price of what people or countries sell (their exports) and what they buy (their imports). If the price of your exports is lower than the price of the goods you import, you have, by definition, *adverse terms of trade;* if the terms of trade worsen over time, that is called *declining terms of trade.* It is entirely possible for a country to make the very best choices possible under the doctrine of comparative advantage, yet end up with adverse terms of trade. From the perspective of classical liberal economists, that result simply reflects the fact that life isn't fair. However, they would also argue that specializing in those products in which you do have a comparative advantage (and reducing your purchase of expensive imports) is still the best *available* option. It offers the best chance to generate the profits necessary to provide capital for a long-term policy of import substitution that would ultimately improve the terms of trade.

Given the ultimate success of the ideas pioneered by Smith and Ricardo, it would be easy to jump to the conclusion that they must have been quickly and easily adopted. Nothing could be further from the truth. While *The Wealth of Nations* went through five editions before Smith's death in 1790, it wasn't until the late 1840s that mercantilist policies were repealed in Britain. Repeal would take even longer, and have a much shorter life, on the European continent. The reason is simple. Just as the idea of the sovereign state was around a long time before it was accepted as a guiding principle in the peace negotiations at Westphalia, laissez-faire capitalism's triumph would have to wait until the underlying conditions changed and the key actors who believed in it were able to build winning domestic and international coalitions.

The Impact of the Industrial and Financial Revolutions

Changes in the economic and political conditions of Europe began to undercut mercantilist ideas during the late eighteenth century. As mentioned earlier, the beginnings of the Industrial Revolution in the late 1700s undermined the mercantilist assumptions that wealth could not be created and that shared economic growth was thus impossible. The economic growth generated by the Industrial Revolution also exposed the inadequacy of relying on specie money in international trade. There

terms of trade A comparison of the price of the products countries export and import.

simply wasn't enough gold and silver to sustain increasing levels of economic activity. In response to this problem, governments began to print paper money and authorize private financial institutions to create their own bank notes, which could be used in exchange and as reserve assets. This **Financial Revolution** ended mercantilism's monetary system and breached the mercantilist division between internal economic transactions (in which a variety of commodities and currencies could be used for exchange) and international trade (where deficits had to be paid in specie).[7]

This financial transformation raised the question of what backing existed to support the value of paper money and other credit instruments. The initial solution was to back paper money with precious metals. Governments linked their paper currencies to defined amounts of gold or silver, which they would pay on demand to those who preferred to hold the specie rather than the paper currency. Britain was the first major trading country to move away from *bimetallism* (a reliance on both gold and silver) to an exclusively **gold standard** in 1819. (Those who enjoy the history of words may be interested to learn that the first paper currency on a gold standard, the English pound sterling, derives its name from the time when it was backed by sterling silver.) A full-fledged international gold standard would not exist until the 1870s, when Germany, France, and the United States all went on gold.[8]

These changes undercut both the logic of mercantilism and its economic and political base. New actors appeared who wanted to replace mercantilism with liberal-capitalist arrangements and had the political assets necessary to demand that their preferences be taken seriously. The next question was whether those groups could build winning coalitions.

The Triumph of Free-Trade Coalitions

By their very nature, coalitions involve political combinations that connect factions with different preferences in a common enterprise. The nature of those combinations varied across Europe.

Britain   In Britain, the first major country to adopt free-trade policies, factions interested in ending mercantilism coalesced with a broad range of other actors. This process of coalition building benefited from major changes in the structure of Parliament and electoral laws. Prior to the 1830s, Parliament was made up of three groups: the nobility and representatives of the clergy in the House of Lords, and representatives of all the rest of Britain's citizens in the House of Commons. Since the House of Lords had equal legislative powers to Commons, having a legislative chamber restricted to the nobility and the high clergy greatly protected the interests of the great landowners and other members of the economic elite. But the system was even more undemocratic than it appeared because of the restrictions on the right to vote for members of the Commons. Less than 5 percent of adult males met the property and income levels required to vote, and nominations for almost half the seats were controlled by local aristocrats. The abuses in some of these electoral districts were so flagrant that they were called "rotten boroughs." Still another large block of seats—estimated at one hundred as late as 1793—was controlled by government payoffs orchestrated by the Treasury Department.

The 1832 Reform Act marked the beginning of the end for this system. The Act expanded suffrage and, even more important, altered the way electoral districts were

Financial Revolution The introduction of bank notes, paper money, and other credit instruments in the late eighteenth and early nineteenth century that ended the reliance on specie and—along with the Industrial Revolution—marked the beginning of the end of mercantilism.

gold standard An international monetary system in which the national currencies used in interstate transactions are backed by a promise to redeem them in gold on demand.

drawn to put the emphasis squarely on representing people rather than economic interests and geographical localities. With the new rules in place, the size of the electorate expanded rapidly, doubling in 1867 and reaching virtually universal male suffrage in 1884 (women got the franchise in 1918). Even before the implications of the 1832 rules had fully played out, the Reform Act changed the distribution of political power in Parliament. It decreased the number of electoral districts controlled by landed aristocrats and shifted the emphasis from representing historic geographical boroughs to representing people. As a result, the Act immediately increased the representation of towns populated largely by the newer commercial classes and signaled that future electoral success would depend on getting the votes of a far larger percentage of the population.[9]

With these institutional changes in constituency politics and the domestic policy-making arena, free-trade supporters were able to coalesce with factions that favored labor, workplace, and tax reform. The coalition with tax reformers was particularly important, because the success of these reformers in changing the tax system made it possible to generate enough revenue to eliminate or reduce tariffs and other mercantilist sources of revenue. These core coalition members received additional support in the 1840s from those who believed trade in foodstuffs needed to be deregulated to reduce the suffering in Ireland created by the potato famine. Even though this incentive for freeing trade would lapse in time, the resulting coalition became so strong that Parliament not only repealed the most important mercantilist policies (the Corn Laws and the Navigation Acts) in the late 1840s, but it also sustained a winning coalition in favor of free trade until the Great Depression increased support for protectionist policies in the early 1930s.

The spread of free trade to the other principal trading states in Europe reinforces the conclusion that linkage politics played a central role in moving countries in and out of policies that favored free trade.

France   The early efforts of French physiocrats to free agricultural trade from protectionist tariffs had resulted in some policy changes in the late 1700s, but the effects of those changes on prices generated so much opposition from wealthy landowners that the political climate swung back toward protecting agricultural prices by controlling trade. As for the manufacturing sectors, the Industrial Revolution began decades later in France than in Britain and, once underway, moved far more slowly. Consequently, while British manufacturing interests were pushing for free trade to promote their exports, French manufacturers were far more likely to regard protection as necessary to enable their infant industries to compete with imports.

There were exceptions to this general picture of opposition to free trade by agricultural and manufacturing groups in France. Manufacturers of luxury goods (including perfumes and jewelry) in Paris wanted the increased access to foreign markets that free trade could create, as did producers of wine and goods made of silk. With these and other groups supporting them, free-trade advocates continued their efforts, but they were not able to form a winning coalition. What finally brought France into the free-trade camp were the preferences of Emperor Napoleon III (also known as Louis-Napoleon), who was Napoleon Bonaparte's nephew. He became president of France after the turmoil created by the 1848 revolts in Paris led to the end of the monarchy and the birth of the Second Republic. Then, in a *coup d'état* (an illegal overthrow of an existing government, usually by factions within the regime's military), Louis-Napoleon unilaterally tore up the democratic constitution in 1851,

9.4 ENDURING PATTERNS

The impact of varying beliefs about just relationships

If people value creating and sustaining legitimate relationships and if they think a political process and the outcome it produces are just, they are more likely to accept that outcome, even if they would have preferred something else. If they think either the outcome or the process is unjust, they are far more likely to oppose it.

The impact of linkage politics

World politics is driven by the interaction of international, factional, and constituency politics.

Opposing and Promoting Free Trade

Actors' reactions to differences in their preferences and relative power varies with their beliefs about the importance and nature of just relationships. Beliefs about the importance and nature of just relationships *internationally* are, moreover, frequently anchored in domestic politics.

As the short review of the movement toward free trade in Britain, Germany, and France in the mid-nineteenth century suggests, British free trade policies were more firmly anchored in domestic politics than those of either France or Germany. British attitudes were also connected to an intellectual perspective—liberalism—that made claims about the moral and ethical superiority of free trade. As you will see in the next section of this chapter, French and German policy makers moved away from free trade quickly, while the British held on until the Great Depression of the 1930s.

The intensity of Third World opposition to free trade in the 1960s and 1970s (see Chapter 10) was increased by the belief that the international economic system established after World War II was illegitimate because most of Africa and Asia was still colonized then, and by the fact that it was domestically unpopular.

---

thus ending the Second Republic, and declared himself emperor in 1852. Under the new constitution he imposed, the emperor alone had the authority to make binding treaty commitments.

All these pieces came together in an 1860 treaty between France and Britain that established free trade as French policy. Intent on expelling Austria from the Italian peninsula, Napoleon III decided to intervene on the side of Italians who were fighting to unify the separate states on the Italian peninsula into a single country. The British government opposed his plans to intervene but were willing to acquiesce in exchange for a treaty that moved France from protectionist policies to free trade. Under the 1852 constitution, Napoleon III could make and implement that deal without parliamentary support.

The German States   A similar pattern can be seen in the movement of Prussia (and, after unification, Germany) toward free trade. The dominant political group in Prussia during the mid-nineteenth century was the *Junker* class, landed aristocrats whose principal source of revenue was the sale of grains grown on their large estates. The Junker-dominated Prussian government had developed a comparatively low set of tariffs that were designed to generate adequate tax revenue without discouraging either exports of grain or imports of manufactures.

These underlying economic and financial incentives for leaning toward free trade were reinforced by foreign policy incentives after Bismarck became chancellor of Prussia in 1862. He was intent on reducing Austrian influence in the German Confederation (the loose intergovernmental organization of German-speaking states established at the Congress of Vienna) as part of his drive to unify the small German states under Prussian control. Consequently, he used a policy of tariff reductions as a means of undercutting Austria's economy and drawing the small German states (which were part of a customs union called the *Zollverein*) closer to Prussia. Given this overall strategy, Bismarck was quick to follow France's 1860 free-trade treaty with Britain with an 1863 treaty between France and Prussia that substantially reduced tariffs.[10]

The Brief Consensus in Favor of Free Trade Unravels

The international and domestic incentives that supported Bismarck's preference for free trade continued during the first years after German unification. Indeed, Bismarck governed with the support of a free-trade, laissez-faire parliamentary coalition from 1871 to 1878. In the mid-1870s, however, industrial and agrarian support for free trade collapsed in Germany. These coalitions unraveled under the economic pressures created by the 1873 industrial depression, the rapid increase in grain imports made possible by improved rail transport from Russia, and by the development of transatlantic steamship routes. These economic incentives were not enough by themselves to produce a return to protection. The final, and critical, piece in the puzzle was Bismarck's conclusion that the central government needed additional sources of revenue to maintain Germany's military capabilities. The liberal coalition on which he relied refused to raise consumption taxes on food and other necessities to pay for increased military spending. Determined to obtain more revenue, Bismarck took advantage of two separate attempts on the Kaiser's life in 1878 to raise the specter of both a domestic and international security threat. Blaming the assassination attempts on socialists, he dissolved the parliament to try for a conservative electoral victory. With that victory in hand, he dropped his free-trade coalition partners for an alliance with industry and agriculture that would vote in favor of higher taxes for increased military spending. The payoff was a return to protectionist trade policies in 1879.

France also returned to protection in the early 1880s. Once again, the reasons are to be found not simply in the economic incentives for supporting this policy option but also in linkage politics. The empire ended when Napoleon III was captured during the Franco-Prussian war in 1870. After years of political turmoil and debate, the Third Republic was founded in 1878. Unlike the empire, the Third Republic featured a strong parliament and a weak executive. Given a strong parliament and the prevailing distribution of political power among factions that opposed and supported free trade, the result was swift—a return to protection.

The return of Germany and France to protection by the 1880s shows that even though a large number of changes in domestic and international coalitions need to take place to produce major shifts in foreign economic policy, those shifts are not always stable and self-reinforcing. Germany and France's return to protection also shows that the mid-nineteenth century consensus on free trade was really quite short-lived. Free-trade looks like an enduring legacy of this period only if one focuses on Britain. Finally, it is important to note that these changes in economic policy had important implications for governments' views of their security requirements. At midcentury, liberal economic thinkers believed that free trade would reduce the level of military conflict by revealing an underlying harmony of interests in world politics and economics. Indeed, the assumption that a harmony of interests existed—if it were only recognized—was so strong among mid-nineteenth century economic liberals that many of them were pacifists.

However, by the end of the nineteenth century liberal pacifism and the belief in a harmony of interests had been badly shaken by events on the European continent. British free traders worried that German unification and France's return to protection were weakening Britain's export industries so much that its security, as well as its economy, was being put at risk. As we discussed in Chapter 6, these fears aggravated existing security concerns. They also poisoned the overall diplomatic climate in the thirty years before World War I by encouraging the growth of competitive nationalism—justified by the pseudoscientific claims of Social Darwinism, which were especially popular in Britain—and by increasing the incentives for colonial expansion. Taken together, these changes led European policy makers to adopt an increasingly competitive, conflict-filled approach to political economy and security systems as the nineteenth century drew to a close.

At the same time as Europe's political economy was being transformed during the nineteenth century, Europe's place in the world economy was changing in dramatic ways. Those changes produced a distinctive, and historically unprecedented, period in the evolution of the European-centered global political economy.

The Eurocentric System's High-Water Mark

Europe's mercantilist state builders created a Eurocentric global political economy during the 300-year-long period of expansion between the late 1400s and late 1700s known as the old colonialism. As we discussed in Chapter 7, the main impetus for expansion was the effort to find alternative trade routes to India and China. It is also important to remember that during the mercantile period, Europe had no significant economic or military advantages over the major civilizations in India and China other than in navigation. As a result, when European explorers and traders arrived in Asia, they had to request, rather than demand, an opportunity to trade. In the mid-1700s, little in the relative positions of Europe and Asia had changed. One hundred years later, little in the economic and political relationships between Europe and the rest of the world looked the same.

A Revolution in Global Patterns of Productivity, Output, and Trade

Table 9–1 brings the transformation into sharp—and very stark—focus. Part (a) of Table 9–1 shows that as late as 1750, Europe's share of the world's total manufacturing output was substantially smaller than China's (23.2 percent as compared to 32.8 percent) and about equal to that of the Indian subcontinent. Indeed, Europe's share was only about one-third of the total for what later came to be called the Third World (Africa, Asia, Latin America, and the Middle East). By 1900, Europe's share

TABLE 9–1   GLOBAL PATTERNS IN MANUFACTURING, 1750–1900

	(a) RELATIVE SHARES OF WORLD MANUFACTURING OUTPUT, 1750–1900						(b) PER CAPITA LEVELS OF INDUSTRIALIZATION, 1750–1900 (RELATIVE TO U.K. IN 1900 = 100)					
	1750	1800	1830	1860	1880	1900	1750	1800	1830	1860	1880	1900
(Europe as a whole)	23.2%	28.1%	34.2%	53.2%	61.3%	62.0%	8	8	11	16	24	35
United Kingdom	1.9	4.3	9.5	19.9	22.9	18.5	10	16	25	64	87	100
Habsburg Empire	2.9	3.2	3.2	4.2	4.4	4.7	7	7	8	11	15	23
France	4.0	4.2	5.2	7.9	7.8	6.8	9	9	12	20	28	39
German States/Germany	2.9	3.5	3.5	4.9	8.5	13.2	8	8	9	15	25	52
Italian States/Italy	2.4	2.5	2.3	2.5	2.5	2.5	8	8	8	10	12	17
Russia	5.0	5.6	5.6	7.0	7.6	8.8	6	6	7	8	10	15
United States	0.1	0.8	2.4	7.2	14.7	23.6	4	9	14	21	38	69
Japan	3.8	3.5	2.8	2.6	2.4	2.4	7	7	7	7	9	12
Third World	73.0	67.7	60.5	36.6	20.9	11.0	7	6	6	4	3	2
China	32.8	33.3	29.8	19.7	12.5	6.2	8	6	6	4	4	3
India/Pakistan	24.5	19.7	17.6	8.6	2.8	1.7	7	6	6	3	2	1

Source: Paul Kennedy, *Rise and Fall of the Great Powers* (New York: Random House, 1987), p. 149. Reprinted by permission of HarperCollins Publishers Ltd © Paul Kennedy, 1987.

of world manufacturing had risen from 23.2 to 62.0 percent, while the Third World's share had fallen from 73.0 to 11.0 percent. The only big gainer outside of Europe in this period was the United States, which rose from one-tenth of one percent in 1750 to 23.6 percent in 1900, thereby surpassing Britain (18.5) and Germany (13.2), the two most industrialized European states. With this kind of explosive growth in industrial output in North America and Europe, Japan—famous for the industrializing efforts of its rulers after the Meiji Restoration in 1868—had to grow rapidly in the last part of the nineteenth century simply to maintain its relative share at 2.4 percent.

Driving these massive changes in relative shares of world manufacturing output were immense increases in industrial productivity in Europe and North America. As Part (b) of Table 9–1 shows, per capita levels of manufacturing output were essentially identical in Europe and Asia in 1750. By 1900, Europe's industrial sector was about *seventeen* times more productive than the Third World. Britain, Europe's most industrialized country, had an industrial output that was *fifty* times higher. Germany, in second place in Europe in 1900 after passing France and closing rapidly on Britain, was *twenty-five* times higher.

Europe's Industrial Revolution was supported by an ongoing revolution in agricultural production. Indeed, many economists believe that relatively closed economies need high agricultural productivity to create the conditions for industrial growth. (Even with the colonial trade established during the mercantilist period, Europe's economy was still largely self-contained in the late eighteenth and early nineteenth centuries.) Agricultural workers have to produce a substantial surplus over their own subsistence needs if industrial workers and the cities that grow up around them are to be fed. Moreover, in a period when limitations in transportation made it very difficult to ship bulky manufactured goods and commodities great distances, industry needed a vibrant agricultural sector to help create an internal market large enough to purchase the goods it produced. After all, the overwhelming majority of the population—and, thus, the potential consumers for industrial goods—still lived on the farm.

The magnitude of Europe's jump in agricultural productivity comes through clearly in the comparative data. Prior to the eighteenth century, agricultural areas in Europe did not produce much more per acre than did prime land in the tropics. By 1900, British farmers were producing well over twice as much per acre as farmers in the tropics. Moreover, technological improvements in agricultural equipment enabled British workers to farm more acres than their tropical counterparts, with the result that the productivity of British farmers was six to seven times higher. The differences in agricultural productivity were even greater in Canada and the United States, where the larger size of the areas open to cultivation enabled farmers to use machinery to even greater advantage.[11]

Europe's revolutions in agricultural and industrial productivity radically altered the global political economy. Europe became a source of capital for international investment that had no historical precedent. This financial transformation was reinforced by a major change in trade patterns. By the middle of the nineteenth century, world trade began to show a stark specialization: Some countries had a comparative advantage in the export of manufactured products, while others had a comparative advantage in primary products from agriculture, mining, and other extractive industries.

Looking for the Sources of Change

As the numbers in Table 9–1 on shares of world manufacturing output show, the major shift in the relative positions of Europe and the rest of the world occurred between 1750 and 1880. The timing is significant both for what it tells us about economic history and for what it implies for modern debates about the origin of

Upon his arrival in Japan, 1853, Admiral Perry met with members of the Bakufu (the Tokugawa Shogunate's administration). His ultimatums led to the 1858 Unequal Treaties opening Japan to foreign trade, making him highly unpopular with the Japanese. Matsuo Taseko's poems about Perry's arrival called upon a divine wind to sweep him and all foreigners from Japan's shores.

Europe's wealth and the Third World's poverty. There are two key points to recognize and remember. First, this shift occurred well before the resurgence of colonial expansion. The partition of Africa, and the New Imperialism more generally, did not begin until the 1880s. Second, this shift in Europe's position in the global economy occurred before trade between Europe and the rest of the world was of much aggregate economic significance. While trade during the mercantile period made many individuals and governments rich, it was not a significant factor in overall economic activity prior to the second half of the nineteenth century. The nineteenth-century revolution in industrial output and global trade patterns occurred *before* there was a large volume of trade between industrialized areas and the tropics.

As W. Arthur Lewis, a noted specialist in political economy, reports: "As late as 1883, the first year for which we have a calculation, total imports into the United States and Western Europe from Asia, Africa, and tropical Latin America came only to about a dollar per head of the population of the exporting countries."[12] Early European industrializers didn't need imports from these areas, because most of the raw materials they needed were available in Europe up until the end of the 1800s. Moreover, any significant growth in the overall magnitude of world trade had to wait for improvements in the transportation of bulky and heavy goods. Railroads began to be built in the Third World in the 1860s. Transportation rates from Third World ports fell significantly only after the introduction of large numbers of iron-hulled steam ships in the 1870s.

Once this revolution in transportation had occurred, policy makers and entrepreneurs in Africa, Asia, and Latin America were in a position to get involved in these increasing levels of world trade in either of two ways: as exporters of raw materials, foodstuffs, and other primary products to the industrializing regions in the world, or as exporters of manufactured goods. Moreover, because manufacturing in the late nineteenth century did not require levels of capital or skills that were beyond their capabilities, there was no technical reason why industrialization could not take place. Exports from tropical areas to the industrialized areas of Europe and North America did grow significantly—at about 4 percent a year for the three decades before World War I—but remained almost exclusively in primary products.[13] Why they did is one of the most hotly contested questions in economics, history, and political science. We lean toward an interpretation that looks at how economic and political factors were entwined in linkage politics.

Part of the reason was clearly external and political: European colonial administrators actively discouraged, and sometimes even viciously suppressed, indigenous manufacturing enterprises. The British suppression of indigenous textile manufacturing on the Indian subcontinent is, for instance, justly infamous. However, the European countries' economic advantages over their colonies also involved factors that had more to do with agricultural productivity and their relative ability to industrialize than their ability to suppress or control others. Capitalist ideas and institutions had been growing in Europe for at least a century before the transportation revolution gave non-European actors the option of exporting bulky manufactured items to Europe. Moreover, a century of growth in agricultural and industrial productivity had given Europe the ability to feed a large industrial work force, far more capital for investment than was the case in most areas outside of Europe and North America, and immensely advantageous terms of trade. The tentative conclusion that these factors may have played more important roles than colonialism in generating Europe's economic takeoff is supported by another interesting fact: Tropical areas that were not colonized in this period showed much the same specialization in primary goods as those that were.

Whatever conclusions one draws about the origin of Europe's great edge in being able to produce and export manufactured goods in the nineteenth century, it's clear that differences in the terms of trade helped sustain the patterns in global trade generated by Europe's massive edge in both agricultural and industrial productivity. The vast differences in the price of the manufactured products exported by Europe and the primary products exported by much of the rest of the world created highly adverse terms of trade for much of Africa, Asia, Latin America, and the Middle East. The adverse terms of trade created by the difference in prices between manufactured goods and agricultural products kept incomes lower in non-industrial areas and created **balance-of-payments problems,** which occur when the aggregate value of the payments, gifts, and capital that flow out of a country is greater than the aggregate value of the payments, gifts, and capital coming in.

Tropical countries also suffered adverse terms of trade problems *within* the agricultural sector as a result of the substantial differences in productivity. The differences were particularly pronounced in foodstuffs, and food prices set limits on the prices that could be charged for other agricultural exports. Lewis offers the following example:

> Low productivity in food set the . . . terms of trade. . . . A farmer in Nigeria might tend his peanuts with as much diligence and skill as a farmer in Australia tended his sheep, but the return would be very different. The just price, to use the medieval term, would have rewarded equal competence with equal earnings.

balance-of-payments problem   A situation in which the aggregate value of the payments, gifts, and capital that flow out of a country is greater than the aggregate value coming in.

But the market price gave the Nigerian for his peanuts a 700-lbs.-of-grain-per-acre level of living, and the Australian for his wool a 1600-lbs.-per-acre level of living, not because of marginal utilities or productivities in peanuts or wool, but because these were the respective amounts that their cousins could produce on the family farms.[14]

The effects of these differences in agricultural productivity on the terms of trade were exacerbated by population movements at the end of the nineteenth century. During this period about fifty million Indians and Chinese emigrated in search of a better standard of living than they could find in their homelands. Most settled in the tropical regions of Africa, Asia, and the Pacific. Adding such a large number of laborers to these areas drove down wages and prices still further, which increased the attractiveness of building more plantations and mines. By contrast, the effect of immigration into the United States and other areas with high industrial and agricultural productivity was quite different. During the same period as the migration of Indians and Chinese was taking place, roughly the same number of Europeans emigrated to North America, Argentina, Chile, Australia, and South Africa. Their pay, however, reflected different market forces. With those higher wages, they had more money to spend on manufactured goods, so the whole process of economic growth accelerated.

When combined with the adverse terms of trade between primary products and manufactured goods, these differences in the terms of trade for agricultural products had devastating results. In principle, specializing in the export of agricultural goods and other primary products can generate enough profits to develop a successful industrial sector. In practice, the adverse terms of trade within the agricultural sectors of many tropical areas reduced profits below the level needed to industrialize. As Lewis concludes:

> Given this difference in the . . . terms of trade, the opportunity that international trade presented to the new temperate settlements was very different from the opportunity presented to the tropics. Trade offered [Europe and] the temperate settlements [in North America and other areas] high income per head. . . . The . . . terms available to the tropics, on the other hand, offered the opportunity to stay poor—at any rate until such time as the labor reservoirs of India and China might be exhausted.[15]

These linked international and domestic economic conditions created few attractive options during this period for policy makers outside of Europe and North America interested in industrialization. But it is also important to note that the areas that lagged far behind in industrialization usually faced political as well as economic impediments to developing competitive manufacturing sectors. Such areas were usually governed by political elites whose primary economic base was in agriculture and who, more often than not, regarded industrialization as a threat. The importance of policy makers' preferences can be seen in the different experiences of Argentina and Australia. In the middle of the nineteenth century these countries had strikingly similar economic profiles. They even relied on the same commodities for their export earnings. In spite of these similarities, their economic paths after 1850 were quite different. Australia used export earnings from agriculture to promote import substitution (building domestic industries to make products that were previously imported) and to industrialize; Argentina's elites did not use earnings from agriculture to industrialize. The key difference was political: Argentina's politics were dominated by a landed aristocracy; Australia's by an urban elite.[16] The crucial role of political choice also comes through clearly in Japan. Japan's rush to industrialize came after the Meiji Restoration brought a pro-industrial coalition into the government. Europe provides still more examples of the impact of politics on the rate of industrialization: Manufacturing was not nearly as strong in central and southern Europe, areas that were governed by elites dependent on agriculture.

While this combination of economic and political factors provides a plausible linkage-politics interpretation for the origins of the changes that occurred in the global political economy during the nineteenth century, debates about the causes of this transformation in Europe's position in the global economy continue to this day. Perhaps even more important for our understanding of world politics in this period, these debates became as much a part of the politics of international economics as did the changes themselves. Controversies about Europe's role in the global economy were, moreover, inescapably connected to controversies about the effects of the changing political economy *within* Europe.

Escalating Controversies on the Eve of World War I

While issues of political economy have been central to the evolution of world politics since the earliest mercantilist state builders and the beginnings of the interstate system, the decades immediately before World War I saw an increase in the number of issues that generated sustained controversies. At the same time as nineteenth-century pressures for democracy and nationalism were leading to expansion of suffrage and rapid growth in the number of factions involved in policy making, industrialization was changing Europe from a predominantly agrarian and largely rural society to an increasingly urban one. Those changes generated a massive shift in constituency politics at the same time as they placed a whole new set of domestic issues on policy makers' agendas. Those controversies—over tax policy, social reform, and workplace legislation—rapidly became entangled with the most prominent international issues of the period. Colonial expansion and the pre-World War I arms races cost immense amounts of money. Those costs were intrinsically controversial; they also sharply reduced policy makers' ability to allocate money to domestic purposes. Those constraints generated a debate about who was benefiting from the new imperialism and intensified ongoing controversies about the fairness of the tax structure.

Similar patterns in linkage politics intensified debates over foreign economic policy. The debate between advocates of free trade and protection was not simply a debate over economic doctrine; it was also a debate over which sectors of the domestic economy would benefit. Meanwhile, the growth in international finance and the movement from specie to paper currencies backed by a gold standard raised questions about where the financial surplus would be invested and how the domestic economy would be affected by the adjustments needed either to maintain or alter exchange rates. Cutting across all these questions was the intensifying debate among supporters of capitalist arrangements, reformers, and Marxists. These issues and the ways in which they were connected give this period a very distinctive flavor.

The transformation in constituency politics and the movement toward more democratic institutions affected the way all these issues played out. While there were many detours along the way (such as the collapse of the Second Republic in France and its replacement by Napoleon III's empire), the overall trend during the nineteenth century was toward universal male suffrage and increased parliamentary control over executive decision making. The rapid transformation of Europe's political economy during the nineteenth century changed the nature of the voters and the issues they cared about at the same time as these electoral and institutional changes made their preferences matter. Industrialization, for instance, drew large numbers of people off the farms and out of the villages in which their families had lived for generations into rapidly booming cities with few social services or safety nets and often squalid living conditions. In 1850 Britain was the only country in the world where the Industrial Revolution and urbanization had reached a level where less than 50 percent of the work force was in agriculture. By World War I, much of Western Europe was well on the way toward an urban, industrial economy. This transformation was so vast and sudden (Germany urbanized so fast that it went from a majority of the population living in rural areas to a majority living in urban areas in only about fifty years) that it shook the foundations of daily life and politics throughout Europe. The way these changes played out varied with the distinctive mixes of international and domestic incentives that confronted policy makers in different countries.[17] The following description of the situation in Britain provides a snapshot of the general situation:

> The two or three decades before 1914 witnessed an increasingly heated debate upon the proper ends and priorities of national policy, this debate being provoked both by the rise of Labour and by the rise of external challenges. It was, moreover, not a debate on which the different aspects of policy could be dealt with separately. The arms race impinged on government finance, and that upon taxation, and that upon social policy and the domestic political constellation; the "social question," in its turn, could also affect spending and taxation, and have impacts on external policy; the furious quarrels about tariffs, or about direct versus indirect taxation, were immediately related to the arms race, social reforms, and the "threat" to capital, and so on. Armaments policy and foreign policy and taxation policy and social policy all hung together.[18]

Debates about Trade, Monetary, and Adjustment Policies

Attacks on the existing political economy came from all directions and ideological persuasions. Within the political mainstream, advocates of free trade and advocates of protection dueled over the implications of different trade policies for long-term growth and tax policy. Meanwhile, the movement toward a gold standard in the 1870s led to charges by the French and the Germans that British policy makers were using the uniquely central role of the pound sterling in the gold standard system to pursue British financial and political interests at the expense of everyone else who depended on the international monetary system. Modern political economists agree with the general thrust—if not all the details—of this critique, summarized by Robert Gilpin:

> The classical gold standard did not function automatically. . . . [Nor did] the international monetary system under the classical gold standard . . . operate impersonally. . . . [Both were] organized and managed by Great Britain; and the City of London [Britain's financial district], through its hegemonic position in world commodity, money, and capital markets, enforced the "rules of the system" upon the world's economies. The integration of national monetary

systems with the London financial market endowed Great Britain with the ability to control to a considerable degree the world's money supply . . . [and] manage . . . world monetary policy. . . . The monetary system under the gold standard was thus a hierarchical one, dominated by Great Britain and . . . [managed in a way that] was not politically symmetrical in its effects on various national economies.[19]

Because of the greater visibility of trade and tax policy, the debates over free trade and protection were more intense than the debates over international monetary policy, which are rarely visible enough to escape the offices of policy makers and financial experts. However, while the management of the gold standard was less visible to the general public, it had significant effects on the growth rates of different countries and the distribution of income across different social groups within European societies. For instance, British money managers in "the City" were determined to maintain the value of the pound relative to gold so that it would continue to be the most desirable currency, not only in trade and international financial transactions but also as a reserve asset. (As we discuss in Chapter 10, U.S. policy makers had similar incentives to maintain the value of the dollar relative to gold after it became the leading international currency after World War II.) The problem was that maintaining the price of the pound relative to gold frequently involved *deflation*—slowing economic growth.

While many believe managing the value of a country's currency by using deflationary **adjustment policies** produces long-term benefits that are widely shared by different groups within a country, there is no doubt that in the short run there are clear winners and losers. Wealthier classes benefit because protecting the value of the currency protects the value of investments denominated in the country's currencies. But people whose incomes depend on wages are hurt because slowing down a country's economy lowers wages and increases unemployment.

While deflationary adjustment policies are hard on workers, they reinforce the value of that country's currency relative to gold (or any other international standard) in two ways. When a country's economy is suffering from *inflation* (when the prices, or nominal value, of a country's goods and services are rising faster than their real value), foreigners will want to buy fewer products from that country for the simple reason that its prices are higher. A fall in demand for products from any particular country simultaneously reduces the attractiveness—and, hence, the value—of its currency. Deflating an economy reverses the process; lowering prices increases the attractiveness of the goods and raises the value of the currency in which those goods are priced.

Deflationary policies can increase the international strength of a country's currency, even when economic growth has not created inflation. Under conditions of economic growth, consumers buy more imports, which sends more of the country's currency abroad in exchange for the goods purchased. Assuming its gold reserves haven't changed, the outward flow of a country's currency will reduce the ratio of its gold holdings relative to the value of the currency in the possession of foreigners (who, under the gold standard, have the right to demand gold in exchange for the money they hold). The more money being held abroad relative to a country's gold reserves, the greater the downward pressure on its value. Deflationary policies can reverse this weakening by reducing imports and, hence, the flow of money abroad.

The distribution of political power in Britain before World War I produced a winning coalition in support of deflationary adjustment policies that hurt the working class and benefited investors and the financial markets, even as domestic politics

adjustment policies
Government monetary and fiscal policies that can promote either inflation or deflation; often used to try to affect the international price of national currencies.

9.5 ENDURING PATTERNS

The connection between preferences and power
The more incompatible actors' preferences, the more strategically important their relative power positions.

The impact of varying beliefs about just relationships
If people think either an outcome or the political process that produced it is unjust, they are far more likely to oppose it.

The impact of linkage politics
World politics is driven by the interaction of international, factional, and constituency politics.

Labor, Deflation, and Predatory Pricing

In the decades before World War I, British working class groups and their political allies opposed using deflationary adjustment policies to maintain the international price of the pound. They opposed it not only because it increased unemployment and lowered wages, but also because they believed the political process that produced those outcomes was illegitimate. Given the incompatible objectives between those who supported such deflationary adjustment policies and those who opposed them, the outcome came down to relative political power and who could build a winning coalition. More often than not, labor lost.

In the early 1980s, many unions in the United States argued that their members were losing jobs because international competitors were selling cars and other products in the United States at prices that were below a fair profit level. The argument that domestic jobs were being lost to foreign competitors because of predatory pricing enabled supporters of a more aggressive U.S. policy to protect U.S. workers to make a claim based on legitimacy as well as self-interest. In this case, U.S. workers—unlike their British counterparts before World War I—found powerful allies in corporations who believed their survival was at stake. The resul was a winning coalition that pushed the executive to demand changes in the trade practices of other countries.

---

produced winning coalitions for tax and pension reform that helped workers. Debates about these policy choices created controversies within the political mainstream at the same time as radical reformers and revolutionaries were stepping up their attacks on the mainstream.

J. A. Hobson—A Radical Reformer's Critique

One of the most famous radical reformers in this period was J. A. Hobson, a journalist and political economist who argued that the growing political power of financial interests had caused the new imperialism and was leading the world toward war.

In 1902 Hobson published *Imperialism, A Study*, the first major attempt to identify the origins of the surge in colonial expansion at the end of the nineteenth century. Hobson argued that this new imperialism was qualitatively different from the old colonialism, that the areas acquired were predominantly colonies of occupation (as opposed to settlement), and that the race to acquire areas involved many more states and a dangerously high level of competition.

Hobson concluded that no genuine national interest was driving colonial expansion, that special interests had usurped national policy making and were manipulating it in pursuit of private gain. He argued that the large financial houses were the "governor of the imperial engine." Unable to find profitable sources of investment at home, they manipulated both public opinion and the government in an effort to acquire colonies that could generate profitable sources of investment abroad.

> While the manufacturing and trading classes make little out of their new markets, paying, if they knew it, much more in taxation than they get out of them in trade, it is quite otherwise with the investor. It is not too much to say that the modern foreign policy of Great Britain has been primarily a struggle for profitable markets of investment. To a larger extent every year Great Britain has become a nation living upon tribute from abroad, and the classes who enjoy this tribute have had an ever-increasing incentive to employ the public policy, the public purse, and the public force to extend the field of their private investments. . . . The direct influence exercised by great financial houses in "high politics" is supported by the control which they exercise over the body of public opinion through the Press. . . . The play of these forces does not openly appear. They are essentially parasites upon patriotism.[20]

To explain the drive to invest abroad, Hobson created what has come to be called an **underconsumptionist thesis.** He argued that owners were continuing to pay workers subsistence wages even as great increases in their productivity generated enormous profits. While that exploitation created short-term gains for owners, it kept workers' disposable income so low that domestic aggregate economic demand could not grow fast enough to create attractive opportunities for those profits to be reinvested at home. Desperate to find opportunities for profitable investments abroad, financial interests threw their political weight behind imperial expansion. Hobson believed that if nothing were done to break the power of financial interests and end the competition for empire, democracy would be fatally undermined and the world would be drawn into a series of wars as colonizers fought over the partition of China and other areas in Asia and Africa. Hobson's solution flowed directly from his analysis of the origins of the problem. He called for radical economic and political reform within Europe to increase the wages of the working class and to reduce the power of investors over government policy. He also suggested that existing colonies be put under international trusteeship and prepared for eventual independence.

Hobson's argument had an extraordinary effect on contemporary politics in Europe. As is frequently the case with critiques that galvanize political movements and recast the terms of public debates, he was right in some aspects of his argument and grievously off-target in others. His analysis of the effects of underconsumption on the concentration of profits in the hands of industrialists and large financial houses is

underconsumptionist thesis An interpretation of patterns in domestic and foreign investment that stresses the negative effects on domestic aggregate economic demand—and thus on the incentives to increase domestic investment—created by keeping workers' wages far lower than their productivity justifies.

still regarded as insightful, as is his emphasis on the massive increase in the export of capital in this period.

However, he was off-target on two central aspects of the linkages between domestic and international politics and their effects on the global political economy. First, most of the capital exported by Britain during this period did not go to the colonies acquired during the new imperialism (there were continuing and quite heavy investments in India, but the British had been involved there long before the end of the 1800s). Instead, it went to the other industrialized countries in Europe, North America, and settlement colonies such as Australia and New Zealand. The second great weakness in Hobson's account lies in his assertion that British foreign policy was controlled by the large investment houses. While these firms certainly had some influence, he provides no evidence of influence on the scale that his argument requires. What remains is an "argument by assertion" tainted by anti-Semitism:

> [The great financial houses] form the central ganglion of international capitalism. United by the strongest bonds of organization, always in closest and quickest touch with one another, situated in the very heart of the business capital of every State, controlled, so far as Europe is concerned, chiefly by men of a singular and peculiar race, who have behind them many centuries of financial experience, they are in a unique position to manipulate the policy of nations. No great quick direction of capital is possible save by their consent and through their agency. Does anyone seriously suppose that a great war could be undertaken by any European State, or a great State loan subscribed, if the house of Rothschild and its connexions set their face against it?[21]

The Growing Popularity of Marxism

To the voices of Hobson and other radical reformers were added calls for revolution by followers of Marx. Beginning with the *Communist Manifesto* (published with Friedrich Engels in 1848) and continuing until his death in 1883, Karl Marx developed a grand theory of the evolution of economic systems. As we explained in Chapter 2, Marxism argues that changes in people's relationships to the means of production drive the evolution of economic systems, the political systems that develop in response to those changes in the structure of the economy, and the very ways in which people conceptualize the world around them. Marx believed that the world evolved through a dialectical process. A *dialectic* is a process of development (and reasoning) in which progress occurs through stages. In each stage there is an ordered development of thesis, antithesis, and synthesis (a new and superior thesis that resolves the previous contradiction between thesis and antithesis). In Marx's hands, the dialectic became an analysis of economically driven change in which one set of internally consistent economic relations (a synthesis) would develop internal contradictions (an antithesis) and class conflicts that would lead to a revolution. Out of that revolution would come a new synthesis which would, over time, develop its own set of internal contradictions and eventually collapse in still another revolution. Marx believed that capitalism was a historically necessary phase in this dialectical process, but also that it would end in a communist revolution. Under communism, capitalism—and, along with it, private property, class conflict, and exploitation—would disappear, to be replaced by an egalitarian and utopian society.

Marx did not spend much time analyzing either the specific nature of this utopian society or the particular steps that would be needed to produce a successful overthrow of the capitalist system. The absence of any detailed guidance on a revolutionary strategy probably reflected his expectation that the spread of capitalism would result in the overwhelming majority of the population being pushed down into a badly exploited working class (called the *proletariat*), while the remaining capitalist exploiters were reduced to such a small number that revolution would appear all but inevitable. Whatever the reason, and irrespective of Marx's claim that the result was historically inevitable, many of his followers were not willing to wait on history. The result was a rapid escalation of the perceived stakes attached to decisions involving the global political economy. Those stakes would grow even higher after World War I.

World War I and the Specter of Revolution

The Russian government collapsed in March 1917 under the combined weight of the cost of World War I and decades of incompetence and autocratic rule by the tsar. Alexander Kerensky's provisional government, which had promised democracy and a continuation of the fight against Germany, then fell to Lenin and the Bolsheviks in November 1917. Lenin promised to expand the communist revolution beyond the new Soviet Union and build a new world order without imperialism, war, or states. The seriousness with which this promise was viewed in the West can be seen in the announcement of Wilson's Fourteen Points in January 1918 (which were explicitly designed as an alternative to the Leninist vision of the post-war world) and the decision by the British, French, and Americans to intervene in the Russian civil war in 1918 (some U.S. troops stayed until 1920). Fears were further heightened by the political chaos in Germany—which included attempts to create Soviet-style republics—after the armistice in November 1918.

Given the scope of this fear—plus the central role of Lenin's ideas in Third World attitudes about imperialism during the decolonization process and the Cold War—it is important to invest some time in understanding the core of Lenin's analysis of imperialism.

Lenin's Interpretation of Imperialism

In an analysis that borrowed heavily from both radical and revolutionary critics of capitalism, Lenin argued that imperialism was a distinctive phase in the historical development of capitalism. In his words:

> Imperialism is capitalism in that stage of development in which the dominance of monopolies and finance capital has established itself; in which the export of capital has acquired pronounced importance; in which the division of the world among the international trusts has begun; in which the division of all territories of the globe among the great capitalist powers has been completed.[22]

Soviet art portrayed Lenin as a charismatic figure courageously leading the masses toward revolution and social justice.

When one disassembles this long sentence into its separate steps, the following sequence emerges: Lenin argued that free-trade capitalism was anti-colonial at its peak in the 1860 to 1870 period. However, after 1870 industrial monopolies began to dominate the economies of the principal capitalist countries. These industrial monopolies were then taken over by banking monopolies. The union of industrial and banking monopolies—with the banks in the driver's seat—created **finance capitalism.** After 1903 finance capitalism became, according to Lenin, the very foundation of economic life. It was this transition from free-trade to monopoly capitalism between 1870 and 1903 that led to the partition of the world.

Lenin built on Hobson's under-consumptionist thesis, but changed it from an argument for radical reform to a call for revolution. He argued that the development of finance capitalism had produced an "enormous 'superabundance of capital'" that could not be profitably invested at home.[23] The stage of imperialism was reached when the entire world had been partitioned in an effort to find profitable sources for investment. With the pressure to expand continuing unabated, the capitalist powers would then be driven into wars of imperialist redivision. World War I was, Lenin claimed, the first war of imperialist redivision. With luck, the costs of the war would lead to a worldwide communist revolution. If not, further wars of imperialist redivision would inevitably follow until capitalism collapsed.

Lenin's argument played a crucial role in the evolution of the Marxist intellectual tradition and affected many of the arguments about the global political economy in the twentieth century. While Lenin's assumption that capitalism had a natural tendency toward concentration that would ultimately lead to revolution is entirely consistent with Marx, Lenin added at least two critical amendments to Marx: the concept of finance capitalism (which Lenin took from an Austrian economist named Rudolph Hilferding), and the idea that finance capitalism would lead to the partition of the world. These amendments provided an explanation for why the revolution predicted by Marx had not yet occurred (the stage of imperialism had bought some extra time), while promising that the communist revolution was still inevitable (but in Lenin's amended version, only after recurring wars of imperialist redivision).

Why wouldn't capitalism save itself through reform? Lenin's answer is a classic example of a *tautology* (an argument by definition):

> It goes without saying that if capitalism could develop agriculture, which today lags far behind industry everywhere, if it could raise the standard of living of the masses, who are everywhere still poverty-stricken and underfed, in spite of the amazing advance of technical knowledge, there could be no talk of a superabundance of capital. This "argument" the petty-bourgeois critics of capitalism [such as Hobson] advance on every occasion. But if capitalism did these things

finance capitalism A term popularized by Lenin that refers to the union of banking and industrial monopolies.

While Western fears of communism were often exaggerated or manipulated for political reasons, Soviet propaganda provided support for those fears by stressing worldwide revolution. The caption in this 1919 poster reads: "You have nothing to lose but your chains, but the world will soon be yours."

Museum of the Revolution, Moscow/Bridgeman Art Library, London.

it would not be capitalism; for uneven development and wretched conditions of the masses are fundamental and inevitable conditions and premises of this mode of production. As long as capitalism remains what it is, surplus capital will never be utilized for raising the standard of living of the masses.[24]

As one can see in this example, tautologies are circular. The conclusion is the same as the starting point. Capitalism is incapable of reform because it is in the nature of capitalism that it can't be reformed. This tautology is, moreover, the second central tautology in Lenin's argument. The first is embedded in the definition of imperialism: "imperialism *is* capitalism in that stage of development . . . " Defining imperialism as a stage of capitalism makes it inevitable that capitalism is guilty of causing imperialism. Asserting that capitalism is incapable of reform simply compounds one tautology with another.

Arguments by definition may be meaningful as statements of faith, but they are not very useful from the perspective of systematic inquiry. The reason is simple. For the relationship between capitalism and imperialism to be a valid question, the two concepts must be different. Put differently, it must be possible for capitalism and imperialism to be *unrelated* for it to be interesting to ask how they are *connected*. Cause and effect must be different things. A doctor tells you nothing if she says the cause of your disease is the disease.

Lenin's argument provides several other examples of classic analytical flaws that are summarized in the box "*A Closer Look:* Lenin's Predictions." Taking some time to understand them will not only help you understand Lenin's arguments better; it will also give you some general tools for evaluating assertions about cause and effect.

Schumpeter's Response to the Argument That Capitalism Caused Imperialism

Analytical errors are not, of course, the exclusive property of any particular ideological perspective. In 1919, Joseph Schumpeter, one of the most famous economists in this period, published the first major attack on the argument that capitalism caused imperialism. In *Imperialism and Social Classes*, Schumpeter argued that true capitalism was pacific and promoted rational long-term behavior. Imperialism, in contrast, was the "objectless disposition on the part of a state to unlimited forcible expansion." Imperialism was generated by political, not economic, forces. Schumpeter argued that the vestiges of the old warrior classes from pre-industrial Europe had maintained their political power through the European aristocracy, and that the subculture of these social classes emphasized militarism for its own sake. These classes had drawn capitalism from its natural course, perverted it with militarism, and turned it into a system of state-protected export monopolies. Ultimately imperialism would end, not because capitalism had been overthrown but because its true nature had triumphed.

The problem is that Schumpeter's argument is every bit as much an argument by definition as Lenin's. If imperialism is "objectless," it is by definition irrational. Since capitalism is defined as being inherently rational, it cannot generate "objectless" choice. This tautology is supported by a second: True capitalism is inherently peaceful; imperialism is militaristic.

While in retrospect there is an amusing symmetry in having both sides of the debate about the relationship between capitalism and imperialism anchored by tautological arguments, there was nothing amusing about the sentiments and fears that drove the growing controversies about capitalism. In Europe, the costs of the war and the economic dislocations that followed it produced real pain and anger that sustained a search for a simple explanation of what had gone wrong. In the colonies, the experience of alien rule and exploitation sustained a similar search. Whatever its intellectual shortcomings, Lenin's arguments—and the Marxist intellectual tradition more generally—provided the most visible and compelling critique of capitalism available. It had, in effect, a "corner on the market." It promised, moreover, inevitable victory. Poorly designed from the perspective of systematic inquiry, it was brilliantly designed as a statement of faith and a call to arms. For these reasons, many nationalist leaders in Third World countries became enamored with Marxism and Lenin's interpretation of imperialism. Subsequently, arguments from the Marxist tradition became one of the primary intellectual weapons in the struggle against European colonialism.

The combination of these revolutionary ideas and the actual communist revolution in Russia that led to the creation of the Soviet Union energized critics of capitalism at the same time as it deeply worried mainstream politicians and their supporters. It formed the backdrop for the debates about the global political economy during the interwar years and lay the foundation for the attempt to preempt revolution with the Bretton Woods system after World War II.

A Closer Look

Lenin's Predictions

Lenin's best-known prediction is the claim that recurring wars of imperialism will "inevitably" bring about a communist revolution. This claim can be unpacked into two subparts: (1) the claim that wars of imperialist redivision are inevitable; (2) the claim that sooner or later one of these wars will generate a communist revolution.

There is a sense in which any claim about cause and effect that stipulates the *necessary and sufficient conditions* under which a predicted outcome will occur has a cast of inevitability about it. A *necessary* condition is a stipulated condition that must occur before the predicted outcome can occur but is not enough in and of itself to produce the outcome. A *sufficient* condition is a stipulated condition that will by itself produce the outcome. A "necessary and sufficient" condition is, therefore, one that not only must occur if a predicted outcome is to follow but also is enough to generate that outcome by itself. All necessary and sufficient conditions have a cast of inevitability about them because they assert that the predicted outcome *will occur* if the conditions are met. They are also still in a form that allows for contradictory evidence. The problem with Lenin's argument is that two of the central "if-then" parts of the argument are framed in ways that do not allow for the presentation of contradictory evidence. Consider the argument supporting his conclusion that wars of imperialist redivision are inevitable:

> Therefore, [it is] in the realities of the capitalist system . . . [that] "inter-imperialist" or "ultra-imperialist" alliances, no

matter what form they may assume, whether of one imperialist coalition against another, or a general alliance embracing *all* the imperialist powers, are *inevitably* nothing more than a "truce" in periods between wars. Peaceful alliances prepare the ground for war, and in their turn grow out of wars; the one is the condition of the other, giving rise to alternating forms of peaceful and non-peaceful struggle out of *one and the same* basis of imperialist connections and the relations between world economics and world politics.[a]

By asserting that the same conditions can generate either war or peace, Lenin subverts the critical "if-then" step that is central to distinguishing questions for inquiry from matters of faith.

He follows a similar approach in his discussion of the partition of the world, the defining condition for the onset of the stage of imperialism. He asserts that there are three different forms that partition can take: a formal colony taken and held by force; a semi-colony (a formal sphere of influence in which, while the area is still independent and unoccupied, its rulers feel compelled to follow the instructions of foreign advisers); and an area subject to informal commercial control through the influence of foreign investors. One might think that it mattered whether imperialism arrived at the point of a bayonet or with an offer of a loan, but Lenin claimed it did not.

> The question as to whether these changes [that lead to the partition of the world] are "purely" economic or *non*-economic (e.g., military) is a secondary one, which does not in the

Conclusion

The evolution of the international economic system was driven by European beliefs and practices from the mercantilist state builders of the Renaissance, through the growth of liberal capitalist ideologies between the 1770s and the 1840s, to the return of protection and the advent of the new imperialism in the 1880s. The decades right before World War I were the high-water mark of the Eurocentric political economy. World War I irretrievably altered the position of Europe within the global political economy. Britain and France, the world's principal sources of capital for international investment before the war, came out of the war so deeply in debt that they needed to look to other countries—principally the United States—for capital to fund new investments and pay their bills. As a direct result, Britain would no longer be able to stay on the gold standard or to manage the international monetary system by itself. Even as these changes shifted the distribution of financial power away from Europe and toward the United States, the costs of the war altered the strategic relationship between Europe and its colonies. The result would be a tumultuous eight decades in the evolution of the global political economy.

least affect the fundamental view on the latest epoch of capitalism. To substitute for the question of the *content* of the struggle . . . the question of the *form* of these struggles . . . (today peaceful, tomorrow war-like, the next day war-like again) is to sink to the role of a sophist.[b]

Since we know that European capital was exported during this period, asserting that imperialist partition exists even if there is no forceful occupation has the effect of allowing imperialism to predict all the possible known outcomes.

The fundamental point, once again, is that systematic inquiry requires meaningful "if-then" statements. Tautologies are meaningless "if-then" statements because the outcome is built into the starting point. Saying that imperialism can produce war or peace—or that the defining conditions for partition can be met simply by the export of capital, which we already know took place—trivializes the "if-then" connection by declaring all the evidence that can contradict the argument out-of-order.

There are parts of Lenin's argument that are written in ways that permit one to introduce counter-evidence. Perhaps the most important are the assertions that industrial monopolies will be taken over by banking monopolies (thereby creating finance capitalists), and that finance capitalism will generate an enormous superabundance of capital that will be invested abroad. England and France were the only two major capital exporters in the period before World War I. Neither fit Lenin's conditions for monopoly finance capital. Indeed, in Britain the banks and industry were on opposite sides in one of the most controversial debates of the day—whether to drop free trade for protection. Industry backed protection; the banks backed free trade. Germany, on which Lenin based most of his examples of finance capitalism, does provide a reasonably good fit with the defining characteristics of finance capitalists. But, and it is a very large "but," economic growth in Germany was so high that there was a shortage of capital. Belgium and the Netherlands had domestic monopolies that looked very much like finance capitalists, but neither were significant exporters of capital, and both were free-trading throughout the period—hardly what one would expect from finance capitalists interested in partitioning the world. As for Russia, the Austro-Hungarian Empire, and Italy, they were capital importers.

Finally, there is World War I itself. According to Lenin, World War I was the first war of imperialist redivision. Why, then, were the two biggest capital exporters on the same side?

[a]V.I. Lenin, *Imperialism, the Highest Stage of Capitalism* (New York: International Publishers, 1977), p. 119.
[b]Ibid., p. 75.

Key Terms

mercantilism	physiocrats	terms of trade
specie	laissez-faire	Financial Revolution
balance of trade	free trade	gold standard
tariffs	harmony of interests	balance-of-payments problems
subsistence farming	division of labor	adjustment policies
transactions demand	absolute advantage	under-consumptionist thesis
reserve asset	comparative advantage	finance capitalism

To The Reader   A CHAPTER SUMMARY and QUESTIONS FOR REVIEW are available at **www.prenhall.com/lamborn**

CHAPTER 10

The Global Political Economy from World War I to the Present

World War I marked a critical turning point in the evolution of the global political economy. While growing international and domestic controversies in Europe were creating internal cracks in the system, the global political economy was still a Eurocentric system in 1914. By the war's end, Europe needed the financial and productive capacity of the United States to rebuild and sustain international trade and finance. Neither side, however, successfully worked through the implications of this new strategic situation. European policy makers wanted to continue to manage the system, even though they didn't have the power to do it. Meanwhile, policy makers in the United States, who had the power to lead an international effort to manage the system, rejected the very idea.

By the end of World War II, the preferences of U.S. policy makers had changed dramatically. They were now convinced that U.S. leadership was absolutely essential in order to build an international economic system compatible with U.S. values and the structure of its domestic economy. However, while they were now committed to leading, they would have to contend with opposition from the Soviet Union and the fears of leaders in many post-colonial societies that the U.S.-led Western economic system was a not very subtle mask for continued exploitation. It wasn't until the 1990s that growing acceptance of market economies around the world began to create a more truly global sense that the system was legitimate. As we discuss in Chapter 11, only a few short years later that claim was, in its turn, under attack because of growing fears about the effects of globalization.

The End of the Eurocentric System

While the rapid industrialization of the United States and Japan between 1865 and 1914 had begun to break Europe's hold on world manufacturing output, Europe continued to dominate international trade and finance before World War I. Britain and France were the two largest sources of capital in the international markets. Britain's uniquely essential position under the gold standard resulted in a situation in which the international monetary system was essentially managed from the City of London. Moreover, the distribution of political power in Britain made it possible for policy makers to follow their preferences, which were to adjust the domestic economy in ways that supported the role of the pound sterling as the principal currency in the international monetary system.

The pre-World War I global political economy thus represented a remarkable picture of reinforcing conditions in the three central arenas of world politics: international, policy-making, and constituency. In the international arena, global patterns in trade, finance, and money were dominated by Europe. *But what did European dominance actually mean?* There were no regional organizations to make policy in this period; the governments of independent states made policy. Hence it was British dominance of the international monetary system that added the potential for purpose—and management—to the regional dominance of Europe in the global economy. However, while the strategic situation in the international arena created the potential for management, whether that potential was achieved depended on the preferences of policy makers and what the domestic context made possible. During this period Britain was governed by policy factions that disagreed about many things, but not about the role of the pound in the international monetary system. With the international and policy-making arenas fitting together neatly, the only remaining piece in the puzzle was British constituency politics. This piece dropped into place as well.

While there were strong differences of opinion about whether Britain should maintain its commitment to free trade or go protectionist, elite constituencies of all the major parties supported continuing the central role of the pound in the international monetary system. Meanwhile, mass constituencies—especially the working class groups that were hurt by deflationary policies designed to maintain the value of the pound—had very little impact on the development of monetary policy. The difference in political influence can partly be explained by the fact that it is far more difficult for non-experts to track the effects of monetary policy. It is also important to know that the structure of the British political system gives a unified cabinet an extraordinary level of control over Parliament and insulates British policy makers from opponents of established economic policies. But there was far more to the absence of mass constituency impact on monetary policy than these two factors. As we discussed at the end of the last chapter, in the decades before World War I, constituency politics in Britain was dominated by high-stakes debates about tax and social welfare policy. Those debates not only kept the focus away from monetary policy; they also gave working class groups and their allies a string of significant victories.[1]

The Effect of World War I

All those pieces changed as a result of the war. The gold standard went first, because continuing to offer gold for national currencies would simply create opportunities for economic warfare. (Later, spending for the war pushed the amount of currency in circulation far beyond the level of gold available to back it; at that point, even if governments had wanted to be on a gold standard, they would not have been able to manage it.) Fixed rates of exchange also disappeared, and the principal currencies began to **float,** with their relative values set by international currency markets rather than formal intergovernmental agreement. In a *managed* float, governments work together to try to keep the value of their currencies within a particular range. In a *free* float there is no government intervention at all. The movement from fixed exchange rates to floating currencies introduced substantially more uncertainty into international economic decisions, because there was no longer any assurance that the price of foreign currencies needed for transactions and investment would remain stable.

Even more significant than the temporary wartime changes in foreign economic policy were the effects of the war on domestic economic policy. The costs of the war were mind boggling. As Paul Kennedy explains, "When [one adds to the destruction of property on the continent] the shipping losses, the direct and indirect costs of mobilization, and the monies raised by the combatants . . . the total charge becomes so huge as to be virtually incomprehensible: in fact some $260 billion." In an effort to put the magnitude of this number in context, Kennedy cites another scholar's estimate that the costs of the war "represented about six and a half times the sum of all the national debt accumulated in the world from the end of the eighteenth century up to the eve of the First World War."[2]

The magnitude of these costs led governments to abandon any pretense of laissez-faire economic policy in their drive to mobilize their domestic economies behind the war effort. Reflecting on the war's effects, Robert Gilpin describes its

float   A situation in which the relative values of national currencies are set by international currency markets.

impact this way: "In order to fight the war, every [European] government had to mobilize the entire liquid wealth of its economy. Through taxation and especially through borrowing, the state acquired control over the resources of the society."[3]

This transformation in domestic economic policy had two profound political results. First, it radically altered the relationship between policy makers and their constituents. The classic, nineteenth-century liberal notion that economic and political life operated in different spheres collapsed. With its collapse, policy makers began to lose the intellectual basis for much of their autonomy in foreign economic policy. Choices that were previously regarded as "nonpolitical" became inescapably political. The magnitude of the perceived stakes was driven even higher by the growing fear of communism after the Russian Revolution in 1917. Communism's critique of capitalism—and its claim that revolutions such as the one that occurred in Russia were inevitable—deeply frightened policy makers in Western Europe and North America. In this context, any failures in government economic policy were viewed as giving communists ammunition in their war on capitalism. These changes in constituency politics were intensified by a second transformation in the politics of economic policy. With a wider range of perceived options confronting policy makers—and the stakes attached to those choices climbing ever higher—it became harder to build stable coalitions.

These changes in the domestic environment for choice would have made it difficult for European policy makers to maintain their role in managing the global political economy even if nothing else had changed as a result of the war. But the war also fundamentally altered Europe's international position. Europe's manufacturing output was 23 percent lower in 1920 than in 1913; it did not regain its pre-World War I levels until about 1925. By 1925, in contrast, the manufacturing output of the United States was 48 percent higher than in 1913.[4] The shift away from Europe and toward the United States was even more striking in international finance. As mentioned above, Britain and France were the largest sources of investment capital in the world before the war. Herbert Feis, one of the most prominent historians of this period, estimates that in 1914 fully one-quarter of all British investment was abroad. Even more striking, income from those foreign investments generated about 10 percent of Britain's total national income. France was only slightly behind, with one-sixth of its total investment and 6 percent of its national income. Germany, a distant third in foreign investment because of the high internal demand for capital, was still earning about 3 percent of its national income on foreign investments. Feis reports: "Almost all of the foreign investments of Great Britain, France, and Germany . . . were either sold to pay for the expenses of the First World War or destroyed or depreciated."[5] The combination of these losses and the need to borrow still more money turned Britain and France from the world's largest creditors into two of the largest debtors. Hoping to recover some of these costs from Germany, the victors forced the new regime (the Weimar Republic) to accept responsibility for $31.5 billion in war reparations, to be paid at the back-breaking rate of $500 million a year.

While Europe fell deeply into debt as the result of the war, the United States was transformed from a debtor country into the world's largest creditor. Before the war, the United States owed $3 billion to foreign creditors; after the war, the tables had been turned, and foreigners owed U.S. banks $3 billion.[6] The sudden centrality of U.S. capital markets made the dollar the key currency in the international monetary system, a change that was reinforced after the war when the United States was the only major state able to return to the gold standard in 1919.

10.1 ENDURING PATTERNS

The connection between preferences and power
The stronger actors' power positions, the more strategically important their preferences.

The impact of risk-taking
People are less willing to run political risks in support of policy choices as their control over choice and implementation declines. However, as their control over choice and implementation declines, they become more indifferent to policy failure—as long as policy failure is not politically dangerous.

The impact of linkage politics
World politics is driven by the interaction of international, factional, and constituency politics.

U.S. Monetary Policy after the Two World Wars and the End of Bretton Woods

After World War I, the radical change in relative economic power of Britain and the United States made the preferences of U.S. policy makers of critical strategic importance in any attempt to manage the international monetary system. Linkage politics created both domestic and diplomatic incentives for U.S. policy makers to reject an active role in international monetary management.

After World War II, U.S. preferences were again of critical strategic importance. This time linkage politics created strong incentives for active involvement, including, as we discuss later in this chapter, a period of unilateral management from the late 1940s through the 1950s.

The domestic risks of playing a leading international role gradually increased through the 1960s. At the same time, the ability of U.S. policy makers to unilaterally manage the system disappeared. The combination of rising domestic political risks and declining international control made U.S. policy makers much more averse to running political risks in support of international monetary policy, leading to the Nixon administration's decision to end the Bretton Woods system in the early 1970s. Subsequently, throughout the 1970s and 1980s, U.S. policy makers frequently refused to follow through on politically risky agreements reached at multilateral conferences.

The Effect of U.S. Policy Preferences

U.S. policy makers had a very different view of government's role in international capital movements and monetary policy than their European counterparts, who preferred direct management. French governments had pushed investors to prop up the regime in Russia from the signing of the defense treaty against Germany in the early 1890s to the communist revolution in 1917, with the result that fully one-quarter of all French foreign investment was in Russia at the outbreak of the war.[7] British officials had worked hard to manage the gold standard and the pound's role in the international monetary system. U.S. policy makers, by contrast, adopted a hands-off policy both on access to U.S. capital markets and on the role of the dollar.

While it may seem counterintuitive, the passive stance adopted by U.S. policy makers toward the new role for the dollar in the international monetary system in the postwar period was actually one of the most competitive options available to them. First, keeping government out of the capital markets made U.S. funds even more attractive to foreign borrowers than they would have been on purely economic grounds. Second, refusing to be drawn into an effort to manage the international monetary system made the dollar more powerful relative to the pound and the franc. It would have taken sustained international coordination between U.S. and British policy makers for the pound to return to its prewar position. While the head of the Federal Reserve Bank in New York worked informally with the head of the Bank of England in an effort to coordinate policies in the late 1920s, there was no formal co-operation at the level of the two governments.

It is not clear whether this failure to coordinate was part of an intentional effort to enhance the role of the dollar or simply reflected the preferences of U.S. officials for a hands-off approach. The European suspicion that it was intentional is strengthened by the record of overtly competitive behavior by U.S. administrations throughout the 1920s in pressuring the British and French for increased access by U.S. companies to markets and resources in British- and French-held areas in the Middle East, Africa, and Asia. It is also the case that there is little reason to believe that U.S. and British preferences were close enough to promote agreement on a new multilateral arrangement. The British government was just as determined to restore the pound to its prewar standing as the U.S. government was uninterested in subsidizing a return to British financial hegemony. On the other hand, the passive approach to the role of the dollar in the international monetary system may have simply been the result of ideological preference and ignorance of its potential effects on international monetary stability. This interpretation is supported by two crucial facts. First, U.S. policy makers were as worried as their European counterparts about the growing specter of communism. Given that shared fear and the obvious value of prosperity in undercutting the threat from the left, awareness of the ramifications of U.S. monetary policy for economic growth and political stability in Europe would have created incentives for a more sustained and cooperative diplomatic strategy in foreign economic policy. The conclusion that laissez-faire ideology and ignorance is the more likely explanation for U.S. choices is supported by a second fact: U.S. policy makers paid almost no attention to the international role of the dollar when they reacted to the crash of Wall Street in 1929.

Whatever the underlying motives, the effect of those choices is clear: They accelerated the decline of Europe's position in the global economy at the same time as they prevented the construction of any new arrangements that could replace the European-dominated ones. The result was a decade of drift followed by a decade of disaster.

The 1920s and 1930s: Drift and Disaster

As we mentioned at the beginning of this chapter, policy makers in the interwar period were caught in a very difficult situation both internationally and domestically. In the years immediately after World War I, Europeans continued to disagree about the relative merits of free trade and protection. The disruptive effects of this continuing disagreement about trade were worsened by radical changes in international finance and the structure of the monetary system. Britain and France were now deeply in debt to the United States. In the case of Britain, the size of the war debt was so large that the government had to allocate between 30 and 44 percent of total central government expenditure to debt repayment between 1920 and 1930. Britain was, consequently, no longer capable either of returning to a gold standard or managing the international monetary system. Absent the ability of one country to lead, any new arrangements would require building sustained coalitions, but the key actors' preferences weren't compatible. Britain might be willing to build a coalition in which the United States subsidized a return of British ascendancy, but a junior role could hardly be attractive to U.S. policy makers. In principle, the magnitude of the shift toward the United States created another option—U.S. leadership—but that was foreclosed by U.S. preferences for a hands-off approach to international monetary policy.

Without either leadership or the basis for sustained coalitions, the principal countries in Europe faced a strategic situation in which they had to pull together a mix of temporary agreements and individual initiatives. The problems this international environment created were compounded by a very small margin for error domestically. British and French constituency groups demanded that their governments provide a new range of services and subsidies without raising taxes. How? By making Germany pay. German policy makers, meanwhile, desperately worked to manage the international aftermath of defeat—including the reparations—while building a new republic in a domestic arena torn by communists on the left and militarists on the right.

The historical record is dreary. In Britain, a brief postwar economic boom was followed by an abrupt collapse in 1921. British exports fell over 50 percent between 1920 and 1921. In June 1921, 23 percent of the work force (over two million people) was unemployed. Over a million would stay on the "dole" until the Great Depression drove the numbers even higher.[8] The Genoa Conference of 1922 tried to bring back some stability to international trade and finance by suggesting a gold-exchange standard under which countries would try to overcome the problem created by not having enough gold to put their own currencies back on the gold standard by holding another country's gold-backed currency as a reserve asset. The pound was the obvious candidate for this role, but the British were not able to go back on gold until 1925.[9]

Without an effectively implemented agreement on money and with international trade still fluctuating wildly, French officials pushed even harder for deliveries of reparations from Germany in an effort to meet their constituents' demands for jobs, services, and reconstruction. The strain on the German economy was immense. The mark, which had an exchange rate of 4.2 marks to the dollar in 1914, sank to 1800 marks to the dollar in January 1923. When Germany tried to meet its economic problems by suspending payments, the French budget deficit climbed steeply. The French response was to invade one of the most economically significant areas in Germany—the Ruhr valley—in early 1923. Germany's response was to call on workers in the Ruhr to strike while continuing to pay them wages. The result was the infamous German hyperinflation. By the fall of 1923 the German exchange rate was 4.2 *trillion* marks to the dollar.[10] With their citizens' savings wiped out and the mark worthless, the government capitulated, promising to find some way to resume reparation payments.

The solution, interestingly enough, would come from the United States. While U.S. policy makers had no interest in becoming involved in international monetary management, there was widespread concern that the French were pushing Germany

The German hyperinflation in 1923 lowered the value of the mark so much that the Berlin housewife shown in this photograph used marks to light her stove.

too hard. Secretary of State Charles Evans Hughes not only believed that Europe's economic recovery required a viable Germany; he also feared that the new regime might either collapse or be driven toward the Soviets. These international incentives were reinforced by domestic incentives: Repayment of French and British war debts to United States banks depended on Germany's ability to pay reparations. To soften up the French for a compromise on German reparations, Hughes pressured France for repayment of their war debt to the United States. When they were unable to raise the necessary capital, he suggested a conference to address the interrelated problems of reparations and war debt. Significant for what it says about executive-legislative relations in the United States, Hughes insisted that the conference be run as a private effort by U.S. bankers to avoid having to involve Congress. The result was the 1924 Dawes Plan, in which a $200 million loan was floated to help Germany resume reparations payments. In exchange for this subsidy, the French had to agree to cut Germany's obligation in half.[11]

The Dawes Plan ended the immediate economic crisis in Germany, and reparations continued to flow until the Great Depression struck. The Dawes Plan did not, however, herald the beginning of a more cooperative, coalition-building phase in managing the international economy. When Britain finally went back on the gold standard in 1925, it set the exchange rate of the pound at its pre-World War I level. While symbolically satisfying, that level was far higher than the current economic conditions allowed. In Britain, the result was a fall in wages, massive unemployment, and the General Strike of 1926. France's reaction to its neighbor's plight was to increase the pressure on the pound by selling some of their holdings and demanding payment in gold.

The inability to coordinate policies in pursuit of jointly acceptable outcomes reached its height—or, should one say, its depth—after the stock market crash in October 1929. To cover their losses in the stock market, U.S. banks called in many of their loans and cut back sharply on new ones. The problem was that all these sensible-sounding moves ignored the central role of the dollar in the international monetary system. Calling in loans stripped other countries of their dollar holdings and dried up the international capital market. The result was a collapse in demand, compounded by Germany's announcement that it could no longer pay reparations, which in turn led to a moratorium by Britain and France on the repayment of their war debts to the United States.

This downward spiral was worsened by a round of protectionist tariffs that reduced trade still further. The most infamous of these was the Smoot-Hawley tariff passed by the U.S. Congress in 1930. Designed to protect U.S. farmers and industries by reducing imports, it instead produced a round of retaliatory increases that cut U.S. exports 69 percent. By the middle of 1932, world trade was down by one-third, and many countries' industrial production was cut in half.[12] These results were so catastrophic that the Smoot-Hawley tariff gave protectionist policies a bad name in many circles, much as the "lessons of Munich" continue to haunt appeasement policies today.

How governments responded to the collapse of international arrangements for money, trade, and capital varied with the preferences of policy makers and what the internal political climate made possible. The British, for instance, were still governed by policy coalitions that were deeply committed to rebuilding the pound's international role. Thus it was that a Labour government chose to reduce unemployment benefits, with unemployment already at 25 percent of the labor force, in

The British decision to return to the pre-World War I price of gold greatly worsened unemployment and led to a major confrontation between organized labor and the government as a strike by coal miners escalated into the General Strike of 1926.

The effects of the Great Depression spread beyond investors to individuals in the middle and working classes. In 1930, a line of unemployed workers stretched along an entire city block in New York City.

an effort to reallocate enough money to maintain the existing exchange rate for the pound. In spite of those efforts, Britain was forced off the gold standard in 1931.

The collapse of the gold standard was followed by a series of independent steps designed to protect the economies of the different key states in the international economic system. Britain led at the Ottawa Conference in 1932 with two high-profile decisions: the end of free trade and the creation of both a trade and monetary bloc (called the *sterling bloc*) with its colonies and dominions (former colonies such as Canada and Australia). The United States followed with a dollar bloc, and the French, who were able to stay on the gold standard, a *franc bloc*.

Several attempts were made to pull back from the brink during the early 1930s, but they failed either because international coalitions could not be built or because there was not enough domestic support. For instance, 64 countries attended an international economic conference in London in June 1933 to discuss reestablishing fixed exchange rates, tariff reductions, reparations, and war debt. The conference ultimately collapsed when President Franklin Roosevelt could not decide on a policy approach that either bridged or suppressed the differences that divided the competing factions in the U.S. delegation. U.S. policy began to move in a more coherent direction in 1934 after Secretary of State Cordell Hull succeeded in winning the internal battle to advise the president. An ardent free-trader, Hull built a coalition that got the U.S. Reciprocal Trade Act through Congress in 1934. The act authorized the executive to negotiate treaties that would reduce tariffs up to 50 percent. In the same year Congress authorized the creation of the Export-Import Bank, designed to promote U.S. exports by providing loans to foreign buyers. These moves were then followed in 1936 with the Tripartite Agreement, in which Britain, France, and the United States—all increasingly worried about the threat from Hitler—agreed to work together to reestablish currency convertibility.[13]

While the Reciprocal Trade Act and the Tripartite Agreement signaled movement toward a more active role for the United States in international economic matters, it was more an indication of the direction in which U.S. policy makers were

The Great Depression was triggered by the effects of the 1929 New York stock market crash on the economic relations connecting the United States and Europe. Its effects, however, were global. Economies in Africa and Asia—now tied closely to the global economy as the result of European and North American colonialism and other forms of political and economic expansion—suffered badly, even though the sources of the Depression lay entirely outside of their control. This photo shows a man carrying his starving mother in Hunan, China, during a famine.

likely to go after World War II than it was the beginning of a sustained move to use foreign economic policy to try to end the Great Depression. The authority granted to the president under the Reciprocal Trade Act was not used to negotiate many reciprocal tariff reductions. As for the role of the dollar in the monetary system after the 1936 agreement, the U.S. government simply set gold at $35 to the ounce and let other countries do what they wanted in response. The decision to get deeply involved in managing the international economic system came only with World War II. The result was the Bretton Woods system.

The Bretton Woods System

The Bretton Woods system refers to a series of agreements on post-World War II international monetary, credit, and trade arrangements that were reached at a conference held in Bretton Woods, New Hampshire, in July 1944, in the midst of the war. While representatives from 44 states attended the conference, the major agreements were negotiated by the representatives from Britain and the United States. They were convinced that they had to prevent a repeat of the economic mistakes of the interwar period that had thrown the world into depression, increased the appeal of extremist ideologies from both the political right and left, and ultimately contributed to the outbreak of war.

The Key Goals, Norms, and Institutions

The Bretton Woods agreement called for the creation of a fixed-exchange rate, gold-standard system after the war. The goal was to create a system that would promote economic growth and trade by establishing a stable set of conditions for currency convertibility while still leaving countries enough flexibility in their domestic economic policy to achieve different country-specific goals and manage internal political demands. Given the level of destruction around the world and the central financial role of the United States in economic recovery, it was expected that initially the dollar would have to play a critical role in moving the world toward a gold standard. While the British hoped to move the pound back on gold quickly, in the immediate postwar period most countries would have to use dollars to meet their international obligations.

Once the immediate period of postwar reconstruction was past, the negotiators at Bretton Woods expected a new intergovernmental organization—the International Monetary Fund (IMF)—to take over the management of the international monetary system. The IMF was charged with three principal responsibilities: to establish rules and procedures for currency convertibility (including facilitating agreement on any changes in the fixed exchange rates); to provide technical help on currency issues (particularly for countries that had limited staff expertise); and to provide short-term financial assistance to help countries overcome temporary balance of payments problems.

The last objective was regarded as particularly crucial. Balance of payments problems arise when the value of what countries import is substantially in excess of the value of their exports. In that situation, countries must be able to pay the difference between what is bought and what is sold in currencies that sellers are willing to accept. However, if countries buy a lot more than they sell—with the result that they pump too much of their currency abroad—sellers may begin to worry about the value of the money they are being asked to accept and demand payment in currencies that have more value in international money markets. If a country does not have enough of those more desirable currencies to buy what it wants, the resulting balance of payments problem may result in a decline in international trade as sellers begin to refuse to accept any more of the would-be importer's currency.

The IMF was designed to address this problem in the following way. When countries joined the IMF they had to make a contribution composed of a mix of gold (if they had any), their national currency, and other currencies that were backed by gold (called **hard currencies**). When faced with a temporary balance of payments problem, member countries could borrow up to 25 percent of their contribution a year for a maximum of five years, for a total of 125 percent. Moreover, all of the help would come in the form of hard currencies useful in international transactions. The IMF would have to approve any requests for help and was expected to establish conditions for withdrawals that would lessen the underlying problems that had created the balance-of-payments deficit in the first place. This provision came to be called the **principle of conditionality.** Decisions would be reached by a special majority requiring an 80 percent positive vote in a voting system where each member's votes were weighted by their contribution. These provisions were designed to give the United States—expected to be the principal source of funds in the postwar period—a veto over all decisions.

The work of the IMF was to be supported by two other organizations: the International Bank for Reconstruction and Development (IBRD, also known as the World Bank) and the International Trade Organization (ITO). The IBRD was to have the same sort of weighted voting as the IMF but was to specialize in a different task: providing loans for capital projects that would aid reconstruction and development. The ITO was to promote the movement of the international economic system toward free trade. The ITO also had some provisions designed to encourage development in non-

hard currencies
Currencies that have a relatively stable value in the international currency market; until 1971, when the gold standard was abandoned, the term denoted currencies backed by gold.

principle of conditionality
The requirement that countries take steps to reduce the sources of their balance-of-payments problems before the IMF provides short-term aid.

industrial countries that members of the U.S. Senate opposed on the grounds that they would hurt U.S. companies and allow too much government intervention in the market. As a result of those controversies, the ITO was the one piece of the Bretton Woods agreements that was not implemented. Its responsibility for moving the world toward free trade was assumed by what was originally intended to be simply a temporary executive agreement: the General Agreement on Tariffs and Trade (GATT). Negotiated in 1947, GATT grandfathered existing protectionist measures while establishing free trade as the long-term goal. Tariff reductions were to be negotiated on a reciprocal basis according to the Most Favored Nation Principle (MFN). The *principle of reciprocity* guaranteed that countries that had the most attractive markets—the ones other countries most wanted to gain access to for their exports—would have the most leverage in the negotiations. The *most favored nation principle* established the rule that whatever reductions one gave the "most favored nation" had to be given to everyone. In short, MFN established the rule that everyone had to be treated the same.

Assessing the Support for the Bretton Woods System

Since there were only about 60 states in the world in 1944, the 44 that sent representatives to Bretton Woods represented a huge percentage of the total (especially when one subtracts Germany, Italy, and Japan—who were on the Axis side—states that were unable to attend because of the war, and small states such as Nepal that had little impact on interstate politics). The breadth of the attendance suggests a remarkable level of backing for the substantive goals of the postwar international economic system and the role of the United States in making it work.

The level of support was simultaneously real and misleading. It was real because the Depression and the spread of fascism during the 1930s had convinced many policy makers and constituency groups that reaching an agreement on trade and the international monetary system was a necessary prerequisite for sustained economic growth and political stability. In particular, the Bretton Woods agreement symbolized the U.S. commitment to become actively involved in managing the global political economy after World War II. It also symbolized recognition by European policy makers that it was no longer possible to sustain a purely Eurocentric system.

However, the appearance of widespread international support is also misleading for three important reasons. First, most of the representatives at the conference were there more to observe and acquiesce to an agreement worked out between the United States and Britain than to debate the fundamental terms. Second, while the supporters of the emerging economic system represented a large percentage of the existing state system, most of the Third World was still colonized. Third, even though Stalin sent representatives, it soon became clear that the Bretton Woods plan for the postwar global political economy was fundamentally incompatible with the Soviet Union's command economy.

Moreover, while the governments that supported the Bretton Woods agreement were determined not to repeat the mistakes of the 1930s, it remained to be seen whether they could successfully manage the competing international and domestic pressures that would be generated by a fixed-exchange-rate, gold-standard system and the movement toward free trade. Before World War I, policy coalitions that supported free trade and the gold standard had been willing and able to sustain those preferences even when the necessary adjustment policies hurt groups in their own countries. With the major shift in economic capabilities from Europe to the United

World Politics and the Individual

John Maynard Keynes: Changing Capitalism to Save It

No individual was more intimately connected with the evolution of the global political economy between the end of World War I and the creation of the post-World War II Bretton Woods system than John Maynard Keynes. Indeed, in the mid-twentieth century some called him the "savior of capitalism."

As you review the discussion at **www.prenhall.com/lamborn**, look for the reasons Keynes objected to Britain's return to the gold standard in 1925. What do his objections have to do with his understanding of Britain's international situation relative to the United States and to his critical evaluation of several of the core assumptions of laissez-faire capitalism? In the 1930s Keynes's analysis of the origins of the Great Depression and the proper role of government in promoting economic growth led him to suggest a new way to organize a capitalist political economy. What were a few of the central pieces of the Keynesian revolution? Finally, look for ways in which Keynes's personality combined with the linked domestic and international contexts in which he lived to create both the drive and the opportunity to lead a revolution in economic thought and practice.

States after World War I and the incompatibility of French, British, and U.S. preferences, neither the international nor domestic preconditions for a trans-Atlantic agreement on global economic policies were in place during the interwar years. By 1944 the preferences of the key Western governments had converged on a compatible view of how the global political economy should be organized, and the United States had the resources to lead in that direction. What was not at all clear—and, simply could not have been known at that time—was whether this international agreement would be enough. Would the key governments be able to bring their domestic constituents along in the same direction?

The Bretton Woods agreement assumed that governments had enough autonomy in their economic policy making to bridge the domestic and international demands of a fixed-exchange rate, free-trade system. The problem, however, was that any movement toward free trade required dismantling tariff barriers that were in place exactly because powerful domestic groups were advantaged by them. Maintaining a fixed-exchange rate system would, moreover, prevent daily supply-and-demand forces from making incremental adjustments in the exchange value of countries' currencies. In the absence of incremental changes driven by the currency markets, governments would at some point have to make large, politically charged policy choices, either directly, by formally altering their currencies' exchange value, or indirectly, by adjustment policies that changed taxes, the money supply, and government spending. In the nineteenth century, Britain, the key country in the international monetary system, had adjusted its monetary and fiscal (tax and spending) policies to maintain the international position of the pound, even when that involved *deflating* the economy (reducing growth, employment, and wages). The human and economic costs of routinely deflating the domestic economy to maintain exchange rates were no longer considered either acceptable or politically possible. The hope was that the new methods of government intervention in the economy advocated by John Maynard Keynes (see box on page 302) would make it possible to stimulate domestic economic growth enough to achieve full employment even as fixed exchange rates were maintained internationally.

It turned out to be far more difficult to bridge the international and domestic arenas for choice than the makers of the postwar system expected. Moreover, the rapid spread of decolonization through Asia, Africa, and the Middle East fundamentally changed the landscape of world politics, creating a new set of issues and actors that altered the evolution of the global political economy. Oddly, one of the most obvious problems in 1944—the incompatibility of the West's market approach to political economy and the Soviet Union's preference for command economies—created far fewer economic problems for the major market economies in the West than expected. The reason, in retrospect, is clear. While the Soviet bloc developed a competing vision of how political economies should be organized, it moved in a largely self-contained direction until its collapse in the late 1980s. Because the economic systems of the West and the East moved in such different directions, their differences did not prevent the development of the Bretton Woods system.

The isolation of the nonmarket economies (principally the Soviet Union, China, and other communist countries) is starkly evident in Table 10–1. Throughout the entire period from 1960 to 1985, only between 3.5 and 5.8 percent of the industrial market economies' trade—and only between 3.7 and 6.8 percent of the trade from developing countries—went to the nonmarket economies. Meanwhile, the trade between developing countries and the industrial market economies showed substantial, but quite asymmetrical, interdependence. Developing countries depended heavily on their trade with the industrial market economies—between 63.7 and 73.8 percent—while the industrial market economies depended far less on the developing countries—between 18.0 and 25.8 percent.

In the first decades after World War II, the competing views inspired by the Marxist intellectual tradition had a major impact on the politics of international economics in the relationships connecting the West with post-colonial societies throughout the Third World. The economies of post-colonial societies, unlike those in the Soviet bloc, were inescapably tied to the Western system. Given those connections, the preferences of the actors in the Third World had more visible effects on the politics of international economics in the Western system even though their societies had far fewer resources than those that the Soviet Union could mobilize. Suspicious of a system of political economy that they associated with colonialism and exploitation, many Third World leaders were drawn to socialist alternatives.

Consequently, the principal issues involving the politics of global economics between the 1940s and 1990s evolved along two interconnected but distinct story lines. The first is the story of efforts by key actors in the Western system to make "their" system work. The second is the story of the effect of the decolonization of the Third World on efforts to change the global political economy. In one of the most important coincidences in recent history, both these story lines generated controversies in the 1960s and 1970s that went through cathartic transformations in the 1980s at the same time as the end of the Cold War and the collapse of the Soviet Union largely eliminated Marxism as a competing worldview on how the global political economy should be organized.

TABLE 10-1 MARKET SHARES OF WORLD TRADE, 1960–1985

Year	FROM INDUSTRIAL MARKET ECONOMIES			FROM DEVELOPING COUNTRIES			FROM NONMARKET ECONOMIES		
	To Industrial Market Economies	To Developing Countries	To Nonmarket Economies	To Industrial Market Economies	To Developing Countries	To Nonmarket Economies	To Industrial Market Economies	To Developing Countries	To Nonmarket Economies
1960	70.5%	25.5%	3.5%	72.2%	22.3%	4.5%	18.7%	9.3%	72.0%
1961	71.2	24.7	3.6	71.4	22.1	5.4	19.1	12.9	68.1
1962	73.1	23.0	3.6	71.5	22.0	5.4	17.9	14.9	66.9
1963	73.8	22.2	3.6	72.3	21.3	5.3	18.8	14.4	66.2
1964	74.2	21.6	3.9	72.0	21.2	5.6	20.2	14.3	65.1
1965	74.7	21.1	3.9	71.6	21.0	6.6	21.5	14.7	63.3
1966	74.7	20.9	4.1	72.5	20.6	6.0	24.1	15.7	59.8
1967	75.2	20.3	4.2	73.4	20.4	5.3	23.8	15.3	60.4
1968	75.9	19.9	3.9	73.8	20.4	5.2	22.8	15.3	61.7
1969	76.8	19.2	3.7	73.6	20.1	5.4	23.3	15.6	60.7
1970	76.9	18.7	3.7	73.4	20.0	5.7	23.5	15.8	60.5
1971	77.0	18.8	3.6	72.7	21.1	4.9	24.0	15.0	60.8
1972	77.5	18.0	4.0	73.1	20.8	5.1	23.7	14.3	61.3
1973	76.7	18.1	4.5	73.1	21.0	4.9	26.9	15.6	56.6
1974	73.5	21.0	4.9	73.3	21.3	3.7	31.7	16.3	51.1
1975	69.7	24.0	5.8	70.1	23.4	4.8	27.3	15.8	56.3
1976	71.3	22.9	5.3	71.2	22.7	4.1	29.0	15.7	54.7
1977	70.9	23.8	4.7	71.0	23.5	4.2	27.8	17.2	54.5
1978	70.8	23.8	4.9	71.1	23.8	4.4	26.8	18.4	54.5
1979	72.7	22.0	4.9	70.9	24.3	3.7	30.9	17.9	51.7
1980	70.9	23.3	4.9	70.1	24.9	3.7	32.2	18.1	48.8
1981	68.4	25.8	4.7	67.0	27.9	4.0	31.1	20.8	47.5
1982	69.3	24.9	4.5	64.2	29.9	5.0	30.9	21.5	47.0
1983	71.4	22.9	4.5	64.0	29.6	5.2	30.2	20.9	48.6
1984	72.9	21.5	4.4	65.2	28.3	5.3	30.3	20.9	48.5
1985	73.7	20.2	5.0	63.7	27.6	6.8	26.1	22.7	51.2

Source: World Bank, *Commodity Trade and Price Trends, 1987–88* (Baltimore: Johns Hopkins University Press, 1988), p. 7. Original data from *United Nations, Monthly Bulletin of Statistics;* UNCTAD, *Handbook of International Trade and Development Statistics.*

As we discuss at the end of this chapter and analyze more fully in Chapter 11, these transformations have created a new and distinctive context for the politics of global economics as we move into the twenty-first century. To lay the groundwork for that discussion, we now turn to the two principal story lines of the 1940s to 1990s period: the efforts by key actors in the West to manage the system created at Bretton Woods and the efforts by states in the Third World to challenge the system's essential goals and structure.

The Politics of International Economics among the Rich

At any point in time, the issues involving the international monetary system, trade, capital flows, and trans-state business enterprises are all interrelated. Saying "everything is related to everything" is, however, not terribly helpful. Moreover, trying to learn the connections among these issues at the same time as you learn about each one individually is overwhelming. Consequently, we have chosen to review the evolution of each of these major issues separately before discussing how they are interconnected in different time periods. We begin with the politics of money, because the structure of the international monetary system provides a crucial backdrop for all the other issues.

The International Monetary System and the Changing Role of the U.S. Dollar

The Bretton Woods agreement called for a gold-standard and a **fixed-exchange-rate system.** In the years immediately following World War II, the United States was the only major country that had the gold reserves and financial strength to make the system work. Britain tried to go back on a gold standard even more quickly than it had after World War I, and this time the United States helped by forgiving its war debt and providing credits: $3.75 billion in early 1946. The depth of Britain's difficulty in supporting the pound can be seen in what happened to those credits. The 1946 credits were "all but blown away when . . . sterling was made convertible for a few days in August 1947."[14] The magnitude of the balance-of-payments problems facing Britain was clearly beyond the resources of the International Monetary Fund (IMF), which had been designed to provide help for short-term problems once the world economy recovered from the war. As for the International Bank for Reconstruction and Development (IBRD), its total resources in 1946 came to only $570 million.[15]

From Unilateral Management to the Run on the Dollar   With the international monetary system tottering on the brink in 1947, the United States government moved to fill the void. The Marshall Plan provided over $17 billion in grants to countries in Western Europe between 1948 and 1952, including $2.4 billion for Britain. Having lost the earlier credits in a premature effort to return to the gold standard, the British government tried a different tack: "Most of the Marshall Plan credits were promptly deposited in the Bank of England to build up currency reserves."[16] The flow of dollars went far beyond the $17 billion in the Marshall Plan. U.S. spending for security operations such as NATO and the Korean War required massive amounts of expenditures abroad, thereby pumping still more dollars into the international monetary system and increasing the system's *liquidity*, or spending capacity. Moreover, throughout the 1950s, U.S. policy makers encouraged Japan and Western Europe to develop trade and monetary policies that discriminated against U.S. exports as a way to stimulate their own economies. U.S. support for the creation of the European Economic Community (EEC) in 1957 reflected a judgment that the political advantages of a strong Europe vastly outweighed the economic disadvantages of discrimination against U.S. exports by the EEC's *common*

fixed-exchange-rate system   A monetary system in which the relative values of national currencies are set by interstate agreement and remain fixed at those values until a new agreement is reached.

TABLE 10–2	U.S. FOREIGN INVESTMENT (in millions of dollars), 1939–1965[a]		
Year	Total U.S. Foreign Investment	Private Investment	U.S. Government Investment
1939	12,480	12,445	35
1940	12,275	12,195	80
1943	14,170	13,340	830
1944	14,810	13,765	1,045
1945	16,867	14,688	2,179
1946[b]	20,798	15,608	5,190
1947	29,069	16,915	12,154
1948	31,483	18,431	13,052
1949[b]	32,653	19,122	13,531
1950[c]	54,359	19,004	35,355
1955[c]	65,076	29,136	35,940
1960[c]	85,768	49,430	36,338
1965[c]	120,126	81,197	38,929

[a]Sources indicate that figures in this table are "subject to considerable error due to the nature of the basic data."
[b]The totals reported for 1946 and 1949 are not an exact sum of the figures for private and government investment. The error is in the original table.
[c]Beginning in 1950, the figures for U.S. government foreign investment include three new subcategories: gold stocks, IMF subscription, and convertible currencies.

Sources: U.S. Department of Commerce, *Statistical Abstract of the United States 1950*, 71st ed. (Washington, DC: U.S. Government Printing Office, 1950), p. 829; U.S. Department of Commerce, *Statistical Abstract of the United States 1951*, 72nd ed. (Washington, DC: U.S. Government Printing Office, 1951), p. 817; U.S. Department of Commerce, *Statistical Abstract of the United States 1970*, 91st ed. (Washington, DC: U.S. Government Printing Office, 1970), p. 765.

market (an agreement to reduce tariffs and other trade barriers among member countries while maintaining a common tariff policy toward nonmembers).

U.S. foreign investment increased dramatically after World War II. In the first years after the war, most of that increase was a function of U.S. government spending associated with the Marshall Plan and the Cold War. However, by the 1950s private investment abroad was growing rapidly (see Table 10–2).

The infusion of dollars jump-started the international monetary system and helped fuel the dramatic recovery of the world economy between 1945 and 1960. The unique role of the dollar simultaneously encouraged the growth of U.S. investment abroad. U.S.-based corporations, which had been actively involved in Latin America since the late 1800s, became a significant presence outside the Western Hemisphere for the first time as a direct result of the advantages their dollar-denominated assets had in the international economy in the first decades after the war.

For the first fifteen years after the war, the role of the dollar in the international monetary system met the objectives of all the key actors in the Western system. For the United States government, it meant not only the achievement of one of its most important objectives—the creation of a Western-leaning system that would rebuild the global economy and strengthen Western Europe and Japan against the Soviet Union—but also the ability to use U.S. currency to pay for Cold-War expenditures around the world. For recipients of this outflow of dollars, it meant access to foreign exchange that could be used to rebuild their economies and financial reserves without having to go back on gold themselves. The shared objective of a fixed-exchange-rate, gold-standard system was achieved by simply pegging the value of other countries' currencies to the dollar.

But by the late 1950s, the system was in deep trouble. In 1948, the U.S. had gold reserves that were much larger than the total number of dollars held by foreigners: $18.1 billion more in gold than in dollars held abroad. By 1959, the number of dollars held abroad had grown so rapidly that there was almost no surplus of gold over foreign holdings. In 1960, U.S. gold holdings fell below the value of the dollars abroad.[17] The speed with which this change occurred in the ratio of gold reserves to dollars held abroad certainly reflected the magnitude of expenditures abroad by the U.S. government and private citizens since the war. But it soon became apparent that there was a larger, more fundamental problem with the role of the dollar in the monetary system. In 1960, the economist Robert Triffin pointed out that depending on one country's currency to provide international liquidity—enough money for international transactions—while simultaneously expecting that currency to serve as a reserve asset was inherently incompatible with a fixed-exchange-rate, gold-standard system. The rapid collapse in U.S. gold stocks shown in Figure 10–1 reflects the run on the dollar created by the combined effects of the underlying structural problem Triffin identified and the growth in U.S. expenditures abroad.

As is often the case with unintended consequences, the reason is obvious—after the fact. Economic growth creates a natural and inevitable demand for more money for international transactions and savings. Depending on a single country's national currency for those international monetary functions requires that more of that country's currency be held by foreigners than would be the case if that national

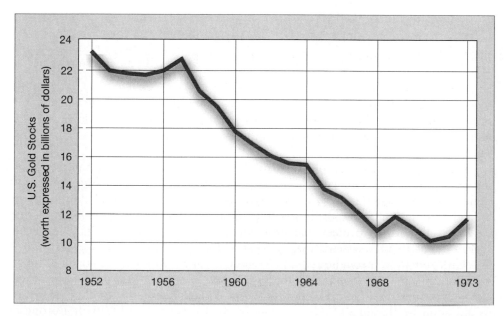

Figure 10–1 **The Run on the Dollar and Declining U.S. Gold Stocks, 1957–1973**
Growing concern about the ability of the United States to honor its obligation under the Bretton Woods gold standard to give foreigners gold in exchange for any dollars they held led to a growing run on the dollar and a rapid decline in U.S. gold stocks.

Source: U.S. Department of Commerce, *Statistical Abstract of the United States* (Washington, D.C.: U.S. Government Printing Office, 1955, 1956, 1961, 1963, 1966, 1968, 1970, 1973).

currency were not also serving as the world's principal international currency. Thus, if the dollar was to serve as the principal international currency, more dollars had to flow abroad than came back. But U.S. dollars held by foreign central banks were—under the Bretton Woods fixed-exchange rate, gold-standard system—redeemable in gold at an internationally established fixed rate. The number of dollars abroad increasingly made that promise unbelievable. The United States could no more solve that problem than medieval alchemists could turn lead into gold.[18]

Triffin's insight, soon called **Triffin's dilemma** in his honor, explained the underlying problem but not the solution. The possibility that the United States might not be able to meet its commitments to back up the dollar with gold at $35 an ounce created concerns both among U.S. policy makers and those who held dollars. Under the norms of the Bretton Woods system, countries faced with this problem were supposed to either cut back on the flow of their currency abroad or devalue. Cutting back on the outflow of dollars would have required a major drop in U.S. commitments abroad. That was acceptable to some of the U.S.'s principal partners. Indeed, President Charles de Gaulle of France tried to force a change in the uniquely favored position of the dollar exactly because he opposed the ability of the United States to use the position of the dollar to fund its policies abroad. Such a cutback, however, was unacceptable to U.S. policy makers.

The option of devaluation was, meanwhile, foreclosed by the central international role of the dollar. Part of the problem was that the dollar was one of the world's principal reserve assets. Consequently, any devaluation would have the effect of destroying the value of savings held in dollar-denominated accounts by exactly the same percentage as the announced devaluation. Perhaps even more fundamentally, the system depended on other countries being able to adjust the value of their currencies by altering their value relative to the announced value of the dollar. This problem became known as the **N-1, or consistency, problem.**

> In a [fixed-exchange rate] monetary system composed of N countries [N stands for the number of countries that are in the system], N-1 countries are free to change their exchange rate but one country cannot change its exchange rate, because its currency is the standard to which all other countries peg their currency values. There is a potential for conflict if everyone tries to exchange their exchange rate in order to improve their competitive advantage or to achieve some other objective; that conflict can be avoided only if one currency value remains fixed relative to all the others.[19]

It was the stability of the dollar that provided a common standard along which other adjustments could be made. Consequently, any devaluation of the dollar was likely to be met by a round of devaluations by other currencies that left everyone in exactly the same position as before.[20]

Taken together, Triffin's dilemma and the N-1 problem created a trap. Depending on a single national currency for international liquidity and savings in a fixed-exchange-rate, gold-standard system would inevitably lead to more dollars being held abroad than U.S. authorities could credibly promise to exchange for gold; but devaluing the dollar to meet that problem was incompatible with its role as the shared standard in the system. It was a situation that called for creative problem solving. Unfortunately, throughout the 1960s policy makers found a lot of band-aids but no solutions. In 1960, responding to the first *run on the dollar* (a situation in which currency speculators sold off large numbers of dollars in anticipation that the dollar would soon be devalued), U.S. officials began to meet monthly with European

Triffin's dilemma   An economic principle that states that relying on one national currency to provide enough money for international transactions, while simultaneously expecting that currency to serve as a reserve asset, will generate unsustainable pressures on its value in a fixed-exchange-rate, gold-standard system.

N-1, or consistency, problem   The benchmark currency in a fixed-exchange rate system cannot solve pressures on the international value of its currency by changing its exchange rate because, being the benchmark, any changes in its value will simply lead to adjustments in all the other currencies.

central bankers in a group called the Bank for International Settlements (BIS), in Basel, Switzerland. Shortly thereafter, finance ministers from the United States, Belgium, Britain, France, Germany, Italy, Japan, the Netherlands, Sweden, and Canada began to meet in what came to be called the Group of Ten.

The End of the Bretton Woods Monetary System   While these international meetings took place, the U.S. government looked for steps that might strengthen the position of the dollar. In 1963, an Interest Equalization Tax was imposed on foreigners borrowing dollars, in an effort to raise costs and reduce the outflow of dollars. The "Kennedy Round" of trade talks in GATT was started in an effort to lower tariffs and increase U.S. exports, thereby increasing U.S. foreign exchange earnings. U.S. corporations were asked to accept voluntary restrictions on capital exports in 1965; the restrictions were made mandatory in 1968 but then dropped altogether in 1974.

The most significant effort to fix the international monetary system during the 1960s was a five-year set of negotiations by the Group of Ten that produced a 1968 agreement to create **special drawing rights (SDRs)** under the International Monetary Fund. Under the original SDR agreement, all members of the IMF were granted an additional line of credit equal to 200 percent of their contribution to the fund. This increase—from a previous ceiling of 125 percent—was designed to create a new form of reserve asset independent of any one country's currency. SDRs were tied to the value of a weighted average of the major currencies in the IMF. It was hoped that SDRs would grow into a new unit of exchange, an international currency that would wean the international monetary system from its dependence on the dollar. The increase in assets created through the SDRs represented about 6 percent of total world reserves.[21]

Looking at the agreement to create SDRs from the perspective of linkage politics and international coalition building, it is relatively easy to see why it was possible to build a winning coalition in support of this attempt to fix the international monetary system. By the late 1960s, U.S. policy makers saw only two options for solving the dollar's problems: unilaterally going off the gold standard or creating a new form of international reserve asset. Going off gold was highly unattractive on both international and domestic grounds. Internationally, it would undercut the position of the United States as the world's preeminent leader on international economic issues. Domestically, it could hardly be anything other than a political liability. The SDR proposal, on the other hand, not only created a new international asset that took pressure off the dollar, it created an asset that the United States could continue to influence through the IMF (where it had enough votes to veto proposals) and the Group of Ten. Meanwhile, the other key actors in the decision (especially Britain and France, but more generally all the members of the Group of Ten) were able—at least symbolically—to reduce the role of the dollar and the unique advantages (along with the unique vulnerabilities) that gave the U.S. government.

While SDRs were a precedent-setting innovation, they simply were not enough to meet the magnitude of the problem. Dollars continued to flow abroad in far greater numbers than the system could tolerate, partly because of private investments by U.S. corporations and individuals, and partly because the Nixon administration continued the practice, begun by President Johnson, of printing money rather than raising taxes to pay for the costs of the Vietnam War. By August 1971, the pressures on the dollar were overwhelming. President Nixon ended the Bretton Woods monetary system by unilaterally taking the dollar off the gold standard. He simultaneously announced a

special drawing rights (SDRs)   A 1968 change in IMF rules that granted member countries an additional line of credit above that merited by the size of their contribution to the fund.

10.2 ENDURING PATTERNS

The connection between preferences and power
The more incompatible actors' preferences, the more strategically important their relative power positions.

The impact of linkage politics
World politics is driven by the interaction of international, factional, and constituency politics.

The Gold Standard and Diplomatic Conflict: 1926–1927, 1971–1973

In the mid 1920s, British policy makers decided to go back on the gold standard. Because it was both domestically popular and signaled their determination to keep London the financial center of the world, British policy makers set the value of the pound at its 1914 level. The French government believed that valuation was far too high and left the franc seriously undervalued. Unable to get the British to agree to a change, the Bank of France tried to force a devaluation by beginning to sell the 70 million pounds it held as part of its reserve assets. The British government countered by threatening to sell 600 million pounds worth of French treasury bills it held as war debt. With neither able to change the other's preferences, Britain's superior power position carried the day.[a]

As the 1960s drew to a close, it was clear that the leading countries in the Western economic system did not have compatible preferences on the question of how they should resolve the pressures on the Bretton Woods monetary system. Those incompatible preferences were, moreover, anchored in linkage politics; areas of possible international agreement were unacceptable to different key actors because of their domestic implications.

U.S. policy makers didn't have the power to impose a solution, but they did have the power to break the existing system. Since the political risks of breaking the system were lower than the risks of continuing to struggle with the existing one, they had domestic incentives to do what their international position made possible—end the commitment to the gold standard and fixed exchange rates.

[a]See Charles P. Kindleberger, A *Financial History of Western Europe* (London: George Allen and Unwin, 1984), pp. 339–41, 358–59.

---

10 percent surcharge (an added tariff) on all imports in an effort to reduce the flow of dollars abroad by shrinking Americans' appetites for foreign goods. Finally, he also imposed a 90-day wage-price freeze. Negotiations throughout the fall led to a new set of fixed exchange rates by December 1971, but even they could not handle the underlying pressures. In February 1973 the U.S. government once again unilaterally devalued the dollar, this time by 10 percent. When follow-up negotiations on a new set of rates failed, the system moved in March to a **free float.** In a "free float," the price of currencies is left entirely to market forces.

free float   A monetary system in which there is no government intervention at all in international currency markets.

After the Fall: Free and Managed Floats; the European Monetary Union
From March 1973 to January 1976, the value of national currencies floated freely according to whatever value they brought in the international currency markets.

World Politics and the Individual

Nixon Ends the Gold Standard: A Really Bad Day at the Office in Europe and Japan

On August 15, 1971, President Nixon announced that the United States would no longer convert foreign-held dollars into gold. As the discussion of this event at **www.prenhall.com/lamborn** shows, U.S. allies in Europe and Asia were stunned by the announcement. When the United States followed up the announcement with demands that those countries accept a set of proposals for solving the problem that they strongly opposed, their surprise turned to anger.

What linked international and domestic incentives encouraged the Nixon administration to play political hardball on this issue? Why, despite the almost unanimous anger and opposition of its allies, did the U.S. position ultimately prevail?

The period was made even more chaotic by the effects of the 1973 to 1974 Arab oil embargo and a four-fold increase in petroleum prices engineered by the Organization of Petroleum Exporting Countries (OPEC), a cartel that controls a large percentage of the world's oil exports. By late 1975 it was clear that, like Humpty Dumpty, the old system could not be put together again. Working under the auspices of the IMF, Britain, the United States, France, Germany, Italy, and Japan worked out an agreement that was announced in January 1976. The agreement had three parts: First, there would be no attempt either to return to a gold standard or to establish an official price for gold. Second, exchange rates would continue to float, but it would be a **managed float** in the sense that the central banks of the principal countries would work closely to keep the float within acceptable ranges. Third, the signatories would work to increase the role of SDRs and the IMF more generally, in creating reserve assets that were not based on an individual country's currency.

Many economic summits have come and gone since 1976, but the managed float is still the central mechanism for handling currency convertibility. While floating currencies have worked better than any perceived alternative, actually managing the float has proved exceptionally difficult. The difficulty in managing the float partly reflects the development of highly sophisticated computerized networks for trading in the international capital markets. By the 1990s trans-state capital movement had risen to a level that was 30 times higher than the value of trade in goods and services.[22] But this change in the structure of capital markets is only part of the problem. More fundamentally, the connection between the international and domestic roles of currencies has been far more difficult for policy makers to bridge than the authors of the Bretton Woods agreement anticipated. This is most clearly the case with the United States, but the U.S. example has encouraged others to think twice before letting their national currencies assume a greater international role. While there have been some recent changes in the 1990s, the initial reaction of German and Japanese policy makers to the upheavals in the 1970s was to make it more difficult for foreigners to increase their holdings of marks and yen in an effort to reduce their exposure to international currency fluctuations.

There was also little interest in following through on the 1976 plan to radically increase the role of SDRs. At 6 percent of total official reserves when they were created, SDRs have dipped slightly to around 5 percent. When this absence of

managed float A monetary system in which governments work together to try to keep the value of their currencies within a particular range.

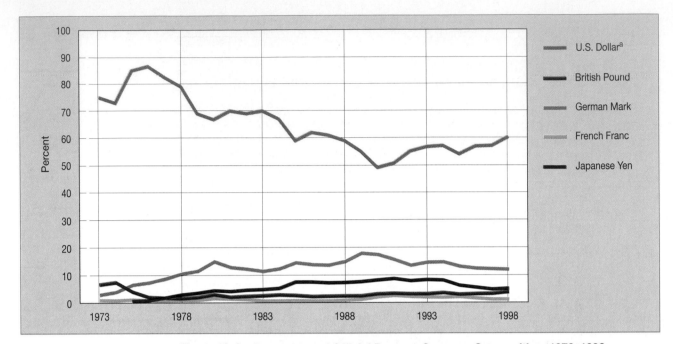

Figure 10–2 **Percentage of Official Reserve Currency Composition, 1973–1998**
While the extent to which countries have relied on the U.S. dollar as a reserve asset has fluctuated since the 1970s, the overall pattern shows only a small decline in the dollar's central role.

[a]U.S. dollars that are included as part of SDRs are included in the figures for the United States.

Notes: (1) Currency reserves are difficult to measure and the final estimates depend heavily on the accounting practices used. In cases in which sources gave significantly different estimates, we have calculated the midpoint of the range; the variation in the reported values is greatest in the figures reported for the U.S.dollar, particularly in the years 1972–1974. (2) Reserve currency percentages for the Swiss franc and the Dutch guilder were very similar to the French franc during this period, ranging between 0.3 percent and 2.7 percent.

Sources: International Monetary Fund, *Annual Report of the Executive Directors for the Fiscal Year Ended April 30, 1975* (Washington, DC: IMF, 1975), p. 39; International Monetary Fund, *Annual Report of the Executive Board for the Financial Year Ended April 30, 1980* (Washington, DC: IMF, 1980), p. 64; International Monetary Fund, *Annual Report of the Executive Board for the Financial Year Ended April 30, 1985* (Washington, DC: IMF, 1985), p. 54; International Monetary Fund, *Annual Report of the Executive Board for the Financial Year Ended April 30, 1990* (Washington, DC: IMF, 1990), p. 67; International Monetary Fund, *Annual Report of the Executive Board for the Financial Year Ended April 30, 1995* (Washington, DC: IMF, 1995), p. 161; International Monetary Fund, *Annual Report of the Executive Board for the Financial Year Ended April 30, 1999* (Washington, DC: IMF, 1999), p. 133.

growth of the SDRs was combined with German and Japanese efforts to restrict the increase in foreign holdings of their currencies, the result was almost inevitable. The dollar's role in global foreign exchange holdings fell from its 1976 high of 86.6 percent but was still at 60.3 percent in 1998 (see Figure 10–2). As a direct result of the continued centrality of the dollar, the domestic politics of foreign policy choice in the U.S. continues to have uniquely significant effects on the shape of any international agreements on managing the float.

The effect of linkage politics on the evolution of the international monetary system can, of course, be seen outside of the United States. Perhaps the most important contemporary example is to be found in Europe. In the late 1970s, the countries in the European Community (EC) decided to create a European Monetary System (EMS) that would both manage currency convertibility within the community and create a new currency unit—the European Currency Unit (ECU)—based on a group of currencies. Basing the ECU on a group of currencies, called a *basket of currencies*, could reduce the role of the dollar without forcing individual countries into a vulnerable position. Later, after the December 1991 Maastricht Treaty called for the transformation of the European Community into the European Union (EU), the goal escalated to the creation of a Monetary Union (MU) by the year 2000.

Several countries, most notably Britain, were led by policy makers who insisted that the Maastricht Treaty allow countries to stay in the EU even if they chose not to participate in the move toward monetary union. However, even in those countries where there was strong support for participating among governmental and private-sector elites, ratification votes held in the 1990s were highly controversial and closely fought. The domestic political problems European policy makers had in their efforts to gain political support for monetary union were strikingly similar to the problems U.S. government officials faced in their efforts to manage the role of the dollar in the 1960s and 1970s. Part of the domestic political problem was symbolic—an emotional attachment to the historical role of national currencies in framing a perception of identity. But there were other issues at stake. While policy makers were enthusiastic, their constituents feared that the adjustments necessary to maintain these international agreements would reduce domestic policy-making autonomy and simultaneously benefit the haves at the expense of the have-nots. The two issues were inextricably linked. The further the ability to influence decisions on domestic economic policy is moved away from national governments, the more those whose political reach is restricted to their ability to pressure governments will be disadvantaged in the bargaining that follows.

In spite of these reservations, a winning coalition in support of the 2000 goal for monetary union was put together in eleven countries: Belgium, Germany, Spain, France, Ireland, Italy, Luxembourg, the Netherlands, Austria, Portugal, and Finland. On January 1, 1999, the euro became an official, shared currency in these countries. (Greece joined the countries allowing the euro on January 1, 2001.) To ease the transition, no banknotes or coins were initially issued. Instead, the debut of the euro was restricted to official transactions, while national currencies continued to be used for daily transactions through 2001. The timetable (now implemented) called for euro-denominated notes and coins to become available for use in January 2002. After only a brief, two-month transition period in which both the euro and national currencies could be used, national currencies were to be withdrawn from circulation by February 28, 2002.

If the euro is successful, it will have significant effects. Regionally, it will signal the end of a long period of state-centered monetary policy in Europe. Internationally, the successful creation of a major regional currency would signal the beginning of a strikingly different global environment for the U.S. dollar.

Trade

While the path from the Bretton Woods conference to the present has taken the international monetary system far from the agreement's original intent, the politics of international trade among the key actors in the Western system have taken a more meandering route. Blocked from the original goal of creating an International Trade Organization (ITO) by opposition within the United States, the essential objective of moving toward free trade moved forward anyway under the auspices of what was supposed to be simply a stop-gap executive agreement, the General Agreement on Tariffs and Trade (GATT). The high point of this initial phase came in 1967, when the Kennedy Round of negotiations under GATT produced an agreement to reduce tariffs on industrial goods by 35 to 40 percent. Then, in the early 1970s, the level of support for free trade fell sharply. It was replaced by a drive to increase exports (called **neomercantilism**) and rising demands that the goal be shifted from free trade to **fair trade.** Advocates of fair trade use the term to mean very different things. On one end of the spectrum are those who argue that the existing system of free trade is really psuedo (or fake) free trade because of government subsidies and the failure to take into account negative externalities—such as the costs of environmental degradation and depleting the world's resources—in the prices charged for goods sold internationally. These critics of existing policies want prices to reflect the *true* opportunity costs of producing goods. Given that goal, this group of fair trade advocates is actually using the term to call for true free trade (in economic theory free trade *should* be built on true opportunity costs). Other advocates of fair trade mean something quite different. For these critics the issue isn't about making the economic system work the way it is supposed to. Instead, it is about protecting a local culture's expectations and distinctive values from market forces. These advocates of fair trade argue that societies ought to be able to control the prices generated by market forces to take into account beliefs about just wages and working conditions. As you might guess, this version of fair trade is more often paired with neomercantilist arguments while the version discussed above is more often paired with environmental concerns.

The sudden drop in the attractiveness of free trade in the early 1970s was partly the result of the economic instability created by the collapse of the Bretton Woods monetary system. Three other factors were also important. The first was a growing focus on unemployment, as the industrial economies went through a period of stagnating growth and high inflation called **stagflation.** Increased exports were widely thought to be one of the best ways to reinvigorate national economies and raise employment levels. The second factor was the perception that structural changes in the patterns of trade were giving Japan and other rising Asian economies an unfair advantage over the United States and Europe. Taken together, these factors stimulated a growing preoccupation with *relative* export shares. The third was the growth in the international environmental movement (see Chapter 13).

With controversies escalating from the 1970s into the 1980s, it seemed that the postwar consensus in favor of free trade was in very real jeopardy. In this climate of anger and recrimination, a new round of talks started under GATT. The negotiations in this Uruguay Round would last from 1987 through April 1994, when an agreement was signed at Marrakesh, Morocco. With that agreement and the grudging ratification of the U.S. Senate, the World Trade Organization (WTO) replaced GATT on January 1, 1995. Fifty years after Bretton Woods, a modern version of the ITO had emerged.

Thus, after a series of detours into neomercantilist controversies, at the beginning of the twenty-first century the international trade system is far closer to the original intent of the Bretton Woods delegates than is the international monetary system. That is particularly surprising, considering how close postwar arrangements came to unraveling in the first years after Bretton Woods.

Postwar Divisions and the Emergence of GATT   The postwar controversies on trade reflected differences that had been papered over at the Bretton Woods conference. While British and U.S. officials had agreed on the general goal of free trade and the importance of grandfathering existing tariffs in place until they could be

neomercantilism   The use of government intervention to promote exports and restrict imports in order to protect domestic employment and wages.

fair trade   A term used by critics of existing free trade practices, including both those who want countries to compete based on true opportunity costs and those who want to alter market forces to reflect local beliefs about just wages and working conditions.

stagflation   A combination of stagnant growth and high inflation.

lowered through reciprocal concessions, they disagreed on two major items. The British wanted to have the right to maintain the imperial trade preferences they had put in place at the Ottawa Conference in 1932. They were also willing to tolerate a wider range of deviation from a pure model of free trade to meet the concerns of countries in Latin America and elsewhere that were interested in more managed approaches to stabilizing export earnings from commodities and promoting industrialization.

At a five-month-long meeting of 57 countries held in 1947 in Havana to hammer out the details of the ITO charter, the negotiated agreement ended up far closer to the British and developing country position than to the U.S. position. The Havana Charter would have promoted international commodity agreements that allowed governments to intervene in markets to promote their exports. It would have also allowed governments to regulate direct private investments and adopt a variety of other arrangements that managed their domestic markets, in an effort to promote import substitution and industrialization. None of these proposals were popular in the United States; they appeared to promote statism and smacked of managed economies. Indeed, they were so unpopular that after waiting for three years in hopes that opposition would decline, the Truman administration gave up on ratification and withdrew the ITO charter from Senate consideration in 1950.

Fortunately, the delegates to the Havana Conference had also agreed on a temporary mechanism for negotiating the movement toward free trade: the General Agreement on Tariffs and Trade (GATT) mentioned earlier. GATT contained none of the controversial provisions for promoting economic development that had doomed the Havana Charter for the ITO; it was also an executive agreement and did not, therefore, require any action by the U.S. Congress to come into force.

GATT established two key norms that were to guide any negotiations for lowering tariff barriers: the **principle of reciprocity** and the **most-favored-nation principle (MFN)**, which establishes a principle of equal and non-preferential treatment in trade. The idea of reciprocity is self-explanatory; it simply stipulated that no country was expected to lower its tariff barriers to the imports of other countries without getting equivalent access in return. The most-favored-nation principle was poorly named but equally straightforward. Under MFN, every member of GATT must be given the same deal as "the most-favored" nation. Of course, as soon as everyone is treated equally, there is no longer a favored nation. While MFN is in that sense a contradiction in terms, the principle of equal and non-preferential treatment it embodies is clear. In addition to the two core principles of reciprocity and equal treatment, GATT established several supporting rules. Export subsidies, price supports, and other techniques designed to increase market share (such as predatory pricing and dumping) were forbidden.

Two important exceptions to these principles were allowed. GATT explicitly allowed regional customs unions and free-trade associations that would, by their very nature, discriminate against nonmembers by offering members a better deal than was generally available. The common market created by the European Community (now the EU) falls under this exemption. A second critical exemption was made for agriculture. Under pressure by the then-powerful agricultural lobby in the United States, a wide range of measures designed to protect agriculture from market fluctuations was allowed under GATT rules. With these controversial issues set aside, the first five rounds of negotiations under GATT between 1947 and 1967 focused on promoting economic growth through the reduction of tariff barriers.

principle of reciprocity
Members of GATT (and now the WTO) are not expected to make concessions on access to their markets unless they receive equivalent access in return.

most-favored-nation principle (MFN) Every member of a multilateral organization must be given the same access to a country's domestic market as the "most-favored-nation."

A large measure of the success of these negotiations can be attributed to the shared commitment to tariff reduction generated by the lessons drawn from the 1930s and the drive to rebuild after the war. The United States played a central role in building the winning coalitions in each round. Given the norm of reciprocity and the **principal supplier rule** that negotiations would be handled by the principal suppliers (defined as countries that produced 10 percent or more of world trade in a particular product), the magnitude of the U.S. economy placed U.S. policy makers at the center of almost every set of negotiations. Getting into the U.S. market was a critical objective of almost all exporters. Under both the norm of reciprocity and the principal supplier rule, that meant negotiating directly with the United States.

U.S. policy makers used this uniquely advantageous strategic position to promote increased trade and economic growth in the non-communist world. At the same time as they negotiated formally reciprocal tariff reductions that provided increased access to U.S. markets for European and Japanese exporters, U.S. officials (as we mentioned earlier) tacitly allowed Japanese officials to maintain non-tariff barriers that protected the Japanese market from U.S. imports and actively encouraged Western Europe to move forward with regional arrangements under the EC that discriminated against U.S. exporters. This discrimination against U.S. exporters seemed a small price, given the magnitude of the perceived stakes during the early Cold War. Moreover, as late as 1955—when European and Japanese recovery was already well under way—the United States still had 23.7 percent of the world's exports.[23] Put colloquially, it was a classic "high gain, low pain" situation. The results were impressive: a 73 percent reduction in tariffs between 1947 and the end of the Kennedy Round in 1967.[24]

The Growth of Neomercantilism The politics of international trade changed dramatically in the 1970s. The economic turbulence created by the end of the Bretton Woods monetary system and the combination of recession and inflation produced by the quadrupling of oil prices in 1973 to 1974 created enormous pressures on policy makers. These pressures coincided with a major restructuring of the distribution of exports in world trade. After watching their exports boom from reconstruction through the 1960s, Europeans watched their relative share begin to drop rather than grow in the early 1970s. U.S. exporters saw an even more dramatic plunge; between 1955 and 1975, the U.S. share in world exports fell about 26 percent.[25] Under free trade principles, this drop in relative share was irrelevant; the appropriate indicator ought to be the growth in absolute, not relative, wealth. The emphasis on relative shares was reminiscent of the perverse, zero-sum principles of mercantilist thought. Moreover, one could argue that from a strictly U.S. perspective, the controversy over the declining U.S. share was doubly perverse. The growth in Europe and Japan's share of world exports represented an immense policy success: The shift in relative shares was the direct and inevitable result of over two decades of U.S. efforts to promote economic growth in Japan and Europe. Thus, while some U.S. policy makers (such as John Connally, secretary of the treasury during the Nixon administration) took an openly neomercantilist position, most U.S. policy makers during the 1970s understood the origins of these changing trade patterns and continued to emphasize the U.S. stake in a liberal world trade system. However, even as that support continued, there was no escaping the fact that the political risks of supporting free trade were rising rapidly.

While the neomercantilist preoccupation with relative economic shares and promoting exports may have been perverse from the historical perspective of U.S.

principal supplier rule
A rule under GATT that negotiations on tariff reductions on a particular product must be handled by countries that produced 10 percent or more of the world trade in that product.

postwar objectives, it had the effect of putting the special arrangements that advantaged Japan and the European Community squarely on the table. The resulting controversies dominated the politics of trade throughout the 1970s and early 1980s. In a series of confrontations, U.S. and European policy makers tried to coerce the Japanese government into "voluntarily" reducing their exports. As many have observed, "in the United States, the typical pattern was a surge in [Japanese] imports, followed by massive filings of unfair trade actions [under GATT and various U.S. laws], followed by pressure on Congress for protectionist legislation, followed, in turn by a negotiated **voluntary export restraint agreement [VER]** as a way to reduce imports without resolving the legal cases and without legislating protection."[26] Similar confrontations occurred between the United States and the European Community, especially over the restrictions the EC's common agricultural program (CAP) imposed on imports of U.S. agricultural products.

These neomercantilist controversies over exports threatened to tear GATT apart. Ironically, by taking the industrialized countries that had benefitted most from the Bretton Woods arrangements to the brink, they also raised the stakes to a point where they created a new agenda for global negotiations under GATT. By the middle 1980s, it was clear that both non-tariff barriers and agriculture would need to be systematically addressed. To these new agenda items were added two other items that had been missing from GATT's original mission: trade in services (as opposed to goods) and rules for handling intellectual property. With no end to the recurring confrontations in sight unless progress was made on these items, a decision was reached at a meeting held in Uruguay in 1986 to launch a new round of negotiations.

Renewed Emphasis on Free Trade: The Uruguay Round of GATT and the Birth of the WTO   The Uruguay Round of negotiations was long   it lasted from 1987 to 1994—and frequently bitter. The final agreement included arrangements for rules and procedures to frame more productive negotiations on agriculture, services, non-tariff barriers, and intellectual property. It also included the provision to replace GATT with a new organization (the World Trade Organization) designed to oversee the implementation of these more comprehensive rules.

In the same period as the Uruguay Round of talks began to make progress, efforts at decreasing trade barriers by encouraging regional agreements moved forward. The European Community became the European Union after the December 1991 Maastricht Treaty. A year later, negotiations among the United States, Canada, and Mexico led to the signing of the North American Free Trade Agreement (NAFTA) in December 1992. Concerns expressed by labor unions over possible job losses to low-income areas in Mexico and environmentalists' fears about the absence of strong environmental protections south of the border were overcome by a coalition that was riding the renewed wave of support among politically powerful groups for open trade in the early 1990s.

The Third World: Life in a System Created and Managed by Others

While the industrialized countries in North America, Western Europe, and Japan were bargaining over ways to improve arrangements for making the global political economy work better, post-colonial societies in Africa, Asia, and the Middle East

voluntary export restraint agreement (VER)   An agreement to reduce exports that is used when policy makers want to maintain a formal position in favor of free trade at the same time as they demand restrictions on foreign access to their markets.

were at best ambivalent about these policy initiatives. They agreed that economic growth was critical and participated in the various GATT negotiating rounds, but they also joined with many countries in Latin America to form coalitions to challenge the system.

Four periods stand out in this process. In the first, which ran from decolonization through the 1960s, Third World leaders concluded that the major pieces of the global political economy worked against them in ways that prevented, rather than encouraged, economic development. It was this period that gave rise to Kwame Nkrumah's arguments about neocolonialism and Raul Prebisch and other Latin American scholars' interpretation of dependency. The second period, spanning roughly the period from the early 1970s to 1979, was a period of high hopes and a concerted challenge to the system's rules, symbolized by the 1974 demand for a New International Economic Order (NIEO) and the 1976 effort to create an Integrated Program for Commodities (IPC). The third period, in the 1980s, brought on an international debt crisis that, along with the failure of the 1970s challenge to the system, brought Third World hopes crashing down into a period of despair even deeper than the bleak period of the 1960s' critique of neocolonialism and dependency. The final period, from the late 1980s to the present, has brought growing stress on economic success through integrating Third World economies into the global market rather than challenging them. We discuss each of these periods in chronological order.

The 1960s Critique: Neocolonialism and Dependency

The Bretton Woods system had been built around a set of interrelated assumptions about politics, economics, and the "normal" state of affairs in the global political economy once the postwar reconstruction had been completed. While there was an expectation that government would have to play a role in balancing the needs of the international systems of trade and money with domestic full employment and growth, the view of government's role was placed within almost two centuries of thought dating to Adam Smith and David Ricardo. It was, of course, an individualistic view that stressed personal liberty and limited government. To these assumptions about political economy were added beliefs about the likely state of affairs after reconstruction, a belief that if the mistakes of the 1930s could be avoided and the communist threat could somehow be overcome, then the principles that guided the Bretton Woods agreement would produce prosperity and freedom.

These views were not widely accepted among the leaders of the independence movements in Africa and Asia. With decolonization, these individuals became the first generation of post-colonial leaders. Nor were they to be long accepted by many in Latin America, where the boom created by being one of the major exporting regions during World War II was to be followed, after the Korean War and the recovery of Europe and Asia, by a long decline through the 1960s. Of the two, the post-colonial critique symbolized by Nkrumah's analysis of neocolonialism was more directly and overtly placed within the Marxist intellectual tradition's rejection of capitalism. There is, however, no doubt that dependency arguments also reflected a fundamental mistrust of capitalism.

Nkrumah and the Attack on Neocolonialism   Kwame Nkrumah gained international stature in the 1950s as the leader of Ghana (formerly the British colony of the Gold Coast), the first black African state to gain independence from colonialism (see the box on Nkrumah in Chapter 7). When he led his people to independence in 1957, Nkrumah promised that formal independence would bring prosperity. By the early 1960s, he had changed his mind. Nkrumah placed his critique of capitalism in the tradition of Marx and Lenin. In a direct reference to Lenin's *Imperialism, the Highest Stage of Capitalism*, he entitled his book-length analysis *Neocolonialism, the Last Stage of Imperialism*. Where Lenin had argued that Marx had failed to anticipate the stage of imperialism, Nkrumah argued that Lenin had failed to anticipate neocolonialism. Nevertheless, as we shall see below, while Nkrumah placed himself in this revolutionary tradition, the solutions he offered reflected more Hobson's preference for radical reform than Lenin's call for revolutionary violence.

Nkrumah defined **neocolonialism** in the following way: "The essence of neocolonialism is that the State which is subject to it is, in theory, independent and has all the outward trappings of international sovereignty. In reality its economic system and thus its political policy is directed from the outside."[27] The aim of this external control, according to Nkrumah, was to exploit, not develop. Furthermore, it was a form of exploitation even worse than colonialism: "neocolonialism is . . . the worst form of imperialism. For those who practice it, it means power without responsibility and for those who suffer from it, it means exploitation without redress."[28]

The stress on economic control as the foundation for political control is entirely consistent with the Marxist tradition. But Nkrumah was a practicing politician, not a theorist. As such, he searched for political solutions. That search would, ironically, take him away from both Marx and Lenin. The tip-off comes early in the introduction to Nkrumah's book. Nkrumah wrote that profits and capital investment were acceptable; the fundamental issue was not profits, it was political power: "The issue is not what return the foreign investor receives on his investments. . . . The question is one of power. A State in the grip of neocolonialism is not master of its own fate."[29]

Nkrumah's analysis of neocolonialism develops along the following lines. He begins by accepting the argument made by Lenin and others that colonialism evolved in the nineteenth century as a means for monopoly capitalism to get enough wealth from the colonies to lessen internal class conflicts within the principal capitalist states. Formal colonial control was simply a tactical change that occurred when the informal control that characterized mid-nineteenth-century laissez-faire capitalism turned out to be inadequate to the task. However, by the end of World War II it was no longer possible to maintain formal empires. As Nkrumah saw it, the prospect of decolonization presented European governments with a major problem: It came at exactly the same time as they were trying to find a way to pay for the new welfare states they were creating to appease workers angered by the cumulative costs of World War I, the Depression, and World War II. The welfare state was necessary to save capitalism, Nkrumah believed, but Europe couldn't pay for it without the continued exploitation of Africa and Asia. The pressures for decolonization made the old colonial structure unsustainable, so the Europeans innovated. Their solution was neocolonialism: Grant formal independence to the colonies while maintaining enough external control to continue the exploitation.

Nkrumah believed that the European colonizers intentionally created nonviable states when they decolonized. By setting up states that were too small and internally divided to be economically viable and politically strong, the Europeans laid the foundation for continuing external control after formal independence. The United

neocolonialism The continued external control and exploitation of post-colonial societies after they have gained formal independence.

States, with its preeminent economic and military position in the Western system in the first decades after World War II, then became the principal agent for sustaining neocolonialism. Nkrumah focused on a wide range of economic, political, and cultural factors that he believed served as the main mechanisms for U.S.-led neocolonial control. He argued that free trade cast post-colonial societies in the role of exporters of primary products and importers of manufactured goods. That division of labor, as we have discussed before, can create very disadvantageous terms of trade and leave primary-product producers vulnerable to wide swings in export earnings as the prices of commodities on the world market fluctuate. (As we discuss below, economist Raul Prebisch's analyses of Latin America make very similar arguments about the dangers countries face when they depend on only a few primary products for their export earnings.) Meanwhile, capital flows and interest rates were dominated by the rich through the banks, government-to-government foreign aid, U.S.-based businesses, and the weighted voting arrangements in the IMF and IBRD.

These economic mechanisms of neocolonial control were reinforced, Nkrumah argued, by political and cultural ones. Intelligence agencies such as the CIA intervened to overthrow leaders who were too independent or left-leaning, and Cold War security needs were used to justify basing troops in Third World countries. At the same time as these overtly manipulative forms of political influence were taking place, the spread of Western culture, religion, and education undermined the ability of people in post-colonial societies to develop independent world views.

Nkrumah offered two strategies for ending neocolonialism: non-alignment in the Cold War and the creation of a Pan-African state. He argued that Third World leaders should refuse to be drawn into the Cold War between East and West. A policy of non-alignment would enable post-colonial leaders to avoid the security arguments used by the United States to drive them into subservient military arrangements. It would also put them in a position where they could play one side off against the other to get aid without strings. (Consistent with this argument, Nkrumah was—along with Tito, Nasser, and Nehru—one of the founders of the Non-Aligned Movement.) Meanwhile, the Pan-African movement would create a country so large that it could industrialize and stand on its own—politically and militarily.

Nkrumah's two political strategies for ending neocolonialism signal his distance from the hard core of the Marxist-Lenist tradition, which stressed revolution as the only solution, but they also raise a perplexing logical question: If the essence of neocolonialism involves external control over the political choices of post-colonial societies, why wouldn't neocolonialists use that control to prevent exactly the choices Nkrumah recommends for ending neocolonialism? It's a question that suggests two quite different answers. People unsympathetic to Nkrumah's interpretation see it as evidence that the idea of neocolonialism is flawed at its core. People sympathetic to the idea go in exactly the opposite direction, pointing out that the Pan-African movement failed and that Nkrumah was overthrown in a coup.

The Growing Visibility of the Dependencia Critique The second major strand of the 1960s Third World critique of the global political economy came out of Latin America—the **dependencia** school of thought. Dependency analysts focused on GATT and the system of international trade, but before we examine their critique of existing trade patterns and rules it is important first to understand why they came to focus on trade as the engine for economic growth. To see why, place

dependencia The Latin American version of the dependency perspective, which argues that global capitalism keeps Third World countries poor by forcing them to specialize in producing commodities and other primary products for export, while importing expensive industrial and high-technology goods from rich countries.

yourself in the position of a Third World policy maker looking around the economic horizon in the early 1960s. Third World countries in this period were overwhelmingly poor and were searching for capital investment and foreign exchange that could be used both to raise the short-term standard of living of their people and promote long-term growth. Moreover, throughout the first half of the twentieth century, the most widely accepted explanations of Third World poverty had been offered by critics of capitalism based in the Marxist intellectual tradition. That perspective and the shared experience of major-power intervention and exploitation created a natural predisposition among Third World leaders to examine the global political economy with great suspicion.

There were, moreover, many opportunities to find evidence that was consistent with the expectation that the system was designed to exploit. Throughout the 1950s, the United States was the principal source of foreign aid, but the U.S. executive branch saw aid principally as a tool to contain communism. Meanwhile, members of Congress frequently demanded that Third World policy makers repay the United States by publicly supporting U.S. diplomatic positions. Finally, most U.S. aid came with economic, as well as political, strings. In an attempt to sell aid domestically, U.S. policy makers had to promise that most of the credits would be spent in the home districts of politically important representatives and senators. As a result, aid recipients frequently had to buy more expensive and often less appropriate U.S. goods as a condition for receiving aid, even in situations in which the aid came in loans that needed to be repaid.

Efforts to find other sources of foreign exchange and capital investment met similar hurdles. U.S.-based trans-state business enterprises (TSBEs) spread rapidly throughout the 1950s as a result of the world's need for capital and the unique role of the dollar. But these businesses typically repatriated most of their profits (**repatriation of profits**) by sending them back to their home country instead of reinvesting them in the host country where they were earned. During this period, TSBEs also frequently meddled in the internal affairs of host countries.

Poor countries could try to avoid the strings that came with TSBEs by going instead to the IMF and the IBRD, but both are run by the rich countries through a weighted-voting system in which the number of votes a country has varies with the size of its contribution. Furthermore, the magnitude of the funds available through these institutions was limited. In the case of the IMF, help was limited to the size of the member's original contribution, which, for poor states, was always small. In the case of the IBRD, there was no link between contributions and the magnitude of aid, but there was a requirement that the funded projects be able to repay the loan with interest. In 1960 this requirement was loosened, and the IBRD moved from an exclusive reliance on **hard loans** (ones in which the project itself had to generate enough profits to repay the loan with interest) to **soft loans** (ones that were offered at concessionary, or below-market, interest rates with very long pay-back periods) offered through the International Development Association. But even then, the amount of funds was quite limited, and Western-trained experts retained the authority to decide who got loans and the conditions that were imposed.

Faced with these obstacles, Third World leaders turned to the United Nations and the General Assembly, where the one-nation, one-vote system gave them a voting majority in 1960 after decolonization had swept through Asia and Africa. In 1960, the General Assembly put Third World development on the global agenda with the announcement of the First Development Decade and the United Nations

repatriation of profits
A situation in which trans-state business enterprises send the profits earned by their foreign subsidiaries back to their home country rather than reinvesting them in the host country where they were earned.

hard loans Loans from multilateral lending agencies that are granted only if the projects in which those loans are invested have the potential to generate profits sufficient to pay the loan back with interest.

soft loans Loans from multilateral lending agencies that are granted with concessionary (below-market) interest rates and very long pay-back periods, typically granted for projects that combine a high social value with a low potential for profit.

Development Program (UNDP). But under UN rules, the funding for these special development programs had to be obtained principally through voluntary contributions, not required assessments. The result was programs funded at a level that was much smaller than the Third World voting majority in the General Assembly had hoped for.

Given these interconnected impediments, Third World leaders came to the conclusion that they would need to *earn* foreign exchange through increased exports. In December 1961, the General Assembly formally passed a resolution entitled "International Trade as the Primary Instrument for Economic Development," which placed the emphasis squarely on trade as the engine of development.[30] The problem was that many Third World policy makers fundamentally disagreed with GATT's goal of free trade and the norms of reciprocity and non-preferential treatment. They argued that free trade and the doctrine of comparative advantage (for a discussion of comparative advantage, see Chapter 9) produced an unequal and unfair division of labor in which Third World countries end up dependent on exports of primary products while they import industrial and high-technology goods.

The data for 1970 in Table 10–3 dramatically illustrates why so many Third World leaders during the 1960s and 1970s were worried that their countries were far too dependent on exports of primary products and had to spend too much of their scarce foreign exchange to import industrial and high-technology goods. In 1970, manufactured goods made up only 24.9 percent of the value of developing countries' exports, while exports of primary commodities and petroleum brought in 75.1 percent of their export earnings. Meanwhile, they used 71.3 percent of the money spent on imports to buy manufactured goods.

Industrial market economies had a very different mix, especially on the export side. While manufactured goods made up only 24.9 percent of developing countries' exports, they were 74.1 percent of the industrial market economies' exports. The differences in the import mix were less dramatic but still clear; manufactured goods made up 59.8 percent of the value of industrial market economies' imports, as compared to 71.3 percent for developing countries.*

According to dependency theorists, specializing in the export of primary products created the following profoundly negative consequences for Third World countries: First, the prices of primary products were notoriously volatile, which produced wild fluctuations in export earnings that lowered the standard of living of the people at the same time as it undermined political stability. Second, the prices of primary products tended to be far lower than the prices of industrial imports, producing adverse terms of trade and balance-of-payments problems. Third, specializing in primary products was expected to produce ever-worsening trade imbalances because of **differential income-elasticity of demand.** While an imposing term, it describes a

---

differential income-elasticity of demand   The expectation that increases in the wealth of poor countries will produce a greater marginal demand for more imports than increases in the wealth of rich countries.

*Table 10–3 also shows two important changes between 1970 and 1984. First, note the massive increase in the cost of importing petroleum after 1970. As we discuss later in this chapter, those increased costs had a major effect on the origins of the Third World Debt Crisis. Second, notice that by 1984 developing countries' exports of manufactured goods had risen from 24.9 percent to 40.1 percent and their imports of manufactured goods had fallen from 71.3 percent to 64.4 percent—a level almost identical to the industrialized world's 61.1 percent. These changes in the composition of imports and exports had important implications, which we discuss in the section "A Watershed Change in Perceived Options: The Late 1980s through the 1990s."

| TABLE 10–3 | VALUE OF PRIMARY COMMODITIES, PETROLEUM, AND MANUFACTURES AS A PERCENTAGE OF TOTAL EXPORTS AND IMPORTS, 1970, 1980, AND 1984, BY REGION AND STAGE OF ECONOMIC DEVELOPMENT |

	PERCENTAGE OF TOTAL EXPORTS			PERCENTAGE OF TOTAL IMPORTS		
	1970	**1980**	**1984**	**1970**	**1980**	**1984**
Developing Countries						
Primary Commodities	55.9%	27.2%	25.9%	21.1%	17.7%	17.6%
Petroleum	19.2	40.2	34.0	7.6	18.8	18.0
Manufactures	24.9	32.6	40.1	71.3	63.5	64.4
Industrial Market Economies						
Primary Commodities	22.4	19.9	17.9	30.3	19.8	17.9
Petroleum	3.5	7.4	7.9	9.9	27.7	21.0
Manufactures	74.1	72.7	74.5	59.8	52.5	61.1

Source: Adapted from World Bank, *Commodity Trade and Price Trends, 1987–88* (Baltimore: Johns Hopkins University Press, 1986). Original source of data: UNCTAD, *Handbook of International Trade and Development Statistics,* and UN, *Monthly Bulletin of Statistics.*

relatively simple idea popularized by the dependencia school: Third World appetites for increased imports from the rich would grow faster with any increase in their income than the appetites of consumers in the developed countries for increased imports from the Third World. *Income-elasticity of demand* refers to how consumers' appetites for purchases change in response to changes in the level of their income. The argument of dependency theorists was that the income-elasticity of demand for imports was higher in the Third World than in the developed industrial economies. This differential demand for imports as incomes rose would exacerbate the negative effects of the adverse terms of trade (created by the fact that the goods and services the Third World imported typically had higher unit prices than their exports), thereby creating deteriorating trade relations over time.

This view led to the conclusion that Third World countries were in a political as well as an economic trap. Specializing in primary products would not only keep them poor; it would undermine their political stability at the same time as their inability to industrialize made it impossible to become military and political powers on the world stage. Given this view, Third World leaders pressed for changes in the rules of international trade throughout the 1960s and 1970s. The first major step in that direction came in 1964 at a meeting held in Geneva under UN auspices. Led by a caucus of Third World states known as the Group of 77, this United Nations Conference on Trade and Development (UNCTAD) created a UN agency designed to study possible changes in the system of trade. Raul Prebisch, one of the most visible scholars associated with the dependencia school of thought in Latin America, was chosen to head the new organization, also called UNCTAD. (The confusion created by giving both the conference and the organization the same name is lessened

10.3 ENDURING PATTERNS

The impact of discounting

People generally prefer current benefits over future benefits and future costs over current costs. Moreover, the less control actors have over policy choice and implementation, the more actors will prefer future costs over current costs and the more they will value current benefits over future benefits.

The Long and Short of It: Workers in the 1960s Dependencia Critique and Today

Throughout the 1960s and 1970s, many Third World policy makers accepted the dependencia argument that free trade was a trap. The political strength of the dependencia interpretation was reinforced by the fact that advocates of free trade could only argue that it would benefit people in the Third World in the long run. In the short run, moving toward free trade would produce painful economic dislocations as protectionist measures were eliminated and government subsidies and welfare programs were reduced. Moreover, that short-run economic pain would take place in an international economic system in which Third World leaders had very little influence.

As we move into the twenty-first century, advocates of increasing globalization argue that it will make workers in the United States and Western Europe better off in the long run. Those workers are, however, being asked to run substantial short-term risks to their economic security in a system in which they have very little influence.

---

somewhat by the practice of using Roman numerals to number the conferences held every four years by the UNCTAD organization. Hence, the first UNCTAD conference became known as UNCTAD I.)

Although UNCTAD's supporters initially had high hopes for the organization, little other than the holding of expensive meetings happened until the early 1970s. Then a series of events created the impression that the Third World might be able to force fundamental change on the system.

The 1970s Challenge

The early 1970s seemed to herald a radical change in the distribution of power in the global economy. The effects of the weakening of the dollar and the collapse of the Bretton Woods monetary system were reinforced by the spread of stagflation and concerns about growing resource scarcity. Then OPEC's ability to quadruple oil prices in 1973 to 1974 provided a dramatic exclamation point that suggested that the Third World suddenly had the rich countries in a bind, and they would have to respond to demands for radical change.

In April 1974, the Sixth Special Session of the General Assembly convened to discuss the implications of these changes. The result was the May 1 Declaration on the Establishment of a New International Economic Order (NIEO). The declaration started with the assumptions that the current system was not only illegitimate and hopelessly flawed but also out of step with changes in the distribution of economic power.

> It has proved impossible to achieve an even and balanced development of the international community under the existing international economic order. The gap between the developed and developing countries continues to widen in a system which was established at a time when most of the developing countries did not even exist as independent States and perpetuates inequality. . . . The present international economic order is in direct conflict with current developments in international political and economic relations. Since 1970 . . . the developing world has become a powerful factor. . . . These irreversible changes in the relationship of forces in the world necessitate the active, full and equal participation of the developing countries . . . in all decisions that concern the international community.[31]

What followed these assumptions was an extraordinary set of demands, starting with proposed changes in how decisions are reached in world politics that, if implemented, would have moved the world toward a one-nation, one-vote format.

> The new international economic order should be founded on full respect for the following principles: . . . Full and effective participation on the basis of equality of all countries in the solving of world economic problems. . . . The right of every country to adopt the economic and social system that it deems appropriate . . . and not be subject to discrimination of any kind as a result. . . . Full permanent sovereignty of every state over its natural resources and all economic activities. . . . No state may be subjected to economic, political or any other type of coercion to prevent the free and full exercise of this inalienable right.[32]

These principles led the way for the following specific demands:

- Paying reparations for colonialism
- Regulating trans-national corporations in the interest of development
- Indexing the price of primary products to the price of manufactured goods
- Changing the international monetary system to promote development
- Encouraging preferential and non-reciprocal treatment in trade
- Increasing the transfer of grants without political or economic strings
- Creating opportunities for access to technology at concessionary rates
- Promoting producer cartels

Needless to say, U.S. officials, like those in most of the developed countries, rejected these demands. However, after boycotting the discussions in the Sixth Special Session, U.S. policy makers agreed to participate in follow-up discussions on the NIEO held in the Seventh Special Session in 1975. Those negotiations established the outline of a possible deal. In exchange for the Third World dropping its most inflammatory demands for "full and equal" participation in all decisions—a demand that, in effect, called for a one-nation, one-vote format for world government—the United States agreed in principle to enter negotiations on active assistance in the area of technology transfers and financial aid plus preferential and non-reciprocal treatment in trade.

The first major test of this agreement took place at UNCTAD IV meetings held in Nairobi, Kenya, in 1976. UNCTAD (the organization) arrived at these meetings with a proposal for an Integrated Program for Commodities (IPC). The announced goal was "global resource management in the interests of the development process . . . to encompass the totality of the commodity problem from production to consumption."[33] It is not surprising that UNCTAD would choose commodities as the engine for export-led growth. Even when one excluded oil, 60 percent of the Third World's total export earnings were generated by commodities. The fact that 80 percent of those sales went to developed countries made it even more attractive.

The problem was that UNCTAD's proposal called for a *buffer stock program* structured around a single common fund that was paid for largely by consumers. In a buffer stock program, surpluses are purchased and stored during times of abundance to keep the price from falling so far that producers are hurt. In times of scarcity, the stored surpluses are sold to increase supply and keep the price from rising so high that consumers are unable to purchase necessary supplies. Buffer stocks are difficult to manage because producers have an incentive to pressure administrators to buy surpluses early (to keep the price from falling) and consumers have an incentive to pressure administrators to sell stored stocks early to increase supply and reduce prices. In the case of the proposed Integrated Program for Commodities, consumers in the industrialized countries suspected that UNCTAD planned to manipulate the buffer stock program to help Third World producers. The proposal was made even more controversial by UNCTAD's demand that the developed countries agree to guarantee funding before agreement was reached on the commodities covered, the formula for contributions, or the management procedures. UNCTAD also refused all requests for clarification and modification. While this strategy probably reflected a concern that clarification would drive wedges between different Third World countries (still known as the Group of 77), it raised suspicions that UNCTAD's real reason for refusing to negotiate modifications was a desire to force a victory for the Third World that would reintroduce the principle of equality (one nation, one vote) in negotiations over the global economy. Given those concerns and basic disagreement over the substance of the proposals, the result was stalemate.

While the negotiations over the IPC stalemated in 1976, it was clear that there were conditions under which the developed countries would agree to offer preferential and non-reciprocal treatment in trade. Significantly, the U.S. and European models for such concessions varied substantially. The U.S. version can be seen in the Generalized System of Preferences (GSP) offered under GATT. Passed by Congress in 1975, GSP authorized the executive to make country- and product-specific arrangements for preferential and non-reciprocal access to U.S. markets. It also established ceilings either by quantity or total value for each product. Finally, it included an escape clause that allowed the U.S. government to end any of these arrangements without prior notice or consultation. It would be hard to imagine a set of arrangements more fully designed to protect the United States against economic losses and maintain its political leverage over recipients.

The European approach was quite different. Following negotiations that lasted over a year, in 1975 the EC signed the Lomé Convention with forty-six states in Africa, the Caribbean, and the Pacific (known as the ACP states). The ACP states got duty-free and quota-free access to the EC; all the EC states were promised in return was MFN status (that is, that they would not be treated worse than anyone else). It is hard to imagine a more preferential and non-reciprocal deal than getting nothing in return for granting complete access to the common market. Moreover, the EC promised to fund the STABEX program, under which the ACP states could apply for either an interest-free loan or a grant if their export earnings fell more than 7.5 percent below the moving average for the preceding four years.

Why such a sweeping agreement? The reasons reflected a combination of political and economic incentives. On the economic side of the ledger, it is important to notice that the Lomé Convention provided access to markets. There were no complicated buffer stock systems that might lead to hidden costs and oversupply. Furthermore, most of the products involved had no European competitors that were disadvantaged by easier access. Finally, the price of the imports would still be set by the market. Any long-term declines in prices would show up in the four-year moving average. Help through the STABEX program would make up only for dips in export earnings around that trend line; it would not change the line itself.

On the political side, the ACP states were helped by the willingness of European states to consider more overt forms of economic management than was the practice in the United States. They were also lucky in timing. Negotiations were already under way when the OPEC oil embargo increased Europeans' sense of vulnerability. But perhaps the most significant underlying political factor could be found in the desire of EC governments to reinforce historic ties established in the colonial period. Seen from that perspective, the Lomé Convention was but another example of the rich offering the poor a handout—a deal designed to legitimize the immense differences in power and prosperity.

The central lesson of the 1970s challenge was, then, that the underlying distribution of economic power had not changed in the dramatic and irrevocable way that the Third World had claimed in the Declaration for a New International Economic Order. Furthermore, while the Europeans would agree to some incremental changes in the international economic system that created mutual benefits for the EC and Third World countries, the United States was unenthusiastic about going even that far. The implications of that message for Third World options would be driven home even more forcefully during the 1980s debt crisis.

The 1980s Third World Debt Crisis

The 1980s Third World debt crisis burst onto the international scene in August 1982 when Mexico announced that it could no longer pay the interest on its international debt. Mexico's problem—$50.4 billion in foreign debt and a **debt service ratio** (the ratio of interest payments to foreign exchange earnings) of 29.5 percent—turned attention to a global problem. Third World debt had risen from $64.4 billion in 1970 to over $600 billion in 1983. The debt-service ratio had, meanwhile, climbed from 13.5 to 20.7 percent. Consider the implications. Over one-fifth of the Third World's total foreign exchange earnings had to be used simply to pay the interest on their foreign debt! Furthermore, much of that foreign debt was in flexible interest rates that moved with the so-called "prime rate" established by Wall Street financial markets. Brazil, with $100 billion in foreign debt, had to find an extra $400 million in export earnings to pay for a 1 percent increase in the interest rate. While countries in Africa had borrowed less heavily in aggregate terms, relative to

debt service ratio   The ratio of interest payments due on foreign loans relative to foreign exchange earnings; since this ratio does not include payments toward the amount borrowed, it measures the ability to service a debt, not repay it.

World Politics and the Individual

Devastated Lives: The Third World Debt Crisis Hits Mexico

The Third World debt crisis had devastating effects on the daily lives of people around the world. In Mexico, the experience was so bleak that the 1980s became known as the "lost decade."

An overview of Mexico's experience during the 1980s debt crisis can be found at **www.prenhall.com/lamborn**. What triggered the sudden decline in Mexico's economy in 1981? How did the sudden collapse of the economy affect urban and rural workers? What policy changes did the IMF demand as the price for help? What were some of the short-run effects of those changes on people's lives?

the scale of their economies they were frequently worse off than the larger Latin American borrowers. Sudan, for instance, had a debt service ratio over 100 percent. The result was 36 debt reschedulings in 1983 alone.

The origins of the Third World debt crisis are a classic example of the dangers of linkage politics when a country is in a vulnerable strategic position in the global economy. Throughout the 1970s, Third World policy makers had political and policy incentives to borrow externally in order to fund deficit spending to finance development and subsidize consumption. The sheer magnitude of the borrowing was risky. Using the money to subsidize consumption rather than promote investments made it doubly dangerous, because it meant these countries had gone deep into debt without significantly increasing their capacity to earn money that could pay off the loans. In the 1980s changing international conditions turned these unwise choices into a full-fledged debt crisis. Consider these developments:

- The massive increase in oil prices engineered by OPEC hurt oil-importing Third World countries even worse than it hurt the industrialized states (see Figure 10–3). Determined not to reduce oil consumption both for political reasons and because cheap energy was regarded as the most promising route to industrialization, Third World countries tried to meet the increased price of oil by borrowing more heavily. Commercial banks in the United States and Europe, awash with deposits from OPEC countries, looked for places to recycle those *petrodollars* profitably. Acting under the false assumption that countries could not go bankrupt, they increased their lending to the Third World.

- Widespread inflation in the industrialized countries in the 1970s created a virtually unprecedented situation in which there were *negative* real interest rates. With inflation higher than interest rates, it actually paid to borrow through most of the 1970s. Then, abruptly, changes in the economic policies of the principal industrialized countries squeezed inflation out of the system and produced a shift to very high positive real interest rates in the early 1980s.

- A recession that began in 1979 in the industrialized countries reduced demand for Third World exports at exactly the time in which the preceding changes had substantially increased their need for foreign exchange earnings.

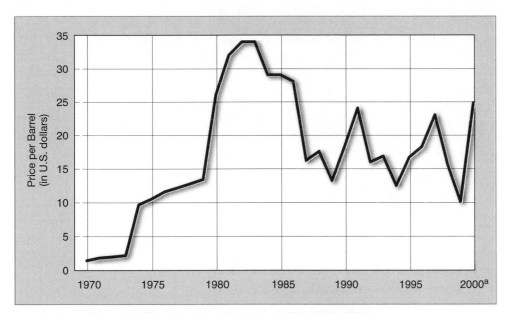

Figure 10–3   Prices for Saudi Arabian Light Crude Oil, 1970–2000

Petroleum is one of the most important commodities in the world economy; it also has some of the most volatile prices. In Figure 10–3 you can see the first (1973–1974) and second (1979–1980) oil shocks that sent tremors throughout the global economy and helped cause the Third World debt crisis. You can also see the 1984–1989 collapse in oil prices that helped much of the world work its way out of the debt crisis. Note, finally, the magnitude of the 1999–2000 increase.

aProjected figure.

Source: U.S. Department of Energy. *Annual Energy Review, 1999* (Washington, DC: U.S. Government Printing Office, 1999), p. 283.

- Finally, the impact of all these externally driven changes was magnified by a steep rise in the value of the U.S. dollar. The increased price of the dollar worsened terms of trade (which meant that the Third World got fewer dollars for each unit sold), increased the price of oil imports (because the international price of petroleum is set in dollars), and raised the cost of debt repayments to U.S. banks.

The decisions to borrow heavily were the responsibility of Third World governments. However, as the list above shows, the debt crisis was triggered by choices and events that were largely outside of their control. Moreover, the strategic vulnerability of Third World countries severely limited their options for getting out of the hole in which they found themselves. Foreign aid always came with strings attached. Under the principle of *conditionality* (which said that the IMF could require that borrowers correct the basic problems that had created the need to seek outside help), the IMF would probably impose unpopular conditions for short-term, balance-of-payments help. Walking away from the IMF wasn't an attractive option either, because private banks were increasingly using the IMF as a gatekeeper—demanding an IMF-approved plan as a precondition for debt rescheduling. As for direct intergovernmental help, except in those situations in which the developed countries maintained strings (such as GSP) or cases that reinforced historic dependency patterns (Lomé), attempts to negotiate preferential and non-reciprocal treatment in trade had failed in the 1970s. *In short, Third World governments were in a terrible strategic situation: What they had the power to do internationally (accept foreign-imposed conditions for help) was unpopular domestically; what was popular domestically (challenge the system), they didn't have the power to do internationally.*

Significantly, both industrial and Third World countries backed out of the debt crisis more by luck than innovative policy choices and coalition building. From mid-1985 to 1990, most of the international conditions that had worsened the debt crisis in the early 1980s swung in the opposite direction: Third World exports increased in response to an economic recovery in the industrial countries; falling interest rates reduced the payments on variable rate obligations; a drop in oil prices reduced the need for foreign exchange; and a fall in the value of the dollar reduced debt payments and oil prices while it improved the terms of trade.

A Watershed Change in Perceived Options: The Late 1980s through the 1990s

Coming hard on the heels of the failure of Third World attempts in the 1970s to demand fundamental changes in the structure and norms of the global political economy, the Third World debt crisis in the 1980s drove home some strategic lessons for policy makers around the world. Policy makers in the industrialized countries were relieved by the failure of confrontational demands for a new international order but were simultaneously sobered by the threat to the international banking system that had been created by the combination of Third World appetites for capital and the often reckless willingness of the big Western banks to lend it. The conclusion was inescapable. Although defeating the 1970s demands for radical change in the global economy had been necessary, there was a shared stake in building mutually acceptable arrangements that would reduce the probability of any future threats to the system on the magnitude of the debt crisis.

At the same time as the appetite for confrontation was decreasing in the industrial countries, Third World leaders were increasingly drawn toward the conclusion that coordination might be better than confrontation. The debt crisis had reaffirmed the strategic vulnerability of the Third World to events and choices well beyond its control, but it had also made it even more inescapably clear that their available options did not include a radical change in the system's arrangements. Those conclusions in turn altered their domestic political calculations. It is one thing to seek domestic political support under banners calling for an attack on neocolonialism and dependency when that seems a credible option. It is quite another when it does not.

These shifts in the incentive-structure built into the context for linkage politics in the Third World were reinforced by a changing of the guard. By the 1980s the last of the generation of Third World leaders that had achieved political prominence during the struggles for decolonization and the first years of independence had died or retired. They had come of age during a period when capitalism was inescapably identified with colonialism, and the Marxist intellectual tradition supplied the most widely believed critique. That generation was now gone from the policy-making arena. With this generational shift, market approaches to growth had a wider audience among policy makers at exactly the point in time when the context for linkage politics had changed. As we have often observed, the success of any diplomatic

10.4 ENDURING PATTERNS

The impact of varying beliefs about just relationships

If people think a political process is just, they are more likely to accept the outcomes it produces—even if they would have preferred something else.

The 1980s Watershed; Anti-Globalization Today

The economic success of the newly industrializing countries (NICs) and the collapse of Marxist alternatives to Western market economies after the disintegration of the Soviet Union lowered the market's perceived procedural illegitimacy in many Third World countries. While questions about outcome legitimacy still remain—as one would expect in a world with such massive international differences in wealth—the inability to effectively tie questions about outcome legitimacy to a competing perspective that challenges the overall legitimacy of the system substantially reduced the ease with which Third World policy makers could build opposition coalitions.

The growth of concerns about globalization in the United States and Western Europe during the 1990s and the first years of the twenty-first century are partly related to the perception that the people who are most adversely affected by globalization don't have a voice in the management of the system. This increasingly widespread sense of procedural illegitimacy makes it easier to build opposition coalitions. However, the absence of a perceived alternative to contemporary market systems makes it difficult to expand those coalitions beyond street demonstrations into government policy-making circles.

---

initiative depends on how policy makers' preferences fit what the international and domestic contexts make possible. In the first decades after decolonization, Third World policy makers' preferences leaned heavily toward the critique embodied in the literature on neocolonialism and dependency. Their domestic context made that approach popular, and the early 1970s seemed to create an international context when it was attainable. The result was confrontation. By the end of the 1980s, policy makers' preferences, the international context, and the domestic incentives had all changed.

This essential transformation in the direction of preferences and the strategic and political incentives for choice was reinforced by two additional factors: the end of the Cold War and the success of some **newly industrializing countries (NICs).** The most famous of the NICs are the four tigers: Taiwan, Singapore, Hong Kong, and South Korea. By the late 1980s, the four tigers had spearheaded a movement toward industrialization and export-led growth that had produced a shift in the composition of Third World exports from 24.9 percent manufactured goods in 1970 to 40.1 percent in 1984 (see Table 10.3). This in turn affected the Third World's share of total world exports in manufactured goods—up to 32 percent in 1993.[34] These increased sales in higher-value manufactured goods generated foreign-exchange earnings that could be used to increase imports. While foreign exchange positions and

newly industrializing countries (NICs) States that show dramatic increases in wealth as they industrialize for the first time.

the ability to buy were badly hurt during the 1980s by the debt crisis, the underlying shift survived and generated an increasingly large stake for large industrialized countries in the health of Third World markets for exports from the richer countries. For instance, by 1993, 42.5 percent of U.S. exports were bought by Third World countries, whereas in 1973, it was 29 percent.[35]

With all these pieces in place, the politics of international economics between rich and poor probably would have shifted substantially in the 1990s even without the end of the Cold War and the collapse of the Soviet Union. There is, however, no doubt that the virtual disappearance of a competing set of ideas about how the global political economy should be arranged and managed reinforced the process of transformation. The result was a watershed in the strategic terms of debate.

Conclusion

The simplest way to make sense of the politics of international economics from World War I to the present is to look for periods defined by distinctive combinations of actors' preferences and what the international and domestic contexts made possible. During the interwar period there was a fundamental mismatch between preferences and power: The actors most interested in managing the international economic system (the British) didn't have the power to achieve their goals; the actors with the ability to lead (public and private policy makers in the United States) preferred not to. From the end of World War II to the late 1950s, the combination of U.S. policy makers' preferences (guided by the hard lessons of the interwar years) and U.S. power in money, finance, and trade produced a period of unilateral management in reconstruction and institution building.

In the late 1950s and early 1960s, the key actors, their relative power, and policy makers' preferences all began to change. The result was a new strategic context for choice and bargaining. The changes occurred first in the international monetary system and in the relations between the developed countries and the post-colonial world. With decolonization, a whole set of new actors crowded onto the stage, actors with distinctively different worldviews than the ones that had guided the postwar institution builders at Bretton Woods. These new actors were deeply influenced by Nkrumah's arguments about neocolonialism and the dependencia analyses of Latin American scholars. They raised questions about the fairness of free trade, the weighted voting systems in the IBRD and IMF, and the role of foreign businesses in their societies. Meanwhile, the success of reconstruction in Europe and Japan changed the issues there as well. There was increasing conflict over the international monetary system and its effects on the ability of U.S. policy makers and corporations to spend money abroad that was printed at home. U.S. policy makers, for their part, felt suddenly disadvantaged by a monetary system that throughout the 1950s had appeared to help them achieve their objectives across a wide range of political and economic issue areas.

The linkage politics of international economics changed yet again in the 1970s. The collapse of the Bretton Woods monetary system and the growth of neomercantilism substantially raised both the diplomatic and domestic stakes of the ways in which the global political economy was arranged and managed. Those changes also appeared to create a strategic opportunity for Third World leaders to challenge the entire system. The result was a decade or more of brinkmanship—both among the industrialized countries over trade and money and between the industrialized countries and the Third World over the nature of the system. The inherent dangers of brinkmanship were then reinforced by the shared scare over the 1980s debt crisis. That crisis led to a difficult period of reevaluation and the late 1980s watershed. Subsequently, when Japan, South Korea, Indonesia, and other key countries ran into difficulty in 1997 to 1998 (see Chapter 11), the question was how to use the IMF and other existing multilateral institutions to address the Asian financial crisis, not how to change the structure of the system. However, the costs of the "solutions" imposed for dealing with the Asian financial crisis soon combined with controversies about a far larger issue—globalization—to shift the linked international and domestic contexts for the politics of international economics once again.

Key Terms

float	managed float	neocolonialism
hard currencies	neomercantilism	dependencia
principal of conditionality	fair trade	repatriation of profits
fixed-exchange-rate system	stagflation	hard loans
Triffin's dilemma	principle of reciprocity	soft loans
N-1, or consistency, problem	most-favored-nation principle	differential income-elasticity of demand
special drawing rights (SDRs)	principal supplier rule	debt service ratio
free float	voluntary export restraint agreement (VER)	newly industrializing countries (NICs)

To The Reader   A CHAPTER SUMMARY and QUESTIONS FOR REVIEW are available at **www.prenhall.com/lamborn**

CHAPTER 11

The Politics of Money, Trade, and Transnational Investment Today

On January 1, 1999, banks in eleven of the fifteen member states of the European Union (EU) began using a new common currency—the *euro*—as a unit of account in their exchanges with one another. While the euro was not scheduled to replace national currencies in everyday transactions until 2002, the January 1999 move signaled the imminent end of a centuries-old period in the international political economy. If all goes as its supporters plan, the euro will soon be one of the world's three major currencies (along with the dollar, and to a lesser extent, the Japanese yen), involved in more transactions than almost any other.

The introduction of the euro symbolized a widespread consensus among government policy makers in Europe that their national currencies were not up to the demands generated by globalization. Given the fact that national currencies such as the French franc and German mark have long been seen as a symbol of statehood as basic and essential as the flag, the introduction of the euro seemed to symbolize an emerging transformation in the role of the state. However, less than a year after European policy makers moved toward the euro to increase the ease with which economic transactions could take place across state boundaries, street demonstrations against globalization began to erupt. A December 1999 protest against the World Trade Organization (WTO) in Seattle was followed by demonstrations at joint meetings of the IMF and World Bank in the spring and fall of 2000 in Washington, DC, and Prague.

The issues raised by the birth of the euro and the spread of street demonstrations against globalization reflect what is distinctive about political economy issues and what is unique about today's linked international and domestic contexts. To make sense of how those enduring patterns and unique contexts have come together, we begin this chapter by exploring what is distinctive about the politics of strategic choice in international political economy, with particular emphasis on issues involving trade, finance, and investment. We then turn to an examination of the contemporary international economic environment and explore such questions as: What do people mean when they talk about economic globalization? How much is it constraining officials' ability to pursue independent economic policies? What specific issues are on today's agenda in international economic affairs?

The Distinctive Nature of Political Economy Issues

Economic issues in world politics involve the production, distribution, and exchange of wealth. To a large extent, these activities have a distinctive purpose and logic of their own. We expect consumers, employees, and investors to seek high prices for what they want to sell and low prices for what they wish to buy. While these incentives often lead to predictable patterns of individual behavior and market outcomes, markets are also shaped by a framework of political rules and choices. To understand economic issues, we thus need to make sense of the political as well as the economic incentives at work. We begin by discussing the nature of political economy, the area of social life in which politics and economics come together.

The Meaning and Study of International Political Economy

While scholars define the term *political economy* in several different ways, we use it in a way that Adam Smith and David Ricardo would easily recognize. **Political economy** is the way in which political choices, institutions, and rules shape and are shaped by markets. A **market** is any arrangement among buyers and sellers that determines the prices and quantities of a good or service.

Political economy issues arise in two major ways. First, controversies arise over regulation. As is true in any domestic economy, the international economy requires rules of the game that tell people what they can and cannot do. These rules help to shape their expectations, strategies, and perhaps their objectives. To operate effectively, people may need to know how much of one currency it takes to buy others; what restrictions, if any, govern how currencies can be bought and sold; and under what conditions actors headquartered in one state are allowed to invest in productive enterprises in other states. When national officials choose the regulatory policies that govern these matters and bargain with other actors about whether global or regional cooperation is possible, political factors enter the equation alongside economic ones. The reason is important: How these issues are resolved often affects the prosperity of different domestic constituencies and can alter policy makers' abilities to achieve their political and policy goals.

These connections lead to the second way in which political economy issues arise. Over time, economic processes can change the preferences and relative power of key actors. For example, from the 1950s through the 1970s, many African and Latin American governments believed that free trade distorted their economic development, undermined their domestic political stability, and reduced their international power across a wide range of important issue areas. In short, politics both shapes and is shaped by international economics and the rules and regimes that regulate economic activity across and within states.

Many questions about world politics and economics can be addressed only if we keep the link between them in mind. For instance, economists have long believed that wealth is created through free trade. Why then do governments often pursue policies that restrain domestic and international markets? As you might expect, political constituencies that would be hurt by open-market policies often have the leverage to veto them. Political and strategic considerations sometimes work in favor of open-market policies. As you saw in Chapters 9 and 10, British leaders during the nineteenth century and U.S. leaders after World War II promoted international trade and financial policies that were quite open by the standards of the time, in part for broad foreign-policy reasons. The key point to remember is that political and market forces continually interact. Political choices and incentives shape the production and distribution of wealth by influencing the location, costs, and benefits of economic activities. State officials, for instance, choose the terms under which foreign capital can enter their countries. Conversely, market forces have major political effects within states and among them.[1] If the euro experiment succeeds, it might lead to even tighter political integration among the EU states.

The interaction among market forces, political incentives, and policy stakes can play out in significantly different ways. For example, protectionist foreign economic policies were much more common before 1945 than they are today. The less protectionist international economic rules in place since the end of World War II have given many trans-state business enterprises (TSBEs) and export-oriented firms a much bigger stake in an open world economy. Many companies now see themselves

political economy The ways in which political choices, institutions, and rules shape and are shaped by markets.

market Any arrangement among buyers and sellers that determines the prices and quantities of a good or service.

as international firms that make and price their products for a global market. One reason the world economy did not move toward higher tariffs during the mid-1970s recessions, as had occurred during the Great Depression, was that globally oriented firms successfully lobbied their governments to keep liberal economic arrangements in place in the face of protectionist political pressures.[2]

Given what we've just said about the close links between politics and markets, you might be surprised that the modern field of international political economy (IPE) is rather new. While there was substantial interest in the relationship between public finance and politics in the generation before World War I, especially in Europe, Western scholars specializing in international politics and international economics had relatively little to say to one another between World War I and the early 1970s, especially in the United States. There were several reasons for this intellectual separation. During the twentieth century, economists have increasingly seen their field as a highly rigorous science designed to analyze market behavior precisely. The development of statistical and game-theory techniques helped them achieve these goals. But these analytic tools came at a price: Much of the political context within which economic behavior takes place was left outside of economists' models.[3]

Meanwhile, for much of the century students of world politics focused their attention elsewhere. To many of them, the crucial issues involved military conflict among the major actors—first World War II, then the Cold War. By comparison, the management of world trade and finance seemed less weighty. This view was reinforced by a bias in the way economic problems were defined, one that probably resulted from the fact that so many economists were American or American-trained. The dollar's dominant role in world finance fostered a mind-set in which the major international economic issues seemed technical rather than political in nature, since the Bretton Woods rules of the game were really not open for discussion or reevaluation.[4] While all of these factors diminished the interest of most U.S. scholars in IPE during this period, policy makers and analysts in the Third World never lost sight of it because of their concern about neocolonialism and dependency.

The intellectual walls between international politics and economics in the United States came down quickly in the early 1970s, sparked by major changes in the world economy. In 1971, President Nixon announced that the dollar would no longer be redeemable for gold to other central banks, ushering in a four-year period of instability in international financial arrangements. Two years later, the Organization of Petroleum Exporting Countries (OPEC) raised the world price of oil substantially and was able to tie it, at least for a short time, to Western policies on Arab-Israeli issues. In 1974 and 1975, Western Europe, Japan, and North America suffered the worst economic downturn since the 1930s, in part because of the "oil shock." Inflation and high unemployment came together, even though prevailing economic theory said they should not. As growth eroded in the industrialized countries, economic issues came to dominate political leaders' attention. Then, as the connections between domestic prosperity and the world economy became more evident, the analytical separation between international economics and politics disappeared. Scholars began to see that political and strategic preferences, choices, and power relationships were linked to economic choices and outcomes, and that the economy was a major issue area in both world and local politics.[5]

With the benefit of hindsight, the analytic separation between world politics and international economics in the United States was highly artificial. Yet it was not surprising considering what was going on at the time. As we have noted many times, people's frameworks for thinking about the world usually reflect developments around them. It was only when the links between economics and politics became too obvious and important to ignore that scholars had strong incentives to rethink the tight boxes in which many of them had kept "political" and "economic" outcomes and processes. Today, international political economy (IPE) is a major part of the study of world politics. Let us now examine five of its distinctive features.

The Tension between Division and Integration

If we think of the international economy as a *system of linked parts*—one in which firms, consumers, and governments are linked by various supply and demand relationships in ways that make the results of their actions interconnected—that system combines major aspects of both *division* and *integration*.[6] The division exists because world politics is built around a system of sovereign states, each of which has complete legal authority over a specific piece of territory. That authority includes the right to regulate all economic activity inside the state's boundaries and, at the extreme, to separate the national economy from the world economy. Although foreign economic policy may be made on the basis of market incentives, governments are under no obligation to do so. For example, subsidiaries of TSBEs can only be set up where permitted by the host state, and once there they must operate according to local law. Since such regulation may channel business activity in directions other than those suggested by supply and demand forces, the existence of sovereign states inevitably impedes some cross-border economic integration that would otherwise occur.

While the incentives to regulate trans-state economic activity are often very strong, the integrative forces within today's global economy nonetheless matter a good deal. Unlike security issues—which are driven by a concern with preserving borders and what is inside them from outside threats—economic issues involve market forces that create incentives to break down the barriers that separate consumers, investors, and firms in one state from those with compatible needs in other states.[7] Many cross-boundary barriers to commerce have indeed been surmounted. Patterns of trade, investment, and production are increasingly trans-state and interconnected. As a result, the prices of comparable goods and services increasingly tend to converge, regardless of where they originate. For example, low relative wage rates in East Asia affect steel and auto production in Pittsburgh and Glasgow by altering production and distribution costs in these globally competitive industries. Then, as firms relocate to take advantage of lower wage rates, they bid them higher. Similarly, financial instability in Asia leads investors to shift their funds out of those countries and into more stable North American markets. These capital inflows then help to drive down local interest rates and spur the creation of new businesses and jobs. To the extent that international and domestic rules allow markets to operate freely, state officials do not manage day-to-day economic activity themselves. In security affairs, governments (and such non-state actors as terrorists) monitor and confront one another directly. In contemporary IPE, states often step into the background and allow the market to operate on its own. Instead of trying to control outcomes directly, governments increasingly see their role as regulators that provide rules that allow economic actors to make their own choices about what, when, and how much to buy and sell.

As this occurs, societies tend to become more interdependent. **Economic interdependence** exists when societies use each others' goods, services, natural resources, and capital. While interdependence is a matter of degree—no society is completely

economic interdependence A condition that exists when two or more people, organizations, or societies depend on each other's goods, services, natural resources, or capital for their continued prosperity.

Despite increasing global economic integration, states today continue to regulate the goods and services that flow across their borders. Customs inspection stations (such as the pictured one in Texas) are the places where national and international trade rules are typically enforced.

autarkic (self-sufficient) economically—there is a lot of room for variation between self-sufficiency and total economic integration. One measure of how connected a state is to the world economy is the proportion of its **gross domestic product (GDP)**—the value of all goods and services produced annually inside a state—that is accounted for by its exports. Overall, this ratio fell substantially between 1913 and 1950, reflecting the disruption produced by World Wars I and II. It then rose dramatically between 1950 and the late 1980s, reflecting the lack of a major world war. But there were major differences across countries: For instance, in 1987, Belgium was by far the most interdependent of the industrial countries, with over 50 percent of its national income derived from exports; the comparable figure for the United States was just over 6 percent.[8]

Interdependence tends to produce two distinct kinds of economic effects.[9] One is **sensitivity,** which refers to how quickly and directly events in one state affect people in other states. The more sensitive countries are to one another, the more difficult it is to confine the effects of economic booms or slumps to the places where they originate. Sensitivity can thus have positive or negative effects. In general, sensitivity interdependence is roughly proportional to the volume of economic interactions that connect citizens and firms in one country with those in other places. In the early 1970s, for instance, the United States and Japan were both sensitive to dramatic increases in the price of imported oil, the effects of which were felt in higher prices for gasoline and longer lines at the pump. Yet Japan was much more sensitive than the United States, since a higher proportion of its fuel consumption came from imports. As a result of the oil price shocks of the 1970s, many major industrial countries tried to reduce or at least control the volume of their net oil imports. As Table 11–1 indicates, some were more successful than others. Italy and France managed to keep imports roughly constant over the last three decades, but the United States and Japan did not.

A second kind of interdependence effect is **vulnerability,** which refers to the difficulty an actor will have in adjusting to changes in its relationship with some other actor(s). Just as the more committed person in a romantic relationship will be hurt

gross domestic product (GDP)   The value of all the goods and services produced annually inside a state.

sensitivity   How quickly and directly events in one state affect people in other states.

vulnerability   How hard it will be for an actor to adjust successfully to changes in its relationship with some other actor(s).

TABLE 11–1   NET OIL IMPORTS,[a] G-8 COUNTRIES, 1970–1997

Country	1970	1975	1980	1985	1990	1995	1997
Canada	4.37	1.5	8.5	−17.9	−15.5	−36.2	−37.1
United States	161.13	310.86	340.3	235.3	376.2	422.5	486.9
Japan	200.64	247.12	251.7	212.1	258.7	275.6	280.3
France	98.92	104.64	114.6	82.2	87.6	86.5	89.6
Germany	125.27	122.54	149.3	120.9	122.7	132.6	137.4
Italy	90.95	91.56	99.4	83.6	91	90.9	89
United Kingdom	106.67	90.96	1.9	−51.6	−11.1	−50.5	−49.1
Russian Federation	N/A	N/A	N/A	N/A	−262	−157.9	−176.1

[a]"Net Oil Imports" refers to the net amount (imports minus exports) of all crude oil, natural gas liquids, refinery feed-stocks, and petroleum stocks and products. Units of measurement are in "Mtoe," million tons oil equivalent.

Sources: Organization for Economic Cooperation and Development, *OECD Environmental Data: Compendium 1999* (Paris: OECD, 1999), p. 207; *OECD Environmental Data: Compendium 1989* (Paris: OECD, 1989), pp. 220–21.

more than the other if the relationship ends, the society that finds it harder to adjust to a change in an economic relationship than its investment or trade partners is more vulnerable. For example, even if two countries import the same share of their fuel needs, one is more vulnerable than the other if it would have to pay higher prices or lay off more workers than the other as it shifted to other suppliers. As this example suggests, a less vulnerable party may be able to impose major costs over one who is more vulnerable. The use of economic sanctions is based on the expectation that another actor will change its policy rather than pay the price of losing trade, capital inflows, and so on. Of course, whether sanctions *can* be used to alter behavior depends on what an actor seeks to achieve and how willing and able the other actor is to resist the coercion.

One often hears today that high levels of interdependence have produced an economically globalized world system. **Globalization** refers to "the increasing integration of national economies into a global one." At the extreme, such integration would essentially eliminate the state as an autonomous economic actor.[10] If this were the case, production, trade, and financial networks would operate according to market dictates alone, and efforts by national officials to make autonomous economic choices would inevitably fail.

As we discuss later in this chapter, there is some disagreement among scholars about the implications of extensive economic interdependence. Here, we simply note that national officials and their constituents are not behaving as if states have lost their relevance as distinct economic and social entities. We thus need to remember that both aspects of the international economic system—division as well as integration—are important, and that one gains insight into IPE issues by noticing how they combine. It helps to remember that each state contains a "slice" of the trans-state system of production, investment, and exchange. Conversely, *national* economies continue to exist because people in different societies often wish to preserve some aspects of their historical distinctiveness and not blend into a homogenous global economy.[11] For this reason, the tension between state and market as organizing social principles is one of the key features of the IPE issue area.

globalization The increasing integration of national economies into a global one and, more generally, the declining meaningfulness of state boundaries in an era characterized by the growing number of global trans-state communication, transportation, and economic networks.

The Strength and Breadth of the Linkages between Domestic and International Politics

A second distinctive characteristic of IPE issues is the strength and variety of domestic-international linkages. The world economy affects people's well-being in a more immediate and direct way than one finds on many security, environmental, and human-rights issues, and the growth in interdependence since the late 1940s has magnified these effects. Once people understand this, they may pressure their governments to act in ways they believe will help them. Pressures to enact protectionist trade policies provide clear examples, but others are present just about every time a consequential foreign economic policy choice is made. For example, Brazilian officials faced a difficult problem in early 1999 as they worked out a strategy to save their currency, the *real*, which had fallen significantly in value on international exchanges. To attract investors willing to buy the currency, which would increase its international value, policy makers needed to raise domestic interest rates to unusually high levels and cut government spending in order to stem inflation. But these measures would almost certainly produce a severe recession and hurt influential domestic constituencies, such as public-sector retirees who would have to pay social security taxes for the first time. Brazil's Congress was thus very reluctant to accept the bitter domestic financial medicine that seemed necessary, despite the country's dire financial situation.[12]

Participation by an Unusually Wide Variety of Actors

A third distinctive feature of IPE issues is that they involve a wide variety of actors, including governments, firms, substate and trans-state policy factions, IGOs, and NGOs. Depending on the matter involved, governments now might bargain with firms as well as other governments, and firms might make coalitions with other firms to enter or dominate national markets.[13] These patterns follow naturally when states give the market some, but not complete, autonomy in economic life. In such cases, governments set and police the rules of the game.

When thinking about rules, policy makers are likely to have domestic and international objectives of their own. Internationally, they're likely to care about the effects of economic policy choices on their country's ability to act effectively abroad. Domestically, they're likely to care about the effect of economic policy choices on their political popularity and their ability to manage the economy effectively. For example, U.S. officials' ability to pursue trade policies based on internationally open markets has been hampered since the 1970s by the breakdown of a domestic free-trade coalition formed in the late 1940s. After World War II, when U.S. industries were the most efficient in the world, it was easy for business and labor groups to support policies that would open U.S. markets to goods and services from a wide variety of countries with the expectation that those countries would reciprocate and increasingly import U.S. products. But as industries in other countries became more competitive and imports began to hurt the position of U.S. businesses—and thus their ability to employ a large, well-paid, industrial work force in the United States—that coalition began to splinter. As a result, U.S. industries and organized labor, especially in the eastern and midwestern sections of the country, pressured Congress and the president for less open trade policies.

Depending on the kind of IPE issue at hand, one thus sees three different kinds of relationships among different types of actors.[14] One involves government-to-government issues; as agents of governments, IGOs are often involved in these as well.

11.1 ENDURING PATTERNS

The impact of varying beliefs about just relationships

If people think a political process is just, they are more likely to accept the outcomes it produces—even if they would have preferred something else.

The impact of risk-taking preferences

People are less willing to run political risks in support of policy choices as their control over choice and implementation declines.

The impact of discounting

The less control actors have over policy choice and implementation, the more actors will prefer future costs over current costs and the more they will value current benefits over future benefits.

The impact of linkage politics

World politics is driven by the interaction of international, factional, and constituency politics.

Selling Free Trade: Britain in the 1840s; the United States in the 1940s, 1970s, and Today

Not surprisingly, selling free trade policies—and, more generally, open markets—to domestic constituencies is far easier when a country's export industries are highly successful. If a country also has politically well-connected groups that believe free trade is part of an approach to political economy that supports democracy and individual freedom, selling those policies will be even easier because supporters will be able to make appeals based on claims about the nature of legitimate relationships.

However, in the absence of a very strong normative commitment to a liberal worldview, trade policies quickly become controversial whenever a country's international position makes it less competitive. It's easy to see why. Opposition by domestic groups that are hurt by the absence of trade protection creates political risks for policy makers. Those risks are in the short term, while the benefits of free trade are in the long term. Moreover, by their very nature, free-trade regimes reduce policy makers' power over outcomes. The less control policy makers have, the more they will want to avoid running political risks and the more they will discount, preferring future costs over current costs and current benefits over future benefits.

The move toward free trade in the mid-nineteenth century was led by Britain; the move toward free trade in the mid-twentieth century was led by the United States. In both instances, pro-free-trade policy makers led countries that had a strong international economic position and politically powerful domestic constituencies that both accepted the normative arguments of liberal capitalism and benefited economically from free-trade regimes.

The move to neomercantilism in the 1970s in the United States suggests how quickly the political calculations of policy makers can change when they are comparing the possible long-term benefits of maintaining a free-trade regime to high short-term political risks. Since globalization creates similar patterns in linkage politics, risk taking, and discounting, one would expect commitments to open markets to be most vulnerable during economic downturns.

These issues involve the definition, revision, and supervision of the rules governing global commerce and finance. They include, among others, controversies over whether a state has, in fact, reciprocated trade concessions made by others as well as disputes about whether a firm or government is violating trade agreements by **dumping** its products, selling them below cost in a foreign market. (Since both cost-accounting standards and the idea of a fair profit vary, it is often hard to reach agreement on whether a particular practice is "dumping.") These government-to-government issues also include questions about whether the list of items subject to multilateral trade agreements should be broadened and under what conditions, and whether a government is honoring commitments to the IMF that were made as a condition of receiving international financial assistance. The case study of Indonesia's and Korea's responses to the Asian financial crises, mentioned later in this chapter, illustrates this kind of IPE issue.

A second group of IPE problems might be called government-to-firm issues. These issues carry high political and policy stakes for specific states, though not for others. They include bargaining over whether foreign investment will be welcomed or allowed in a particular state or region; bargaining over government contracts with foreign firms; acquisition by governments of foreign-produced technology; and the intervention by particular governments in international financial markets.

Firm-to-firm issues make up a third group of IPE problems. These are matters that, as a rule, are of no general political or policy concern to state officials. Instead, they involve firms doing their business within the existing legal and political framework. Noncontroversial corporate alliances, market-sharing plans, and mergers illustrate this group. As many barriers to cross-border trade and investment were loosened or abolished in the 1980s, these relationships became more common and commercially significant.[15]

The Compatibility of Governments' Long-Term Economic Goals in Market Economies

A fourth feature of IPE issues in market economies is that government actors are often not put in competitive relationships with one another. This attribute makes economics quite different from security. In security relations, states that see themselves as adversaries have trouble pursuing mutually beneficial military policies. By contrast, if markets are allowed to operate somewhat autonomously, people in different states can grow wealthier at the same time. Of course, the route to such gains is competition among individuals and firms, and competition produces winners and losers. If no one lost, it would mean that the market was *not* winnowing out the less efficient actors and rewarding those that were doing better. But even though individuals and firms lose, the overall result in a market economy is a shared benefit—increases in the overall level of absolute wealth.

While incentives for states to cooperate in regulating market economies is one of the chief characteristics of IPE, it's important to recognize that over a period of time variations in economic growth can significantly alter the relative power of state and non-state actors across a wide variety of political and economic issues. This possibility creates tension between the assumption of liberal economics that adherence to market principles will lead everyone to be better off in the long run, and competitive concerns that uneven growth could allow the faster-growing state to use its wealth for coercive purposes.

dumping Selling products below cost (or, in some versions, at only a negligible profit) in a foreign market.

Close Functional Interconnections among the Central Issues

A fifth distinctive feature of IPE is that its issues are very closely linked functionally. Policies designed to achieve objectives on one issue tend to affect others directly. Some of these effects may be desired, but others may not. While such functional dependence is not unique to IPE, the interconnections are unusually strong because an economy is a set of linked supply-and-demand relationships. Changes in the price or availability of one commodity or service, including money, typically affect choices and outcomes in other areas. An actor's ability to sustain a strategy in one area, such as trade, thus depends on what is going on in the others, and the strategy in one area invariably affects what is happening elsewhere in the economy. For instance, the inflation level in a country depends partly on the value of its currency relative to other major currencies (since the cheaper it becomes, the more imports cost in the local currency). The currency's value, in turn, is linked to demand for that state's exports.

Three Core Issues: International Trade, Finance, and Foreign Direct Investment

Despite the close interconnections among IPE issues, there is a long tradition of analyzing them in three clusters: international trade, finance (including international monetary policy), and foreign direct investment. After we define the essence of each cluster, we explore how each illustrates the distinctive features of IPE issues more generally.

International Trade

International trade refers to the cross-border movement of goods and services. Economic incentives for trade arise when individuals choose to consume products from abroad that are unavailable, more expensive, or lower in quality at home. It thus reflects what scholars call the world's **production structure**—the set of economic relationships and factors that determine what can profitably be produced for sale in particular locations.[16] While trade can generate a higher standard of living for consumers than they would otherwise enjoy, it may also have negative political and social effects. If unregulated, it can turn states into chronic international debtors, redistribute income across or within nations in ways that people consider unacceptable, and give foreign producers undesired leverage over vulnerable importers. For all of these reasons, international trade policy is highly consequential for just about everyone, and often very controversial.

Before we go further, let us review some of the terms analysts use to discuss trade issues. The **balance of payments** refers to the flow of goods, services, gifts, and other assets between the residents of one state and residents elsewhere in the world during a specific time period (usually a calendar year). A country's **balance on current account** is the portion of the payments balance that deals with the current export and import of goods and services. When a U.S. oil company buys Saudi Arabian crude petroleum, this transaction enters the U.S. current account as a *debit* (purchase) and the Saudi current account as a *credit* (sale). The **balance on capital account** is the part of the payments balance that deals with sales and purchases of stocks,

---

production structure The set of economic relationships that determines what is produced in what locations, for which purchasers, and at what prices.

balance of payments The aggregate value of the payments, gifts, and capital flowing out of a country compared to the aggregate value of the payments, gifts, and capital coming in.

balance on current account The portion of the overall balance of payments that involves the export and import of goods and services.

balance on capital account The portion of the overall balance of payments that involves the sale and purchase of stocks, bonds, and other assets between private individuals and firms in different states.

bonds, and other assets between individuals and firms in different states. It excludes what are called official reserve assets—the stock of foreign currencies and obligations owned by governments—because its purpose is to track market forces rather than government actions and policies. A state's *balance of trade* is the value of its merchandise exports minus its imports. In many states, policy makers want to see a positive balance, even though a negative one might better reflect consumer preferences and comparative advantages. To achieve this goal, they might have to manipulate the price of their currency on international exchanges in a way that others find unacceptable. If some countries are to have a positive trade balance, others must have a negative one.

Let's now consider the kinds of strategic choice problems posed by trade, by examining how trade illustrates the more general features of IPE issues. First, trade patterns reflect both the integrative pressures of a world economy and the forces of separation represented by sovereign states. On the one hand, world trade is freer than at any time since World War I, and perhaps ever.[17] Tariffs are very low by historical standards, quantitative restrictions on goods are disappearing, and trade in services has been liberalized a good deal in recent years. Yet national commercial markets are still more separated than joined. Consider the U.S.-Canadian trade relationship, which has become one of the least regulated in the world as the result of a series of agreements dating back to the 1960s. Close proximity and comparable levels of development mean that communication and transportation costs do not inhibit cross-border exchange much more than long-distance exchanges within each country (such as between Vancouver and Montreal, on the one hand, or Los Angeles and Boston, on the other). However, in spite of these similarities and the official emphasis on reducing barriers between the United States and Canada, trade between a Canadian province and a U.S. state is on average 20 times smaller than trade between two Canadian provinces.[18] As this example suggests, historic national patterns can exert a strong continuing pull even when policy makers favor more open interstate trade. Moreover, many policy makers worry about the negative effects and political fallout that more open trade can create. Removing barriers to trade often leads to short-run losses for some domestic groups while others make short-run gains. Consequently, political leaders usually care about the distributional impact of their trade policies. If certain industries (such as the U.S. footwear sector) suffer due to foreign competition, that could lead to concentrated unemployment and the problems that often come in its wake, including drugs and urban violence. The quality of life may deteriorate so much for certain geographic groups, social classes, and ethnic groups that the overall welfare gains from trade may not be seen as worthwhile. Officials may also want to protect certain industries for reasons of national security (for example, U.S. microelectronics) as well as national culture or pride (French wine and cheese).[19] They may explicitly promote exports or even use *industrial policy*—direct or indirect subsidies to certain industries that they want to protect from foreign competition.

Second, trade exhibits very strong domestic-international linkages. We saw a historical example of this in Chapter 9, namely that mercantilist policies lasted as long as they did because they reflected strongly reinforcing economic and political incentives. Today, **protectionism** is typically practiced in a less overt and more defensive way (so much so that even neomercantilists now tend to call themselves "fair traders"). Still, domestic groups that dislike the distributional effects of open markets typically lobby vigorously against them. Part of the reason these constituencies

protectionism Any government policy or practice designed to shield its national market from external competition.

Before international trade was substantially liberalized beginning in the 1960s, the U.S. footwear industry thrived in many cities in Maine. Vigorous competition from imports made in lower-wage countries has caused many U.S. shoe firms to go out of business, devastating the economic foundations of a number of local communities.

often succeed is that the distributional losses attributable to free trade tend to be much more concentrated than the gains. If shoe factories shut down in New England due to competition from imports, a town or whole region feels the pain intensely. And yet, nationwide, Americans may hardly notice that shoes now cost somewhat less, either because the imports are priced lower or because the few domestic shoe firms that survived had to lower their prices to stay in business.

Third, trade issues typically involve a wide array of domestic and international actors. Almost any trade agreement raises stakes for many domestic groups, and the large role the World Trade Organization plays in the monitoring and enforcement of trade pacts makes it a key actor as well. When the North American Free Trade Agreement (NAFTA) was being considered by the U.S. Congress, for instance, business, agricultural, labor and environmental factions were heavily involved in the lobbying. The anti-NAFTA coalition between labor and environmental groups was based on a belief that foreign producers who have lax environmental laws or fail to enforce those they have can lower their production costs and thereby acquire an unfair competitive advantage in trade. In the NAFTA case, the World Trade Organization (WTO) panels that settle disputes about the application of free-trade rules also came in for criticism. As one lobbyist for a public advocacy group put it, "[trade] rules are set and disputes are settled in an entirely anti-democratic fashion by unelected, unaccountable trade bureaucrats lobbied heavily by industry interests."[20] In recent years, a number of American safety and environmental rules have been ruled as unfair restraints on trade by WTO panels.[21]

Fourth, even though freer trade does have distributional consequences within and across countries, joint gains from trade are possible, and governments can choose to pursue them. If Ricardo was correct, open trade should increase overall wealth over time by forcing producers to concentrate on areas of comparative advantage. Here, the experience of the first six Newly Industrializing Countries (NICs)—Brazil, Mexico, Hong Kong, South Korea, Singapore, and Taiwan—may be revealing. Beginning in the 1970s, their GDPs and exports grew rapidly, even though the

11.2 ENDURING PATTERNS

The effect of the shadow of the future

The more compatible people expect their preferences to become over time, the more cooperative and less power-based their strategic choices are likely to be.

From Dependencia to the NICs in the Third World

In the 1960s, dependencia interpretations argued that the goals of GATT (free trade achieved through reciprocal and non-preferential tariff reductions) would produce long-term stagnation. Given that view, they looked for sources of power that would enable them to challenge existing arrangements.

The success of the NICs' export-led economic growth during the last third of the twentieth century altered many Third World policy makers' view of the shadow of the future. For a brief but important period in the 1990s, the shadow of the future associated with open markets shifted from entrapment and stagnation to an opportunity for growth.

industrialized countries gave them no special trade preferences. Between 1964 and 1985, the NICs' exports to the industrialized countries grew at an average rate of over 23 percent a year, ten points higher than the average for all imports into these countries. As this occurred, each NIC began to create a modern, diversified economy. This led two authors to conclude that "the record of the NICs demonstrates that during the 1970s and 1980s, the world economy was sufficiently open so that even in the absence of any special treatment some poor countries could achieve rapid rates of export and income growth."[22]

Fifth, consider how closely trade is linked functionally to other IPE issues. For example, the ability to export competitively depends in large part on the relative price of one's currency. All else being equal, the cheaper a state's currency, the cheaper its products, and the higher the foreign demand. So from an exporting perspective, it may make sense to have what economists call an **undervalued currency** (one held artificially below what its price would be on an open currency market). And yet, policy makers might see good reasons for rejecting this strategy. They might be concerned that their trading partners will simply devalue their own currencies and wipe out the advantage of an undervalued currency. They might want to keep their currency at—or even above—market value to encourage foreigners to invest or hold government securities denominated in that currency. These complex connections between trade, currency values, and investment create difficult cross pressures, especially in countries in which exports make up a large share of national income.

International Monetary Policy and Finance

International finance, involving monetary transactions across national borders, makes up a second cluster of IPE issues. Since different economies use different

undervalued currency
A term that is used when observers believe the value of a country's currency is below the price it should have in an open international market.

currencies, economic transactions are more complicated across borders than within them. One aspect of international finance is centered in banking centers located in London, New York, Paris, Frankfurt, Tokyo, and Hong Kong. Here, huge quantities of currencies are bought and sold daily, with governments closely monitoring the values of their currencies and perhaps intervening to stabilize those values. Another aspect of international finance is more directly intergovernmental in nature. Here, central bank officials in the major-currency countries and International Monetary Fund (IMF) officials supervise the functioning of the international financial system and at times intervene in a coordinated way to even out market fluctuations. Policy makers often talk about the need to earn **foreign exchange**—those foreign currencies that are accepted as payments internationally or that can be exchanged for such a currency—so they can make purchases abroad, pay for imports, and repay foreign loans. When states experience a serious shortage of foreign exchange, the IMF often steps in to offer assistance and advice.

Again, let us pause to review some key terms. Because currency exchange is central to business across borders, arrangements for setting **exchange rates** are the central problem in international finance. If they wish, policy makers can fix their exchange rates by setting a constant external price, either in gold or another state's currency. This creates a predictable environment for transactions, but it also keeps officials from pursuing an independent monetary policy. At the other extreme, officials can let the exchange rate simply be determined by supply and demand forces. This constitutes a policy of floating exchange rates. As you may recall from Chapter 10, in the mid-1970s the original Bretton Woods rule requiring IMF members to set a fixed exchange rate was abandoned. Since then, countries have been free to set the international price of their currency in a number of ways. As Table 11–2 indicates, there has been a trend toward policies of letting markets have more of an impact on the currency price, although more than one-fourth of all countries still choose to peg their currencies to some other currency unit. Perfectly free floating is rare. Most governments intervene in the foreign exchange markets routinely, either to smooth out short-term fluctuations or to influence the long-term zone (range) in which their exchange rates may freely move (the latter constituting a *managed float*). If an exchange rate badly needs adjustment, a government may set a price it intends to keep for some time. If in the process the exchange rate goes down, this is called a devaluation; if it rises, the currency has been revalued upward.

Consider now how the problems of strategic choice in international finance reflect the same distinctive features of IPE issues. First, even though contemporary international finance reflects very strong integrative pressures, state officials can choose to regulate their exposure to these pressures if they are willing to pay the costs. An average of $1.5 trillion moves each day through the world's currency markets, reflecting the view that growth will be maximized if money is free to seek the highest rate of return across countries. This puts pressure on central bank officials in each state to adopt similar short-term interest rates and systems of financial regulation lest investors find better terms elsewhere. In this sense, the cost of having rules that differ too much from the norm is very high.[23] But there is a reason that our topic in this chapter is the politics of international economics and not just an analysis of world markets. Political leaders may be willing to pay economic costs in order to avoid the extreme sensitivity of being tied closely to potentially volatile international currency markets. In a number of places—including many Asian states as well as Argentina, Hong Kong, Bulgaria, and Estonia—local currencies are anchored

foreign exchange
National currencies that are generally accepted in international trade and finance.

exchange rate The price at which one currency is traded for another.

TABLE 11–2   POST-BRETTON WOODS EVOLUTION IN EXCHANGE RATE SYSTEMS

Type of Exchange Rate Regime[a]	AFRICA			ASIA			MIDDLE EAST AND EUROPE			WESTERN HEMISPHERE			TOTAL		
	1976	1986	1996	1976	1986	1996	1976	1986	1996	1976	1986	1996	1976	1986	1996
Total number of countries participating in exchange rate regimes	40	47	50	17	23	24	17	17	17	26	32	32	100	119	123
Total number of countries pegged to either a single currency or to a basket of currencies	39	34	25	15	14	11	13	11	8	19	21	11	86	80	55
Of those countries participating in pegged regimes (above), those pegged to a basket of currencies[b]	12	15	5	7	9	9	5	6	5	0	2	0	24	32	19
Total number of countries utilizing limited flexibility regimes	0	0	0	1	2	0	2	4	4	0	0	0	3	6	4
Total number of countries utilizing more flexible regimes	1	13	25	1	7	13	2	2	5	7	11	21	11	33	64
Of those countries participating in more flexible regimes (above), those independently floating[c]	0	8	20	0	1	5	1	1	2	0	3	9	1	13	36

[a]Please note that, on this chart, two types of exchange-rate regimes—"pegged to either a single currency or a basket of currencies" and "more flexible"—have been further broken down into subcategories that describe the number of countries that utilize a particular exchange-rate regime within each of these categories. For example, in Africa for 1976, the chart indicates that 39 countries utilized some type of pegged exchange-rate regime, but that 12 of those countries chose to utilize an exchange-rate regime that was pegged exclusively to a basket of currencies rather than an exchange-rate regime that was pegged to a single currency. Similarly, in Africa for 1986, the chart indicates that 13 countries utilized some type of "more flexible" exchange-rate regime, but that 8 of those countries chose to "independently float" as their method of being "more flexible."

[b]This is a subcategory of the "pegged" exchange-rate regime above.

[c]This is a subcategory of the "more flexible" exchange-rate regime above.

Source: *IMF World Economic Outlook: October 1997.* Table 15, "Geographical Distribution of Officially Reported Exchange Rate Arrangements." © International Monetary Fund, October 1997. Reprinted with permission.

tightly to an external currency as a stabilizing device. Although this policy requires the government to maintain enough foreign exchange to back every unit of the local currency, it acts as a stabilizing device should there be massive pressures to sell it.[24]

Second, international financial issues reflect linkage politics, though perhaps less so than trade. Linkage is somewhat more evident on trade issues, both because trade in goods tends to be highly visible and because trade policy typically must be approved by a legislature in democratic countries. Monetary policy, by contrast, is often controlled by central bank officials, who tend to be *relatively* more insulated

While Great Britain decided not to eliminate the pound and adopt the euro as its new currency, controversy over the introduction of the euro continued, as this scene in London in January 1999 (on the first day of international trading in the euro) suggests. While some euro supporters confidently expect that the British will come to regret their decision to keep the pound, others expect that difficulties in making the euro work will create controversy where there was once support.

from day-to-day political pressure. Still, linkage is also evident in international finance. For example, most states choose an international monetary policy of managed floating, since fixing exchange rates forces painful actions when the state faces a trade deficit or an attack by currency speculators who think its value is out of line with the market. In these situations, because policy makers are often reluctant simply to devalue the currency, tough medicine is often prescribed to fix the underlying economic problems. Such measures often include high interest rates (which can induce a recession or choke an economic recovery) and deep cuts in public spending as a way to stem inflation. As we suggested in the introduction to this chapter, the euro will be severely tested during major recessions, when domestic constituencies that advocate lower interest rates will have to convince those worried mainly about inflation that jobs are more important than price stability.

Third, international finance involves a wide array of actors. On a daily basis, the main participants are the thousands of currency traders operating worldwide, working in banks and brokerage firms, who collectively choose which currencies are going up and which are going down in value. As we said earlier, if a government allows its currency's value to be set mainly by the market, it will intervene only to smooth out major zig-zags in the price. When governments do get involved, finance ministry and central bank officials are the major players, though other ministries may also care about the value of the currency, due to the broad effect it has on domestic prices and the competitiveness of a state's exports. When state officials find it impossible to maintain an acceptable value for their currency, the IMF is typically called in. Its officials work with those in commercial banks to put together the rescue packages that have become a common fixture of modern international finance.

Fourth, governments are not put in a distinctively competitive role on international financial issues. When the market is allowed to set exchange rates, it is the individual exporters, importers, institutional investors, and currency traders who compete with one another to buy money cheaply and sell it expensively. And as governments have lost the tremendous advantage in financial information that they used to have over the small firm or currency trader, it has become much easier for people to make cross-national comparisons and to move capital quickly on the basis of very small differences in prices or interest rates.[25] All of this has made it harder for governments to compete directly in international finance, though many non-state actors do so on a continual basis.

Fifth, international financial issues are linked very closely to other IPE issues. If we think of money as a commodity that has a market price (just as soybeans, autos, and computers do), it makes sense that the demand for goods and services made in particular countries depends, other things being equal, on the relative costs of the currencies that must be used to buy them. A currency that is losing value internationally raises the price of that country's imports while lowering the price of its exports. Conversely, a currency that is growing stronger makes it harder to export but lowers the prices of imported goods. Depending on which sectors of the economy benefit from importing and exporting (and the size of the overall inflationary or deflationary effects), a state's overall economic situation can shift quickly and sizably with its exchange rate.

Foreign Direct Investment

Foreign direct investment (FDI) constitutes a third cluster of IPE issues. FDI is a type of international capital flow that transfers part of a firm's managerial skills and knowledge abroad (such as when a TSBE creates a foreign subsidiary). Unlike **portfolio investment**—in which investors finance the construction of new plants or equipment owned by others—FDI involves the creation of a foreign subsidiary, the assets of which are directly controlled by the parent company. If Royal Dutch Shell builds a plant in Indonesia, that is an example of FDI; if investors help build a plant in Indonesia controlled by another firm, that constitutes portfolio investment. FDI has become a major force in fostering greater economic interdependence. Increasingly, firms are producing through a network of foreign subsidiaries for a world market. As a result, fewer of the goods that cross national borders are sold or bought in the usual sense by different actors; more often now they are transferred between different branches of the same trans-state business enterprise (TSBE). As this suggests, FDI has been growing faster than cross-border trade. Between 1985 and 1990, the average annual increase in FDI worldwide was 34 percent, almost three times higher than the average growth in world exports (12 percent).[26]

As with trade and finance, FDI illustrates the five distinctive characteristics of IPE issues. First, it reflects the increasing integration of world markets but also the persistence of territorial divisions in world politics. Since production is now significantly globalized, firm managers can often choose where they will locate particular aspects of the production process. Because capital is mobile and there is a pool of labor in many places that is eager for work, direct investment is very sensitive to shifts in relative production costs across states. Gillette officials, for example, have boasted

foreign direct investment (FDI)   Situations in which a trans-state business enterprise or other actor owns and controls assets in a foreign state.

portfolio investment   The purchase of stocks, bonds, and other financial instruments, in which the enterprises are either owned or operated by others.

Globalized production means that firm managers can split up the production process, moving parts of it that are more labor-intensive to parts of the world where the wage structure is relatively low. Here, at an Intel plant in Penang, Malaysia, workers assemble computer parts, a process that would cost the parent firm much more in the United States or Northern Europe.

that they can easily shift production across countries to avoid wage increases or to adjust to shifts in demand for their products.[27] TSBEs now originate in many different home states—a big difference from the situation just a few decades ago, when most trans-state firms were American or European in origin.[28] At the same time, TSBE subsidiaries are subject to local regulations in the host state. Host governments differ in how much they tax TSBE profits, how firmly they insist that some of the firm's research and development activity take place in the subsidiary located in their country, and how closely they try to regulate capital movements between the subsidiary and outside actors for balance-of-payments purposes. The firm typically has some leverage on such issues, especially if it can plausibly threaten to relocate the local subsidiary elsewhere, taking jobs with it. But the host government also tends to have leverage because the firm's presence represents a sizable investment that the parent company rarely wants to lose or find subject to repeated interference by the host government.

Second, FDI exhibits notable domestic-international linkages. In the firm's home state, workers may object strenuously to the firm's "exporting" jobs to lower-wage countries and even organize boycotts of the firm's products when they are reimported. In the host state, labor-management disputes between a foreign firm and its locally employed workers often assume nationalist overtones. The host state government may then face a set of unpleasant options: If it sides with the workers, it may lose the subsidiary; if it is unsympathetic to the workers' grievances, it will be accused of allowing them to be exploited by foreigners.[29]

Third, FDI issues involve a variety of actors. Consider just a few examples. When a TSBE seeks to enter a foreign market, it must negotiate the terms with the local government. The TSBE's home government may intrude through its choices about how to tax the firm's profits at home and abroad. At times, a local government will require foreign investors to be joined by a local partner in what is called a *joint venture*. At other times, a local government may insist that the TSBE license its technology to local firms if it wants to operate locally. As these examples indicate, FDI issues are perhaps the least "state-centered" of all those discussed in this book, since they necessarily involve some corporate participant as well as a government.

Fourth, while FDI tends to redistribute wealth, it also has the potential to produce broader prosperity. When governments compete to attract FDI, they may offer potential entrants into their market concessions on taxes, requirements that TSBEs employ a certain percentage of local nationals in management positions, and so on. Such competition increases the TSBEs' leverage when they bargain with governments and has probably depressed wages both in the Third World (where many of the subsidiaries locate) and in the older industrialized states (from which many jobs have been "exported"). Yet host societies benefit from FDI in various ways, including an improvement in the local balance of trade that comes through the subsidiary's exports from the host state and an opportunity to acquire new technologies and management skills not otherwise available. For example, FDI into the United States has provided 4.7 million jobs for Americans and generated $4.1 billion in research and development.[30] FDI thus opens up the possibility for broad improvements in living standards due to economic growth, even though it also may heighten some conflicts over distribution of the wealth generated by that growth.

Fifth, FDI is linked closely to other IPE issues. When TSBE executives consider whether to establish a foreign subsidiary, they look at how the exchange rate and the tariff level affect the costs of exporting to that foreign market as opposed to operating inside it. And for governments that want to attract FDI, the tradeoffs can be difficult. They may need to make tax concessions to firms that are considering setting up a plant in their country, in which case the resources available for welfare programs would probably shrink. That might cause domestic unrest that could conceivably outweigh the economic benefits of attracting the production facility.

Two key points seem evident from our discussion so far. Understanding economic issues in world politics forces us to appreciate how political and market incentives are linked. And even though international trade, finance, and investment are distinct problem areas, they share key features that are common to IPE issues as a group. These points can help us analyze some of the key contemporary issues in IPE. Today, it is often claimed that globalization is producing a single world market that has the potential to produce tremendous prosperity, but that it is also robbing policy makers of their ability to manage national economies in distinctive ways. We turn next to a discussion of these claims.

The Contemporary Context for International Political Economy

The most distinctive feature of the world economy is its level of integration, compared even to a few decades ago. Trade barriers are lower, capital is freer to move across borders, and the production of goods and services is increasingly dispersed among branches of parent firms in various states. Does this mean—as one would expect from the perspective of the liberal tradition—that globalization is eroding the functions and capacity of states? It turns out that there is little consensus on this issue. While national markets may be more integrated in some ways than ever before, territorial divisions still matter. National policy makers and their constituents are not acting as if states have no distinctive economic and social purposes. We begin by exploring the implications and limits of globalization. We then examine some of the specific issues on policy makers' agendas that grow out of this phenomenon.

The Impact of Globalization

In 1998, Jeffrey Sachs posed the following question in an article that surveyed current trends in the world economy: "How will national economies perform now that nearly all of the world is joined in a single global marketplace?"[31] The question assumes that globalization has become a pervasive feature of world life and implies that national governments have lost much of their capacity to blunt or channel its effects. What evidence would seem to support such an assumption? Let us consider some illustrative examples in each of the three IPE issue clusters. We can then explore some of the counter-claims that are made about globalization.

On Trade The world economy has become much more integrated in recent decades, thanks to the combined effects of market incentives, global organizations such as GATT and the WTO, and the growing number of regional trade agreements, covering such areas as the Asia-Pacific region, Eastern and Southern Africa, and North America, as well as Europe (see Table 11–3).

The World Trade Organization now is charged with regulating much more than trade in goods, which used to make up most of international commerce. It now oversees the liberalization of trade in services, investment, **intellectual property** telecommunications, and information technology, as well as goods. Moreover, two older economic sectors that used to be heavily protected by governments—textiles and agriculture—are now subject to WTO rules. The WTO's system for settling trade disputes has more teeth in it than the one used under its predecessor organization, the General Agreements on Tariffs and Trade (GATT).[32] Perhaps most illustrative of the trend is the growing impact of trade on the U.S. economy. Historically the United States has been relatively self-sufficient economically, as one would expect of a state of continental size that is well-endowed with skilled labor and raw materials. Yet over the last four decades, U.S. producers have become much more dependent on export markets. During that time, the share of merchandise exports in U.S. manufactured goods has risen from 6 percent to nearly 20 percent.[33]

On Finance and Foreign Direct Investment In finance, the evidence of increasing globalization is even stronger. So much money is traded daily in international markets that governments' ability to counteract market trends is very small, even when they act together. As one writer put it, "the sheer size of the pool of liquid assets available to the private sector is constantly in the minds of national policy makers."[34] Until fairly recently, the creation and use of credit took place mainly within states. Now it takes place largely across states, in markets linked electronically and thus instantaneously. This means that interest rates on comparable securities converge across countries (except for the small insurance premium the borrower pays to cover the risk of losses when currencies are exchanged). As you would expect, the growing dominance of global capital markets limits any government's ability to set interest rates outside the range set by world markets. Local banks and credit markets still exist and serve local customers, but they are much more subject to world market conditions than the reverse.[35]

In FDI, one likewise sees increasing evidence of a genuinely global market. A major reason has been the reduction of controls in many countries over capital movements. Once firms could borrow easily in one country or currency and invest in others, it became much easier to invest abroad.[36] This had often been hard to do between the 1930s and 1980s, when many states maintained tight controls over the

intellectual property
Works of art, literature, and software that are protected by patents, copyrights, and trademarks.

TABLE 11–3 **SELECTED REGIONAL MULTILATERAL TRADE AGREEMENTS**

Name of Trade Agreement or Treaty and Year Signed	Purpose of Trade Agreement or Treaty	Participants or Signatories
APEX (Asia-Pacific Economic Co-operation), 1989	Originally an informal dialogue group established to respond to increasing economic interdependence in the region. It has evolved into the primary promoter of free trade and economic cooperation in the region and between Asia and the rest of the world.	Australia, Brunei, Canada, Chile, China, Hong Kong, Indonesia, Japan, Korea, Malaysia, Mexico, New Zealand, Papua New Guinea, Peru, Philippines, Russia, Singapore, Taiwan, Thailand, Vietnam, United States
ASEAN (Association of Southeast Asian Nations), 1967	Designed to promote cultural, economic, and social cooperation in Asia, to safeguard political sovereignty in the region, and to provide a forum for resolving inter-regional differences	Brunei, Cambodia, Indonesia, Laos, Malaysia, Myanmar, Philippines, Singapore, Thailand, Vietnam
COMESA (Common Market for Eastern and Southern Africa), 1994	Set up to promote regional cooperation in developing natural and human resources via the promotion of a regional trading bloc	Angola, Burundi, Comoros, Congo, Djibouti, Egypt, Eritrea, Ethiopia, Kenya, Madagascar, Malawi, Mauritania, Nambia, Rwanda, Seychelles, Sudan, Swaziland, Uganda, Zambia, Zimbabwe
EU (European Union), 1993 Precursors: ECSC, 1951 EEC, 1958 EC, 1967	Begun by six member countries to promote European economic and social progress, to assert the distinct identity of the EU internationally, to introduce European citizenship, to obtain freedom, security, and justice via the promotion of an internally free market and internal labor mobility, and to build and establish EU law	Belgium, Germany, France, Italy, Luxembourg, Netherlands, Denmark, Ireland, United Kingdom, Greece, Spain, Portugal, Austria, Finland, Sweden
MERCOSUR (Treaty of Asuncion), 1991	Established a common market in South America	Argentina, Brazil, Paraguay, Uruguay
NAFTA (North American Free Trade Agreement), 1992	Established a free trade region between signatories	Canada, Mexico, United States
WTO/GATT (World Trade Organization/General Agreement on Tariffs and Trade), 1998/1986	Set up to further trade liberalization and to expand free trade, especially to less-developed signatories, by reducing or eliminating trade barriers via contractual obligations contained in a single multilateral trade regime (GATT)	140 member states

Sources: COMESA, "Common Market for Eastern and Southern Africa," *COMESA Home Page* (*http://www.comesa.org*); ASEAN, "ASEAN News," ASEAN Main Menu (*http://www.asean.or.id/*; University of Queensland, Australia, "Globalisation: Trade Agreements and Treaties" (*http://www.uq.edu.au/jrn/global/trade.html*, 28 August 2000); SICE (Sistema de Informacion sobre Comercio Exterior), "SICE: Trade Agreements" (*http://www.sice.oas.org/tradee.asp*, 26 August, 2000); Europa, "The ABC of the European Union" (*http://europa.eu.int/*).

exchange of currencies. From the perspective of increasing market integration worldwide, one consequence is striking. So much business is now done between the subsidiaries of the same firm (a practice known as **intra-firm trade**) that less and less trade takes place between separate national economies at all.[37]

What inferences can we draw from these trends? Analysts who see globalization as powerful and pervasive point to several implications. One is that if states want to draw upon outside capital for purposes of financing public debt or long-term investment, they have lost their autonomy to fix the price and availability of money. If interest rates are too low by world standards, capital will flee quickly to places that offer a higher rate of return. If a government sets rates too high, foreign money will flow in, but small domestic firms might not survive. Trade is also likely to be

intra-firm trade Interstate commercial transactions that take place between subsidiaries of the same trans-state business enterprise.

11.3 ENDURING PATTERNS

The connection between preferences and power

The strategic importance of differences in actors' preferences varies with the distribution of power: the weaker an actor's relative power position, the more strategically important the more powerful actors' preferences; the stronger actors' power positions, the more strategically important their preferences.

The impact of linkage politics

World politics is driven by the interaction of international, factional, and constituency politics.

Money and Capital in Four Periods: Whose Preferences Matter?

Before World War I, the preferences of British, French, and German national policy makers had an important effect on exports of capital from their countries' capital markets. The preferences of British policy makers were also important in the management of the international monetary system. In all these cases, how that power was used depended on the incentives created by linkage politics.

After World War I, and also after World War II, the preferences of U.S. policy makers—and the incentives created by linkage politics in the United States—were of crucial significance both in matters of international monetary policy and capital movements.

One of the most intriguing effects of globalization as we move into the twenty-first century is that it appears to be increasing the trans-boundary effects of capital movements and international monetary processes at the same time as the power of any government to manage those issue areas is declining rapidly. Put differently, it has become increasingly hard to figure out whose preferences matter.

---

affected; high foreign demand for a currency will make that state's exports less competitive by raising their local prices. One solution now being discussed is to reintroduce some regulation on what are now largely unregulated capital flows. We examine this issue later in the chapter.

On Domestic Income Inequality and the Marginalization of Labor
Another potential implication of globalization is its effect on income inequality within societies. Here, however, the causal relationships are more complex. In industrialized societies, extensive trade with lower-income countries is said to harm industries that employ low-skill workers by inviting in cheaper imports that compete with their products. (Note, though, that this is what an open market should produce; less efficient producers should be driven out of business by a free market.) Not surprisingly, income inequality has grown in the United States during a period of rapidly increasing globalization over the last two decades. But this result may not be entirely due to open trade. This period has also seen a major introduction of computing into the workplace—an innovation that has profoundly shifted the nature of entire industries and many types of jobs—as well as significant increases in

immigration. By decreasing the number of lower-skilled jobs in the U.S. economy at the same time as an influx of new residents has swelled the pool of less-skilled workers, these developments have hurt the unskilled part of the U.S. labor market. Neither of these developments, however, grows out of trade. Economists estimate that, at most, increased trade with developing countries accounts for 20 percent of the loss in income of low-skilled workers relative to highly skilled workers.[38] Nevertheless, that 20 percent effect is very real to those who feel it, and unemployment and declining real wages have long been linked in the popular imagination with a rush of "cheap imports."

A closely related possible implication of globalization is that it marginalizes the economic and political position of labor within societies at the same time as it undermines governments' ability to maintain a social safety net. In a globalized economy, firms feel pressure to stay competitive in global terms, and governments feel pressure to attract and hold those firms. Both factors tend to diminish workers' bargaining power. Labor is hurt because globalization makes capital more "footloose." If workers become too demanding, a firm can relocate elsewhere. But the proposition must be qualified, since some FDI is hard to relocate. As *The Economist* put it, "once a multi-billion dollar microchip-assembly plant has been built, it tends to stay put, even if government decides to tighten the tax screw a little."[39] Finally, it is argued that because capital and skilled labor can be expected to flee states that tax them too highly, there is downward pressure on tax rates and social-welfare spending. This has been called "the race to the bottom." Welfare programs have become politically more vulnerable since the 1980s, especially in the United States, during a time of rapid globalization. But did the latter cause the former? It may be that people have turned against the welfare state more because they have become disenchanted for ideological reasons with government regulation of the economy than because expensive welfare programs seem to make societies uncompetitive in the world market.[40] Because both factors have been present, it is hard to determine which has been more important.

Even if states were on the defensive before the onslaught of globalization, these arguments suggest that with globalization they have lost much of their capacity to promote social purposes other than accommodating world market forces. But not everyone agrees with these claims. For example, analysts have noted a strong correlation across countries between the degree of exposure to international trade and the extent to which governments that value high social spending are able to allocate money to unemployment insurance, pensions, and family benefits. In the small European countries that are very heavy traders as a share of GDP, the level of social spending is quite high.[41] While one cannot infer a causal link directly from a statistical association, there seems to be a broad consensus about trade in these societies: The discipline of the world marketplace will be accepted, and government, in turn, will fund programs to even out the large income inequalities that would otherwise result from open trade.

Further, in direct contradiction to the "race to the bottom" argument, overall taxes in the European Union actually grew from 41.3 percent of GDP in 1980 to 43.8 percent in 1990 to 45.4 percent in 1996.[42] Since military spending as a share of GDP remained constant or dropped during this period in these countries, these tax data suggest that even though social spending has shrunk in recent years in many places, some states continue to maintain extensive welfare systems. If this interpretation is correct, though the capacity and authority of states to regulate exposure to the world economy may have eroded somewhat, the effects of globalization are still tempered by political and policy choices.

Responses to Globalization

Challenging Globalization through Street Demonstrations   As we have discussed, globalization is not neutral in its impact on individuals, groups, and countries. There are usually winners and losers—both within and across countries—when trade barriers fall, national capital markets become more tightly connected, and business firms increasingly operate branches in different countries. In the United States, for example, globalization during the 1990s was associated with a sustained boom in the country as a whole. Unemployment reached its lowest level in more than twenty-five years, inflation remained low and stable, and stock prices rose substantially during the decade. But these benefits disproportionately rewarded those at the top of the economic ladder. Despite large growth overall, wages and fringe benefits for the average U.S. worker have barely grown since 1973, and people at the bottom of the income distribution have actually seen their wages drop.[43]

Globalization is also associated with non-economic costs that many people find troubling. Although the expansion of foreign direct investment and trade have led to industrialization and growth in many parts of the Third World, environmental regulations are often weak or unenforced in poorer countries, with the result that wastes are discharged into the air or water in ways that would be prohibited in most developed countries. And because the average wage in many Third World countries is very low by developed-country standards, business firms can often demand a much longer work day for much less money than would be possible in a wealthier state. These environmental and economic conditions, some people believe, mean that globalization typically leads to the exploitation of the earth and the local work force in many areas of the world.

Further globalization, then, is likely to be controversial. Union members, environmental groups, and human-rights activists often oppose measures that would lower trade barriers or increase the leverage of international financial institutions on poor countries. Meanwhile, people who work for export-oriented firms and banks that do international lending typically view international economic integration far more positively. At present, globalization's supporters have the upper hand in many of these disputes, both because they usually are far better connected politically and because economic interdependence is fueled by strong technological trends. Air travel moves people and goods more efficiently than ever before. The costs of communication, driven by the electronic revolution, continue to drop. And even though most investment capital remains in its country of origin, large pools of capital can now move so easily around the world that investors shift funds quickly in search of tiny changes in interest rates or profit margins.[44]

Under these conditions, what options are open to those who oppose further globalization? To influence policy agendas, they must try to make the disadvantages that accompany globalization as noticeable and widely salient as possible. This is just what a broad coalition of anti-globalization protesters tried to do a few years ago. Each year, the World Trade Organization (WTO), the International Monetary Fund (IMF), and the World Bank hold separate meetings to set their policy agendas. The IMF and the World Bank also hold a joint annual summit—typically in

A broad coalition of activists assembled in Seattle in December 1999 to disrupt a meeting of the World Trade Organization. Union members, student activists, environmentalists, and human-rights advocates joined to denounce what they saw as a corporate-dominated agenda for international trade and development.

Washington, DC. At a WTO meeting held in Seattle in December 1999, turbulent street protests virtually shut down the conference. The joint IMF-World Bank meeting held in Washington in the spring of 2000 attracted a similarly large and angry group of demonstrators, and the pattern was repeated at joint meetings in Prague in September 2000. The unionists, anarchists, student activists, and environmentalists who participated in these demonstrations might not have agreed on much else, but they all objected to what they saw as narrow, corporate-oriented concerns behind the Bank's and Fund's lending decisions. Lost in this policy agenda, they believe, has been a concern with alleviating the poverty, illness, and environmental problems that plague much of the Third World, and to which they believe international corporations and globalization contribute. Nor did it help, the protestors contended, that the Bank's and Fund's leaders operated largely in secret and were responsive to no elected body.[45]

An NGO known as Global Trade Watch (GTW) played a key role in organizing the anti-WTO protest in Seattle. GTW is one of six subgroups within a larger consumer organization known as Public Citizen, founded in 1971 by Ralph Nader. The website for GTW states that it seeks to lead

> the way in educating the American public about the enormous impact of international trade and economic globalization on our jobs, the environment, public health, safety, and democratic accountability. Global Trade Watch works in defense of consumer health and safety, the environment, good jobs, and democratic decision-making, [all of which] are threatened by the so-called "free trade" agenda of the proponents of economic globalization.[46]

According to GTW's research director, the Seattle demonstration was designed to block any new round of WTO-sponsored tariff-cutting negotiations and to inhibit any expansion of the WTO's authority in the world economy. GTW's campaign, known as "No New Round: Turnaround," energized many grass-roots organizations across national borders, producing 40,000 demonstrators at the Seattle conference. The protest's organizers maintain that they achieved their immediate goals, since no new WTO initiative came out of the Seattle meeting.[47]

GTW's leader, Lori Wallach, became an anti-globalization activist when she found that many of the consumer-protection legislative objectives she was working on for Ralph Nader's organization conflicted with U.S. international trade commitments. Her organization objects both to the substance of WTO, IMF, and World Bank policies and to the ways in which those policies are reached. Substantively, her organization believes that these organizations' free-trade agenda has not benefited those who most need help in the Third World. In addition, Wallach questions the legitimacy of the decision-making process under which many WTO-sponsored market-opening initiatives have been implemented. Wallach believes that the rules governing global commerce should not be made by IGOs staffed by unelected bureaucrats; such rules should instead "be made at a level where people who are going to live with the results can hold decision makers accountable."[48]

The principal strategic question confronting the GTW was where its leaders might find useful sources of power. How could a small NGO get IGOs backed by a broad coalition of wealthy governments and trans-state business enterprises to change their policies? The answer was to organize demonstrations and publicity campaigns that could shift the cost-benefit calculations of the leaders of key governments and IGOs and also educate people who had previously stayed on the sidelines. Wallach said the Seattle demonstrations were like a grass-roots political campaign run on a shoestring. The power, she said, came from the many volunteers who cared deeply about the issues and joined "speakers' pools to go into local colleges, and PTAs, and Rotary Clubs, and neighborhood groups to teach people about the WTO and also get them involved in Seattle."[49] To compensate for its meager financial resources, GTW built a broad coalition of committed activists. Environmentalists, union members, church leaders, consumer advocates, and community activists from several dozen countries joined to try to redefine global integration by changing where its benefits flowed, and at what cost.

The Seattle, Washington, and Prague protests achieved three notable results. First, the sense of inevitability long attached to trade liberalization and market integration was weakened. Second, a network of non-state groups emerged as watchdogs over the IGO and corporate institutions that set the standards for commercial and financial globalization. Just a few years ago, none of this was in place or even imaginable. These two changes produced a third result: The World Bank, IMF, and the WTO have gotten the message sent by the demonstrators and seem to be making adjustments. For instance, soon after taking office early in 2000, the new managing director of the IMF, Horst Kohler, went on a "listening tour" of sixteen developing countries. When he returned, he began streamlining the conditions attached to IMF balance-of-payments loans—conditions poor countries often found socially and politically disruptive. Similarly, James D. Wolfensohn, the head of the World Bank, now admits that many of the Bank's programs have done little to improve the lives of the world's poor. After much debate within the agency, he gave one of the Bank's economists the latitude to write a report that focuses on how the world's poorest people actually live. The report's conclusions strongly challenge orthodox development economics by challenging the premise that all loans should aim to stimulate aggregate national economic growth, even if the poor do not benefit measurably.[50] Implied in this analysis is a broader standard for judging the value of globalization processes in the poorest countries.

These changes create some opportunities for building a productive dialogue, but the gulf between the two groups is profound. Lori Wallach wants to introduce values and decision procedures into international trade, banking, and investment policy that run strongly against modern business culture and the beliefs of international economic civil servants. Indeed, the norms holding her coalition together may be driven more by a deep mistrust of business firms than an inherent distaste for economic globalization.[51]

Moreover, NGOs such as Global Trade Watch may have trouble holding together for as many years as it is likely to take to achieve their long-range goals. Broad coalitions carry a fairly high risk of splintering. Two shared goals have brought the antiglobalization coalition together: a belief that greater accountability and transparency needs to be brought to trade policy making, and a conviction that globalization must be carried out in a way that sustains the environment, helps the poor, and protects workers' rights. While this glue might prove to be strong, it is also possible that different factions in this coalition may ultimately come to seek incompatible goals. Even now, signs of such an outcome can be seen. Labor and anti-poverty activists want more freedom for individual countries to adapt international commercial guidelines to individual national needs. Environmentalists, by contrast, tend to want strong, uniform rules to protect what they consider to be an absolute good.

Over time, such fissures could fracture the antiglobalization coalition. In the short run, however, street demonstrations protesting globalization have increased the political incentives for policy makers in central governments and key IGOs to search for ways to adjust the rules and norms to increase their effectiveness and perceived legitimacy. Capital controls and rules governing foreign direct investment are two places where that effort has been most visible.

Capital Controls   By the mid-1990s, the market for capital was very unrestricted internationally. FDI, portfolio investment, bank loans, bond lending, and other financial instruments had all grown substantially across borders.[52] Then, disaster struck. A collapse of Thailand's currency during the 1997 Asian financial crisis led to massive capital outflows that eventually infected much of Asia, and Russia's banking system collapsed. No less an advocate of market solutions than international financier George Soros suggested that some form of international capital controls might be needed to prevent such problems in the future. He noted that the countries that kept their financial markets closed during these crises weathered them better than those that were more exposed. As he put it, "keeping domestic financial markets totally exposed to the vagaries of international financial markets could cause greater instability than a country that has become dependent on foreign capital can endure."[53]

Financial markets are prone to two problems that get worse when the markets are tightly integrated and sharply responsive to changes in people's confidence levels. First, banks that are not adequately regulated or capitalized (supplied with capital or investment funds) tend to be run imprudently. From the owner or manager's point of view, any profits are theirs, and the government will absorb the losses. With this sense of fiscal irresponsibility, bankers make overly risky loans, and this can lead to major problems if the economy as a whole is in trouble. Another problem is that in a financial panic, each lender is tempted to pull its money out quickly, fearing that if it waits, the borrower will be out of funds. Both of these problems fueled the 1997 Asian financial crisis. Sharp drops in currency values, fueled in part by imprudent lending, led to a decline in investor confidence that spread quickly through the region. The IMF tried to repair the damage, but it did not address the underlying causes of the problem.[54]

Some background is useful at this point. The 1944 Bretton Woods agreement allowed states to impose controls on capital movements that were not directly used to finance current (goods and services) transactions. This preference was widely shared at the time. In an essay titled "National Self-Sufficiency," John Maynard Keynes, a key architect of the IMF, had argued that "finance [should] be primarily national."[55] By this he meant that financial flows between states would be likely to interfere with national management of the economy, which had become critical during the Great Depression and World War II. It was seen as no less important after 1945. Unlike FDI, short-term movements of capital (such as those used to purchase government bonds that have short maturities) are very sensitive to exchange-rate expectations and small differences in interest rates across states. It was well known that even an anticipated change in one of these factors could trigger major inflows or outflows of capital, which would undermine the effectiveness of any policy change. For this reason, many states kept short-term movements of capital under tight control for decades after World War II.* It was only when international capital markets and FDI expanded tremendously in the 1970s that such policies lost their effectiveness. Firms whose operations had become increasingly global could now much more easily evade any national restrictions on capital movements by moving money through their various affiliates. Alternatively, they could decide to build plants and create jobs in places with looser restrictions. Capital controls thus came to be seen as self-defeating, and many governments that had not already done so abandoned them in the 1980s and 1990s. In 1997, an IMF oversight group recommended that the IMF revoke its official approval of capital controls and explicitly urge member states to liberalize their national policies if they had not done so.[56]

Asia's financial crisis in 1997 prompted some policy makers and analysts to reconsider this consensus. Asian leaders had complained that their economies became highly vulnerable to international currency traders at the first sign of trouble. Hard-built prosperity should not be that fragile, many of them said; there is nothing sacred about unimpeded capital flows. One idea, suggested by economist James Tobin, is to impose a tax on all short-term international financial transactions as a way to limit speculative currency purchases (those designed to make a quick profit, rather than to be held over the longer term or used to finance the purchase of goods or services). Chile, for example, imposes a tax on those who want to take earned income out of the country after less than a year. The purpose behind such ideas is clear: to cut back on national exposure to the forces of globalization.

---

*The United States began the post-World War II period with open capital rules. By the end of the 1960s it had been joined by West Germany, Canada, the Netherlands, Sweden, France, Italy, and Belgium. Britain opened its capital markets in 1979, and Australia and New Zealand did so in the 1980s, but Spain, Portugal, Greece, and Ireland did not fully liberalize their capital markets until the 1990s. Latin American states were quite open in the late 1950s and early 1960s but have fluctuated back and forth since that time.

For a number of reasons, American financial actors and government officials dislike the idea of returning to capital controls in any form. Wall Street banks and brokerage firms want to expand into emerging capital markets overseas, which have been growing much faster than the domestic capital market. A return to controls would hinder these plans and would make it difficult for U.S. investors to get the highest available returns on their assets. Executives of U.S.-based TSBEs feel they could move even more easily from place to place worldwide and better compete with foreign firms if their capital transactions were unhindered. And since Americans save such a small share of their income compared to people in other countries, Washington wants the United States to be able to borrow from the rest of the world easily. By contrast, Asian governments now see capital controls as a way to protect their economies from shocks created by massive capital movements, and as high savers they have less need to tap world capital markets freely. Many Europeans worry that their financial systems are too rigid to face free capital flows over the long term and prefer regulated to unregulated markets as a matter of principle.[57] Given these serious disagreements, it is no surprise that "both the theory and practice of capital market liberalization are . . . in limbo."[58] There will probably be some fairly widespread changes in national rules on capital flows as a result of the Asian crisis, but it is not clear what these will be.

Codes of Conduct for Foreign Direct Investment   As with discussions about the desirability of creating rules controlling capital flows, the debate about the value of codes of conduct for foreign direct investment (FDI) is a direct response to globalization. Not long ago, economists used to think about trade and FDI in separate categories; one, in fact, was seen as a functional substitute for the other. Building plants in foreign countries was viewed as a way to jump over their tariff barriers. This was the reason why many U.S.-based TSBEs built factories in Europe in the 1960s: They wanted to get inside the "walls" of what was becoming a common European Economic Community tariff imposed on the outside world. But as tariffs have gradually come down and the production of goods and services has become globalized, trade and FDI are now seen as tightly interrelated. It is common now, as we noted earlier, for a firm's production to be split up across a number of states, which explains why intra-firm trade has grown so much. In addition, some FDI, especially in service industries, is essential for selling to foreign customers. Fast-food restaurants, for example, could not service foreign markets at all without a physical presence inside them. Since it is getting harder to make meaningful distinctions between trade and FDI, and governments now actively compete for FDI as an integral part of their economic development, discussions are intensifying about a global code of conduct for FDI.[59]

You might wonder why there are no comprehensive rules for FDI at the global level, as there are for trade and finance. It has been very difficult to reconcile the competing principles, political interests, and policy objectives that come with having a foreign business presence inside states. For one thing, there have always been two quite different principles for dealing with this problem in international law. One, derived from state sovereignty, holds that governments have exclusive jurisdiction over everything that occurs in their territories. The other emphasizes that states may not discriminate against aliens or injure them or their property, once they are admitted into a state. The international law of investment has alternated between these principles without ever reconciling the tensions between them.[60] Nevertheless, efforts to create global rules for FDI began in the context of bargaining over the creation of the GATT in the 1940s. But it soon became clear that states' positions on the key questions were too far apart for agreement. Similarly, a proposed comprehensive agreement to protect FDI within the Organization for Economic Cooperation and Development (OECD)—an intergovernmental group of twenty-four developed states that collaborates on economic and social issues—never materialized. In the 1970s, the issue again became controversial when a number of developing countries, concerned about the impact and behavior of TSBEs, imposed widespread controls, restrictions, and conditions on their entry and operations.[61] But no comprehensive global code was negotiated, largely because the issue had become so politically charged.

There has been piecemeal progress on such a code. Within the WTO, there have been agreements on three issues. One stops governments from requiring investors to use a minimum level of local inputs in their products (so-called **local content rules**) or requiring them to export from the host state at least as much as they import. Another keeps host states from infringing on investors' inventions and trademark brands. A third opens up domestic markets to investors in services, such as telecommunications or highway construction, but does so only partially. More comprehensive rules have been established on a case-by-case or regional basis. Over 1,600 bilateral investment treaties have been signed so far. As with extradition treaties, they apply to the specific parties, but only to those states. Firms established in one EU country are free to set up shop anywhere else in the Union they wish, and such mobility may in time be granted to firms that are established within the perimeter of NAFTA.[62]

The issue now is whether much stronger rules will become part of the WTO framework, in effect establishing a comprehensive global code protecting FDI. One suggestion would guarantee foreign firms the same treatment within host states as national firms. If carried to its logical extreme, such a rule would mean that foreigners would have the same **right of establishment** as local firms. Another suggested rule would prohibit host states from discriminating among investors from different states with regard to the same products or services. Yet another would establish a global tribunal for settling disputes about either of the other rules.[63] Together, these rules would effectively grant foreign firms the same rights now enjoyed by traders (exporters and importers) under WTO rules. The difference—one that is crucial politically—is that exporters do not have a visible, physical presence in a host state. In effect, such rules would signify that the nondiscrimination norm had trumped sovereignty in regulating global production.

Such ambitious global rules seem to be politically out of reach, at least for now. Efforts within the OECD to build a version of a comprehensive foreign investment code, which some observers saw as a springboard for a comparable agreement within the WTO, died in 1998. Not only were governments unable to agree on how much to liberalize FDI, but a trans-state coalition composed of environmentalists, unions, and other activists denounced the very idea of such an accord. It would, they said, give away too much to business without protecting either workers or the environment. Facing this pressure, political leaders backed away from the agreement.[64] In addition, policy makers in many developing countries fear that too much of their sovereignty would be compromised under the proposed rules. Even the Indian finance minister who began his country's financial liberalization in the early 1990s was skeptical about liberal global rules for FDI: "We are not ready as yet for right of

local content rules
Government regulations in a host country that require foreign businesses to use a minimum amount of products from the host country in the goods they import for sale.

right of establishment
The legal right of a foreign firm to enter, operate, and incorporate under local, host-country law.

11.4 ENDURING PATTERNS

The impact of varying beliefs about just relationships

If people value creating and sustaining legitimate relationships and if they think a political process and the outcome it produces are just, they are more likely to accept that outcome—even if they would have preferred something else. If they think either the outcome or the process is unjust, they are far more likely to oppose it.

The effect of the shadow of the future

The more compatible people expect their preferences to become over time, the more cooperative and less power-based their strategic choices are likely to be. Conversely, the more incompatible people expect their preferences to become over time, the more competitive and power-based their strategic approach is likely to be.

The impact of linkage politics

World politics is driven by the interaction of international, factional, and constituency politics.

Imagining Just Systems: India Today and the United States after World War II

People's notions about justice and legitimate relationships are almost always deeply embedded in their understandings of the historical experiences of people with whom they identify. Those understandings also affect the range of different possible futures they will consider. As a result, it is important to pay close attention to widely spread perceptions of the history of linkage politics for different regions—and groups within those regions—around the world.

As the text suggests, people on the Indian subcontinent evaluate their understanding of just systems of political economy in the context of their colonial experience. Similar concerns about liberal rules for FDI can be found throughout Africa, Asia, the Middle East, and Latin America.

After World War II, U.S. policy makers worked hard to create a system of international political economy in trade, money, and finance that reflected U.S. values and historical experiences. Those values and experiences led to a preference for exactly the type of liberal economic rules that often creates fears of exploitation and vulnerability in those who evaluate systems of political economy through a lens framed by colonialism.

---

establishment. You have to remember our history as a colony. The East India Company came here as a trader and ended up owning the country."[65]

Still, the question of global rules for FDI is unlikely to die. As one scholar put it, "taking no action appears equally undesirable. The growing reach and impact of [TSBE] activities have raised serious political, economic, and social concerns in many countries."[66] Perhaps the OECD states will eventually agree on comprehensive rules

Indonesia's and South Korea's Responses to the 1997 Asian Financial Crisis

For three decades, the economies in East Asia grew at a rate of almost 8 percent a year, more than twice as fast as the best-performing Western industrialized economies. No countries had ever grown so quickly for so long. Then, quite suddenly in mid-1997, economies began to fall apart. An international financial crisis began in Thailand and quickly spread to Malaysia, Indonesia, and South Korea.

The case study on **www.prenhall.com/lamborn** analyzes Indonesia's and South Korea's responses to the crisis. As you will see, the reactions of the political leaders in the two countries were quite different. Look for the likely causes of those different reactions. Did the leaders of the two countries have similar or different mixes of economic and political incentives? Were there important differences in the structure of the political institutions—or in the access of non-governmental actors—that affected the coalitions that formed and the ways in which the crisis played out? What impact did perceptions about the political legitimacy of the key actors have on their ability to influence events?

Finally, consider the role of the IMF in managing this crisis. What do these two cases suggest about the effectiveness and legitimacy of the IMF?

---

that might then be implemented, sector-by-sector, on a global scale.[67] It would seem that globalization is forcing policy makers to deal with the issue, even if it is unclear how they will eventually resolve it.

Conclusion

This chapter examined economic issues in world politics and showed how globalization is affecting the economic context in which national policy is made and firms do business. As we discussed, the effects of globalization on today's world political economy are particularly strong in the areas of trade, international monetary policy, finance and foreign direct investment, and changes in international and domestic income inequality. Given the political as well as economic significance of these areas, it's hardly surprising that globalization has produced a range of responses, running from raucous and widely publicized street demonstrations to high-level discussions of the value of capital controls and codes of conduct for foreign direct investment.

While the politics of international economics in today's world has these distinctive features, they are only the most recent examples of the ways in which markets shape and are shaped by political rules and choices. These relationships reflect one of the most fundamental aspects of IPE as an issue area: the tension between the pressures growing out of market integration and those that stem from political separation. That point leads to the second characteristic of IPE issues that we discussed earlier in the chapter: very strong domestic-international

In Indonesia (at left), the Suharto regime's refusal to make meaningful reforms to deal with the Asian financial crisis led to riots in which over 500 died in Jakarta between May 13 and May 15, 1998. In South Korea, the government in power when the crisis began decided not even to contest a scheduled election. On the day he took office, Kim Dae Jung (elected president on December 18, 1997 and shown at the right at a December 19 ceremony) led a parade of ordinary Koreans through the capital near the financial district to symbolize his commitment to reform.

linkages. As the case study about the 1997 Asian financial crisis shows, a big difference in the Korean and Indonesian responses to the financial crisis was the way in which variations in domestic political constituencies, institutions, and preferences produced different responses to similar external vulnerabilities. One reason was that while both countries had a wide variety of governmental and nongovernmental actors involved, in Indonesia the non-governmental actors were often simply extensions of the families of the ruling political elite. That fundamentally altered the stakes for the government in a way that would not have been true if crony capitalism had been less of a family operation. For these reasons, linkage politics worked out differently across the distinctive domestic contexts of Indonesia and South Korea.

Finally, the Indonesian and Korean cases illustrate two other key aspects of IPE issues. Although the IMF's policy demands were controversial, they reflected a widely held perception that the key international actors had a shared stake in ending the crisis and dealing with its underlying causes. This assumption that governments and non-governmental actors have a shared stake in global prosperity is, as we noted earlier, a key aspect of IPE in market economies. However, given the strong functional linkages across IPE issue clusters, to achieve this goal the response to the crisis had to take into account implications for trade and FDI as well as regional and global finance. This combination produced a very distinct set of patterns in the politics of strategic choice.

Key Terms

political economy
market
economic interdependence
gross domestic product (GDP)
sensitivity
vulnerability
globalization
dumping

production structure
balance of payments
balance on current account
balance on capital account
protectionism
undervalued currency
foreign exchange
exchange rates

foreign direct investment (FDI)
portfolio investment
intellectual property
intra-firm trade
local content rules
right of establishment

To The Reader A CHAPTER SUMMARY and QUESTIONS FOR REVIEW are available at **www.prenhall.com/lamborn**

Human Rights amidst Global Diversity

In October 1998, General Augusto Pinochet, who ruled Chile as a dictator in the 1970s and 1980s, was arrested while in London to undergo surgery. The arrest came at the request of the Spanish government. The arrest warrant, based on the 1984 International Convention against Torture, said that the general was wanted for questioning related to "crimes of genocide and terrorism that included murder." According to Spanish officials, Pinochet ordered the murder and torture of hundreds of Chilean and Spanish citizens while he headed Chile's government. On this basis, Spain requested his extradition. Chilean officials quickly demanded Pinochet's release, arguing that he had diplomatic immunity as a member of the Chilean Senate and had entered Britain on a diplomatic passport.[1]

The Pinochet case surprised the world and quickly captured the attention of diplomats, international lawyers, and the global news media. (The outcome of Spain's extradition request is discussed in the case study "Accountability for Human Rights Abuses"; see page 399.) Not that long ago, the way in which Spain and Britain acted in this case would have been highly unusual. What policy makers did within their state's borders was rarely subject to interference by outsiders. State sovereignty meant that a government's internal behavior was normally a matter of its domestic jurisdiction. The founding members of the United Nations considered internal autonomy so fundamental that they guaranteed respect for domestic jurisdiction at the beginning of the UN Charter, in Article 2. Claims such as Spain's—that a former political leader could be held internationally accountable for human-rights abuses committed while he held office even though he had been granted immunity in his own country for those actions—were rarely made. In one of the few cases where such claims had been vigorously made, Israel asked Argentina to extradite Nazi war criminal Adolf Eichmann to Jerusalem. When the request was rebuffed, Israeli agents kidnapped Eichmann and returned him to Israel for trial, where he was subsequently convicted of genocide during the Holocaust and executed in 1962. The extraordinary lengths to which Israel had to go to take jurisdiction of one of the worst mass murderers in history suggests how little international support there once was for broad human-rights accountability.

That attitude may be changing. Britain's willingness to take Spain's claims regarding Pinochet seriously suggests a growing sensitivity to human rights issues and, at least among some actors, more agreement on how to enforce those rights. Some international legal experts now argue that gross violations of human rights transcend the concerns of the particular states where the abuses were committed. According to the Geneva Conventions signed after World War II and the Nuremberg Principles, under which Nazi officials were tried as war criminals for human rights abuses, there should be no safe haven for flagrant human rights violators. While such norms have existed for several decades, what may be growing is a willingness of more states to enforce them.[2] But not everyone approves of this trend. In addition to those who believe that sovereignty should continue to shield public officials from external scrutiny of their internal conduct, other skeptics worry about the practical implications of the Pinochet case. If, they argue, any former national leader can be charged with human rights abuses by foreigners, the international legal system could be thrown into chaos. But if the Nuremberg Principles are instead applied selectively, it may simply allow strong states to impose their jurisdiction on weak ones.[3]

To help you understand these kinds of problems, we begin this chapter with an overview of the evolution of human rights issues in world politics. We then explore the fundamental questions posed by human rights issues, their characteristic features as problems in strategic choice, and what is distinctive about the context within which international human rights discussions are taking place. We conclude with a discussion of two prominent issues on the contemporary human rights agenda: establishing accountability for past abuses by authoritarian regimes and dealing with crimes against humanity.

The Evolution of Human Rights as an Issue

The idea that all people have rights—a moral claim to treat people in a certain way simply because they are human—has a long history. However, contemporary human rights issues are immensely complicated by the fact that world politics is very much the product of a *particular* history—the expansion of what was originally a European state system to the rest of the world. This historical reality makes European, or more broadly, Western traditions central to the ways in which human rights issues are framed in contemporary world politics. As we shall see, the centrality of Western traditions also creates profoundly troubling questions about the meaning of human rights amidst global diversity.

The Natural Law Tradition Collides with the Emergence of Sovereignty

The Greek Stoics, active around the second and third centuries BC, seem to have been the first group in the Western tradition to argue that people have rights simply because they are human. They criticized the parochialism of the classical Greek *polis*—supposedly an island of civilization surrounded by a sea of barbarians—and suggested the idea of a single city of humankind in which each person's worth is recognized. Roman thinkers built on this foundation by suggesting the possibility of a universal system of laws. Cicero described natural law as being "of universal application . . . we cannot be freed from its obligations by Senate or people, and we need not look outside ourselves for an expounder or interpreter of it. And there will not be different laws at Rome and at Athens, or different laws now and in the future, but one eternal and unchangeable law will be valued for all nations and for all times."[4] Over time, the Roman **jus gentium** (law of peoples), which was developed to deal with disputes between Roman citizens and citizens of conquered areas, came to validate the existence of basic principles of right and wrong that transcend culture, religion, political system, and historical era.

The medieval Catholic Church also claimed that natural law expressed the unity of humankind. Any earthly divisions, such as between church and state, would be resolved at a higher level of divinely inspired law. These ideas ran into resistance when modern states developed in the late Middle Ages. Many princes sought autonomy from the Church, and they sometimes won it. The Church responded by emphasizing a new notion of natural law based more on the individual.[5] According to **natural law,** all people are bound by rules ultimately derived from God (or nature).

jus gentium   The "law of the peoples," originally developed by the Romans in an effort to create a set of universal laws that would apply to relations between Rome and citizens from other societies.

natural law   A tradition that asserts that there are universal principles—usually based in religion but sometimes also in nature—that exist independent of states and the political process.

372 PART FOUR Contested Transnational Obligations

Advocates of natural law argue that states and people are obligated to follow these universal principles whether or not they have consented to be bound by them. This doctrine holds that these duties exist prior to, and independently of, human-made law, known as **positive law.**

The idea of sovereign territoriality, the emerging tradition of **legal positivism,** and the Westphalian bargain that made religion the prerogative of the ruler were, however, in constant tension with such ideals. As a result, while the U.S. Declaration of Independence (1776), the French Declaration of Rights (1789), and the key texts in other political traditions proclaim that the rights of people are inalienable, the ultimate duty to protect these rights is placed in the hands of governments. It would never have occurred to the authors of these texts that such rights could legitimately be scrutinized by outsiders. The contemporary notion that human rights have a universal basis sits very uneasily with the claim that internal autonomy and domestic jurisdiction shield state officials from external scrutiny of their human rights behavior.

As the nineteenth century wore on, the growing popularity of political liberalism combined with seventeenth and eighteenth-century social contract theory (exemplified by Hobbes, Locke, and Rousseau) to provide a non-theological basis for human rights. Both liberalism and natural law claimed that people had natural rights no government could legitimately take away, and that, should that happen, the government could justifiably be removed or overthrown. But liberalism replaced the religious rationale for the existence of universal human rights with one based on the idea that individuals were the ultimate holders of rights and responsibilities.

The liberal tradition provided a broad conceptualization of the basis for human rights claims, but it had little immediate effect on interstate human rights relationships. After World War I, under the auspices of the League of Nations, guarantees were made for ethnic minorities who lived in the former territories of the Austrian Empire. But no League representative could enter these areas or communicate with their people without the host state's permission.[6] The minority guarantees thus became victims of the Westphalian bargain.

International Human Rights Issues since World War II

Human rights landed firmly on the world politics agenda in 1945. The Holocaust convinced officials and citizens in many states that governments' treatment of their citizens now had to be a topic of global concern. Eleanor Roosevelt, who chaired the UN committee that drafted the Universal Declaration of Human Rights, saw this document as a statement of principles that defined "a common standard of achievement for all peoples and nations."[7] In addition to the Declaration, two other key documents eventually resulted from this work: the Covenant on Civil and Political Rights and the Covenant on Economic, Social, and Cultural Rights. While the Declaration was not binding and the two covenants were treaties that required ratification by states before they could go into effect, the three represented a significant landmark in the evolution of human rights as an issue in world politics. Collectively called the International Bill of Rights, these three documents identified a set of universal rights that applied to individuals, not just to national minorities. The post-World War I minority guarantees had been resented by those states targeted for international scrutiny, and those guarantees had conspicuously left out peoples, such as the ethnic Hungarians in Romania, whose plight was of no particular concern to

positive law Laws formally adopted by recognized authorities.

legal positivism A tradition that asserts that states are only bound to honor rules they accept either through formal treaty or long-established custom and practice.

In the late 1940s, Eleanor Roosevelt, widow of President Franklin D. Roosevelt, chaired the group that produced the first comprehensive modern definition of human rights. Mrs. Roosevelt decided early on that this statement would have to be legally nonbinding or many governments would refuse to accept it even in principle.

the major states. It was much harder to object to the global standards contained in the International Bill of Rights on such grounds.[8]

The drafting of the International Bill of Rights did not mean that human rights faced smooth sailing in the post-World War II world. As the Cold War began in the late 1940s, momentum slowed as human rights became an object of contention between the East and West blocs. Western officials accused communist leaders of ignoring civil and political rights. East-bloc officials noted that the West had, at best, a mixed record on social and economic rights. Further multilateral development of international human rights standards was held up by these tensions. The two human rights covenants in the International Bill of Rights were debated by the UN General Assembly in the early 1950s but did not receive Assembly approval until 1966.

Multilateral work on human rights resumed during the 1970s, as the United Nations moved from setting standards to examining how states were implementing them. In 1970, the UN's Economic and Social Council for the first time authorized the Human Rights Commission to conduct confidential investigations of complaints involving a pattern of violations. When the two Human Rights Covenants came into force in 1976, an International Human Rights Committee was set up to monitor how the signatories implemented the covenant dealing with civil and political rights. Meanwhile, public attention tended to focus on the General Assembly, where the human rights debate was open and very partisan. Israel, South Africa, and Chile, all strongly disliked by the Third-World and Soviet-bloc states, were discussed far more often than other alleged violators.

Outside the UN, the principle of multilateral scrutiny was also applied to the Soviet bloc. In 1973, the Conference on Security and Cooperation in Europe (now known as the Organization for Security and Cooperation in Europe, or OSCE) was convened in Helsinki to stabilize East-West relations. Moscow wanted recognition of the territorial and ideological status quo in Europe; in return, the West asked for human rights guarantees. The Helsinki Accords, signed when the Conference concluded in 1975, covered four areas: security in Europe and the Mediterranean; cooperation in economics, science, technology, and the environment; humanitarian

12.1 ENDURING PATTERNS

The connection between preferences and power

The stronger actors' power positions, the more strategically important their preferences.

The impact of varying beliefs about just relationships

Actors' reactions to differences in their preferences and relative power varies with their beliefs about the importance and nature of just relationships. If people value creating and sustaining legitimate relationships and if they think a political process and the outcome it produces are just, they are more likely to accept that outcome—even if they would have preferred something else. If they think either the outcome or the process is unjust, they are far more likely to oppose it.

The impact of linkage politics

World politics is driven by the interaction of international, factional, and constituency politics.

Christians in the Ottoman Empire; Minorities and the Versailles Peace Treaty; the Cold War

From the Serbian revolt of 1804–1817, through the Greek War of Independence in 1821–1829, to the Balkan wars of 1912 and 1913, policy makers in Russia, Austria, Germany, France, and Britain used charges that the Ottoman Empire was violating the human rights of Christians in their Balkan possessions as partial justification for intervening. Though the historical evidence suggests policy makers in those states cared more about pushing the Turks out of Europe than protecting Christians, the human rights argument was immensely popular among domestic constituency groups.

In the post-World War I period, the victorious allies claimed that "the war to end all wars" would bring a new and more just state system that protected the human rights of minorities and promoted democracy and national self-determination. They acted, however, only to protect human rights in the defeated states. Even if they had wanted to police each other—which they did not—policy makers in the winning states did not have the power to impose their views on anyone but the losers. Finally, intervening in the domestic affairs of the enemy was politically popular; turning the mirror toward their own societies was not.

In the post-World War II period, there was a sustained push to promote human rights conventions. However, the politics of strategic choice resulted in human rights issues becoming tools that reinforced the Cold War instead of transcending it.

and human rights issues, as well as the free flow of ideas and information throughout Europe; and procedures for monitoring progress in these areas. Over time, though the Soviet-bloc states tried to interpret the provisions of the Helsinki Accords very narrowly, NGOs and Western states used them to call for a free press and more political liberty in Eastern Europe. These actors now could tell Moscow: "We don't advocate anything you haven't signed." The 1970s also saw human rights emphasized in U.S. foreign policy more than at any time since the administration of Woodrow Wilson. This helped legitimate the issue as a proper topic of international concern.[9]

The 1980s saw more international standard setting and the beginning of a wave of democratization that would continue during the 1990s. Public awareness of human rights also increased during this period. In the early 1970s, media coverage of the issue had been spotty at best, but in part due to its increasing prominence in U.S. foreign policy, media coverage expanded significantly over the next fifteen years.[10] By the end of the decade, power had been transferred to democratic governments in the Philippines, Argentina, Brazil, Chile, South Korea, Pakistan, and Taiwan. The most significant change came in 1989 and 1991, as the Cold War ended and the Soviet empire crumbled. This collapse created a very different international environment for human rights. A convention prohibiting discrimination against women was opened for signature and ratification, and one prohibiting torture was drafted. Human rights NGOs proliferated, which significantly increased global monitoring capabilities. Today, governments' human rights practices—their respect for freedom of expression, association, religion, and so on—are a major issue among as well as within states. For a summary of the major human rights agreements, see Table 12–1.

TABLE 12–1   LANDMARK GLOBAL INTERNATIONAL HUMAN RIGHTS INSTRUMENTS

Treaty	Status	Purpose
Slavery Convention	Entered into force March 9, 1927	States the principle that slavery in all its forms should be abolished.
Universal Declaration of Human Rights	Adopted and proclaimed December 10, 1948	Puts forth a general outline of the principles defining the inherent and inalienable freedoms of all mankind, and the intent to codify those principles and freedoms in international law.
Convention on the Prevention and Punishment of the Crime of Genocide	Entered into force January 12, 1951	States the general principles of the proscription of genocide in any form.
International Covenant on Economic, Social, and Cultural Rights	Entered into force January 3, 1976	Ensures states of their right to pursue economic development consistent with their social and cultural principles and without outside interference from other states.
International Covenant on Civil and Political Rights	Entered into force March 26, 1976	Ensures all individuals within signatory states' jurisdictions their right to life, equality before the law, the rights of freedom of belief, of association, of thought, of conscience, and of religion, and the exercise thereof.
Convention on the Elimination of Discrimination Against Women	Entered into force December 18, 1979	Ensures equality between men and women in law and in fact.
Convention against Torture and Other Cruel, Inhuman or Degrading Treatment or Punishment	Entered into force June 26, 1987	States the principle that there is no justification for torture by the state and that all forms of torture conducted by the state should be abolished.
Convention on the Rights of the Child	Entered into force September 2, 1990	Ensures the special protection of, and the necessity of, separate and special safeguards for the child.

Source: United Nations Office of the High Commissioner for Human Rights, "International Human Rights Instruments" (*http://www.unhchr.ch/html/intlinst.htm*, May 26, 2001).

Three Fundamental Questions about Human Rights Principles

Human rights principles assume that every individual has rights by virtue of being a person—rights that exist regardless of people's status as citizens of some state, family members, workers, or members of any organization.[11] Philosophers, legal theorists, and social scientists agree that claims for human rights are ultimately moral in nature: They are based on how human beings *should* be treated, whether or not they are actually treated that way.

While human rights claims are moral imperatives, their effectiveness depends upon an appeal to some standard of political legitimacy.[12] As we discuss later in this chapter, the multilateral institutions that try to secure compliance with human rights norms typically couch their appeals in terms of political legitimacy, as do governments that promote human rights observance as a foreign policy goal. The state and non-state actors that share beliefs about human rights procedures and outcomes increasingly define their common identities in terms of such agreement. NATO, the EU, and the Organization for Economic Cooperation and Development (OECD) often point out that they admit only democratic states with good human rights records. By contrast, when actors disagree about human rights, they typically make their cases by referring to different, and at times incompatible, notions of legitimacy. Such disagreements are predictable, since the claims that individuals and groups can legitimately make against society constitute one of the most politically sensitive of all governance issues.

In analyzing which actors have what rights, people often debate three questions. First, they ask whether the holders of rights must be individuals, or whether groups can also possess human rights. Second, they ask whether human rights standards are necessarily universal, or whether non-universal standards can also be said legitimately to exist. Third, they ask which potential rights really "count" as human rights. Let us examine each of these questions.

Who Has Human Rights: Groups or Only Individuals?

The argument that only individuals can properly claim human rights derives from the Anglo-Saxon strain of liberal thought. According to this view, it is individuals who typically must be protected from the coercive power of some group, whether it is the state, society, or a tribe. Of course, society has certain rights—or at least responsibilities—with respect to individuals, which may require limits on the exercise of individual human rights. In wartime, for instance, we expect more censorship of military news than otherwise. Individual rights must therefore be balanced by individual duties to society. But assertions that there are collective rights, such as the right of an ethnic group to self-determination (a state of its own), are, from this point of view, incorrect. It is not the group that holds a "right." The right of self-determination should instead be interpreted as the legitimate claim of individual group members to achieve a state.[13]

An opposing view argues that groups as well as individuals have rights. In this view, people have collective as well as individual identities and, as a result, their well-being and dignity depend on the viability of that group identity. For instance, in communal societies structured around village or tribal ties, people's sense of self revolves around the group. The notion of "rights," and especially of "individual rights," is unknown in African languages and has made little headway in traditional Islamic, Hindu, or Buddhist communities. In these places, rights belong to the group, or if individuals can claim them, those rights also carry obligations that individuals owe to that group.[14]

Furthermore, even when rights are not defined communally, individuals' rights can be safeguarded only when groups to which they belong are secure. The cases of genocide against Jews, Armenians, Cambodians, Bosnian Moslems, and Tutsis are familiar. Less well known is that more tribal peoples have been eliminated in the twentieth century than in any other.[15] Even in less extreme cases, advocates of group rights argue that groups must have separate standing to make claims that collective, as distinct from individual, rights have been violated. They point out that the liberal notion that only individuals have rights assumes that people live their lives essentially as isolated individuals, without meaningful group connections. Not only does that view deny people's social nature, it also ignores the fact that individuals cannot enjoy the full range of human possibilities unless the groups they belong to are safe from physical danger and discrimination.[16]

Are Human Rights Universal?

A second fundamental debate about the nature of human rights revolves around the question of whether human rights standards are universal or vary across place and time. This question is difficult to answer, both because it opens up sensitive issues about the history of European expansion and because it forces a choice between two attractive ideas. On the one hand, common norms should protect people wherever they happen to live. On the other hand, human rights norms should reflect the world's diverse cultural traditions, varying group values and development priorities, and the degree to which societies are comprised of sharply antagonistic ethnic groups.

As we explained earlier in the chapter, in the nineteenth and twentieth centuries, the religious rationale for universal human rights norms in the Catholic natural law tradition lost influence and was gradually superseded by the liberal idea that individuals are the ultimate holders of rights and responsibilities. This universalist idea provides the basis for just about every UN document relating to human rights. The preamble to the Universal Declaration of Human Rights, adopted by the UN General Assembly in 1948, notes the "equal and inalienable rights of all members of the human family." Article 2 says: "Everyone is entitled to all the rights and freedoms set forth in this Declaration, without distinction of any kind."[17] More recently, the Vienna Declaration and Programme of Action, adopted at a UN conference in 1993, held that while religious, cultural, and historical differences must be respected, all states have a duty to promote and protect all human rights and fundamental freedoms.[18]

Despite these claims, the argument in favor of non-universal standards is based on the idea that different cultures and historical periods have distinctive views about human rights. Leaders in different states have diverse political and policy agendas, and behind these lie very different national traditions. These preferences and values inevitably color leaders' view of human rights issues. Even in the United States, which is so often identified with universalist norms, views of universality are usually highly selective. Americans generally think of rights as "freedom from" government rather than as "freedom to enjoy" substantive material or other goods. Because their nation was born out of a desire to limit arbitrary government power, and because most citizens had been able to improve their material circumstances, the "inalienable" rights emphasized by Thomas Jefferson and James Madison concerned free speech and free elections rather than rights to food, shelter, and clothing. The result, from a global perspective, is a very narrow conception of fundamental rights.[19] By contrast, Singapore, Malaysia, and Indonesia, among others, maintain that economic development to improve a population's standard of living is a more urgent priority than a free press or free elections.[20]

Thus, many people believe that different cultures have legitimately diverse views about governance and the role of the individual in society, and they recognize that these values imply diverse human rights standards. Bilahari Kausikan, a senior diplomat from Singapore, put these issues squarely on the table in a widely read article in which he asked: "What institutions and which values? The individualistic ethos of the West or the communitarian traditions of Asia? The consensus-seeking approach of East and South-East Asia or the adversarial traditions of the West?"[21] These remarks were part of a debate over whether "Asian values"—which emphasize social harmony, discipline, and strong family and communal ties—validly imply a different notion of rights from those found in the more pluralistic, and at times individualistic, West. Kausikan's position suggests two reasons for cross-cultural disagreements about human rights. First, those who have been victims of colonialism, which was often justified as a way to bring "civilization" to non-Western peoples, often resent human rights lessons from those same Westerners. Such instruction is especially resented when it is not accompanied by what Asians call "self-criticism." As many Asians see it, their societies have developed economically without the social problems found in Western societies, especially the United States: crime, drug abuse, and weak family ties. This makes it natural, as a Japanese writer put it, for "these [Asian] nations to become more confident in their own ways and more critical of the self-righteous and assertive ways of Western, particularly American, diplomacy and NGO [human-rights] activity."[22]

The second reason for cross-cultural disagreements about human rights is even more fundamental: People from different cultural backgrounds may simply disagree about how or by whom rights are created. People from different cultures are likely to assign different meanings or weights to human individuality and autonomy. Anthropologists argue that different cultures bring with them "different modes of thought."[23] One's notions of the intrinsic worth of the individual, the individual's rights and duties in society, and the purposes and duties of government are all, to some extent, culture-bound. We've seen that traditional African cultures have no notion of individual rights as such. One South African writer, in characterizing what she called her "umbilicals," said: "You are not left to be merely your private self: you represent others or others represent you, so that you are ever conscious of [the] relative status, classification, interdependent relationships in terms of which your conduct is being judged."[24] People socialized in communal cultures tend not to view human rights in individualistic terms, since that standard puts a much lower value on the "interdependent relationships" they cherish.

Which Rights Count?

As you can see, there is wide disagreement about who has rights and whether those rights are universal or particular to distinctive cultures and countries. On paper, at least, there is more agreement about the third question: Of all the claims that could be asserted as rights, which ones "really" count? Most states have given an authoritative answer to this question in adopting the Universal Declaration of Human Rights, the International Covenant on Civil and Political Rights, and the International Covenant on Economic, Social, and Cultural Rights. The two covenants elaborate the provisions in the Universal Declaration and have the legal force of treaties. The Universal Declaration, which does not carry the obligations of a treaty, provides, among other things, for a guarantee of the life, liberty, and security of each person; for equal protection under the law; protection against racial, sexual, and other forms of discrimination; protection against slavery and torture; the guarantee of a fair trial and protection against arbitrary arrest; the right of every person to move freely within his or her country, emigrate, and return; the right to freedom of speech, association, and religion; the right to take part in the government of his or her country, directly or through representatives; the right to own property, work, and receive Social Security; and the right to food, clothing, education, and health care. By the early 1990s, over ninety states had ratified the two covenants.

Two qualifications should be noted. While almost every state has approved the list of rights in the Universal Declaration, many routinely violate these rights and resist international scrutiny of their human-rights behavior. In addition, as we've seen, officials in different states prioritize these rights differently. Those in the wealthy states usually emphasize civil and political rights, while those in the poor world emphasize economic and social rights. There has been dialogue on these often starkly opposed positions. At the 1993 Vienna Human Rights Conference, the United States and other developed countries conceded "an inalienable right to development" for the first time. No obligations to assist that development, however, were noted as binding on the wealthy states.

Four Distinctive Features of Human Rights Issues

Human rights issues have four distinctive features from the perspective of the politics of strategic choice. First, human rights issues arise due to conflicting interpretations of legitimacy. Second, more than any other issue in world politics, human rights questions evoke cultural and political diversity. Third, a wide variety of actors are key players on human rights issues. Fourth, when human rights become an issue among states, sovereignty is challenged, if not undermined.

These four distinctive features create great challenges in the politics of strategic choice on human rights issues. The belief that promoting justice *ought* to be a high priority in international politics is a necessary precondition for claims about human rights violations to become important trans-national issues. However, doing anything about human rights abuses requires building a coalition that includes actors with the power to influence the outcomes. That makes the preferences of states and other international actors that have relevant sources of power more strategically important than the preferences of weaker actors, which immediately undercuts the claims to universality that are at the heart of human rights issues.

This essential problem in the politics of strategic choice is complicated by the fact that choices of international actors are almost always affected by linkage politics. Building coalitions among policy factions and between those factions and their key constituents complicates human rights issues in two important ways. First, it makes it likely that factions interested in building a coalition to act on human rights will frequently need to get political support from factions who rank human rights lower than the pursuit of other policy preferences. Making policy side-payments to get those actors on board will often make human rights policies look like smoke screens for special interests. This problem in factional politics is reinforced by constituency politics. Getting constituents to back human rights initiatives usually requires appealing to important national, cultural, or religious symbols. Those symbols are likely to be anchored in the *distinctive* history of the social groups key constituents identify themselves with, once again undercutting the claim for universality.

Conflicting Interpretations of Legitimacy

When people take action to claim their rights or the rights of those they want to protect are endangered, they challenge existing institutions, practices, or norms.[25] Such challenges are typically based on a notion of legitimacy that contradicts existing practices. For example, when Westerners living in the Persian Gulf state of Abu Dhabi condemned the government's practice of first crucifying convicted murderers and then executing them by a firing squad, their purpose was not to question the men's guilt. They argued that such torture is morally indefensible even if the men are guilty. The legitimacy of the practice is defended by the local inhabitants—both public officials and ordinary citizens—who claim that rough treatment of criminals and public executions deter crime at a time when the Gulf states face social instability in the form of millions of temporary workers and other expatriates. In any case, they argue, how *we* deal with this matter is *our* business. We punish convicted criminals according to *our* laws, which are based on Islamic law.[26]

What distinguishes human rights from other world politics problems is that conflicting interpretations of legitimacy are not just associated with the issue; they largely create it. In the areas of security, international economics, and the environment, how actors react to differences in their preferences and power positions depends in part on whether they believe others' purposes are legitimate. In the human rights area, actors focus much more centrally on what they believe to be legitimate behavior; their objectives stem from judgements about the way a government should treat its citizens. In mid-1999, a Kurdish rebel leader was put on trial by Turkey for treason. He was allowed only limited access to his lawyers under very controlled conditions. When spokesmen for two human rights NGOs called this "an atmosphere of intimidation," they challenged the legitimacy of Turkey's methods for dealing with a dreaded, longstanding insurgency.[27] These kinds of judgements make ethics and values central to the very meaning of human rights as an issue area.

The controversy over "Asian values" further illustrates the centrality of normative judgements in human rights matters. In maintaining that Asia has different human rights standards from those in the West, Kausikan makes two major points. First, many Asians don't want their societies to resemble those in the West. They prefer a society in which individuals do not define their rights in opposition to the state, and one in which authority is treated with deference. Both notions are alien to U.S. culture, if somewhat less so to the rest of the West. Second, in societies that are ethnically heterogenous, underdeveloped, and not well integrated, the state may at times need to operate with a heavy hand. "Good government," Kausikan claims, may require detention without trial to deal with military rebels or religious extremists, or curbs on press freedoms to avoid fanning ethnic hatreds or social divisions.[28] Representatives of the Western tradition typically reject both claims. Zbigniew Brzezinski, who was national security adviser in the Carter administration, asserts that human freedom and respect for the individual are universal values, and that Asians who argue differently will find that, as their societies develop, people will demand such behavior. Similarly, the director of Human Rights Watch/Asia argues that Kausikan's view rationalizes arbitrary state power, which is likely to be used more broadly against dissent than its defenders acknowledge.[29]

It's hard to find mutually acceptable compromises when people challenge the legitimacy of each others' views about the nature of human rights. For instance, over 137 million women in at least 28 African countries have had parts of their genitals removed surgically as a cultural rite. Supporters argue that the practice is no more harmful than male circumcision and is a valid expression of African tradition. Reacting to a government effort to ban the practice, the supreme spiritual leader of Senegal's Toucouleur people said: "I would rather die than be forced to stop doing what I believe in." Opponents call the practice female genital *mutilation*. They say that many of the women who are subject to it detest it, that it is involuntary, and that people trying to escape it should have a right to permanent asylum on grounds of persecution.[30] Resolving such differences is next to impossible, and even finding middle ground is difficult.

Cultural and Political Diversity

As the examples above suggest, people's ideas about legitimacy function within normative communities. Such communities can be global, but more often they coincide with national, subnational, or trans-national groups in which people share a culture. Since many cultures hold distinctive values about people's rights and obligations, human rights conflicts provide a prism through which we can observe many examples of cultural and political diversity.

Turkish leaders, for example, are fighting a protracted battle with groups that want to express more freely the society's Islamic culture. After winning a seat in parliament in 1999, a woman was denied her seat because she wears an Islamic head

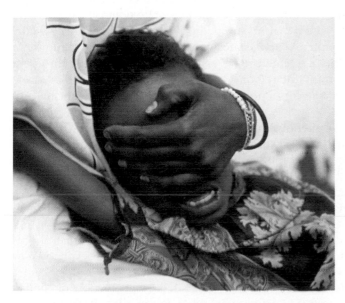

Many African teenage girls, such as the one pictured here, are subjected to a surgical procedure to remove part of their genitals. From a Western point of view, the practice is barbaric, but from the perspective of some traditional African cultures, this practice is a valid expression of a distinctive cultural tradition.

scarf, which is prohibited in government buildings and schools. The prime minister accused her of "challenging the secular principles of the Turkish state" by using her head scarf as a political symbol and said that "she will not be permitted to reappear [in parliament] like that." After female university students were kept from taking end-of-semester exams for wearing head scarves, protests erupted and were put down forcibly by the police.[31] To opponents, the head scarf is a provocative challenge to secular democracy, a key element of Turkey's modern political culture. To committed Muslims, the ban on the head scarf denies their rights and delegitimizes a core element of their identity.

Societies that absorb many immigrants often find their tolerance stretched by practices that challenge local human rights norms. In Maine, a refugee from Afghanistan had his son taken away by authorities when neighbors saw the man kiss the boy's penis. In traditional Afghan culture, the practice is an expression of parental love, but in the West it is seen as child abuse. The boy was returned home, but only after the case went to the State Supreme Court. As the United States experiences the largest wave of immigration since the early twentieth century, Americans must decide whether they can accept practices including involuntarily arranged marriages, disciplinary techniques such as shaming, and cultural initiation ceremonies involving piercing, genital alterations, and other forms of scarification.[32]

Involvement of a Wide Variety of Actors

The third key feature of human rights issues from the perspective of the politics of strategic choice is the wide number and variety of state and non-state actors that get involved. Moreover, the types of roles that state and non-state actors play, as well as the reasons that prompt them to get involved, vary in significant ways.

States are centrally involved in international human rights issues because each state, through its constitution and other laws, defines the rights and obligations of its people. Designating these rights and duties is a core aspect of sovereignty. Only when individuals or groups are dissatisfied at the national level are regional or global human rights norms invoked. Furthermore, even though other actors are involved in placing human rights issues on world political agendas, state policy makers are the ones who ultimately decide which matters are authoritatively dealt with regionally or globally. As in the environmental area, states make such decisions in three ways: by negotiating human rights agreements; by taking responsibility for enforcing those agreements; and by joining the regional and global IGOs that also play a role in agenda setting, collective rule formation, and the monitoring and assessment of existing rules.

IGOs perform two basic functions in the human rights area: *promotion* and *protection*. IGOs promote human rights within forums where those issues are discussed, international standards are set, and the standards are publicly disseminated. Global meetings, such as the 1968 International Conference on Human Rights in Tehran and the 1993 United Nations World Conference on Human Rights, are the most inclusive forums for discussing such issues. By adopting treaties and opening them for state ratification, the UN General Assembly has helped to set standards and socialize actors to accept them. Each piece of the International Bill of Human Rights was drafted through UN bodies; in fact, little human rights standard setting is now done outside an IGO framework.

Protection has both a direct and indirect aspect. Direct protection of human rights by IGOs is rare, since states mainly perform this function. It occurs most often when a UN representative, such as the High Commissioner for Refugees, acts under the authority of applicable treaties or with the consent of some state to implement internationally approved policies. Indirectly, IGOs hold hearings on human rights cases, publish lists of violations and violators, and bargain behind the scenes to solve specific rights-related problems. For example, the states that are parties to the UN Covenant on Civil and Political Rights elect an expert committee to review state reports and hear private petitions (from people whose states have accepted an optional protocol to the Covenant accepting such action). This committee takes instructions neither from states nor other UN bodies, but reports to the UN General Assembly through the UN Economic and Social Council (ECOSOC). Since it was created in 1978, it has assertively promoted human rights while cooperating where possible with the states involved. Its members have questioned many states about their reports and policies and have referred troubling cases to higher UN bodies.[33]

In recent decades, human rights NGOs have mushroomed and become far more visible. Only 53 NGOs attended the 1968 Tehran Conference in their status as consultants to the UN's ECOSOC. For the 1993 Vienna Conference, 248 came as consultants and 593 were listed as conference participants. The increased numbers reflect more NGO participation from poor states and more representation of local interests and issues.[34] Amnesty International alone has a million members worldwide and claims to have supporters in 162 states and territories.[35]

But what do NGOs *do* to promote human rights? Their main concerns are to minimize torture, murder, and the forced disappearances of dissenters. To accomplish these goals, they engage in research and monitoring, grass-roots pressure and mobilization, direct lobbying at the governmental and intergovernmental level, observation of trials, visits to detention centers, and direct provision of goods and services to actors that need them.[36] NGOs are often more committed to collecting data on human rights conditions than are governments. They may also be able to act more credibly in interpreting and sharing that information, since private organizations have no foreign policy axe to grind.[37] For example, in May 2001, when the United States lost its seat on the UN's Geneva-based Human Rights Commission for the first time since 1947, Amnesty International called the action "part of an effort by nations that routinely violate human rights to escape scrutiny."[38] Except in Europe and the Americas, where fairly developed regional regimes exist, more human rights reporting is done by NGOs than by IGOs or governments.[39] In the 1960s and 1970s, Amnesty International was a pioneer in seeking out information about political prisoners. Today, many other NGOs are also involved. Taking advantage of the global wave of democratization, which has made many governments more supportive of human rights and less inclined to cover up past abuses, many of these groups are now trying to gather information about murder, torture, and other abuses perpetrated by authoritarian governments over the past few decades. The lowered costs of international communication in the electronic age have also helped NGOs to carry out this task. Hours after the first gunfire in the January 1994 Chiapas rebellion in southern Mexico, human rights activists had sent out many e-mail messages to interested parties. The resulting media attention and influx of NGO personnel into the area seems to have sharply limited the government's ability to respond coercively.[40]

NGO officials also engage in lobbying at the grass-roots, governmental, and intergovernmental levels. Amnesty International developed the tactic of intensive letter-writing campaigns on behalf of prisoners of conscience, directed at the captor government as well as others that were assumed to have influence on it. Along with other NGOs, Amnesty International has played a key role in keeping the spotlight on the growing problem of torture.[41] More recently, Physicians for Human Rights and Human Rights Watch helped initiate a global campaign to ban anti-personnel land mines, putting an issue on the international agenda that had not been there at all. Many governments were indifferent to the human costs of land mines, and the United States wanted no part of such a ban. The resulting treaty was perhaps the clearest victory in years for an NGO-assembled international coalition. In addition, NGOs have worked to establish an international criminal court and to end the use of children as soldiers.[42]

Like NGOs in other issue areas, human rights NGOs monitor state behavior and lobby government and IGO officials. Amnesty International and the International Commission of Jurists at times send observers to watch trials that are considered politically motivated. The hope is that their presence will deter miscarriages of justice and, if that fails, that information can be gathered for later use. Officials from the International Committee of the Red Cross (ICRC), which is known as the unofficial protector of international humanitarian norms, have observed trials, most often when the accused is a prisoner of war or otherwise falls under the provisions of the Geneva Conventions on War.[43] ICRC representatives also visit prisons and try to improve conditions. Only the ICRC has received widespread permission for systematic prison visits, in part because its direct concern is limited to prisoners' treatment, not the reasons for their detention.

Finally, NGOs focusing on humanitarian issues directly assist victims of war, genocide, and natural disasters. These groups have roots mainly in the wealthy states, which have the largest private, nonprofit sectors. More goods and services are transmitted by private U.S. humanitarian agencies than by the U.S. government. Still, the humanitarian disasters of the 1990s have taxed even these resources. The director of the U.S. Committee for Refugees argues that more could be done to help Rwandan officials reconstruct their country's broken judicial system, and more could be done to help them build jails to detain those accused of genocide.[44]

Domestic pressure groups are also actively involved in international controversies about human rights. They tend to be passionate about the issue, and their involvement can create political stakes and risks for officials. "Our clout comes from our linkage to public opinion," as one activist put it.[45] In recent years, the Christian right in the United States has mobilized support to protect foreign Christians from persecution and has argued in favor of mandatory economic sanctions against states that persecute religious minorities. The pressure on U.S. policy makers is strong; indeed, no other Western society lets its human rights policy be driven so much by domestic religious groups as does the United States.[46] China, for example, has been targeted by the U.S. religious right as an especially bad human rights offender for its harsh treatment of Christians who try to practice their religion. This example also illustrates how domestic-international linkages operate from the outside-in when it comes to human rights.

As this review suggests, the wide variety of domestic and international actors with a stake in human rights issues has two major effects on how human rights issues play out in world politics. First, the sheer number of the actors involved and the distinctiveness of the roles they play make it hard to ignore human rights issues and difficult to negotiate and implement human rights agreements. Second, the involvement of a wide range of state and non-state actors reinforces an essential dilemma of human rights issues: How does one square an international commitment to human rights with the principle of sovereignty?

12.2 ENDURING PATTERNS

The impact of risk-taking preferences

The higher the expected value people attach to an outcome, the higher the political risks they will be willing to run to achieve it.

The impact of discounting

The higher the expected value actors attach to achieving a specific policy outcome, the less their choices will be affected by discounting. The less control actors have over policy choice and implementation, the more actors will prefer future costs over current costs and the more they will value current benefits over future benefits.

The impact of linkage politics

World politics is driven by the interaction of international, factional, and constituency politics.

Taking Risks for Human Rights: NGOs, States, and IGOs

Reporting on human rights violations in authoritarian states and ones torn by political violence is dangerous. So, too, is providing humanitarian relief in countries such as Afghanistan or Somalia, which have seen long periods of civil war.

The prominence of NGOs in many of these dangerous human rights activities partly reflects the distinctive incentive structure produced by the politics of strategic choice. It's almost a truism to observe that the people who join human rights NGOs place a very high value on promoting human rights. While the sources of that commitment are often very personal, their high level of commitment makes participants both more willing to run political risks in pursuit of their objectives and more

willing to accept current costs to achieve future gains. Finally, the high degree of similarity in the values of people in human rights NGOs greatly simplifies the linkage politics in such organizations.

Policy makers in states and IGOs are almost always more conflicted than people in NGOs when their efforts to protect human rights collide with the norm of sovereign territoriality. IGOs and states also have to assemble far more complex and unstable coalitions—ones composed of policy factions and constituency groups with a far wider variety of preferences and values—before they can act in meaningful ways.

The Continuing Tension between Human Rights and State Sovereignty

Under norms that have prevailed since the seventeenth century, any outside scrutiny of the way in which a government treats its citizens can be viewed as an assault on the state's sovereignty. As we saw in earlier chapters, the Treaty of Westphalia gave European rulers complete control over their states' religious affairs. Over time, that deal evolved into the principle of *internal legal autonomy*. This principle holds that no outside entity can lawfully control what goes on inside a sovereign state; in other words, governments have a monopoly on public authority within their states' boundaries. Under traditional international law, these ideas meant that individuals and groups within states had no internationally recognized rights and duties. A ruler might treat his people humanely if, for example, he felt bound to do so by natural law, but he was under no explicit international obligation to do so. The Westphalian bargain meant that each ruler recognized the others' internal jurisdiction, in return for which his own was legitimized.

This bargain had both benefits and drawbacks. By ruling interference in other states' internal affairs out of bounds, it helped prevent one source of social instability. If state A can interfere with the right of officials in state B to govern B's own citizens, B's society may be destabilized. And because sovereignty oriented European diplomacy during the eighteenth and nineteenth centuries toward relations among states rather than toward the system of rule within them, small states were shielded from a certain amount of bullying at the hands of larger states on internal matters.

The Holocaust chipped away the absolutist view of sovereignty. Just as a growing concern about family violence has led governments to get more involved in matters that used to be the exclusive business of the head of the family, the unprecedented human rights crimes of the World War II era increased support for international scrutiny of states' human rights behavior.[47] In principle, every member of the United Nations has accepted human rights scrutiny. Even though the UN must refrain from intervening in matters that are "essentially within the domestic jurisdiction of any state" (Article 2, section 7 of the UN Charter), UN members pledge "universal respect for, and observance of, human rights and fundamental freedoms for all without distinction as to race, sex, language, or religion" (Article 55). If Article 55 is taken seriously, does it mean that individuals as well as states now have meaningful, internationally recognized rights? Acceptance of the UN Charter and the International Bill of Rights suggests the answer is yes—that, as Robert Jackson put it, "human beings have normative standing in international relations independent of their status as subjects or citizens of particular sovereign states."[48]

The unprecedented terror to which European Jews and many other victims were subjected during the Holocaust began to erode the absolute notion of sovereignty. For many people, these crimes were personified by Adolf Eichmann, who directed implementation of the Holocaust, a systematic plan that led to the murder of more than 6 million Jews. Shown here on trial in Jerusalem in 1961, Eichmann was convicted and executed the following year.

On this basis, it has been argued that systematic cruelty justifies outside action in response to states' internal behavior.[49] If this standard were applied systematically, the Westphalian bargain would be outmoded. But it is unlikely to be applied systematically anytime soon. States, not peoples or individuals, are members of the United Nations, and it is their governments to which IGOs answer. The drafters of the UN Charter rejected a provision that would have given the UN the authority to *protect* rather than just *promote* human rights. Aside from genocide, which is covered by a specific treaty, there is no legally accepted definition of what would constitute truly massive violations of human rights. Even in the case of genocide, there is no international enforcement mechanism, nor does the Genocide Convention discuss how the crime might be prevented.[50] Still, the absolutist view of sovereignty is more controversial than ever, which explains why human rights has become such a central issue in contemporary world politics.

The Strategic Context Today

Progress has been made over the last few decades in setting and monitoring international human rights standards, and the spread of democracy and market economies since the 1980s means that these norms face less opposition than before. Implementing these standards, however, often remains problematic. Many officials still resist outside scrutiny of their human rights behavior. Even in cases of shocking abuses, prevention and enforcement mechanisms remain weak, as indicated by three cases of genocide in the 1990s: two in the Balkans, one in Rwanda. In this section, we first survey the changing strategic context for human rights issues, focusing on the growth of trans-state standards, increasing global scrutiny, the growing role of NGOs and IGOs, and continuing problems with implementation. We then examine the two most widely discussed contemporary issues: establishing accountability for past abuses by members of authoritarian regimes and dealing with crimes against humanity.

Today, more states are more open than ever before to dissent, international oversight of their internal practices, and at least the promise that they will protect basic human rights. Three overlapping developments have produced these results. The end of the Cold War erased major ideological and political disagreements about human rights, and the wave of democratization that began in the 1980s reinforced these developments. The revolution in communication technologies and globalization also helped knock down some barriers that once shielded states and trans-state business enterprises from human rights scrutiny. But the cultural rifts and socioeconomic problems that hold back progress on human rights have not disappeared. The glass is half-full or half-empty, depending on which part of the picture seems more important.

The end of the East-West competition and the collapse of most Marxist governments has softened somewhat the dispute about individual as opposed to collective rights. For example, the 1993 Vienna Declaration on Human Rights embraces economic, social, and cultural rights, the right to development, the rights of refugees and internally displaced persons, the rights of minorities, and the rights of women, as well as the traditional list of civil and political rights that protect individuals. Paragraph 4 of the Declaration states that "the promotion and protection of *all* human rights is a legitimate concern of the international community." Paragraph 5 states: "All human rights are universal, indivisible and interdependent, and interrelated."

This implies, for example, that free speech and a free press may help in the fight against hunger, just as much as an adequately fed and housed population can lay the basis for a more pluralistic, tolerant community. Paragraph 8 identifies democracy, development, and a respect for fundamental [civil and political] freedoms as mutually reinforcing.[51] At least at the level of rhetoric, these provisions suggest that ideological arguments about rights are narrowing. During the Cold War, the idea that democracy and basic human rights are mutually reinforcing was much more controversial.

If this idea is correct, we would expect to see human rights records improve as states democratize. This has happened in some places. In Asia, progress toward political liberalization in South Korea, Taiwan, and Indonesia has led to the installation of governments with far greater respect for human rights. In Europe, few governments still claim that human rights violations are entirely a matter of domestic jurisdiction. Now that the former East-bloc states in Central and Eastern Europe have joined the European Human Rights Convention, the European Court of Human Rights could effectively become the constitutional court of Europe as a whole.[52] Africa and Latin America present more complex human rights pictures. In Africa, formal democratic procedures—political parties, elections, and various news media—have become common. But elections are often fraudulent, and incumbents often harass or imprison opponents and try to silence public protests. In Latin America, multiparty democracies now exist in most states, though the inability of the police and courts to control crime in many places has led to an increase in police brutality and limited defendants' rights.[53]

How can we make sense of this complex data? Jack Donnelly distinguishes between three levels of progress toward the protection of human rights. When a state "liberalizes," abuses decline and at least some previously excluded groups are allowed to participate in political life. A second stage, "democratization," involves universal suffrage, governments that are in fact (not just in name) responsive to the public, and truly competitive politics. A "rights-protective" government goes further; it makes the protection of all rights guaranteed in the International Bill of Rights a central goal.[54] Only in relatively few states have rights-protective governments become the rule, and democratization is tenuous in many more. While quite a few states have liberalized and some have democratized over the past ten to fifteen years, the deeper culture of respect for human rights has yet to take root in many of them.

There are, however, some reasons to be cautiously optimistic. Political, economic, and technological changes have opened up the world considerably. As Thomas Friedman put it, we have gone from a world built around "division and walls" to one built around "integration and webs."[55] In a divided, walled-off world, human rights abusers had a convenient ideological rationale for denying citizens their rights and could often hide behind the walls to escape scrutiny. Neither device is as effective today, and outsiders' abilities to monitor internal conditions have also improved. As a result, human rights scrutiny by states, IGOs, and NGOs has become more penetrating and systematic.

Of course, globalization has not touched every society to the same extent. But it has made access to the world market economy on preferred terms, often in the form of EU or WTO membership, into a strong inducement for most political leaders, one that governments can, if they wish, use as leverage to improve applicants' human rights records. Finally, anyone with a computer and Internet access can now communicate easily with much of the rest of the world, particularly with NGOs that specialize in human rights. By chipping away at governments' ability to control information and communications, an integrated, "webbed" world could eventually have far-reaching implications for the way people are treated.

These changes have also made TSBEs fair game for human rights activists who want to stop what they see as the exploitation of labor. For example, TSBEs are under increasing pressure to justify cozy arrangements with abusive governments and their treatment of workers in poor countries. Firms used to ignore such criticism with the claim that they were not political actors. But the effective economic sanctions against South African apartheid in the 1980s forced many firms to leave that country and showed that they can be vulnerable to public pressure on human rights. More recently, Texaco, Amoco, Levi Strauss, Eddie Bauer, PepsiCo, and Liz Claiborne left Myanmar after harsh criticism of their willingness to do business with such a repressive government. After similar criticism, Reebok pledged not to use child labor or forced labor, and for the past decade has made annual awards to human rights campaigners. Royal Dutch Shell, stung by criticism for doing business with Nigeria's military government, responded by consulting with human rights and church groups, and they later published a set of business principles that mentioned human rights for the first time. Shell's spokesman cautioned that "we're business people, not experts on human rights." TSBEs have tried to win acceptance of industry-wide codes of human rights conduct so that particular firms will not be placed at a competitive disadvantage for good behavior on this issue. But widespread public concern in the wealthy countries about sweatshop conditions and infringements of political and civil rights have made the issue a sensitive one for firms, and one not likely to disappear.[56]

Alongside these developments, the UN-based human rights regime has been strengthened. During the Cold War, the Human Rights Commission operated in secret, at the insistence of states anxious to preserve their internal autonomy and avoid embarrassment. Its annual meetings are now public, and states with poor human rights records come in for strong criticism. Efforts by China and other targets to tone down the criticism suggest that the targets take it seriously. To improve its battered human rights reputation, China signed the Covenant on Civil and Political Rights in 1998. As happened to the Soviet Union after the Helsinki Accords, this commitment gives outsiders and domestic activists a standard by which to measure the Chinese government's behavior and some leverage to demand changes.[57] The Commission also appoints experts to report on problem areas such as torture, extrajudicial executions, arbitrary detentions, and religious intolerance, as well as conditions in specific states. These experts operate independently of governments and by the UN's authority. Their annual reports to the Commission keep a spotlight on serious issues and on uncooperative governments.

IGO scrutiny may be particularly useful to other actors who are trying to stop human rights abuses. As one of the Human Rights Commission's outside experts put it, "It's not the UN that can change things directly. It's groups in the country itself. International monitoring gives these forces, both non-governmental and within government, some support."[58] Likewise, the Commission's public hearings give NGOs access to the governments being investigated they might not otherwise have. The tough questions posed by Commission members at these hearings often come from NGO-supplied information.[59]

Unfortunately, this pressure is unlikely to be effective against actors that are indifferent or hostile to human rights. Turkish leaders facing what they consider a terrorist Kurdish secessionist movement freely use torture against their prisoners.

Saddam Hussein would almost surely massacre his Shiite minority population were it not for the no-fly zone imposed by Western aircraft. China, Myanmar, and many other states routinely jail political dissidents. Mass killings, torture, or forced disappearances have also occurred in recent years in Rwanda, Bosnia, Haiti, Liberia, and Cambodia.

As this discussion of the contemporary strategic context suggests, policy makers in both state and non-state actors face major challenges in promoting human rights. We turn next to an examination of attempts to implement human rights standards through multilateral regimes and foreign policy.

Human Rights Regimes in Action

Setting and Monitoring Multilateral Standards

Multilateral human rights regimes exist at two levels in contemporary world politics: a global regime based on United Nations declarations, and additional regimes in a few geographic regions. Both the global and regional regimes reflect the principle that states' conduct toward their people should promote and protect human dignity. Unlike international regimes in other issue areas, there is no implicit or explicit assumption of reciprocity in behavior. States are pledged to uphold these principles regardless of what the other parties do.

The norms of the UN-based regime are found in the human rights statements and treaties accepted by states: the International Bill of Rights and the Conventions on Prevention of Genocide, Elimination of Racial Discrimination, and so on. Their provisions are implemented under the auspices of the UN Human Rights Commission and the Human Rights Committee. The Human Rights Commission has played a key role in regime development and can investigate confidentially complaints of systematic human rights violations. The Human Rights Committee consists of eighteen experts who supervise the implementation of the International Covenant on Civil and Political Rights by reviewing periodic reports from states on their compliance with its provisions.

Despite success in setting human rights standards, when it comes to enforcement the UN-based regime is very weak. Before a situation can even get to the full UN Commission, it must go through three levels of preliminary scrutiny. Once it gets to the full Commission, the process is slow, since the body meets just once a year. These delays make it hard to bring the full procedures into operation sooner than two years after a complaint is received. Cooperation with the Human Rights Committee is entirely voluntary. Nothing requires a state whose record is being reviewed to answer any particular questions or provide any specific information, and states may take years to respond. Zaire's initial report was due in 1978 and was not delivered until 1987. The Committee's mandate, moreover, is limited to the states that have become parties to the Covenant. These loopholes help us understand why the regime failed to prevent the ethnic cleansing of the 1990s. UN organs can do almost nothing directly to change state behavior since violators have no fear of real penalties.[60] This weakness does not, however, mean that the regime lacks any value, since negative publicity may induce policy makers to curb some human rights abuses.

If states have the option of joining a global regime, what is the rationale for separate, regionally based regimes? The UN Charter notes that states can use regional mechanisms to carry out UN principles (Article 52) and that the Security Council may do so as well (Article 53). Regional arrangements are useful when the states in some region have stronger shared purposes or a sense of common legitimacy than the international community as a whole. This is now true in Western Europe, and it may be true some day in Latin America and Africa.

The twenty-three (mainly Western European) states that constitute the Council of Europe belong to the strongest human rights regime in the world. Acting on the basis of a 1949 human rights convention, the European Court of Human Rights, the regime's supreme judicial body, reviews complaints that come directly from individuals. Since the late 1980s, it has assumed a steadily more prominent role within the European Union (see Table 12–2). Although the Court has no way to enforce its decisions directly, no European government has openly defied a ruling. Bad human rights performers are typically shunned by other regime members; Spain and Portugal were kept out of the Council of Europe until they shed their fascist governments, and Turkey and Greece have been suspended during periods of military rule. Under a 1987 treaty dealing with torture and degrading punishment, a special committee is authorized to visit any place within the territory of any party to that treaty where even one person might be detained. Nowhere else are such intrusive

TABLE 12–2	**NUMBER OF INDIVIDUAL APPLICATIONS LODGED WITH THE EUROPEAN COURT OF HUMAN RIGHTS**					
Year	Provisional Files	Applications Registered	Decisions Taken	Applications Declared Inadmissible or Struck off the List	Applications Declared Admissible	Decisions to Reject in the Course of the Examination of the Merits	Judgments Delivered by the Court
1955–1982	22158	10210	9458	9251	297	8	61
1983	3150	499	436	407	29	0	15
1984	3007	586	582	528	54	0	18
1985	2831	596	582	512	70	0	11
1986	2869	706	511	469	42	0	17
1987	3675	860	590	559	31	0	32
1988	4108	1009	654	602	52	0	26
1989	4900	1445	1338	1243	95	0	25
1990	4942	1657	1216	1065	151	0	30
1991	5550	1648	1659	1441	217	1	72
1992	5875	1861	1704	1515	189	0	81
1993	9323	2037	1765	1547	218	1	60
1994	9968	2944	2372	1789	582	1	50
1995	10201	3481	2990	2182	807	0	56
1996	12143	4758	3400	2776	624	0	72
1997	12469	4750	3777	3073	703	1	106
1998	16353	5981	4420	3658	762	0	105
1999	20399	8396	4250	3519	731	0	177
TOTAL	153921	53424	41794	36136	5654	12	1014

Source: European Court of Human Rights, *Survey of Activities, 1999* (Strasbourg: Council of Europe, 1999), p. 50.

human rights inspections accepted. The strong sense of shared values that makes such a regime possible is illustrated by the regime's impact on national political reforms. New constitutions in Spain, Portugal, and Greece were written to conform with the regime's standards, and rulings of the European Court have prompted changes in domestic legislation in such states as Britain, France, Germany, Ireland, and Austria.[61]

The regional regimes in Latin America and Africa are considerably weaker. The Inter-American Court of Human Rights has decided only two cases. The Inter-American Commission of Human Rights, similar in authority to the comparable UN body, receives about five hundred complaints a year. Although its decisions are usually ignored, the Commission has performed an important monitoring function. Its series of reports in the 1970s and 1980s on the repressive situation in Chile helped to launch and energize the international campaign against the Pinochet government. Argentina and Chile devoted a lot of diplomatic effort in the 1970s and 1980s to avoid this public criticism. The African regime is even more impotent. An eleven-member Commission on Human and People's Rights is limited to discussing general situations of rights abuses, rather than specific cases, and even then can do so in depth only when the Organization of African Unity (OAU) approves such an investigation through its Assembly of Heads of State and Government.[62]

Clearly, the level of commitment to multilateral human rights norms depends on the underlying societal support for such values. The European regime, whose members share a culture strongly influenced by liberalism, is much stronger than the global one; the Latin American regime is about as strong as the global regime; and the African one is much weaker. There are, moreover, no regional regimes in Asia or the Middle East. Common experience in a human rights regime may deepen the social values the regime tries to foster, but it cannot create those values from scratch.

Human Rights and Foreign Policy

As we've seen, implementation of human rights norms—even when those norms involve multilateral regimes—ultimately requires the actions of states. This fact often leads to a foreign policy question: How much weight, if any, should a state place on helping foreign nationals whose rights are violated by their governments? The question is difficult even when leaders or citizens care about the issue.

There are two reasons a government might pursue an active human rights policy. First, a political leader's moral beliefs may push him or her to do so. If people feel strongly that preventable injustices are occurring, they may want to speak out or take direct action, whether the targets of that criticism like it or not. As president, Jimmy Carter chose to criticize openly the human rights policies of several governments allied to the United States. He paid for this choice with criticism in return—from domestic U.S. constituencies friendly to those governments as well as those governments themselves. On the other hand, many lives might have been saved if people had taken action in the early stages of the Holocaust or the ethnic cleansing that occurred in the Balkans during the 1990s.

Second, a foreign policy that takes normative considerations seriously may please important domestic constituencies. As Henry Kissinger put it, "a nation will evaluate a policy in terms of its domestic legitimization, because it has no other standard of judgment."[63] Americans cite the Declaration of Independence and the Bill of Rights to claim that rights such as free speech and free press are self-evident everywhere.

12.3 ENDURING PATTERNS

The impact of varying beliefs about just relationships

If people value creating and sustaining legitimate relationships and *if they think a political process and the outcome it produces are just, they are more likely to accept that outcome, even if they would have preferred something else.*

The effect of the shadow of the future

The more compatible people expect their preferences to become over time, the more cooperative and less power-based their strategic choices are likely to be.

The impact of linkage politics

World politics is driven by the interaction of international, factional, and constituency politics.

The European Court of Human Rights and the Inter-American Court of Human Rights

The Council of Europe has the most effective contemporary multilateral human rights regime. Between 1955 and 1999, the European Court of Human Rights delivered 1014 judgments. Its effectiveness reflects the value key European actors and their constituents attach to human rights and, perhaps even more significantly, their widely shared understanding of the nature of legitimate relationships. The fact that many Europeans expect their preferences to become even more compatible over time decreases the strategic value of stressing the ability—the power—to oppose trans-national norms. Finally, both of these considerations simplify the linkage politics issues associated with facilitating the work of trans-state human rights institutions.

Latin American human rights regimes exist in a far less supportive environment. As a result, the Inter-American Court of Human Rights has decided only two cases.

A policy that promotes such rights tends to have a built-in reservoir of U.S. public support. However, many groups within the United States that support the export of U.S. human rights values are simultaneously suspicious of multilateral institutions, regarding them as a potential threat to U.S. sovereignty. The domestic incentives are far simpler for policy makers in states such as the Scandinavian countries, which base more of their foreign policy on working within international regimes. Their human rights policy builds upon domestic support for multilateralism as a broad foreign policy strategy.

While these motivations can produce incentives for foreign policy makers to promote human rights—and there are some examples of significant accomplishments, such as the international effort to end apartheid in South Africa—foreign policy makers also often have strong incentives not to make human rights promotion a key objective. Unlike NGOs, states have many competing goals—often too many to take on any single goal in a completely consistent way. Human rights

C A S E   S T U D Y

Human Rights and Trade in U.S. Policy toward China

The Clinton administration came into office in 1991 promising there would be no "business as usual" with authoritarian regimes that violated basic human rights. If that meant using trade as a lever to coerce compliance, the administration promised to do it—even in cases as difficult and politically sensitive as U.S. trade with China.

However, as the case at **www.prenhall.com/lamborn** shows, the administration dramatically reversed course in May 1994 and, in October 2000, President Clinton signed legislation granting China permanent normal trading relations. Look for how this case exemplifies the four distinctive features of human rights issues: the impact of conflicting interpretations of legitimacy; the complications created by cultural and political diversity; the involvement of a wide variety of state and non-state actors; and the tension between the desire to promote human rights and the continuing claims of state sovereignty. Ask yourself one of the key questions that dominated the debates in the United States: Are we more likely to change human rights practices by becoming engaged in a country (often called *constructive engagement*) or by using a "carrots-and-sticks" approach to entice cooperation?

NGOs can afford to be single-minded in trying to free political prisoners because, unlike many states, they do not have security or trade stakes in the target state.

Since few states have the luxury to pursue human rights issues single-mindedly, three problems tend to affect the incentives of foreign policy makers interested in human rights. First, their efforts to change the behavior of other states are likely to fail. Policy makers that want to curb human rights abuses in another state tend to find that they have few usable tools. For reasons we've noted, normative arguments focused directly on the offense tend to fall on deaf ears in the target government. Because any policy tool except moral argument is not clearly tied to the abuses, such instruments may appear illegitimate to third parties as well as the target state.[64] No matter what other tool is used, the effect is often just to escalate the dispute. As we have emphasized, political leaders usually view human rights criticism as a challenge to their internal position and sovereignty. It is almost always resisted and may, for that reason, lead to harsher treatment for dissidents. The few cases in which pressure has worked should not, in this view, cloud the many in which it had little effect or even a negative result.

A second problem is related to the first. Public criticism of the way another state treats its people tends to "raise international emotional temperatures" and makes it harder to cooperate with that state on other issues.[65] The case study of U.S.-Chinese relations bears out this point. President Clinton gave up an effort to use trade as a lever on China's human rights behavior because Washington also had important security concerns at stake in its relationship with Beijing. The implication is that to get along with others, one must avoid criticizing them on sensitive issues, especially when very different standards of legitimacy are involved.

A third problem grows out of the first two. Because it is difficult to change other states' human rights behavior, states' actions tend to be inconsistent across cases.

They often single out small or isolated states and avoid those with which they have more to lose. For example, it is easier for the United States to single out such targets as Myanmar than to exert pressure on China. Vice President Al Gore thus promised, if elected president, to promote human rights values when the price is low, but to be tactful when dealing with countries that can damage American interests.[66] Although it is hard to achieve, consistency on this issue is important. It helps to build international legitimacy and makes the targets of human rights criticism less able to characterize it as unbalanced.

What might one expect foreign policy makers to do when there are good reasons to act and not act? If policy makers care about human rights, they could work to strengthen multilateral mechanisms that might reduce their need to rely on bilateral diplomacy. When states confront each other directly over human rights, their prestige tends to become directly engaged, and the substance of the issue tends to receive less emphasis.[67] Global mechanisms that apply uniform standards would lessen this problem. But as we saw, the strongest multilateral regimes contain states that already share common human rights values, something not found globally. So as more societies democratize, it might be possible to move toward more uniform standards, thus reducing the need to rely on bilateral measures.

In the meantime, two notable problems are on the human rights agenda. One involves coming to terms with the past abuses of authoritarian regimes in a way that promotes reconciliation. A second involves strengthening or creating international mechanisms for dealing with the most serious human rights abuses. The 1990s saw some of the worst genocide the world has witnessed since World War II; ensuring that the guilty are punished and future such incidents are dealt with is a major problem.

Two Prominent Issues on the Human Rights Agenda

Establishing Accountability for Past Abuses by Authoritarian Regimes

Over the past two decades, a number of societies have begun difficult and often painful transitions from authoritarianism to democracy. The phenomenon has been worldwide in scope. Much of Latin America and East-Central Europe has been involved, along with parts of East Asia and Africa. The pain involves coming to terms with tremendous crimes perpetrated within one's own society. Just as Germans had to accept responsibility for perpetrating the Holocaust, Russians, Afrikaners (White South Africans descended from Dutch settlers), and Argentines, among many others, have had to acknowledge that their governments committed terrible abuses, including murder, unlawful or arbitrary detention, forced disappearances, pervasive racial discrimination, and denial of many other human rights. Societies in these situations face a dilemma. Coming to terms with the abuses requires that perpetrators be identified and publicly held accountable. Doing this requires carefully unearthing the relevant facts, most of which were buried long ago. Yet too long or deep a search may inflame old wounds, turn the perpetrators of yesterday's injustices into today's martyrs, and defeat the purpose. Finding a just and workable solution to this dilemma is one of today's major human rights problems.

A just solution matters because how accountability is established sets much of the public tone for the new democratic institutions. Consider the example set by the

Bishop Desmond Tutu became famous throughout the world for his opposition to South Africa's system of racial segregation, known as apartheid. After majority rule was instituted in the early 1990s, he favored a policy of reconciling whites and blacks.

retribution   The principle that wrongdoers should suffer in proportion to the suffering they have caused others.

restoration   The principle that the primary response to human rights abuses should be an effort to achieve social peace through material and nonmaterial compensation that "makes victims whole."

Czech Republic. A parliamentary commission was charged with exposing the identities of those who served as informants for the former communist government. Estimates of the number of people involved run as high as 150,000. Although democratization has succeeded in many other respects, the commission has not even tried to ensure that the accused receive due process. Instead, people are denounced and presumed guilty without being able to see the evidence against them. These procedures are defended in two ways: Those who helped the old regime should taste some of their own medicine, it is argued; and any chance of a communist resurgence, which would presumably draw largely on people who worked for the communist government, must be squelched.[68] But these procedures lead to two problems. They could turn former informants into martyrs, especially if those individuals had been coerced into disclosing such information to the authorities. It also sets a precedent that the ends justify the means. Democratic institutions can operate undemocratically if people demand certain outcomes loudly enough. There is no procedural legitimacy in such a solution, and democracies depend on a perception that their procedures are legitimate.

How then can procedural legitimacy be established? Philosophers, theologians, and legal theorists who have pondered the issue of just punishment note the tension between two core principles, retribution and restoration. **Retribution** focuses on establishing personal responsibility for wrongdoing and implies that the punishment should fit the crime; wrongdoers should suffer in proportion to the suffering they have caused others. Seen through this lens, any other penalty is held to be unjust, since only retribution makes the offender(s) "pay." **Restoration** focuses on healing. Instead of trying to settle scores by punishing the guilty, it asks how social peace can best be restored. To achieve this end, it emphasizes "making victims whole" through various forms of material or nonmaterial compensation, not on making the guilty suffer as an end in itself.[69]

South Africa has become a modern laboratory for restorative justice in the form of the South African Truth and Reconciliation Commission (SATRC). It is designed to come to grips with the bitter legacy of apartheid, which was systematically applied between 1948, when the white-minority Afrikaner government took power, and 1994, when that system of rule was finally dismantled and everyone was given the franchise. The idea behind the SATRC is that accountability without vengeance can lead to forgiveness for wrongdoing, producing social peace between the black majority and the whites that have remained in the country. Bishop Desmond Tutu finds the rationale for restorative justice in the African concept of *ubuntu:*

> *Ubuntu* says I am human only because you are human. If I undermine your humanity I dehumanize myself. You must do what you can to maintain this great harmony, which is perpetually undermined by resentment, anger, [and a] desire for vengeance. That's why African jurisprudence [legal theory] is restorative rather than retributive.[70]

Even before the SATRC began taking testimony in April 1996, 2,700 people had asked for amnesty. Under the rules, perpetrators would confess and then be pardoned; victims would tell their stories of abuse, perhaps receive modest reparations, and then forgive the perpetrators.[71] No blanket amnesty for all human rights offenders was planned. Amnesty was explicitly refused to those who committed the worst crimes, and those who did not come forward to confess were subject to normal prosecution by the regular courts. Still, the overriding idea was forgiveness as a route to reconciliation. Some who have opposed this idea argue that it actually works against social healing. Because it denies what they call the "human need for justice and retribution," they claim that it fosters frustration and resentment that the guilty have escaped too easily.[72]

The SATRC seems gradually to have produced the kind of disclosures that were desired. For example, in May 1999, three years after the hearings began, Eugene de Kock described the methods of a counter-terrorism unit he headed from 1985 to 1993. During that period, the unit was responsible for kidnapping, torturing, and killing at least seventy anti-apartheid guerrillas. The purpose of de Kock's testimony was, of course, amnesty. But his testimony strongly suggested that the unit acted on orders of the highest political authorities—President P. W. Botha and Botha's successor, F. W. de Klerk. Both men denied the charges, though significant evidence indicates their culpability.[73] When the SATRC began its hearings it was feared that only low-level operatives would come forward and confess, and that high-level leaders would never be tied to specific crimes. The "truth," in other words, might remain hidden. But that has not happened, even if those ultimately responsible at the time have not admitted guilt. The past has been exposed.

The results have convinced some who initially were skeptical about non-retributive justice. One foreign observer changed his mind because "South Africa has gained far more than it lost by pardoning its demons. The truth has proved a potent antidote to revenge."[74] In any case, reconciliation seems to have been necessary to move beyond white-minority rule peacefully and decisively. South Africa's interim constitution, which paved the way for black-majority rule, was essentially a peace treaty. In return for a peaceful end to apartheid, it promised the conditional amnesty. This was why Bishop Tutu and Nelson Mandela, the anti-apartheid hero who became the first president of the new South Africa, made forgiveness a matter of patriotic duty.[75]

Could a similar approach work elsewhere? It may be that the conditions in South Africa in the early 1990s won't be found in many other places. At that time, the white-minority government still held power, and whites had to be induced to surrender it peacefully. Tutu's use of *ubuntu* to legitimize the bargain was thus critical. By contrast, the Latin American democratic transitions of the 1980s and 1990s were largely made without directly confronting the issue of accountability for human rights abuses. Chile's Pinochet claims immunity for any acts he committed as president and has never apologized for anything. In Argentina, a comprehensive and generous policy of monetary compensation has been available to the victims and victims' families who suffered from the tortures and disappearances that took place in the 1970s. But families are told little about what is known of their loved ones' fates, and the military and security forces have never been forced to account for their crimes.[76] Similarly, when Hugo Banzer was overthrown as Bolivian leader in 1978, the kidnapping, torturing, and killing that his government apparently coordinated with Pinochet were swept under the rug. Banzer was elected democratically as Bolivia's president in 1997. When Pinochet was arrested in London in 1998, human rights activists, journalists, and even some members of Banzer's own governing coalition began charging him with complicity in thirty-six deaths. Now his presidency's legitimacy is seriously undermined, and Bolivians, like Chileans, must suddenly come to grips with a past they have tried to repress.[77]

The lesson might be that transitions from authoritarian to democratic rule are especially fragile when systematic human rights abuses have been committed.

Nevertheless, full disclosure and conditional amnesty might work *if* they are both pursued openly during and after the transition. Delay risks an outcome such as Bolivia's or Argentina's. If these issues are handled properly, it would seem to facilitate the transition from authoritarianism. If they are mishandled or ignored, dealing with the unfinished business later is likely to be especially difficult.

Dealing with Crimes against Humanity

Also on today's human rights agenda is the question of how to deal with **crimes against humanity**, which include systematic murder, torture, rape, forced resettlement, and enslavement. Under international law, as reaffirmed in the Nuremberg and Tokyo trials after World War II, crimes against humanity are subject to **universal jurisdiction**, which means that any state can try a person charged with them.* On this basis, Pinochet was detained in Britain, pending the outcome of the extradition requests; the ruling held that the Spanish allegations constituted crimes against humanity. Despite the progress in identifying internationally recognized human rights norms since World War II, no permanent international mechanism exists to try those charged with crimes against humanity.

Why is such a mechanism needed if jurisdiction for these crimes is universal? Few states exercise their legal right to try these cases. Doing so requires major investments of time, money, and diplomatic as well as political capital. When crimes have been committed in another state, even obtaining the evidence needed to mount an effective case may be too large a job for any one country. We saw that there are good reasons for states to avoid pressing human rights concerns as a foreign policy goal; to try or even hold a foreigner for crimes committed elsewhere brings on further costs and risks. In principle, nearly everyone wants to see justice done, but few will pay the costs. Crimes against humanity thus require an international institution that can help solve the problems of applying uniform standards, obtaining and sharing the necessary information, and enforcing the verdicts.

These longstanding problems were brought vividly to life by many wars during the 1990s. As we saw in Chapter 8, over the last decade ethnic conflict has become more widespread and barbaric. Civilians have often been the primary target, in many cases because the aggressors wanted their land or have been taught that their victims were inferior to them. The conflicts between ethnic Serbs and Bosnian Muslims, Serbs and Albanian Kosovars, and Hutus and Tutsis in Rwanda have been particularly vicious. In these cases and others, civilians were murdered, raped, tortured, and forced from their homes. In the Balkans, 750,000 Bosnian Muslims were driven from their homes in 1992, and one million ethnic Albanians were expelled from Kosovo during just a few weeks in 1999.[78] In just three months, 500,000 Tutsis were killed in Rwanda.

Although very little was done during these wars to stop the crimes, several efforts were later made to bring the perpetrators to justice. The UN Security Council established the International Criminal Tribunal for the Former Yugoslavia in 1993, and in 1994 it set up a second tribunal to try those responsible for the genocide in Rwanda. By mid-2001, the Yugoslav tribunal had initiated trials in twenty-six cases,

crimes against humanity
Human rights abuses that are so extreme that they are regarded as a crime against all the people in the world.

universal jurisdiction
Crimes that may be investigated and prosecuted by any state.

---

*Air and sea piracy are also in this category.

Accountability for Human Rights Abuses in Authoritarian Regimes: The Pinochet Case

Augusto Pinochet Ugarte . . . appears to be one of the main [persons] responsible . . . [for] creating an international organization that conceived, developed, and carried out a systematic plan of illegal detentions (abductions), tortures, forcible transfers of persons, murders, and/or disappearances of many people, including citizens from Argentina, Spain, the United Kingdom, the United States, Chile, and other countries. These actions were carried out in different countries in order to . . . exterminate the political opposition and many people, for ideological reasons.

From the second arrest warrant for Augusto Pinochet

In October 1998, a Spanish investigative magistrate named Baltasar Garzon indicted former Chilean president Augusto Pinochet for human rights abuses that occurred while he was president in the 1970s and 1980s. Garzon asked the Spanish government to request that Pinochet be extradited from Britain to stand trial in Spain. As you read the case at **www.prenhall.com/lamborn**, look for the legal principles Garzon used to make the case for the extradition and for the legal principles that guided the British debates on how to respond. With those principles before you, consider why this case may turn out to be a significant landmark in the evolution of international law.

Garzon's actions were enthusiastically supported by human rights groups, but the key states involved—Britain, Chile, and Spain—felt cross-pressured by the Pinochet case. Some of that cross-pressuring reflected the continuing tension between human rights principles and the principle of sovereign territoriality. Explore the ways this case reveals that tension. Also look for the distinctive mixes of international and domestic incentives that confronted policy makers in Britain, Spain, and Chile.

---

and thirty-eight people accused of war crimes were being held in detention awaiting disposition of their cases. International arrest warrants had been issued for another twelve people, including Slobodan Milosevic, the former president of Yugoslavia. Milosevic's apprehension in Spring 2001, accomplished with the help of the newly elected democratic government in Serbia, was considered a major achievement for the tribunal and for war-crimes accountability more generally.[79] In February 2001, three Bosnian Serbs were convicted of rape and sexual enslavement during the Bosnian War. This marked the first time a war crimes tribunal had ruled that rape was a crime against humanity.[80] As of May 2001, the International Criminal Tribunal for Rwanda had initiated action in forty-five cases. Eight of these cases resulted in sentences, though some were still at the stage of appeals.[81] One of these cases was especially noteworthy. In September 1998 the Rwandan prime minister at the time of the massacres became the first person in history to be sentenced for the internationally recognized crime of genocide.[82]

As important as these steps are, they remain ad hoc, which leads to two problems. Ad hoc tribunals require specific choices to activate, and there is no guarantee that

12.4 ENDURING PATTERNS

The impact of risk-taking preferences

The higher the expected value people attach to an outcome, the higher the political risks they will be willing to run to achieve it. People are less willing to run political risks in support of policy choices as their control over choice and implementation declines. However, as their control over choice and implementation declines, they become more indifferent to policy failure—as long as policy failure is not politically dangerous.

The impact of discounting

People generally prefer current benefits over future benefits and future costs over current costs. Moreover: The lower the expected value actors attach to achieving a specific policy outcome, the more their choices will be affected by discounting; the less control actors have over policy choice and implementation, the more actors will prefer future costs over current costs and the more they will value current benefits over future benefits.

The impact of linkage politics

World politics is driven by the interaction of international, factional, and constituency politics.

Yugoslavia Disintegrates: European and American Responses

Trying to protect victims of human rights abuse while the abusers are still powerful is dangerous and costly to the would-be protectors (though not, of course, to the victims). Those dangers and costs produce substantial short-term political risks, risks that are often greater than the value policy makers in states and IGOs attach to protecting human rights. The multilateral nature of trans-state coalitions makes running high political risks even less attractive.

When Yugoslavia disintegrated in the early 1990s, European governments got involved far sooner than the United States because the humanitarian issues were reinforced by greater security stakes and more supportive public opinion. The Clinton administration finally committed U.S. troops to humanitarian and peacekeeping efforts only when changing military conditions on the ground reduced the level of the threat to peacekeepers at the same time as continued media coverage of human rights atrocities dramatically increased the political risks of continued inaction.

---

those choices will be made in future cases. In both the Rwandan and Yugoslav cases, U.S. support for the tribunals was an effort to compensate for inaction while the crimes were underway.[83] Ad hoc tribunals also forfeit whatever deterrent effect a standing body would have on future conflicts. We cannot know how significant that effect would be, but it should not be discounted entirely. One message being sent by the Yugoslav and Rwandan indictments to people who commit crimes against humanity is "you can't hide." But it is a mixed message, since without a standing tribunal, the likelihood that universal jurisdiction will be exercised is highly unpredictable.

In 1999, Swiss lawyer Carla del Ponte was appointed chief prosecutor for the UN's war crimes tribunals on Yugoslavia and Rwanda. These tribunals vigorously upheld the principle that sovereignty cannot be used to shield people accused of war crimes and other crimes against humanity. Yet many human-rights activists and international lawyers believe that a permanent International Criminal Court is needed to further strengthen this precedent.

An initiative that would go beyond ad hoc procedures is the International Criminal Court (ICC), now awaiting ratification by sixty states before it can come into being. The ICC will be a standing body that can investigate and prosecute genocide, other crimes against humanity, and war crimes when state authorities fail to do so. A largely independent prosecutor will be able to investigate allegations of such crimes on the basis of information from victims and other reliable sources, without the requirement that a state or the UN Security Council approve the referral. The ICC statute attempts to bridge the tension between the principle of universal jurisdiction and the principle of state sovereignty. The discretion and powers of the prosecutor will be somewhat limited; some limits will be placed on the obligations of states to cooperate with the Court; and the Court must have its jurisdiction approved in specific cases, either from the state on whose territory the crimes were committed or the state in which the accused is a national. Even with these concessions to sovereignty, the statute outlines plans for a fairly strong institution. As of May 2001, 139 states had signed the Rome statute that would establish the ICC, though only thirty-two of the required sixty states had ratified it.

The United States is one of the states that so far has refused to approve the ICC statute. Although the United States publicly supported an ICC during the four-year period in which the statute was hammered out, fears that U.S. military personnel would be subject to unjustified indictment proved impossible to overcome. Despite its strong human rights rhetoric and support for the ad hoc Yugoslav and Rwandan tribunals, the Clinton administration opposed any court that could indict U.S. citizens without prior U.S. approval. The administration refused to change its position despite concessions in the statute on a number of key points. National security was written in as a legitimate reason to refuse cooperation with the court, superior military orders became a valid defense against prosecution, limits were imposed on the prosecutor's discretion, and two opportunities for states to appeal the court's jurisdiction were included.[84] Adamant opposition from the Pentagon and strong misgivings on Capitol Hill were apparently responsible for the U.S. stance, which put Washington alongside Iran, Iraq, China, Libya, Algeria, and Sudan in rejecting the ICC.[85]

Can the ICC succeed without the United States? Human rights activists say that its international support guarantees that it will come into existence. Pessimists argue that whether or not it formally exists, its effectiveness depends on widespread acceptance of universal jurisdiction. Without the United States on board, they say that cannot be achieved.[86] The optimists seem to have a better argument here. Washington's concern is that its citizens not be at any risk of prosecution. Unless the Pentagon abandons its own rules of conduct in war, which closely follow the key provisions of the several Geneva Conventions on Conduct in War, there would be little chance of an American soldier or pilot being indicted in any case.[87] Only if Washington were unhelpful to ICC officials in cases in which it its citizens were not parties would there then be a problem. In these cases, it is hard to see why any U.S. administration would frustrate the work of an institution that nearly every one of its allies strongly endorses if it had no direct stake in the outcome. The ICC would thus seem headed for eventual success, with or without the United States. American support is preferable, since it would increase the likelihood that the Court could get jurisdiction of those indicted, and that effective pressure might be put on holdouts to similarly comply with ICC operations. Such support might be obtained over time if the Court developed a set of working procedures in which U.S. officials could have confidence.

In sum, the idea that perpetrators of human rights abuses should be held responsible for their actions has gained a lot of ground in recent years. If the South African and ICC experiments succeed, important precedents will be set in this area. Still, it is up to key states to decide how much support they give to enforcing international human rights standards, either at home or in other states. Policy discretion has by no means been removed from human rights issues.

Conclusion

The notion that all people have rights just by virtue of their humanity is an old one in political thought but a fairly new and revolutionary one in political practice. It is certainly so in world politics. Not long ago, the idea that the British government would seriously consider carrying out a judge's order that a former Chilean president and current senator be detained and extradited to a third country for acts committed in Chile while he was president would have left observers dumbfounded. It is still a surprise as we enter the twenty-first century, though less so than it would have been even a few decades ago.

We need to be careful, however, not to exaggerate these changes. First, the definition and implementation of human rights is a controversial, high-stakes policy and political issue within and among states. Second, while the idea that outsiders can authoritatively challenge a state's internal behavior implicitly challenges the Westphalian bargain, we should not confuse the enhanced legitimacy of internal human rights monitoring or scrutiny with the ability to enforce global standards. World politics continues to be built around a state system, and it is states, not peoples or individuals, to which IGOs answer. We should not forget that the drafters of the UN Charter deliberately chose to give the organization authority only to "promote," not "protect," human rights. The idea that human rights have a universal basis does seem to be growing, especially where the most serious abuses are concerned. But that idea sits very uneasily alongside the sovereignty to which most states still cling, and major differences among cultures also limit agreement on truly universal human standards.

Key Terms

jus gentium
natural law
positive law

legal positivism
retribution
restoration

crimes against humanity
universal jurisdiction

To The Reader   A CHAPTER SUMMARY and QUESTIONS FOR REVIEW are available at **www.prenhall.com/lamborn**

CHAPTER 13

The Politics of International Environmental Issues

The earth's tropical forests are rapidly disappearing, and many of its animal species are vanishing along with them. These forests, located in equatorial Latin America, Africa, and Asia, cover between 6 and 7 percent of the Earth's land surface (an area the size of the lower 48 U.S. states). But they once were much larger. Scientific data suggests that tropical forests at one time covered between 12 and 16 percent of the Earth's land surface. Most of the destruction has occurred since 1950. According to a 1991 estimate by the Food and Agriculture Organization, .9 percent of the remaining tropical forests disappear each year (6.8 million acres annually). If current rates of tropical deforestation and forest degradation continue, scientists estimate that up to half of the animal species that once lived in these forests will be gone by the middle of the twenty-first century. This loss of species would be the largest extinction of life on Earth in *65 million years*.[1]

As a biological possibility, this is astonishing. But why do we discuss it in a world politics book? Just like security and economic problems, international environmental problems directly affect people's lives. For example, vanishing forests have an impact on people's livelihoods and physical well-being. Forests act as giant sponges, slowing down water that runs off from mountains to farmland or cities below. By slowing soil erosion, forests help to conserve productive soil. Forests also affect the Earth's climate; 50 to 80 percent of the moisture in the air above tropical forests comes from trees that move water up through their root systems and then evaporate it into the atmosphere as water vapor. When forested areas are destroyed, rainfall in those areas drops, causing soils to lose nutrients and eventually wash away. The result can be a sparse grassland on which nothing much will grow, or even a desert.[2]

Yet even if we grant that these are serious problems, are they *political* in nature? Not that long ago, few political leaders paid much attention to environmental issues, and when those issues did get on policy agendas, that tended to happen within individual societies. Before 1980, few world politics books mentioned the environment at all. But the pressures generated by a growing population and industrialization have moved environmental issues much higher on political and policy agendas across as well as within states. As this chapter shows, people often disrupt the natural environment, typically for economic reasons. Other people, including those who live in other states, may want to slow or halt such damage, some of which may affect them directly. In many cases, the actors agree neither about the extent of the environmental damage nor who should take responsibility for halting it. Furthermore, sharp North-South divisions about the outcomes and processes of the global economy tend to intensify these disputes. These factors have combined to create a highly politicized set of environmental issues in contemporary world politics.

This chapter begins by exploring how political and natural forces combine to create a distinctive type of world political problem. We introduce the five core environmental issues: air pollution, water pollution, desertification and deforestation, global warming, and biological diversity. We then examine the distinctive features of environmental controversies from the perspective of the politics of strategic choice. In this section, we look particularly at the incentives that push actors toward denial and delay in dealing with the environment. The political effects of these incentives are reinforced by the difficulty scientists have in identifying the important

When populations grow rapidly, problems such as waste disposal, air pollution, and insufficient water tend to worsen as well. As this photo of an apartment house in Ho Chi Minh City, Vietnam, suggests, in recent decades, several Third World cities have come close to bursting at the seams with people.

ecosystem A spatially bounded habitat within which plant and animal species interact with each other and with the chemical and physical processes that sustain life.

global commons The atmosphere and open-access areas that are shared by all states but possessed by none.

gross world product (GWP) The total value of goods and services produced worldwide.

thresholds in ecological processes. The discussion that follows explores how these distinctive political and scientific problems affect contemporary efforts to manage environmental problems through international regimes, population control, debt-for-nature swaps, and strategies for sustainable development.

When Nature and Politics Collide

Environmental issues emerge when people alter atmospheric, water, animal-life, or plant-life conditions in ways that are believed to cause harm. It wasn't long ago that the (mis)use of natural resources was regarded as a purely local concern. The long-term scientific and political implications of that (mis)use for regional and global **ecosystems** were not well understood. Recently, it has been recognized that environmental damage can cross borders, adversely affecting neighboring states and the **global commons,** open-access areas such as the oceans or Antarctica that are shared by all states but possessed by none. This recognition has led to the environment becoming an important issue in world politics.

The Impact of Population Growth and Rising Consumption

The underlying source of environmental problems has been the recent yet explosive growth in population and per capita consumption. In the year 1000, there were about 265 million people in the world—roughly the population of the present-day United States. By 1700, that number had grown to 615 million; by 1800 the world had 900 million people; by 1900, the number was 1.63 billion; by the mid-1960s, despite two world wars, the world's population had reached 3.33 billion. By 2000, it had passed 6 billion, and it is projected to be 10 billion by the middle of the twenty-first century. Consider what just one country, and that by no means the world's largest, can contribute to this growth. If Nigeria's population continues to grow at the present rate, it will exceed the present population of the entire world in just a little over a century. In a world of finite resources, problems that may have been tolerable with fewer people become much more serious with many people. While sanitation was poor during the Middle Ages, there were relatively few people at that time, and they consumed relatively little. As Michael Nicholson put it, it "did not much matter how much mess [people] made except very locally. Its impact was too small to make much difference."[3]

Stress on the world's environment increased when people began to consume more on average *as well as* multiply faster. Per capita **gross world product (GWP)**—the total value of goods and services produced worldwide divided by the world's population to measure average production per person—began to rise significantly during the nineteenth century as a result of the Industrial Revolution, and that growth has accelerated. While the world's population doubled between 1950 and 1987, per capita GWP doubled between 1950 and 1975.[4] More people produce more wear and tear on the Earth's water, air, and other natural resources, even if overall living standards—and thus per capita consumption—don't improve. But with people everywhere seeking higher living standards, consumption of the Earth's resources should continue to accelerate even faster than the growth in population. For example, if China's citizens (one of every six in the world) begin to use refrigerators, autos, and other manufactured goods at the current Western level, stress on the world's air quality and climate will dramatically increase.

Environmental Problems Become International Political Issues

By itself, environmental stress doesn't create a political issue. Actors must first view protection of the Earth as a human problem that can be addressed by humans. To make the environment an international political issue, people must also see how such problems are linked across states and believe that joint action is needed to solve them.

For most of history, the environment was not seen this way. Weather, water, and wildlife were seen as background conditions to be accepted, rather than as issues that humans could shape by their actions. Consequently, the damage that uncontrolled economic activity did to the natural environment received little attention. In recent decades opinion has shifted, as increases in the speed, diversity, and scale of human activities have begun visibly to damage the Earth. Through advances in scientific research, the causes of events such as the disappearance of animal species and global warming have become better understood. While there is much that science still can't tell us about the environment, and many actors often dismiss the available research if it is anything less than conclusive, the growth in environmental knowledge has helped to place these issues into forums where people can address them politically.[5]

The environment typically becomes a political issue in the presence of recognized negative **externalities** (sometimes called spillover effects). Externalities occur when firms or individuals impose involuntary costs or benefits on bystanders—that is, parties uninvolved in a particular behavior or transaction.[6] When you pay a barber for a haircut, only the two parties involved are affected by the transaction. But bystanders sometime become unintended parties to other people's activities, either positively or negatively. Some years ago, one of the authors of this book lived above a bakery. Six days a week he awoke to the smell of freshly baked breads and rolls. The wonderful aroma cost him nothing; it was a byproduct of the baker's daily routine. Now imagine living near an airport or a paper mill; the loud noise or unpleasant odor is an externally imposed cost. Or imagine living in Malaysia, Singapore, or Thailand and suffering from the air pollution caused by the burning of forests hundreds of miles away in Indonesia. These are all examples of externalities. The actors who produce these effects on bystanders don't calculate those costs unless their incentives are shaped by some type of regulation. Within societies, governments may choose to regulate harmful externalities. Many governments have restricted strip mining, the emission of pollutants into the air, lakes, and rivers, and the way hazardous wastes are handled. But such problems are harder to deal with politically across states.

Environmental issues did not appear on international agendas until the late 1960s. *Silent Spring*, a 1962 book by Rachel Carson, helped to launch the modern environmental movement by showing that the widespread use of pesticides would create health hazards. Carson's book was soon joined by other works that offered similar kinds of apocalyptic environmental warnings. They focused on the population explosion, the negative byproducts of industrialization, and the likely limits to industrial growth.[7] Out of these works and others like them, a concern about ecological carrying capacities was created. Several major accidents also focused public

externalities Involuntary costs and benefits imposed on people as the result of the actions (usually the provision of a good or service) of others.

attention on environmental issues. Smog in Britain in 1953 killed 3,000 people in one month and led the government to introduce a clean air act in 1956. Serious oil spills a few years later off the British and the U.S. coasts caused both governments to tighten rules governing the operation of oil tankers. The discovery of DDT in Antarctic penguins was an issue by the early 1970s. The 1985 chemical devastation of the Rhine River and the 1986 Chernobyl nuclear accident reinforced this growth of environmental awareness. As such problems attracted media coverage, environmental groups in developed countries put pressure on policy makers, demanding action. They began by focusing on national issues and remedies but came to believe that many of the problems were international in scope.[8]

The United Nations Conference on the Human Environment, convened in Stockholm in 1972, helped to define the environment as a world political issue in its own right. Up to that time, functional IGOs had been created to manage issues such as international trade, finance, security, health, and development, but none had been formed to deal with *acid rain* (the acid that forms in precipitation due to the emission of sulfur dioxide and nitrogen oxide wastes into the air), hazardous waste disposal, or resource conservation. The conferees at Stockholm changed that by launching the United Nations Environmental Program (UNEP), designed to stimulate international cooperation on these sorts of issues. UNEP was given few financial resources to achieve this goal. But it benefitted from having highly motivated policy entrepreneurs as leaders—such as Mustafa Tolba, who played a critical role in the development of the 1987 Montreal Ozone Protocol. Over time, UNEP became a forum and clearinghouse that gave environmental scientists, activists, and policy specialists a way to reinforce one another's concerns and their influence on ecological issues within their own countries. During the 1970s, many governments established ministries or departments to deal specifically with environmental issues. In 1972 only 26 states had such bureaus; a decade later, the number was 144.[9]

During the 1980s, the international environmental agenda grew, with increasing concern focusing on global environmental threats such as climate change, irreversible species loss, and large-scale desertification.[10] In the same decade, the many implications of these possible environmental threats began to be widely discussed in terms of sustainable development. As presented in *Our Common Future*, the 1987 Report of the World Commission on Environment and Development (known as the Brundtland Report for the commission chair, Norwegian Prime Minister Gro Harlem Brundtland), **sustainable development** calls for promoting forms of economic development that are compatible with future as well as present needs. At the time, this approach marked a key shift in people's thinking about the relationship between economics and ecology. Until the 1980s relatively few people argued that economic development had to accommodate environmental limits. The Brundtland Report began a discussion of these issues that continues to this day. It gained credibility in the eyes of many people because it appeared around the time that a hole in the atmospheric ozone layer had been found and global warming was emerging as a serious problem.

The impact of growing concern about sustainable development on the prominence of international environmental issues in the 1980s was reinforced by the 1986 explosion of the Chernobyl nuclear reactor in the Ukraine, which spread radioactive fallout across Europe. Atmospheric radiation levels in Finland rose to ten times their normal amounts; in Paris, the level of radioactive fallout ten days after the accident was as high as it had been during the most intense phase of nuclear-weapons testing

sustainable development
Organizing economic activity to promote economic growth and protect the environment; emphasizes the importance of identifying and respecting environmental limits.

When environmental accidents occur, the damage to air, water, and soil spreads without regard to state boundaries. The explosion of the Soviet nuclear reactor at Chernobyl in 1986 increased atmospheric radiation levels as far west as Sweden, Italy, and France. In an effort to slow the contamination, helicopters were called in to drop 5,000 tons of material on the reactor.

in 1963.[11] Yet neither Soviet nor Russian authorities ever took responsibility for the damage.*

Five Core Issues

Air Pollution   Before the Industrial Revolution, fresh air was essentially a free good almost everywhere. Air pollution—the presence of chemicals in the atmosphere that harm living things and other materials—has changed that. Most pollutants enter the atmosphere through the burning of fossil fuels by factories and power plants and from motor vehicles. In cities such as Mexico City and Sao Paulo, motor vehicles cause 80 percent or more of the air pollution. According to the World Health Organization, at least 1.1 billion people live in cities in which the air is unhealthy. In addition to hurting humans, air pollution damages streams, takes nutrients from the soil, and endangers wildlife.[12] In the rich countries, national and regional rules now restrict the type of motor fuels that can be used, the efficiency with which motor vehicles must use them, and the industrial waste that can be emitted into the air. But such rules are often weak or absent in poor states, many of which are industrializing with obsolete technologies little cleaner than those used by the rich states a few generations ago.

---

*Under international law, governments are obligated to take adequate steps to control sources of pollution that cause damage across state boundaries. This rule is based largely on the *Trail Smelter* arbitration case, in which a tribunal awarded the United States damages for pollution suffered from a Canadian smelter. In practice, though, this precedent has not been very useful in claims between states. Governments have preferred to use civil courts to try to seek redress for the effects of transboundary pollution rather argue their cases before international arbitration panels. See Patricia W. Birnie and Alan E. Boyle, *International Law and the Environment* (Oxford: Oxford University Press, 1992), pp. 89–90, 393–94.

Water Pollution Water quality constitutes a second issue cluster. Water pollution produces changes in water quality that harm living organisms or otherwise make water unsuitable for desired purposes. Some contamination of oceans, lakes, and rivers is unintentional. Runoff from cities located near ocean or lake shores and from nearby farms and industries eventually finds its way into the oceans. Oil spills can kill fish and seabirds and make water unfit for recreation. Other contamination is intentional. Hazardous wastes, sewage, and garbage have long been dumped from coastal communities into the seas under the belief (or excuse) that the vastness of the oceans would allow small amounts of waste to disintegrate and disappear.[13] Water pollution also endangers adequate supplies of clean drinking water. More than 70 percent of the Earth is water, but much of it is frozen at the North and South Poles or is salt water that is unfit for drinking. Nonsalt water that is available for human use is found in lakes, rivers, and above-ground or underground reservoirs. Acid rain and air pollution can make water in the above-ground sources unfit to use, and many pollutants that have infected surface supplies and the soil have seeped into underground supplies, rendering them unfit as well. A 1995 World Bank study found that contaminated water causes about 80 percent of the diseases in poor countries and kills about ten million people every year.[14]

Desertification and Deforestation Desertification and deforestation form a third, linked set of issues because both erode fertile soils. **Desertification** involves a decline in the productive potential of arid (dry) or semi-dry land of 10 percent or more. Very severe desertification involves at least a 50 percent drop in land productivity. Organic matter in soil is easily washed away by water or wind, especially if soils have been over-grazed. High population growth rates and economies limited mainly to agriculture have forced increased use of marginal farmlands in many poor areas. These cultivation pressures do not necessarily produce deserts, but they can strip vital minerals from the soil, destroying once-productive crop lands. In 1984,

desertification Formally defined as a 10 percent decline in the productive potential of arid and semi-arid land.

As this photo of a spreading desert in Egypt suggests, desertification can have a devastating effect on people's lives. Once-fertile lands need not, however, become actual deserts to have their use as sources of food for humans, animals, and soils depleted.

the UNEP reported that 35 percent of the Earth was in some danger of desertification.[15] Deforestation, discussed at the beginning of the chapter, contributes to the problem by changing precipitation patterns, making once-fertile land more arid.

Global Warming   We discuss efforts to deal with global warming in detail in the case study on U.S. policy toward the Kyoto Protocol (see page 421). The problem of global warming arises from the emission of greenhouse gases into the atmosphere. The natural greenhouse effect helps keep much of the Earth warm enough to support life; without it, it is estimated that the Earth's average temperature would be about 33 degrees Centigrade colder than it is now.[16] But an excess of these gases in the atmosphere traps too much heat. Global concentrations of greenhouse gases have increased by nearly 30 percent during the last century. During that time, an increase between 0.3 and 0.6 degrees Centigrade in the Earth's mean surface temperature has also been observed, a development that scientists have characterized as "not entirely natural in origin."[17]

Biological Diversity   A fifth cluster of issues has to do with biological diversity—the variety of types of living organisms found in different habitats. As we said earlier in this chapter, if tropical forests keep disappearing at the present rate, we will soon experience the largest extinction of species in 65 million years. Even a small loss of habitat can lead to a major loss of species. Biologists estimate that when a natural habitat is reduced to a tenth of its original size, the number of species eventually drops by one-half. Aside from the obvious loss in the aesthetic richness of the natural world, such an impact on the living creatures we share the globe with raises normative issues about our responsibilities to coexist rather than destroy. But we also have a very practical stake in biodiversity. Many of the species being lost and the ecosystems they inhabit provide the basis for medicines, industrial chemicals, crops, fibers, and petroleum substitutes. Such products provide hundreds of millions of dollars a year to the world economy.[18]

Distinctive Features of Environmental Issues

The Political Incentives for Denial and Delay

Each of the key strategic incentives in this area pushes actors toward denying that the problem exists or delaying meaningful action to deal with the underlying problems. For actors to make progress on environmental issues, five such incentives must typically be overcome.

The Impact of Discounting   First, state officials often discount heavily any benefits that might stem from dealing with environmental issues. Recall that when people evaluate the incentives attached to policy options, they discount costs and benefits over time, typically preferring to receive benefits sooner and pay costs later. For environmental policies to succeed, costs must often be paid now for benefits that will come (if they come at all) later. Consider the problem of global warming. The major greenhouse pollutant is the carbon dioxide produced by burning oil, coal, and, to a lesser extent, natural gas. To deal with global warming, many people would have to cut their use of carbon-based fuels, principally by driving less and finding other ways to heat buildings. As *The Economist* put it, "a quick, enforced switch to non-polluting alternatives would savagely cut people's living standards."[19] The costs would be unpopular, and even then temperatures would probably not stabilize quickly. Under these conditions, it is often an easy choice to avoid paying the costs, even if that means that the benefits will not be produced. Future environmental benefits tend to be discounted especially heavily in poor states. As one analyst put it:

> For the poor who worry about whether they will be able to survive tomorrow, contemplating the impact of their actions upon conditions one hundred or even thirty years hence must seem an irrelevant luxury. Cutting down and burning trees or other non-sustainable activities may seem the only way to ensure immediate survival regardless of the long-run damage inflicted upon the biosphere.[20]

Counterfactuals and the Tragedy of the Commons Environmental benefits often appear as *undesired outcomes that don't occur*. The fact that people think they must pay high costs (for example, in the form of changing their driving habits) to protect the environment and then may not be able to *see* a positive environmental result raises both an analytical and a political problem. The analytical problem is that it is hard to demonstrate that there is an environmental benefit when the benefit comes in the form of preventing something bad from happening. How, after all, can one be sure that it would have happened if nothing were done? The political problem is that those who support costly environmental policies are then forced to justify sacrifices through a **counterfactual argument**.

Counterfactual arguments can be made either about the past or the future. If they are about the past, they suggest that things would be different today if something different had been done in the past. If they are about the future, they suggest that today's choices will alter what the future brings. The problem is that the choice not taken can never produce the predicted results. For example, how can one demonstrate conclusively that "if the League of Nations had developed an effective collective security system, German aggression in the 1930s could have been prevented." Similarly, how can one persuade skeptics that "if we had instituted mandatory ceilings on motor vehicle emissions a decade ago, the Earth's temperature would not have risen X degrees since that time."

People often speculate about what "might have been." But counterfactual arguments are not conclusive, since they lay out scenarios that are literally *counter to known facts*. We rarely know "what might have been" had one different thing occurred because such scenarios do not allow us to do a controlled experiment. This is a procedure in which every other relevant variable in some situation is held constant (controlled) so that the precise impact of the one factor we want to test can be determined. If two groups of patients of similar ages and medical conditions are given different drugs, the effect of the difference can be assessed because the people in the two groups are the same in every other pertinent way. But it is impossible to do controlled experiments in most areas of public and foreign policy, making it tricky to argue counterfactually in this area.

Counterfactual arguments are especially shaky when knowledge about cause and effect in some area is incomplete. Even if a controlled experiment could be done in these cases, we would not know which variables would have to be held constant. For example, scientists do not know how much temperatures will rise if carbon-based gases continue to escape into the atmosphere, since they do not know what other factors may also contribute to global warming. They are also unsure what the precise

counterfactual argument
An argument that explores what *might* have happened *if* some central factor had been different.

consequences in various parts of the world will be of any climate changes that do occur.[21] This uncertainty helps opponents of costly environmental policies resist such measures. Lacking evidence that specific damage will occur without specific preventive measures, environmentalists may be open to the charge that their arguments are just speculative counterfactuals.

These first two political features contribute toward **collective action problems** on many environmental issues. Collective action problems occur when individual actors (which can be persons, states, or firms) have no incentive to contribute toward some **collective (public) good.** A collective good is *indivisible*, meaning that if it is provided at all, it must be supplied to everyone; it cannot be parceled into individual portions. It is also *nonexcludable*, meaning that no one can be kept from using it, even if the person doesn't help provide it. Public television is an example. It is available free to all people within the viewing area who have a TV set, whether or not they contribute toward the costs of producing the shows. **Private goods**—those that are divisible and excludable—are quite different. Admission to a sports event is denied to those who don't pay (excludability), and at times even to those who want to attend but for whom no space is available (divisibility). By contrast, **free-riding** is predictable behavior where collective goods are involved. It occurs when actors consume a good without contributing toward its provision or upkeep because they cannot be individually charged for its use.

People are especially unlikely to contribute if they discount heavily any benefits the good provides and if those benefits consist of bad things that don't happen. If many actors follow this logic, the good will only be provided minimally, if at all. Within societies, governments solve collective action problems by imposing taxes for public projects such as toxic waste cleanup and defense. Those problems are harder to deal with internationally since there is no government that can force actors to pay to solve them.

In 1968, the biologist Garrett Hardin suggested that overuse of a common pastureland by short-sighted herdsmen—called the **tragedy of the commons**—is a good metaphor for the free-riding so often seen on environmental issues. Hardin asks us to imagine a pastureland next to a rural village on which all the local herdsmen can graze their cattle. For economic reasons, each wants to keep as large a herd as he can. This behavior poses few problems as long as tribal wars and disease keep the numbers of men and animals below the land's **carrying capacity**—the level beyond which some resource will be depleted for healthy, productive use. When that threshold seems to be approaching, Hardin argues, each herdsman must consider how he prefers to use the disappearing resource. Is it better to help maintain the commons for future use by holding down the size of his herd? Or should he emphasize his own short-term welfare, in which case the commons will disappear faster? The benefits of selling one more animal would be his alone, but the benefits of preserving the commons would be shared with other herdsmen today and with future generations. According to Hardin, the herdsman, seeking to maximize his individual gains, will choose what appears to him to be the "only sensible course": add another animal. Other herdsmen do the same, with the result that the *collective* good—preservation of the commons for future generations—cannot be maintained.[22] Such behavior may even have a biological basis. Perhaps humans have been programmed genetically to survive as a species by putting themselves and their families first, their tribe (or state) second, and the rest of the world a very distant third.[23]

collective action problems Problems that occur when people have no incentive to help pay for the provision of a collective (public) good.

collective (public) good A good or service (usually a benefit, but the logic also applies to costs, sometimes called "public bads") that cannot be withheld from any member of a group once it is provided to a single member of that group.

private good A good or service that can be possessed or consumed by an individual without making it available to others.

free-riding A situation that occurs when actors consume a collective good without helping to pay for it.

tragedy of the commons Situations in which people have an incentive to increase their consumption of a collective good even though that increased consumption will significantly reduce either the quality or supply of the good.

carrying capacity The level of use beyond which an ecosystem or other natural or human system can no longer sustain itself.

The Amazon rainforest is home to many plants and animals. When loggers find it profitable to cut down the trees, they destroy irreplaceable habitats for much wildlife, such as these macaws in the Tampobata River region of Peru.

Does the tragedy-of-the-commons metaphor help us analyze contemporary environmental problems? Consider what a logger gives up if he refrains from cutting down one tree in a forest. Sold as timber, the tree is worth about $590; if not cut down, it provides about $196,250 worth of benefits in the form of oxygen, soil fertility, and control of soil erosion over its lifetime.[24] While these benefits are over 300 times greater than the lumber's market value, they do little to help the logger right now. Since logging is a competitive business, it will be hard for him to resist cutting down the tree. To take another example, so many whales were killed between 1925 and 1975 that eight of the eleven major species became commercially extinct.[25] Similarly, the San Pedro River, which flows from Mexico into Arizona and is a breeding spot for 220 bird species, is in danger of drying up because groundwater pumping for agriculture and urban development is draining the wells that feed it. As a free-flowing river in the dry American Southwest, its loss would be a major ecological setback.[26] In each of these cases, some part of the ecosystem has been damaged because individual actors have chosen short-term rewards rather than behavior that would preserve the long-term collective good.

We should not assume that capitalism is uniquely prone to these problems. While businesses in a market economy may find it profitable to impose pollution on others in the absence of regulation, governments can identify and hold them accountable for such damage through taxes or other penalties. As we discuss in the case study on environmental projects in Brazil and Hungary cited at the end of the chapter, it was much harder to assign such responsibility for environmental damage in the communist states that used to rule Eastern Europe. Because industrial enterprises in those countries were publicly owned, there was no effective ecological watchdog over them. The legacy today in these societies is many dead rivers and heavily polluted industrial districts.[27]

Different Views of Just International Solutions   A third political feature of international environmental issues is that the standards actors use for evaluating what is "just" are highly contested. As Malaysian Prime Minister Mahathir Mohamad put it:

> We know that the 25 percent of the world['s] population who are rich consume 85 percent of its wealth and produce 90 percent of its waste. Mathematically speaking, if the rich reduce their wasteful consumption by 25 percent, worldwide pollution will be reduced by 22.5 percent. But if the poor 75 percent reduce consumption totally and disappear from this earth altogether, the reduction in pollution will only be 10 percent.[28]

These attitudes reflect a point we made in Chapters 10 and 11: People in rich and poor societies evaluate international economic procedures and outcomes differently. There is thus a wide North-South gulf on what we might call "environmental justice." This gulf has held back implementation of a treaty to help prevent further global warming.

A Multiplicity of International Actors   Involvement by a wide variety of actors is a fourth political feature of international environmental issues. States are involved because policies on such matters as population growth rates, forest management, and energy use are ultimately worked out and implemented at the national level. Moreover, even though other actors are also involved in placing environmental issues on world political agendas, state policy makers are the ones who ultimately

ENDURING PATTERNS

13.1

The impact of varying beliefs about just relationship

If people value creating and sustaining legitimate relationships and *if they think a political process and the outcome it produces are just, they are more likely to accept that outcome—even if they would have preferred something else. If they think either the outcome or the process is unjust, they are far more likely to oppose it.*

The impact of discounting

People generally prefer current benefits over future benefits and future costs over current costs. However, the higher the expected value actors attach to achieving a specific policy outcome, the less their choices will be affected by discounting. The less control actors have over policy choice and implementation, the more actors will prefer future costs over current costs and the more they will value current benefits over future benefits.

The impact of risk-taking preferences

The higher the expected value people attach to an outcome, the higher the political risks they will be willing to run to achieve it. People are less willing to run political risks in support of policy choices as their control over choice and implementation declines.

The Montreal Ozone Protocol and the Kyoto Protocol on Climate Change

It is hard to build trans-state coalitions to address international environmental issues not only because it usually requires people to pay now to receive benefits later—which is politically risky—but also because policy makers differ in their view of just international outcomes. Enforceable international agreements can increase policy makers' willingness to take political risks and lower the impact of discounting by giving them more control over policy choice and implementation. However, the key political factor in overcoming the effects of discounting and political risks on choice would appear to be the value actors attach to achieving the goal. That value is, moreover, very much tied to normative issues: what *ought* to be our responsibilities to future generations.

Support for the 1987 Montreal Protocol on Substances that Deplete the Ozone Layer was difficult to build because of the sheer number of actors involved, but it had special advantages from the perspective of the politics of choice. The major TSBEs that manufactured the substances that were to be phased out had developed economically workable substitutes, and many key constituency groups were convinced that further depletion of the ozone layer would increase the chances that people alive today would develop dangerous skin cancers. The existence of viable substitutes dramatically dropped the anticipated short-term economic costs of environmental regulation; reducing the risks of skin cancer simultaneously created the promise of short-term benefits.

Opposition within the United States to the Kyoto Protocol reflected the belief that adopting its limits would impose significant short-term economic costs in exchange for only the distant possibility of long-term benefits. The conviction that those costs were unjust because the Protocol asked too much of the rich countries and too little of the Third World increased opposition still further, especially in the United States.

decide which issues are dealt with authoritatively at the international level. They do this in three major ways: by negotiating international environmental agreements; by taking responsibility for enforcing those agreements and, if necessary, amending international regulations; and by joining the international governmental organizations (IGOs) that also play a role in agenda setting, collective rule formation, and policy implementation on environmental issues.

IGOs are key actors in this area because they help to frame, implement, and monitor environmental activity. Part of their impact comes through **agenda setting.** IGO officials bring issues to the attention of governments and then help keep those matters in the spotlight. Mostafa Tolba, the head of the United Nations Environment Program (UNEP), personally focused attention on the hole in the atmospheric ozone layer and then forged the consensus that led to the Montreal Ozone Protocol.[29] IGOs also serve as forums for multilateral diplomacy on ecological issues—the places where actors meet to bargain. The UNEP convened the negotiations that led to most of the key environmental treaties of the 1970s and 1980s, including accords on the ozone layer, the control of movements of hazardous wastes across state boundaries, and preservation of diverse biological species.[30] Collecting and circulating environmental information is another IGO function, one especially valuable to states and NGOs that lack the resources to uncover such data on their own. UNEP's Earthwatch program includes systems that monitor deforestation and desertification. The Global Environmental Monitoring System (GEMS) collects and distributes data on air and water quality. IGOs also affect environmental policy by influencing national development plans. The various multilateral development banks, including the World Bank, now include environmental impact criteria in the way they assess lending projects.

Like IGOs, NGOs help to get issues on officials' agendas. At the 1992 Earth Summit, in addition to the 172 delegations representing states, some 15,000 representatives of over 2,000 environmental NGOs attended. Before governments were ready to do so, many of these activists wanted to negotiate a treaty to control greenhouse gases.[31] In 1990, the presence of NGO leaders at the annual Group of Seven economic summit meeting helped keep environmental matters on the agenda, despite U.S. opposition.[32] NGOs provide information or arguments to sympathetic actors. Most of the substantive preparation for the 1992 Earth Summit was coordinated by NGOs.[33] Some NGOs work closely with IGOs to develop environmental policy. After several U.S. NGOs lobbied the World Bank to pay more attention to the ecological effects of its projects, World Bank officials invited NGOs to consult on these matters.[34] Because their members tend to be highly motivated, NGOs often help monitor compliance with international agreements once those agreements are in place. Greenpeace has energetically reported violations of treaties to control the dumping of hazardous wastes.[35]

The North-South split over legitimate relationships and outcomes often divides environmental NGOs in the rich states from those in the poorer states. Northern-based NGOs tend to argue that the way societies grow in the future must be controlled. Southern-based environmental NGOs focus on the problems noted by Prime Minister Mohamad: overconsumption in the North, poverty in the South, and a tendency for trans-state business enterprises (TSBEs) that pollute to shift their base of operation from the North to the South.[36]

Close links between the environment and economic development have made TSBEs key actors on environmental issues. TSBEs with no attachment to local

agenda setting The process by which issues become identified as topics worthy of analysis and action by policy makers.

Conference diplomacy, at which problems are discussed in the context of multilateral international meetings, has become a familiar feature of world politics in the last few decades. Here, delegates are assembled for the 1992 Earth Summit in Rio de Janeiro.

communities may act in ways that bring on tragedy-of-the commons problems. Residue from mines has polluted rivers and bays, and agribusinesses have polluted crop lands with pesticides. In some areas, foreign-owned cattle ranching firms buy land cheaply, farm it intensively for a short time, and then abandon it once it has been stripped of grass or nutrients.[37] TSBEs also tend to get involved in environmental politics when they see important business issues at stake. For example, they often try to weaken or delay environmental regulations they feel hurt their profits or market position. In the early 1980s, before U.S. chemical firms decided to pursue substitutes for chlorofluorocarbons (CFCs), which were used in refrigerants and aerosols, they held up progress toward global rules that would require other technologies by reducing efforts to find substitutes for them.[38]

The Impact of Linkage Politics   Each of the political features of international environmental issues noted so far tends to be magnified by a fifth: linkage politics. Even if leaders are willing to invest in costly policies, their constituents may not want to do so for any of the reasons we've discussed. For example, the Food and Agriculture Organization (FAO), a UN specialized agency, was designated as the lead agency for the Tropical Forest Action Plan (TFAP). The TFAP was designed to deal with deforestation by investing resources in forest regeneration. But FAO officials steered most of the investments into commercial timber development, not forest conservation or sustainable use, since their key constituents were governments' forestry departments. The forestry departments, in turn, promoted the sale of timber, which meant cutting down as many trees as possible. When environmental NGOs monitoring the TFAP tried to change these incentives by removing the program from the FAO's Forestry Department, the FAO's director-general resisted the suggestion.[39] The tragedy of the commons was thus reinforced across actors and arenas.

It can be hard to build policy coalitions when so many players must be on board. But policy entrepreneurs may find ways to assemble a coalition out of the various possibilities. At a key point in the bargaining over a treaty to ban CFCs, UNEP head

Mustafa Tolba took personal responsibility for brokering a compromise. Acting as the representative of the Southern states that sought compensation from the North for giving up the inexpensive CFC technology, the Egyptian-born Tolba brought the factions together. States whose firms had a major presence in the CFC market, who had shown interest in the ozone issue, and who provided geographic balance were invited to a closed session to hammer out a draft treaty with Tolba. With Tolba "delivering" the poor states and the United States sympathetic from an early stage, the Europeans—initially reluctant except for Germany to give up CFCs—were brought along.[40]

Functional Interdependence and Threshold Effects

Along with the political features discussed in the last section, environmental issues are defined by a distinctive set of physical processes. As Garrett Hardin's metaphor of the commons indicates, one of the most important is the existence of physical thresholds, or carrying capacities, beyond which an ecosystem or life form cannot be sustained. Particular species can exist only within certain physical and chemical conditions known as *tolerance ranges*. Changes in climate, in nutrients found in the soil or water, or in air pollution beyond these limits trigger **threshold effects.** For example, certain pollutants in water are organic wastes that bacteria decompose. Because the bacteria use up oxygen dissolved in the water as they do this, organic waste beyond a certain level degrades water quality by stripping it of so much oxygen that fish will die.[41]

In some cases, scientists know where these thresholds are, and those limits are fairly stable. The quantity of oxygen-demanding wastes in water may be precisely measured, giving ecologists some sense of when a lake is becoming dangerous to fish. In other cases, scientists may not know where or how stable these physical limits are. Unstable thresholds tend to result when multiple physical or chemical agents interact in an ecosystem. For example, the amount of phosphorous a lake can absorb depends on what other substances have been dumped in it and on the species that inhabit it. The policy problems created by the instability of many environmental thresholds are thus compounded by the fact that there are usually multiple causes for that instability. These difficulties are then intensified still more by the close functional connections among different ecological processes. Forests affect precipitation, which affects the quality of vegetation and soil, which affects the animal species that can be sustained.

Consider the process of global warming. Deforestation increases the greenhouse gases that trap heat near the Earth's surface by leaving more carbon dioxide in the atmosphere instead of allowing it to be ingested through trees. Tropical deforestation also leads to higher levels of nitrous oxide, which stays in the atmosphere for over a century and traps 230 times as much heat per molecule as carbon dioxide. Global warming has been linked to increased rainstorms (since at higher temperatures more moisture evaporates) and smog formation. It could thus produce flooding and degrade air quality.[42]

These multiple links imply that the thresholds defining ecologically sustainable activity can be crossed in several ways. For instance, topsoil becomes prone to desertification in seven ways: (1) overgrazing on arid or semiarid land; (2) deforestation without reforestation; (3) surface mining without land reclamation; (4) irrigation techniques that lead to land erosion; (5) salt buildup and waterlogged soil; (6) farming

threshold effects   The point at which the nature of a relationship between two or more variables changes and, thus, "crosses a threshold."

13.2 ENDURING PATTERNS

The connection between preferences and power

The stronger actors' power positions, the more strategically important their preferences.

The effect of the shadow of the future

The more compatible people expect their preferences to become over time, the more cooperative and less power-based their strategic choices are likely to be.

"Spaceship Earth," Scientific Proof, and Politics

During the 1970s, environmentalists coined the phrase "Spaceship Earth" as part of their campaign to convince people that everyone in the world was dependent on the ecological health of the Earth for their survival. From the perspective of the politics of strategic choice, it was an effort to redefine people's understanding of the shadow of the future in the hope that an image of shared vulnerability would increase the incentives to cooperate in making choices to protect the environment. While the image was both apt and strategically astute, polluters—much like cigarette makers—have an incentive to challenge the scientific basis both for any predicted damage created by their products and for any suggested remedies. Demanding proof before regulation appears completely reasonable, but—as we discussed in Chapter 3—over half a century ago philosophers of science demonstrated that it is impossible to *prove* any scientific proposition about cause and effect to be universally true. All scientists can do is accumulate a body of interrelated theoretical arguments and evidence that is sufficiently overwhelming that scientists regard a particular interpretation as a settled question, one for which there is no reasonable basis for continued dispute. People who have a stake in avoiding regulation have strong incentives to ignore this point and demand the impossible—proof—even as they read data and theoretical arguments in self-serving ways. Since the actors whose preferences matter most are the ones who have the power to alter outcomes, the outcomes of these debates about the shadow of the future on environmental policy vary with the ambiguity of the scientific research and the political power of polluters.

In May 1984 the European Commission presented a proposal requiring that cars manufactured in the European Community meet tougher emissions standards. Automobile manufacturers in France, Great Britain, and Italy convinced their governments to oppose the new rules, but the German government supported the move and used its power within the Community to push the regulations through within a year. There was a greater political consensus about the scientific evidence on the dangers of air pollution in Germany where acid rain was visibly destroying cherished forests in politically important regions. The German automobile industry also supported requiring tighter emissions standards because installing catalytic converters was necessary to their sales in North America.

In stark contrast, the demand for scientific proof has created an immense roadblock to action on global warming in the United States. Part of the reason can be found in the great complexity of the science: It is extraordinarily difficult to identify threshold effects in the functionally linked ecological processes that affect global temperatures. The difficulty in anticipating the impact of innovation on the development of environmentally friendly strategies for economic growth simultaneously makes it hard to evaluate claims about the impact of environmental regulation on the economy. These complexities provide many strategic opportunities for opponents to the Kyoto Protocol—who are currently exceptionally well-placed politically—to attack the credibility of scientific studies about the relationship between pollution and global warming.

on land with unsuitable soil; (7) soil compacting by farm machinery and cattle hoofs.[43] As the population grows and pressure on forests and farmland grows with it, tragedy-of-the-commons scenarios are likely through a number of these paths.

These scientific complexities reinforce the political incentives for actors to delay in confronting ecological issues. Consequently, threshold effects often sneak up on people. The problem is that once thresholds are crossed, the results may be irreversible. For instance, members of an animal species might be lost gradually due to over-hunting to a point where, suddenly, too few members with enough genetic variation are left to produce sustainable populations. Florida panthers and the African cheetah have suffered this fate.[44] The distinctive features of environmental issues reviewed in this section make efforts to manage environmental problems in a world of states exceptionally challenging.

Efforts to Manage International Environmental Problems

The Growth of International Environmental Regimes

Managing international environmental problems often involves the use of an **international regime.** Regimes are the principles, norms, rules, and decision-making procedures states use to deal with issues of common concern. They emerge when states want to collaborate on a problem in more than an ad hoc way, but will not surrender their sovereignty to a supranational body in order to do it. A marine pollution regime, for instance, has existed since the 1970s. It is based on the principle that oil, sewage, and radioactive materials are dangerous in water; it is thus necessary to control certain activities of governments, ship operators, and ship owners. General norms of behavior regulate what may be thrown into the oceans. Based on treaties such as the 1972 London Convention on Dumping, specific rules indicate, for example, how tankers must be cleaned to keep the oceans healthy. They also provide mechanisms for settling disputes about the meaning of the rules.[45]

Regimes are often established by multilateral agreements, of which more than 140 existed in the environmental area in the early 1990s.[46] These regimes deal with a wide variety of issues, including wildlife conservation, transboundary air pollution, ocean pollution, transboundary shipments of hazardous wastes, and protection of the atmospheric ozone layer (see Table 13–1).

Another method for managing such problems is what lawyers call **soft law**—agreed-upon guidelines for preferred behavior that do not have the force of binding legal obligations. UNEP has developed a good deal of soft law in the area of sustainable development. Soft law has the benefit of registering a degree of international consensus in areas where the support needed to create binding agreements is lacking. It then can provide a basis for multilateral treaties if such support develops at some later time.

These management efforts have had a mixed record of success. There have been some notably effective environmental regimes, such as the Mediterranean Action Plan (Med Plan). Begun in 1975 to deal with marine-based sources of pollution, it now also covers land-based sources that directly influence industrialization policies and includes as members all states that share the Mediterranean shoreline. Getting poor states such as Algeria and Egypt, which initially opposed the plan as a barrier

international regime An agreed-upon set of principles, norms, rules, and procedures for coordinating multilateral action in an issue area.

soft law Formal multilateral agreements that do not have binding legal obligations.

C A S E   S T U D Y

The United States, Global Warming, and the Kyoto Protocol

Evidence of possible global warming began to appear in the 1970s. Since that time, growing concerns about climate change have collided with fears that policies designed to protect the atmosphere would reduce economic growth, imperiling the profits of businesses at the same time as it drove down wages and reduced the ability of the poor in the Third World to boot-strap their way out of poverty.

As the case at **www.prenhall.com/lamborn** explains, after years of contentious debate, the 1997 Climate Change Convention held in Kyoto, Japan, produced a plan (called the Kyoto Protocol) for reducing emissions thought to be causing global warming. The question then was whether the Protocol would be ratified. Had the agreement reached at Kyoto really managed to bridge the differences between rich and poor states, workers and employers, environmental activists and government policy makers?

What were the major international fault lines at the conference? How were these divisions affected by linkage politics—the connections between policy makers' international agendas and the political risks generated by factional and constituency politics?

Recall two basic points about power and the politics of choice. First, the sources of power can vary with the issues and actors involved. Second, the norms and procedures (the regimes) in specific venues—as well as general concerns about building relationships that will be regarded as mutually legitimate—can affect the way power is used. How do these principles help explain the bargaining at Kyoto and the outcomes of the debates about ratification?

Finally, put all these pieces in the politics of strategic choice together for the United States. Once you have, make a counterfactual argument. Look for the piece that you think would have produced the biggest shift in U.S. policy—and the overall outcome—if the key facts in that specific piece had been different.

---

to their development, to join France and Italy is seen as a key achievement.[47] Other successes include a regime regulating transboundary air pollution, an agreement that prevents the mining of Antarctica's minerals for fifty years, and the hazardous wastes agreement. But some problem areas are only weakly regulated, if at all. The global marine-pollution control regime neglects land-based pollutants and is notably weaker than the Med Plan. The 1973 Convention on Trade in Endangered Species set up a worldwide system of reporting and trade sanctions to curb the traffic in such endangered species as the African cheetah, but a loophole allows states with an interest in certain species to opt out of the controls.

What explains this record, one that has been characterized as "extremely patchy"?[48] In a world of sovereign states, unwilling governments cannot be forced to cooperate. As we have seen, political leaders often worry about the costs and risks of environmental protection. Such concerns loom especially large in the South, where poverty, not a clean environment, is seen as the key problem. The notion of sustainable development, to which we turn next, has been used to try to bridge the tensions between environmental and economic objectives.

TABLE 13-1   SELECTED INTERNATIONAL ENVIRONMENTAL ACCORDS

Issue Area	Accord	Date Signed
Conservation of Biological Diversity	Rio Declaration	June 3–14, 1992
	World Charter for Nature	1982
Deforestation	International Tropical Timber Agreement	January 26, 1994
	International Tropical Timber Agreement	November 18, 1983
Desertification and Land Cover Change	United Nations Convention to Combat Desertification in Those Countries Experiencing Serious Drought and/or Desertification, Particularly in Africa	September 12, 1994
	United Nations Conference on Desertification (UNCOD) Plan of Action to Combat Desertification and General Assembly Resolutions 29-9	August 1977
Global Climate Change	Rio Declaration	June 3–14, 1992
	United Nations Framework Convention on Climate Change	May 9, 1992
Population Dynamics	Rio Declaration	June 3–14, 1992
Stratospheric Ozone Depletion	Adjustments and Amendment to the Montreal Protocol on Substances That Deplete the Ozone Layer	November 23–25, 1992 June 29, 1990
	Montreal Protocol on Substances That Deplete the Ozone Layer	September 16, 1987
	Vienna Convention for the Protection of the Ozone Layer	March 22, 1985
Trade/Industry and the Environment	Sanctions against Environmental Illegal Activities	February 12, 1998
	Rio Declaration	June 3–14, 1992
Transboundary Air Pollution	Convention on Environmental Impact Assessment in a Transboundary Context	February 25, 1991
	Convention on Long-Range Transboundary Air Pollution	November 13, 1979
Treaties Law	Vienna Convention on the Law of Treaties	May 23, 1969

Source: CIESIN, "ENTRI Menu of Treaty Texts Organized by Subject," May 2, 2001 (*http://sedac.ciesin.org/pidb/texts-subject.html*).

Debates about Sustainable Development

The idea of sustainable development represents an effort to harmonize human activities and the natural world. The potential environmental effects of rapid economic growth become clear when we look at what has happened in East Asia since the 1970s. As we saw in Chapters 10 and 11, growth in that region has been about double the world's average for most of the past few decades. But this growth has come at a price. Nine of the world's fifteen cities with the highest levels of air pollution are in East Asia. A fifth of all land in the region covered by vegetation has suffered soil degradation due to overgrazing and erosion that has resulted from some of the highest deforestation rates in the world. Half to three-quarters of the coastlines and marine protected areas in East Asia are threatened by notable loss of species.[49]

Integrating environmental standards into people's economic choices requires a major change in worldview. It used to be taken for granted that the market (or the government in command economies) would maximize social welfare as long as people had progressively more or better goods and services to consume. It was

13.3 ENDURING PATTERNS

The connection between preferences and power

The stronger actors' power positions, the more strategically important their preferences.

The impact of linkage politics

World politics is driven by the interaction of international, factional, and constituency politics.

Ratifying Kyoto: The United States and Japan

As we stressed in Chapter 3, it is important to remember that the sources of actors' power vary with the issues and actors involved. In cases where actors have ongoing relationships with established norms and institutions, actors' relative power positions can also be affected by the norms and rules within those relationships and institutions.

Under the rules agreed upon at the 1997 conference, the Kyoto Protocol will go into effect only after it is ratified by countries that produced 55 percent of the covered emissions in 1990. With the United States—the world's largest source of greenhouse gases emissions—refusing to ratify the agreement, Japan's preferences became critical because, without Japan on board, it would be almost impossible to get to 55 percent. On October 29, 2001, a conference on implementing the Kyoto Protocol began in Morocco. With the international spotlight on Japan, senior Japanese officials reported that they found themselves in a very difficult position. While Japanese public opinion was in favor of the treaty, Japanese industrialists had begun to lobby hard against it, arguing that with the United States not participating, they would be at a competitive disadvantage.*

*Andrew C. Revkin, "U.S. Taking a Back Seat in Latest Talks on Climate," *New York Times*, October 19, 2001, p. A5.

---

further assumed that the supply of natural resources is infinite or can be supplemented by substitutes, and that waste disposal will not be a major problem even as consumption grows. But environmentalists have increasingly challenged what they consider the narrow definition of "social welfare" implied in this view. From an economic standpoint, welfare is viewed entirely in terms of material consumption, aside from any environmental costs. Sustainable development, by contrast, begins from the premise that economic growth must be planned to conserve the Earth's stock of resources and its broader ecological support systems.

Two kinds of equity left out of traditional economic models are stressed. One is **intergenerational equity**—the idea that future generations have a right to a healthy planet and the use of scarce resources. The other kind of equity involves calls for international environmental justice. This principle holds that while poor states must be developed in ways that do not deplete their ecosystems, wealthy states must help by cutting unnecessary and wasteful consumption.[50] Both notions of equity challenge the kinds of behavior that leads to tragedy-of-the-commons problems. They imply policies that encourage ecologically responsible production and consumption choices—choices that will leave the environment in no worse (and perhaps better) condition for future generations than it is today.

intergenerational equity
The principle that economic growth should be promoted in ways that protect both the economic and environmental interests of future generations.

For these reasons, sustainable development has become a central focus of discussion among development specialists and environmentalists. It was the idea behind the 1992 Rio Conference on Environment and Development, a highlight of which was the adoption of Agenda 21, a broad set of goals intended to deal with world poverty in an ecologically sound way. Agenda 21 addresses (1) the quality of life for individuals and communities; (2) efficient use of natural resources; (3) protection of the global commons; (4) sustainable policies regarding land, communities, and transportation; and (5) management of chemicals and waste. By integrating environmental concerns into development planning, it is assumed that the basic needs of the world's poor can be met, overall living standards can rise, and the ecosystem can be protected.[51] In short, no drastic trade-offs must be made between "growth" and "nature." Officials who built international environmental regimes previously had often dealt with issues through separate, narrow treaties to minimize the political barriers to cooperation. Sustainable development implies a more holistic approach in which the environmental implications of many controversial activities must be managed simultaneously.[52]

The desire to avoid difficult choices has, however, robbed sustainable development of a widely shared meaning. One author counted at least seventy different formulations of the concept in various publications.[53] There is no working consensus across groups about what needs to be sustained, for whom, and for how long. Even those who support the general idea of reconciling growth and nature disagree on basics. Consensus is difficult to achieve partly because scientists haven't established certainty about the ecological consequences of various activities. Policy makers must also balance the political demands generated by different economic and environmental constituencies. Some actors care most about the survival of future human generations; others care more about how growth can be sustained at present levels for as long as possible; still others care most about the survival of wildlife and natural habitats.[54]

These disagreements appear within both the rich states and poor states and especially across the North-South divide. As we've seen, the environmental movement emerged out of concern for ecological sustainability in the developed North. But even with generally high living standards, people often resist making economic sacrifices for nature's sake. When the Dutch government fell in 1988 after proposing a series of environmental initiatives that included removal of a popular transportation subsidy, politicians elsewhere took notice.[55] And Richard Darman, a former director of the U.S. Office of Management and Budget, expressed a feeling shared by many of his fellow citizens when he said: "Americans did not fight and win the wars of the twentieth century to make the world safe for green vegetables."[56]

In the South, people's interpretations of sustainability are filtered through their economic pressures and their views about Northern demands that they make costly adjustments for the sake of the environment. Immediate needs tend to take priority over environmental concerns when people are poor. For example, while fishermen are urged to preserve coral reefs (the oceans' tropical forests), Filipino villagers dynamite or pump arsenic into the reefs to force the fish to surface. Even though they know that their actions deprive future generations of food and the beauty of the reefs, they feel unable to afford a long time horizon.[57] The incentives to cut down trees provide still another example of the pressures in poor countries to meet short-term needs. Over the past two decades, developed and developing countries have managed their forest resources in strikingly different ways. Wealthier countries have increased

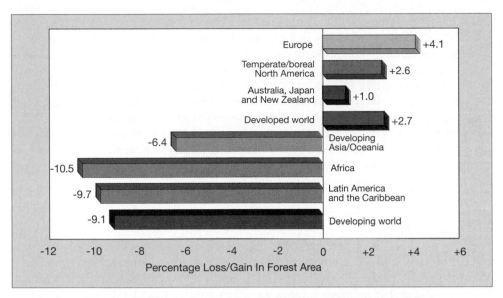

Figure 13–1   **Percent Change in Forest Area, by Region and Developmental Tier, 1980 to 1995**

Note: Data exclude the countries of the former Soviet Union.

Source: Food and Agriculture Organization (FAO) of the United Nations, *State of the World's Forests 1999* (Rome: FAO Information Division, 1999), Figure 2.

their forest acreage. Poorer countries, seeing timber as a resource that can alleviate poverty, have reduced their forest lands. Figure 13–1 shows the percent change in forest area by region between 1980 and 1995.

The middle classes can afford a longer time horizon than people dependent on fishing and lumbering for survival, but they too often choose current consumption or growth over conservation. They hope to achieve living standards comparable to those in the developed world—if not for themselves, then for their children. Environmental policies that sacrifice growth are unlikely to win their support. The message to the North has been clear since the Stockholm Conference: Environmental protection is a luxury that the poor countries can afford only after they are developed.

Poverty need not lead to environmentally short-sighted behavior. Poor people adopt sustainable use strategies when their economic circumstances make that necessary or attractive. For example, when Cuba was a part of the Soviet bloc, Cuban farmers emulated Eastern European practices. They abandoned traditional, natural farming methods and turned to pesticides and fertilizers. When those chemicals were no longer available, agricultural yields at first fell, and pests devoured much of what was left. More recently, farmlands have been weaned away from chemicals. Crop rotation, inter-planting of corn and sweet potatoes, and other natural methods have been brought back, and many farmers now earn up to twice the average wage.[58]

Since the 1992 Rio Earth Summit, about 100 countries have prepared national sustainable development strategies. As part of the trend toward economic deregulation worldwide (discussed in Chapter 11), much has been learned about the kinds of incentives that can help harmonize growth and environmental protection. Relatively more emphasis than before is placed on plans using existing markets or creating new markets to regulate behavior, as opposed to banning or otherwise regulating what people can and cannot do. One being considered would allow greenhouse gas emission rights to be traded internationally, with the countries able to cut emissions compensating somewhat for those less able to do so. These strategies represent a "work in progress," according to a recent World Bank report, but they also reflect an underlying optimism that tragedy-of-the-commons scenarios can be prevented, or at least their effects softened, through flexibility and experimentation.[59]

However one views sustainable development, two problems loom large for poor states trying to square this circle. Rapidly growing populations reinforce poverty and increase the strain on natural resources, and high external debt burdens make it hard to escape the constraints of poverty and pursue ecologically sound growth.

Population Control

Population control is an issue that has long been seen as central to environmental sustainability: too many people chasing limited food, water, and usable living space. More than two centuries ago in *An Essay on the Principle of Population*, Thomas Malthus argued that population tends to increase faster than food supply, with disastrous consequences unless the rate of growth can be controlled. Hardin's tragedy of the commons is the modern version of this same argument; unless population growth can be limited, tolerable living conditions will become unsustainable.

How close is humankind to unsustainable population levels? The answer depends on the carrying capacity of people's environments. Unlike other animals, humans can use technology to increase an area's carrying capability, at least for a while. Irrigation and chemicals can boost crop yields; forests can be cut down to provide income and living space. But inescapable ecological constraints are likely to be reached at some point. As we saw earlier in this chapter, world population levels have skyrocketed in this century. Many indications suggest that carrying capacities have been reached, especially in the South. It is estimated that 7 percent of usable topsoil (24 billion tons) is lost *each year* from the world's farmland. A rate one-tenth as high would be unsustainable over the long run in terms of feeding and providing income to people.[60] Many regions already suffer from a shortage of fresh water. The most seriously affected areas—the Middle East, northern India, much of China, and parts of Africa—are those in which populations are growing rapidly. Some of these regions also have histories of violent conflict. The World Bank's vice president for the environment thus predicted that "the wars of the next century will be over water."[61] In recent years, a major increase in world food production has been achieved through irrigation. Much of that water has come from underground supplies accumulated during the ice age. As those supplies are used up—or in industrialized areas have become polluted with toxic chemicals—once-fertile agricultural land is increasingly being taken out of production. As a result, world food production, which grew on a per capita basis from 1950 through the mid-1980s, is now lagging.[62]

All of these problems are evident today in China, the world's most populous country. Even if the government's one-child-per-couple policy remains in place, China's population is expected to grow by three hundred million over the next twenty years—an increase greater than the present U.S. population. In a society still largely inhabited by peasants, population pressures are leading to a major loss of arable land. Over the next decade the erosion of topsoil, its degradation due to use of artificial fertilizers over extended periods, and the expansion of urban settlements and transportation networks are projected to wipe out 10 percent of usable crop land. With the population increase expected during that time, productive farmland is expected to drop by 25 percent per capita. As this takes place, more and more people will migrate to China's cities, where overcrowding, pollution, and lagging public services are putting a strain on the government and undermining the communist government's political legitimacy.[63]

Third World policy makers have more control over outcomes on population-control issues than they do on many other socioeconomic issues. In the developed states, population growth reached **replacement levels** (zero or only small net growth) decades ago. By contrast, in many Southern countries, population growth rates remain quite high—often 3 to 4 percent a year. Because the key to solving this problem lies within Third World societies, the international institutions that deal with population matters have given Third World policy makers a substantial voice in creating a loose international regime to deal with this issue. While emphasizing that rapid population growth is a barrier to development and that Southern governments should provide information on family planning to their people, these institutions leave it to individual states to decide what their population objectives will be. For obvious reasons, there are no specific global rules specifying desired population growth rates.[64]

Nevertheless, a wide variety of international actors care about population control, and a number of international institutions have been active on population issues. They include IGOs such as the United Nations Population Fund and population units of the World Bank and various specialized agencies of the UN; the International Planned Parenthood Federation, an NGO that receives much of its funding from governments; and bilateral aid agencies in a number of countries, such as the U.S. Agency for International Development. Beginning in the 1960s, these institutions helped knit together the loose regime described above, in part because the economic development doctrines of the time emphasized that population control would lead to growth and help promote political stability in the Third World.

These institutions have influenced national population policies in three ways. They have increased the salience of these issues at the national level. By tying population control to the broader developmental missions of the World Bank and the UN system, these organizations have helped to legitimize family planning programs within Third World societies. Birth control is now widely seen as beneficial to these nations individually and to the world as a whole, and not just as a preoccupation of the rich countries. These institutions have also helped governments support research on fertility attitudes and behavior, acquire the equipment to carry out population policies, and monitor the impact of the policies. Finally, they have helped provide governments with the resources to carry out those programs, including training programs for health professionals, family planning facilities, contraceptives, and public information programs to educate people about the importance of family planning.[65]

Some progress is being made in limiting population growth. A 1990 study estimated that family planning programs over the past several decades have reduced the world's population by more than 400 million from what it would otherwise be. Such a conclusion is based on significant fertility declines in a number of Third World countries. In Indonesia, fertility dropped by 46 percent between 1971 and 1991; in Morocco, it dropped by 31 percent between 1980 and 1991. In Bangladesh, one of the world's poorest countries, fertility rates declined by 21 percent between 1970 and 1991. Demand for contraception in these states rose dramatically during the 1970s and 1980s, stimulated by a number of trends. One is a decline in death rates. By increasing the number of children that survive, pressure is put on family

replacement levels
The birth rate at which populations will neither increase nor decrease in size.

13.4 ENDURING PATTERNS

The impact of varying beliefs about just relationships
If people think either an outcome or the process that produces it is unjust, they are far more likely to oppose it.

The impact of linkage politics
World politics is driven by the interaction of international, factional, and constituency politics.

Politics and Population Control

International efforts to promote population control are complicated by the fact that attitudes about the legitimacy of population control—and different methods to achieve it—vary across cultures and religions. The magnitude of these cultural and religious complications is increased by the fact that international efforts to coordinate population control measures are often seen as intrinsically illegitimate because they involve foreign interference in intensely personal choices of great moral sensitivity.

In the United States, government policy on international efforts at population control varies with which party is in office. Democratic administrations—with more powerful pro-choice constituencies—tend to support international efforts that involve some forms of birth control. Republican administrations—with more powerful anti-abortion constituencies—tend to oppose international efforts unless they expressly forbid any initiatives that can be seen as supporting abortion.

In much of India, efforts by IGOs and NGOs to promote family planning frequently run into opposition based on concerns about foreign interference, cultural and religious reservations, and concerns about the effect of empowering women to control reproductive choices.

resources, encouraging people to have fewer children. The greater ease with which ideas can spread from urban into rural areas has made information about birth control more accessible. Better education, moreover, has made women more informed about reproductive choices.[66]

But it is too soon to conclude that the population control battle has been won. Even if the worldwide rate of population growth were to drop to the replacement level of 2.1 children per couple, the current global population could still double before it stabilizes at about 12 billion sometime in the twenty-first century. A world population twice the size of the present one, concentrated largely in poor Third World states, would seriously threaten the carrying capacity of ecological systems. Further, if fertility were to remain even 5 percent higher than replacement level, according to a UN analysis, the world's population would reach 21 billion in the year 2150—more than three times what it is today.[67] Consequently, even though a tragedy-of-the-commons outcome in this area is less certain than it was a generation ago, it still could come to pass.

Debt-for-Nature Swaps

Another effort to manage international environmental problems involves debt-for-nature swaps, an idea that helps poor countries escape crushing debt while also enhancing the environment. Beginning in the late 1970s, developing countries accumulated huge external debt burdens, mainly to pay for expensive imported oil. Large loans were negotiated with multinational banks, at times with little concern for how they would be repaid. As international interest rates rose in the 1980s to finance the U.S. trade and budget deficits, the Third World debt burden became even harder to bear. A 1 percent increase in interest rates, for instance, can increase the annual repayments of the largest borrowers by up to five billion dollars. By 1990, Third World debt had risen to almost half of its collective Gross National Product, and more than 40 of those states had debts valued at more than 2.75 times their annual foreign exchange earnings. This led to drastic reductions in living standards in the poorest countries. In Uganda, for example, $3 per person has been spent annually in recent years on health care, while $17 a year per capita has been spent on servicing international debt.[68]

Debt-for-nature swaps help to foster sustainable economic development in such cases. They involve canceling part of a country's external debt in return for a specific pledge by the debtor to preserve the environment. This idea recognizes that debt burdens and environmental deterioration are often linked in poor countries. Their economic situations are often so desperate that governments turn a blind eye to the destruction of tropical forests, the exploitation of nonrenewable resources such as oil and other minerals, and ranching that depletes the grazing land, since these activities are a source of hard currency. Hard currency is attractive to the governments because it can be used to service their debt. Debt-for-nature swaps give Third World policy makers more incentives to focus on conservation priorities over the long term by removing a short-term source of burden on their treasuries and export income. Conservation International, a Washington, DC-based NGO, initiated the first debt-for-nature swap with Bolivia in 1987. As of mid-1997, 45 projects in 17 countries have generated over one billion dollars in environmental investment funds.[69]

Such agreements are typically reached through a specific sequence of steps. The investor (for example, an environmental NGO) agrees with an indebted country to initiate a debt-for-nature exchange. The investor then identifies donors (foundations, banks, or governments) that will put up the funds to buy the debt. Contacts are then made in international financial markets to identify from whom and at what price the debt can be purchased. The investor and the debtor then agree on how much hard-currency debt will be forgiven in return for some amount of local currency devoted to specific environmental activities. Only then does the investor buy the debt, which is exchanged for funds to be used for the stipulated project(s). As this process unfolds, the investor and donor must walk a fine line between getting a tangible result for their efforts and appearing to interfere in the debtor state's internal affairs.[70] Those results can, however, be environmentally valuable. Costa Rica has participated in six debt-for-nature swaps, exchanging almost $80 million in forgiven debt in exchange for about $44 million devoted to preserving national parks, the creation of a National Biodiversity Institute, reforestation, and the protection of endangered species. In Poland, the first debt-for-nature exchange involved cleaning up a polluted river. In the Philippines, forgiven debt has been earmarked to protect tropical forests, which declined by 55 percent between 1960 and 1985.[71]

C A S E S T U D Y

A Tale of Two Environmental Protest Movements

Hydroelectric projects increasingly generate opposition from environmentalists. In cases where people have to be relocated to make room for the dams and reservoirs, these projects also provoke opposition from human rights activists. In these conflicts, environmental and human rights groups frequently find themselves in a struggle with governments and well-financed economic interests who argue that hydroelectric power provides one of the cleanest and best ways to promote economic growth.

In Brazil, a coalition of non-governmental actors who opposed the Balbina project didn't have the political leverage to stop or significantly change the project, with disastrous effects on the people in the Waimiri-Atroari tribe and on many others whose ways of life depended on the river's free flow. Initially, the exact opposite appeared to have happened to the Gabcíkovo-Nagymaros project to rechannel the Danube River. There, a coalition of non-governmental actors led protests that prompted the Hungarian government to announce the suspension of the project in 1989.

As you read the case study on these two environmental protest movements on **www.prenhall.com/lamborn**, look for ways in which linkage politics in the Balbina case placed groups that supported the project in a strategically powerful position. Then look for the ways in which dramatic shifts in the linkage politics of Europe during 1988 and 1989 suddenly placed Hungarian opponents of the Gabcíkovo-Nagymaros project in a strategic position where they could build a blocking coalition.

Finally, look for "the rest of the story" on the Gabcíkovo-Nagymaros project. How do the same general principles in the politics of choice that explained the 1989 success of the project's Hungarian opponents help explain the subsequent impasse with the Czech Republic, which was in a position to divert the Danube into a new channel unilaterally and had plenty of incentives—because of domestic politics—to do so?

Debt-for-nature swaps originated in the mutual incentives of the international conservation movement and heavily indebted Third World countries. Over the long term, given the enormous poverty and environmental challenges the world faces, these incentives can be expected to grow stronger. But conservationists and Third World policy makers recognize that innovative financing arrangements are needed to realize these mutual interests. The Heavily Indebted Poor Countries (HIPC) Debt Initiative, announced at the 1996 meeting of the International Monetary Fund and the World Bank, could provide such an opportunity. It began a process of debt relief for up to 41 of the world's neediest states. For the first time, creditors agreed to reduce the debt burdens of eligible countries that promise to make demonstrable progress in reducing poverty, reforming their social policies, or reorganizing their economies along more efficient lines. This notion of "social conditionality"—a close cousin of the IMF's conditionality policies for its financial assistance—could easily be expanded to include sustainable development policies that would target key environmental concerns. Debt-for-nature exchanges could be negotiated on a case-by-case basis to achieve these ends. Especially in cases where ecosystems are in imminent danger, such programs have a chance of winning the financial and political support to succeed.[72]

In sum, sustainable development is an attractive idea, since it suggests that the Third World can escape from poverty without major environmental costs. But this attempt to square the circle has robbed the concept of a widely shared meaning. From the Stockholm Conference onward, Southern officials have insisted that the environment be discussed in a context that includes questions of poverty, North-South inequality, and development. The South expects the North to accept much more responsibility for the difficulties poor states face. Officials in poor states want the North to consume less, so that the South can ultimately consume more. From the vantage point of Northern policy makers, neither demand is reasonable.[73] Until either these perspectives change or some as yet undiscovered way to bridge these differences is found, continued stalemate is likely on environmental issues that demand major sacrifices from either North or South.

Conclusion

This chapter examined environmental issues in world politics, focusing on the way in which political incentives and ecological constraints shape choices and outcomes. Even though most actors understand that the physical carrying capacities of ecosystems are being exceeded in many areas, costly delays in dealing with the underlying problems occur over and over again. This tragedy-of-the-commons pattern is "tragic" because ecological thresholds, if crossed, can lead to great, and at times irreversible, damage. If tropical forests are lost, the species that lived in them can never be recovered; if the Earth heats up too much, valuable farmland and living space will eventually be under water. Out of concerns such as these, environmentalists have created a major issue area in contemporary world politics.

It is tempting to ask whether people can learn how to avoid these thresholds before it is too late. From an ecological perspective, this is surely necessary. Nevertheless, the political incentives that encourage delay and denial will have to be addressed—and trans-state coalitions built when strategic opportunities present themselves—for the outcomes to be different. Achieving environmentally sustainable development is as much, if not more, a political and a socioeconomic issue as it is an ecological one.

Key Terms

ecosystems
global commons
gross world product (GWP)
externalities
sustainable development
desertification
counterfactual arguments

collective action problems
collective (public) good
private goods
free-riding
tragedy of the commons
carrying capacity
agenda setting

threshold effects
international regime
soft law
intergenerational equity
replacement levels

To The Reader   A Chapter Summary and Questions for Review are available at **www.prenhall.com/lamborn**

Mercantilism	Struggle between Pope and Holy Roman Emperor stalemates 1356	c. 1000-1300 Feudalism undermined by increased trade	*Old Colonialism*
	Machiavelli writes *The Prince* 1513	1492 Columbus sets sail	
	Reformation begins 1517	1526 Vienna beseiged by Ottoman Empire	
	Wars of Religion 1618-48	1648 Peace of Westphalia	*Classical Balance of Power*
	Hobbes publishes *Leviathan* 1651		
	Ottoman Empire begins retreat 1699		
Industrial and Financial Revolutions		1776 *Wealth of Nations* published	
	French Revolution 1789	1792 French Revolutionary and Napoleonic Wars begin	
	Britain outlaws slavery 1807	1815 Concert of Europe begins	
	Britain ends mercantilism 1846-49	1848 *Communist Manifesto*	
		1848-53 Concert of Europe unravels	
	German unification 1871	1879-81 Germany and France drop free trade	*New Imperialism*
Controversies about free trade v. protectionism	Peak of Bismarckian alliance system 1887		
		1914-18 World War I	
	Lenin writes *Imperialism* 1916	1917 Russian Revolution	
	League of Nations established 1919		
	Collective security fails 1930s	1929 Depression begins	
		1939-1945 World War II	
	Bretton Woods Conference 1944	1945 UN Established	*Decolonization*
	Truman accepts containment 1946	1947 GATT	*Cold War*
	Universal Declaration of Human Rights 1948		
	EEC 1958	1964 UNCTAD Founded	
Accelerating globalization	Bretton Woods system ends 1971-73	1972 Stockholm Conference on the Environment	
	NIEO Declaration 1974	1980s Third World Debt Crisis	
	USSR disintegrates 1991	1995 WTO replaces GATT	
	Kyoto Conference on Climate Change 1997		
	September 11 attacks 2001	2002 Euro goes into general circulation	

Enduring Patterns across Unique Contexts

In Chapter 1, we said: "the 'facts' of world politics are many and complex. To understand world politics, you will have to learn many of those facts: the distinguishing characteristics of particular historical periods, the substance of the issues, the nature of the actors, and the specific ways in which international and domestic politics are interconnected across different time periods, issues, and actors."

In Chapters 4 to 13, you have seen the "facts" of world politics change across issues, actors, and time. Environmental and human rights issues look different from issues involved in the quest for security and the politics of trade, money, and investment in international economics. You've also seen that the actors involved in these issues show immense variation, from NGOs and other non-state actors through IGOs and coalitions that claim to speak for the state. There is, finally, almost a bewildering variety in the key facts across time and place. World politics looked different when the state emerged in medieval Europe. It looked different when international and domestic politics came together to produce mercantilist colonial expansion and classical-balance-of-power politics. The social, political, and economic transformations between the late eighteenth and mid-nineteenth centuries transformed world politics once again, producing the death of mercantilism and classical balance of power as well as the birth of the Bismarckian synthesis and the rise of the new imperialism. The twentieth century changed world politics yet again, with the sudden growth in the prominence of the United States in security systems and the global political economy, the end of colonialism, the acceleration of globalization, and the rising—but hotly contested—demands for increased trans-state obligations in promoting human rights and protecting the environment.

If you are going to make sense of world politics, you need to learn its central "facts." However, as we also emphasized in Chapter 1, "the facts of world politics—the issues, contexts, and actors—are only part of the story. The other part of the story is finding *patterns* in the facts." In Chapter 3 we suggested that the politics of strategic choice provided the broadest stretch of common ground—the biggest and most versatile set of intellectual tools—for finding patterns that could help introductory students make sense of world politics. As we explained in that chapter, we were drawn to that conclusion because, sooner or later, all the worldviews we discussed in Chapter 2 and all the major substantive issues in world politics get around to real people making hard choices under conditions of strategic interdependence.

In this chapter we revisit the principles introduced in Chapter 3 and review examples of how those enduring patterns in the politics of strategic choice helped make sense of the immense variety of human experiences discussed in Chapters 6 to 13. We make no claim that this review is comprehensive. Indeed, aspiring to comprehensiveness would be repetitive, boring, and ultimately counterproductive. The goal, instead, is simply to remind and reinforce, to provide some focus that might help as you reflect on the substantive and theoretical questions that energize your individual efforts to make sense of world politics today and tomorrow.

The Connection between Preferences and Power

As you will recall, the first basic political principle is quite simple.

> *The strategic importance of power varies with the compatibility of actors' preferences. The strategic importance of differences in actors' preferences varies with the distribution of power.*

The nature of these connections can be expressed in four straightforward statements:

- *The more incompatible actors' preferences, the more strategically important their relative power positions.*
- *The more compatible actors' preferences, the less strategically important their relative power positions.*
- *The weaker an actor's relative power position, the more strategically important the more powerful actors' preferences.*
- *The stronger an actor's relative power position, the less strategically important the weaker actors' preferences.*

When applying these patterns to specific cases, it's important to remember that political power is always embedded within human relationships, and that the sources of actors' power in those relationships vary. They vary with the substance of the issues and preferred outcomes, the nature of the actors involved, their relationships, existing norms and institutions, and the context. It's also important to remember that, while actors' relative power may be affected by the relative scale of their capabilities, capabilities and power are *not* synonymous. Actors with very few capabilities can, if the situation is right, be placed in a quite powerful position.

For all these reasons, political power is always *relative* power—relative to a particular set of actors and outcomes. It is meaningful to talk about an actor's relative power position within a relationship. It is *not* meaningful to conceptualize political power as an individual attribute or possession that exists outside of a relationship.

What if actors' preferences are *about* power? Significantly, in such a case the strategic interdependency of power and the compatibility of actors' preferences still holds. Having one actor gain in power relative to another creates a political problem only to the extent that those redistributive effects (changes in actors' relative power) are incompatible with the second actor's preferences. The notion that people will sometimes support efforts by others to gain power may seem counterintuitive, but it is a fundamental aspect of many political choices. Even in international politics, where one would expect people to be highly sensitive to questions of relative power, policy makers in one country will occasionally support efforts by other governments to increase their power. For instance, since at least World War II, British leaders have often welcomed the growth of U.S. economic and military strength, even as Britain's has declined dramatically, because U.S. goals have been seen as largely compatible with Britain's.

Because the sources of power vary across different combinations of issues, actors, and relationships, it is entirely possible that an actor's most effective response to another actor's attempt to increase one dimension of power may lie in manipulating a *different* form of power. For instance, an actor faced with a deteriorating military situation may find that it has few attractive options for improving its relative military position but does have the ability to alter the intentions of the militarily stronger actor in ways that would make the existing distribution of military power less dangerous. Thus it was that British foreign policy makers in the late nineteenth and early twentieth centuries decided that the massive gap between U.S. and British economic and military capabilities made befriending the United States essential to British security.

With these points in mind, let's turn to how this first set of enduring patterns helps us understand aspects of the politics of choice across a wide range of issues, actors, and historical periods. The easiest way to do that is to break the theoretical relationship connecting preferences and power into its subparts.

The Strategic Impact of Variation in Actors' Preferences

The more incompatible actors' preferences, the more strategically important their relative power positions.

Wars are obvious examples of this pattern, but it also comes through clearly in diplomatic systems designed to deal with security and political economy issues in peacetime, as well as cases involving human rights and the environment. Machiavelli stressed power and redistributive effects because he assumed that all men were bad and would act viciously whenever the strategic context created an opportunity to succeed. As its name suggests, the classical-balance-of-power system also focused on the relative power of its key states, but—and it is an important *but*—the strategic implications of the key actors' conflicting preferences over the distribution of territory and subjects were softened by a shared commitment to preventing preponderance and maintaining the system. Consequently, in classical-balance-of-power diplomacy, one finds a far greater willingness to form flexible alliances in pursuit of those common objectives than one finds in the dog-eat-dog world of Renaissance Italy, where there was no such shared commitment. One also finds a far greater willingness to accept the possibility that acting cooperatively within those alliances might result in adverse redistributive effects (an increase in another state's power relative to your own).

This strategic principle can also be seen in Bismarck's post-unification alliance system and, more generally, in his commitment to *machtpolitik* (power politics) and *realpolitik*. Bismarck's strategic approach reflected his assumption that Europe was divided by enduring conflicts in actors' preferences that could be managed only by pre-targeted, standing alliances designed to deter the stronger and restrain the weaker. And while the substance of the issues dividing the key actors in Bismarck's time look different from the issues that divided the United States and the Soviet Union during the Cold War, the conclusion that the incompatibility of the actors' preferences made relative power positions critical is essentially identical. Indeed, in some ways the situation was worse during the Cold War. While the conflicting preferences that divided Europe in the late nineteenth century were crosscutting and overlapping (hence Bismarck's intricate web of alliances), the conflicts during the Cold War were reinforcing (hence the polarized alliance structure of NATO versus the Warsaw Pact).

The same essential pattern can be seen in diplomatic systems designed to deal with issues of international political economy. The mercantilist system stressed relative power because it assumed that wealth could only be discovered and not created. Given that assumption, shared economic growth was impossible. The result was zero-sum economic competition. The neomercantilist trade policies of the 1970s and 1980s focused on power because of the assumption that one needed to increase

German Chancellor Otto von Bismarck, U.S. President Harry Truman, and British Prime Minister Margaret Thatcher all constructed security policies that emphasized power because they assumed their countries' principal foreign adversaries were led by people with incompatible preferences. However, unlike Bismarck and Truman—whose assumptions of incompatible preferences led to power-based strategies throughout their terms in office—Thatcher shifted to a more collaborative, less power-based strategy when she came to the conclusion that Mikhail Gorbachev had more compatible objectives than previous Soviet leaders.

relative export shares to promote domestic employment and earn foreign exchange. Third World demands for one-nation, one-vote decision making during the 1960s and 1970s (symbolized most boldly by the call for a New International Economic Order) reflected the strategic judgment that the incompatible views of the rich and poor meant that the distribution of power would determine which view prevailed.

While the sources of power could hardly be more different, the same relationship between the incompatibility of actors' preferences and the strategic importance of power can be seen in cases involving environmental and human rights issues. Throughout the 1990s, U.S. and Chinese policy makers expressed very different views about human rights. Given those different preferences, the outcome depended on what power made possible. When U.S. trade policy turned out to be too weak a lever to move Chinese policy, it was the Clinton administration that changed direction. In the debates on implementing the Kyoto Protocol on global warming, it was the United States that found itself on the diplomatic defensive, with the preferences of U.S. and European policy makers far apart. This time the United States was the one in a position to say "no" and did. (For more information on these two cases, see the website for this book: *www.prenhall.com/lamborn.*)

> *The more compatible actors' preferences, the less strategically important their relative power positions.*

On the security side, the Concert of Europe (especially after Britain withdrew) is a good example of a situation in which the compatibility of key actors' international and domestic goals led them to downplay their relative power positions and focus instead on their combined ability to achieve shared goals. They worked together to restore the old legitimizing principles from the classical-balance-of-power system and to prevent radical change in domestic economic, political, and social arrangements. The effects of Gorbachev's policies provide a second example of this principle. Gorbachev got Soviet policy coalitions to reframe their understanding of Soviet interests in a way that suddenly made Soviet preferences compatible with those of policy makers in the West. This reframing led to the collapse of the arms race, the end of Soviet control in Eastern Europe, and the end of the Cold War.

There are also several important examples of this theoretical relationship in political economy. Mercantilism was attacked by Adam Smith partly because he rejected the zero-sum competition implied by its assumption that wealth could not be created. The strategic importance of relative power fell even lower with David Ricardo's idea of comparative advantage, which placed the emphasis on pursuing what an individual or country did best, rather than on what they did relative to others. Classic laissez-faire free trade ideology takes this perspective to its logical conclusion, positing a harmony of interests between the pursuit of individual wealth and the economic good of the whole. This reasoning implies that states' relative import and export balances do not matter as long as those patterns of exchange reflect the choices of specific producers and consumers. In such a world, it is Smith's famous "invisible hand" that guarantees desirable results, not states' relative power.

The relationship between the increasing compatibility of actors' preferences and the decreasing strategic importance of power also lies at the very heart of the growth of human-rights regimes in Europe today. The effectiveness of the European Court of Human Rights depends on an unusual willingness to de-emphasize questions of interstate power. That willingness clearly reflects the growing compatibility of the views of key actors in participating states on the meaning and importance of human rights.

The Strategic Impact of Variation in Actors' Power Positions

The last section looked at the relationship between preferences and power by starting with variations in the compatibility of actors' preferences. Here we reverse the process and begin with variations in actors' power positions.

> *The weaker an actor's relative power position, the more strategically important the more powerful actors' preferences.*

Weak states know this theoretical relationship all too well. The classical-balance-of-power system was built to achieve the objectives of the policy makers in the major military powers. Small states were either objects of desire or used to rebalance the system in the process of reciprocal compensation. Their situation wasn't much better during the Concert of Europe, as Metternich and his coalition partners intervened throughout Europe to quash political change. It got worse—at least for the small states in the German Confederation—when Bismarck decided to create a unified Germany under Prussian control in the 1860s. The League of Nations' collective security system was the first to announce that the strong would pay attention to the preferences of the weak, but the League's failure to protect China and Ethiopia in the 1930s showed it was a hollow promise.

Meanwhile, outside of Europe, the same theoretical relationship played out through the long history of colonialism. During the old colonialism, indigenous civilizations in the Western hemisphere were defeated and occupied not simply because they were weaker. The more fundamental cause is to be found in the stronger actors' preferences. Europeans coveted the weaker civilizations' possessions (if they had gold and silver) and their climatically attractive lands. The post-Napoleonic lull in the acquisition of formal colonies reflected a change in the composition of the key actors and Britain's declining appetite for empire after the experience with rebellion in North America, the abolition of slavery, and the end of mercantilism. The resurgence of expansion during the new imperialism was made possible by the effect of the Industrial Revolution on relative power positions, but it was the combined effect of multiple economic and strategic incentives—plus the bogus justifications created by racism and Social Darwinism—that produced a widely shared preference for imperial expansion.

Great power asymmetries do not always produce catastrophes for the weak. The United States was virtually an economic hegemon immediately after World War II, but its preferences led to decisions such as the Marshall Plan and the willingness to accept trade discrimination from Europe and Japan that produced outcomes compatible with the goals of policy makers in many weaker states in the Western system. The same cannot, of course, be said of the fit between U.S. preferences and those in many post-colonial societies. Before the collapse of communism in the Soviet Union, socialist economic arrangements were far more attractive than capitalist ones to leaders in many post-colonial societies. However, those leaders were unable to change the preferences of U.S. policy makers for market economic systems built on the movement toward free trade and reciprocal and non-preferential treatment. Unable to change the preferences of the United States and too weak to challenge the system of international political economy that the U.S. championed, leaders of Third World countries who disagreed with the United States found themselves in the position described by Thucydides two millennia ago: "For you know as well as we do that . . . the strong do what they will and the weak suffer what they must."[1] This example leads to the last enduring pattern involving the relationship between preferences and power.

> *The stronger an actor's relative power position, the less strategically important weaker actors' preferences.*

Because this point is simply the mirror image of the preceding one, the examples in that section could be easily be rewritten to show this facet of politics. For example, colonizers could disregard the preferences of those they subjugated as long as they had the power to enforce their will against actual and anticipated resistance. Rather than listing more such examples, let's consider a related, but far more intriguing, question: When might a more powerful actor *want* to pay attention to the preferences of weaker actors? Two important situations come to mind. One is a function of the second political principle; the other of the third.

The Impact of Varying Beliefs about Just Relationships

The first political principle defines an essential feature of the strategic situation actors confront when they consider any particular issue. However, how actors evaluate the implications of differences in their preferences and relative power positions on any specific issue depends on how "fair" they believe the relationship is overall—*if*

Working decades apart on different continents with different adversaries, both Martin Luther King, Jr., and Mahatma Gandhi realized that appealing to a sense of what is just can be one of the most important sources of strategic leverage available to disadvantaged and exploited groups. That strategy will, of course, work only if their adversaries have a moral conscience.

fairness matters to them. More specifically, the connection between power and the compatibility of actors' preferences varies with the importance actors attach to creating or sustaining legitimate relationships, their beliefs about legitimate procedures and outcomes, and their perception of how legitimate or just their existing relationships are.

> *If people value creating and sustaining legitimate relationships* and *if they think a political process and the outcome it produces are just, they are more likely to accept that outcome—even if they would have preferred something else. If they think either the outcome or the process is unjust, they are far more likely to oppose it.*

The diversity of the world's cultures and group identities is interwoven with wide differences in people's sense of the historical record, the nature of their current situations, and their aspirations for the future. As a result, it is exceptionally hard to build shared notions of legitimate procedures and outcomes in world politics. Both the fact that it is difficult and the fact that it sometimes happens make the impact of varying beliefs about just relationships an important part of the politics of strategic choice.

The Political Connections between Process and Outcome Legitimacy

As we discussed in Chapter 3, judgments about the legitimacy of relationships reflect two distinct dimensions: the *process* by which particular outcomes are reached and the *substance* of the outcomes (who got what). The political implications of process legitimacy and outcome legitimacy are intertwined.

> *The lower the perceived legitimacy of a political process, the greater the political significance of outcome legitimacy. The lower the perceived legitimacy of an outcome, the greater the political significance of process legitimacy.*

The patterns in this piece of the second principle can be analyzed either by looking at cases in which there are trade-offs between process and outcome legitimacy—which is the way it is expressed above—or by looking at situations in which the two dimensions reinforce each other. The U.S. demand that European leaders decide how to use the bulk of the Marshall aid money is an example of a situation in which procedural and outcome legitimacy reinforced each other in positive ways. The Europeans not only got the money they needed for reconstruction after World War II—an outcome they liked—they also got to decide how it was spent. On the reinforcing but negative side, recall the hostility with which Third World leaders attacked the structure, norms, and institutions of the Western political economy in the 1960s to 1980s. That hostility was due to more than their opposition to any specific economic and political outcomes. As they asserted in the declaration calling for a New International Economic Order, Third World leaders regarded the prevailing arrangements as procedurally illegitimate because (with the exception of the states in Latin America) almost all had still been colonies during the period in which the system was organized.

Examples of situations in world politics in which increased process legitimacy helps offset the negative political effects of illegitimate outcomes are hard to find for the simple fact that process legitimacy is in short supply in interstate politics. Recall, however, the way in which the visible success of the Four Tigers and other Newly Industrializing Countries (NICs) combined with the collapse of communism's appeal in the 1980s and early 1990s to substantially increase the perceived legitimacy of the market as an organizing principle. Those events appear to have reduced opposition to free-trade regimes, even as the market continues to produce outcomes that are, in many cases, still highly unattractive.

Claims about what is fair are, of course, frequently colored by people's preferences for particular outcomes. People whose relative power position is weak on a particular issue often sense that their best chance to affect the outcome is to change the preferences of the strong by appealing to shared standards about what is just. In his campaign to eject the British from India in the 1930s and 1940s, Mahatma Gandhi made it clear that his strategy of nonviolence was designed to change British preferences by demonstrating that their policies in India were inconsistent with their own fundamental values about what was just. Nonviolence was, therefore, simultaneously morally right and strategically astute. Martin Luther King, Jr.'s leadership of the U.S. civil rights movement during the 1960s in the United States represented a similar combination of moral imperatives and strategic shrewdness. Such a strategy will work, however, only if its advocates are right in their assessments of their adversaries' values, or if there is a third party that will intervene. Gandhi and King were successful partly because they guessed right about the level of violent suppression of dissent that British and U.S. citizens were willing to accept to preserve the status quo.

Significantly, it is not just the weak who make appeals to community standards about just procedures and outcomes. Rich or militarily strong states at times seek to build international or domestic support for policies they have the capacity to implement on their own. They do so to defuse opposition and facilitate the achievement of their goals. For instance, during both the Korean and Persian Gulf wars, U.S. policy makers cited United Nations approval as a key indicator of the legitimacy of U.S. involvement in the conflict.

As the examples above suggest, claims about what is just are made by both challengers and defenders of the status quo and by both the weak and the strong. Consequently, it is important to look for variation in actors' beliefs about the importance

A summit meeting of the member governments of the European Union (EU) is shown at left. One of the most unusual aspects of the transformation of the European Economic Community (EEC) into the EU is the growing emphasis on using agreements about individual issues to build a stronger set of overall political relationships. This pattern is one of the best contemporary examples of the significance of the second political principle (the impact of varying beliefs about the nature and importance of just relationships) on the politics of strategic choice.

and nature of legitimacy and then assess how that variation affects the strategic situations in which people find themselves.

When People Don't Value Existing Relationships

If people don't value creating and sustaining legitimate relationships—or if they think a particular set of outcomes or procedures is illegitimate—then they are even more likely to challenge situations that don't fit their preferences. The absence of any commitment to building legitimate relationships greatly worsened the pathologies of the Italian state system during the Renaissance and increased the number of atrocities associated with European colonial expansion. The existence of competing universal principles sustained the centuries-long conflict between popes and Holy Roman emperors during the Middle Ages and the struggle between Catholics and Protestants that culminated in the Thirty Years' War. Even though many limited wars continued to take place during the classical-balance-of-power period, the agreement on a set of legitimizing principles at Westphalia lowered the magnitude of the violence and lay the foundation for a somewhat higher level of trust and longer time horizons. A return to competing universals—this time between the Westphalian principles and the demand for nationalism and democracy—then led to the lingering and violent death of the Old Order (and, with it, the classical balance of power) during the one hundred years between the French Revolution and the rise of the Bismarckian system at the end of the nineteenth century. It also, as we have mentioned many times, accelerated the late 1940s' ratcheting up of the Cold War and then helped sustain it for forty years. Different views about the nature of legitimate economic relationships were also at the center of the debates between rich and poor about trade in the 1960s and 1970s. Today, different understandings of legitimate relationships are one of the biggest sources of conflict between the West and Islamic states. Different views about just relationships are also at the center of the debates between rich and poor states about environmental issues.

When People Do Value Existing Relationships

If political actors value legitimacy and *also see their relationships as just, they will at times accept procedures and outcomes that adversely affect them.* These conditions are demanding, but the fact that they can occur is illustrated by the transformation in the diplomacy connecting the key actors in Western Europe. Nowhere is this clearer than in the relationship between France and Germany. After Bismarck defeated France in the Franco-Prussian War and then annexed the provinces of Alsace and Lorraine, policy makers in the two countries showed little, if any, desire to invest in creating a set of mutually legitimate relationships. Several arms races and two world wars later, the willingness to invest in an effort to create legitimate relations changed dramatically. The evolution of democracy in West Germany, shared membership in an anti-Soviet alliance, and a joint commitment to the success of the European Community laid the foundation for collaboration based on shared principles and mutual consent. As a result, over the last several decades, French and German leaders have often subordinated efforts to achieve specific objectives to the goal of building a deep and durable set of relationships as part of the European Union.

For instance, in the early 1990s the French government backed away from its preferred position in negotiations on grain imports into Europe after Germany and Britain argued that French opposition to the deal was undercutting Europe's overall international relationships. The British and French agreed to German desires to recognize Slovenia and Croatia—despite their concern that it would worsen the conflict as Yugoslavia disintegrated—in order to help develop a unified European policy. In the Maastricht negotiations on creating the European Union, the Germans and the French acceded to Britain's desire to have the flexibility to opt out of some EU provisions in an effort to respond to British notions of legitimate trans-state relations.

It is important to note that the theoretical relationship in the second political principle frames the problem of peaceful change in a significantly different way than the world federalists and functionalists framed their critique of the state system after World War II (see Chapter 7). From their theoretical perspective, the problem was the absence of a supranational authority that could enforce particular outcomes. From our theoretical perspective, the problem is the absence of a commitment to a larger community whose shared goals and principles could inspire individual actors to accept outcomes they don't like. The same problem is evident today in states in which warring ethnic or linguistic factions do not see value in building or sustaining a community that might transcend or at least soften their differences.

It follows, therefore, that the critical issue is variation in three factors: (1) the extent to which the key actors are committed to building and sustaining trans-state communities; (2) the extent to which actors who share that commitment agree on the substance of legitimacy; and (3) the extent to which existing relationships (including both their process and outcome dimensions) are perceived to have reached those standards. These are demanding conditions, but they are conditions that are logically compatible with the existence of a system of sovereign states. If they are met, decentralized systems have a good chance at handling peaceful change and collective conflict management. Moreover, it is at least equally possible that one could fail on all three in a world governed by a supranational authority.

We are, however, getting ahead of ourselves. To assess the probability that a particular diplomatic system will succeed, we need to *connect* the theoretical relationships in all five of the political principles. That being the case, we had best first finish the review of the individual pieces.

The Effect of the Shadow of the Future

The first two principles give you a picture of the strategic context in one arena at one point in time. But what if actors expect that some of the key variables are likely to change? People pay attention not only to how power, preferences, and issues of legitimacy are related today but also to how they expect these factors to evolve over time. This aspect of choice is called "the shadow of the future" to symbolize the notion that different anticipated futures cast different shadows on choice. How far people look into the future—their time horizons—and what they see within those time horizons affect their understandings of the strategic situation confronting them.

Different judgments about the shadow of the future are central to many environmental issues. Will the continuation of current economic practices lead to global warming, or will technological changes solve the problem without any significant changes in lifestyles? Different shadows of the future are also key considerations in debates about the role of supranational institutions in human rights. Will maintaining the principle of sovereign territoriality increase opportunities for legitimate expressions of democracy and diverse, but legitimate, judgments about the nature of justice, or will it simply provide continued protection for elite exploitation? The debate in the 1990s over whether the expansion of economic ties between the United States and China should be tied to an improved record on human rights and political liberties turned on contrasting judgments about the future. If you thought that economic growth would empower reform-minded groups, then it made sense to increase U.S. investment and trade (called a policy of *constructive engagement*). If you thought that Chinese elites were unlikely either to change their preferences or allow themselves to be replaced by reformers, then it made sense to focus on more competitive, power-based strategies for weakening their political position.

Different judgments about the possibility of creating jointly acceptable outcomes over time are at the center of many contemporary security controversies. If you believe that Arab nationalists will be satisfied with the return of the Golan

The Golan Heights overlooks Israel at one of its narrowest and most militarily vulnerable points. The question of whether Israel should return the Golan Heights to Syria in exchange for a declaration of peace hinges on different estimates about the shadow of the future. Will Syria honor such a pledge? If yes, the trade may well be worth it. If not, then Israel will be in a far worse military position in the future than it is now.

(Rina Castelnuovo/*The New York Times*)

Heights to Syria and the surrender of the West Bank to the Palestinians, then you are far more likely to think it makes sense for Israel to risk a trade of land for peace. If you believe that Israeli and Arab preferences will remain fundamentally incompatible over time, then you will think it is important for Israel to hold on to those areas to protect against attack.

Seeing the World as a Place Fit for Diffuse or Strict Reciprocity

How people view the shadow of the future affects more than individual policy choices. It also affects people's overall bargaining strategies and worldviews. People who believe there is a high probability of creating stable, jointly acceptable relationships are more likely to follow a cooperative strategy. What might such a cooperative strategy look like? In relationships characterized by *diffuse reciprocity*, people help each other out without keeping score. Thus, the Amish don't ask what their neighbor has done for them lately when a barn needs to be built; they organize a community barn raising. A system of diffuse reciprocity is harder to build in world politics than in individual relationships and small communities, where the bonds that connect individuals are usually more intimate and durable. Nevertheless, transnational relationships can vary in ways that either move policy makers closer toward a system that approximates diffuse reciprocity or drive them in the opposite direction. For instance, the intense collaboration between the United States and Britain during World War II, followed by their decades-long cooperation during the Cold War, produced something closer to diffuse reciprocity between those two countries than one often sees in international politics.

The possibilities for creating diffuse reciprocity depend on actors simultaneously having long time horizons, common values, and shared preferences. What happens to bargaining strategies and worldviews when actors' time horizons are short or they are uncertain about how long they will need to deal with another actor? In such cases, people are likely to resist making concessions that do not produce immediate benefits. A relationship based on *strict reciprocity* is an example of this pattern. Strict reciprocity exists when the parties in a relationship keep score about who is owed what by whom. When people are unsure about how long a relationship will last, or when they expect the strategic interactions with another person to end sooner rather than later, they are likely to keep a running tally of who has done what for whom in order to make sure that they're not on the short end when the relationship breaks off.

What happens when the time horizons stay long but the perceived compatibility of the actors' preferences and values decreases? If you think another person's values and preferences are incompatible with yours, trust is dangerous, and the longer you have to deal with them, the more dangerous it is. The notion that the world is full of people whose goals make them too dangerous to trust is, as we mentioned above, closely identified with the classical realist tradition. Machiavelli argued:

> Whosoever desires to found a state and give it laws, must start by assuming that all men are bad and ever ready to display their vicious nature, whenever they may find occasion for it. If their evil disposition remains concealed for a time, it must be attributed to some unknown reason; and we must assume that it lacked occasion to show itself; but time, which has been said to be the father of all truth, does not fail to bring it to light.[2]

If you assume that time will not fail to bring man's vicious nature to light, then the further you look into the future, the more important it becomes to guard against defections. If you make different assumptions about the compatibility of actors' preferences, the plausibility of realism fades, and strategies of either strict or diffuse reciprocity become more attractive.

Variations on a Theme: Examples from the Historical Record

Just as the historical record shows many examples of the first two principles in the politics of strategic choice, it provides instances of the third. Consider cases that fit the following pieces of the third principle.

> *The less stable the strategic context, the more actors' estimates of the strategic implications of different policy options will vary with the length of their time horizons.*

Unstable strategic contexts are notoriously difficult to read. Variations in the length of actors' time horizons simply make the problem worse. The impact of these differences on policy making is more pronounced the larger the number of factions that need to be on board to form a winning coalition. The reason is simple: The larger the number of factions, the greater the likely variation in decision makers' time horizons and perceptions. The strategic environment in Renaissance Italy was wildly unstable, and Machiavelli argued in favor of choice by a single individual, the Prince. In stable environments, he supported mixed government. Classical-balance-of-power Europe was more stable than Italy was in Machiavelli's time, but by modern standards it still suffered from a high level of unpredictable threat. The process of agreeing on when a state might be moving into a position where it could, at some time in the future, become a preponderant power was simplified by autocratic rule. The sovereign's guesses about the future might be wrong, but decisions would be made based on those guesses. The failures of collective conflict management in the democratic age are partly due to the difficulty in getting key factions in large policy-making coalitions to see the same futures.

> *The more incompatible people expect their preferences to become over time, the more competitive and power-based their strategic approach is likely to be.*

Machiavelli assumed incompatible preferences and emphasized power. Classical-balance-of-power statesmen assumed a high degree of conflict over territory but a shared commitment to maintain the system (to avoid falling back into a war of all against all) and to prevent preponderance. Thus, while they paid close attention to their relative power when it came to specific conflicts, they also tried to keep conflicts limited and to collaborate when that seemed possible. The leaders of the Concert of Europe presumed increasingly compatible preferences among the key states' rulers but increasingly incompatible preferences with domestic factions advocating democracy and nationalism. As a result, power was downplayed in interstate relations and emphasized in domestic interventions. Bismarck assumed enduring rivalries domestically and internationally and, consequently, made decisions in both arenas based on power. In the 1930s, Churchill and Chamberlain disagreed about the possibility of creating mutually acceptable arrangements with Hitler: Chamberlain thought it possible and de-emphasized power; Churchill thought it impossible and supported rearmament. After World War II, Truman's advisers were split between those who thought U.S.-Soviet preferences might turn out to be compatible over time (the Kennan-Marshall faction) and those that thought they would move further apart (the Nitze-Acheson faction) as the wartime collaboration against Hitler faded further into the past. A similar debate over the possibility of a future convergence was central to factional differences during the Reagan and Bush administrations about whether to cooperate with Gorbachev.

One can see the same differences in political economy. Power-centered systems—such as mercantilism and the Third World's demand for a one-nation, one-vote system in the UN resolution demanding a New International Economic Order—presupposed incompatible preferences over time. In stark contrast, GATT presupposed converging preferences as tariffs were dismantled and the world moved to free trade. It therefore stressed reciprocity and non-preferential treatment. This example leads to another possible pattern in the ways in which the shadow of the future can affect the politics of strategic interaction.

The longer the time horizons of actors who believe there is a high probability of creating stable, jointly acceptable relationships, the more likely it is that they will follow a cooperative strategy (such as one designed to create a system of diffuse reciprocity).

As we said above, one doesn't see this pattern very often in world politics. We have, however, covered two important examples. One, which we have just touched on, was the Western effort to build stable, jointly acceptable economic relationships after World War II; in this case, the question was not "who paid whom what," but rather how to make the system work. The Concert of Europe provides a second example. While the leaders of the Concert approached their ideological enemies quite competitively, they appear to have behaved toward each other with striking indifference for the strategic implications of shifts in their relative power positions. The Prussian king relied on Metternich, the Austrian chancellor, for advice on how to handle domestic problems with radical opponents of the regime. The Austrians once used Russian troops in Austria to suppress a rebellion. This mutual aid resembles the image of diffuse reciprocity in a tightly knit community; when help is needed, the community responds, and help arrives. The point is not to keep score or count who owes what to whom; the point is to get it done.

It is important to recognize that it's not just the length of the time horizon that produces diffuse reciprocity. It is length *combined* with the substance of actors' expectations—the belief the long-term outcomes and procedures will be legitimate and jointly acceptable. Long time horizons paired with different expectations produce different strategic implications.

The longer the time horizons of actors who believe there is a low probability of creating stable, jointly acceptable relationships, the more likely it is that they will follow a strategy designed to minimize the risks attached to possible defections.

Depending on how bad one expects the future to be, there are two common options for dealing with this situation. If actors expect things to be really bad, they should avoid collaborative behavior as much as possible to minimize the dangers of being double-crossed. In its extreme form, this leads to Machiavelli's advice for survival in Renaissance Italy and to Stalin's preference for either controlling actors or, when that was not possible, avoiding any long-term collaboration. In a less extreme form, this pattern can lead to a strategy in which actors who are willing to collaborate in pursuit of specific objectives but uncomfortable about "unsecured" trust over the long haul demand a policy of strict reciprocity. During the 1970s, Soviet and U.S. decision makers came to believe that an unrestrained nuclear arms race between them was both dangerous and a waste of money. The result was several significant nuclear arms control agreements. But because neither side really trusted the other, the accords were carefully limited as to what they regulated, and each side carefully observed the behavior of the other to make certain the agreements—and the underlying principle of strict reciprocity—were being followed.

It is time to pause briefly and see where we are in this review. As we have mentioned before, the first political principle defines the strategic situation in the issue specifically at hand. The second connects that issue to a larger process of strategic interaction that defines the nature of the actors' relationships. The third examines how actors expect these two linked processes of strategic interaction to change over time. Taken together, these first three principles drive the strategic incentives built into the situation actors confront in a single political arena. However, people *vary* in how they *react* to strategic incentives. That leads us to the fourth political principle.

The Impact of Risk-Taking Preferences and Discounting

Making Risky Choices

Political and Policy Risks   As we stressed in the introduction to the politics of strategic choice in Chapter 3, strategic choices are, by their nature, risky choices. They are risky in two senses. First, the outcomes that result from strategic choices are seldom certain. There is almost always some chance that people will not achieve their goals even if they choose the best option available and implement that choice as effectively as possible. Second, strategic choices usually involve an investment in resources, time, and political capital. Strategic choices, therefore, carry both a policy risk and a political risk. *Policy risk* refers to the probability that actors' substantive goals will not be achieved even if their policy choices are implemented effectively. *Political risk* refers to the likelihood that policy choices will have adverse effects on actors' political positions—on their ability to make and sustain their preferred policy choices.

You can identify the policy risks attached to options for achieving specific international outcomes by analyzing how the first three principles come together in the international arena:

- Who are the key actors in any effort to achieve this specific international outcome?
- What are their preferences and relative power positions?
- How much importance do they attach to sustaining legitimate relationships, and how legitimate do they believe existing procedures and outcomes are?
- How does the shadow of the future affect the attractiveness of each actor's options?

Answering these questions will give you a good idea of the *level* (the size) of the policy risks of each option. The level of the political risks attached to those options can then be estimated by asking the same questions of the two other arenas that affect world politics: the policy-making arena within which factions try to put together winning coalitions in support of their preferred policy choices; and the constituency arena that connects those factions to their key political supporters and constituents.

In sum, when talking about international politics, the international arena generates the policy risks, and the policy-making and constituency arenas generate the political risks. The fourth principle in the politics of strategic choice examines how actors are likely to *react* to the level of policy risks generated by the international situation and the level of political risks generated by factional and constituency politics. Actors' risk-taking preferences—their willingness to accept different levels of political and policy risks—will vary with the value they attach to achieving a specific policy outcome and how much control they have over a policy choice and how it is implemented.

Discounting　How people react to political and policy risks also depends on when the costs and benefits attached to those risks are expected to arrive. As we explained in Chapter 3, people generally prefer to get the benefits of a choice quickly and to defer the costs as long as possible. Consequently, actors typically discount costs (including political risks) and benefits (including preferred policy outcomes) over time, generally preferring current benefits over future benefits and future costs over current costs. When people discount, they adjust the value of costs and benefits depending on when they arrive. Benefits people have to wait for are valued less than those they can get right away. Costs that people can defer look less costly.

It is easy to choose the best available strategic option when the policy and political incentives reinforce each other, and the benefits come early. Options that offer a high probability of achieving actors' policy objectives while simultaneously decreasing their political risks are as close to being "no-brainers" as strategic choices get. The choice will, of course, be more difficult if the best available option has only a low probability of success, or if the costs come early and the benefits late. But even in these cases, people are likely to make the decision to go ahead if doing nothing is perceived to be worse than taking the only available chance to achieve valued objectives. Policy makers can get to this point in two quite different ways. If the political risks of failure are very small, even low-probability options may be worth pursuing. The odds of winning the jackpot in a state lottery are terribly small, but so too are the investment and the political risks of purchasing a handful of tickets. Since many people see lotteries as their only opportunity to get rich, and few people are likely to be ostracized by family and friends for taking the chance, why not try?

The situation is quite different when the costs of failure are high. People are highly unlikely to put their life's savings on the line in a lottery. But what if the situation people are currently facing—the status quo—is both utterly incompatible with their policy preferences and dangerous to their political survival? If the status quo is highly unattractive, the cost of doing nothing may seem greater than the risk of acting, even if the only option that appears to offer a way to escape the current situation has only a small probability of long-term success. In such a situation, options that are likely to fail at some point in the future may look better than standing pat, especially if those options front-load the benefits while deferring the costs of failure.

For instance, the governing coalition in Japan in 1941 estimated U. S. military capabilities as being eight to ten times greater than their own. However, the key people in that coalition also believed that the only available diplomatic options for preserving the peace would require foregoing their most highly valued foreign policy objectives and produce domestic rebellion. The war was expected to produce immediate

The Japanese decided to attack Pearl Harbor in 1941 even though they estimated U.S. military capabilities to be eight to ten times greater than their own. Among other factors, this decision was affected by the fact that the perceived peaceful alternatives were likely to come at a huge immediate political and policy cost with almost no immediate benefit. Given how most people discount costs and benefits over time, having those massive costs come early while the benefits come late increased the political leverage of factions within the Japanese government who preferred attack over capitulating to U.S. demands.

political and foreign policy benefits. Failure, though likely if the United States chose to fight long enough to win, was three or four years away. Consequently, the current costs of standing pat were seen as far worse than the long-term risks of bombing Pearl Harbor and fighting a war with the United States. In October 1941, Prime Minister Fumimaro Konoye argued that the decision to attack Pearl Harbor in a few weeks should be reconsidered, that the great difference in military capabilities between the United States and Japan made war too dangerous. General Hideki Tojo, then war minister and soon to succeed Konoye as prime minister, adamantly disagreed. Referring to a well-known temple that bordered a dangerous ravine, he argued that "there are times when we must have the courage to do extraordinary things—like jumping, with eyes closed, off the veranda of the Kiyomizu Temple!"[3]

Patterns in Actors' Reactions to Risk and Discounting

As these examples suggest, actors' reactions to the level of political and policy risks they confront in different strategic situations varies with how they value achieving gains versus preventing losses, their risk-taking preferences, and how they discount costs and benefits over time. Consider first these assumptions about risk-taking preferences:

- *The higher the expected value that an actor attaches to a policy outcome, the more willing that actor will be to invest resources and political position in an effort to achieve that goal.*
- *The less control they have over policy choice and implementation, the less willing coalition members will be to take political risks in an effort to achieve coalition policy goals.*
- *The less control they have over policy choice and implementation, the more indifferent coalition members will be to policy failure—if policy failure isn't politically dangerous.*

If these assumptions are correct, using them to identify actors' risk-taking preferences will help explain why people react the way they do to the level of policy risks generated by the international strategic context and the level of political risks generated by the contexts for factional and constituency politics. People's reactions also reflect how they discount costs (including political risks) and benefits (including preferred policy outcomes) over time. People generally prefer current benefits over future benefits and future costs over current costs. This preference is reinforced by the fact that waiting to receive benefits creates a risk that those benefits will never arrive. The exact way in which actors discount costs and benefits varies with the following factors:

- *The higher the expected value actors attach to achieving a specific policy outcome, the less their choices will be affected by discounting.*
- *The less control they have over policy choice and implementation, the more actors will prefer future costs over current costs and the more they will discount future benefits relative to current benefits.*
- *The higher the immediate political risks of preferred policy options, the more willing actors will be to defer policy benefits in exchange for a reduction in current political risks.*

Intriguing patterns emerge when you put these pieces together. Front-loading the costs and delaying the gains goes directly against the incentive to discount—to prefer future costs over current costs and current benefits over future benefits. The fourth political principle suggests that this pattern is less likely to happen when actors have a high degree of control over policy choice and implementation and when the value they attach to the outcome is so high that it weakens the incentive to discount. Meanwhile, these factors also increase actors' willingness to run political risks to achieve policy objectives. Consequently, when they occur, they simultaneously drive down the attractiveness of discounting and increase the willingness to take short-term risks in pursuit of long-term gains.

This pattern is exactly what one finds in the classical-balance-of-power period in Europe, a period of autocratic rule in which the sovereigns feared both a return to a pre-Westphalian war of competing hegemonies and a Hobbesian war of all against all. While the level of political risks facing the autocratic sovereigns of this period was usually substantially lower than the level of political risks facing policy makers in Renaissance Italy and during the Wars of Religion, war was still a risky enterprise. Moreover, the classical-balance-of-power system expected actors to pay the costs of war in anticipation that those immediate costs would produce long-term benefits: preserving the system and preventing preponderance. The assumptions about risk-taking preferences and discounting in the fourth principle suggest that the level of control exercised by these autocrats made it easier for them to accept the political risks created by their willingness to pay now to achieve benefits later.

Significantly, these requirements are exactly what one does *not* find in the linked domestic and international contexts in which policy makers struggled to implement the League of Nation's collective security system or in more recent situations that involved efforts to organize other types of collective conflict management systems. Consider the comparison between collective security and classical balance of power. While the goals of the two systems are fundamentally different—preserving universal peace versus preventing preponderance—collective security requires discounting and risk-taking patterns strikingly similar to those in classical balance of power. Policy makers in both systems had to be willing to pay high immediate costs that were politically risky in pursuit of long-term benefits that were of limited political value. Each long-term goal (preventing preponderance, lessening the probability of war) was of limited political value not only because the benefits lay in the future, but also because those benefits would come in the form of counterfactuals, outcomes that didn't happen. The League's enforcers of collective security didn't value the outcomes highly enough to adjust their discounting accordingly. Meanwhile, the growth of democracy increased the level of political risks at the same time that it drove down policy makers' willingness to run those risks.

Notice that in both these systems the incentives created by actors' risk-taking preferences and their willingness to discount costs and benefits reinforced each other. In the case of balance of power, the reinforcing incentives helped support the system; in collective security the reinforcing incentives cut the other way, undermining the system. It does not, of course, have to work out that way. These theoretical relationships can also push in opposite directions. Recall the evolution of U.S. policy making during the early years of the Cold War. While the value policy makers attached to achieving their goals encouraged them to downplay the incentive to discount and increased their willingness to run political risks, the number of factions they had to get on board to make and sustain policy pushed in the opposite direction. Cross-pressured, U.S. policy factions in the executive branch tried to reduce the level of political risks by magnifying the sense of perceived threat. They also showed a preference for altering the decision-making environment in ways that increased their control by decreasing congressional influence over the choice and implementation of politically risky policies.

The impact of these patterns can also be seen in issues involving the environment and political economy. Trying to prevent global warming involves paying high short-run costs in an effort to achieve long-run benefits. Free-trade policies ask more of policy makers than neomercantilist policies because the logic of free trade asks people to accept the short-run costs of making themselves vulnerable to foreign competition in exchange for gaining the long-run benefits of eliminating protectionist trade restrictions. That is exactly the opposite of what the logic of discounting typically leads people to prefer. Given the first discounting assumption, one would expect these effects to drop the more ideologically committed one is to free trade, but the willingness to accept short-term costs as an investment in long-term success can be undermined by higher political risks and having to make choices in political arenas that require large and complex policy coalitions. The combination of recession and inflation (stagflation) produced a dramatic jump in the political risks of free trade policies in the 1970s. Since the structure of the U.S. political system encourages policy factions to be politically risk averse and policy risk acceptant, the result was a swing away from free trade to neomercantilism.

As this example suggests, increases in the level of short-term political risks can produce a dramatic reversal in the willingness to accept short-term pain to get long-term gain, even in a country where policy makers have a strong commitment to the goal of free trade. It is little wonder then, that in the 1950s to 1980s Third World leaders were hostile to the suggestion of free-trade advocates in rich countries that they should accept far higher short-term costs to get even more deferred and problematic benefits.

The Impact of Linkage Politics

As we have emphasized from the very outset of the book, world politics involves linkages across multiple political arenas: political interactions among international actors (whether individuals or organized groups), factional politics within each actor (if the actors are coalitions), and constituency politics (the relationships between policy factions and their mass and elite constituencies).

> *The connections across international politics, factional politics, and constituency politics affect the strategic context in each arena, the level of the stakes and risks policy makers confront and how they react to them, the choices actors make, and the outcomes (given those choices).*

The effects of these cross-arena linkages run in two directions: from the international arena into factional and constituency politics; and from those two domestic arenas into international politics. During the classical-balance-of-power period, the interstate consensus in support of dynastic rule increased the domestic legitimacy of autocratic sovereigns. At the same time, the absence of democratic institutions increased policy makers' ability to act on their estimates of relative military power, to make and break alliances quickly, to practice reciprocal compensation, and to make war in pursuit of balance-of-power's principal diplomatic objectives. After the French Revolution and the Napoleonic wars, domestic pressure led autocratic rulers in the Concert of Europe to redefine their understanding of the nature of the primary threats in world politics. They moved away from Britain's emphasis on preventing a repeat of Napoleon's drive for hegemony and toward preventing any radical changes in domestic political and economic arrangements. At the same time, international support for restoring the Old Order facilitated the Concert's efforts to suppress domestic reformers.

Both the classical balance of power and the Concert of Europe provide examples where the "in-out" and "out-in" linkages reinforced policy makers' desire and ability to achieve preferred outcomes. The League of Nations' collective security system is a classic example of linkages that undercut both. Even in an ideal environment, collective security systems create a tension between the international requirement that help arrive quickly and automatically and the domestic requirement of consultation and political support. The antiwar sentiment of the 1920s and 1930s made it almost impossible for British and French policy makers to guarantee that they would fulfill their international responsibilities at the same time as the international context produced the most difficult kind of threats for collective security systems to handle—challenges by major powers (Germany, Japan, and Italy).

Similar patterns in linkage politics can be seen in political economy. Mercantilism provides an example of reinforcing linkages. The highly competitive world of interstate trade (suppressing imports, promoting exports, authorizing privateers to prey on shipping, competing for colonial empires) was entirely compatible with the drive to increase the state's domestic political and economic control. Policy making in post-colonial societies in the 1950s to 1980s provides the analogue to the negative linkages of collective security. What Third World policy makers had the power to do internationally (accept IMF and GATT rules) wasn't popular domestically; what was popular domestically (successfully challenging those rules), they didn't have the power to do internationally.

Since every issue discussed in Chapters 6 to 13 is analyzed from a linkage politics perspective, we could continue these examples almost indefinitely. Rather than do that, we will simply reiterate a basic point: Look for cross-arena linkages whenever you analyze any issue area, case, or historical period. To do that well, you will need to be sensitive to another fundamental point: *It's how the pieces in the five political principles come together that really counts.* If you want to identify the distinguishing features of different periods or figure out why some strategies work and others fail, look for how the separate theoretical relationships in the politics of strategic interaction *combine*.

Conclusion

As we said at the outset of this chapter, the organization of this book reflects a judgment that the best way to begin an exploration of world politics is to combine an understanding of the key "facts" of world politics with a set of intellectual tools that cultivates what appears to be the largest available patch of common ground: the politics of strategic choice. Tools designed to cultivate this common ground should help you see how each worldview discussed in Chapter 2 can contribute to a better understanding of world politics when the issues it emphasizes and the assumptions it makes fit your values, interests, and the linked international and domestic contexts in the period and area of the world you want to understand. Perhaps even more important, these tools should help you use a theoretically informed understanding of the past to make sense of the world around you and to assess its impact on your life's choices today and tomorrow.

Faculty and students interested in taking a closer, more theoretical look at the key concepts in an approach that emphasizes the politics of strategic choice will find the next two chapters of particular value. We then conclude with a chapter that considers how you might use what you have learned—with or without Chapters 15 and 16—to consider what the future might hold.

To The Reader   QUESTIONS FOR REVIEW are available at
www.prenhall.com/lamborn

Getting to Choice
Preferences, Power, and Perception

The process of strategic interaction in world politics is driven by actors' choices. Those choices are, in turn, driven by the ways in which actors' preferences, relative power, and perceptions combine. This chapter takes a closer look at these three concepts and how they shed light on the politics of choice.

The first section explains what it means to say that actors have preferences and make purposive choices. The second section expands on our earlier discussions of power, one of the most important yet misunderstood concepts in politics. The chapter's third section examines what people actually see when they look at the distribution of power and preferences. It explains the concepts of perception and misperception—what actors notice about their strategic environment and how they make inferences from that information. Finally, the fourth section explores some of the most important sources of variation in actors' preferences and perceptions: differences in culture, group identity, norms, and institutions; differences in the search process that actors use to identify and evaluate options; variations in the standards actors use to judge success and failure; variations in people's reactions to when costs and benefits arrive; differences in actors' time horizons (how far they look into the future); and variations in how they respond to risks.

Preferences and the Concept of Purposive Choice

What does it mean to say that actors have preferences and make purposive choices? People can have goals without articulating or perhaps even considering what they would be willing to sacrifice to achieve them. *Preferences*, as we use the term, refers not to abstract wants but to a set of specific alternatives that an actor has ordered from most to least attractive. Because the alternatives an actor perceives may conflict with one another on some dimensions, establishing a preference ordering may require making trade-offs among valued outcomes.

Officials in the People's Republic of China have, for example, long maintained that one of their principal purposes is to reunite the entire Chinese nation. The reincorporation of Hong Kong (which had been ruled by Great Britain for a century and a half) into China in July 1997 was a step toward achieving this purpose; the reincorporation of Macao (an area on the southern coast of China that Portugal had ruled since the sixteenth century) in December 1999, another. Reincorporation of Taiwan, if that occurs, would be one more such step. However, while Chinese officials were able to persuade Great Britain and Portugal to return Hong Kong and Macao, the situation they face regarding Taiwan is more complex. Taiwan is, for all practical purposes, an independent state, not a colonial possession, and its people are unlikely to accept reunification with the mainland peacefully unless political freedom there increases substantially. If this assumption is correct and Chinese officials continue to desire that Taiwan rejoin the mainland without having to fight a war to acquire it, they will at some point have to decide which they *prefer:* maintenance of their existing authoritarian system or a significant change in that system that would make reunification attractive to the people on Taiwan.

As this example illustrates, the idea of preferences implies an ability to order (prioritize) a set of possible outcomes from most to least attractive. To use information about actors' preference orderings to explain their choices, it must be appropriate for analysts to make the following two assumptions about actors' preferences. First, it must be appropriate to assume that the actors can reduce their assessments of the relative attractiveness of the outcomes they want to achieve to a *single comparable dimension*. Actors can *begin* with multiple dimensions of value, but they must be able to combine them into a single overall evaluative dimension that can be used to order the relative attractiveness of different options. Second, it must be appropriate to assume that the actors' choices among their ordered options are **transitive**. To say that choices are made *transitively* simply means that if an actor prefers option *a* over option *b* and option *b* over option *c*, then *a* is preferred over *c*. Unless actors' choices among ordered options are transitive, we cannot say that their preferences and choices are connected in a logically consistent way.

As we discussed in Chapter 3, actors have two kinds of preferences: preferences over outcomes and preferences over the particular policies or instruments they can use to achieve those outcomes. Preferences over outcomes reflect the value an actor attaches to certain specific states of the world. U.S. officials, for example, strongly prefer: (1) an internationally cooperative, steadily democratizing China, to (2) an internationally cooperative China that is not becoming more democratic, to (3) an internationally uncooperative (that is, aggressive) China.[1] Yet in a situation where outcomes are interdependent, actors' policy choices depend not just on the particular state of the world they prefer, but also on what they think others will do regarding that issue. In other words, how one values various outcomes is one necessary ingredient—but not the only one—in explaining preferences over policies and the specific policies that officials choose.

Comparing Purposive Choice to Commonsense Notions of Rationality

We can now specify more precisely what is meant by **purposive choice** and explain its relationship to the idea of *rationality*. Purposive choice simply assumes that actors can order their preferences over different policy options, and once they have done that, choose transitively from among those ordered options so as to maximize their expected satisfaction. To some, rationality means no more than that actors make purposive choices.*

However, many more people use *rationality* to refer not simply to purposive choice given ordered options, but also to the wisdom of actors' preferences and the quality of the process by which they identify and evaluate options for achieving their goals. It's easy to understand why this is so. The commonsense notion of **rationality** suggests the careful and thoughtful pursuit of wise and moral objectives. Given this common use of the word, people are typically very uncomfortable describing immoral or poorly informed choices as being rational. While this reluctance is understandable, the tendency to embed judgments about the wisdom or morality of actors' goals and the quality of their search and evaluation procedures into the idea of rationality creates a great deal of confusion. Immoral values, such as systematic plans to commit genocide, can lead to purposive behavior. Similarly, poorly informed decisions can reflect transitive choices among the rank-ordered options actors perceive.

transitive choice
Situations in which actors who have ordered their preferences choose consistently among those ordered preferences.

purposive choice
Situations in which actors choose transitively (consistently) among ordered preferences so as to maximize their expected satisfaction.

rationality In casual, everyday usage refers to choices made after a comprehensive evaluation of all the possible options for achieving a worthy goal.

*Much of the contemporary "rational choice" work in political science follows this minimal version of purposive choice. See, for example, the work of Bruce Bueno de Mesquita.

Adolf Hitler is one of the most universally recognized symbols of evil in the Western world. But does that mean that his choices were *irrational?* The answer is surely "yes" if one is using either commonsense notions of rationality or the more restrictive term *substantive* rationality because both focus on the wisdom and morality of actors' goals. However, to argue that Hitler was *instrumentally* rational, all you have to assume is that Hitler had preferences, and that he chose among his perceived options in a way that he thought would maximize his expected satisfaction.

Consequently, scholars prefer to avoid common usage meanings of rationality and distinguish between three different types of rationality: *substantive* rationality, which focuses on the quality and worthiness (the substance) of actors' goals; *comprehensive* rationality, which focuses on how systematically and thoroughly (how comprehensively) actors search for options and evaluate the ones they see; and *instrumental* (or *procedural*) rationality, which simply assumes that people choose transitively from among the ordered options they perceive so as to maximize their expected satisfaction (given their values). Given these distinctions, we suggest using these terms with great care. In those cases where it is appropriate to assume that actors can order their perceived options, we suggest using the unambiguous term (purposive choice) and avoiding the ambiguous one (rational choice) when you are trying to explain actors' choices given their preferences and perceived options. Having done that, you are then free to talk directly about the morality of actors' values—or the quality and wisdom of the process they use to identify and evaluate options—when that is your primary concern. When the term "rationality" is used by others, you need to be aware of the distinctions among substantive, comprehensive, and instrumental rationality and look for ways to unpack and clarify the exact points they are making.

Defining purposive choice and its relationship to the commonsense notion of rationality clears the way for evaluating the very real and significant variation in how self-consciously and thoroughly people assess options and select policies. Some policy makers deliberate more methodically than others, and some situations, such as crises that could lead to major wars, presumably induce officials to evaluate the available policy options very carefully, regardless of those officials' individual beliefs and decision-making styles. Even though people's beliefs and the way they notice and evaluate incoming information can affect the specific policy option that is chosen, variation in these factors does not in most cases affect the essence of purposive or goal-oriented behavior. In characterizing political actors as purposive, we assume only that people have preferences that they care about achieving. We believe that this is a reasonable assumption if one sees politics as the attempt to achieve interdependent outcomes.

It is also important to recognize that people can use a variety of yardsticks to define what success means in achieving their goals. Some try to maximize their net assets; others try to minimize net losses. We leave open the issue of which criterion of success people choose and simply note here that either is consistent with the notion of purposive action. We return to this issue later in the chapter.

Social Choice: When the Actors Are Coalitions

So far, we have assumed that the actors who make choices are either individuals or factions. Imagine now that the actors are instead coalitions. What does the idea that actors have *preferences* mean when the actors are coalitions as opposed to unitary actors such as individuals or factions? Choice by coalitions is called **social choice.** Recall the definitions of faction and coalition from Chapter 3. A faction is a group of people with a single set of preferences over outcomes (ends) and identical preferences over policies (the best available means to achieve those ends). A coalition is a group of factions that has different ends but who choose to act together temporarily because they happen to agree on a specific policy. Coalitions often need to give some of their members pay-offs, called *side-payments*, to keep them on board.

The commonsense notion of *purpose* takes on different meanings in coalitions and factions. Because members of a faction have identical preferences over outcomes and also agree on the policy instruments that are most likely to produce those outcomes at acceptable costs and risks, the meaning of purpose is unambiguous when the actors are factions. On the other hand, because coalitions are composed of factions with different preferences over outcomes, and thus are not **unitary actors**, the meaning of purpose here is more complex and ambiguous. What brings together the factions in a coalition (in spite of their different preferences over outcomes) is agreement on policies that each member sees as useful instruments for achieving their different objectives. The members of coalitions thus have some shared preferences (about means) as well as some different preferences (about ends that go beyond the scope of the coalition's shared policy choices). Consequently, while it is meaningful to talk about a coalition's purposes (because its members share common policy preferences), it is important not to lose sight of the fact that they simultaneously disagree about some other objectives.

An example will illustrate this point. An alliance is a military coalition designed to deter, defend against, or coerce a common enemy. The United States, Britain, and the Soviet Union (USSR) formed such a coalition during World War II. While political leaders in each of these states, particularly the USSR, had international objectives that were at odds with those of the other two allies, they agreed that Nazi Germany represented *the* supreme threat to them all. So even though Japan had some major successes early in the war and America's position in the Pacific was very vulnerable after the attack on Pearl Harbor, they agreed to focus on defeating Germany completely before they finished off Japan. This alliance decision, made early in the war, set the framework for virtually all others that followed.[2] However, the basis for that coalition disappeared with Hitler's defeat. Not surprisingly, the two Western states could not sustain agreement with the Soviets once that threat disappeared.

Paying attention to this essential difference between factions and coalitions will enable you to anticipate the conditions under which coalitions may fall apart over time. But the essential difference between factions and coalitions also reveals

social choice   Choices made by coalitions.

unitary actors   Actors that have a single set of preferences over both outcomes and policies; individuals and factions are, by definition, unitary actors, but coalitions are not.

other—and less intuitively obvious—potential sources of inconsistent choice by coalitions. Factions, like individuals, have transitive preferences. Coalitions, because they are composed of factions with different preferences over outcomes, may produce *intransitive* choices; that is, coalitions may agree that option *a* is more attractive than option *b*, and that *b* is better than *c*, but end up opting for *c* over *a*. When factions' preferences don't combine to produce a clear winner, coalitions can produce choices that do not reflect any internally consistent set of preferences.

Consider a hypothetical example of intransitive choice by coalitions that is based on a very real event, the Cuban Missile Crisis. In October 1962, U.S. policy makers discovered that the Soviet Union was deploying a large number of missiles in Cuba that could hit targets throughout most of the continental United States. The perceived options quickly boiled down to three: a blockade to seal Cuba off from further Soviet military deliveries while U.S. and Soviet leaders negotiated a settlement; an air strike to destroy the missile sites; or a full-scale invasion to eliminate both the missiles and the Castro regime. What would happen if the decision had depended on forming a winning coalition among three factions with the following preferences?

Faction #1: Prefers *air strike* over *invasion* over *blockade*

Faction #2: Prefers *blockade* over *air strike* over *invasion*

Faction #3: Prefers *invasion* over *blockade* over *air strike*

In this hypothetical scenario, each faction can order its individual preferences such that if *a* is preferred to *b* and *b* is preferred to *c*, then *a* is preferred to *c*. However, while each faction would make individual choices among the perceived options transitively (consistently), they may not be able to form a winning coalition whose choices reflect transitive preferences. Consider how this problem might occur. If the choice is between the air strike and the invasion, Factions #1 and #2 form a coalition that wins a majority in favor of the air strike. If the choice is between the air strike and the blockade, #2 and #3 form a coalition in favor of the blockade. Given a choice between the blockade and the invasion, #1 and #3 form a coalition that chooses an invasion. However, when the preferences of all three factions are weighted equally in a majority vote, and they consider the three options two at a time, the invasion option loses to the air strike, which loses to the blockade, which loses to the invasion, which loses to the air strike, and so on, producing no resolution of the issue.

Some decades ago, Kenneth Arrow, an internationally famous economist and choice theorist, showed that when three or more unitary actors have preferences over three or more alternatives but make choices between pairs of those alternatives, they may produce an intransitive outcome for the group as a whole, even though each unitary actor (each faction) has transitive preferences.[3] One of the easiest ways to understand Arrow's insight about when such problems can occur is to compare the "merry-go-round" scenario above with a set of preference orderings that produces a clear, transitive choice. Consider the outcome if the three factions had instead had the following preference orderings:

Faction #1: Prefers *air strike* over *invasion* over *blockade*

Faction #2: Prefers *blockade* over *air strike* over *invasion*

Faction #3: Prefers *invasion* over *air strike* over *blockade*

Here, given a choice between the air strike and the invasion, Factions #1 and #2 can form a coalition in favor of the air strike. Given a choice between the air strike and the blockade, #1 and #3 can agree on the air strike. And given a choice between the invasion and the blockade, #1 and #3 can agree on an invasion. But notice that the invasion option loses to the air strike option when those two are compared. This means that a coalition favoring the air strike cannot be defeated by any other coalition (assuming that the rules allow two of the three factions to outvote the third). As a result, given the set of factional preferences outlined just above, the group as a whole *can* produce a transitive choice.

What is the crucial difference in these two sets of preference orderings that leads to such different results? In the first example, #1 prefers air strike > invasion > blockade. This preference ordering makes sense if one is determined to destroy the missiles but is sensitive to the level of casualties and the risks of a larger war. (The blockade is last because it would not by itself necessarily have removed any missiles already in Cuba. Of the two options that are designed to take out the missiles directly, the air strike is preferred because it leaves open the possibility that a larger military operation will not be needed.) Faction #2 prefers blockade > air strike > invasion. That makes sense (is purposive) if one is most concerned with the level of casualties and the risk of war. Given those preferences, a policy maker would want to begin with the least forcible of the options, working up from there only if the less forcible options fail. Faction #3's preference orderings do not, however, seem to make much sense. It prefers the *most* forcible option (invasion) to the *least* forcible option (blockade) to the *middle* option (air strike). Faction #3's preferences simply do not seem to fit on the same evaluative dimension as the preferences of Factions #1 and #2. In the second example, by contrast, all of the factions appear to be arranging their preferences along the same dimension. Thus, in the second scenario, even though Faction #2 is concerned most about the risks of a larger war, and #1 and #3 care more about being certain that the missiles will be removed, all share the same dimension along which they order their preferences for the different options.

We can only make sense of the preferences of Faction #3 in the first example if we assume that more than a single dimension is being used to order the preferences. What might it be? One possibility (again speaking entirely hypothetically) is that while Faction #3 is composed of people who share the belief that force is likely to be needed to remove the missiles directly, international incentives (getting rid of the missiles) weren't the only ones driving their preference orderings. One possibility is that their policy preferences reflected domestic institutional incentives. If a military operation to remove the missiles were chosen, they wanted land forces to be used so that in future decisions about military roles and missions the Army would get an "acceptable" share of the total resources. Of the three options, only an invasion of Cuba simultaneously met their domestic and their international objectives. However, if an invasion were not chosen, the domestic dimension of the choice dropped out, and the leaders of this faction ordered the remaining two options solely on the international dimension, preferring the less forcible to the more forcible option.

It turns out that the problem of intransitive social choice we have identified is not a problem if—but only if—three conditions are fulfilled.[4] One is that the actors (the factions in a coalition) arrange their preferences along the same single evaluative dimension. While factions can start with a concern for multiple factors—such as the probability of removing the missiles and the level of casualties in the Cuban Missile Crisis example—they must be able to reduce those multiple considerations to one final dimension along which the perceived options can be rank-ordered. A second precondition for transitive choice by coalitions is that the factions' preference orderings are "single-peaked": all the actors have one alternative that they favor more than any other. Third, their preferences must decline steadily (*monotonically*) as one moves away from this single, best option. As we have seen, Faction #3 in the first example did not satisfy any of these conditions. The result was a pattern of intransitive choice among the three options.

We can summarize our discussion about preferences in coalitions by making five points. First, a coalition is a set of factions that agree on a particular policy choice but see that shared choice as part of a strategy to achieve *different* combinations of ends. Second, as a direct result of the first point, there is no guarantee that coalitions will be stable over time (as, for example, in the Anglo-American-Soviet World War II alliance), since their differing preferences over objectives may at some point lead them to disagree about policy choices. Third, coalitions often need to give their members side-payments to keep them in the coalition. Those side-payments may produce internally inconsistent policy choices that increase the chances of failure. For instance, before World War I, the key factions governing Germany agreed that it would be dangerous if France were able to build anti-German alliances that included Britain and Russia. However, as the price of continuing in the coalition, one faction demanded policy side-payments that antagonized Britain, and the other demanded a side-payment that antagonized Russia. As a result, the coalition succeeded in staying in office, but at the price of adopting a set of foreign policies that was internally inconsistent and more likely to fail.

Fourth, even without the problem of side-payments, because the factions in a coalition may order their preferences on multiple dimensions (as Faction #3 did in the first hypothetical scenario about the Cuban Missile Crisis), there is no guarantee that coalitions will make transitive choices from among ordered preferences in a way that fits our commonsense notion of purpose. Fifth, because factions within coalitions are simultaneously involved in a process of strategic interaction internally (to hold the coalition together) and externally (to achieve coalition policy preferences), it is possible that policy compromises made to hold the coalition together may decrease the chances that coalition members will achieve their international objectives (as was the case during the Carter administration, when linkage politics made it difficult to sustain coherent policies toward the Soviet Union and the Third World).

The potential effects of linkage politics and differences in factions' preferences over outcomes on the stability of coalitions will, of course, always be with us. As for the potential for intransitive choices by coalitions, it can occur in any situation of multidimensional choice, or when actors are unable to order their preferences monotonically around a single most-preferred outcome. Multidimensional choice is likely to be quite common in world politics because individuals and factions may be trying to achieve desired outcomes with respect to political and policy risks at the same time. Thus, what may easily appear counterintuitive—intransitively ordered social choices from a group composed of members who individually act purposively—is understandable if we assume that actors may care simultaneously about more than a single dimension.

A Closer Look at What It Means to Be Powerful

As defined in Chapter 3, *power* is the ability to increase the likelihood of achieving a desired outcome. Power is *always* an aspect of particular relationships. Because power is embedded in particular relationships, it is never simply a bundle of resources or capabilities. Instead, the sources of power vary across different issues**, actors, and time periods.[5]

As a result, what functions as a power resource in one situation may be useless or even counterproductive in others. For example, massive military resources allowed the United States to devastate huge sections of Vietnam, but they could not help U.S. leaders achieve their political goals in that country during the 1960s and early 1970s. Possession of nuclear weapons seems to deter others from nuclear attack, but these weapons are completely ineffective in helping political leaders break down trade barriers in other states. Why is political power so context-specific? Unlike money, political power is not highly *fungible*—that is, something that can be used for a wide variety of purposes. Money is very fungible; one does not need different types of money (only different amounts) to buy different goods and services. But the kind of resources one needs to change the likelihood of achieving desired political outcomes depends on who is trying to get whom to do what. Consequently, actors need different resources depending on what it is they want to do and whose behavior they need to affect to accomplish that goal.[6]

These points have several implications for the way we think about power. First, it is not meaningful to characterize particular actors as "great powers," "small powers," and so on, apart from some relationship these actors have with others and some set of objectives their leaders want to achieve. Of course, such terms are common. We often hear that we live in a "one superpower world" with the collapse of the Soviet Union, or that some state is "becoming a regional power." Yet the fact that the United States now faces no other state with a comparable amount and range of potentially useful resources says little about what U.S. leaders can get other actors to *do* in specific strategic situations.

Second, we cannot characterize particular kinds of resources as either effective or ineffective sources of power without specifying the conditions under which they will be used. It has been argued, for instance, that "hard" (coercive) resources such as military force are losing effectiveness in achieving political objectives in world politics, as compared with "soft" ("cooptive") resources such as the attractiveness of one's culture, ideology, and political institutions. According to this argument, military conquest has become relatively more costly with the declining tolerance for military casualties in many societies. It has thus become more efficient, under a fairly wide range of strategic conditions, for actors to change others' behavior by making one's goals seem legitimate rather than by using pressure.[7] Yet, as we saw throughout Chapters 6 to 13, it has always been easier for leaders to achieve their objectives if they can persuade others that those ends are legitimate. In this sense, any resource that helps one actor to shape another's preferences *may* be an effective source of power. To determine whether a resource will be an effective source of power, we must first specify who is trying to get whom to do what. That holds regardless of whether the resource is "soft" or "hard."

Third, actors' *willingness* to use available sources of power will vary with the importance they attach to achieving their goals. Consider, for instance, a situation in

---

**What is meant by an *issue* can vary. For instance, if the term is used to describe a very broad area such as trade policy, then it is possible that an actor could be influential in that general issue area while still unable to prevail on a specific bargaining issue, such as oil prices, within that area.

which an actor is a target of coercive diplomacy. As we discussed in Chapter 8, coercive diplomacy uses force and threats of force to produce a change in the target's behavior. Nevertheless, the target may be so motivated to achieve his objective, as were North Vietnamese leaders during the Vietnam War, that his incentives may remain unchanged even if he is very weak militarily relative to the actor that is trying to coerce him. As this suggests, the extent to which one of the parties is more determined to prevail, *relative to the other*, is a key factor in determining whether the coercer or the target wins in such a test of wills.[8]

Fourth, even if an actor wants to increase his or her power relative to another actor, whether that goal produces conflict between them depends heavily on what the two want to achieve. Consider two possibilities. *If* actors have highly compatible preferences *and* are committed to building a relationship that both see as legitimate, one might even *want* the other to be politically powerful as a way to further their common agenda. As we have pointed out, British-American relations since World War II have illustrated such a relationship. Harold Macmillan, who was resident minister for Britain in Africa during the war (and a future prime minister), suggested to a colleague during that period that Britain could often expect to achieve its objectives by being a dutiful junior partner to the Americans: "this way you could often get them to do what *you* wanted, while they persuaded themselves that it was really all their idea!"[9] By 1957, ties between the two governments were so close that U.S. diplomats were instructed that the general rule against disclosing classified information to foreigners did not apply to their British colleagues.[10]

What if one actor wants to increase its power relative to another, but the target of this action does *not* like it? In this type of situation, the target might choose to respond by manipulating the same form of power. Arms races illustrate this possibility. Arms races involve a competitive peacetime increase in weapons by two states or coalitions that grows out of conflicting purposes and their fears of each other.*** Alternatively, the target's most effective response may involve using a different form of power. For example, by the late 1960s many Arab political leaders had become very frustrated that they could not defeat Israel, a tiny country, on the battlefield. In order to increase international pressure on Israel, they tried manipulating the availability of oil exports, of which they have a very large proportion of the world's supply. In 1973, in return for stopping a major global oil embargo that they had begun, Arab oil exporters demanded that the United States and other industrialized oil importers change their diplomatic and military policies toward Israel, which they regarded as too friendly. While the United States did not change its behavior as a direct result of this pressure, there was widespread speculation at the time that the embargo could conceivably have had such an effect.

***This paraphrases the definition of Samuel Huntington in "Arms Races: Prerequisites and Results," in C. J. Friedreich and S. E. Harris, eds., *Public Policy*, Vol. 8 (Cambridge, MA: Graduate School of Public Administration, Harvard University, 1958), p. 41. For two reasons, definitions of arms races usually specify that they occur in peacetime. One is to allow analysts to determine the possible relationship (if any) between an arms race and the onset of a war. Another is that during a war, one would expect the parties to be acquiring arms quickly to use against the adversary. What makes an arms race distinct from a wartime situation is that this competition goes on when the parties are not actually engaged in combat.

Common Problems with Measuring and Conceptualizing Power

Despite the key role of power in political analysis, people have often misconceptualized and mismeasured it. The nature of power itself, as we have noted, is often misunderstood. Consider such common questions as these: "Why was the United States, which was *so much more powerful than North Vietnam*, unable to defeat it?" "Why was the Soviet Union, which was *so much more powerful than the Afghan freedom fighters*, unable to defeat them?" These questions assume that some generic source(s) of power always leads to success, regardless of the context. One analyst took this assumption so far as to derive a formula for the "strength of nations." It consisted of the sum of population, territory, economic and military assets, and "the will to pursue national strategy."[11]

What this approach—and the general tendency to treat power as an attribute of actors—ignores is that the relevant sources of power depend on the issue and the actors involved, and may be arena specific. Moreover, the link between power and preferences may be affected by norms, time horizons, and the institutions in which actors operate. In the Vietnam and Afghan wars, military assets were important, and the United States and the USSR both had major advantages over their opponents in this area. But other assets also mattered in these encounters, including disparities in the intensity of preferences. North Vietnam and the Afghan resistance fighters cared more than their opponents about prevailing in the conflicts (judging by the greater relative costs they were willing to bear) and operated with longer time horizons. As we discussed in Chapter 14, German and French leaders now think about their relative power positions on virtually every issue on their agendas in terms of the common norms they share as democracies, committed members of the European Union (EU), and members of NATO. In thinking about the links between preferences, power, and policy choices, remember that the *situation* determines the relevant sources of power.

Two other problems, both of which derive from the nature of power as a relationship that occurs among actors, concern its measurement. First, power may at

The sources of power vary with the issues and actors involved. Saudi Arabia, with its vast oil fields, has substantial influence over the world price of oil.

times be exercised without any *visible* attempts to do so. When this occurs, one actor may get his or her way at the expense of another because the second actor does not even challenge the first. The analytic problem is that there may be little, if any, direct evidence that the second actor's preferences were constrained by those of the first. For example, Third World leaders may be just as unhappy today about their terms of trade with the industrialized countries as they were in the early 1970s. The relative absence of *overt* demands for major changes in international economic rules and institutions since then does not necessarily mean that power is irrelevant in this situation. It may only mean that would-be challengers to the existing rules of the economic game are so convinced that they would fail that they do not even bother to try. Second, one can easily overestimate the weight of one particular actor's power in some situation if others pursued the same objective at the same time.[12] In this type of situation, determining how much the one actor's resources mattered in producing the outcome may be difficult. For example, the fact that Russia acquiesced to NATO's enlargement in the late 1990s was often said to result from intense U.S. pressure. Yet this assumption likely exaggerated the impact of American wishes, efforts, and resources. Britain, Germany and other NATO members *also* strongly supported the policy, which made it even more difficult for Russia to block it.

How can we get around these measurement problems? The first requires research into the preferences of the key actors to determine how much they conflict. If preferences are compatible, no actor needs power to get its way. Even if their preferences are substantially incompatible, the actors disadvantaged by the status quo may choose not to invest in a challenge for the reasons noted above.[13] The evidence on this point is likely to be at least somewhat ambiguous and difficult to trace, but it may be obtainable. (The problem here is one of explaining a non-event, something that is inherently difficult to do.) Somewhat easier is the problem of discerning the impact of one actor in achieving an outcome when others also worked to produce it. Here, experts may be used to estimate the relative power positions and contributions of various actors when they formed an implicit or explicit coalition. Such expertise, for example, has been used to estimate which interstate alignments are likely to succeed in post–Cold War Europe, and what the future of Hong Kong is likely to be under the control of China.[14]

Another problem concerns variations in actors' ability to mobilize and allocate relevant resources. In some political systems, leaders can fairly readily mobilize those resources, while doing so in others is harder. These differences can have a major impact on outcomes. Israel, for instance, has far fewer people and a much smaller economy than its antagonists do collectively, but produces a far more effective military. In France, even though the executive since 1958 has had substantial policy flexibility, the number of politically mobilized groups with a vested interest in existing patterns of budgetary allocation has made it difficult for officials to move significant resources from one purpose to another.[15] Imagine that, as an analyst, you have decided what kinds of power resources are relevant to some actor in dealing with some issue. How then can you assess whether leaders will actually have these assets available to them? To answer this question, you need information on the policy and political incentives and risks created by various resource options. Recall also that leaders' risk-taking behavior depends on how much they care about an objective as well as the policy and political risks attached to it. Once you know these things, you can begin to estimate how successful leaders will be in extracting the necessary resources.

Strategic skill matters. The United Nations Environment Programme (UNEP) did not have many political assets when Mostafa Tolba became its executive director, but Tolba's strategic vision and diplomatic skill placed UNEP at the center of a successful and precedent-setting agreement—the 1987 Montreal Protocol—to reduce substances that depleted the ozone layer.

The Effect of Strategy

Still another analytical issue concerns the effect of strategy on policy outcomes. At times, a good strategy—that is, a suitable plan for using resources in pursuit of policy objectives—may contribute as much to success as the exact mix or amount of resources. Conversely, having the "right" resources does not imply that leaders will use them effectively to alter the probability of getting what they want. Consider two contrasting examples. In the decades between 1870 and 1914, Germany was in a difficult strategic position, sandwiched between two actual or potential enemies, France and Russia. In spite of that underlying geopolitical problem, during the decades Bismarck was in power, Germany pursued an effective strategy of keeping its potential enemies off balance and disunited. As the diplomatic failures of his successors suggest, Bismarck's achievements had much to do with a clever strategy and fairly little to do with the country's underlying resources. By contrast, although U.S. foreign policy has exhibited some striking successes, it has often been plagued by a tendency to substitute resources for a kind of "Bismarckian strategic skill" in dealing with problems.[16] Simply put, actors' material resources—their capabilities—are a necessary but rarely a sufficient condition for the effective exercise of power.

Being able to use the concepts of power and preferences comfortably is crucial if you want to be able to evaluate the strategic situation confronting actors in world politics and explain the *consequences* of their choices. However, to explain the *origins* of choice, you need to know what the actors themselves see. To explain choice, how the actors involved see a given situation is even more important than the "objective facts" themselves.

The Strategic Significance of Actors' Perceptions and Misperceptions

Policy makers' strategic assessments and the way they frame their available options depend on their *perception*—on how they notice and evaluate incoming information—about the world around them. A mistaken perception—a *misperception*—occurs when actors fail to notice what is present, think they see something that is not present, or draw an incorrect inference from a piece of data that is accurately noticed. While the concept of a misperception is clear, it is frequently difficult to get agreement on when a misperception has occurred because analysts often disagree among themselves both about what is there to be noticed and what the correct inference is.

Whether or not their perceptions are accurate, what people "see" or believe about the world directly shapes their preferences and the policy options they believe are useful.[17] As Louis Halle, a long-time observer of U.S. foreign policy making, put it, people's choices reflect "the *image* of the external world" in actors' minds. "[To] the degree that the image is false," he said, "no technicians, however efficient, can make the policy that is based on it sound."[18] It's crucial, therefore, to pay close attention to actors' perceptions and misperceptions when they survey the strategic landscape.

Unfortunately, to use the idea of a mistaken perception, we must be able to identify not only what actors perceive (their *psychological environment*) but also what is really there to be perceived (their *operational environment*). The problem is that

Before September 11, 2001, the World Trade Center did not look like an environment in danger of an immediate security threat. Even after the attacks on the World Trade Center and the Pentagon, few people perceived sorting mail to be a dangerous job.

distinguishing between actors' operational and psychological environments is often a difficult and tricky process. In many cases, the evidence needed to make a clear judgement is unavailable. Equally basic, stipulating what is really there in a strategic environment requires a well-developed theory of situational incentives.

Because both the empirical and theoretical requirements for systematically stipulating what is "really" there in the operational environment are so difficult to meet, scholars and other analysts who want to use the idea of misperception typically make a more-or-less plausible *ex post argument* (an argument after the fact) that actors misjudged their environment in some respect. Such arguments often involve showing that other actors in the exact same situation (perhaps other members of the same cabinet who had access to the same data) were able to perceive the situation more accurately than the actor in question. While these efforts frequently yield very intriguing insights, the ad hoc ways in which they are developed also makes them very prone to error. Consequently, we recommend that you pay close attention to your theoretical assumptions about the nature of situational incentives whenever you try to identify correct and incorrect perceptions. If you do, you will find the concept of misperception to be of considerable value. You will also find a large literature on the types and consequences of perceptual errors on which you can draw for ideas and insights.[19]

While immensely varied, the literature on misperception emphasizes the effects of people's beliefs about how politics works, their images of other actors, their hopes and fears, their cognitive limits, and the guidelines they use to draw conclusions from limited or ambiguous data. As we mentioned in Chapter 3, errors that are the result of actors' beliefs, images, and cognitive limits are called "unmotivated" or "cold misperceptions." Errors that stem from people's emotions or their desire to make the world fit their preconceived notions are called "motivated" or "hot misperceptions."

Unmotivated (Cold) Misperceptions

The principal sources of *unmotivated (cold) misperceptions* can be found in people's beliefs and their images of the world around them—which create frameworks that form and organize perceptions—and in the effects of cognitive limits on the ways people process information and use shortcuts to understanding. A **belief** is some causal or factual assumption about politics or social life. Realists, for example, believe that international cooperation results mainly from a shared sense of threat, while liberals believe that other shared purposes can also foster cooperation. A **belief system** is a more-or-less organized set of assumptions about some issue. As we discussed in Chapters 10 and 11, many believe the terms of trade are biased against Third World exports (often raw materials or semi-processed goods) and favor the exports of developed states (often finished or high-technology goods). This belief is nested within a *system* of linked assumptions about which states and policy coalitions dominate the international economy and thus can set terms of trade from which they benefit.

The effects of actors' belief systems on perception are frequently reinforced by the images they hold. An **image** is a person's beliefs about some specific actor that affect his or her predictions about the other's behavior.[20] As Mikhail Gorbachev made major changes in Soviet policies during the late 1980s, for instance, U.S. leaders slowly adjusted their image of him, from very suspicious to much less so, which led to much better relations with the USSR.

Actors' perceptions are also affected by their cognitive limits. **Cognitive limits** refers to the difficulties people have in processing all the information potentially available to them. Those difficulties strongly incline people to use various mental shortcuts as mental filters in deciding what evidence to take seriously, what inferences should be drawn from that evidence, and what choices should follow from those inferences. In these respects, policy makers behave the way we all do in our daily lives. We all view the world through various beliefs, images, and analogies that simplify and make life's many complexities manageable. As a result, people have a strong tendency to see what they expect and want to see.

One of the most important consequences of people's cognitive limits is their tendency to rely on various **choice heuristics**—"rules of thumb" used to generalize from limited data. One example is the "availability heuristic."[21] It is used to evaluate the frequency or probability of some event on the basis of how easily examples come to mind. If, for instance, someone asks officials who deal with foreign assistance how often governments run into internal political problems as a result of the conditions the IMF puts on loans, they might consider how many recent meetings they have attended on this issue, or whether they have recently heard about any reports of such cases. Often, use of this heuristic will yield a good answer to the question. When examples of something come easily to mind, it is likely that they are indeed plentiful. But people often fail to consider other factors that may have made such examples easy to recall. The officials in this example may have a deep interest in this particular issue and thus pay special attention to it, or several prominent examples of problems with IMF conditionality may just have happened to arise recently, making them easy to recall. Choice heuristics provide an easy-to-use strategy for dealing with complex questions. But precisely because they are easy to use, they often invite misuse, and thus can affect people's judgments and perceptions.

Another kind of judgmental heuristic is the use of a historical analogy. Such analogies are examples drawn from the past that guide actors in diagnosing a problem or

belief A causal or factual assumption about politics or social life.

belief system An interrelated set of causal and factual assumptions about some aspect of the world.

image A person's beliefs about a particular actor.

cognitive limits Variations in people's ability to process and evaluate all the information potentially available to them.

choice heuristics The mental shortcuts people use to generalize from the data they perceive.

evaluating options for dealing with it. As with any analogy, the case is chosen because it resembles the present situation in some key respects. But if, as is quite likely, it also differs from the present situation in key ways, using it may lead to a misperception. For example, when Egypt moved troops across the Suez Canal into the Sinai desert in May 1967, Israeli officials did not worry at first. They likened the situation to an episode in 1960, when Egypt moved troops across the Sinai to Israel's border to demonstrate diplomatic support for Syria. Egypt did not initiate hostilities at that point, and instead withdrew its forces a few weeks later. But the inference that Egyptian leaders had a similar objective in 1967 was wrong; the 1967 troop movements were a prelude to the Six-Day War.[22]

As you think through these concepts and examples, bear in mind that because people's cognitive capabilities are limited, they need mental shortcuts (such as choice heuristics) and cognitive organizing devices (such as beliefs and images) to function. At the same time, those shortcuts and organizing devices can lead to errors in noticing and evaluating information. They can also affect actors' objectives and preferred policy options. First, they influence the "facts" that people consider relevant—the ones actors look for, notice, and remember. During unrest in the Dominican Republic in 1965, for example, U.S. officials were so afraid "another Castro" would gain control in the Caribbean that they failed to notice that the internal Dominican situation was nothing like that in Cuba just before Castro took power. The Dominican insurgency lacked a single charismatic leader like Castro, and there was no popularly based guerrilla movement, as there had been in Cuba. As one account put it, "all of these facts were forgotten, or probably not known."[23] None of these facts was, however, inherently difficult to discern at the time. U.S. officials missed these facts because they had such a specific and potent image of what a "Caribbean revolution" would look like that it was difficult for them to focus on what was actually taking place.

Second, once people have firm assumptions or expectations about some situation, a great deal of contrary evidence is needed to change their minds. A steady stream of evidence that challenges their views is rarely enough; overwhelming evidence that comes in big, unmistakable chunks is usually needed.[24] This helps us understand why many conflicts in world politics are so hard to resolve. To get from conflict to cooperation, actors frequently have to change their images of each other, and as we've seen, this is difficult to do.

Third, beliefs and images shape objectives and preferred policy options by making people more likely to favor one possible interpretation of ambiguous data rather than other, equally plausible interpretations. For example, actors tend to see others' behavior as more centralized, more coordinated, and less haphazard than it actually often is.[25] Consider two illustrative cases. At the height of the Cuban Missile Crisis, U.S. officials had trouble convincing Soviet leaders that a U-2 reconnaissance plane that flew over their country's airspace truly was lost, rather than on a spying mission, even though the former was correct. Chinese officials may have entered the Korean War in part because they assumed threatening rhetoric from lower-level Japanese and U.S. officials reflected the views of top policy makers, which it did not.[26]

While it is easy to criticize mistakes after the fact, remember that people need to simplify the situations they confront to make sense of them. In terms of these two examples, because actors can rarely be certain of others' intentions, they often believe it is prudent to assume that another actor's observed words and actions reflect a coherent pattern of intentions and behavior. And since each actor tends to assume that others share this belief, all public actions, except those that are clearly accidental, are usually assumed by outsiders to reflect a highly coherent, coordinated strategy.[27] As we discussed in Chapter 4, this assumption is often wrong. In practice, governments are rarely unitary actors. Political leaders may therefore miss many opportunities to exploit, or at least explore, factional or other internal disagreements about policy within other actors.

Motivated (Hot) Misperceptions

Motivated (hot) misperceptions grow out of people's hopes and fears rather than an intellectual need for simplifying beliefs, images, and heuristics. While the sources are different, hot errors produce many of the same results as cold ones.

Stalin's behavior before Germany attacked the Soviet Union in 1941 illustrates a motivated misperception. Stalin knew that Hitler was a bully and detested Marxist regimes. But once the Germans and Soviets concluded a nonaggression agreement in 1939, Stalin, who desperately wanted to avoid a major war, tried hard to work things out with Germany. He convinced himself that Hitler might try to bully him but would surely not launch an unprovoked, surprise attack. So when German troops began massing adjacent to the USSR's western frontier in the Spring of 1941 and Stalin received credible intelligence reports that an invasion was imminent, he concluded that the buildup simply foreshadowed a tough set of German demands. When Germany invaded the USSR in June, the Soviets were unprepared, and Stalin was so shaken that he dropped from sight for several days.

Not surprisingly, these two sources of perceptual error can become intertwined. For example, in 1962 British leaders began to suspect that U.S. officials would not produce and sell them the Skybolt missile, which the British desperately wanted. At that time, British policy makers saw Skybolt as the only way to preserve the useful life of their strategic bomber force. While U.S. officials had pledged to make Skybolt available to London *if* the United States chose to produce the missile for its own use, a U.S. decision to go ahead with production was never a certainty. By 1962, British officials had ignored many hints that U.S. leaders were about to cancel the project and that Washington expected the British to propose an alternative.[28] As this example illustrates, even when people's hopes or fears make important "facts" unattractive to notice and contemplate, a serious failure to do so means that a cold error (seeing only what one expects to see) is essentially facilitating the hot one (seeing what one wants to see).[29]

In conclusion, it's crucial to remember that people's choices are driven by their perceptions. Those perceptions typically reflect a combination of what is really there to be perceived, their prior expectations (based on their beliefs and images), the tools they have developed to manage their cognitive limits, and their emotional needs. When it comes to predicting choice, what matters is how the *actors* see the situation. When it comes to explaining the *consequences* of their choices—the outcomes of strategic interaction—understanding the kind and degree of *mis*perception can be critical.

The Origins of Actors' Preferences and Perceptions

It's clear that actors' preferences and perceptions have a profound impact on the politics of strategic choice. That leads to an obvious question: How much is known about the origins of people's preferences and their cold and hot misperceptions? The answer, unfortunately, is that scholars know a lot more about the implications of variations in actors' preferences and perceptions than they know about their origins. But while scholars do not know nearly as much as they would like about the origins of actors' preferences and perceptions, they are following up a wide range of intriguing leads.

Group Identity

Actors' preferences and perceptions reflect the social groups that are important to them. In high school, your self-image and view of others may have been colored by the outlook of your circle of friends. Something comparable can occur in politics. It happens most visibly when one looks at the effects of different cultures and long-established national identities, but people's objectives and policy preferences may also be affected by the experiences they share with others in the same profession, such as health care workers in the World Health Organization (WHO), or with others working on a common task, such as military officers who must decide how to carry out a delicate peacekeeping mission. Scholars interested in the effects of group identity on preferences and perceptions emphasize that even though groups often grow out of already existing shared interests or values, such groups can alter their members through *socialization*. To socialize someone is to teach that person what it means to be part of a particular group. Socialization often produces a shared identity through which oneself and others are viewed. Groucho Marx made a joke of this in saying "I wouldn't join any group that would accept me as a member!"

Constructivism, which we discussed in Chapter 2, places particular stress on the impact of groups on actors' identities, preferences, and perceptions. It makes two main points.[30] First, actors' identities and objectives are "socially constructed." In other words, people's understandings of who they are—as well as what they consider legitimate and want to achieve—often grow out of their social environment. Second, the social relationships in which actors are embedded affect their perceptions of their strategic situation and their interpretations of others' actions.

Think, for instance, of Turkey. Is it chiefly an Islamic (Eastern) or a European (Western) society? Turkey is now undergoing an "identity crisis" over this very issue. Turks are overwhelmingly Islamic, but unlike many people in other Islamic societies, many of them believe that their society should be officially secular, not theocratic. In contemporary political terms, a strong emphasis on secularism would shape Turkish identity along more Western than Eastern lines. If Turkey were to be admitted to the EU—a goal long sought by Turkish leaders—that would be likely to reinforce a Western orientation. But the EU is hesitant about admitting Turkey to membership, largely because many Europeans believe that an Islamic society is not "Western" enough to fit comfortably in their group. As a result, Turks' national identity is now closely connected to Turkey's relationships with other societies. For example, if Europe decisively rejects Turkey as an economic and social partner, Turkish factional leaders and their key constituencies might choose to embrace other Islamic societies much more explicitly than they have before.

One only has to look at the mid-twentieth-century transformation of Germany to see an intriguing historical example of the effects of changing domestic and international relationships on group-defined identities, norms, and understandings and wonder, in turn, about the effects of those changes on people's strategic assessments and objectives. Germany invading its immediate neighbors is literally unthinkable today. However, as you consider this example and its possible implications for the different paths Turkey might take, remember that feelings of shared community are *especially* strong among contemporary EU members. One would not expect Turkey, sitting as it does at the juncture between the West and Islam, to develop as strong a sense of shared group identity even if it were admitted to the EU. However, from a constructivist point of view, the effects of the cross-pressuring created by those complex combinations of social relationships are exactly the sorts of processes to which students of world politics should be paying far more attention.

Institutions and Norms

Institutions can also affect actors' preferences and perceptions. An IGO's members, for instance, might specify that only practicing democracies with acceptable human-rights records are eligible to participate. This is now the expectation of the Organization for Security and Cooperation in Europe (OSCE) and NATO, and it has provided NATO members with some leverage to ensure that Poland, the Czech Republic, and Hungary continue their market and political reforms after they joined the alliance in 1999. Politically significant norms can also exist at the level of individual states (for example, the strong rejection of nuclear weapons in every Scandinavian country), or within particular substate factions (such as the American religious groups who pressure Congress to withhold U.S. financial support from any international agency or program that facilitates abortions). The same applies to institutions. Think of the UN General Assembly, a national parliament, and a local school board. In each case, membership implies a certain shared set of purposes and conduct toward other members. Whenever people have regularized expectations about behavior, it is likely that norms and institutions are present.

Norms are "shared expectations about appropriate behavior held by a community of actors."[31] Unlike values, which simply identify some desirable state of the world, norms indicate how people should actually behave in order to produce those conditions. We can find evidence of norms in two ways. One is through patterns of behavior that we could not easily explain without them. It is difficult, for instance, to explain much of the costly multilateral humanitarian intervention of the last decade in places such as Somalia and Rwanda *other* than through a norm that says that citizens of failed states should not be left to starve or be slaughtered.[32] Another source of evidence that a norm exists is through some explicit statement of what the behavioral expectations are. Many IGOs have such statements in their founding treaties. For example, members of the World Trade Organization (WTO) are expected to make trade concessions to others when they receive such concessions from them. This norm, in fact, is the basic expectation on which the WTO is based.

In Chapter 5, we defined *institutions* as "persistent and connected sets of rules (formal and informal) that prescribe behavioral roles, constrain activity, and shape expectations."[33] In other words, an institution is a set of mutually acceptable practices for achieving an agreed norm or set of norms. It promotes those norms by helping to coordinate people's expectations about outcomes and behavior. Institutions can be formal, as in IGOs and NGOs, or informal, as in the coordination that routinely occurs among the leaders of central banks as they try to keep exchange rates among the major currencies within stable ranges. The practices that constitute particular institutions thus reflect but also help to shape the way people think about

norms Moral rules (freely accepted obligations based on people's understanding of right and wrong) that are widely accepted within a community.

preferred outcomes and policy tools. For example, without the International Energy Agency (IEA)—an IGO that provides for mandatory sharing of oil supplies among members if any of them suffer shortfalls—oil-consuming states might be more vulnerable to producers' embargoes than they are now. As a result, IEA members are more likely to be able to resist politicization of the world oil economy than they might be otherwise.

We can make these points more generally: *Institutional norms can affect all of the variables in the process of politics*. These include power, preferences over outcomes and policies, risk-taking preferences, and time horizons. Consider a few examples. First, in the UN, the permanent members of the Security Council (SC) have a veto, while in the General Assembly (GA) there is no veto. For that reason, SC members' policy preferences are necessarily constrained according to what Russia, the United States, France, Britain, and China will accept. There is no such constraint on preferences in the GA, where, as we discussed in Chapter 5, members often are indifferent to what actually happens within the institution itself; they use their speeches principally to legitimate policies that take effect elsewhere. Second, there seems to be a strong—although implicit—global norm forbidding nuclear attack against a non-nuclear actor.[34] It is often seen as significant that nuclear weapons have never been fired against an opponent since their use in the closing days of World War II, and that today even nuclear threats by states against non-nuclear countries have virtually disappeared.[†] Such a norm effectively requires nuclear-weapons states to possess non-nuclear forces for essentially all security purposes other than as a deterrent to a nuclear, chemical, or biological attack. Finally, the existence of the IEA allows its members to take strategic risks (such as, for instance, supporting Israel over Arab opposition) that they might not take if they were more immediately vulnerable to the effects of an oil embargo.

Given the ways in which institutionalized norms can affect actors' strategic assessments and objectives, we might ask how and when they originate. What are the sources of IGOs, international legal rules such as diplomatic immunity, and such *international regimes* (the values, norms, and specific rules that govern particular issue areas in world politics) as the international trade and monetary regimes? In brief, norms and institutions tend to come about in three ways. One possible route is through asymmetric power relationships. This process can take place when actors with dominant military or economic assets "invest" some of those assets in creating networks of institutions and norms that help to order international life. After World War II, the United States fostered liberal trade policies, largely as a way to fuel growth that would help strengthen an anticommunist coalition. Those liberal norms and rules, however, have largely endured beyond the Cold War and are the basis today for the WTO.

Norms can also emerge multilaterally when a number of actors come to view them as useful instruments for pursuing their objectives. Diplomatic immunity arose

---

[†]The one exception is threats of or actual use of nuclear weapons to retaliate for the use of nuclear, biological, or chemical weapons by some state or other actor. During the Persian Gulf War, President Bush was careful not to rule out a nuclear strike if Iraq used other weapons of mass destruction, and this threat may have helped deter Saddam Hussein from such an act. Similar deterrent threats were made by India and Pakistan when the crisis over Kashmir and cross-border terrorism seemed to bring them to the brink of war in the spring of 2002.

in Renaissance Italy because reliable communication among political units was impossible so long as emissaries were not free to move unhindered across boundaries. Today, the norm that precludes threatening to use nuclear weapons against non-nuclear states reflects a similar convergence of purpose across a large number of states. Finally, political entrepreneurs may succeed in "selling" an institutional solution to some problem, especially if that actor can credibly claim good causal knowledge of how to produce a desired effect.

Variation in the Process Used to Identify and Evaluate Options

As we discussed earlier in this chapter, the human mind is a limited information-processing mechanism. These cognitive limits make it impossible for people to search comprehensively for options to deal with any but the simplest decision problems.[35] Consider, for instance, two quite different strategies for identifying and evaluating options. In one, you **optimize**—that is, you search for the "best" policy option. In the other, you **satisfice.** Here, you search until you find an option that is "good enough." In other words, once you find an acceptable option, you stop searching for others, even if some other option might produce a better outcome.

The issue then is *how much* actors are willing to invest in identifying and evaluating different options. How wide a range of options do they try to identify? How carefully do they evaluate the relative merits of the options they identify? The fact that search and evaluation processes are limited rather than comprehensive does not mean that people act carelessly. On the contrary, people typically search for and evaluate alternative policy options in a purposeful way, though they do so within the bounds of limited information and often much uncertainty.[36] To act in such a purposive manner requires three decisions. Officials must: (1) determine the number of policy options that will be identified in a given situation; (2) decide how those options will be evaluated; and (3) decide how those options should be reevaluated over time as new information becomes available.[37]

The choices that people make on these matters vary widely. With regard to Step #1, decision makers could search their memory and seek a wide range of suggestions from advisers to generate a broad variety of feasible options, or they could stop searching for options once they found one that was acceptable. In between, there is room for a somewhat more rigorous search process than the stereotype of satisficing suggests. Regarding Step #2, decision makers could try to specify all of their objectives, rank each option they have identified in terms of how well it is likely to accomplish each goal (with due regard for the relative importance of each objective), and then make side-by-side comparisons of each option with regard to each objective. On the other hand, they might try simply to specify whether each option that happens to be identified is adequate for the most important objectives. Alternatively, they might decide to evaluate some options carefully, even if they did not try to find the *best* option across *all* their objectives.

Some analysts advocate an *incremental* decision strategy for carrying out tasks #1 and #2. Such a strategy assumes that, in practice, policy changes often involve only marginal alterations from an existing policy. With this in mind, officials who use an incremental strategy limit the search for options to those that differ only slightly from the status quo. They may do so because more fundamental change on some issue is politically difficult, or because they lack the information or theoretical

optimize   To search for the best possible option available.

satisfice   A search process in which actors look for options and evaluate the ones they see only until they find an option that meets a minimum standard.

knowledge to consider options that would change policy in more far-reaching ways. An incrementalist strategy considers carefully only those consequences of policy options that can be calculated fairly readily and precisely.[38]

Finally, with respect to Step #3, an actor could reexamine each of the available options repeatedly as new information becomes available, making periodic side-by-side comparisons of each pair. Another possibility is to evaluate each of the options in a more limited set *until* one of them is deemed acceptable. Alternatively, an actor could periodically reevaluate a few selected options more carefully over time, while ignoring the others after an initial evaluation.[39]

Four major factors affect how rigorously people will search for and evaluate policy options. Most important is how much one cares about an issue. People are most careful about decisions when they have a high stake in some outcome. You probably selected a college more carefully than you have chosen any specific courses once you arrived there (even this one!), since one's choice of a college usually matters more. Second, it matters how much time one has to decide. In international crises, for instance, policy makers typically have only a limited amount of time to make high-stakes choices. This often causes stress, which may interfere with an actor's ability to make distinctions among alternative options.[40] Third, some people are more skilled in organizing and conducting search and evaluation procedures than others. We would expect these people, for reasons of their own comparative advantage, to search for and evaluate options rather carefully. Fourth, it matters how much people are constrained by the organizations in which they operate. As we noted in discussing

Large organizations such as the U.S. State Department and the Central Intelligence Agency (shown here at a joint briefing) depend on standard operating procedures (SOPs) to get routine work done. But when the unexpected happens, SOPs usually produce inferior results, such as when surveillance techniques used to identify security threats during the Cold War continued to be used even after the Cold War had ended and the nature of the threats changed. Capable policy makers and their advisers know the limitations of SOPs and often try to look "outside of the box" when new situations occur. The problem is not simply that good new ideas are usually hard to come by; it's also that ignoring SOPs and taking individual initiative place the political risks of failure squarely on the shoulders of the innovator.

bureaucratic politics in Chapter 4, people's responsibilities within particular organizations (either governmental, intergovernmental, or trans-state) may influence their policy positions. One reason may be that people within one organization need to act in ways that those in other organizations can anticipate, since much of their work may involve close coordination with people in other organizations. And if people identify strongly with an organization, that sentiment may influence how thoroughly they search for alternative policy options and how closely they scrutinize the likely consequences of those options, especially when the agency's welfare or their own professional interests within it seems to be at stake.

This type of satisficing is common when organizations have developed highly routinized ways of carrying out specific tasks. These routines are called **standard operating procedures** or **SOPs.** SOPs are well-rehearsed and well-accepted procedures that people use to carry out repeated activities. They serve to minimize uncertainty about appropriate behavior in certain types of situations and spare organizations the costs of improvising various policies when one is believed to be sufficient. For example, militaries of allied states often undertake joint exercises to prepare them to deter or fight wars. In the course of such exercises, officers need to exchange intelligence data with their counterparts in other states' militaries. SOPs typically are developed to regulate such exchanges by answering the following kinds of questions: With whom in other militaries do we (military officers) share sensitive information? Under what conditions? Who makes decisions about exceptions to these guidelines?

As this example suggests, SOPs have several effects on organizational search and evaluation procedures. First, they tell people what to expect in performing their tasks and specify the criteria of good task performance. SOPs tell officers, for instance, when other militaries engaged in joint exercises have received the type and amount of data that they need. Second, by indicating who must coordinate behavior with whom, SOPs affect how members of an organization relate to other organizations. Finally, SOPs affect the range of options that an organization's members consider in making decisions. If a new state joins a set of exercises, the military organizations involved in it will probably decide what intelligence to share with the newcomer by using or modifying existing SOPs.[41]

Paradoxically, SOPs suggest that thoughtful, goal-oriented people can purposively choose to remain relatively ignorant of a wide range of policy options. SOPs allow organizations to act cost effectively in performing routine tasks by avoiding a need to improvise new procedures continually. In this way, they stabilize organizations and their personnel on a day-to-day basis.[42] Yet by searching for and assessing options only selectively, satisficing procedures often carry a price. In the case of SOPs, that price is rigidity. To have a fairly small set of available, well-rehearsed procedures means that organizations may not "know" how to act in any but highly routine situations. In crises, for instance, policy makers may have little choice but to accept existing SOPs as their feasible options, regardless of whether those routines make sense in that situation. On the other hand, adopting those SOPs may have made good sense at one time, especially if those responsible for an organization expect the SOPs to work well in typical situations. Any change, then, is effectively a risky choice, with people typically preferring to postpone costs (expensive search and evaluation processes) and enjoy benefits (a fairly predictable decision environment) while they can. This, of course, is consistent with the notion of purposeful political action.

standard operating procedures (SOPs) Well-established and routine procedures people use to carry out repeated activities.

Differences in Relative Power and the Assessment of Options

Not surprisingly, actors' relative power positions affect their assessments of policy options and purposes. Actors powerful enough to achieve their purposes fairly easily are likely to find that objectives or policies that would not otherwise be attractive may become so. However, the ability to achieve goals easily can create its own special risk: a tendency to ignore the significance weaker actors attach to maintaining legitimate relationships.[‡] Contrast this situation with the one facing actors who, while powerful enough to have a chance of achieving some objective, are aware that they face major opportunity costs and some risk of failure. Here, actors' assessments of their options will depend on how much they value the outcome in spite of the costs and risks. These first two situations are, in their turn, both different from a third possibility, namely, that actors' relative power position will be so poor that it prevents them from considering some purpose or option at all. Examples of how each of these three situations affects actors' assessments of their options follow.

Political leaders may have so many resources relative to other actors that even very ambitious objectives and policies can become attractive to them. For about twenty years after World War II, the United States was in this situation regarding several key issue areas. Its nuclear-weapons advantage over the Soviet Union was so great (meaning that the United States could inflict much more nuclear damage on the USSR than the reverse) until well into the 1960s that U.S. leaders confidently "extended" the deterrent umbrella of American nuclear weapons over Western European territory. Although they knew that the United States would suffer tremendous nuclear damage in a major war with the Soviet Union,[43] their margin of nuclear superiority seemed to make it unlikely that the Soviets would start or provoke such a war. Nuclear weapons, moreover, were inexpensive as compared to the non-nuclear forces that would have been required to offset Soviet forces. Providing a "nuclear umbrella" to their European allies thus became a relatively cheap, low-risk option. Similarly, America's relative economic capabilities were so large during this same period that U.S. leaders could afford to pursue foreign economic policies toward Europe and Japan that strengthened the Western bloc as a whole at the expense of purely American economic welfare. Until well into the 1960s, the United States enjoyed overwhelming advantages in foreign-exchange reserves, exports, and research and development expenditures over every other state. Cushioned by these assets, U.S. leaders accepted a high degree of Japanese protectionism during the 1950s and 1960s and tolerated an exchange rate that made it artificially easy for Japan and U.S. European allies to export to the United States. These policies were attractive because growth and political stability in Europe and Japan were major U.S. objectives, and one-sided U.S. trade concessions made them easy to achieve.[44]

If the resources available to political leaders give them a small margin for error, we would expect that to affect their objectives and preferred policy options.

[‡]The Nonproliferation Treaty (NPT) illustrates this point. The NPT seeks to limit the number of states possessing nuclear weapons to those that had a nuclear capacity in the late 1960s, when the treaty was negotiated. It seems U.S. officials have rather consistently failed to recognize the hostility that this distinction between nuclear "haves" and "have nots" has created. Indian officials have repeatedly spoken about the resentment they feel regarding such a double standard.

Whenever resources are limited relative to some objective, taking an action implies **opportunity costs.** Such costs can be defined as "the highest valued alternative (or opportunity) that must be forsaken in choosing the course of action."[45] Many foreign-policy debates revolve around the desirability or feasibility of paying certain opportunity costs to achieve some objective. Such costs can involve either material resources or a decision to bypass a policy that poses fewer risks. For example, once the USSR achieved nuclear parity with the United States in the late 1960s (meaning that the United States could no longer destroy enough Soviet nuclear weapons in a first strike to avoid devastation of the U.S. homeland), the policy of extending the U.S. nuclear umbrella over Europe became riskier and more controversial. By the early 1980s, four former high-level U.S. officials were urging American leaders to withdraw their commitment to use U.S. nuclear weapons first, even in the event of a major war in Europe. For these officials, the risk of U.S. nuclear devastation had become too large an opportunity cost, even if a policy based on a refusal to pay it could be expected to harm U.S. relations with its major allies.[46] Although U.S. officials refused to take this advice, citing the risks to relations with key allies, this option became more respectable after the United States lost the clear nuclear superiority that it had a decade or two before.

By contrast, once the U.S. economic advantage over Europe and Japan began to erode in the 1960s, there were tangible consequences for U.S. foreign economic policy. By the 1970s U.S. officials were more vigorously protecting specific industries, more aggressively promoting U.S. exports, and more strongly protesting "unfair" foreign trade practices than they had been a decade earlier. They were also increasingly unwilling to tolerate an exchange rate that hurt the U.S. balance of payments. None of these policies was new, and U.S. leaders did not stop promoting liberal, multilateral, economic exchange. But as America's resource margin over its economic partners changed, so did the overall balance of U.S. economic actions toward them.[47]

Actors' relative power position may even keep them from considering certain policy options at all. It is interesting to compare the actions of many Third World leaders over time in calling for major changes in the international economic system. As we explained in Chapter 10, from the early 1960s through the mid-1970s, many of these leaders demanded changes in the institutions and the norms that govern world trade. They argued that since many Third World countries' terms of trade had deteriorated even as the industrialized countries had grown richer, the basic economic rules should be tilted more in the poorer countries' favor. They rejected the idea that international markets should set prices on their own, since doing so had led to worse terms of trade, and they urged adoption of trade rules that allowed the richer countries to discriminate actively in favor of the poor countries (for example, by allowing Third World products to enter developed states at lower tariff rates than those that were exported from developed states). It is probably not a coincidence that the demands peaked between 1973 and 1976. This was at a time when stagflation, concern about the scarcity of oil and other resources, and the international weakness of the dollar made the developed countries seem particularly weak, while the example of the OPEC oil embargo made the less developed states appear relatively strong. By the 1980s, when the Third World was burdened by huge international debts and Marxism had collapsed as an effective competing ideology, Third World states had much less leverage on international economic issues, and these demands virtually ceased.

opportunity costs The level of lost opportunity when actors choose one option over another; the bigger the forgone value, the higher the opportunity cost.

Variation in the Meaning of Success and Failure

Defining the "success" of a policy choice implies two major questions: direction and distance. Concerning *direction*, is a successful policy one that achieves gains or one that prevents losses? Scholars have taken several positions on this question. Many expected-utility theorists (especially those in microeconomics) assume that when people make choices they try to maximize their expected utility in terms of *gains in net asset levels*. This means that they try to do as well as they can, relative to the status quo, within the limits of what they consider an acceptable level of risk.[48] **Prospect theory** makes different assumptions. It assumes that people care more about *avoiding losses* than they do about making gains, even when the value of what is at stake is identical. People therefore *do not* act as if these two types of results are equally useful. They can be expected to take greater risks to avoid losses than to make gains.[49] Prospect theorists would expect, for instance, that people would be more unhappy about losing twenty dollars than they would be happy over finding twenty dollars. From this perspective, political leaders can be expected to be loss-averse in making policy choices. An official would, for instance, be expected to take greater risks to prevent an alliance from weakening than to strengthen it.

Scholars have debated this issue vigorously, most often assuming that political leaders *always* act either to minimize losses or maximize net assets. In our view, this is not a very useful debate. Instead of arguing about whether leaders *always* act to minimize losses or maximize net assets, we should examine the standards decision makers actually use. All the participants in this debate assume that leaders behave purposively, however they define the direction of success. In other words, officials are seen as trying to do the best they can, even in the presence of the cognitive constraints that keep them from making optimal decisions. What is important here is that attempting *either* to maximize net assets *or* avoid losses is consistent with the

prospect theory
A scholarly tradition that assumes people are more concerned with preventing losses than achieving gains.

Map 15–1   Prospect Theory and Different Ways of Looking at the Boundaries of the United States
Prospect theorists emphasize the importance of the reference points people use to identify losses. Most U.S. citizens will look at a map of the United States and see an almost natural border. Some Mexican nationalists may look at the same map and see lost territories. As this map shows, the areas Mexico lost include almost all of modern Texas, New Mexico, Colorado, Arizona, Utah, Nevada, and California.

notion of purposive action. When you analyze policy makers' reactions to their situations, you should keep both of these possibilities in mind and try to determine—rather than simply assume—the direction in which actors define policy success.

The second question that must be answered to define the success of a policy concerns *distance*. How good must a "good policy" be? Three criteria are typically used to answer this question. One is to satisfice, to search only until you find an option that is "good enough." As the definition of satisficing suggested, it is not so much about the choices actors make as it is about the quality and comprehensiveness of their search for options. Emphasizing this point is important because the concept of purposive behavior assumes that people who are able to order their perceived options from most to least attractive will choose the best option they perceive. People who engage in satisficing behavior are still purposive; they just don't invest heavily in identifying and evaluating a wide range of options. Instead, they stop looking for options when they find one that they consider satisfactory. When might actors satisfice in their search for options? One likely situation is one in which the international and domestic risks of making a poor decision are low. Since finding and evaluating more options is frequently costly, it may be prudent to satisfice when the political and policy stakes attached to a choice are low.

Another possible standard for success is to do what one always does in that situation—that is, fall back on an existing SOP. As we discussed, SOPs can be cost-effective, given the costs of more rigorous searches for options. When they are well chosen, they also can provide built-in safeguards against lax or dangerous procedures. During the Cuban Missile Crisis, some of the greatest risks of undesired military escalation occurred when existing SOPs were ignored.[50] SOPs are indispensable for military operations, especially those that involve coordinating large, complex forces. For example, just prior to the Gulf War in 1991, U.S. leaders had only one contingency plan available for dealing with a military emergency in that part of the world. It had originated in the early 1980s, when the Joint Chiefs of Staff drafted a set of plans to fight the Soviet Union or Iran if either threatened the Gulf oil fields. At that time, those were the states believed most likely to threaten Western oil supplies. The plans included detailed transportation and logistics procedures for moving a large military force to the Gulf and preparing it to fight. While the opponent differed in 1991 (Iraq), U.S. leaders felt comfortable with the existing plan, which accomplished the key task of putting the troops in the right place. Most important, officials did not want to improvise when they were responsible for achieving a complex task during a crisis.[51]

Sometimes, however, only the best will do. When the international or domestic risks of choosing poorly are high, officials will want to evaluate as thoroughly as they can each plausible option. They may end up choosing an existing SOP in such situations; even so, they will most often want to be briefed in detail on what procedures have been prepared and what their implications are likely to be, so that those procedures can be modified or bypassed if that is necessary.[52] Furthermore, policy makers will reject incremental alterations of existing policy if their own preferences push them toward large-scale reexamination of the status quo. One cannot evaluate changes as fundamental as President Nixon's trip to China in 1972, which ended over twenty years of intense hostility between the two states, or Mikhail Gorbachev's decision to allow the Warsaw Pact to crumble, without appreciating that some strategic situations and sets of incentives do *not* call for a satisficing choice.

Discounting and the Length of Actors' Time Horizons

Policy choices often have effects that last for years, if not decades, down the road, and these implications can affect the choices that people make today. The degree to which they do so depends on two major factors. One is actors' time horizons, defined as the time period they consider relevant when they look into the future. All else being equal, the longer a future one sees, the more heavily expectations about that future will weigh in present-day choices. For example, states that have been the key participants in major wars typically try to agree on a new set of basic norms in world politics once those conflicts have ended. The Treaties of Westphalia, the Congress of Vienna, the Treaty of Versailles that ended World War I, and the agreements between the major members of NATO and the Soviet Union regarding German reunification in 1990 are examples. At these historical moments, something like a "constitution" to govern interstate relations is often worked out. Historically, the state with the largest military and economic resources has often invested at such times in building IGOs and norms of international conduct that will to some extent constrain the way it uses its power capabilities, in return for others' agreement to be similarly bound by those institutions and rules. Britain did this in 1815 when it helped form the Concert of Europe; the United States did so in 1945 (for the non-communist countries). At such times, the largest state typically sees a long future within which it wants to bind states to certain international norms. Yet political leaders at times seem to disregard the potential consequences of their actions. As we saw in Chapter 6, French nobles weakened their long-term political position by accepting the king's offer to buy their way out of their military duties. In doing this, the nobles undercut the perceived legitimacy of the privileges they enjoyed, which had been justified by their military role in protecting the faith.

How far one looks into the future may vary with what one looks at. Politicians who are focused on the next election may be fairly indifferent to what happens after that. Yet specific issues may require a tighter deadline. Budgetary decisions are usually tied to legislative appropriations cycles. Decisions about buying or developing weapons systems typically take into account the useful life of those systems and the expected procurement actions of likely adversaries and allies. A schedule for making other types of policy decisions may depend on the timing of meetings of such IGOs as the IMF or the UN General Assembly, since governments need established policies to participate effectively in these institutions. Finally, the procedural norms within a political system may shape expectations about time horizons. For example, controversial policy issues are dealt with very deliberately in Japan since each relevant policy faction must sign off on an option before it is considered seriously.[53]

A second factor involves discounting. As we discussed in Chapters 3 and 14, people usually prefer current benefits over future benefits and future costs over current costs. To "discount" is to convert the anticipated costs and benefits over time to their estimated present value. Suppose someone who wants you to paint a house asks you to do the job now but wait to be paid for six months. Assume also that payment at the promised time can be counted on. In deciding whether to accept the job, you will convert the promised payment to its present value, probably by subtracting the opportunity costs you must pay for waiting. You might decide that the relevant cost is the interest you could have earned on the money over six months; it could also be the interest you will have to pay over that time on a credit-card balance that you could pay off now if you were paid immediately for doing the job. Similarly, if leaders consider taking an unpopular action today, such as raising taxes in order to accomplish a goal in the future (such as improving their country's military), they will assess how much that outcome is worth in today's terms. The more they discount that value (because the costs must be paid before the benefits arrive), the less likely they are to choose it, even if they consider it likely that the policy would succeed.

Variation in Actors' Risk-Taking Preferences

Recall that strategic choices carry both *policy risks* (the likelihood that one's substantive goals will not be achieved, even if a policy is carried out effectively), and *political risks* (the likelihood that policy choices will weaken one's political position). People's reactions to the risks they face can have a major impact on their choices. Let us review the factors that affect people's risk-taking preferences. First, when political and policy risks reinforce each other, actors' strategic choices are likely to be easy; they will tend to avoid the options that are risky in both senses and choose those with low risks. On the other hand, all else being equal, when political and policy risks push in opposite directions, the higher the political risks attached to options with a low policy risk, the likelier it is that policy makers will prefer options that allow them to trade an increase in the level of policy risks for a decrease in the level of political risks. Thus, leaders may prefer certain tactics that would not be optimal from a foreign-policy standpoint because they can shore up their strength with a key domestic faction or constituency.

Second, the higher the expected value people place on achieving some outcome, the greater the political risks they will be willing to assume to pursue it. During the 1980s, Mikhail Gorbachev was willing to accept the political risk that the Soviet Communist Party would lose some of its authority because he believed that the USSR's then-current political system was broken beyond repair. A leader less committed to such a policy objective might well have been more political-risk averse.

Third, the level of political risks people will accept depends in part on how much control they have over policy choice and implementation. Actors may be willing to take risks if they can control the process; it is quite a different matter to take risks if control is in others' hands. For instance, a finance minister may be willing to take high political risks to achieve an objective in which he or she strongly believes, while a lower-level official in the same ministry is less likely to do so. This helps us understand why SOPs typically constrain actors' behavior more at lower than at higher levels of an organization's hierarchy.

Fourth, how people trade off these two kinds of risks also depends on how quickly they feel compelled to act. If either political or policy risks threaten to rise quickly, a policy that increases the other type of risk might become more acceptable than under other conditions.

These patterns can help us make sense of choices that might, on their face, otherwise seem hard to understand. In Chapter 6 we saw why German statesmen took a series of actions at the turn of the twentieth century that had the effect of strengthening the ties between Russia and France, even though these policies made it likelier that Germany would have to fight a two-front war. They did so because key political factions believed that the available alternatives had even higher risks. Similarly, in 1980 President Carter approved a plan to rescue the U.S. hostages held in Iran, even though the plan could easily fail. Carter did so because the very visible plight of the hostages, coupled with the recent Soviet invasion of Afghanistan, was creating an impression that he was a victim of forces he could not control. That, in turn, was weakening him politically at home as well as abroad during an election year.[54]

Risk-taking preferences can thus help us understand how political actors define success and search for options. If they care a lot about achieving some outcome, they are likelier to define success in ways that encourage them to take very high personal and political risks. Terrorists who physically endanger themselves to achieve their objectives are one (admittedly extreme) example of this pattern. But if actors are fairly indifferent about achieving some outcome, and especially if they are politically risk-averse, they will tend to find satisficing preferable to a more exhaustive search for the best option. It is often said that organizational procedures and cultures are rigid. Whether this is so depends on the political and policy incentives of organizational leaders. If they are satisfied with existing policy and seek mainly to preserve or enhance their political position, the conventional wisdom will be correct. But if either factor changes, organizational policies and norms could become less stable.

Conclusion

In this chapter we surveyed a wide number of possible sources of actors' preferences and perceptions, including: differences in culture, group identity, norms, and institutions; differences in the search process that actors use to identify and evaluate options; variations in actors' understandings of the meaning of success and failure; variations in people's reactions to when costs and benefits arrive; differences in actors' time horizons (how far they look into the future); and variations in how they respond to risks. How these factors affect actors' preferences and perceptions takes us to the heart of political action. As we said at the outset, the process of strategic interaction in world politics is driven by actors' choices. Those choices are, in turn, driven by actors' preferences, relative power, and perceptions. This chapter provided a closer look at these three foundational concepts. The next chapter focuses on how they combine to affect strategic choice and interaction.

Key Terms

transitive choice	belief system	satisfice
purposive choice	image	standard operating
rationality	cognitive limits	procedures (SOPs)
social choice	choice heuristics	opportunity costs
unitary actors	norms	prospect theory
belief	optimize	

To The Reader   A CHAPTER SUMMARY and QUESTIONS FOR REVIEW are available at **www.prenhall.com/lamborn**

CHAPTER 16

The Process of Strategic Choice and Interaction

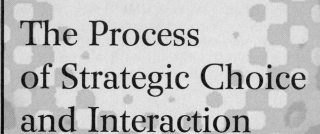

The theoretical approach in this book has stressed the politics of strategic choice and the linkages between domestic and international politics. We have chosen this approach because we believe that, when they are combined, choice under conditions of strategic interdependence and linkage politics create the broadest stretch of common ground available for introducing students to world politics.

Strategic choice is a special kind of purposive choice. As we explained in Chapter 15, purposive choice refers to situations in which actors order their preferences and choose transitively from among those ordered options. Purposive choices take on a *strategic* character when actors' choices reflect not just their own goals, but also their expectations about *others'* likely choices. A vote in an election is purposive, but not strategic, if the actor wants to express her preferences for a particular outcome but does not expect her vote to influence either the electoral outcome or the actions of others. That is typically the case for secret ballots cast by individual voters in national elections. Votes by factions on governing boards of IGOs or NGOs are, in contrast, almost always designed to affect either the outcome or the perceptions of other actors.

People are likely to behave strategically either when they want to affect the choices of others or when they believe that their ability to achieve their preferred outcomes depends both on their choices and the choices of others (that is, when they have partial but incomplete control over the outcomes). In a situation of strategic interaction, all of the actors are behaving in this way. They make their choices *independently*, but the outcomes are *interdependent* because no actor individually controls the outcomes.

The outcomes generated by a process of strategic interaction are thus the combined result of all the key actors' choices. When you ask your boss for a raise, the outcome depends both on your actions (such as the effectiveness of any appeals you can make about the fairness of your request) and those of the boss (such as whether she or he has the ability to delay any action, bargain down the amount of the increase, and so on). Similarly, whether the leaders of two states in the midst of a crisis go to war will depend not just on what each one wants to achieve, but on what each expects the other to choose. Strategic choice is choice *given* people's objectives *and* their expectations about *others'* likely choices. Actors derive their expectations about other people's behavior by putting themselves in the others' shoes—by deciding how they would behave if they had the others' objectives, faced the same political and policy risks, and so on.[1] Strategic interaction characterizes a situation in which all the actors are assumed to be behaving strategically in this sense. Each is trying to achieve his or her purposes in the presence of others who are doing the same thing, and who therefore will affect the outcome.

Linkage politics is the second central focal point in our theoretical lens. The ways in which actors evaluate the strategic situation they confront is typically affected by linkage politics and a concern for bridging the preferences of a variety of state and non-state actors. The cross-arena linkages that connect international politics, the factional politics of policy-making coalitions, and constituency politics affect both the international issues on actors' agendas and how they deal with

Widespread street demonstrations against globalization provided a backdrop for the Group of Eight summit meetings held in Genoa, Italy, in July 2001. While one of the major purposes of the demonstrations was simply to state the demonstrators' policy position, there was another, and potentially far more important, goal: to force the governments in the Group of Eight, the World Bank, International Monetary Fund, and the World Trade Organization to accept the protestors as meaningful political actors in this issue area. If the demonstrators could create a situation of *strategic interdependence*, then they would have become meaningful political actors, even if the governments of the Group of Eight did not want to formally recognize their role.

those issues. For instance, some trade-offs across issue areas (such as minimizing human rights concerns with a trading partner in order to ease business relations with that state) may be made largely to ease one's domestic political risks. When constituencies are powerful and easily mobilized, these groups may have both the desire and ability to impose high costs on policy makers who make choices they dislike.

Examining the process of strategic interaction and the ways in which it is affected by linkage politics will not tell us everything we want to know about world politics. Perhaps most important, such an approach cannot tell us *why* actors want to achieve certain outcomes. It is exactly because that is such a fundamental part of understanding politics that we discussed a wide range of ideas about the origins of actors' preferences and perceptions in Chapter 15. However, given some reliable information on actors' preferences, power, and perceptions over outcomes, a focus on strategic choice and interaction will help you understand both why actors choose particular policy options and whether those policies are likely to be effective.

Chapter 16 thus complements what you learned in Chapter 15. There you took a closer look at the foundational concepts of preferences, power, and perceptions. Now we discuss how these pieces fit together. We begin with a brief overview of the principal stages in the process of strategic choice and interaction. We then turn to a discussion of the ways in which preferences, power, and perception combine in the international arena to affect the strategic—or *situational*—incentives for choice. Since many scholars believe game theory provides one of the most useful ways to evaluate the effect of different situational incentives on choice, we follow with an explanation of game theory and the value and limitations of using it to identify situational incentives. The chapter concludes with a discussion of the effects of linkage politics.

Unpacking the Process of Strategic Choice

It's useful to break the process of choice and strategic interaction into six analytically distinct steps. They can be summarized as follows:

1. Actors' Preferences over Outcomes   An approach that focuses on strategic choice assumes that actors can identify the relative value of the goals they would like to achieve. For example, how important to Chinese leaders is reunification with Taiwan? How committed are certain political leaders to the creation of a world criminal court that would have broad jurisdiction to try people accused of serious humanitarian crimes, regardless of their nationality or their government's consent? Keep in mind that Step #1 consists *only* of identifying how actors order the outcomes (the ends) they want to accomplish. This process is distinct from the evaluation of the policies (the means or instruments) by which these ordered preferences might be achieved.

2. Actors' Evaluations of the Strategic Situation   Here actors try to understand the strategic situation they confront. Such a task involves certain cognitive (mental) processes, such as perception (noticing and evaluating incoming information about the world) and the use of one's particular beliefs about the world or specific actors to discern or interpret their power or preferences and to make judgments about cause and effect in politics. Leaders may "see" either more or less hostility from leaders in another state than the others feel toward them. In other words, people can *mis*perceive the strategic context in more or less serious ways, and this may have consequences for their policy preferences.

3. Actors' Searches for Policy Options   Given their understanding of the strategic situation they confront, actors must first identify the policy options (or means) available for achieving their preferred outcomes. As we discussed in Chapter 15, the thoroughness of this search process varies with how much they care about the issue at hand, how much time they have to decide, how well they use their skills in organizing themselves to make such choices, and how constrained they are by the organizations in which they operate. Much of the real work of matching perceived ends and means lies in this search process.

4. Actors' Evaluations of the Relative Attractiveness of the Perceived Options   Actors' evaluations of the policy options they perceive will vary with the thoroughness and quality of the evaluation process they use. Their evaluations also will vary with the value they attach to achieving gains versus avoiding losses and the standard they use for judging success. Some actors, for instance, may be committed to identifying the best option available given time constraints and the cost of the search and evaluation process. Others may settle for an option that is merely satisfactory (in the sense that it meets a minimal threshold). Finally, actors' evaluations will vary depending on how they discount costs and benefits over time and how they react to the perceived political and policy risks attached to different options.

5. Actors' Strategic Choices, Given Ordered Policy Options   This is the step in which a policy option is selected. In many ways it is the simplest stage, because theories of purposive choice assume that actors will choose transitively once they have rank-ordered their perceived options from most to least attractive.

Strategic choices thus reflect people's perception of the strategic situation they confront within and across political arenas, their evaluation of the options they see as available to deal with the situation, and the way they react to the expected consequences of those options. When these variables are seen as stable or moving within predictable ranges, actors' policy choices are likely to remain stable as well. For example, U.S. policy toward the Soviet Union remained remarkably stable between 1950 and 1990 for the simple reason that the mix of incentives in the international, policy-making, and constituency arenas were seen as stable. This explains why, even in an international environment that differed in some key respects from that of the late 1940s (including the visible fragmentation of what was originally thought to be a monolithic Marxist-Leninist system), U.S. policies of containing Soviet expansion remained, as one historian put it, "extraordinarily" durable into the early 1980s.[2] Significant policy changes, by contrast, typically reflect major changes either in actors' objectives or in their perceptions of the strategic situation and available options. It's also possible that actors' preferences for different policies could be affected by changes in their discounting behavior and the way they react to the perceived risks of different options.

6. The Implications of Actors' Choices for Strategic Interaction   People's choices reflect calculations about the choices they expect others to make as well as their own objectives. Taken together, these separate choices generate a process of strategic interaction that can produce a wide variety of anticipated and unanticipated outcomes; it can also change actors' preferences, relative power, and perceptions over time.

It is the outcomes of these interaction processes that determine whether policy makers can actually achieve their purposes. For example, will two governments pursuing protectionist policies begin a trade war or achieve some compromise short of that outcome? Will a government that is bargaining with a trans-state business firm on terms for entry into that state's market be able to reach agreement on those terms? Will two governments in a crisis escalate to war or dampen down the conflict without war? As in any bargaining situation, the outcome will depend not only on how each actor understands the strategic situation—including the degree of compatibility of objectives, relative power positions, and attachment to common norms—but also on each actor's risk-taking preferences, time horizons, and tendencies to discount costs and benefits. As we discussed above, misperceptions of any of these factors are likely to produce policies that will fail to achieve the actor's objectives.

Two additional points should be kept in mind as you consider the process of choice and strategic interaction in politics. First, while this six-step summary breaks the process into analytically distinct components, that does not mean that people always take each discrete step. For example, officials in organizations at times skip Steps #3 and 4 because their policy options have been defined for them in advance by organizational leaders across categories of situations that are considered "typical." As we discussed in Chapter 15, such "standard operating procedures" may be cost-effective, considering the time and effort it could take to find other ways to achieve the organization's goals. All that we assume about these steps in the choice process is that actors can get to ordered preferences over policy options in some way (that is, that they can accomplish Steps #1 to 4). How (and how well) they do that varies a good deal.

Second, while these six steps are analytically distinct, they need not occur in precisely this sequence. For example, Step #2 (actors' evaluations of the strategic context) or Steps #3 and 4 (identifying and evaluating options) could lead actors to reexamine their goals (Step #1). Similarly, Step #6 (the outcomes of strategic interaction) could change the strategic environment in a way that induces actors to reevaluate their goals or search for different policy options.

However actors approach the tasks summarized in these six steps, their evaluation of the strategic environment they confront and their available policy options affects everything else they do related to choice. That evaluation depends, in turn, on how their preferences, relative power, and perceptions combine.

Evaluating the Strategic Incentives for Choice

It is important to remember that the international strategic environment—and the situational incentives for choice it generates—is shaped by the way the first three political principles *combine*. Recall that the strategic importance of actors' relative power position depends on the compatibility of their preferences over outcomes. The more incompatible their objectives, the more strategically important their relative power; the more compatible their objectives, the less it matters who is more powerful. By the same reasoning, the political significance of differences in actors' preferences depends on their relative power positions because relative power affects who can control outcomes. Thus, the weaker an actor's relative power, the more strategically important the stronger actor's preferences; the stronger an actor's power, the less important are the weaker actor's preferences. In sum, the ability to increase the probability of getting one's way in some situation *defines* relative power, while the difference between what one wants and what others want indicates the *importance* of relative power in that situation.

Differences in people's preferences and power positions on specific issues are evaluated in terms of their assessments and preferences about legitimate relationships. Recall that the higher the value people place on legitimate relationships *and* the more legitimate they believe their existing relationships to be, the more likely they are to accept policy outcomes and decision procedures that adversely affect their short-term policy preferences and power positions within those relationships. In other words, the more people care about dealing "fairly" with others and believe that their own relationships are "fair," the likelier they are to accept less in some exchanges than they would otherwise.

Two important results follow from this. First, strong concerns about legitimacy can constrain officials' actions by ruling out some policy options that they might otherwise consider attractive. For instance, if policy makers and their constituents believe, as the first President Bush often said, that their state's armed forces should be put in "harm's way" *only* when there is no perceived alternative to using force, those officials' flexibility in dealing with foreign-policy crises will be sharply limited, as compared with officials who consider using military force in a wider variety of situations. Second, a concern for legitimacy can shape people's broader views about what a "good society" should look like, both within states and across them. Since World War II, for example, political actors in North America and Western Europe have concluded that under *no* imaginable circumstances would they go to war with one

The success of NATO's peacekeeping efforts in Bosnia (at left) and of U.S. and British nation-building efforts in Afghanistan after the installation of the interim government led by Hamid Karzai depends not only on military capabilities but also on whether the people in those countries regard those roles as legitimate. If the perceived legitimacy of these missions collapses, soldiers assigned to them can quickly become targets, as was the case in Somalia in the early 1990s. The same essential strategic patterns affect international economic and environmental issues. When trans-state business enterprises fund massive lumbering projects in Third World countries (at right), the strategic situation they confront will vary dramatically depending on whether key local actors regard such lumbering as a legitimate business activitiy.

another. Although this choice first emerged because there were no specific reasons for states in these groups to fight one another and they faced a common adversary during the Cold War, a rejection of war among them has since became part of these states' basic identities as members of these groups. To be a member in good standing of such a community requires adherence to this standard of proper behavior.

The first two principles in the politics of strategic choice capture strategic relationships at single points in time. They represent a snapshot (or a series of discrete snapshots if multiple time points are considered one by one), not a video. Yet people pay attention not just to how preferences, power, and issues of legitimacy are related today, but also to how they expect these factors to evolve over time. People's judgements about the length of time they will continue to interact with other actors—and the way in which power, preferences, and issues of legitimacy will combine and play out during that anticipated period—"cast a shadow" back onto the present, affecting how people make decisions in the present. Different anticipated futures thus help to create distinct incentives for choice.

If people's time horizons are long, their behavior in the present will be shaped by calculations about developments that may or may not occur quite far down the road. For example, in 1965, when U.S. leaders were deciding to expand their military involvement in Vietnam, an assistant to Defense Secretary McNamara suggested that 70 percent of the U.S. aim in expanding participation in the war was "to avoid a humiliating U.S. defeat (to our reputation as a guarantor)." Only 30 percent of the U.S. objective, in this interpretation, was to help the South Vietnamese people enjoy a free way of life without fear of aggression.[3] This meant that U.S. leaders were prepared to fight a war not because they believed that the immediate situation demanded it, but because they feared that if they did not, other peoples and leaders down the road would not trust U.S. security commitments and might defect to the communist bloc.* During the Cold War, virtually all U.S. foreign policy makers considered this a very bad outcome. By contrast, if people's time horizons are short, their present behavior will be largely unaffected by events that might come later. For example, much of the opposition to expensive policies to deal with global warming, acid rain, and other international environmental problems rests on the view that future conditions do not justify such sacrifice now. In such situations, people are likely to discount fairly heavily any future benefits of dealing in the present with difficult environmental problems.

Consider next the impact of variation in people's expectations about how compatible their substantive objectives and norms will be over whatever length of time they are looking into the future. The more compatibility people see when they look into the future, the more cooperative and the less power oriented their strategies for dealing with other actors will be. Conversely, the less compatibility they see down the road, the more they will assume that they must rely on power to achieve their goals. This is a major issue now for U.S. officials when they consider their future relationship with China. Many specialists on Chinese politics see a future in which China's leaders will mainly cooperate with their neighbors and avoid using or threatening force to achieve their goals. Such a scenario does not assume that China will become a democracy but does assume that its policy coalitions will not be dominated by ultra-nationalist factions. Yet such factions could become dominant within Chinese policy coalitions, in which case direct confrontations between China and Japan, Taiwan, and other Asian states would become more likely.[4] Under these circumstances, U.S. policy toward China would be likely to become much more competitive and power-driven. Thus, debates about America's China policy largely turn on which scenario people expect.

Analysts who talk about the shadow of the future at times make claims about actors' behavior based on broad characterizations of the underlying issues. One such argument contends that it is harder for actors to cooperate on security issues than on economics because the shadow of the future in the two issue areas is very different. In economics, according to this argument, actors expect their relationships to continue indefinitely, since neither side can eliminate the other or suddenly force a change in the nature of the game. Actors are thus inclined to cooperate on economics in the present to make future benefits likely. In military-security affairs, by contrast, actors can conceivably use force to eliminate others.[5] This argument suggests that it is more dangerous to make concessions that could increase one's relative vulnerability on security than on economic issues. Such arguments should be treated cautiously. Conquest does occur in world politics, but it is rare. Only once since 1945 has one state absorbed another by force, and in this case (Iraq's invasion of Kuwait in 1990)

---

*Many critics of the Vietnam War disputed the assumption that U.S. credibility in future, unrelated conflicts would depend on U.S. actions in Vietnam. They argued that future credibility would depend much more on the specific issues at stake in a particular situation. For a discussion of these kinds of beliefs (although in this case in the context of U.S. commitments in Europe), see Joseph Lepgold, *The Declining Hegemon: The United States and European Defense, 1960–1990* (New York: Praeger, 1990), pp. 153–56.

Amish communities provide well-known examples of diffuse reciprocity within a society, and nothing symbolizes that ethic more than a community barn raising, where people come without pay or the expectation of a specific reward to help a farmer put up a new barn. International politics is much better known for a norm of strict reciprocity.

the action was reversed. In assessing either the length of actors' time horizons or the compatibility of their preferences, one must focus on the specific issues and parties involved.

We conclude this discussion of the shadow of the future by making three points. First, the less stable the strategic context, the more that people's estimates of it will vary with the length of their time horizons. Thus, if actors' preferences, relative power positions, or attachment to shared norms are shifting rapidly or unpredictably, it becomes important in analyzing policy choices to know how far into the future they are looking. Second, the longer the time horizons of actors who believe that others will continue to share their substantive preferences and norms, the likelier it is that they will seek to create a system of **diffuse reciprocity.** Diffuse reciprocity is a type of relationship in which people do not "keep score" about what they give to and receive from others, but instead offer and take concessions from one another based on the parties' needs. Very close interstate alliances or tight links among non-state actors (such as terrorist organizations that frequently share intelligence and cooperate on specific operations[6]) illustrate such a relationship. Third, to the extent that actors are uncertain about how long they will deal with others, how long some issue will be on their agendas, or how much others share their preferences, they will hesitate to make concessions unless they are repaid quickly and comparably. Such a relationship is one of **strict reciprocity.** Here actors keep close track of who gives what to whom, and whether commitments are precisely implemented. Arms control illustrates this pattern; actors rarely cut their weapons arsenals unless others do so simultaneously and in equal measure.

diffuse reciprocity
A relationship in which people help each other out without keeping track of who gave what to whom.

strict reciprocity A relationship in which people help each other out only as long as they are repaid quickly in comparable amounts.

game theory A theoretic approach to identify situational incentives by analyzing variations in the compatibility of actors' preferences and the effects of strategic interaction over time.

Using Game Theory to Identify Strategic Incentives

Game theory is one of the most widely used theoretical approaches for identifying situational incentives. It can be used given information on the distribution of actors' preferences, their perceptions, and their expectations of the different paths along which a process of strategic interaction might develop over time. Game theory can be of great help, but it also has important limitations. It does not deal directly with differences in actors' relative power (though, as we discuss below, game theory has been connected with estimates of power in expected utility approaches). It also bypasses the issue of where preferences over outcomes come from in the first place. It thus captures key pieces of the politics of strategic interaction while setting aside other pieces that are equally fundamental. This section discusses the assumptions and nature of game theory and some commonly used game models. We conclude by spelling out the value as well as the limitations of this analytical approach.

The Simplifying Assumptions of Game Theory

As an analytical framework, game theory makes a number of assumptions. First, outcomes are assumed to reflect interdependent strategic choices. Recall that politics, according to the definition used here, involves interdependent choices among purposive actors. Second, actors are assumed to be unitary and purposive. While purposive behavior is central to the way we view the process of politics, the assumption of unitary actors is more problematic. By definition, this assumption applies to factions, but it can be problematic for coalitions. Groups can be treated as unitary actors only if their members have preference orderings that produce transitive choice. As we discussed in Chapter 15, this means that preferences must fall along a single dimension, be single-peaked, and decline steadily as one moves away from the single best option. Third, actors are assumed to be able to rank-order (from best to worst) all the policy options they have identified given their preferences over outcomes. In other words, it is assumed that each actor can rank-order the relative **utility**—the relative value—they attach to each possible outcome.** The complete array of these rank-ordered utilities is called a *payoff matrix*. Fourth, given an estimate of the relative utilities actors attach to different outcomes, actors do not differ in their abilities to identify and assess strategies. Fifth, while actors are assumed to be purposive, the extent to which their purposes conflict varies across situations. Some games are called *zero-sum* (what one actor loses another gains) and thus assume completely opposed preferences. Others, called *non-zero-sum* games, focus on *mixed-motive* situations, where the parties have compatible as well as opposed preferences. Here the parties can gain or lose at the same time. Politics usually involves non-zero-sum situations. Sixth, the type of games we examine carry the assumption that agreements among actors are not enforceable. This is important in international politics, where there is no legal authority to enforce actors' agreements.[7] Seventh, unless one specifically assumes that different games are linked, game-theoretic applications implicitly assume that choice reflects the single game identified in the payoff matrix.

These assumptions allow analysts to evaluate how actors *would* make interdependent policy choices, *if* the simplifying assumptions of game theory approximate the actual situation. For instance, game theory explains whether actors are likely to reach an **equilibrium outcome** and what it will look like. An equilibrium outcome is one that the actors have no incentive to change unilaterally, given their current preferences. Being able to identify equilibrium outcomes is very useful when analyzing

utility   The value an actor attaches to a particular outcome.

equilibrium outcome   An outcome in which none of the actors in a strategically interdependent situation has an incentive to make unilateral changes.

**In some versions of game theory, it is assumed that actors can assign an actual value (called a *cardinal utility*) to each outcome. In this introduction we make the far less demanding assumption that they can rank-order the values.

strategic choice. It makes it possible to tell what outcomes, if any, are stable under current circumstances. Equilibria do *not* necessarily indicate what is ethically desirable, balanced from the point of view of all the actors, or likely to persist indefinitely.[8]

As we mentioned above, game theory usually does not deal directly with possible differences in actors' relative power. Instead, it typically assumes either that the actors have equal power or that power is folded into utilities by increasing the value of those options for which actors' resources are useful, and decreasing the value of those options that actors' power positions put them in a poor position to achieve.

To keep this introduction to game theory as simple as possible, we consider situations involving just two actors. We begin with games that assume actors interact only once. Such models depict what are called *non-iterated* games. We then consider the strategic implications that arise in *iterated* games, ones that last more than one round.

Well-Known One-Round Games

The Prisoner's Dilemma, Chicken, and Stag Hunt are perhaps the most well-known and widely used games in the study of international politics. They describe three mixed-motive situations that capture a variety of important and interesting political situations.

The Prisoner's Dilemma   Imagine two criminals (A and B) who are guilty of murder and several lesser crimes. They have agreed that if they are ever caught, neither will "rat" on the other. However, now they have been caught, and the police—who have only enough evidence to convict them of one of their minor crimes—are trying hard to create incentives for the prisoners to confess to murder. The two are placed in separate rooms and prevented from communicating. While the police acknowledge that both will get a light prison term on the lesser charges if neither confesses to the murder, the police also make an offer that they hope will be too good to refuse: If one confesses before the other, he will go free while the other receives a life sentence for the murder. If both confess at the same time, each will get a moderate sentence.

Both actors rank-order their options from 1 to 4, with 1 being the most preferred and 4 being the least preferred. Rank-ordering actors' preferences doesn't tell you *how much* more (or less) one option is valued than another (to do that you would need to be able to measure the intervals between each place in the ranking). It simply indicates that they prefer the one ranked first the best, the one ranked second the next best, and so forth. In this case, all you know is that each prisoner prefers going free the most, a light prison sentence second, a moderate sentence third, and a life sentence last (fourth). Even with information this limited, looking systematically at how actors rank-order different possible outcomes can tell you quite a bit about the strategic incentives confronting them in a particular situation.

In the strategic situation outlined in the Prisoner's Dilemma, the combination of the two actors' preference orderings produces the payoff matrix in Figure 16–1. Prisoner A is called the "row actor," since we read his strategic options along the rows, and prisoner B is called the "column actor," since we read his choices down the columns. (Actor A's rank-orders of the utilities attached to each option are represented by the red number; B's are indicated by the blue number.)

Consider the situation confronting Prisoner A in Figure 16–1. As we have explained, while Prisoner A can rank-order his preferred outcomes (with 1 being most

Figure 16–1   **The Prisoner's Dilemma**

*"Sucker's Payoff"

preferred and 4 least), the particular outcome he will actually get depends not only on his choice but also on the choice of Prisoner B, over whom he has no control and with whom there can be no binding agreements. Prisoner A thus analyzes the attractiveness of his options in the following way: If Prisoner B chooses not to confess, would Prisoner A prefer a strategy of confessing or not confessing? Since 1 represents his most-preferred option (and 2 his second most), clearly he would prefer a strategy of confessing if B chooses not to confess. But what if B were to confess? If B confesses, then A is also better off confessing, because a strategy of confessing produces the third ranked outcome, while the don't-confess strategy produces the worst outcome of the four. When cooperation produces the worst possible outcome in a strategic situation, it's called a **"sucker's payoff."**

Given this analysis of the incentives attached to the different options confronting Prisoner A, his best strategy is clear. No matter what B chooses to do, A is better off confessing. When an actor's best choice is the same regardless of what the other actor chooses, he is said to have a **dominant strategy.** The problem in the Prisoner's Dilemma game is that *both* prisoners have a dominant strategy to confess. As a result, the dual-confession outcome (bold type in Figure 16–1) is a stable equilibrium outcome whenever actors are confronted with this situation in a single-round game. The irony—the *dilemma* in the single-play Prisoner's Dilemma game—is that both actors rank the equilibrium outcome only third best and know they would have received the second-best outcome if they had cooperated in a shared strategy of not confessing. But neither follows this jointly cooperative strategy, since both have dominant incentives to confess.

We see these characteristics whenever there are strong individual incentives not to cooperate, but the actors would all be better off *if* they cooperated. Consider states with conflicting security preferences. Each would like to find a way to avoid spending money acquiring weapons that don't add to its security, but each also fears that if it doesn't spend money on more weapons and the other does, its security will deteriorate. In this situation, both would benefit from an arms control agreement, because it would provide security at a lower cost. But as attractive as that outcome is, it is only second best. What each would prefer the most is the opportunity to improve its security by buying more weapons while the other refrained from doing so. Given this preference ordering, it is very hard for actors to believe that they can afford to trust

sucker's payoff
A situation in which the actor who cooperates is double-crossed and receives the worst possible outcome.

dominant strategy
A situation in which actors have a strategic option that remains their best available choice no matter what the other actors choose; when actors do *not* have a dominant strategy, it's hard to decide which option to choose because their best option varies with the choices others make.

Figure 16–2 **Chicken**

		Driver B	
		Swerve	Don't swerve
Driver A	Swerve	2, 2	3, 1
	Don't swerve	1, 3	4, 4

that the others will honor an arms control agreement. As in the one-round Prisoner's Dilemma game, each has a dominating strategy: No matter what the others choose, it is better to break any arms control agreement than it is to honor it. The result is an arms race in which neither side gains any increased security.

Chicken The game of Chicken asks us to imagine a situation similar to the one made famous by the James Dean movie *Rebel Without a Cause*. In the original version of the game, two teenage drivers want to demonstrate their toughness to gain additional prestige among their peer group. To do that, they challenge each other to a dangerous game of intimidation in which they race their cars toward each other from opposite directions. If one swerves and the other does not, the former is a "chicken," the latter a "hero." If both swerve simultaneously, each suffers a slight but equal loss in reputation. If neither swerves, each will be badly hurt or killed in the resulting collision.***

Given the assumed values of the actors, the best possible result is to drive straight ahead while the other "chickens out" and swerves. The second best outcome is to swerve simultaneously; no one loses face (relative to the other), and no one gets hurt. The third best is to swerve while the other drives straight; better to lose face than to be killed or maimed. The worst outcome is to have both call the other's bluff and have a collision. The payoff matrix is shown in Figure 16–2.

Notice that the game of Chicken creates a different set of incentives for choice than does the Prisoner's Dilemma. While Driver A would prefer the don't-swerve strategy if he were certain that B was going to swerve (it would give him his most preferred outcome), Driver A would prefer to swerve if he were convinced that B would not swerve. Although it would only give him his third-ranked choice, that's still better than the fourth. Because Driver A's preferred choice *varies* with B's choice, Driver A does not have a dominant strategy. Meanwhile, Driver B is faced with exactly the same set of cross-pressures as he considers which option is best for him.

***As those who have seen *Rebel Without a Cause* know, in the movie the game of Chicken is played by driving toward a cliff, with the first person who stops his car or jumps out the chicken. The incentives produced by the game structure are the same; just imagine a race toward a cliff rather than toward a head-on collision and substitute "stop first" for "swerve" and "stop second" for "don't swerve."

Game theory helps us understand not only these conflicting incentives, but also the implications of this cross-pressuring for actors' likely choices. While each actor has an incentive in the Chicken game to act *as if* he will stand firm (not swerve), the danger of acting on that strategy is that one could end up with a collision—the worst possible outcome. In such a situation, it is generally considered prudent (but, unlike the situation in which both sides have dominant strategies, by no means certain) to choose a strategy that will minimize the worst possible outcome. This strategy is called a **minimax strategy** (for *minimizing* the *maximum* worst result). If Driver A chooses to swerve, the worst possible result is ranked third best; if he chooses not to swerve, the worst possible result is ranked dead last at fourth. Since coming in third is "less bad" than coming in fourth, the swerve option represents a preference to achieve the minimax outcome.

The Chicken game helps us to interpret choices in **brinkmanship** situations. These are cases in which one actor can gain at the other's expense if the other actor backs down, but mutual intransigence leads to mutual disaster. U.S. Secretary of

minimax strategy
Choosing the option that minimizes the maximum worst result that can occur; often recommended in situations in which actors do not have a dominant strategy.

brinkmanship   A strategy in which actors threaten shared disaster in an effort to force other actors to capitulate.

In the game of Chicken, actors manipulate the risk of shared disaster in an effort to make the other person capitulate. The extreme danger inherent in such brinkmanship strategy leads game theorists to advocate a minimax strategy in which the actors accept less than they want in order to avoid ending up with the worst possible outcome—shared disaster when they go over the brink. In the classic James Dean movie *Rebel Without a Cause*, Dean faces a rival for dominance among their teenage peers (at left) and agrees to a game of Chicken in which the two race cars toward a cliff to see who will chicken-out first to avoid going over the brink. In the movie, both try to jump at the last moment, but only Dean gets out and his challenger goes to his death. Many analysts and the general public thought Kennedy and Khrushchev were also involved in a game of Chicken (at right) during the Cuban Missile Crisis, with nuclear war the outcome if they went over the brink. Domestic politics led Kennedy to demand that Khrushchev agree to a deal in which he appeared to capitulate, but secret documents revealed years later show that Kennedy also made concessions in an effort to end up with a jointly acceptable, minimax outcome that ended the threat of war.

State Rusk captured their flavor when, after Soviet leaders withdrew their missiles from Cuba, he said "We were eyeball to eyeball, and the other fellow just blinked."

Stag Hunt A third well-known game, called Stag Hunt, asks us to imagine this situation: A group of hunters gathers to trap a stag (a deer). To succeed, all the hunters must participate. Each will eat plentifully if they capture a deer. If one person runs away from the group to catch a rabbit, he will eat lightly (assuming he catches the rabbit), but none of the others will eat at all since it takes the entire group to trap a deer. If all the hunters break away at the same time to chase rabbits, they each have some chance to eat lightly, but it is unlikely that all of them will catch a rabbit, both because all the activity may scare the rabbits away and because it is unlikely that enough rabbits will be found for all of them.

Since they are all hungry and prefer venison to rabbit (not to mention a big meal to a small one), each hunter has this preference ordering: (1) stay with the group and hunt deer to have a chance to eat well; (2) defect from the group to try to catch a rabbit while others stay with the group; (3) chase rabbits simultaneously with everyone else; (4) stay with the group while some other hunter(s) leaves (which means you are likely to end up with neither the deer nor the rabbit). The payoff matrix, simplified to portray two hunters, is shown in Figure 16–3.

Note again the absence of a dominant strategy. If Hunter A thinks Hunter B is going to try to trap the stag, he is better off cooperating in the stag hunt (Outcome 1). However, if Hunter A thinks Hunter B is likely to go off on his own to trap a rabbit, then he is better off chasing rabbits too, because if B is chasing rabbits, A will get the fourth—and worst—outcome if he stays in the stag hunt.

The strategic incentives in the payoff matrix for Stag Hunt can be interpreted in different ways. Some argue that actors will defect at the first chance (go off on their own to try to get the rabbit) in order to avoid the "sucker's payoff" (staying to trap the stag while others defect to go after the rabbit).[9] This reasoning assumes that people's willingness to cooperate in this situation is low because the costs of being wrong about others' intentions is too high. Others, however, have a different interpretation, arguing that this situation provides stronger incentives to cooperate in the hunt for the stag than to defect and go after the rabbit. The probability of getting

Figure 16–3 **Stag Hunt**

		Hunter B	
		Try to trap stag	Try to trap rabbit
Hunter A	Try to trap stag	1, 1	4*, 2
	Try to trap rabbit	2, 4*	3, 3

* "Sucker's Payoff"

the rabbit acting alone must be far higher than the probability of getting the deer acting together for there to be an incentive to defect, since all the hunters prefer deer to rabbit and more food to less. Thus, if one assumes that the probabilities of bagging the two animals are comparable, the expected value of capturing the deer—and, hence, the value of cooperating over defecting—would be much greater. (Expected value is calculated by multiplying the utility of an outcome by the assumed probability of obtaining it.)

As the ambiguous strategic incentives in this situation suggest, trying to predict choice when there isn't a dominant strategy can lead one to look for considerations outside of the game that might affect actors' choices. For instance, people's willingness to run risks to cooperate might depend on how much intrinsic value they place on cooperation, or whether there is some other game linked to this one that might give one of the hunters an incentive to defect. Perhaps one of the hunters is training a younger person in rabbit hunting; perhaps one is reluctant to cooperate because other group members took advantage of him on some other issue. In sum, unless one makes some additional assumptions, it is hard to say whether one-round Stag Hunt situations create greater incentives to cooperate or defect.

The problem of maintaining economic sanctions illustrates Stag Hunt situations in world politics. To isolate states that they believe have violated international norms, governments at times institute such economic sanctions as *embargoes* (a refusal to sell to the target) or *boycotts* (a refusal to buy from the target). Actors often feel cross-pressured by the incentives they face in such situations. Honoring the sanctions is analogous to the shared objective of cooperating with the other hunters and then enjoying a big meal of venison. Yet no one wants to be a "sucker" in this situation. This would occur if a government honored sanctions at some economic cost while others did business under the table with a target government—an outcome similar to remaining ready to trap a deer while all the other hunters chase rabbits. No government can be certain it will not be a "sucker" if it honors the sanctions, since the economic incentives to defect may be high (a state enforcing sanctions is likely to pay higher prices to get needed goods and services).

At this point, we need to move away from the assumption that the actors interact only once (that the game has only one round). The problem of maintaining economic sanctions in the presence of incentives to defect is typically one that goes on over some period. If sanctions are to work in changing a target's behavior, they typically do so only over a period of time, as the target pays continued economic costs of isolation. Even more important, being willing to invest in actions designed to reinforce international norms suggests that one is looking to the future as well as the present, that actors are concerned about more than one round. Thus, if we want to explain the increasing use of sanctions in world politics as an alternative or complement to the use of force, we need to understand how the sanctioning actors' time horizons might allow them to see that a shared goal can be reached, but *only* if they persevere in behavior from which it may at times seem tempting to defect. We thus move on to a discussion of games that involve multiple choices over time.

Iterated Games

Assuming that the parties expect to face each other just once may not be very realistic. If the actors instead assume that they are likely to face the same other actors repeatedly under comparable conditions, an **iterated game** model becomes

iterated game   A game that has multiple rounds; iterated games frequently have dramatically different strategic incentives than the one-round versions.

appropriate. Iterated games have two important advantages over one-round gains: They make it possible to examine the effect of expectations about the future (the shadow of the future) on present choices; they make it possible to examine the process of strategic interaction over multiple rounds.

Much of world politics consists of iterated encounters in such issue areas as bargaining over trade agreements, arms control, and the debt rescheduling that occurs periodically between major multinational banks and debtor governments. But the extent to which iteration can help actors cooperate depends on the strategic circumstances. In Prisoners' Dilemma situations, repeating the game makes defection (for instance, cheating on arms control agreements) unrewarding, since any short-run gains are outweighed by the mutual punishment resulting from the other party's defection.[10] Even if the parties cannot, for some reason, communicate effectively through words, a repeated Prisoners' Dilemma lets them *see* that defection will simply invite others to defect as well.

Incentives to cooperate are also likely to be reinforced when Stag Hunt games are iterated. This type of situation is often called an "assurance game." The actors want to cooperate (note that mutual cooperation is both parties' strongest preference) and will presumably do so if they think that others will as well. Thus, especially in small groups where the parties can closely observe one another's behavior, sustained cooperation is highly likely, given a basic similarity of preferences. Policy makers are often urged to begin a search for international agreements among a small group of like-minded actors, since such actors will be likelier to agree on outcomes *and* be better able to reassure one another about compliance.[11]

In Chicken, by contrast, iteration can produce quite different incentives to choose competitive versus cooperative strategies depending on the destructiveness of the jointly competitive outcome. As a result, iteration does not produce a clear and unambiguous strategy in Chicken. In a strategic situation in which the jointly competitive outcome carries acceptable (even if highly unattractive) costs, over multiple rounds actors might decide they have to stand firm in the face of repeatedly competitive behavior by the other side in order to show the resolve that is assumed to be useful in future encounters. Russian officials were intransigent during the July 1914 crisis in part because they felt they had let their ally, Serbia, down in the 1908 Bosnian crisis by being too accommodating. Similarly, after U.S. officials felt they had been "pushed around" by Soviet leaders at a 1961 summit meeting, they believed that they needed to "take a stand somewhere." That "somewhere" turned out to be Vietnam.[12]

On the other hand, in situations in which the jointly competitive outcome would produce unacceptably high costs, such as in crises involving weapons of mass destruction, iteration is likely to have the opposite effect. The destructiveness of the jointly competitive outcome (both refuse to swerve) in a game of nuclear brinkmanship is so bad that there are immense incentives to assure that it *never* happens. Trying to make sure that a particular outcome never happens over multiple rounds involves minimizing the cumulative probabilities. Because cumulative probabilities are calculated by multiplying the probabilities of the outcomes in each round, the numbers get small fast. A 90 percent probability of successful brinkmanship in one round becomes a 53 percent probability of success over six rounds. This prospect is obviously not a very attractive one if the game is nuclear brinkmanship.

These kinds of calculations assume that policy makers are unitary actors and can afford to set aside concerns that arise within domestic arenas and focus on

Many analysts believe arms control agreements provide a classic example of how strategic incentives change when one moves from a one-round Prisoner's Dilemma to an iterated game. Game theory suggests that all the actors in a one-round Prisoner's Dilemma have an incentive to break prior agreements to cooperate. However, in multiple-round (iterated) games, any cheating can be punished, and the prospect of retaliation creates incentives to honor agreements. The decision of the Bush administration in the fall of 2001 to end the Antiballistic Missile Treaty so the United States could try to build a national missile defense would appear to run counter to the expected effects of iteration on the stability of arms control agreements, but at the time of the decision Russia had very few attractive options for retaliation. Without a credible way to punish the United States, the impact of iteration on the strategic incentives to cooperate dropped dramatically.

the international stakes and risks attached to one set of possible outcomes. The calculations become far more complex when the actors are coalitions and domestic political risks are a major factor. For instance, iterated Prisoners' Dilemmas require a **mixed strategy** in which an actor's choices depend on what the other actors did in the previous round of the game. If they defected, you defect; if they cooperated, you cooperate. This strategy is relatively easy to follow when a unitary actor is making the choices, but it is often hard to get agreement on pursuing mixed strategies when the actors are coalitions. On arms control, for instance, hawks may not believe they are actually seeing cooperation even when it is there, while doves may have a bias toward seeing cooperation even when it is absent. Mixed strategies may create varying political risks for different factions, further complicating the possibility of a coherent, long-term strategy. These observations suggest that we need to be careful to evaluate the limitations and value of game-theoretic approaches systematically.

The Limitations and Value of Game-Theoretic Approaches

As you've seen, game-theoretic models can often provide a good sense of what actors' basic policy options look like, given information on the actors' preferred outcomes. But we should pause here to recall what these models omit. First, the relative power of actors interested in a particular set of issues affects their ability to achieve their goals and the policy options they consider in trying to achieve those goals. To get a complete understanding of the strategic situation that the actors confront, we must add power to the compatibility of actors' preferences. Second, actors'

mixed strategy A strategy in which actors vary their choice to cooperate or compete in each round of an iterated game depending on what the other actors did in the preceding round.

evaluations of the implications of the strategic situation they confront varies with their beliefs about the importance and substance of establishing and maintaining legitimate relationships. If we want to understand actors' strategic situations in light of the relationships they have with other actors, we must add this "larger game" involving commitments to justice and shared norms. Third, when assessing the effects of situational incentives on choice, what really matters is what actors perceive. As the example of the different ways in which political hawks and doves are likely to read evidence of cooperation suggests, motivated misperceptions (as well as the problems created by unmotivated misperceptions) can affect the value of any theory of strategic incentives that analysts use to stipulate what is really there. Fourth, world politics is almost always linkage politics. Therefore, if we are to understand the linked strategic situations actors face in world politics, we need to add the connections between international politics and the coalition-building games in the other arenas (such as the policy-making and constituency arenas). Finally, actors' *reactions* to the mix of incentives they confront in a game-theoretic payoff matrix will vary with their risk-taking preferences and how they discount costs and benefits over time.

These observations suggest two possible ways to use game theory to improve our understanding of strategic choice and interaction. One can either use game theory as it was originally developed and then add the crucial pieces of the politics of strategic choice that were left out, or one can add the missing pieces first. If the missing pieces are added first, the meaning and value of the payoff matrix changes. In this revised role, the payoff matrix reflects actors' preferences over policy options, *given* their perceptions of the distribution of power, the implications of the issue at hand for the legitimacy of ongoing relationships, the incentives created by linkage politics, and reactions to risk and discounting. Of course, this means that one's estimates of the payoffs will be harder to derive because this approach requires both information and theories that are external to game theory.

In spite of these difficulties, since the mid-1980s game theory has begun to be used in this way by scholars interested in the origins and outcomes of strategic choice in world politics. The most significant and promising research program in this area has been pioneered by Bruce Bueno de Mesquita. This research program has developed far more sophisticated game-theoretic models than the three simple ones explained earlier and uses detailed information from area experts to estimate the values of the key variables in those models. Significantly, evaluations of the predictive ability of Bueno de Mesquita's models by U.S. government agencies in a variety of systematic tests and experiments have concluded that its predictions of actors' choices and the outcomes of strategic interaction are accurate more than 90 percent of the time. This success rate is even more striking when one notices that the model has been used across a broad range of issue areas and state and non-state actors.[13]

Of course, even if one enhances game-theoretic models to get a more complete picture of the variations in the situational incentives confronting actors in different contexts, it is important to remember that much remains to be done to fill out our understanding of world politics. We very much need a companion set of theories that explain the origin and evolution of actors' preferences, perceptions, and power. Finally, it is important to remember that while good theory is critical, it can't do the job alone. There is no substitute for detailed knowledge of particular issues, actors, and time periods if we are to answer questions about world politics.

Adding Political Incentives into the Mix

The first three political principles focus on the strategic incentives generated by actors' perceptions of how key actors' preferences and relative power combine in the international arena and how they are likely to develop over time. We began with the international arena because the primary purpose of a text on world politics is to explain strategic choice and interaction in the international area. However, while there may be occasions in which actors make choices based solely on the situational incentives they perceive in the international arena, it is far more characteristic for world politics to reflect a process of linkage politics in which international, factional, and constituency politics continually shape one another.

It is time, therefore, to add the political incentives generated by factional and constituency politics into the mix. It's obvious that factional politics within policy-making coalitions and constituency politics affect the level of political risks attached to different policy options. But how can those risks be identified and estimated? Fortunately, the same principles that can be used to identify the situational incentives in the international political arena can be used to identify the strategic situation in the political arenas in which factional and constituency politics take place. An analysis of the strategic situations in the policy-making arena and the constituency arena can be used to identify the political risks arising out of factional and constituency politics, just as we have been using an analysis of the strategic situation in the international arena to evaluate the probability that different policy options will succeed or fail internationally.

What actors can create dangerously high political risks for policy factions? Politically powerful actors in the policy-making and constituency arenas who have incompatible preferences, regard existing relationships to be illegitimate, and expect their opposition to produce a more attractive shadow of the future than doing nothing and staying on the political sidelines. In short, to assess the *level* of the political risks attached to different policy options, you use the same enduring patterns in the politics of strategic choice you used to make sense of international politics to analyze the key factions in the policy-making arena and the key constituencies in the constituency arena.

Once you've identified the magnitude of the political risks attached to different options, the next step is to use the patterns in the fourth principle—which describes the sources of variation in actors' risk-taking preferences and how they discount costs and benefits—to evaluate how policy makers are likely to react to the mix of policy and political risks they perceive.

As we have discussed, some of the sources of variation in how actors discount and react to risk are driven by the differences in the *value* individual actors attach to their preferred outcomes, while others depend on the *context* within which policy choices are made and implemented.

- *The higher the expected value that an actor attaches to a policy outcome: (1) the more willing that actor will be to invest resources and political position in an effort to achieve that goal; and (2) the less their choices will be affected by discounting.*

- *The less control they have over policy choice and implementation: (1) the less willing coalition members will be to take political risks in an effort to achieve coalition policy goals; (2) the more indifferent coalition members will be to policy failure—if policy failure isn't politically dangerous; (3) the more actors will prefer future costs over current costs; and (4) the more they will discount future benefits relative to current benefits.*

While the value actors attach to different outcomes is hard to know without studying them individually, the context within which policy coalitions are made and broken often varies with the political structure and norms of the policy-making and constituency arenas. Consequently, an evaluation of those two arenas can provide important clues about how policy makers in particular state and non-state actors are likely to discount costs and benefits and react to different levels of political risk. In the U.S. political system, for instance, policy must pass through multiple "veto points" as it moves through the executive, Congress, and perhaps the courts. These points typically create many opportunities for factions with relevant political resources to block policy initiatives or demand significant concessions, and the large number of mobilized constituency groups and intense media scrutiny frequently create incentives to do exactly that. These contextual factors provide strong incentives for U.S. policy factions to heavily discount the costs and benefits of policy options and to avoid running high political risks—*unless* they attach a very high value to achieving their preferred outcome.

Anticipating how actors are likely to react to the mix of incentives they perceive is the last crucial step in making sense of strategic choice. Put those patterns together with some reliable information on actors' preferences, power, and perceptions, and you will be better able to analyze both why actors choose particular policies and whether those policies are likely to be effective.

Conclusion

Strategic choice theories assume that people see the world in strategic terms, that they can order their preferences, and that they choose transitively from the perceived options for achieving those ordered preferences. These are not very demanding assumptions, but there are likely to be situations in which people don't think strategically even though they are choosing under conditions of strategic interdependence. There are also likely to be situations in which the things people value are valued for reasons that are so different that they cannot find ways to reduce those separate dimensions to a single preference ordering. Finally, while information on actors' preferences, perceptions, and power are critical if you are to use strategic choice approaches, it's often very hard to get that information—partly because the data is simply very difficult to come by, but more fundamentally because a lot of foundational theoretical work remains to be done on the origins of actors' preferences and perceptions.

These are important limitations. It is also important not to lose sight of the fact that there are many other approaches to understanding world politics that offer valuable insights. But even with these reservations and limitations understood and acknowledged, we still are drawn to the conclusion that a focus on linkage politics and choice under conditions of strategic interdependence gives you the most widely applicable set of tools for making sense of world politics across a broad range of actors, issues, and historical periods. It does that both because choice under conditions of strategic interdependence is a central piece of politics, and because this approach is organized theoretically in a way that will help you remember that to understand world politics you need to differentiate between what is *unique* in politics—the distinctive aspects of particular actors, issues, cultures, and historical periods—and what is *enduring*—the patterns in how real people react to the politics of strategic choice.

Key Terms

diffuse reciprocity
strict reciprocity
game theory
utility

equilibrium outcome
sucker's payoff
dominant strategy
minimax strategy

brinkmanship
iterated game
mixed strategy

To The Reader   A Chapter Summary and Questions for Review
are available at **www.prenhall.com/lamborn**

What Will the Future Hold?

At the beginning of this book we promised that you would be able to make sense of world politics if you combined an understanding of what is distinctive about the different issues, actors, cultures, and historical periods—the unique contexts—in world politics with an appreciation for enduring patterns in the politics of strategic choice. For centuries, the quest for security and international economics dominated world politics. The environment was a purely local issue, if that, and human rights had been largely a matter of unchallenged domestic jurisdiction since the seventeenth century. However, during the last fifty years, international concern about the environment and human rights has grown dramatically, creating two "new" central issues in world politics. Consequently, to understand what policy makers and ordinary citizens care about in world politics today, you need to be familiar with the new agenda as well as the traditional one.

But what about the future? When pondering what the future might hold in these four issue areas, we find it useful to start with some reflections on what makes the environment, human rights, security, and international political economy distinctive from the perspective of the politics of strategic choice. After that, we review today's "unique contexts"—the contemporary strategic situation in each issue area. With those before us, we then identify a series of "what-if" questions that explore several different scenarios for what the future might hold.

Reflections on the Distinctive Characteristics of the Central Issues

When one looks closely at the ways in which the politics of strategic choice plays out in issues involving the environment, human rights, international political economy, and security, it becomes increasingly clear that each issue area confronts actors with a distinctive mix of strategic incentives.

Security

Security issues involve the threat, use, or control of force. Security problems can have a distinctively "unforgiving" nature; if actors make choices that turn out badly, the errors can have negative and often irreversible consequences. Consequently, security issues typically confront leaders and citizens with very high-stakes choices. Moreover, force is seldom threatened or used unless the actors involved believe their objectives are incompatible. Unfortunately, security issues also often lack much transparency, and security dilemmas can make actors even more fearful of one another than they need to be "objectively." When we find situations in which subjective fears are intense because the actors perceive the stakes to be very high but find reliable information about motives and capabilities hard to obtain, we are likely to find situations in which the politics of strategic choice dominate policy makers' attention in a way one seldom sees in other issue areas.

The International Space Station is, in many ways, a symbol of the future. It symbolizes the future partly because it is in space and looks futuristic, but more importantly because its multilateral collaborative spirit appears to suggest positive responses to the globalization of world politics. Without denying that symbolic value, it is important to recognize that the January 1998 agreement among fifteen countries to build the station represented a complex mix of international incentives, factional politics, and side-payments to important constituency groups. The context of world politics may change, but the patterns in the politics of world politics endure.

International Political Economy

International political economy issues arise when political choices, institutions, and rules shape, and are shaped by, trans-state market forces. These issues feature a strong tension between two different kinds of social forces: division and integration. Market forces create incentives to break down any barriers that separate consumers, investors, and firms in one state from those with complementary economic preferences elsewhere. But state officials may want to maintain political barriers that protect important constituents from the resulting competition or to maintain a distinct way of life in their societies. As we saw in Chapter 11, debates about globalization illustrate judgments about the relative impact and utility of these two forces. Economic issues are also characterized by tight functional linkages. It is hard to deal with a trade problem without also confronting monetary and foreign-investment problems. Because economic issues so immediately involve people's well-being, domestic-international linkages are very strong. As a direct result, a wide variety of domestic, state, and non-state actors have strong incentives to become players on these issues. However, although international economic issues produce many cross-arena linkages and energize a wide variety of actors, when market forces are allowed to operate with considerable autonomy, government actors can often avoid direct competition with one another. Unlike security, international economics is not inherently preoccupied with preserving the meaningfulness of borders and the distinctiveness of the activities that go on within them. But because policy making by the leaders of sovereign states is still central to international efforts to manage the world economy, borders still matter. Consequently, the tension between the forces of integration and division remains the most characteristic feature of this issue area.

The Environment

International environmental issues arise when people alter atmospheric, water, animal-life or plant-life conditions in ways that are seen to cause harm, and when those that are concerned about this damage seek international solutions. As we saw in Chapter 13, environmental issues exhibit political characteristics that make it very hard to build coalitions that can successfully address environmental problems. Because ecological processes are closely linked, policies designed to deal with environmental issues such as air pollution, global warming, and desertification invariably affect each other. Moreover, the possible benefits of collective action tend to be heavily discounted because perceived benefits appear as undesired future outcomes that *don't occur*. The politics of strategic choice in this issue area is further complicated by the fact that standards of legitimacy are highly contested across the North-South divide. There are also a wide variety of actors involved, and there are strong cross-arena linkages. All these considerations push people toward delay and denial in dealing with the underlying problems. However, while these political factors encourage delay, ecosystems are subject to limits on carrying capacity; the environment can take only so much damage before key physical thresholds are crossed. The popularity of sustainable development as a goal is based on the premise that wiser use of the Earth's resources can slow down the environmental doomsday clock. Even so, there is little agreement on what sustainable development means or who should pay for it. For all these reasons, the most characteristic feature of the environment as an issue area is the extent to which the combination of incentives and the context for choice make it hard to find solutions and easy to find the many political and ecological paths to undesirable outcomes.

Human Rights

Human rights issues arise in world politics when someone asserts a claim that people in some other state must be treated in a certain way, and the local authorities disagree. Such claims assume that every person has rights no government can take away. Because these issues involve claims about just treatment that are deeply controversial, they exhibit four distinctive features: first, they are created by conflicting interpretations of legitimacy; second, more than any other world-politics issue, they evoke cultural and political diversity; third, a wide variety of actors are key players, with an especially important role for IGOs in setting standards and NGOs in monitoring state behavior; and, fourth, they challenge the Westphalian bargain under which sovereignty gave state policy makers virtually unchallenged internal autonomy. The passion and sensitivity human-rights issues evoke make them increasingly visible and controversial in world politics, as the deterioration in U.S.-China relations during the 1990s, the atrocities in Yugoslavia and Rwanda, and the Pinochet case all illustrate.

Some Similarities and Differences That Matter

Because each of these issue areas typically presents distinctive strategic incentives and contexts for choice, comparing them gives you a sense of the kinds of situations actors face in a given area. On the environment, for example, actors typically must have a long time horizon to care about the issue at all because, except for toxic waste disposal, most of the problems become crises only in the long term. Meanwhile, there are many short-term costs associated with preventing those long-term problems. Building coalitions to address most environmental problems thus requires finding people who have long time horizons, are willing to pay short-term costs to achieve long-term benefits, and who can find ways to overcome the collective action problems that are common to most environmental policy solutions. Few people have such long time horizons, and even those who do may object to paying the costs to deal with those problems today, long before any highly diffuse benefits might be evident.

The strategic incentives are typically very different for proponents and opponents of vigorous human rights standards. Proponents tend to see abuses *today* and often proceed from a moral code that makes action an imperative. Those who are criticized similarly tend to see their sovereignty and domestic political control under immediate challenge. And while collective action problems are central to environmental issues, those problems tend not to arise in the human rights area, except in cases in which a coalition imposes economic sanctions on a human rights abuser.

Issue areas can also vary significantly with the importance actors attach to sustaining legitimate relationships and the standards they use for judging whether particular relationships are legitimate. For example, reciprocity is a common standard by which actors define their mutual rights and obligations. Many norms are based on a fairly strict notion of reciprocity: I will behave a certain way *if* you do so too. This standard makes sense when actors share an objective but want to minimize the risk that some parties won't keep their word. Such fears are common in economics, the environment, and security. Here the strategic incentives typically create mixed-motive situations in which the parties have incentives both to cooperate and to compete. As a result, bargaining on these issues tends to be based on defined, mutually contingent responsibilities. But strict reciprocity is beside the point when actors perceive an unconditional *moral* claim to behave a certain way. Human rights illustrates such situations. Here the relevant question is not "What has the other actor done for me?" but "What is morally right in this situation?" If actors care about human rights, they will act in ways they consider legitimate, regardless of what the other actors have done for them.

As Chapters 6 through 13 show, the international and domestic contexts for choice and the strategic incentives for choice can vary significantly across different historical periods. As we enter the twenty-first century, those contexts and incentives appear to be shifting in new and interesting ways.

Reflections on the "Unique Contexts" of Contemporary World Politics

World politics today is characterized by a unique mix of issues and linked international and domestic contexts. The efforts to deal with global terrorism after the September 11 attacks—and its implications for the historically complicated and often difficult relations between the Western and Islamic worlds—have cut across the continuing echoes produced by the end of the Cold War, globalization, the growing variation in the meaningfulness of political boundaries, and the increasing importance of non-state actors.

Continuing Echoes from the Cold War's End

While the Cold War lasted, it constrained and channeled international conflict and cooperation in strong and predictable ways. Military and economic relationships were organized largely within the two major blocs. Across the major East-West fault line, there was competition and at times intense conflict on security, economic, and human rights issues. Just as important, the Cold War dominated many policy makers' attention and the world politics agenda as a whole. Few international issues were perceived or addressed independently of actors' stakes on the major Cold War issues.

The fall of the Berlin Wall and the breakup of the Soviet Union reshuffled international security and economic relationships by removing the major fault line that had separated East and West. From the late 1940s to the late 1980s, most security issues were seen in a global perspective. Local problems and disputes were often seen as unimportant in their own right. For many people, how security problems in Southeast Asia, Latin America, and Africa affected the perceived credibility of American and Soviet commitments took priority. With the end of the global competition between the United States and the Soviet Union, security commitments and relationships became increasingly regionalized and ad hoc through the 1990s. The Desert Storm coalition that fought Iraq in 1991 was assembled entirely ad hoc. Japan began to fashion an independent defense strategy for the first time since before World War II. With the United States withdrawing hundreds of thousands of the troops it had stationed in Western Europe between the early 1950s and early 1990s, the European members of NATO began discussions about forming an independent military force under the European Union.

The impact of these changes on the growing regionalization of security issues during the 1990s was reinforced by the ways in which ethnic conflict and regional security disputes—such as the Indian-Pakistani security rivalry, the Arab-Israeli conflict, and the Taiwan issue—became more tied to local conditions, unconstrained by the threat or promise of Soviet or American involvement. Meanwhile, as we discuss in the next section, economic relationships have evolved in the opposite direction, toward globalization. By eliminating Marxism as a viable economic alternative to capitalism, the end of the Cold War permitted a truly *global* world economy to form for the first time. The Czech Republic, for forty years a front-line bastion of the Soviet bloc, is actually liberalizing its economy more thoroughly than many Western European countries.

The end of the Cold War also reshuffled the world politics agenda in more indirect ways by allowing space for newer issues to enter the spotlight and changing the way others are framed. Although the environment had been on the international agenda since the early 1970s, Cold War preoccupations helped to crowd it out of sustained, high-level policy attention in many places. After years of simmering on the back burner, environmental accords have become more ambitious, and global debates about them have become more intense since the late 1980s. International conversations about human rights have also been altered in similar ways. The Holocaust generated a lot of discussion about universal human rights standards immediately after World War II, but momentum toward codifying these norms and encouraging more intense scrutiny of states' practices stalled during the Cold War, as each side used human rights as a weapon against the other. With those strategic impediments gone, the 1990s witnessed a flurry of discussions about universal standards in areas such as genocide, crimes against humanity, and civil and political rights.

In sum, the Cold War so completely dominated world politics and demanded observers' attention that for over a decade after its end observers could not quite decide what had replaced it. Symptomatic of that indecision was the tendency to label the period simply the "post–Cold War period," which characterized world politics more by what it *wasn't* than what it *was*. The extraordinary reshuffling of global diplomatic relationships after the September 11 terrorist attacks may result in a reframing of key policy makers' understandings of what's important in world politics today. We consider that possibility when we talk about a range of "What if?" scenarios later in the chapter. Before doing that, however, we need to get the other central dimensions of today's unique contexts on the table.

Accelerating Globalization

As we discussed in Chapter 11, globalization refers to the rapid growth in world-wide communication and transportation and to the expanding and deepening worldwide linkages among markets, which many people believe is leading to the emergence of a single world market. One need not go quite that far to note that economic interdependence, particularly in monetary relations, is at an all-time high. Changes in prices, interest rates, and currency values in one place affect those elsewhere particularly quickly, and more and more countries are affected by them. Trade has also been powerfully affected by globalization. With trade barriers at historic lows, less competitive producers lose out quickly to those who can make comparable goods or provide comparable services more cheaply or reliably. To ordinary citizens as well as bankers and policy makers, globalization makes the world "smaller" than before. Fewer areas and economic activities are unconnected to global markets, and those that do remain outside tend to develop more slowly.

But these connections carry a price tag. Globalization produces international market pressures for societies to reduce government regulation of the economy; to alter business, labor, and environmental practices that are seen as economically inefficient; and to respond quickly to international economic cues. In some ways, these "outside-in" influences are comparable to the effects that the Cold War had on a wide range of state policies, from research and development priorities (heavily tilted in certain states to military rather than civilian projects), to science and foreign language education (emphasized in some places as a way to prepare people to compete against the adversary), to immigration policies (shaped, in the United States, by a preference for admitting emigrants from communist rather than noncommunist countries). From a liberal economic perspective, reducing government regulation and adapting to fast-moving international markets are the right things to do. Yet there is a downside as well. Liberal economic policies reward those most able to compete and hurt those least able to compete. This is why globalization is associated with rising income inequality within many countries, especially the United States, even while growing economic interdependence makes those societies wealthier overall.

Globalization also makes it increasingly difficult to manage cultural differences and to create space for distinctive local customs and beliefs about legitimate relationships. We see these difficulties in the reemergence of the controversies created by different visions of "just relationships" in Western and Islamic societies. We see it in concerns about the global reach of U.S.-dominated media and popular culture. And, on a far more micro level, we see it in the concerns of individual communities—from ones as different as those in the Amazon basin to small-town America—that globalization will overwhelm cherished ways of life.

Increasing Variation in the Meaningfulness of Political Boundaries

Another distinguishing feature of contemporary world politics is an increasing differentiation in the meaningfulness of political boundaries across issue areas. Security issues reinforce the importance of boundaries, as they always have. When security is an issue, protection depends on boundaries that separate "them" from "us." By contrast, economic interdependence undermines the political significance of borders, especially for those actors best able to compete in a globalized world economy. While people who trade and invest heavily across borders usually don't want to give up their distinctive national identities, globalization makes those identities less meaningful in at least two ways. In a globalized economic system, one's economic opportunities are less constrained than otherwise by one's nationality, and national officials have less flexibility to pursue distinctively different national economic policies.

Environmental issues show a third variant in the meaningfulness of borders. Environmental issues are inherently trans-border in effect, but they have no impact as such on the political importance of borders. Since the effects cut across borders, the benefits of environmental protection are public goods—free and open to all. The costs of such protection, however, must be paid by specific actors. Since the costs are highly political, the distinctive strategic situations in this area reflect the impact of discounting and collective action problems. It will thus be difficult to build winning coalitions in this issue area.

Human-rights issues create yet another variant because they cut both ways when it comes to the meaningfulness of boundaries. When people make claims based on universal human-rights standards, the Westphalian bargain is directly challenged. But this overt challenge is tempered by the counter-claims often made on grounds of cultural distinctiveness and sovereignty. When cultural distinctiveness is invoked, it is argued that there are no universal standards; when sovereignty is invoked, it is argued domestic jurisdiction rules any such interference out of bounds.

The Growing Importance of Non-State Actors

The rising numbers and impact of non-state actors is a fourth distinctive feature of the contemporary period. IGOs and NGOs are now major participants in agenda setting, bargaining, and monitoring state policies, and TSBEs are key participants in the international economy. This is hardly surprising. The more open national economies are, the easier it is for TSBEs to operate. The more that local actions of any kind have effects that carry across borders, the more we can expect IGOs to deal with the common problems. To the extent borders decline in significance and it becomes easier to build trans-state coalitions, NGOs have growing incentives to form and participate in international policy making. Indeed, there is a synergistic relationship between the meaningfulness of borders and the role and impact of non-state actors. The more porous national borders become—or the less incompatible the policies of state actors—the more "political space" there is for IGOs and NGOs to build effective roles by providing forums, serving as potential brokers, and acting as watchdogs over national policies.

These reflections on the distinctive features of contemporary world politics make it tempting to ask "What comes next?" Will sovereign borders become less meaningful over time, or could a backlash against globalization occur? Many people would like to know the answers to such questions. Of course no one has a crystal ball, so we cannot literally predict the future. What we can do is sketch out some scenarios about what the future could bring under various plausible sets of conditions.

What Might Be Next? Thinking Contingently (*If* These Facts, *Then . . .*)

As we have noted in this book, people typically develop insights about world politics inductively, by generalizing from the specific issues and historical periods they care about. This sort of inductive reasoning creates significant problems when people think about the future, since there is a tendency to assume that today's facts indicate stable trends. Observers' surprise at the sudden end of the Cold War reflected an assumption that the incentives that had been stable on both sides for decades would continue indefinitely. Similarly, when the elder President George Bush said in the early 1990s that the end of the Cold War promised a "new world order" in which aggression would be regularly punished, he was extrapolating the successful war against Iraqi aggression in Kuwait into a trend. To avoid overgeneralizing from individual cases or periods, we need to ask questions more deductively—to put our questions in the form of *contingent statements* that connect assumptions about the facts with theoretical statements that identify the likely implications of those facts.

Contingent statements take the following form: *If* the facts in some situation are X, *then* our understanding of the enduring patterns in the politics of strategic choice would lead us to expect Y (a particular outcome). Proceeding in this way will allow you to use the general principles of politics we've examined in this book to explore real-world issues about what the future is likely to hold.

About the Quest for Security

The lack of a single, global rivalry in the first decade after the end of the Cold War produced a more regionalized international security environment. Regional problems such as the breakup of Yugoslavia, the deteriorating Arab-Israeli peace process, and African wars were dealt with largely on their own terms, rather than through the stakes and commitments produced by involvement in a much larger, longstanding conflict. The September 11 attacks reintroduced a global security agenda.

The British- and U.S.-led campaign to eliminate terrorist networks with a global reach may end up affecting far more than people's level of security against terrorism. Most fundamentally, it has put a spotlight on the relationship between the West and Islamic societies and the political significance—and manipulation—of religion and culture. Less fundamental but still of great importance has been its effect on U.S.-Russian relations which, by late fall 2001, had radically improved. Those improvements had effects across a wide variety of areas, including even a major shift in the negotiations over the Bush administration's plans to move forward with a national missile defense. It also altered the U.S. relationship with Pakistan and India and the political ramifications of the Arab-Israeli conflict. Meanwhile, efforts to block terrorists' access to money led to new regulatory policies on banking that may have wider implications for stopping money laundering by a wide range of criminal organizations.

In some ways, this situation is one remarkably like the beginning and the end of the Cold War, situations in which the strategic environment was fluid enough that the choices made by policy makers could really alter fundamental aspects of particular historical periods. *If* the West is able to find a way to convince large numbers of Moslems that the war against terrorism is not a war against Islam, *then* some aspects of the centuries-old collision between Western and Islamic societies may reach new, more mutually acceptable resolutions. *If* that happens, and *if* the campaign against global terrorist networks is successful, *then* resolving the conflict between Israelis

If the close ties between President Bush and Hamid Karzai, head of the interim government in Afghanistan, can serve as the beginning of a more mutually legitimate set of relations between the West and Islamic societies, then the strategic context within which controversies in the Middle East play out is likely to change. However, Bush's decision to characterize Iraq and Iran as part of the "axis of evil" complicates the West's continuing effort to make a convincing case that its campaign against terrorism and "rogue states" is not an attack on Islam.

and Palestinians is likely to become a very high priority for the United States and a number of other key actors.* These positive effects of a successful campaign are likely to be reinforced by a consolidation of the new U.S.-Russian relationship and expanded U.S. contacts in the Near East and South Asia.

There is, of course, the other set of possibilities: that the campaign will go badly and that the West's argument that it is not attacking Islam will be rejected. *If* those things happen, *then* far more than security against terrorism will be put at risk.

China's relationships with its neighbors also have the potential to reshuffle global security questions. What if China were to be seen as a much larger threat than it is today? What if it became much more overtly aggressive toward Taiwan, began asserting its other territorial claims in Asia more forcefully, and began building a state-of-the-art nuclear arsenal? *If* such events came to pass, *then* the present U.S. strategy of trying to "engage" China almost certainly would come to an end. This strategy is based on the assumption that the United States can cooperate with China on trade and some security issues where the international incentives overlap, while trying to coax Chinese leaders gradually out of aggressive incentives on issues where their preferences diverge. *If* the events above occur—and especially if they all occur around the same time, suggesting a movement toward fundamentally less compatible objectives—*then* the U.S. strategy of engagement will be seen to have failed. Moreover, *if* the relationship continues to deteriorate and China develops a modern nuclear arsenal, U.S. leaders and citizens might feel directly threatened. In that case, mutual nuclear deterrence is likely to become a day-to-day issue in the relationship, as it was in U.S.-Soviet relations during the Cold War.

However, even under these conditions, it is unlikely that Sino-American relations would resemble the Cold War. For one thing, there was a strongly ideological dimension to the Cold War, especially in the first few decades when Soviet-style Marxism was seen by many people around the world as attractive, and the fear of ideological contagion helped to drive U.S. containment policies. Today, few people outside China find its version of Marxism attractive, and the one powerful set of symbols Chinese leaders have to employ—Chinese nationalism—is by definition not exportable. Further, at least for the foreseable future, China will not be able to project its conventional military capabilities far from its own territory, as Soviet leaders could do during the 1970s and 1980s. So, even *if* China were to become a much bigger security threat to its neighbors and the United States, a conflict on the scale and intensity of the Cold War is unlikely. But we would be likely to see a major, enduring security rivalry that could have far-reaching implications for China, the United States, and much of the rest of Asia.

About the International Political Economy

Globalization has produced a situation in which fewer and fewer national economies are unconnected to international markets. Goods, services, information, and money

---

*Pressure on the United States to resolve the conflict between Palestinians and Israelis could also grow in exactly the opposite sequence. *If* the campaign against terrorism were not going as well as hoped and *if* complaints that it was anti-Islamic were becoming more widespread or credible, *then* a jointly acceptable peace between Israel and the Palestinians could be seen as a necessary precondition both for building legitimate relationships between the West and Islamic states and for effectively prosecuting the campaign against global terrorism.

move across borders at levels and, in the case of money, at speeds that are historically unprecedented. According to the current conventional wisdom, staying out of the global economy sharply increases the likelihood that firms will lose out to foreign competitors and that nations will fail to prosper. However, unreservedly joining the global economy often requires difficult domestic adjustments. So far, the conventional wisdom commands a healthy consensus worldwide, and the trend is with the "joiners." But what if there were a major backlash against globalization? In that case, a return to much more closed national economies is quite possible.

What could trigger such a backlash? *If* the Asian economic crisis returns, *then* the region-wide consensus in favor of economic openness could unravel. For two decades, Asia had the world's fastest growing economies, largely due to greatly increased intraregional trade, high direct foreign investment, and liberal policies on capital controls. All of that could be reconsidered if the lesson people draw from the crisis is that too much economic openness creates bigger problems than too much government regulation. They might draw that lesson if, for instance, they conclude that substantial capital controls are necessary to prevent societies from being vulnerable to the decisions of international investors or currency speculators. Alternatively, *if* Latin America experiences a comparable economic meltdown, a similar scenario could begin to play out in the Americas. Over the last two decades, Mexico, Chile, Brazil and a number of the states in the region have substantially liberalized their economies and jumped on the globalization bandwagon. But many of these countries have huge and precarious debt-to-earnings ratios, which make their currencies vulnerable to attack by speculators. Brazil experienced a devastating currency crisis in 1998 and 1999, and could easily do so again. Argentina experienced an even worse financial meltdown in 2001 and 2002. *If* several countries within the region have simultaneous crises, sentiment could turn sharply against financial openness. The movement toward free trade could be affected as well. In the 1990s, President Clinton announced that a key U.S. objective by the second decade of the twenty-first century was a free trade area that would include the entire Western hemisphere. President Bush's early policy statements suggest that his views are compatible with that objective. *If* prevailing sentiment moves at least somewhat toward economic closure, that objective could be delayed or its ambitiousness curtailed.

A major backlash against globalization *could* also be sparked by political developments that originate within particular countries. For policy makers to pursue policies that link their economies tightly to world markets in a sustained manner, they need to minimize the political risks that such policies typically produce. Those risks stem from opposition on the part of economic factions that fear their incomes will drop or their jobs will disappear, and from other groups that fear a loss of "traditional"—that is culturally differentiated and insulated—ways of life. As we've discussed, tight economic interdependence often creates fault lines within societies between those who prosper under internationally open policies and those who are hurt by them. Over time, those fissures could become politically unsustainable. In the United States, incomes and overall wealth have become much more unevenly distributed over the last few decades; the media has been full of stories about new multimillionaires and their conspicuous consumption. At some point a policy coalition *might* take power that is determined to right these perceived wrongs by bringing back trade restrictions or closer regulation of foreign investment. In this scenario, globalization could be at risk not because it failed to make society wealthier and more productive overall; it would be at risk because groups that viewed the

Although the United States and the International Monetary Fund played active roles in trying to manage the 1997 Asian financial crisis, both stood aside in early 2002 when Argentina went through an economic meltdown that brought down a succession of governments and sent protestors into the streets. If the effects of this meltdown can be contained within Argentina—as the U.S. government and the IMF say it can—then leaving Argentina to suffer with little outside help may make national policy makers much more reluctant to borrow heavily abroad. However, if the damage cannot be contained within Argentina, or if other countries run into similar problems, then the focus is likely to shift toward problems with the international economic system, increasing pressure for taking a close look at controls on foreign direct investment and international capital movements.

distribution of that wealth as illegitimate had the incentives and ability to mobilize successfully around an agenda of fundamental change.

About the Environment

In the environmental area, people tend to avoid dealing with the underlying problems until there is a local disaster or some critical ecological threshold is crossed. Because ecosystems have finite carrying capacities, such thresholds may soon be reached if present levels of economic activity are sustained or increased. What is likely to happen to the politics of international environmental issues if a disaster occurs or a critical threshold is crossed?

First, consider what is likely to happen *if* some discrete event produces an ecological disaster that has intense, devastating effects in some country or region. The Exxon Valdez oil spill and the explosion of the Chernobyl nuclear reactor provide historical examples. Another nuclear reactor *could* explode; toxic waste being transported from one community or country *could* spill or contaminate ground water; an obsolete chemical factory *could* explode or catch on fire. The possibilities, in fact, are nearly endless. The effects of such accidents would be localized but could be profoundly catalytic politically. It is hard to imagine how Russia could have a productive relationship with the countries to its west if its nuclear or chemical facilities posed international dangers, and its leaders were unable or unwilling to clean up the problem or take reasonable steps to prevent similar problems in the future. These accidents could also spur regional or global efforts to deal with the underlying problems.

Second, consider what might happen *if* some ecological process produced effects that harmed specific groups, and *if* those groups were able to mobilize against the groups that they believed to be responsible for the problem. The twenty-first century could well see wars over access to drinking water—a plausible scenario *if* population pressures and desertification continue. Similarly, the destruction of the Amazon rainforest *could* mobilize and radicalize indigenous peoples against the farmers, ranchers, and TSBEs who, in their eyes, are destroying their villages and livelihoods. While such conflicts are likely to remain localized, they could catalyze action from state policy makers as well as NGOs and IGOs that see a stake in the problem.

Third, consider what might happen *if* ecological thresholds that have truly global implications were crossed. The hole in the atmospheric ozone layer *could* begin growing again, despite the drastic reduction in the use of CFCs. Global warming *could* become a serious practical problem, causing the kinds of damage discussed in Chapter 13. Population pressures *could* cause problems that would be seen as truly global in scope, such as devastating, frequent famines. In such cases, we are likely to see far more concerted international action to deal with the underlying problems than we do now.

All three of these scenarios are likely to shift the mix of incentives for choice in ways that overcome the two central barriers to effective environmental policies: the impact of collective-action problems and the effects of discounting on choice. Regardless of whether it is a major environmental accident, a local war generated by devastating ecological changes, or the crossing of a major ecological threshold with truly global implications, the benefits of environmental action would move from the future to the present. Actors are far more likely to agree to pay the price when the problem is real and immediate rather than hypothetical, even with the prior knowledge that some environmental thresholds may be irreversible once crossed. Absent

This satellite picture shows the growing hole in the ozone layer over Antarctica between 1970 and 1993. If the hole grows larger, or if some other dramatic and visible evidence of possible global warming emerges, then international pressure on the United States to rethink its opposition to the Kyoto Protocol—and, more generally, its opposition to any significant multilateral action to prevent global climate change—is likely to increase. However, the Bush administration's domestic political base includes many groups that staunchly support the administration's position. Unless domestic political incentives change, it is unlikely that increased international pressure will produce a change in U.S. policy.

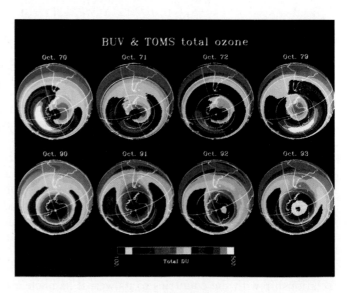

one of these catalysts, we would not expect any change in the incentives for delay that typically characterize environmental policy making.

About Human Rights, Sovereignty, and the State System

The contemporary situation in the human rights area also suggests an interesting set of what-if questions about the future. Human-rights issues are currently subject to two strong but opposing pressures. On one side are the pressures created by the growing belief that there are universal human rights standards. On the other side are the pressures created by opposition from political leaders who assert that sovereignty rules out interference in their state's internal affairs and from those who claim that distinct cultures can interpret the notion of "rights" in distinct ways. At the moment, the proponents and opponents of universal rights are in something of a global stalemate. How might this stalemate be resolved? In a general sense, the answer may lie in the fate of the worldwide movement toward democracy, a trend that began in the 1980s and continued vigorously during the 1990s.

One could posit two scenarios built around different contingent statements about the course of global democratization. *If* the trend toward democracy stalls and some major countries such as China continue to oppose an emphasis on universal standards, the stalemate could continue for a long time. Some regions would move forward, but others would make no progress or even slide backward. Universal standards are enforced by a supranational court in the European Union (EU). That strong a regime is unlikely to be replicated elsewhere for the foreseeable future, but more limited progress could be made in regions such as Latin America, where democratization is proceeding and limited efforts are being made to overcome the legacy of past abuses. Overall, though, the effect would be to continue the global debate inconclusively.

On the other hand, *if* democratization continues to spread globally, *if* there is a growing consensus on the substance of a set of universal human-rights norms, and *if*

The trial of Slobodan Milosevic for crimes against humanity began in February 2002 at the International War Crimes Tribunal in The Hague. The ability of the international community to hold Milosevic accountable is only one of the challenges facing those who would promote human rights by making the claim of universal jurisdiction at work in the Milosevic case. The other challenge is to demonstrate that it is not just the victors who can demand justice. To show that, claims of atrocities against the Serbs after their defeat will need to be investigated as thoroughly as the atrocities Serbs committed in Bosnia and Kosovo.

political leaders who mistreat their people can be regularly held accountable for their actions—perhaps, in the worst cases, by an International Criminal Court—*then* some truly important, even profound changes could take place in world politics. Under these conditions, incentives to redraw territorial boundaries to put different ethnic groups in different states *may* drop somewhat over time, since there would be less difference across states in how individuals and groups are treated. *If* these conditions could be simultaneously satisfied, multiethnic states may become more stable and viable, since minorities and majorities would enjoy the same basic rights, and the problem that leaders have in credibly promising to treat minorities well would diminish. In short, credible universal human rights norms would facilitate and stabilize democratic, multiethnic societies.

The implications of this second scenario are important, and at the same time, counterintuitive. Under the conditions outlined in the preceding paragraph, universal human-rights standards and sovereignty become mutually reinforcing rather than incompatible. This would indeed take us a long way from the Westphalian bargain, which was crafted precisely to *prevent* external interference in internal affairs. But the Westphalian bargain, like any other bargain, was a product of *its* specific historical conditions. Were democratization to deepen and spread internationally, the conditions of the mid-seventeenth century—a lack of popular rule and an international system that legitimated autocracy—would be reversed. With that, a new bargain, forged around international legitimation of universal human-rights standards and democracy, *could conceivably* emerge in its place. If it does, the context of world politics will have changed in truly significant ways.

A Last Word

These reflections on what the future might hold conclude this introduction to world politics as it moves into the twenty-first century. We have one parting comment. In Chapter 1, we said that the ultimate goal of this book is to give you a set of intellectual tools for understanding world politics that you can apply for yourself. That goal reflects our belief that the best test of textbooks and teachers is their ability to make themselves expendable by liberating students to think creatively and systematically on their own. Whether we have met that test is not for us to decide, but neither is our success or failure under our complete control. We hope that you use the ideas we've presented—along with those of others and your own—to think creatively and systematically about important and interesting problems in world politics.

To The Reader   QUESTIONS FOR REVIEW are available at **www.prenhall.com/lamborn**

Notes

Chapter 1

1. Thomas Hobbes, *Leviathan* (Baltimore: Penguin Books, 1974), p. 186. Spelling has been modernized.

2. Karen W. Arenson, "A Generation Unfamiliar with Feeling Vulnerable," *The New York Times*, September 14, 2001, p. A22.

3. For thumbnail sketches, see Cathal J. Nolan, *The Longman Guide to World Affairs* (White Plains, NY: Longman, 1995), pp. 158–59, 440–42. For country-by-country military casualties, see J. David Singer and Melvin Small, *The Wages of War, 1816–1965: A Statistical Handbook* (New York: Wiley, 1972).

4. Raymond Vernon and Debra Spar, *Beyond Globalism* (New York: Free Press, 1989), p. 100.

5. U.S. Department of Commerce, Bureau of the Census, Ethnic and Hispanic Branch, "Total and Foreign-Born U.S. Population." Available on the U.S. Immigration and Naturalization Service website: *http://www.ins.usdoj.gov/ graphics/aboutins/statistics/ 308.htm.*

6. Diana Jean Schemo, "Turmoil in Brazil," *The New York Times*, January 16, 1999, p. A1.

7. Walker Connor, "When Is a Nation?" *Ethnic and Racial Studies* 13, no. 1 (January 1990): 91–103.

8. "Demography and the Politics of Identity in the Russian Federation," special issue of *Anthropology and Archeology of Eurasia* 34, no. 1 (Summer 1995): 94.

9. David Welsh, "Domestic Politics and Ethnic Conflict," in Michael E. Brown, ed., *Ethnic Conflict and International Security* (Princeton: Princeton University Press, 1993), p. 45.

10. Mostafa Rejai and Cynthia H. Enloe, "Nation-States and State-Nations," *International Studies Quarterly* 13, no. 2 (June 1969): 151–53.

11. Ibid., p. 44.

Chapter 2

1. Robert G. Gilpin, "The Richness of the Tradition of Political Realism," *International Organization* 38, no. 2 (Spring 1984): 290.

2. Kenneth N. Waltz, *Theory of International Politics* (New York: McGraw-Hill, 1979), p. 117.

3. Thucydides, *History of the Peloponnesian War*, ed. M. I. Finley, trans. Rex Warner (Harmondsworth, England: Penguin, 1972), p. 49.

4. Thucydides, *The Peloponnesian War* (New York: Modern Library, 1982), p. 351.

5. François de Callières, *On the Manner of Negotiating with Princes* (South Bend, IN: University of Notre Dame Press, 1963), p. 111.

6. Kautilya, *Essentials of Indian Statecraft*, ed. T. N. Ramaswamy (New York: Asia Publishing House, 1962), p. 109.

7. Hans J. Morgenthau, *Scientific Man vs. Power Politics* (Chicago: The University of Chicago Press, 1946), pp. 191–92. See also Morgenthau's "Six Principles of Political Realism," in Hans J. Morgenthau, *Power Among Nations: The Struggle for Power and Peace*, 5th ed. (New York: Knopf, 1973), pp. 4–15.

8. Niccolò Machiavelli, *The Prince*, ed. Quentin Skinner and Russell Price (Cambridge: Cambridge University Press, 1988), p. 54.

9. Henry Kissinger, "In the Middle East, Clashing Concepts of Peace," *The Washington Post*, June 26, 2000, p. A19.

10. Thomas Hobbes, *Leviathan*, ed. C. B. Macpherson (Baltimore: Pelican Books, 1968), p. 161. For the discussion of the right of nature, see p. 189.

11. Kenneth N. Waltz, *Man, the State, and War: A Theoretical Analysis* (New York: Columbia University Press, 1959), pp. 224–38.

12. Kenneth N. Waltz, "Realist Thought and Neorealist Theory," in Charles W. Kegley, Jr., ed., *Controversies in International Relations Theory: Realism and the Neoliberal Challenge* (New York: St. Martin's Press, 1995), pp. 74–81.

13. Michael W. Doyle, *Ways of War and Peace: Realism, Liberalism, and Socialism* (New York: Norton, 1997), p. 19.

14. Ibid., p. 209. See also Michael Howard, *War and the Liberal Conscience* (London: Temple Smith, 1978), p. 11.

15. Stanley Hoffmann, *Duties Beyond Borders: On the Limits and Possibilities of Ethical International Politics* (Syracuse, NY: Syracuse University Press, 1981), p. 8.

16. The next three paragraphs draw on Mark W. Zacher and Richard A. Matthew, "Liberal International Theory: Common Threads, Divergent Strands," in Kegley, *Controversies in International Relations Theory*, pp. 120–37.

17. Norman Angell, *The Great Illusion: A Study of the Relation of Military Power to National Advantage* (New York: G. P. Putnam's Sons, 1913), p. 35.

18. Richard N. Cooper, "Economic Interdependencies and Foreign Policy in the Seventies," *World Politics* 24, no. 2 (January 1972): 179.

19. Immanuel Kant, *Principles of Lawful Politics: Immanuel Kant's Philosophic Draft Toward Eternal Peace*, trans. Wolfgang Schwarz (Aalen, Germany: Scientia Verlag, 1988), p. 67.

20. For a good sample of this literature, including work that challenges the "inter-democratic peace" argument on realist

grounds, see the articles reprinted in Michael E. Brown, Sean M. Lynn-Jones, and Steven E. Miller, eds., *Debating the Democratic Peace* (Cambridge, MA: The MIT Press, 1996).

21. Michael Doyle, "Liberalism and World Politics," *American Political Science Review* 80, no. 4 (December 1986): 1151–69; John M. Owen, "How Liberalism Produces the Democratic Peace," in Brown et al., *Debating the Democratic Peace*, pp. 116–54.

22. This position is associated with the English School of liberal thinkers. For a classic statement of this argument, see Hedley Bull, *The Anarchical Society: A Study of Order in World Politics* (New York: Columbia University Press, 1977). For a review of the literature on this point, see Barry Buzan, "From International System to International Society: Structural Realism and Regime Theory Meet the English School," *International Organization* 47, no. 3 (Summer 1993): 327–52.

23. Robert Keohane, *After Hegemony: Cooperation and Discord in the World Political Economy* (Princeton: Princeton University Press, 1984).

24. Doyle, *Ways of War and Peace*, p. 211.

25. Tom Bottomore, "Marxism," in Mary Hawkesworth and Maurice Kogan, eds., *Encyclopedia of Government and Politics*, Vol. I (London: Routledge, 1992), p. 155.

26. Robert L. Heilbroner, *The Worldly Philosophers* (New York: Simon & Schuster, 1953), p. 136.

27. Doyle, *Ways of War and Peace*, p. 326.

28. James E. Connor, ed., "Introduction," *Lenin on Politics and Revolution* (New York: Pegasus Books, 1968), p. xxv; Doyle, *Ways of War and Peace*, pp. 342–46.

29. Connor, "Introduction," p. xxv.

30. Theotonio dos Santos, "The Structure of Dependence," *American Economic Review* 60 (May 1970): 231. See also Immanuel Wallerstein, *The Modern World-System: Capitalist Agriculture and The Origins of the European World-Economy in the Sixteenth Century* (New York: Academic Press, 1976), p. 232.

31. This summary draws on Tony Smith, "The Underdevelopment of the Development Literature: The Case of Dependency Theory," *World Politics* 36, no. 2 (July 1979): 249–51.

32. Robert Cox, "Social Forces, States, and World Orders," in Robert O. Keohane, ed., *Neorealism and Its Critics* (New York: Columbia University Press, 1986), p. 207. This paragraph also draws on Andrew Linklater, "The Achievements of Critical Theory," in Steve Smith, Ken Booth, and Marysia Zalewski, eds., *International Theory: Positivism and Beyond* (Cambridge: Cambridge University Press, 1996), pp. 279–81.

33. Cox, "Social Forces, States, and World Orders," p. 208.

34. "The Poor Who Are Always With Us," *The Economist*, July 1, 2000, p. 46.

35. Smith, "The Underdevelopment of the Development Literature," p. 252; J. Samuel Valenzuela and Arturo Valenzuela, "Modernization and Dependency: Alternative Perspectives in the Study of Latin American Underdevelopment," *Comparative Politics* 10, no. 4 (July 1978): 546.

36. Alexander Wendt, "Anarchy Is What States Make of It: The Social Construction of Power Politics," *International Organization* 46, no. 2 (Spring 1982): 397.

37. John Gerard Ruggie, "Introduction: What Makes the World Hang Together? Neo-Utilitarianism and the Social Constructivist Challenge," in John Gerard Ruggie, *Constructing the World Polity: Essays on International Institutionalization* (London: Routledge, 1998), p. 33; Jeffrey T. Checkel, "The Constructivist Turn in International Relations Theory," *World Politics* 50, no. 2 (January 1998): 326.

38. Wendt, "Anarchy Is What States Make of It," p. 398.

39. Jeffrey Goldberg, "The Education of Holy Warriors," *The New York Times Magazine*, June 25, 2000, pp. 34, 35, 70.

40. Among other sources, see Anthony Giddens, *The Constitution of Society* (Berkeley: University of California Press, 1984); Peter L. Berger and Thomas Luckman, *The Social Construction of Reality: A Treatise in the Sociology of Knowledge* (New York: Anchor Books, 1966); Nicholas Greenwood Onuf, *World of Our Making: Rules and Rule in Social Theory and International Relations* (Columbia, SC: University of South Carolina Press, 1989), pp. 52–65; Alexander E. Wendt, "The Agent-Structure Problem in International Relations Theory," *International Organization* 41, no. 3 (Summer 1987): 355–61.

41. Ruggie, "Introduction," pp. 11–12.

42. Martha Finnemore, *National Interests in International Society* (Ithaca, NY: Cornell University Press, 1996), p. 2.

43. Ibid.

44. Ruggie, "Introduction," p. 4.

45. Checkel, "The Constructivist Turn in International Relations Theory," p. 340.

46. Jacqui True, "Feminism," in Scott Burchill and Andrew Linklater, eds., *Theories of International Relations* (New York: St. Martin's Press, 1995), p. 212.

47. J. Ann Tickner, "Identity in International Relations Theory: Feminist Perspectives," *The Return of Culture and Identity in IR Theory* (Boulder, CO: Lynne Rienner, 1996), p. 148.

48. Jan Jindy Pettman, "Gender Issues," in John Baylis and Steve Smith, *The Globalization of World Politics: An Introduction to International Relations* (Oxford: Oxford University Press, 1997), p. 484.

49. Christine Sylvester, "The Contributions of Feminist Theory to International Relations," in Steve Smith, Ken Booth, and Marysia Zalewski, eds., *International Theory: Positivism and Beyond* (Cambridge: Cambridge University Press, 1996), pp. 263–67.

50. Ibid., p. 264.

51. Cynthia Enloe, *The Morning After: Sexual Politics in the Post–Cold War Era* (New York: Routledge, 1993), p. 16.

52. Sylvester, "The Contributions of Feminist Theory to International Relations," p. 266.

53. Christine Sylvester, *Feminist Theory and International Relations in the Postmodern Era* (Cambridge: Cambridge University Press, 1994), pp. 40–41.

54. Sandra Harding, *The Science Question in Feminism* (Ithaca, NY: Cornell University Press, 1986), p. 171.

55. Erica Goode, "Response to Stress Found That's Particularly Female," *The New York Times*, May 19, 2000, p. A22.

56. J. Ann Tickner, "A Critique of Morgenthau's Principles of Political Realism," in Robert J. Art and Robert Jervis, *International Politics: Enduring Concepts and Contemporary Issues*, 5th ed. (New York: Addison Wesley Longman, 2000), pp. 25–26.

57. Ibid., p. 24.

58. Waltz, *Man, the State, and War*; Waltz, *Theory of International Politics*.

59. For a discussion of this approach, see Robert Jervis, *Perception and Misperception in International Politics* (Princeton: Princeton University Press, 1976), p. 17.

Chapter 3

1. *The Politics of Aristotle*, ed. and trans. Ernest Barker (London: Oxford University Press, 1958), pp. 5–6.

2. Tom Tyler, "Justice and Leadership Endorsement," in R. Lau and D. Sears, eds., *Political Cognition* (Hillsdale, NJ: Lawrence Erlbaum Associates), pp. 257–78.

3. Harold and Margaret Sprout, "Environmental Factors in the Study of International Politics," in James N. Rosenau, ed., *International Politics and Foreign Policy*, rev. ed. (New York: Free Press, 1969), p. 45.

4. William C. Wohlforth, "Scholars, Policy Makers, and the End of the Cold War," in William C. Wohlforth, ed., *Witnesses to the End of the Cold War* (Baltimore: Johns Hopkins University Press, 1996), p. 267.

5. The analysis in the next two sections of this chapter is based on Alan C. Lamborn, "Theory and the Politics in World Politics," *International Studies Quarterly*, 41, no. 2 (June 1997), pp. 187–214.

Chapter 4

1. Alan James, *Sovereign Statehood* (London: Allen & Unwin, 1986), chap. 2; Daniel Philpott, "Sovereignty: An Introduction and Brief History," *Journal of International Affairs* 48, no. 2 (Winter 1995): 356.

2. Richard Ullman, "Local Sovereignty, Global Responsibility, and Yugoslavia's Wars," remarks delivered at a conference, "Local Sovereignty and Global Responsibility," Humboldt University, Berlin, December 12, 1996.

3. *Empirical* as opposed to *juridical* statehood is discussed in Robert H. Jackson, *Quasi-states: Sovereignty, International Relations, and the Third World* (Cambridge: Cambridge University Press, 1990), pp. 21, 23–24, 51–53.

4. Kalevi J. Holsti, *The State, War, and the State of War* (Cambridge: Cambridge University Press, 1996), pp. 119, 90.

5. Jackson, *Quasi-States*, pp. 21–26.

6. Kenneth H. F. Dyson, *The State Tradition in Western Europe* (New York: Oxford University Press, 1980), pp. 34, 113, 136. The quoted phrase is from Jean Bodin, *The Six Books of a Commonwealth* (Cambridge, MA: Harvard University Press, 1962), p. 84. This work was originally published in 1576.

7. Richard Falk, "Sovereignty," in Joel Krieger, ed., *The Oxford Companion to the Politics of the World* (New York: Oxford University Press, 1993), p. 851.

8. Edward Vose Gulick, *Europe's Classical Balance of Power* (New York: Norton, 1955), pp. 67–69.

9. Dyson, *The State Tradition in Western Europe*, p. 137.

10. Gordon A. Craig and Alexander L. George, *Force and Statecraft*, 3rd ed. (New York: Oxford University Press, 1995), pp. 52–53.

11. Richard G. Lipsey, Peter O. Steiner, Douglas D. Purvis, and Paul N. Courant, *Microeconomics*, 9th ed. (New York: Harper & Row, 1990), p. 317. See also Jeff Worsham, Marc Allen Eisner, and Evan J. Ringquist, "Assessing the Assumptions: A Critical Analysis of Agency Theory," *Administration and Society*, 28, no. 4 (February 1997): 419–40.

12. See Waldo Heinrichs, *Threshold of War* (New York: Oxford University Press, 1988), pp. 78, 166–69; Sean Dennis Cashman, *America, Roosevelt, and World War II* (New York: New York University Press, 1989), pp. 65, 67–68; Warren F. Kimball, *Forged in War* (New York: William Morrow, 1997), pp. 98–99.

13. Robert D. Putnam, "Diplomacy and Domestic Politics: The Logic of Two-Level Games," *International Organization*, 42, no. 3 (Summer 1988): 438–39.

14. "AFL-CIO to Fight Renewal of China Trade Benefits," *Los Angeles Times*, April 14, 1994, p. A7; Edward Friedman, "The Challenge of a Rising China: Another Germany?" in Robert J. Lieber, ed., *Eagle Adrift: American Foreign Policy at the End of the Century* (New York: Longman, 1997), p. 217.

15. "The Hollowing of a Threat," *The Washington Post*, May 12, 1994, pp. A1, A23.

16. Alexander L. George, "Domestic Constraints on Regime Change in Foreign Policy: The Need for Policy Legitimacy," in Ole R. Holsti, Randolph M. Siverson, and Alexander L. George, eds., *Change in the International System* (Boulder: Westview, 1980), pp. 233–36.

17. "Shalikashvili Defends Use of 'Smart Mines,'" *The Washington Post*, August 29, 1997, p. A33; "U.S. Dispatches Team to Discuss Mine Treaty," *The Washington Post*, August 17, 1997, p. A23.

18. For a fuller discussion, see Alan C. Lamborn, *The Price of Power* (Boston: Unwin Hyman, 1990), chap. 6.

19. Hans Morgenthau, *Politics Among Nations*, 5th ed. (New York: Knopf, 1978), pp. 5–10.

20. Alexander L. George and Robert O. Keohane, "The Concept of National Interests: Uses and Limitations," in Alexander L. George, *Presidential Decisionmaking in Foreign Policy: The Effective Use of Information and Advice* (Boulder:

Westview, 1980), pp. 217–37. For a somewhat similar argument, see James N. Rosenau, "National Interest," in David Sills, ed., *International Encyclopedia of the Social Sciences*, Vol. 11 (New York: Macmillan, 1968), pp. 34–40.

Chapter 5

1. Bruce Cronin, "International Law," in Herbert Kritzer, ed., *Legal Systems of the World: A Political, Social, and Cultural Encyclopedia* (Santa Barbara, CA: ABC-CLIO, 2002), p. 5.

2. Anthony Clark Arend, *Legal Rules and International Society* (Oxford: Oxford University Press, 1999), pp. 16–20.

3. Louis Henkin, *How Nations Behave: Law and Foreign Policy*, 2nd ed. (New York: Columbia University Press, 1979), pp. 47, 51–52.

4. M. N. Shaw, *International Law*, 3rd ed. (Cambridge: Cambridge University Press, 1991), pp. 15–16.

5. Shaw, *International Law*, p. 23.

6. Antonio Cassese and Andrew Clapham, "International Law," in Joel Krieger, ed., *The Oxford Companion to the Politics of the World*, 2nd ed. (Oxford: Oxford University Press, 2001), p. 41.

7. Robert O. Keohane and Craig N. Murphy, "International Institutions," in Mary Hawkesworth and Maurice Kogan, eds., *Encyclopedia of Government and Politics* (New York: Routledge, 1992), p. 871.

8. Inis Claude, *Swords into Plowshares*, 4th ed. (New York: Random House, 1971), p. 21.

9. Union of International Associations, *Yearbook of International Organizations, 1996–1997*, 33rd ed. (Munich: K. G. Saur, 1996), p. 1685.

10. Keohane and Murphy, "International Institutions," p. 872.

11. Clive Archer, *International Organizations* (London: Allen & Unwin, 1983), pp. 44, 46.

12. Lawrence Ziring, Robert Riggs, and Jack Plano, *The United Nations*, 3rd ed. (New York: Harcourt Brace, 2000), p. 99.

13. "Security Council Puts Sanctions on Angola's UNITA," *The Washington Post*, August 29, 1997, pp. A31, A33.

14. *Yearbook of International Organizations*, p. 1684.

15. This discussion draws upon Joseph Lepgold, "North Atlantic Treaty Organization," in Bruce W. Jentleson and Thomas G. Paterson, eds., *Encyclopedia of U.S. Foreign Relations*, Vol. 3 (New York: Oxford University Press, 1997), pp. 265–76.

16. Colin Mackerras, *East and Southeast Asia: A Multidisciplinary Survey* (Boulder, CO: Lynne Rienner, 1995), p. 555.

17. Thomas Friedman, "Indonesian Balancing Act," *The New York Times*, April 21, 1997, p. A25.

18. Mackerras, *East and Southeast Asia*, p. 565.

19. See Mark Zacher, "International Organizations," in Joel Krieger, ed., *The Oxford Companion to the Politics of the World* (New York: Oxford University Press, 1993), pp. 451–53.

20. Ibid., p. 451.

21. Inis Claude, "Collective Legitimization as a Political Function of the United Nations," reprinted in Friedrich Kratochwil and Edward Mansfield, eds., *International Organization: A Reader* (New York: HarperCollins, 1994), p. 192.

22. Richard Benedick, *Ozone Diplomacy* (Cambridge, MA: Harvard University Press, 1991), pp. 6, 71–72, 86, 155, 161.

23. Sonia Mazey, "European Integration," in Hawkesworth and Kogan, *Encyclopedia of Government and Politics*, pp. 1144–45.

24. John McCormick, *The European Union: Politics and Policies*, 2nd ed. (New York: Westview Press, 1999), p. 232.

25. Mazey, "European Integration," p. 1146.

26. George Ross, "European Union," in Krieger, *The Oxford Companion to the Politics of the World*, p. 269.

27. Ibid.

28. Ibid.

29. Thomas Christiansen, "European and Regional Integration," in John Baylis and Steve Smith, eds., *The Globalization of World Politics*, 2nd ed. (Oxford: Oxford University Press, 2001), p. 503.

30. Mazey, "European Integration," p. 1150.

31. Christiansen, "European and Regional Integration," p. 503.

32. Ross, "European Union," p. 270.

33. Ivo H. Daalder and Michael E. O'Hanlon, *Winning Ugly* (Washington, DC: The Brookings Institution, 2000), pp. 132, 137, 138, 141.

34. Well over 60 percent of respondents claim to support such a goal. See Juan Diez Medrano, "The European Union: Economic Giant, Political Dwarf," in T. V. Paul and John A. Hall, eds., *International Order and the Future of World Politics* (Cambridge: Cambridge University Press, 1999), p. 157.

35. Bill Seary, "The Early History: From the Congress of Vienna to the San Francisco Conference," in Peter Willetts, ed., *The Conscience of the World: The Influence of Non-Governmental Organisations in the UN System* (London: Hurst and Company, 1996), pp. 17–18.

36. *Yearbook of International Organizations*, p. 1685; Harold K. Jacobson, *Networks of Interdependence: International Organizations and the Global Political System*, 2nd ed. (New York: McGraw-Hill, 1984), p. 10.

37. John W. Kingdon, *Agendas, Alternatives, and Public Policies* (Boston: Little, Brown, 1984), pp. 3–4.

38. Gareth Porter and Janet Welsh Brown, *Global Environmental Politics*, 2nd ed. (Boulder, CO: Westview Press, 1996), p. 53.

39. Peter Willetts, "Consultative Status for NGOs at the United Nations," in Willetts, *The Conscience of the World*, pp. 44, 46.

40. Lee Hockstader, "How Did We Deserve This?" *The Washington Post Magazine*, August 17, 1997.

41. Willetts, "Consultative Status for NGOs," pp. 48–49.

42. Leon Gordenker and Thomas G. Weiss, "Devolving Responsibilities: A Framework for Analysing NGOs and Services," *Third World Quarterly* 18, no. 3 (1997): 446–48.

43. Joan E. Spero and Jeffrey A. Hart, *The Politics of International Economic Relations*, 5th ed. (New York: St. Martin's Press, 1997), p. 97.

44. H. Jeffrey Leonard, "Multinational Corporations and Politics in Developing Countries," *World Politics* 32, no. 3 (April 1980): 456.

45. Ibid.

46. Felician A. Foy and Rose Avato, compilers and eds., *Catholic Almanac, 1997* (Huntington, IN: Our Sunday Visitor Publishing Division, 1997), pp. 333–68.

47. David W. Ziegler, *War, Peace, and International Politics*, 7th ed. (New York: Addison-Wesley, 1997), pp. 155–58.

48. "The Secret Agent," *The Economist*, August 20, 1994, p. 13.

49. Roy Godson and William J. Olson, "Global Ungovernability and the Threat from Organized Crime," paper delivered at the 1994 Annual Meeting of the International Studies Association, Washington, D.C., p. 6.

50. Phil Williams, "Transnational Criminal Organizations and International Security," *Survival* 36, no. 1 (Spring 1994): 96–100.

51. Jane Connors, "NGOs and the Human Rights of the Women at the United Nations," in Willetts, *The Conscience of the World*, pp. 165–73.

52. Jack N. Behrman, *Some Patterns in the Rise of the Multinational Enterprise* Research Paper No. 18 (Chapel Hill: University of North Carolina, Graduate School of Business Administration, 1969), p. 61.

53. Thomas N. Gladwin and Ingo Walter, *Multinationals Under Fire* (New York: John Wiley and Sons, 1980), pp. 193–96.

54. Peter Hebblethwaite, *Paul VI* (New York: Paulist Press, 1993), pp. 215–16.

Chapter 6

1. Joseph Strayer, *On the Medieval Origins of the Modern State* (Princeton: Princeton University Press, 1970), pp. 4, 12; Hendrik Spruyt, *The Sovereign State and Its Competitors* (Princeton: Princeton University Press, 1994), pp. 3–6, 28, 176–80.

2. Garrett Mattingly, *Renaissance Diplomacy* (Boston: Houghton Mifflin, 1971), pp. 56–57.

3. Jacob Burckhardt, *The Civilization of the Renaissance in Italy* (London: Penguin Books, 1990), p. 28.

4. Niccolò Machiavelli, *The Prince and the Discourses* (New York: Modern Library, 1950), p. 528.

5. Ibid., p. 53.

6. Ibid., pp. 61, 117.

7. Ibid., pp. 61, 118.

8. Ibid., p. 9.

9. See Adam Watson, *The Evolution of International Society: A Comparative Historical Analysis* (New York: Routledge, 1992) chaps. 15, 16. See also David Kaiser, *Politics and War* (Cambridge, MA: Harvard University Press, 1990), chap. 1.

10. Some scholars take a position different from the one expressed here. Steven Krasner, for instance, argues that because powerful actors frequently violate norms such as the ones adopted at Westphalia, norms are of little significance in world politics. See Stephen D. Krasner, "Compromising Westphalia," *International Security* 20, no. 3 (1995–1996): 115–51.

11. Thomas Hobbes, *The Leviathan* (Baltimore, MD: Penguin Books, 1968), pp. 161, 185–6, 184, 186.

12. Kaiser, *Politics and War*, 1, pp. 141; see also Edward Vose Gulick, *Europe's Classical Balance of Power* (New York: Norton, 1967).

13. M. S. Anderson, *The Rise of Modern Diplomacy, 1450–1919* (New York: Longman, 1993), pp. 45, 46.

14. François de Callières, *On the Manner of Negotiating with Princes* (South Bend, IN: University of Notre Dame Press, 1963), p. 97.

15. Ibid., pp. 11, 31–32, 110.

16. Hans J. Morgenthau, *Politics Among Nations*, 2nd ed. (New York: Knopf, 1954), p. 200.

17. Gulick, *Balance*, p. 24.

18. Kaiser, *Politics and War*, pp. 215–28.

19. Gulick, *Balance*, pp. 256–57; Henry Kissinger, *A World Restored* (Boston, MA: Houghton Mifflin, 1957), pp. 234–35.

20. Kissinger, *Restored*, chaps. 11–14; see also Gulick, *Balance*, chap. 12.

Chapter 7

1. D. K. Fieldhouse, *The Colonial Empires* (New York: Dell Publishing, 1966), pp. 131, 136.

2. Quoted in William Langer, *The Diplomacy of Imperialism* (New York: Knopf, 1972), p. 84.

3. Quoted in Langer, *Imperialism*, p. 88.

4. Stefan T. Possony, "Peace Enforcement," *Yale Law Journal* 55, no. 5 (1946): 929.

5. Paul F. Diehl, *International Peacekeeping* (Baltimore: The Johns Hopkins Press, 1993), pp. 17–21; Gerald J. Mangone, *A Short History of International Organization* (New York: McGraw-Hill, 1954), pp. 143–54.

6. Quoted in Bruce Russett, "Redefining Deterrence Theory: The Japanese Attack on Pearl Harbor," *Journal of Peace Research* 2 (1967): 99.

7. John Lewis Gaddis, *We Now Know: Rethinking Cold War History* (Oxford: Oxford University Press, 1997), pp. 13–14, 15.

8. The comparison of U.S. and Soviet capabilities in the two preceding paragraphs is based on data from the following sources: George Forty, *United States Tanks of World War II in Action* (Dorset, U.K.: Blandford Press, 1983), chap. 1; George Forty, *World War Two Tanks* (London: Osprey, 1995), chap. 4; Richard Natkiel, ed, *Atlas of Maritime History* (New York: Facts on File, 1986), p. 247; Edgar O'Ballance, *The Red Army: A Short History* (New York: Praeger, 1964),

pp. 189–91; Elisworth L. Raymond, *Soviet-American Comparative Statistics; USSR War Losses* (Ithaca, NY: Cornell University Press, 1949), pp. 2–9; Steven L. Rearden, *The Formative Years. Vol. I: 1947–1950* (Washington, DC: Historical Office of the Office of the Secretary of Defense, 1984), Table 4; Joshua Stoff, *Picture History of World War II American Aircraft Production* (New York: Dover Publications, 1993), pp. 175; U.S. Department of Commerce, *Statistical Abstract of the United States, 1948*, 69th ed. (Washington, DC: U.S. Government Printing Office, 1948), pp. 226–29; U.S. Department of Commerce, *Statistical Abstract of the United States, 1950*, 71st ed. (Washington, DC: U.S. Government Printing Office, 1950), pp. 210–13; *World Book Encyclopedia*, Vol. 14 (Chicago: World Book, 2000), p. 89.

9. John Herz, "Idealist Internationalism and the Security Dilemma," *World Politics* 2 (1950): 157.

10. The following two paragraphs are drawn from Alan C. Lamborn, "Theoretical and Historical Perspectives on Collective Security," in Joseph Lepgold and Thomas Weiss, eds., *Collective Conflict Management and Changing World Politics* (Albany: State University of New York Press, 1998).

11. Inis L. Claude, Jr., *Power and International Relations* (New York: Random House, 1962), pp. 162, 164.

12. Inis L. Claude, *Swords into Plowshares*, 4th ed. (New York: Random House, 1972), p. 156.

13. Charles A. Kupchan, "The Case for Collective Security," in George W. Downs, ed., *Collective Security Beyond the Cold War* (Ann Arbor: University of Michigan Press, 1994), p. 48.

14. Hans J. Morgenthau, *Scientific Man versus Power Politics* (Chicago: Phoenix Books, University of Chicago Press, 1965), pp. 191–94.

15. Ibid., p. 193.

16. Ibid., p. 194.

17. Ibid., pp. 198–203.

18. John Foster Dulles, *War or Peace?* (New York: Macmillan, 1950), pp. 2, 3, 5–6, 8, 16, 252.

19. Gaddis, *We Now Know*, pp. 30, 116, 120, 204, 290.

20. Melvyn P. Leffler, *A Preponderance of Power: National Security, the Truman Administration, and the Cold War* (Stanford, CA: Stanford University Press, 1992); Robert Jervis, "The Impact of the Korean War on the Cold War," *Journal of Conflict Resolution* 24, no. 4 (December 1980).

21. Leffler, *A Preponderance of Power*, p. 13.

22. John Lewis Gaddis, *Russia, the Soviet Union, and the United States*, 2nd ed. (New York: McGraw-Hill, 1990), pp. 189–90.

23. Gaddis, *We Now Know*, p. 205.

24. Ibid., p. 293.

25. Walter LaFeber, *The American Age* (New York: Norton, 1994), pp. 468–76.

26. Leffler, *A Preponderance of Power*, p. 103; see also James A. Nathan and James Oliver, *United States Foreign Policy and World Order*, 3rd ed. (Boston: Little, Brown, 1985), p. 53.

27. Quoted in Nathan and Oliver, *United States Foreign Policy*, p. 54.

28. Quoted in LaFeber, *The American Age*, p. 475.

29. Nathan and Oliver, *U.S. Foreign Policy*, pp. 60–61.

30. Ibid., p. 62.

31. Quoted in Jerel Rosati, *The Politics of United States Foreign Policy* (New York: Harcourt Brace Jovanovich, 1993), p. 395.

32. LaFeber, *The American Age*, p. 473.

33. Quoted in Nathan and Oliver, *United States Foreign Policy*, p. 101.

34. Ibid., pp. 102–3.

35. Ibid., p. 124.

36. Mohammad Yahya Nawroz and Lester W. Grau, "The Soviet War in Afghanistan" (Fort Leavenworth, KS: Foreign Military Studies Office, 1995). Available at *http://call.army.mil/call/fmso/fmsopubs/issues/waraf.htm*

37. See Samuel P. Huntington, "Arms Races: Prerequisites and Results," in Carl Friederich and Seymour Harris, eds., *Public Policy* (Cambridge, MA.: Harvard University Press, 1958).

38. Andrew Bennett, "Patterns of Soviet Interventionism, 1975–1990," in William Zimmerman, ed., *Beyond the Soviet Threat* (Ann Arbor: University of Michigan Press, 1992), pp. 105–27.

39. William Zimmerman and Deborah Yarsike, "Mass Publics and New Thinking in Soviet and Russian Foreign Policy," in Zimmerman, *Beyond the Soviet Threat*, pp. 3–20.

40. Philip Roeder, "Dialectics of Doctrine: Politics of Resource Allocation and the Development of Soviet Military Thought," in Zimmerman, *Beyond the Soviet Threat*, pp. 71–104.

41. Allen Lynch, "Changing Elite Views on the International System," in Zimmerman, *Beyond the Soviet Threat*, p. 32.

Chapter 8

1. Stephen M. Walt, "The Renaissance of Security Studies," *International Studies Quarterly* 35, no. 2 (June 1991): 212.

2. Arnold Wolfers, "National Security as an Ambiguous Symbol," in Arnold Wolfers, *Discord and Collaboration* (Baltimore: Johns Hopkins University Press, 1962), p. 150.

3. Robert Jervis, "Cooperation Under the Security Dilemma," *World Politics* 30, no. 2 (January 1978), p. 174; Wolfers, "National Security as an Ambiguous Symbol," p. 158.

4. Deborah Sontag, "Israel Rethinking Stand in Lebanon," *The New York Times*, November 28, 1998, pp. A1, A6.

5. Jervis, "Cooperation Under the Security Dilemma," p. 175.

6. Wolfers, "National Security as an Ambiguous Symbol," p. 151; William R. Keylor, *The Twentieth Century World: An International History*, 3rd ed. (New York: Oxford University Press, 1996), pp. 83–84.

7. Wolfers, "National Security as an Ambiguous Symbol," pp. 151, 158.

8. Barry Buzan, *People, States, and Fear*, 2nd ed. (Boulder, CO: Lynne Rienner, 1991), pp. 112–16.

9. Lawrence Freedman, "The Concept of Security," in Mary Hawksworth and Maurice Kogan, eds., *Encyclopedia of Government and Politics*, Vol. 2 (New York: Routledge, 1992), p. 732; Buzan, *People, States, and Fear*, p. 112.

10. This discussion draws on Robert Jervis, "Security Regimes," *International Organization* 36, no. 2 (Spring 1982): 358–60.

11. Ibid., p. 359.

12. For an argument that overoptimism about the enemy's capabilities is a major triggering cause of war, see John G. Stoessinger, *Why Nations Go to War*, 7th ed. (New York: St. Martin's Press, 1998), pp. 209–12.

13. John Herz, *International Politics in the Atomic Age* (New York: Columbia University Press, 1959), p. 231.

14. Freedman, "The Concept of Security," p. 732.

15. Lawrence Freedman, "International Security: Changing Targets," *Foreign Policy* 110 (Spring 1998): 48.

16. Freedman, "The Concept of Security," p. 733.

17. Robert J. Art, "To What Ends Military Power?" *International Security* 4, no. 4 (Spring 1980): footnote 2, 5–6.

18. Walter Slocombe, "The Countervailing Strategy," *International Security* 5, no. 4 (Spring 1981): 20–24.

19. Kenneth N. Waltz, "More May Be Better," in Kenneth N. Waltz and Scott Sagan eds., *The Spread of Nuclear Weapons: A Debate* (New York: Norton, 1995), p. 24.

20. Thomas C. Schelling, *Arms and Influence* (New Haven: Yale University Press, 1966), p. 72.

21. Art, "To What Ends Military Power?" p. 7.

22. Frederic S. Pearson, *The Global Spread of Arms: Political Economy of International Security* (Boulder, CO: Westview, 1994), p. 139.

23. Thomas C. Schelling and Morton H. Halperin, *Strategy and Arms Control* (McLean, VA: Pergamon-Brassey, 1985), p. 2.

24. Ibid., p. 2.

25. Robert Jervis, "Arms Control, Stability, and Causes of War," *Political Science Quarterly* 108, no. 2 (Summer 1993): 243–44.

26. Michael R. Gordon, "U.S. to Use Its Missile Warning System to Alert Russians to Launchings Worldwide," *The New York Times*, September 2, 1998, p. A9.

27. Teena Karsa Mayers, *Understanding Weapons and Arms Control: A Guide to the Issues*, 4th ed. rev. (Washington, DC: Brassey's (U.S.), 1991), p. 84.

28. Stuart Croft, *Strategies of Arms Control: A History and Typology* (Manchester, UK: Manchester University Press, 1996), p. 154.

29. Steven Lee Meyers, "Pentagon Ready to Shrink Arsenal of Nuclear Bombs," *The New York Times*, November 23, 1998, pp. A1, A10.

30. Raymond Aron, *Peace and War: A Theory of International Relations* (Garden City, NY: Anchor Books, 1973), p. 125.

31. Michael Mandelbaum, "Is Major War Obsolete?" *Survival* 40, no. 4 (Winter 1998–1999): 21–26.

32. Michael Hirsch, "Calling All Regio-Cops," *Foreign Affairs* 79, no. 6 (November/ December 2000): 6.

33. Randall Forsberg, William Driscoll, Gregory Webb, and Jonathan Dean, *Nonproliferation Primer: Preventing the Spread of Nuclear, Chemical, and Biological Weapons* (Cambridge, MA: The MIT Press, 1995), p. 13.

34. John F. Sopko, "The Changing Proliferation Threat," *Foreign Policy* 105 (Winter 1996–1997): 9; Richard K. Betts, "The New Threat of Mass Destruction," *Foreign Affairs* 77, no. 1 (January/February 1998): 27.

35. Joanna Spear, "Arms and Arms Control," in Brian White, Richard Little, and Michael Smith, eds., *Issues in World Politics* (New York: St. Martin's Press, 1997), pp. 113–14.

36. Sopko, "The Changing Proliferation Threat," p. 7.

37. Bradley Graham and Dana Priest, "U.S. Targets Sites Crucial to Weapon-Making," *The Washington Post*, December 17, 1998, pp. A29, A31.

38. "Bombs, Gas, and Microbes," *The Economist*, June 6, 1998, p. 24.

39. Glenn E. Schweitzer, "A Multilateral Approach to Curbing Proliferation of Weapons Know-How," *Global Governance* 2 (1996): 25–26.

40. Betts, "The New Threat of Mass Destruction," p. 35.

41. Richard A. Falkenrath, "Confronting Nuclear, Biological, and Chemical Terrorism," *Survival* 40, no. 3 (Autumn 1998): 55.

42. Ibid., pp. 50–53.

43. Donald Snow, *Distant Thunder: Third World Conflict and the New International Order* (New York: St. Martin's Press, 1993), p. 128.

44. Michael E. Brown, "Causes and Implications of Ethnic Conflict," in Michael E. Brown, ed., *Ethnic Conflict and International Security* (Princeton: Princeton University Press, 1993), p. 5.

45. Ibid., pp. 4–5.

46. Stephen Ryan, "Nationalism and Ethnic Conflict," in Brian White, Richard Little, and Michael Smith, eds., *Issues in World Politics* (New York: St. Martin's Press, 1997), p. 161; Ted Robert Gurr and Barbara Harff, *Ethnic Conflict in World Politics* (Boulder, CO: Westview Press, 1994), p. xiii.

47. A good example of the process by which regime illegitimacy can lead to ethnic war is found in V. P. Gagnon, Jr., "Ethnic Nationalism and International Conflict: The Case of Serbia," *International Security* 19, no. 3 (Winter 1994–1995): 130–66.

48. Ryan, "Nationalism and Ethnic Conflict," pp. 158, 166–67.

49. *Preventing Deadly Conflict: Final Report With Executive Summary* (New York: Carnegie Corporation, 1997), p. 6.

Chapter 9

1. Robert Gilpin, *The Political Economy of International Relations* (Princeton: Princeton University Press, 1987), pp. 119–21.

2. D. K. Fieldhouse, *The Colonial Empires* (New York: Dell Publishing, 1966), p. 33.

3. Jacob Viner, "Power versus Plenty as Objectives of Foreign Policy in the Seventeenth and Eighteenth Centuries," *World Politics* 1, no. 1 (October 1948): 10.

4. Mark Bradley, *Liberal Leadership, Great Powers and their Challengers in Peace and War* (Ithaca, NY: Cornell University Press, 1993), chap. 2.

5. See the discussion in Viner, "Power versus Plenty."

6. Gilpin, *Political Economy*, p. 174.

7. Ibid., p. 122.

8. Benjamin J. Cohen, "A Brief History of International Monetary Relations," in Jeffry A. Frieden and David A. Lake, eds., *International Political Economy*, 3rd ed. (New York: St. Martin's Press, 1995), p. 210.

9. For a discussion of these changes, see Anthony H. Birch, *The British System of Government*, 8th ed. (London: HarperCollins, 1991), pp. 33–37.

10. For information on the international and domestic incentives that produced the movement toward free trade in Britain, France, and Germany, see Charles Kindleberger, "The Rise of Free Trade in Western Europe, 1820–1875," *Journal of Economic History* 35, no. 1 (1975): 20–55.

11. W. Arthur Lewis, *The Evolution of the International Economic Order* (Princeton: Princeton University Press, 1978), pp. 9–10, 14–15.

12. Ibid., p. 5.

13. Ibid., p. 12.

14. Ibid., pp. 17, 19.

15. Ibid., pp. 18–19.

16. Ibid., p. 25.

17. For some examples of the variation, see Alan C. Lamborn, *The Price of Power: Risk and Foreign Policy in Britain, France, and Germany* (Boston: Unwin & Hyman, 1991).

18. Paul Kennedy, *The Realities Behind Diplomacy: Background Influences on British External Policy, 1865–1980* (Boston: Allen & Unwin, 1981), pp. 48–49.

19. Gilpin, *Political Economy*, p. 124.

20. J. A. Hobson, *Imperialism: A Study* (Ann Arbor: University of Michigan Press, 1965), pp. 53–54, 59–60, 61.

21. Ibid., pp. 56–57.

22. V. I. Lenin, *Imperialism, the Highest Stage of Capitalism* (New York: International Publishers, 1977), p. 89.

23. Ibid., p. 62.

24. Ibid., pp. 62–63.

Chapter 10

1. See Stephen Blank, "Britain: The Politics of Foreign Economic Policy, the Domestic Economy, and the Problem of Pluralistic Stagnation," *International Organization* 31, no. 4 (1977): 673–721; Alan C. Lamborn, *The Price of Power* (Boston: Unwin Hyman, 1991), chap. 7; and John Ruggie, "International Regimes, Transactions, and Change: Embedded Liberalism in the Postwar Economic Order," *International Organization* 36, no. 2 (1982): 379–415.

2. Paul Kennedy, *The Rise and Fall of the Great Powers* (New York: Random House, 1987), p. 279.

3. Robert Gilpin, *The Political Economy of International Relations* (Princeton: Princeton University Press, 1987), p. 128.

4. Kennedy, *Rise and Fall*, p. 280.

5. Herbert Feis, *Europe, the World's Banker, 1870–1914* (New York: Norton, 1965), pp. xi, 14–16, 47–48, 72.

6. Walter LeFeber, *The American Age*, 2nd ed. (New York: Norton, 1994), p. 341.

7. Feis, *The World's Banker*, p. 52.

8. Felix Gilbert and David Clay Large, *The End of the European Era, 1890 to the Present*, 4th ed. (New York: Norton, 1991), p. 203.

9. Gilpin, *Political Economy*, p. 129.

10. Gilbert and Large, *The End of the European Era*, p. 195.

11. LeFeber, *The American Age*, pp. 344–45.

12. Kennedy, *Rise and Fall*, p. 329.

13. Gilpin, *Political Economy*, pp. 131–31.

14. "Clement Attlee," *The Economist*, November 11, 1989, p. 26.

15. Joan Spero and Jeffrey Hart, *The Politics of International Economic Relations*, 5th ed. (New York: St. Martin's Press, 1997), p. 11.

16. David Ashford, *Policy and Politics in Britain* (Philadelphia: Temple University Press, 1981), p. 103.

17. Spero and Hart, *Politics of International Economic Relations*, p. 14.

18. Gilpin, *Political Economy*, pp. 134–35.

19. Ibid., p. 138.

20. Ibid., pp. 137–38.

21. Spero and Hart, *Politics of International Economic Relations*, p. 16.

22. Ibid., p. 27.

23. Raymond Vernon and Debra Spar, *Beyond Globalism: Remaking American Foreign Economic Policy* (New York: Free Press, 1989), p. 47.

24. Spero and Hart, *Politics of International Economic Relations*, p. 57.

25. Vernon and Spar, *Beyond Globalism*, p. 47.

26. Spero and Hart, *Politics of International Economic Relations*, pp. 72–73.

27. Kwame Nkrumah, *Neocolonialism, the Last Stage of Imperialism* (New York: International Publishers, 1965), p. ix.

28. Ibid., p. xi.

29. Ibid., p. x.

30. Resolution 1707 (XVI), reprinted in Dietrich Rauschning, Katja Wiesbrock, and Martin Lailach, eds., *Key Resolutions of the United Nations General Assembly, 1946–1996*

(Cambridge, UK: Cambridge University Press, 1997), pp. 228–29.

31. Resolution 3201 (S-VI), reprinted in Rauschning, Wiesbrock, and Lailach, *Key Resolutions*, p. 311.

32. Rauschning, Wiesbrock, and Lailach, *Key Resolutions*, p. 311.

33. Robert L. Rothstein, *Global Bargaining: UNCTAD and the Quest for a New International Economic Order* (Princeton: Princeton University Press, 1979), p. 49.

34. Spero and Hart, *Politics of International Economic Relations*, p. 231.

35. Ibid., p. 234.

Chapter 11

1. Robert Gilpin, *The Political Economy of International Relations* (Princeton: Princeton University Press, 1987), pp. 8–10.

2. Helen V. Milner, *Resisting Protectionism: Global Industries and the Politics of International Trade* (Princeton: Princeton University Press, 1988), pp. 239–41.

3. Susan Strange, "International Economics and International Relations: A Case of Mutual Neglect," *International Affairs* 46, no. 2 (April 1970): 308; Jeffry Frieden and David A. Lake, "Introduction: International Politics and International Economics," in Jeffry Frieden and David A. Lake, eds., *International Political Economy: Perspectives on Global Power and Wealth*, 3rd ed. (New York: St. Martin's Press, 1995), p. 3.

4. Strange, "International Economics and International Relations," p. 308.

5. Frieden and Lake, "Introduction," p. 4.

6. Barry Buzan, *People, States, and Fear*, 2nd ed. (Boulder, CO: Lynne Rienner, 1991), pp. 230–34.

7. For an interesting discussion of defense as the goal of keeping some other group (*them*) out of an actor's (*our*) territory, see William R. Polk, *Neighbors and Strangers: The Fundamentals of Foreign Affairs* (Chicago: University of Chicago Press, 1997), chap. 3.

8. Helen V. Milner and Robert O. Keohane, "Internationalization and Domestic Politics: An Introduction," in Robert O. Keohane and Helen V. Milner, eds., *Internationalization and Domestic Politics* (Cambridge, UK: Cambridge University Press, 1996), pp. 10–13.

9. These two paragraphs draw on a distinction made in Robert O. Keohane and Joseph S. Nye, Jr., *Power and Interdependence* (Boston: Little, Brown, 1977), pp. 12–19.

10. The quoted phrase comes from Helen Milner, "International Political Economy: Beyond Hegemonic Stability," *Foreign Policy* 110 (Spring 1998): 119. See also Linda Weiss, *The Myth of the Powerless State* (Ithaca, NY: Cornell University Press, 1998), pp. 168–69.

11. Buzan, *People, States, and Fear*, pp. 232–33.

12. Anthony Faiola, "Brazil, IMF Agree on Economic Framework," *The Washington Post*, February 5, 1999, p. A27.

13. John M. Stopford and Susan Strange, *Rival States, Rival Firms: Competition for World Market Shares* (New York: Cambridge University Press, 1991), p. 2.

14. See Alan Russell, "Trade, Money, and Markets," in Brian White, Richard Little, and Michael Smith, eds., *Issues in World Politics* (New York: St. Martin's Press, 1997), pp. 57–60.

15. Ibid., pp. 59–60.

16. Susan Strange, *The Retreat of the State* (New York: Cambridge University Press, 1996), p. 44.

17. "World Trade," *The Economist*, October 3, 1998, p. 3.

18. John McCallum, "National Borders Matter: Canada-U.S. Regional Trade Patterns," *American Economic Review* 85, no. 3 (June 1995): 616. For a more extensive discussion of this question, see John F. Helliwell, *How Much Do National Borders Matter?* (Washington, DC: Brookings Institution, 1998).

19. Bruce E. Moon, *Dilemmas of International Trade* (Boulder, CO: Westview, 1996), pp. 8–10.

20. William P. Avery, "Domestic Interests in NAFTA Bargaining," *Political Science Quarterly* 113, no. 2 (Summer 1998): 289.

21. "World Trade," p. 22.

22. Milner and Keohane, "Internationalization and Domestic Politics," p. 11.

23. Andrew Leyshon, "Dissolving Difference? Money, Disembedding, and the Creation of 'Global Financial Space,'" in P. W. Daniels and W. F. Lever, eds., *The Global Economy in Transition* (Essex, UK: Longman, 1996), p. 77; Paul Blustein, "Currencies in Crisis," *The Washington Post*, February 7, 1999, p. H14.

24. Blustein, "Currencies in Crisis."

25. Daniel Yergin and Joseph Stanislaw, *The Commanding Heights* (New York: Simon & Schuster, 1998), p. 155.

26. Strange, *The Retreat of the State*, pp. 46–47.

27. Richard E. Caves and Ronald W. Jones, *World Trade and Payments: An Introduction*, 4th ed. (Boston: Little, Brown, 1985), p. 192; Frederic S. Pearson and Simon Payaslian, *International Political Economy* (Boston: McGraw-Hill, 1999), p. 223.

28. Strange, *The Retreat of the State*, p. 50.

29. Pearson and Payaslian, *International Political Economy*, p. 249.

30. Theodore H. Moran, "Trade and Investment Dimensions of International Conflict," in Chester A. Crocker, Fen Osler Hampson, and Pamela Aall, eds., *Managing International Chaos* (Washington, DC: United States Institute of Peace, 1996), p. 157.

31. Jeffrey Sachs, "International Economics: Unlocking the Mysteries of Globalization," *Foreign Policy* 110 (Spring 1998): 97.

32. "World Trade," p. 4.

33. "The World Economy," *The Economist*, September 20, 1997, p. 23.

34. The quoted passage is from Russell, "Trade, Money, and Markets," p. 49; see also Charles Lipson, "International Finance," in Joel Krieger, ed., *Oxford Companion to Politics of the World* (New York: Oxford University Press, 1993), p. 303.

35. "The World Economy," p. 24; Susan Strange, "The Erosion of the State," *Current History* 96 (November 1997): 365.

36. Strange, "The Erosion of the State," p. 367.

37. Russell, "Trade, Money, and Markets," p. 50.

38. Sachs, "International Economics," pp. 107–8; Dani Rodrik, "Sense and Nonsense in the Globalization Debate," *Foreign Policy* 107 (Summer 1997): 20.

39. "The World Economy," p. 30.

40. For a lively discussion of this argument, see Yergin and Stanislaw, *The Commanding Heights*.

41. Rodrik, "Sense and Nonsense in the Globalization Debate," pp. 25–26; Geoffrey Garrett, "Global Markets and National Politics: Collision Course or Virtuous Circle?," *International Organization* 52, no. 4 (Autumn 1998): 812–18.

42. "The World Economy," p. 33.

43. Gary Burtless, Robert Z. Lawrence, Robert E. Litan, and Robert J. Shapiro, *Globaphobia: Confronting Fears About Open Trade* (Washington, DC: Brookings Institution, 1998), pp. 1–4.

44. Burtless et al., *Globophobia*, p. 6.

45. Joseph Kahn, "International Lenders' New Image: A Human Face," *New York Times*, September 26, 2000, p. A5.

46. See "More About Public Citizen" (*www.citizen.org/newweb/more_about.htm*).

47. Interview with the Research Director, Global Trade Watch, October 21, 2000.

48. Moises Naim and Lori Wallach, "Lori's War," *Foreign Policy* 118 (Spring 2000): 34.

49. "Lori's War," 50.

50. "International Lenders' New Image," p. A5.

51. Naomi Klein, "Rebels in Search of Rules," *New York Times*, December 2, 1999, p. A35.

52. Sachs, "International Economics," p. 103.

53. Quoted in "The Crisis of Global Capitalism," *Newsweek*, U.S. Edition, December 7, 1998. (*web.lexis-nexis.com/univer...5= db7fe516158acd6f90043c88e5dcd92*).

54. Sachs, "International Economics," pp. 104–5.

55. Ibid., pp. 102–3.

56. John B. Goodman and Louis W. Pauly, "The Obsolescence of Capital Controls? Economic Management in the Age of Global Markets," *World Politics* 46, no. 1 (October 1993): 50, 52–59; Barry Eichengreen, "The Asian Financial Crisis: The IMF and Its Critics," *Great Decisions 1999* (New York: The Foreign Policy Association, 1999), p. 27.

57. Robert Wade, "The Coming Fight Over Capital Flows," *Foreign Policy* 113 (Winter 1998–99): 45–52.

58. Sachs, "International Economics," p. 106.

59. "World Trade," pp. 10, 13; United Nations Conference on Trade and Development, *World Investment Report 1996: Investment, Trade, and International Policy Arrangements* (New York and Geneva: United Nations, 1996), p. 129.

60. *World Investment Report 1996*, p. 132.

61. Ibid., p. 132.

62. "World Trade," p. 13.

63. Ibid.

64. Ibid.

65. Ibid., pp. 13–14.

66. John M. Kline, "Business Codes and Conduct in a Global Political Economy," in Oliver F. Williams, ed., *Global Codes of Conduct: An Idea Whose Time Has Come* (Notre Dame, IN: University of Notre Dame Press, 1999), p. 6.

67. "World Trade," p. 14.

Chapter 12

1. Clifford Krauss, "Britain Arrests Pinochet to Face Charges by Spain," *New York Times*, October 18, 1999, pp. A1, A12; T. R. Reid, "Pinochet Extradition Case to Proceed in Britain," *Washington Post*, April 16, 1999, p. A30; Ricardo Lago and Heraldo Munoz, "The Pinochet Dilemma," *Foreign Policy* 114 (Spring 1999): 26–27.

2. Krauss, "Britain Arrests Pinochet to Face Charges by Spain."

3. Lago and Munoz, "The Pinochet Dilemma," p. 27.

4. Quoted in J. R. Vincent, *Human Rights and International Relations* (Cambridge, UK: Cambridge University Press, 1986), p. 21.

5. Ibid., pp. 22–23.

6. Seyom Brown, *International Relations in a Changing Global System*, 2nd ed. (Boulder, CO: Westview Press, 1996), p. 97.

7. Quoted in Brian Urquhart, "Mrs. Roosevelt's Revolution," *New York Review of Books*, April 26, 2001, p. 34.

8. Gidon Gottlieb, *Nation Against State* (New York: Council on Foreign Relations Press, 1993), pp. 30–31.

9. Jack Donnelly, *International Human Rights*, 2nd ed. (Boulder, CO: Westview Press, 1998), pp. 9–10; Aryeh Neier, "Human Rights," in Joel Krieger, ed., *The Oxford Companion to the Politics of the World* (Oxford: Oxford University Press, 1993), p. 401.

10. Michael Posner, "Rally around Human Rights," *Foreign Policy* 97 (Winter 1994–95): 137.

11. See William F. Felice, "The Case for Collective Human Rights: The Reality of Group Suffering," *Ethics and International Affairs* 10 (1996): 47; Vincent, *Human Rights and International Relations*, p. 13; Donnelly, *International Human Rights*, p. 18; Hedley Bull, "Human Rights and World Politics," in Ralph Pettman, ed., *Moral Claims in World Affairs* (New York: St. Martin's Press, 1979), p. 79.

12. Jack Donnelly, *Universal Human Rights in Theory and Practice* (Ithaca, NY: Cornell University Press, 1989), pp. 14–15.

13. Ibid., pp. 145, 147.

14. Adamantia Pollis, "Human Rights," in Mary Hawkesworth and Maurice Kogan, eds., *Encyclopedia of Government and Politics*, Vol. 2 (London: Routledge, 1992), pp. 1332–33.

15. Felice, "The Case for Collective Human Rights," p. 58.

16. Ibid., pp. 49, 50, 57.

17. "Universal Declaration of Human Rights, 1948," reprinted in Ian Brownlie, ed., *Basic Documents on Human Rights*, 3rd ed. (Oxford: Oxford University Press, 1992), pp. 21, 22.

18. Paul Lewis, "Differences Are Narrowed at UN Talks on Rights," *New York Times*, June 21, 1993, p. A7 (emphasis added).

19. Felice, "The Case for Collective Human Rights," p. 49.

20. Alan Riding, "Human Rights: The West Gets Some Tough Questions," *New York Times*, June 20, 1993, p. E5.

21. Bilahari Kausikan, "Asia's Different Standard," *Foreign Policy* 92 (Fall 1993): 35.

22. Onuma Yasuaki, "Toward an Intercivilizational Approach to Human Rights," in Joanne R. Bauer and Daniel A. Bell, eds., *The East Asian Challenge for Human Rights* (Cambridge, UK: Cambridge University Press, 1999), p. 107, also pp. 104–6.

23. Adda B. Bozeman, *The Future of Law in a Multicultural World* (Princeton: Princeton University Press, 1971), p. 14.

24. Noni Jabavu, *Drawn in Colour: African Contrasts* (London: Murray, 1960), p. 51, quoted in Bozeman, *The Future of Law in a Multicultural World*, p. 97.

25. Donnelly, *Universal Human Rights in Theory and Practice*, p. 14.

26. "Arabian Punishment: Preserving Values," *The Economist*, September 13, 1997, p. 46.

27. Stephen Kinzer, "Kurd's Trial Draws Attention to Turkish Court," *New York Times*, May 31, 1999, p. A7.

28. Kausikan, "Asia's Different Standard," pp. 36, 38.

29. Zbigniew Brzezinski, "The New Challenges to Human Rights," reprinted in James M. Lindsay, ed., *Perspectives: Global Issues* (Boulder, CO: Coursewise Publishers, 1998), pp. 154–55; Sidney Jones, "'Asian' Human Rights, Economic Growth, and United States Policy," *Current History* 95, no. 605 (December 1996): 420.

30. "Female Genital Mutilation: Is It Crime? Is It Culture?" *The Economist*, February 13, 1999, p. 45; Ginger Thompson, "No U.S. Asylum for Woman Threatened with Genital Cutting," *New York Times*, April 25, 1999, p. NE27.

31. Amberin Zaman, "Head Scarf Debate Gets More Intense in Turkey," *Washington Post*, May 5, 1999, p. A25.

32. Barbara Crossette, "Testing the Limits of Tolerance as Cultures Mix," *New York Times*, March 6, 1999, pp. A15, A17.

33. David P. Forsythe, *The Internationalization of Human Rights* (Lexington, MA: D.C. Heath, 1991), pp. 57–58, 62–63.

34. Ann Marie Clark, Elisabeth J. Friedman, and Kathryn Hochstetler, "The Sovereign Limits of Global Civil Society: A Comparison of NGO Participation in UN World Conferences on the Environment, Human Rights, and Women," *World Politics* 51, no. 1 (October 1998): 9.

35. "About Amnesty International," May 19, 1999 (*www.amnesty.org/aboutai/index.html*).

36. Aryeh Neier, "Asia's Unacceptable Standard," *Foreign Policy* 92 (Fall 1993): 46; David P. Forsythe, *Human Rights in World Politics* (Lincoln: University of Nebraska Press, 1983), pp. 66–70.

37. Forsythe, *Human Rights in World Politics*, p. 67.

38. Barbara Crossette, "U.S. Is Voted Off Rights Panel of the U.N. for the First Time," *New York Times*, May 4, 2001, p. A12.

39. Craig Murphy, *International Organization and Industrial Change: Global Governance Since 1850* (Oxford: Oxford University Press, 1994), p. 191.

40. Jessica T. Mathews, "Power Shift," *Foreign Affairs* 76, no. 1 (January-February 1997): 54.

41. Forsythe, *The Internationalization of Human Rights*, p. 73.

42. Human Rights Watch, *Human Rights Watch World Report 1999* (New York: Human Rights Watch, 1998), p. xv; "Human-Rights Law: The Conscience of Mankind," *The Economist*, December 5, 1998, p. 13.

43. Forsythe, *Human Rights in World Politics*, p. 68.

44. Ibid., p. 70; Roger P. Winter, "How Human Rights Groups Miss the Opportunity to Do Good," *Washington Post*, February 22, 1998, p. C2.

45. Forsythe, *Human Rights in World Politics*, p. 131.

46. Michael Ignatieff, "Human Rights: The Midlife Crisis," *New York Review of Books*, May 20, 1999, p. 61.

47. Michael Ross Fowler and Julie Marie Bunck, *Law, Power, and the Sovereign State* (University Park, PA: Pennsylvania State University Press, 1995), p. 136.

48. Robert H. Jackson, "International Community Beyond the Cold War," in Gene M. Lyons and Michael Mastanduno, eds., *Beyond Westphalia: State Sovereignty and International Intervention* (Baltimore: Johns Hopkins University Press, 1995), p. 68.

49. Fowler and Bunck, *Law, Power, and the Sovereign State*, p. 138.

50. Catherine Guicherd, "International Law and the War in Kosovo," *Survival* 41, no. 2 (Summer 1999): 21.

51. See *Vienna Declaration and Programme of Action*, U.N. GAOR, World Conference on Human Rights, 48th Session, 22nd plenary meeting, U.N. Doc. A/CONF.157/24 (Part 1) (1993), cited in Thomas Buergenthal, "The Normative and Institutional Evolution of Human Rights," *Human Rights Quarterly* 19, no. 4 (November 1997): 713–14.

52. Buergenthal, "The Normative and Institutional Evolution of International Human Rights," pp. 715–16.

53. Human Rights Watch, *World Report 1999*, pp. 6–7, 91–94, 153, 225.

54. Jack Donnelly, "International Human Rights After the Cold War," in Michael Klare and Yogesh Chandrani, eds., *World Security*, 3rd ed. (New York: St. Martin's Press, 1998), p. 248.

55. Thomas Friedman, "A River Runs Through It," *New York Times*, May 25, 1999, p. A31.

56. "Human-Rights Law," *The Economist*, pp. 14–15.

57. Ibid., p. 6.

58. Ibid.

59. Ibid., p. 7.

60. Jack Donnelly, "State Sovereignty and International Intervention: The Case of Human Rights," in Lyons and Mastanduno, *Beyond Westphalia*, pp. 125–29.

61. Ibid., pp. 132–33.

62. Ibid., pp. 133–36.

63. Henry Kissinger, *A World Restored* (Gloucester, MA: Houghton Mifflin, 1973), p. 328.

64. Donnelly, "International Human Rights After the Cold War," pp. 246–47; Jones, "'Asian' Human Rights," p. 425.

65. Ian Clark, *The Hierarchy of States: Reform and Resistance in the International Order* (Cambridge, UK: Cambridge University Press, 1989), p. 45.

66. See "A Suitable Target for Foreign Policy?" *The Economist*, April 12, 1997, p. 15. The quotation is from "America's Next President?" *The Economist*, May 22, 1999, p. 24.

67. Ann Kent, "China and the International Human Rights Regime: A Case Study of Multilateral Monitoring, 1989–1994," *Human Rights Quarterly* 17, no. 1 (February 1995): 1.

68. Donnelly, "International Human Rights After the Cold War," p. 249.

69. The two positions are summarized in David Little, "A Different Kind of Justice: Dealing with Human Rights Violations in Transitional Societies," *Ethics and International Affairs* 13 (1999): 65–68.

70. Quoted in Little, "A Different Kind of Justice," p. 69.

71. "South Africa Looks for Truth and Hopes for Reconciliation," *The Economist*, April 20, 1996, p. 33.

72. Little, "A Different Kind of Justice," pp. 65, 74.

73. "Senior Officer Admits Role in Killing Foes of Apartheid," *New York Times*, May 25, 1999, p. A8.

74. David Goodman, "Unfinished Work," *Washington Post*, May 30, 1999, p. B4.

75. "South Africa Looks for Truth and Hopes for Reconciliation," p. 33; Goodman, "Unfinished Work."

76. Juan E. Mendez, "Accountability for Past Abuses," *Human Rights Quarterly* 19, no. 2 (May 1997): 263.

77. Clifford Kraus, "Bolivian's Dark Past Starts to Catch up with Him," *New York Times*, March 14, 1999, p. A3.

78. Roger Cohen, "Tribunal Is Said to Cite Milosevic for War Crimes," *New York Times*, May 27, 1999, p. A12.

79. "Fact Sheet on ICTY Proceedings," International Criminal Tribunal for the former Yugoslavia, April 18, 2001 (www.un.org/icty/glance/profact-e.htm).

80. Barbara Crossette, "A New Legal Weapon to Deter Rape," *New York Times*, March 4, 2001, p. W5.

81. "ICTR Detainees—Status on 9 May 2001," International Criminal Tribunal for Rwanda (www.ictr.org/ENGLISH/factsheets/detainee.htm).

82. James C. McKinley, Jr., "Ex-Rwandan Premier Gets Life in Prison on Charges of Genocide in '94 Massacres," *New York Times*, September 5, 1998, p. A4.

83. David P. Forsythe, "Human Rights Policy: Change and Continuity," in Randall B. Ripley and James M. Lindsay, eds., *U.S. Foreign Policy After the Cold War* (Pittsburgh: University of Pittsburgh Press, 1997), p. 279.

84. Human Rights Watch, *World Report 1999*, p. 470.

85. Jeremy Goldberg, *What Happened in Rome?* Senior Honors Thesis, Georgetown University, Spring 1999, pp. 38–45.

86. Human Rights Watch, *World Report 1999*, p. 472; Ignatieff, "Human Rights," p. 62.

87. "Human-Rights Law," *The Economist*, p. 13.

Chapter 13

1. Gareth Porter and Janet Welsh Brown, *Global Environmental Politics*, 2nd ed. (Boulder, CO: Westview Press, 1996), p. 12; G. Tyler Miller, Jr., *Environmental Science: Working with the Earth*, 7th ed. (Belmont, CA: Wadsworth Publishing, 1999), pp. 453–54. Some estimates of the rate of destruction are even higher. Biologist E. O. Wilson estimates that tropical rain forests are disappearing at a rate of 2 percent a year (twice the 1991 FAO estimate), an area equal to the state of Florida. See E. O. Wilson, "Is Humanity Suicidal?" *New York Times Magazine*, May 30, 1993, p. 28.

2. Miller, *Environmental Science*, pp. 441–42.

3. Michael Nicholson, *International Relations: A Concise Introduction* (New York: New York University Press, 1998), p. 157. The world population figures come from John Vogler, "Environment and Natural Resources," in Brian White, Richard Little, and Michael Smith, eds., *Issues in World Politics* (New York: St. Martin's Press, 1997), p. 232; and from Anne H. Ehrlich, "Toward a Sustainable Global Population," in Dennis C. Pirages, ed., *Building Sustainable Societies* (Armonk, NY: M. E. Sharpe, 1996), p. 152. The statistic on Nigeria's population is from Wilson, "Is Humanity Suicidal?" p. 6.

4. Porter and Brown, *Global Environmental Politics*, p. 3.

5. Barry Buzan, *People, States, and Fear*, 2nd ed. (Boulder, CO: Lynne Rienner, 1991), pp. 131–32; Evan Luard, *The Globalization of Politics* (New York: New York University Press, 1990), pp. 70–71.

6. Paul A. Samuelson and William D. Nordhaus, *Economics*, 15th ed. (New York: McGraw Hill, 1995), p. 32.

7. See Paul Ehrlich, *The Population Bomb* (New York: Ballantine, 1968); Donella H. Meadows, et al., *The Limits to Growth* (New York: Universe Books, 1972); Lester R. Brown, *World Without Borders* (New York: Vintage Books, 1972).

8. Luard, *The Globalization of Politics*, pp. 72–73.

9. Seyom Brown, *New Forces, Old Forces, and the Future of World Politics* (New York: Harper Collins, 1995) p. 190. Peter M. Haas, "Making Progress in International Environmental Protection," in Emanuel Adler and Beverly Crawford, eds., *Progress in Postwar International Relations* (New York: Columbia University Press, 1991), p. 279.

10. Chris Brown, *Understanding International Relations* (New York: St. Martin's Press, 1997), pp. 232–33.

11. Brown, *New Forces, Old Forces*, p. 193.

12. Miller, *Environmental Science*, pp. 248–50; Craig Timberg, "Gore Sets Goal to Rid Parks of Air Pollution," *Washington Post*, April 23, 1999, p. A15.

13. Anne Kelleher and Laura Klein, *Global Perspectives: A Handbook for Understanding Global Issues* (Upper Saddle River, NJ: Prentice Hall, 1999), p. 109.

14. Ibid., p. 110; Miller, *Environmental Science*, p. 316.

15. Kelleher and Klein, *Global Perspectives*, p. 112.

16. Thomas F. Homer-Dixon, "Physical Dimensions of Global Change," in Nazli Choucri, ed., *Global Accord: Environmental Challenges and Environmental Responses* (Cambridge, MA: MIT Press, 1993), pp. 50–51.

17. *Climate Change 1995: A Report of the Intergovernmental Panel on Climate Change* (www.ipcc.ch); "The Long Road to Kyoto," *FACSNET Climate Change History #33* (www.facsnet.org).

18. Wilson, "Is Humanity Suicidal?" p. 28; Miller, *Environmental Science*, p. 76.

19. "Stay Cool," *The Economist*, April 1, 1995, p. 11.

20. Vogler, "Environment and Natural Resources," p. 231.

21. "Reading the Patterns," *The Economist*, April 1, 1995, pp. 65–67; Miller, *Environmental Science*, p. 276–77.

22. Garrett Hardin, "The Tragedy of the Commons," *Science* 162 (December 1968): 1244–45.

23. Wilson, "Is Humanity Suicidal?" p. 26.

24. Miller, *Environmental Science*, p. 442.

25. Ibid., p. 506.

26. Jon Christensen, "In Arizona Desert, a Bird Oasis in Peril," *New York Times*, May 4, 1999, p. D5.

27. Brown, *Understanding International Relations*, p. 232.

28. Mahathir Mohamad, "Statement to the UN Conference on Environment and Development," in Ken Conca and Geoffrey Dabelko, eds., *Green Planet Blues: Environmental Politics from Stockholm to Kyoto*, 2nd ed. (Boulder, CO: Westview, 1998), p. 325.

29. Richard Benedick, *Ozone Diplomacy* (Cambridge, MA: Harvard University Press, 1991), p. 6.

30. Porter and Brown, *Global Environmental Politics*, p. 42.

31. Mark R. Amstutz, *International Ethics* (Lanham, MD: Rowman and Littlefield, 1999), p. 171; Jessica T. Mathews, "Power Shift," *Foreign Affairs* 76, no. 1 (January-February 1997): 55.

32. Barbara J. Bramble and Gareth Porter, "Non-Governmental Organizations and the Making of U.S. International Environmental Policy," in Andrew Hurrell and Benedict Kingsbury, eds., *The International Politics of the Environment: Actors, Interests, and Institutions* (Oxford: Oxford University Press, 1992), p. 313.

33. Amstutz, *International Ethics*, p. 171.

34. John McCormick, "The Role of Environmental NGOs in International Regimes," in Norman J. Vig and Regina S. Axelrod, eds., *The Global Environment: Institutions, Law, and Policy* (Washington, DC: Congressional Quarterly Press, 1999), p. 65.

35. Porter and Brown, *Global Environmental Politics*, pp. 56–57.

36. McCormick, "The Role of Environmental NGOs in International Regimes," p. 60.

37. Kellcher and Klein, *Global Perspectives*, p. 112.

38. Porter and Brown, *Global Environmental Politics*, p. 62.

39. Ibid., p. 45.

40. Benedick, *Ozone Diplomacy*, pp. 72, 85.

41. Miller, *Environmental Science*, pp. 80, 316–17.

42. Sara Hoagland and Susan Conbere, *Environmental Stress and National Security* (College Park, MD: Center for Global Change, University of Maryland, 1991), pp. 17, 20; Miller, *Environmental Science*, p. 274.

43. Miller, *Environmental Science*, 359–60.

44. David S. Maehr, *The Florida Panther* (Washington, DC: Island Press, 1997); P. M. Gros, "Status of the Cheetah Acinonyx Jubztus in Kenya: A Field-Interview Assessment," *Biological Conservation* 85 (1998): 137.

45. Vogler, "Environment and Natural Resources," p. 239.

46. Nazli Choucri, "Environmentalism," in Joel Krieger, ed., *The Oxford Companion to the Politics of the World* (New York: Oxford University Press, 1993), p. 269.

47. For a good account of the Med Plan, see Haas, "Making Progress in International Environmental Protection," pp. 285–305.

48. Vogler, "Environment and Natural Resources," p. 241.

49. Vinod Thomas and Tamara Belt, "Growth and the Environment: Allies or Foes?" in Robert J. Griffiths, ed., *Annual Editions: Developing World, 98/99* (Sluice Dock, Guilford, CT: Dushkin, 1998), p. 176.

50. Porter and Brown, *Global Environmental Politics*, pp. 23–27.

51. Daniel Sitarz, ed., *Agenda 21: The Earth Summit Strategy to Save Our Planet* (Boulder, CO: Earthpress, 1994), pp. 28–29.

52. Andrew Hurrell, "International Political Theory and the Environment," in Ken Booth and Steve Smith, eds., *International Relations Theory Today* (University Park, PA: The Pennsylvania State University Press, 1995), pp. 142–43.

53. Thaddeus J. Trzyna, ed., *A Sustainable World: Defining and Measuring Sustainable Development* (Sacramento: California Institute of Public Affairs, 1995), p. 23, footnote 1.

54. Sharachachandra M. Lele, "Sustainable Development: A Critical Review," in Conca and Dabelko, eds., *Green Planet*

Blues, p. 253; Alex Farrell and Maureen Hart, "What Does Sustainability Really Mean?" *Environment* 40, no. 9 (November 1998): 7.

55. Jim MacNeill, Peter Winsemius, and Taizo Yakushiji, *Beyond Interdependence: The Meshing of the World's Economy and the Earth's Ecology* (New York: Oxford University Press, 1991), p. 107.

56. Uday Desai, "Environment, Economic Growth, and Government in Developing Countries," in Uday Desai, ed., *Ecological Policy and Politics in Developing Countries* (Albany: State University of New York Press, 1998), p. 4.

57. H. Sterling Burnett, "The Developed versus the Developing," in Griffiths, ed., *Annual Editions: Developing World, 98/99*, p. 180.

58. Desai, "Environment, Economic Growth, and Government in Developing Countries," p. 3; "Fidel's Sustainable Farmers," *The Economist*, April 24, 1999, p. 34.

59. *Five Years After Rio: Innovations in Environmental Policy*, Environmentally Sustainable Development Studies and Monographs Series No. 18 (Washington, DC: The World Bank, 1997).

60. Ehrlich, "Toward a Sustainable Global Population," p. 153.

61. Quoted in Gail Robinson and William Sweet, "Environmental Threats to Stability: The Role of Population Growth," in *Great Decisions 1997* (New York: Foreign Policy Association, 1997), p. 58; Ehrlich, "Toward a Sustainable Global Population," p. 154.

62. Ehrlich, "Toward a Sustainable Global Population," pp. 154–55.

63. Jack A. Goldstone, "Imminent Political Conflicts Arising from China's Population Crisis," in Daniel H. Deudney and Richard A. Matthew, eds., *Contested Grounds: Security and Conflict in the New Environmental Politics* (Albany: State University of New York Press, 1999), pp. 247–49.

64. Barbara B. Crane, "International Population Institutions: Adaptation to a Changing World Order," in Peter M. Haas, Robert O. Keohane, and Marc A. Levy, eds., *Institutions for the Earth* (Cambridge, MA: The MIT Press, 1994), pp. 353–54, 359, 390.

65. Crane, "International Population Institutions," pp. 389–93.

66. This data can be found in William K. Stevens, "Poor Lands' Success in Cutting Birth Rate Upsets Old Theories," *New York Times*, January 2, 1994, pp. 1, 8.

67. Stevens, "Poor Lands' Success in Cutting Birth Rate Upsets Old Theories."

68. *Debt for Nature: UNESCO Environment Brief* No. 1 (1991), p. 3; Gary C. Bryner, "Agenda 21: Myth or Reality?" in Vig and Axelrod, p. 169.

69. Conservation International, "The Greening of International Finance: Ten Years of Debt-for-Nature Swaps," Washington, DC, undated mimeo; Conservation International, "Debt-for-Nature Swaps: Exchanges to Date," undated mimeo.

70. UNESCO, *Debt for Nature*, p. 5.

71. Ibid., pp. 7, 13.

72. See Conservation International, "The Greening of International Finance," pp. 4–5.

73. Lawrence E. Susskind, *Environmental Diplomacy* (Oxford: Oxford University Press, 1994), p. 21; Vogler, "Environment and Natural Resources," p. 233.

Chapter 14

1. Thucydides, *The Peloponnesian War* (New York: Modern Library, 1982), p. 351.

2. Niccolò Machiavelli, *The Prince and the Discourses* (New York: Modern Library, 1950), p. 117.

3. John Toland, *The Rising Sun* (New York: Bantam Books, 1970), p. 128.

Chapter 15

1. Stephen S. Rosenfeld, "The Most-Favored China Policy," *Washington Post*, October 10, 1997, p. A25.

2. Maurice Matloff, "Allied Strategy in Europe, 1939–1945," in Peter Paret, ed., *Makers of Modern Strategy: Machiavelli to the Nuclear Age* (Princeton: Princeton University Press, 1986), pp. 683–85.

3. See Kenneth Arrow, *Social Choice and Individual Values*, 2nd ed. (New York: Wiley, 1963), pp. 19–21, for the original theorem and proof of this argument. For a less technical presentation of the argument, see William H. Riker and Peter Ordeshook, *An Introduction to Positive Political Theory* (Englewood Cliffs, NJ: Prentice Hall, 1973), pp. 84–94.

4. Bruce Bueno de Mesquita, David Newman, and Alvin Rabushka, *Red Flag Over Hong Kong* (Chatham, NJ: Chatham House, 1996), pp. 165–66.

5. Robert Dahl, "Power as the Control of Behavior," in Steven Lukes, ed., *Power* (New York: New York University Press, 1986), pp. 41–46; David A. Baldwin, "Power Analysis and World Politics: New Trends versus Old Tendencies," *World Politics* 31, no. 2 (January 1979): 161–94.

6. Baldwin, "Power Analysis and World Politics," pp. 163–75.

7. Joseph S. Nye, Jr., "The Changing Nature of World Power," *Political Science Quarterly* 105, no. 2 (Summer 1990): 177–92.

8. Alexander L. George and William E. Simons, "Findings and Conclusions," in Alexander L. George and William E. Simons, eds., *The Limits of Coercive Diplomacy*, 2nd ed. (Boulder, CO: Westview, 1994), pp. 281–82.

9. Alistair Horne, *Harold Macmillan, Vol I: 1894–1956* (New York: Viking Penguin, 1988), p. 160.

10. Robert M. Hathaway, *Great Britain and the United States: Special Relations Since World War II* (Boston: Twayne Publishers, 1990), pp. 50–51.

11. Ray S. Cline, *World Power Trends and U.S. Foreign Policy for the 1980s* (Boulder, CO: Westview, 1980), chap. 2.

12. Karl W. Deutsch, *The Analysis of International Relations*, 3rd ed. (Englewood Cliffs, NJ: Prentice Hall, 1988), chap. 3.

13. Peter Bachrach and Morton S. Baratz, *Power and Poverty: Theory and Practice* (Oxford: Oxford University Press, 1970), pp. 47–51.

14. For examples, see Joseph Lepgold, Bruce Bueno de Mesquita, and James Morrow, "The Struggle for Mastery in Europe, 1985–1993," *International Interactions* 22, no. 1 (1996): 41–66; de Mesquita, Newman, and Rabushka, *Red Flag Over Hong Kong*.

15. Alan C. Lamborn, *The Price of Power* (Boston: Unwin Ayman, 1991), chap. 9.

16. See Colin S. Gray, *Weapons Don't Make War: Policy, Strategy, and Military Technology* (Lawrence, KS: University Press of Kansas, 1993).

17. Robert Jervis, *Perception and Misperception in International Politics* (Princeton: Princeton University Press, 1976), pp. 14–15.

18. Louis Halle, *American Foreign Policy* (London: G. Allen, 1960), pp. 316–18, quoted in Alexander L. George, *Presidential Decisionmaking in Foreign Policy* (Boulder, CO: Westview Press, 1980), p. 55 (emphasis in original).

19. See, among others, Jervis, *Perception and Misperception*; Robert Jervis, "Hypotheses on Misperception," *World Politics* 20, no. 3 (April 1968): 454–79; George, *Presidential Decisionmaking in Foreign Policy*, chap. 3; James F. Voss and Ellen Dorsey, "Perceptions and International Relations: An Overview," in Eric Singer and Valerie Hudson, eds., *Political Psychology and Foreign Policy* (Boulder, CO: Westview, 1992), pp. 3–30; Michael D. Young and Mark Schafer, "Is There Method in Our Madness? Ways of Assessing Cognition in International Relations," *Mershon International Studies Review* 42 (1998): 63–96; Philip E. Tetlock and Charles B. McGuire, Jr., "Cognitive Perspectives on Foreign Policy," in G. John Ikenberry, Jr., *American Foreign Policy: Theoretical Essays* (New York: HarperCollins, 1996), pp. 536–54.

20. Robert Jervis, *The Logic of Images in International Relations* (Princeton: Princeton University Press, 1970), p. 5.

21. Susan T. Fiske and Shelley E. Taylor, *Social Cognition*, 2nd ed. (New York: McGraw-Hill, 1991), pp. 381–91.

22. Yaacov Vertzberger, *The World in Their Minds* (Stanford: Stanford University Press, 1990), pp. 300–301.

23. Abraham Lowenthal, *The Dominican Intervention* (Cambridge, MA: Harvard University Press, 1972), pp. 154–55.

24. Jervis, "Hypotheses on Misperception," p. 456.

25. Jervis, *Perception and Misperception in International Politics*, pp. 319–26.

26. Ibid., p. 326.

27. Raymond Cohen, *Theatre of Power* (London: Longman, 1987), p. 20.

28. Richard Neustadt, *Alliance Politics* (New York: Columbia University Press, 1970).

29. Richard Nisbett and Lee Ross, *Human Inference* (Englewood Cliffs, NJ: Prentice Hall, 1980), p. 228.

30. See, among other works, Alexander Wendt, "Anarchy Is What States Make of It," *International Organization* 46, no. 2 (Spring 1992): 391–425; Michael Barnett, "Institutions, Roles, and Disorder: The Case of the Arab States System," *International Studies Quarterly* 37, no. 3 (September 1993): 271–96; Martha Finnemore, *National Interests in International Society* (Ithaca, NY: Cornell University Press, 1996).

31. Finnemore, *National Interests in International Society*, p. 22.

32. Martha Finnemore, "Military Intervention and the Organization of International Politics," in Joseph Lepgold and Thomas G. Weiss, eds., *Collective Conflict Management and Changing World Politics* (Albany: State University of New York Press, 1998).

33. Robert O. Keohane and Craig N. Murphy, "International Institutions," in Mary Hawkesworth and Maurice Kogan, eds., *Encyclopedia of Government and Politics* (New York: Routledge, 1992), p. 871.

34. Richard Price and Nina Tannenwald, "Norms and Deterrence: The Nuclear and Chemical Weapons Taboos," in Peter J. Katzenstein, ed., *The Culture of National Security* (New York: Columbia University Press, 1996), pp. 134–43.

35. This point has been discussed in many books and articles and has been documented in thousands of laboratory experiments. See, among other works, Herbert A. Simon, *The Sciences of the Artificial*, 2nd ed. (Cambridge: MIT Press, 1981), chap. 3; James G. March and Herbert A. Simon, *Organizations* (New York: Wiley, 1958), chap. 6; David W. Miller and Martin K. Starr, *The Structure of Human Decisions* (Englewood Cliffs, NJ: Prentice Hall, 1967), p. 62.

36. Simon and March, *Organizations*, 140; Robert W. Jackman, "Rationality and Political Participation," *American Journal of Political Science* 37, no. 1 (February 1993): 279–90; Herbert A. Simon, *Administrative Behavior*, 3rd ed. (New York: Free Press, 1976), pp. xxviii–xxx, Herbert A. Simon, "From Substantive to Procedural Rationality," in Spiro J. Latsis, ed., *Method and Appraisal in Economics* (Cambridge, UK: Cambridge University Press, 1976), pp. 130–31.

37. Irving L. Janis and Leon Mann, *Decision Making: A Psychological Analysis of Conflict, Choice, and Commitment* (New York: Free Press, 1977), pp. 29–30.

38. David Braybrooke and Charles E. Lindblom, *A Strategy of Decision* (New York: Free Press, 1963), chap. 5.

39. This paragraph draws heavily on Janis and Mann, *Decision Making*, pp. 29–30.

40. Ole Holsti, "Crisis Decision Making," in Philip E. Tetlock et al., eds., *Behavior, Society, and Nuclear War*, vol. I (New York: Oxford University Press, 1979), pp. 31–32; Janis and Mann, *Decision Making*, p. 22.

41. Richard Cyert and James G. March, *A Behavioral Theory of the Firm* (Englewood Cliffs, NJ: Prentice Hall, 1963), pp. 101–12.

42. Ibid., p. 103.

43. Richard K. Betts, "A Nuclear Golden Age? The Balance Before Parity," *International Security* 11, no. 3 (Winter 1986–1987): 3–32.

44. Stephen D. Krasner, "American Policy and Global Economic Stability," in William P. Avery and David P.

Rapkin, eds., *America in a Changing World Political Economy* (New York: Longman, 1982), pp. 29–38.

45. David A. Baldwin, "The Costs of Power," *Journal of Conflict Resolution* 15, no. 2 (June 1971): 146.

46. See McGeorge Bundy, George F. Kennan, Robert S. McNamara, and Gerard Smith, "Nuclear Weapons and the Atlantic Alliance," *Foreign Affairs* 60, no. 4 (Spring 1982): 753–68. For one among many responses to this article, see Karl Kaiser, Georg Leber, Alois Mertes, and Franz-Josef Schulze, "Nuclear Weapons and the Preservation of Peace: A German Response to No First Use," *Foreign Affairs* 60, no. 5 (Summer 1982): 1157–70.

47. Krasner, "America Policy and Global Economic Stability," pp. 38–43.

48. Bruce Bueno de Mesquita, David Newman, and Alvin Rabushka, *Forecasting Political Events: The Future of Hong Kong* (New Haven: Yale University Press, 1985), p. 20.

49. Daniel Kahneman and Amos Tversky, "The Psychology of Preferences," *Scientific American* 246 (1982): 16–173; Jack S. Levy, "An Introduction to Prospect Theory," in Barbara Farnham, ed., *Avoiding Losses/Taking Risks: Prospect Theory and International Conflict* (Ann Arbor: University of Michigan Press, 1994), pp. 10–15.

50. David A. Welch, "The Organizational Process and Bureaucratic Politics Paradigms," *International Security* 17, no. 2 (Fall 1992): 126–27.

51. Robert Woodward, *The Commanders* (New York: Simon & Schuster, 1991), pp. 220–21, 247; Welch, "The Organizational Process," p. 124.

52. Welch, "The Organizational Process," p. 128.

53. Raymond Cohen, *Negotiating Across Cultures* (Washington, DC: United States Institute of Peace Press, 1991), p. 92.

54. Peter G. Bourne, *Jimmy Carter* (New York: Scribner, 1997), p. 459; Betty Glad, *Jimmy Carter: In Search of the Great White House* (New York: Norton, 1980), p. 470.

Chapter 16

1. Thomas C. Schelling, "Strategic Analysis and Social Problems," in Thomas C. Schelling, *Choice and Consequence* (Cambridge, MA: Harvard University Press, 1984), pp. 205–6.

2. John Lewis Gaddis, "Containment: Its Past and Future," *International Security* 5, no. 4 (Spring 1981): 74.

3. "McNaughton Draft for McNamara on 'Proposed Course of Action,'" March 24, 1965, Document #96, *The Pentagon Papers* (New York: Bantam Books, 1971), p. 432.

4. Edward Friedman, "The Challenge of a Rising China: Another Germany?" in Robert J. Lieber, ed., *Eagle Adrift: American Foreign Policy at the End of the Century* (New York: Longman, 1997), pp. 241–42.

5. Robert Axelrod and Robert O. Keohane, "Achieving Cooperation Under Anarchy: Strategies and Institutions," in Kenneth A. Oye, ed., *Cooperation Under Anarchy* (Princeton: Princeton University Press, 1986), p. 232.

6. For an interesting example of such alleged cooperation across a number of Middle East and African States, see "U.S. Has Moved to Contain Wealthy Bombing Suspect," *Washington Post*, August 13, 1998, pp. A1, A27.

7. This category of games is called "noncooperative," although one of the major questions in analyzing world politics is whether actors' preferences create incentives for them to cooperate.

8. James D. Morrow, *Game Theory for Political Scientists* (Princeton: Princeton University Press, 1994), p. 8.

9. Kenneth Waltz, *Man, the State, and War* (New York: Columbia University Press, 1959), pp. 167–68.

10. Robert Axelrod, *The Evolution of Cooperation* (New York: Basic Books, 1984); Robert O. Keohane, *After Hegemony* (Princeton: Princeton University Press, 1984), pp. 75–78.

11. Robert O. Keohane and Joseph S. Nye, Jr., "Two Cheers for Multilateralism," *Foreign Policy* 60 (Fall 1985): 158.

12. Walter LaFeber, *America, Russia, and the Cold War, 1945–1992*, 7th ed. (New York: McGraw-Hill, 1993), p. 223.

13. For a discussion of the model and its success rate, see Bruce Bueno de Mesquita, David Newman, and Alvin Rabushka, *Red Flag Over Hong Kong* (Chatham, NJ: Chatham Publishers, 1996), p. 70 and Appendix B. For examples of its use in the security area, see Bruce Bueno de Mesquita and David Lalman, *War and Reason: Domestic and International Imperatives* (New Haven, CT: Yale University Press, 1992). For examples of its use in economic and environmental issue areas, see Bruce Bueno de Mesquita and Frans N. Stokman, eds., *European Community Decision Making* (New Haven, CT: Yale University Press, 1994), chaps. 4, 6, 8.

Glossary

absolute advantage An assumption that every country will have one or more products that it can either make better or sell cheaper than any international competitor.

adjustment policies Government monetary and fiscal policies that can promote either inflation or deflation; often used to try to affect the international price of national currencies.

agenda setting The process by which issues become identified as topics worthy of analysis and action by policy makers.

arms control Multilateral efforts to mutually limit the development, deployment, or use of weapons.

balance of payments The aggregate value of the payments, gifts, and capital flowing out of a country compared to the aggregate value of the payments, gifts, and capital coming in.

balance of trade The net value of exports minus imports; a positive balance of trade is called a favorable balance of trade.

balance on capital account The portion of the overall balance of payments that involves the sale and purchase of stocks, bonds, and other assets between private individuals and firms in different states.

balance on current account The portion of the overall balance of payments that involves the export and import of goods and services.

balance-of-payments problem A situation in which the aggregate value of the payments, gifts, and capital that flow out of a country is greater than the aggregate value coming in.

balancing A diplomatic strategy of allying with the weaker side during a conflict to form a blocking coalition that could prevent the strongest states from becoming too powerful.

band-wagoning A strategy of allying with the stronger side during a conflict.

belief A causal or factual assumption about politics or social life.

belief system An interrelated set of causal and factual assumptions about some aspect of the world.

biological weapons Weapons made of microorganisms that cause lethal or disabling diseases.

brinkmanship A strategy in which actors threaten shared disaster in an effort to force other actors to capitulate.

bureaucratic politics A situation in which the preferences and choices of government policy makers are driven by their desire to protect the interests of the agency they represent and advance their personal political power.

capabilities The size of an actor's economic or military resources.

carrying capacity The level of use beyond which an ecosystem or other natural or human system can no longer sustain itself.

chemical weapons Gaseous, liquid, or solid chemicals used to poison, asphyxiate, or disable large numbers of people.

choice heuristics The mental shortcuts people use to generalize from the data they perceive.

classical balance of power A decentralized system for managing interstate conflict that emerged in Europe after the Peace of Westphalia.

classical realism A worldview based on the assumption that the principal sources of conflict in politics lie in human nature because people are self-interested, competitive, and power hungry.

coalition A group of two or more factions (or individuals) with different preferences over outcomes (ends) but compatible preferences on a specific set of policies that they agree to cooperate with each other to achieve.

cognitive limits Variations in people's ability to process and evaluate all the information potentially available to them.

collective action problems Problems that occur when people have no incentive to help pay for the provision of a collective (public) good.

collective (public) good A good or service (usually a benefit, but the logic also applies to costs, sometimes called "public bads") that cannot be withheld from any member of a group once it is provided to a single member of that group.

collective security A diplomatic system designed to promote peace and guarantee the security of its members by promising help for any member who is attacked; unlike standard military alliances, which target actors outside the alliance, collective security systems are designed principally to deter aggression within the community.

comparative advantage A doctrine that asserts that every economic entity (whether it is a person, company, or country) will be better off in the long run if it specializes in producing what it can do best, even if others can produce the same goods more efficiently.

compellence (or coercive diplomacy) The use or threatened use of force to make actors change their behavior.

constituency arena The collection of relationships and strategic contexts within which policy factions interact with their mass and elite constituencies—the actors whose support those factions need in order to continue in the role of policy maker.

constituency politics The relationships and interactions that connect policy-making factions with their constituents and political backers.

containment A term originally used to refer to the U.S. policy of preventing Soviet territorial expansion during the Cold War; the term has increasingly been used to refer to any strategy designed to keep a threat isolated (contained) within its current territory.

counterfactual argument An argument that explores what might have happened if some central factor had been different.

crimes against humanity Human rights abuses that are so extreme that they are regarded as a crime against all the people in the world.

critical theory A research approach that advocates using an understanding of the interrelationships among values, ideas, observation, and the structure of society to change the world in ways that will help the poor and politically weak.

cyberterrorism The destruction of computer-based information and communication systems.

debt-service ratio The ratio of interest payments due on foreign loans relative to foreign exchange earnings; since this ratio does not include payments toward the amount borrowed, it measures the ability to service a debt, not repay it.

defense The use of force to physically stop an ongoing or imminent attack.

dependencia The Latin American version of the dependency perspective, which argues that global capitalism keeps Third World countries poor by forcing them to specialize in producing commodities and other primary products for export, while importing expensive industrial and high-technology goods from rich countries.

dependency perspective An interpretation of economic development that views capitalism as responsible for keeping the countries of the Third World poor by forcing them to specialize in producing commodities and other primary products for export while importing expensive industrial and high-technology goods from rich countries.

desertification Formally defined as a 10 percent decline in the productive potential of arid and semi-arid land.

deterrence Threats of force to prevent actors from doing something they would otherwise do; for deterrence to work, there must be *both* a credible threat and a jointly acceptable peaceful alternative.

dialectical materialism Marx's theory that changes in people's relationships to the means of production drive the evolution of economic systems, the political systems that develop in response to those changes in the structure of the economy, and the ways in which people conceptualize the world around them.

differential income-elasticity of demand The expectation that increases in the wealth of poor countries will produce a greater marginal demand for more imports than increases in the wealth of rich countries.

diffuse reciprocity A relationship in which people help each other out without keeping track of who gave what to whom.

disarmament Efforts to eliminate a particular type of weapon. Used by itself, the term typically refers to multilateral efforts toward mutual disarmament; when single states decide to disarm, regardless of what other actors do, it's called unilateral disarmament.

discounting People's tendency to prefer current benefits more than future benefits and future costs more than current costs; they are likely to accept a higher cost in exchange for delaying when it has to be paid and a smaller benefit in exchange for receiving it sooner.

division of labor A situation in which people specialize in different economic roles and activities.

dominant strategy A situation in which actors have a strategic option that remains their best available choice no matter what the other actors choose; when actors do not have a dominant strategy, it's hard to decide which option to choose because their best option varies with the choices others make.

dual-use technologies and products Technologies and products designed for peaceful uses in civilian life that can be easily converted into weapons.

dumping Selling products below cost (or, in some versions, at only a negligible profit) in a foreign market.

economic interdependence A condition that exists when two or more people, organizations, or societies depend on each other's goods, services, natural resources, or capital for their continued prosperity.

ecosystem A spatially bounded habitat within which plant and animal species interact with each other and with the chemical and physical processes that sustain life.

empirical sovereignty An actor's ability to make an effective internal claim to sovereign control within the boundaries of a state.

equilibrium outcome An outcome in which none of the actors in a strategically interdependent situation has an incentive to make unilateral changes.

ethnic communities (sometimes called nations) Groups of people who believe they have a common ancestry, history, and culture; usually, ethnic communities also share an attachment to a particular territorial homeland and a commitment to promote a shared future as a distinctive community.

exchange rate The price at which one currency is traded for another.

externalities Involuntary costs and benefits imposed on people as the result of the actions (usually the provision of a good or service) of others.

faction A group of actors who have identical preferences over both outcomes and policies.

factional politics Interactions of policy-making factions within international actors.

fair trade A term used by critics of existing free trade practices, including both those who want countries to compete based on true opportunity costs and those who want to alter market forces to reflect local beliefs about just wages and working conditions.

feminist tradition A worldview and research approach that focuses on the origins and effects of socially constructed gender identities and roles; feminist interpretations argue that a more fully feminist understanding of world politics will lay the groundwork for more just social, political, and economic arrangements.

finance capitalism A term popularized by Lenin that refers to the union of banking and industrial monopolies.

Financial Revolution The introduction of bank notes, paper money, and other credit instruments in the late eighteenth and early nineteenth century that ended the reliance on specie and—along with the Industrial Revolution—marked the beginning of the end of mercantilism.

fixed-exchange-rate system A monetary system in which the relative values of national currencies are set by interstate agreement and remain fixed at those values until a new agreement is reached.

float A situation in which the relative values of national currencies are set by international currency markets.

foreign direct investment (FDI) Situations in which a trans-state business enterprise or other actor owns and controls assets in a foreign state.

foreign exchange National currencies that are generally accepted in international trade and finance.

free float A monetary system in which there is no government intervention at all in international currency markets.

free trade A policy that eliminates government controls and taxes on interstate trade.

free-riding A situation that occurs when actors consume a collective good without helping to pay for it.

functionalism An intellectual tradition that assumes that the state system is the principal cause of war and that if apolitical, non-state actors could help people meet their basic human needs, the state system would ultimately become irrelevant and disappear, creating a more just and peaceful world.

game theory A theoretic approach to identify situational incentives by analyzing variations in the compatibility of actors' preferences and the effects of strategic interaction over time.

global commons The atmosphere and open-access areas that are shared by all states but possessed by none.

globalization The increasing integration of national economies into a global one and, more generally, the declining meaningfulness of state boundaries in an era characterized by the growing number of global trans-state communication, transportation, and economic networks.

gold standard An international monetary system in which the national currencies used in interstate transactions are backed by a promise to redeem them in gold on demand.

gross domestic product (GDP) The value of all the goods and services produced annually inside a state.

gross world product (GWP) The total value of goods and services produced worldwide.

hard currencies Currencies that have a relatively stable value in the international currency market; until 1971, when the gold standard was abandoned, the term denoted currencies backed by gold.

hard loans Loans from multilateral lending agencies that are granted only if the projects in which those loans are invested have the potential to generate profits sufficient to pay the loan back with interest.

harmony of interests A doctrine that assumes individual and community interests coincide; frequently serves as the basis for assertions that liberating actors to pursue their individual goals is compatible with achieving what is best for the community as a whole.

image A person's beliefs about a particular actor.

institutions Organized sets of rules that structure people's roles, expectations, and behavior.

intellectual property Works of art, literature, and software that are protected by patents, copyrights, and trademarks.

intergenerational equity The principle that economic growth should be promoted in ways that protect both the economic and environmental interests of future generations.

international actor Any individual, faction, or coalition that attempts to achieve objectives across the boundaries of two or more countries.

international arena The collection of interstate and trans-state relationships and strategic contexts within which international politics takes place.

international intergovernmental organizations (IGOs) Formal international institutions with an ongoing administrative structure that have states (and only states) as members.

international law Rules designed to regulate the interstate activities of state and non-state actors.

international non-governmental organizations (NGOs) International organizations created by private individuals and groups.

international politics Trans-border actions of state and non-state actors.

international regime An agreed-upon set of principles, norms, rules, and procedures for coordinating multilateral action in an issue area.

interstate politics The interactions of states.

intra-firm trade Interstate commercial transactions that take place between subsidiaries of the same trans-state business enterprise.

involuntary defection A situation in which policy makers are unable to honor an agreement even though they want to.

iterated game A game that has multiple rounds; iterated games frequently have dramatically different strategic incentives than the one-round versions.

juridical (legal) sovereignty The right under international law and custom to make choices free from the legally binding control of other actors either within or outside the state.

jus gentium The "law of the peoples," originally developed by the Romans in an effort to create a set of universal laws that would apply to relations between Rome and citizens from other societies.

laissez-faire A policy that calls for government nonintervention in the economy, except for the essential minimum required to protect security and establish the legal bases for free exchange.

legal positivism A tradition that asserts that states are only bound to honor rules they accept either through formal treaty or long-established custom and practice.

legal rules Binding obligations created by a formal political process that identifies both the substance of the laws and the governmental agencies that have the right and responsibility to enforce them.

levels of analysis Different points on a scale of social or natural aggregation at which behavior can be observed and assessed.

liberalism Traditionally, a worldview that emphasizes finding ways to promote individual liberty and to identify and achieve common objectives that create joint gains.

linkage politics Ways in which choices and outcomes in one particular political arena are affected by what goes on in other arenas.

local content rules Government regulations in a host country that require foreign businesses to use a minimum amount of products from the host country in the goods they import for sale.

"loose nukes" problem Fears that nuclear material and weapons developed by states will fall into the hands of terrorists.

managed float A monetary system in which governments work together to try to keep the value of their currencies within a particular range.

market Any arrangement among buyers and sellers that determines the prices and quantities of a good or service.

Marxism A worldview that uses an economic and historical analysis of the evolution of class conflict called dialectical materialism to identify the origins of revolution, peace, and justice.

mercantilism A set of beliefs about political economy that assumed that wealth could only be discovered, not created, and that the best way to accumulate wealth was in precious metals.

minimax strategy Choosing the option that minimizes the maximum worst result that can occur; often recommended in situations in which actors do not have a dominant strategy.

misperception Error caused by the failure to notice something that is present or by an incorrect inference about something that is accurately noticed.

mixed strategy A strategy in which actors vary their choice to cooperate or compete in each round of an iterated game depending on what the other actors did in the preceding round.

moral rules Freely accepted obligations based on people's understanding of right and wrong, which are not enforceable by political authorities unless they are supported by a companion set of legal rules.

most-favored-nation principle (MFN) Every member of a multilateral organization must be given the same access to a country's domestic market as the "most-favored-nation."

motivated (hot) misperception An error created by an individual's emotions or the desire to make the world fit preconceived notions.

N-1, or consistency, problem The benchmark currency in a fixed-exchange rate system cannot solve pressures on the international value of its currency by changing its exchange rate because, being the benchmark, any changes in its value will simply lead to adjustments in all the other currencies.

nation A group of people who share a common identity as a social entity.

national interest The idea that all the people in a state have some core collective concerns.

nationalism The feeling members of a group have when they perceive themselves as having a common identity based on a shared past and a commitment to a shared future.

natural law A tradition that asserts that there are universal principles—usually based in religion but sometimes also in nature—that exist independent of states and the political process.

neocolonialism The continued external control and exploitation of post-colonial societies after they have gained formal independence.

neofunctionalism An intellectual tradition that shares the functionalist assumption that the state system causes war, but which also holds that because strategies to provide basic human needs are inescapably political, states must be given political incentives to rely on non-state actors.

neomercantilism The use of government intervention to promote exports and restrict imports in order to protect domestic employment and wages.

neorealism (also called **structural realism**) A worldview based on the assumption that the anarchic nature of the interstate system is the principal source of conflict in world politics.

new imperialism A period of renewed colonial expansion that began around 1880.

newly industrializing countries (NICs) States that show dramatic increases in wealth as they industrialize for the first time.

Non-Aligned Movement A coalition of countries founded in 1955 that advocated remaining neutral in the Cold War.

norms Moral rules (freely accepted obligations based on people's understanding of right and wrong) that are widely accepted within a community.

nuclear weapons Weapons that use an atomic fission or fusion process to create enormous heat and blast effects that destroy and irradiate targets.

objective security Actual, as distinct from perceived, security; an actor is objectively secure if no one wants to attack it, or if it can deter a threatened attack, or if it can defeat an actual attack at an acceptable cost.

old colonialism The period of European colonial expansion that began in the late 1400s and lasted until the Napoleonic wars.

operational environment The setting in which an actor's choice is actually taking place.

opportunity costs The level of lost opportunity when actors choose one option over another; the bigger the forgone value, the higher the opportunity cost.

optimize To search for the best possible option available.

outcome legitimacy The perceived legitimacy of a particular result, as distinct from the process by which that result was achieved.

perception The process of noticing and evaluating incoming information.

physiocrats A group of eighteenth-century French economists who argued that government-imposed taxes and regulations on trade were both a violation of the natural order and counterproductive.

policy-making arena The collection of relationships and strategic contexts within which factions form coalitions that can act in the name of an international actor.

policy risk The probability that actors' substantive goals will not be achieved even if their policy choices are implemented effectively.

political economy The ways in which political choices, institutions, and rules shape and are shaped by markets.

political risk The probability that policy choices will hurt actors' political positions.

portfolio investment The purchase of stocks, bonds, and other financial instruments, in which the enterprises are either owned or operated by others.

positive law Laws formally adopted by recognized authorities.

power Actors' ability to increase the probability that their preferred outcomes will occur.

preemptive attack Situations in which actors, believing they are about to be attacked, strike first to gain a military advantage.

preferences A set of alternatives that an actor has ordered from most to least attractive.

preferences over outcomes The relative attractiveness of different ends, as opposed to the methods by which those ends might be achieved.

preferences over policies The relative attractiveness of the different means (or instruments) by which a specific end (or goal) can be achieved.

preponderance (or hegemony) A situation in which one state is so strong that it can dominate all the others.

principal-agent problems Difficulties that arise either when agents have trouble identifying the wishes of their principal, or when principals have difficulty getting their agents to do what they want.

principle of conditionality The requirement that countries take steps to reduce the sources of their balance-of-payments problems before the IMF provides short-term aid.

principle of effective occupation An agreement among European colonizers to recognize the claim of whichever colonizer first gained control over a specific piece of Africa, which set off a scramble to partition Africa as quickly as possible.

principle of reciprocity Members of GATT (and now the WTO) are not expected to make concessions on access to their markets unless they receive equivalent access in return.

principal supplier rule A rule under GATT that negotiations on tariff reductions on a particular product must be handled by countries that produced 10 percent or more of the world trade in that product.

private good A good or service that can be possessed or consumed by an individual without making it available to others.

private international law The interstate rights and duties of individuals and other non-governmental actors.

process legitimacy The perceived legitimacy of the procedures or means by which an outcome is reached.

production structure The set of economic relationships that determines what is produced in what locations, for which purchasers, and at what prices.

prospect theory A scholarly tradition that assumes people are more concerned with preventing losses than achieving gains.

protectionism Any government policy or practice designed to shield its national market from external competition.

psychological environment Actors' mental image of the world around them, sometimes quite different from their operational environment.

public international law The legal rights and duties of sovereign states.

purposive choice Situations in which actors choose transitively (consistently) among ordered preferences so as to maximize their expected satisfaction.

rationality In casual, everyday usage refers to choices made after a comprehensive evaluation of all the possible options for achieving a worthy goal.

realism A worldview that assumes incompatible goals and conflict are the defining features of politics and therefore argues that actors must focus on relative gains, relative power, and security.

reciprocal compensation The practice of reshuffling the territory of smaller states to rebalance the distribution of military power after wars.

repatriation of profits A situation in which trans-state business enterprises send the profits earned by their foreign subsidiaries back to their home country rather than reinvesting them in the host country where they were earned.

replacement levels The birth rate at which populations will neither increase nor decrease in size.

reserve asset Money and other financial assets set aside as savings.

restoration The principle that the primary response to human rights abuses should be an effort to achieve social peace through material and nonmaterial compensation that "makes victims whole."

retribution The principle that wrongdoers should suffer in proportion to the suffering they have caused others.

right of establishment The legal right of a foreign firm to enter, operate, and incorporate under local, host-country law.

risk-taking preferences Actors' willingness to take a chance that either their political or policy objectives may not be fully achieved.

rogue states Countries whose leaders appear to be trying to acquire weapons of mass destruction to aid terrorists or challenge existing international norms and institutions.

satisfice A search process in which actors look for options and evaluate the ones they see only until they find an option that meets a minimum standard.

second-strike nuclear forces Nuclear weapons designed and deployed in ways that make it possible for them to survive a surprise nuclear attack.

security dilemma A situation in which one actor's efforts to increase its security decreases the security of others, even when the first actor's choices reflected defensive motives.

sensitivity How quickly and directly events in one state affect people in other states.

shadow of the future The ways in which people's guesses about what the future may hold affect their judgments about the relative attractiveness of the different choices they are considering.

side-payments Concessions (or payoffs) given to members of coalitions to entice or reward cooperation.

social choice Choices made by coalitions.

social constructivism An approach that focuses on how people's identities, ideas, and goals are affected by their participation in social groups during particular historical periods and how their socially constructed understandings and perceptions in turn shape the ways in which political cooperation and conflict are organized.

Social Darwinism (also called *natural history*) A pseudoscientific adaptation of Darwin's ideas about evolution, natural selection, and survival of the fittest that argued that civilization advanced through the struggle of race against race and nation against nation.

social identity traditions Research approaches that assume individuals' self-images, values, preferences, and perceptions are principally determined by the characteristics of the groups to which they belong.

soft law Formal multilateral agreements that do not have binding legal obligations.

soft loans Loans from multilateral lending agencies that are granted with concessionary (below-market) interest rates and very long pay-back periods, typically granted for projects that combine a high social value with a low potential for profit.

sovereign territoriality A legal and political principle that asserts a claim to final authority within the territorial boundaries of a state and denies the legitimacy of any higher authority outside the state.

sovereignty A legal and political principle that asserts a claim to final authority within the territorial boundaries of a state and denies the legitimacy of any higher authority outside the state.

special drawing rights A 1968 change in IMF rules that granted member countries an additional line of credit above that merited by the size of their contribution to the fund.

specie Money coined in precious metals, usually gold or silver.

stagflation A combination of stagnant growth and high inflation.

standard operating procedures (SOPs) Well-established and routine procedures people use to carry out repeated activities.

state A form of political organization that claims the exclusive right to govern a specific piece of territory.

strategic choice Choices made when people both believe that their ability to achieve their goals depends on the choices of other actors and evaluate the relative attractiveness of their options based on what they prefer and what they expect others to do.

strategic interaction A situation in which actors are involved in a sequence of interdependent strategic choices.

strategic interdependence A situation in which the outcomes generated by each individual's choices and actions depend on the choices and actions of the others.

strategic vulnerability The inherent weakness or strength of an actor's situation if it is attacked; actors that are vulnerable may still be relatively secure if no powerful actors want to attack them.

strict reciprocity A relationship in which people help each other out only as long as they are repaid quickly in comparable amounts.

subjective security Actors' perceptions about how secure they are.

subsistence farming An agricultural system in which food is grown for the personal use of the farmer and for exchange in local markets; implies that farmers are able to produce little, if any, beyond what is necessary to survive.

sucker's payoff A situation in which the actor who cooperates is double-crossed and receives the worst possible outcome.

superpowers A term coined in the late 1940s to characterize the military capabilities of the United States and the Soviet Union, which dwarfed those of any other state.

sustainable development Organizing economic activity to promote economic growth and protect the environment; emphasizes the importance of identifying and respecting environmental limits.

suzerain systems Hierarchically arranged networks of semi-autonomous political entities; in which none of the rulers—not even the highest ranking—is sovereign.

tariffs Government-imposed taxes on imports.

terms of trade A comparison of the price of the products countries export and import.

terrorists Individuals or groups who use violence or the threat of violence against innocent bystanders to achieve political purposes.

theory An intellectual tool for examining questions about the world systematically through a number of linked "if-then" assertions about cause and effect.

threat A situation of impending danger when an actor has both the power and intent (expressed or implied) to harm another.

threshold effects The point at which the nature of a relationship between two or more variables changes and, thus, "crosses a threshold."

time horizons How far people look into the future when assessing the possible implications of a choice they are considering.

tragedy of the commons Situations in which people have an incentive to increase their consumption of a collective good even though that increased consumption will significantly reduce either the quality or supply of the good.

transactions costs The direct cost of reaching and implementing an agreement, whether those costs are financial, political, or human.

transactions demand The varying need (demand) for money as a medium of exchange.

transitive choice Situations in which actors who have ordered their preferences choose consistently among those ordered preferences.

transparency An outsider's ability to know what an actor is doing quickly enough to make well-informed choices.

trans-state actors (TSAs) Private individuals, groups, and organizations located in two or more states that maintain their relationships without depending on government organizations and channels of communication.

trans-state business enterprises (TSBEs) Business firms with headquarters in one state and affiliates in at least one other state; also called multinational corporations (MNCs) or transnational corporations (TNCs).

trans-state criminal organizations Networks of criminal activities in two or more states.

trans-state politics The actions of non-governmental actors that have effects that cut across state boundaries.

trans-state religious organizations Religious groups that organize across state boundaries to promote their faith.

Triffin's dilemma An economic principle that states that relying on one national currency to provide enough money for international transactions, while simultaneously expecting that currency to serve as a reserve asset, will generate unsustainable pressures on its value in a fixed-exchange-rate, gold-standard system.

underconsumptionist thesis An interpretation of patterns in domestic and foreign investment that stresses the negative effects on domestic aggregate economic demand—and thus on the incentives to increase domestic investment—created by keeping workers' wages far lower than their productivity justifies.

undervalued currency A term that is used when observers believe the value of a country's currency is below the price it should have in an open international market.

unitary actors Actors that have a single set of preferences over both outcomes and policies; individuals and factions are, by definition, unitary actors, but coalitions are not.

universal jurisdiction Crimes that may be investigated and prosecuted by any state.

unmotivated (cold) misperception An error created by cognitive (mental) limits on an individual's ability to process information.

utility The value an actor attaches to a particular outcome.

voluntary defection A situation in which policy makers decide not to honor an agreement even when they could.

voluntary export restraint agreement (VER) An agreement to reduce exports that is used when policy makers want to maintain a formal position in favor of free trade at the same time as they demand restrictions on foreign access to their markets.

vulnerability How hard it will be for an actor to adjust successfully to changes in its relationship with some other actor(s).

weapons of mass destruction (WMD) Nuclear, biological, and chemical weapons capable of killing enormous numbers of people.

world federalists Those who argue that the best way to create a more peaceful and just world is to create a federal system of world government in which existing sovereign states take on reduced roles analogous to states in the United States.

worldview A distinctive way of understanding political life that includes a set of central concerns that its advocates believe are defining aspects of political life as well as a set of cause-and-effect assumptions about how the political world works.

Photo Credits

CHAPTER 1 UN/DPI Photo/James Skovmand, *1*; Dufka/Getty Images Inc.-Hulton Archive Photos, *5*; SuperStock, Inc., *19 (left)*; Mike Yamashita/Woodfin Camp & Associates, *19 (right)*

CHAPTER 2 Rob DeGeorge, *31 (Peace button)*; Frent Collection/Corbis, *31 (Communist Press button)*; Museo del Prado, Madrid, Spain/A.K.G., Berlin; SuperStock, *33*; Courtesy of the Library of Congress, *35*; Bettmann/Corbis, *40*; Anti-Slavery International, *42 (left and right)*; AP/Wide World Photos, *44*; Homer Sykes/Woodfin Camp & Associates, *49*

CHAPTER 3 IISD/ENK-Leila Mead/IISD International Institute for Sustainable Development, *55*; Bettmann/Corbis, *59 (left)*; Owen Franken/Corbis, *59 (right)*; © 1995 Walterson/Dist. by Universal Press Syndicate, *61, 67, 69*

CHAPTER 4 SuperStock, Inc., *76*; AP/Wide World Photos, *82*; Culver Pictures, Inc., *84*; Michael Elazier, Congressional Black Caucus, June 1999, *89*; AP/Wide World Photos, *92*

CHAPTER 5 AFP/Corbis, *96*; UN/DPI Photo, *106*; AP/Wide World Photos, *125 (left and right)*; Reuters/Toshiyuki Aizawa/Getty Images Inc.-Hulton Archive Photos, *129*

CHAPTER 6 The Granger Collection, *131*

CHAPTER 7 Bettmann/Corbis, *164*

CHAPTER 8 Peter C. Brandt/Getty Images Inc.-Stone, *223*; Bill Foley/Woodfin Camp & Associates, *226*; Sahm Doherty/TimePix, *232*; Corbis, *247*

CHAPTER 9 Naples Docks, Italy, artist unknown, 14th century, Capodimonte Museum, Naples/Theartarchive, *257*; Andrew Butler/The National Trust Photographic Library, *259*; Courtesy U.S. Naval Academy Museum, *275*; The Granger Collection, New York, *285*; Russian propaganda poster celebrating 1st May: "You have nothing to lose but your chains, but the world will soon be yours," Museum of the Revolution, Moscow/Bridgeman Art Library, London, *286*

CHAPTER 10 Stone/Getty Images Inc.-Stone, *290*; Corbis, *296*; Getty Images Inc.-Hulton Archive Photos, *297*; Library of Congress, *298*; AP/Wide World Photos, *299*

CHAPTER 11 AFP/Corbis, *334*; Barry Johnson/Getty Images, Inc.-Liaison, *339*; EPA-Documerica, *346*; AP/Wide World Photos, *350*; Shepherd Sherbell/Corbis/SABA Press Photos, Inc., *352*; Paul Conklin/PhotoEdit, *359*; AP/Wide World Photos, *367 (left and right)*

CHAPTER 12 AFP/Corbis, *369*; Franklin D. Roosevelt Library, *373*; AP/Wide World Photos, *381*; Getty Images Inc.-Hulton Archive Photos, *386*; AP/Wide World Photos, *396*; AP/Wide World Photos, *401*

CHAPTER 13 AP/Wide World Photos, *404*; Karen Kasmauski/NGS Image Collection, *406*; AP/Wide World Photos, *409*; Georg Gertzer/Photo Researchers, Inc., *410*; Art Wolfe/Photo Researchers, Inc., *414*; Antonio Ribeiro/Getty Images, Inc.-Liaison, *417*

CHAPTER 14 Ralph Mercer/Getty Images Inc.-Stone, *432 (background)*; Hader/Corbis, *436 (left)*; Library of Congress, *436 (center)*; Getty Images Inc.-Hulton Archive Photos, *436 (right)*; Library of Congress, *439 (left)*; Information Service of India, *439 (right)*; Chamussy/SIPA Press, *441*; Rita Castelnuovo/The New York Times, *443*; National Archives and Records Administration, *449*

CHAPTER 15 Wei Yan/Masterfile Corporation, *454*; Hulton-Deutsch Collection/Corbis, *457*; Minosa/Scorpio/Corbis/Sygma, *464*; AP/Wide World Photos, *466*; New York Convention & Visitors Bureau, *467 (left)*; Getty Images Inc.-Stone, *467 (right)*; Roger Ressmeyer/Corbis, *475*

CHAPTER 16 Galen Rowell/Corbis, *484*; Pizzoli Alberto/Corbis/Sygma, *486*; Wade Goddard/Corbis/Sygma, *490 (left)*; Michael Nichols/NGS Image Collection, *490 (right)*; SuperStock, Inc., *492*; Photofest, *497 (left)*; Ralph Crane/TimePix, *497 (right)*; TimePix, *501*

CHAPTER 17 Pawel Kopcznksi/TimePix, *506*; NASA/Johnson Space Center, *507*; AP/Wide World Photos, *514, 517*; NASA/Goddard Space Flight Center, *518*; AP/Wide World Photos, *519*

Index